INTERNATIONAL LAW: A CANADIAN PERSPECTIVE

(SECOND EDITION)

by

L.C. GREEN, LL.B., LL.D., F.R.S.C.

Honourary Professor of Law
University Professor, University of Alberta

Textbook edition of Title 81 of
The Canadian Encyclopedic Digest
(Ontario) Third Edition

1988
THE CARSWELL COMPANY LIMITED

Canadian Cataloguing in Publication Data

Green, L.C. (Leslie Claude), 1920-
  International law

2nd ed.
Includes bibliographical references and index.
ISBN 0-459-31981-7

1. International law. 2. International law —
Canada. I. Title. II. Title: Canadian encyclopedic
digest, Ontario. 3rd ed.

JX68.G74   1988   341   C88-093749-1

To G.S.
Teacher and Friend

Preface to the First Edition

This monograph is directed to Canadian students as well as to those practitioners who may need to know the Canadian approach to particular issues in international law. It may also be useful as a reference guide for governmental officials and diplomats wishing to know the Canadian attitude on points of interest to them in their official duties.

This publication was originally prepared as the title International Law in the Canadian Encyclopedic Digest. Initially, an abbreviated version of the author's International Law Through the Cases (4th ed., 1978, Carswell/Oceana) was attempted; hence the reference in the table of cases. In preparing the manuscript, however, it soon became clear that the materials in the casebook were both too extensive and too narrow, for in that work non-Canadian material is paramount. As a result, the original idea of abbreviating the casebook was abandoned, and it was decided instead to seek out Canadian judicial decisions or official statements of understanding on relevant international law issues.

With these ends in view, citations of doctrinal material have been kept to a minimum, although an effort has been made to include relevant writings by Canadian authors or in Canadian publications. Non-Canadian materials are included when they express the law in a manner that is either universally accepted or may be considered compatible with Canadian practice or approach.

Readers interested in further Canadian doctrinal sources should refer to Christian Wiktor's Canadian Bibliography of International Law, prepared under the auspices of the Canadian Council on International Law.

I should like to thank the publishers, who have been responsible for preparing the table of cases and the index, and my secretary, Mrs. Darlene Nosko, who coped willingly with all my typing errors.

L.C. Green
Edmonton, December 1983

Summary of Contents

Classification

All references are to paragraph numbers.

List of Abbreviations

A & E. .... Adolphus and Ellis's Reports (King's Bench,
Great Britain), 1834-40
A.C. .... Appeal Cases (Great Britain), 1891-
A.I.R. .... All India Reporter, 1914-
A.J.I.L. .... American Journal of International Law
All E.R. .... All England Reports, 1935-
A.L.J.R. .... Australian Law Journal Reports, 1958-
Anglo-Amer. L.R. .... Anglo-American Law Review
Ann. Dig. .... Annual Digest of Public International Law Cases, 1919-49
App. Cas. .... Appeal Cases (Great Britain), 1875-90
B.F.S.P. .... British and Foreign State Papers, 1812-
B.Y.B.I.L. .... British Year Book of International Law
Beav. .... Beavan's Reports (Rolls Court, Great Britain), 1838-66
Bee .... Bee's Admiralty Reports (United States), 1792-1809
Black. .... United States Supreme Court Reports, 1861-2
Blatchf. .... Blatchford's U.S. Circuit Court Reports, 1845-87
Burr. .... Burrow's Reports (King's Bench, Great Britain), 1757-71
C.B. (N.S.) .... Common Bench New Series (Great Britain), 1856-65
C.C.S.D.N.Y. .... Circuit Court, Southern District, New York, 1827-47
C.F.P. .... Canadian Federal Papers
C.L.B. .... Commonwealth Law Bulletin, 1975-
C.M.L.R. .... Common Market Law Reports, 1962-
C.M.R. .... Court Martial Reports (United States), 1951-
C.T.S. .... Consolidated Treaty Series (ed. C. Parry)
C.Y.B.I.L. .... Canadian Year Book of International Law
Can. T.S. .... Canada Treaty Series, 1928-
Ch. .... Chancery Reports (Great Britain), 1891-
Cmd. .... Command Papers (Great Britain), 1919-56
Cmnd. .... Command Papers (Great Britain), 1957-
Co. Rep. .... Coke's Reports (Great Britain), 1572-1616
Cowp. .... Cowper's Reports (King's Bench, Great Britain), 1774-8
Cranch .... United States Supreme Court Reports, 1801-15
C. Rob. .... C. Robinson's Admiralty Reports (Great Britain), 1774-8
D.L.R. .... Dominion Law Reports (Canada), 1912-
Dall. .... Dallas's United States Supreme Court Reports, 1754-1800
Dods. .... Dodson's Admiralty Reports (Great Britain), 1811-22
E.C.J. .... European Court of Justice
E.C.R. .... European Court Reports, 1954-
E.R. .... English Reports, 1220-1865
Ex. D. .... Exchequer Division Reports (Great Britain), 1875-80
F. .... Federal Reporter (United States), 1880-1924
F. 2d .... Federal Reporter, Second Series (United States), 1924-
F. (J.C.) .... Fraser, Justiciary Cases (Scotland), 1898-
F.C. .... Federal Court (Canada), 1971-
F. Supp. .... Federal Supplement (United States), 1932-
Fed. .... Federal Reporter (United States), 1932-

Forr. .... Forrest's Exchequer Reports (Great Britain), 1800-1
G.A.O.R. .... General Assembly Official Records
GATT .... General Agreement on Tariffs and Trade
G.L.R. .... Ghana Law Reports, 1960-
Ga. .... Georgia Reports (United States), 1846-
H.M.S.O. .... Her (His) Majesty's Stationery Office (Great Britain)
H.R.L.J. .... Human Rights Law Journal
Hackworth .... Digest of International Law, 8 vols. (1940-1944)
Hague Recueil .... Recueil des cours de l'Académie de droit international
Hudson Int. Leg. .... Hudson International Legislation, 9 vols. (1931-50)
I.A.C. .... Immigration Appeal Cases
ICAO .... International Civil Aviation Organization
I.C.J. Rep. .... International Court of Justice Reports, 1947-
I.C.J.Y.B. .... International Court of Justice Year Book
I.C.L.Q. .... International and Comparative Law Quarterly
I.L.M. .... International Legal Materials, 1962-
I.L.O. .... International Labour Organization
I.L.R. .... International Law Reports, 1950-
I.T.R. .... Industrial Tribunal Reports (Great Britain), 1966-
I.Y.B.H.R. .... Israel Year Book on Human Rights
Imm. A.R. .... Immigration Appeal Reports, 1981-
Ind. Y.B.I.A. .... Indian Year Book on International Affairs
K.B. .... King's Bench (Great Britain), 1901-52
L.J.K.B. .... Law Journal King's Bench Reports (Great Britain), 1831-1949
L.N.T.S. .... League of Nations Treaty Series, 1920-45
L.Q.R. .... Law Quarterly Review
L.R.T.W.C. .... Law Reports of the Trials of War Criminals, 1947-49
Ll. R. .... Lloyd's Reports (Great Britain) 1919-
M.A.T. .... Mixed Arbitral Tribunals (Recueil des décisions), 1921-30
M.L.R. .... Military Law Reporter (United States), 1973-
Malayan L.J. .... Malayan Law Journal
Malloy, Treaties .... Treaties, Conventions, etc., between the
                                United States and Other Powers, 1776-1909, 1910
Martens, Nouveau Recueil Général .... Nouveau Recueil de Traités, 1908-
Martens, Recueil .... Recueil de Traités, 1817-35
Mod. L.R. .... Modern Law Review
Moore, International Arbitrations .... History and Digest of International
                        Arbitrations to which the United States has been a Party, 1898
NATO .... North Atlantic Treaty Organization
N.R. .... National Reports (Canada), 1974-
N.S.W.L.R. .... New South Wales Law Reports (Australia), 1862-
N.Y.S. .... New York Supplement Reporter, 1888-
N.Z.L.R. .... New Zealand Law Reports, 1883-
O'Connell, Vols. 1-2 .... O'Connell, D.P., International Law
                                                          (2 vols., 2d ed., 1970)
Oppenheim, Vols. 1-2 .... Oppenheim, L., International Law
                (ed. H. Lauterpacht, vol. 1, 8th ed., 1955; vol. 2, 7th ed., 1952)
O.R. .... Ontario Reports (Canada), 1931-
Ottawa L.R. .... Ottawa Law Review
P. .... Probate Reports (Great Britain), 1891-
P.C.A. .... Permanent Court of Arbitration

4

P.C.I.J. .... Permanent Court of International Justice
P.D. .... Probate Division Reports (Great Britain), 1875-90
Pet. .... Peters' United States Supreme Court Reports, 1828-42
Q.B. .... Queen's Bench Reports (Great Britain), 1891-1901, 1952-
Q.B.D. .... Queen's Bench Division Reports (Great Britain), 1875-90
Que. R.P. .... Québec Rapports de Pratique (Canada), 1898-
R.I.A.A. ...... United Nations, Reports of International Arbitral Awards, 1948-
R.I.I.A. .... Royal Institute of International Affairs
R.P.C. .... Reports of Patent, Design and Trade Mark Cases, 1985-
R.S.C. .... Revised Statutes of Canada
S.A.L.R. .... South African Law Reports, 1908-
S.C. .... Reports of the Supreme Court of the Cape of Good Hope
S.C.R. .... Supreme Court Reports (Canada), 1876-
S.C.R. .... Supreme Court Reports (India), 1950-
S.R. & O. .... Statutory Rules and Orders (Great Britain)
Schwarzenberger, Vols. 1-4 .... Schwarzenberger, G., International Law
            as applied by International Courts and Tribunals (vol. 1, 3rd ed., 1957;
                              vol. 2, 1968; vol. 3, 1976; vol. 4, 1986)
Series A .... P.C.I.J. Judgments and Orders, 1922-30
Series A/B .... P.C.I.J. Advisory Opinions, Judgments and Orders, 1931-40
Series B .... P.C.I.J. Advisory Opinions, 1922-30
So. 2d .... Southern Reporter, Second Series (United States), 1941-
Spinks .... Spinks' Prize Cases (Great Britain), 1854-6
St. Tr. .... State Trials (Great Britain), 1163-1820
T.I.A.S. ..... Treaties and Other International Acts Series (United States), 1950-
T.L.R. .... Times Law Reports (Great Britain), 1841-1952
U.B.C.L.R. .... University of British Columbia Law Review
U.N.C.I.O. .... United Nations Conference on International Organization
UNESCO .... United Nations Educational, Social and Cultural Organization
U.N.G.A. .... United Nations General Assembly
U.N.S.C. .... United Nations Security Council
U.N.T.S. .... United Nations Treaty Series, 1946-
U.N.W.C.C. .... United Nations War Crimes Commission, Law Reports
                              of Trials of War Criminals, 1947-9
U.N.Y.B.H.R. .... United Nations Year Book on Human Rights
U.S. .... United States Supreme Court Reports, 1875-
U.S.C. .... United States Code
U.S. Digest .... Digest of United States Practice in International Law, 1973-
Ves. Jr. .... Vesey Junior's Chancery Reports (Great Britain), 1789-1816
W.C.R. .... Hudson, M.O., World Court Reports (4 vols., 1934-43)
W.L.R. .... Weekly Law Reports (Great Britain), 1953-
Wall. .... Wallace's United States Supreme Court Reports, 1865-76
Wheaton .... Wheaton's United States Supreme Court Reports, 1816-27
Whiteman, Vols. 1-14 .... Whiteman, M.M., Digest of International Law
                              (14 vols., 1963-73)
W. Rob. .... W. Robinson's Admiralty Reports (Great Britain), 1838-52
Y.B.I.C.J. .... Year Book of the International Court of Justice
Y.B.I.L.C. .... Year Book of International Law Commission
Y.B.W.A. .... Year Book of World Affairs

Table of Cases

All references are to paragraph numbers.

[**Publisher's Note**: For further reference, see L.C. Green's casebook, International Law Through the Cases (4th ed., 1978), which reproduces, in edited form, many of the cases cited below.]

7

TABLE OF CASES

Table of Statutes

All references are to paragraph numbers.

TABLE OF STATUTES

Table of Treaties and Related Documents

All references are to paragraph numbers.

47

I Foundations of International Law

1. NATURE AND SOURCES OF INTERNATIONAL LAW

§1 It is the essence of public international law that it operates across state boundaries and, broadly speaking, the same rules and principles are accepted as binding by all states and operate to govern their relations inter se. Moreover, there is no legislature, compulsory judicial system or police force on the international level, and the interrelationship between international law and international politics[1] is such that one is inclined to be sympathetic towards those who maintain that 'International Law is that thing which the evil ignore and the righteous refuse to enforce.'[2] On the other hand, there can be no doubt that in their relationships among themselves, states do in fact appeal to legal principles, use legal language, refer to legal writings and, even in times of economic stress, maintain a legal service attached to their foreign ministries, and acknowledge the existence at The Hague of an International Court of Justice, to which they may have recourse if they wish. Even national judges, who are not normally called upon to deal with issues arising between states, acknowledge the existence of international law as a legal system. Thus, Lord Alverstone C.J. found it possible to adopt[3] the definition of Lord Russell of Killowen in an address in 1896:[4] "What, then, is international law? I know of no better definition of it than it is the sum of the rules or usages which civilised States have agreed shall be binding upon them in their dealings with one another."

1. See, e.g., Kaplan and Katzenbach, The Political Foundations of International Law (1961).

2. Leon Uris, Exodus (1958), p. 498.

3. *West Rand Central Gold Mining Co. v. R.*, [1905] 2 K.B. 391 (D. C.).

4. (1896) 19 Reports of American Bar Assn. 253, address reprinted under title "International Law," (1896), 12 L.Q.R. 11.

§2 It is, therefore, essentially, a law based on the consent of states.[5] As a result of the agreement produced by this mutual consent, the states concerned comply with the rules and usages in question and recognize that failure to do so is a breach of the law which opens the way to those remedies that international law makes available. When Lord Russell spoke and Lord Alverstone gave his statement judicial authority, it was still possible to regard international law as a system of an interstate character, but in the years that have elapsed, the nature of international society has changed. There now exists a vast array of international organizations which enjoy a legal personality distinct from the states creating them. Moreover, a variety of business corporations have direct dealings with states and are frequently as powerful as any state. These organizations and corporations act on the international stage and their relations then tend to be governed by international rather than national law. Moreover, some organizations have been created by international agreements which possess jurisdiction even over private individuals and the latter as well as the states creating the organizations in question, such as the European Community, become subject to international law. Today, therefore, international law may be defined as "that body of rules and principles which States and other entities enjoying legal personality and operating on the international scene recognize as necessary for the maintenance of peace and good order among themselves, and habitually obey in order to maintain and preserve that good order".[6]

5. See, however, Charney, "The Persistent Objector Rule and the Development of Customary International Law" (1985), 56 B.Y.B.I.L. 1.

6. See Green, Law and Society (1975), p. 173, or (1962), 14 Univ. of Toronto L.J. 176 at 193.

§3 Since international law knows no international frontiers, it is not uncommon to find the judges in any particular case citing doctrine, that is to say literature, regardless of the nationality of the writer,[7] and this is particularly true of those writers who constitute what are generally described as the classicists of international law.[8] They also refer to judicial decisions regardless of the country whose court has rendered the decision in question,[9] and in certain circumstances will even examine agreements between foreign states in order to establish the existence of a universally established rule.[10] On occasion, when it is argued that there is a new rule in nascendi, courts will look to the judicial and state practice of foreign states to ascertain the extent to which that trend may be regarded as accepted.[11]

7. See *Rose v. R.*, [1947] 3 D.L.R. 618 (Que. K.B.), per Bissonnette J. citing Pradier-Fodéré and Martens; *Ref. re Power of Municipalities to Levy Rates on Foreign Legations and High Commissioners' Residences* (Foreign Legations Case), [1943] S.C.R. 208 (S.C.C.), per Duff C.J. citing Vattel, Hurst, Hall; see also, Tascherau J. in *Ref. re Exemption of U.S. Forces from Proceedings in Cdn. Criminal Cts.* (Foreign Forces Case), [1943] S.C.R. 483 (S.C.C.).

8. See series of Classics of International Law (Grotius, Vattel, Pufendorf, etc.) published by Carnegie Endowment for Int. Peace and reprinted by Oceana Publications Inc. See also, *R. v. Keyn* (The Franconia) (1876), L.R. 2 Ex. D. 63.

9. See *Cashin v. R.*, [1935] Ex. C.R. 103 (Ex. Ct.); *St. John v. Fraser-Brace Overseas Corp.*, [1958] S.C.R. 263 (S.C.C.); see also, *Foreign Legations Case, ante.*

10. *Foreign Forces Case, ante,* per Tascherau J. citing agreements between U.K. and France, U.S. and France, U.S. and Belgium.

11. *Congo (Republic) v. Venne,* [1971] S.C.R. 997 (S.C.C.); *Zodiack Int. Products Inc. v. Polish People's Republic* (1977), 4 B.L.R. 179 (Que. C.A.); *The Philippine Admiral,* [1976] 2 W.L.R. 214 (P.C.); *Trendtex Trading Corp. v. Cental Bank of Nigeria,* [1977] 2 W.L.R. 356 (C.A.); see also, Schreuer, "Some Recent Developments in the Law of State Immunity" (1978) 2 Comparative Law Yearbook 215; Emanuelli, "L'immunité souveraine et la coutume internationale: de l'immunité absolue à l'immunité relative?" (1984) 22 C.Y.B.I.L. 26. U.N., Materials on Jurisdictional Immunities of Statutes and their Property (1982).

§4 While it is generally asserted that international law is of universal application and equally recognized by all states, it cannot be ignored that some rules of the system are in fact not acknowledged by all states.[12] It may be that a particular treaty is only binding upon two states parties thereto[13] and as such creates particular law for them alone. However, such a treaty must not purport to create rules which are derogatory of those principles of international law which are regarded as constituting jus cogens[14] and binding upon all at all times,[15] nor must it seek to create rights or impose duties upon a third state without that state's consent.[16] In addition to such particular treaties, there may be some the parties to which are so numerous that the treaties in question are considered as creative of general international law. This is true when the rule created by the treaty has not been accepted by a major power.[17] When there are few non-parties and no major power is included among them the treaty may be considered to have created universal international law and be binding on all, including non-parties.[18] Finally, states within a geographic region may create laws for themselves which deviate from the rules of international law which are generally recognized.[19] Such regional international law does not apply to any state outside the region, nor to any state having business in the region or with any member of the region unless it agrees to be so bound.

12. See Green, "Is There a Universal International Law Today?", (1985) 23 C.Y.B.I.L. 3.

13. Most extradition treaties, e.g., that between Canada and the U.S., C.T.S. 1976, No. 3, or Canada and Sweden, C.T.S. 1976, No. 8.

14. Law binding irrespective of the will of individual states.

15. See Vienna Convention on the Law of Treaties, 1969, 8 I.L.M. 679, to which Canada acceded in 1970, but which did not come into force until 1980, Art. 53: "A treaty is void if, at the time of its conclusion, it conflicts with a peremptory norm of general international law. For the purposes of the present Convention, a peremptory norm of general international law is a norm accepted and recognized by the international community of States as a whole as a norm from which no derogation is permitted and which can be modified only by a subsequent norm of general international law having the same character". By Art. 64, "if a new peremptory norm of

general law emerges, any existing treaty which is in conflict with that norm becomes void and terminates." The Treaty provides no example of such a norm, but it is becoming generally accepted that the basic principles in the field of human rights are such, while Geneva Convention III on Prisoners of War, 1949, 75 U.N.T.S. 135 expressly forbids the parties from making any agreement which would detract from the rights of prisoners, and the prisoners themselves are unable to renounce any of the rights conferred upon them by the Convention (Arts. 6 and 7 respectively). See §349.

16.   See Art. 34. See §308.

17.   Thus the Geneva Convention on the Continental Shelf, 1958, 499 U.N.T.S. 311, which Canada ratified in 1970, has not been accepted by the Federal Republic of Germany, and though it had been accepted by 39 states by the time of its judgment, the International Court of Justice in the *North Sea Continental Shelf Cases,* [1969] I.C.J. 3 refused to apply its demarcation procedures as against that state.

18.   This appears to have been the attitude of the International Military Tribunal at Nuremberg in regard to Hague Convention IV of 1907 concerning the Laws and Customs of War on Land and the 1929 Geneva Convention on the Treatment of Prisoners of War (*Nuremberg Judgment* (1946), Cmd. 6964, 48, 64-65). On the other hand, although the Geneva Gas Protocol, 1925, received over 40 accessions, including all the major European powers, it was not ratified by the U.S. until 1975, and prior to that date the U.S. maintained that the Protocol was, despite the number of acceptances and its own original signature, not binding upon that country. The general opinion among writers, however, including American (e.g., Greenspan, The Modern Law of Land Warfare (1959), p. 357), was that gas warfare was in fact illegal. Reference should also be made to the advisory opinion of the International Court of Justice on *Reparation for Injuries Suffered in the Service of the United Nations* (the Bernadotte case), [1949] I.C.J. 174, in which it was held that "fifty States, representing the vast majority of the [then] members of the international community, had the power, in conformity with international law, to bring into being an entity possessing objective international personality, and not merely recognized by them alone, together with capacity to bring international claims . . . whether or not the defendant State is a member of the United Nations" and regardless of its recognition by such state. This should be compared with the finding of the Permanent Court of International Justice in its advisory opinion concerning *Status of Eastern Carelia* (1923), 1 W.C.R. 191, when it held that the League of Nations had no competence to discuss a matter concerning a non-member which refused to recognize the competence of the League, but in this case, the non-member in question was the Soviet Union.

19.   See, for example, discussion on American international law as it concerns diplomatic asylum in the *Asylum Case* (Colombia/Peru), [1950] I.C.J. 266, particularly the judgments of Judges Alvarez and Read (290 and 316); and on 'African law' as opposed to 'the public law of Europe', the separate opinion of Vice-President Ammoun in the *Namibia Case* (South-West Africa), [1971] I.C.J. 16, 86. See also, Snyder and Sathirathai, Third World Attitudes toward International Law, 1987; and the jurisprudence of the European Communities Court, the European Court of Human Rights and the Inter-American Court of Human Rights.

§5   Since there is no supreme sovereign in international law, for in the eyes of the law all states are equal,[20] and there is no legislative body with authority to enact treaties,[21] no compulsory judicial tribunal[22] with power to issue a judgment in absentia[23] or before which states are obliged to appear and lacking any international police force or other enforcing body,[24] it is often claimed that international law lacks the characteristics of a legal system and cannot be regarded as law.[25] In their practice, however, states clearly indicate that they recognize the need for an international legal system and constantly enter into discussions for the drafting of new statements of what they regard to be the law. Moreover, the Charter of the United Nations commits the General Assembly,[26] that is to say the totality of members, "to initiate studies and make recommendations . . . encouraging the progressive development of international law and its codification"[27] and to that end an International Law Commission was established in accordance with Article 22 of the Charter. This body has, in fact, been responsible for drafting many of the most important treaties that have been adopted since 1945.[28] Furthermore, when queries arise as to whether a state may take certain action or whether action taken by another and directed at the interests of the former may legitimately be taken, consultations are held with legal advisers[29] who express their opinions in legal terminology,[30] and such opinions may form the basis for protests or demands for compensation equally expressed in legal language,[31] and they may even form the basis for a claim being made by one state against another before the International Court of Justice,[32] or some specially created tribunal.[33]

20. In practice this is reflected in the organization of the United Nations; see §§ 413-421. In the General Assembly, where all members of the United Nations are represented, each state, regardless of size or power, has one vote. In the Security Council, all have agreed that five of the members shall possess the right of veto. Prima facie, this is incompatible with sovereign equality (see Article 2(1) of the Charter). In fact, however, it is as a result of the exercise of this sovereignty that the members have agreed that, in certain circumstances, these five will possess a power that the others lack. This is no different from the position under every treaty whereby the parties freely undertake to limit the exercise of their sovereignty in the manner required to enable the treaty to operate. See Vattel, Le Droit des Gens (1758), Preface, s. 18, Carnegie tr., p. 7: "Since men are by nature equal, . . . Nations, which are composed of men and may be regarded as so many free persons living together in a state of nature, are by nature equal and hold from nature the same obligations and the same rights. Strength or weakness, in this case, counts for nothing. A dwarf is as much a man as a giant is; a small Republic is no less a sovereign State than the most powerful King."

21. The International Law Commission is only empowered to draft conventions, and even when the General Assembly adopts a treaty, it is only by virtue of ratification or accession by states that the treaty can become law. Resolutions of the General Assembly, even when expressed in compulsive language, are only recommendations; see separate opinion of Judge Lauterpacht in advisory opinion on *South-West Africa — Voting Procedure,* [1955] I.C.J. 67, 115. Decisions of the Security Council are only binding when they relate to enforcement measures under Chapter VII of the Charter (Art. 25).

22. The International Court of Justice is available to those States which agree to have recourse to it. By Article 36 of the Court's Statute states may declare in advance that they will accept the jurisdiction of the Court for all disputes or only for those of a particular kind. The jurisdiction thus optionally accepted is frequently referred to as 'compulsory'. See §§400-412.

23. It is when jurisdiction has been created by virtue of a treaty providing for compulsory judicial settlement (see *Re U.S. Diplomatic and Consular Staff in Tehran* (Provisional Measures), [1979] I.C.J. 7), or because of a declaration under Art. 36 of the Statute (see note 22, *ante*) or when a defendant country acknowledges its acceptance of jurisdiction in some other way (see *Corfu Channel* (Preliminary Objection) (U.K./Albania), [1948] I.C.J. 15, that the court can give a judgment in absentia.

24. By Art. 94(2) of the Charter, a successful party to an action before the International Court of Justice may, if the other party fails to comply with the judgment, refer the matter to the Security Council which *may* then decide to take steps to enforce the judgment (italics added).

25. Austin regarded international law as 'law improperly so-called' or 'positive morality'. There is, of course, no reason why his definition of 'law properly so-called' should be regarded as exhaustive and of universal application; see Williams, "International Law and the Controversy Concerning the Word 'Law'," (1945) 22 B.Y.I.L. 146.

26. Art. 13(1)(a).

27. Progressive development envisages the creation of new law, while codification refers to the consolidation of existing law and the spelling out in treaty form of what has previously been regarded as customary law.

28. E.g., the 1958 treaties on the Law of the Sea, the 1961 Convention on Diplomatic Relations, the 1969 Convention on the Law of Treaties, etc.

29. See Merillat, Legal Advisers and Foreign Affairs (1964).

30. See, e.g., McNair, International Law Opinions (1956); see, also, the section on Canadian Practice in International Law as Reflected Mainly in Statements of the Department of External Affairs in the C.Y.B.I.L.

31. See, e.g., Can. Claim against U.S.S.R. for damage caused by Cosmos 954, FLA-268, Jan. 23, 1979, FLA-813, Mar. 15, 1979, 18 I.L.M. 899, 909.

32. E.g., *Re U.S. Diplomatic and Consular Staff in Tehran,* [1979] I.C.J. 7, [1980] I.C.J. 3.

33. See *The I'm Alone* (Canada/U.S.) (1933/1935), 3 R.I.A.A. 1609 (Can.-U.S.: Special Joint Comm.); *Trail Smelter Arbitration* (Canada/U.S.) (1938/1941), 3 R.I.A.A. 1905 (Arbitral Trib.).

§6 In addition, states have agreed over the centuries that certain acts by private individuals constitute crimes as defined by international law, which crimes become amenable to trial and punishment by any state into whose hands the offender may fall,[34] and occasionally they have established special international tribunals for the trial of such offenders.[35] Further, individual states have sometimes embodied into their criminal codes reference to offences as defined by international law, without any further attempt at national specification.[36] Finally, in recent years states have entered into treaties condemning certain acts as criminal and, in the absence of an international criminal court,[37] the parties to those treaties have undertaken to amend their criminal codes in order to assume jurisdiction over such offences.[38]

34.   The best known instances are piracy jure gentium, i.e. by the law of nations (see *The Le Louis* (1917), 2 Dods. 210 (H.C. of Admiralty), and *Re Piracy Jure Gentium*, [1934] A.C. 586 (P.C.)), and war crimes. See §§189-213 and 359-382.

35.   E.g., the International Military Tribunals at Nuremberg and Tokyo.

36.   See Canadian Criminal Code, R.S.C. 1970, c. C-34, s. 75(1): "Every one commits piracy who does any act that, by the law of nations, is piracy." See also references to war crimes and crimes against humanity; Act to amend the Criminal Code, the Immigration Act, 1976 and the Citizenship Act, S.C. 1987, c. 37. See also 18 U.S.C. 1051-2 as applied in the *Achille Lauro* incident, 1985, 24 I.L.M. 1509 at 1556-7.

37.   See, e.g., League of Nations Convention for Creation of an International Criminal Court, 1937, 7 Hudson, Int. Leg., 878, of which no ratification was ever deposited by any state; U.N. Draft Statute for an International Criminal Court, 1954, 9 U.N. G.A.O.R., Supp. 12, 23 (reproduced in Williams, International Criminal Law (1978), p. 900; Gingold, "An International Penal Code: Why, How and When", (1976) 24 Chitty's Law J. 350; Green, "An International Penal Code — NOW?" (1976) 3 Dalhousie Law J. 560 and "New Trends in International Criminal Law", (1981) 9 I.Y.B.H.R.; Bassiouni, International Criminal Law (3 vols. 1986-87).

38.   See, e.g., Convention on the Prevention and Punishment of Crimes against Internationally Protected Persons, including Diplomats, 1973, 1035 U.N.T.S. 167, Art. 3, ratified by Canada 1976; Hague Convention for Suppression of Unlawful Seizure of Aircraft, 1970, 860 U.N.T.S 105, Art. 2; Criminal Code, s. 6 [am. S.C. 1972, c. 13, s. 3; 1974-75-76, c. 93, s. 3]; ss. 76.1-76.3 [en. S.C. 1972, c. 13, s. 6]; Genocide Convention, 1948, 78 U.N.T.S. 277; Criminal Code, s. 281.1 [en. R.S.C. 1970, c. 11 (1st Supp.), s. 1]. See also Criminal Law Amendment Act, S.C. 1985, c. 19; Williams, "The Criminal Law Amendment Act 1985: Implications for International Criminal Law", (1985) 23 C.Y.B.I.L. 226. See §§189-213.

§7   Since international law lacks a legislature, it becomes binding upon states only by virtue of their consent.[39] The clearest expression of such consent having been given is to be found in treaties[40] to which the state in question has become a party. However, while treaties are the clearest expression of such consent, there are also unwritten sources[41] which may be cited as evidence of the law.

39.   See §4 on particular, general, universal and regional international law. See also, *The S.S. Lotus* (France/Turkey), (1927), 2 W.C.R. 20, 35: "International law governs relations between independent States. The rules of law binding upon States emanate from their own free will as expressed in conventions [—this term is used in international law as a synonym for treaties—] or by usages generally accepted as expressing principles of law and established in order to regulate the relations between the co-existing independent communities with a view to the achievement of common aims. Restrictions upon the independence of States cannot therefore be presumed"; *West Rand Central Gold Mining Co. v. R.*, [1905] 2 K.B. 391 at 401 (Div. Ct.) *per* Lord

Alverstone C.J.: international law "rests upon a consensus of civilised States, not expressed in any code or pact, nor possessing, in case of dispute, any authorised or authoritative interpreter; and capable, indeed, of proof, in the absence of some express international agreement, only by evidence of usage to be obtained from the actions of nations in similar cases in the course of their history." Insofar as judicial settlement is concerned, see the similar approach of the Permanent Court of International Justice in its advisory opinion on *Status of Eastern Carelia* (1923), 1 W.C.R. 191 at 204: "It is well established in international law that no State can, without its consent, be compelled to submit its disputes with other States either to mediation or arbitration, or to any other kind of pacific settlement." As to the International Court of Justice, see *Application for Revision and Interpretation of the Continental Shelf Case* (Tunisia/Libyan Arab Jamahiriya), [1985] I.C.J. 192 at 216: "It is of course a fundamental principle that 'The consent of States, parties to a dispute, is the basis of the Court's jurisdiction in contentious cases' (*Interpretation of Peace Treaties,* [1950] I.C.J. 65 at 71. It follows, first, that parties to treaties or special agreements are free to make their consent to the seisin of the Court, and hence the Court's juridsiction, subject to whatever pre-conditions, consistent with the Statute, as may be agreed between them; and, secondly, that in principle a State may validly waive an objection to jurisdiction which it might otherwise have been entitled to raise." See §§404-411. See, however, Charney, "The Persistent Objector Rule and the Development of Customary International Law" (1985), 56 B.Y.B.I.L. 1.

40.   It makes no difference to the nature of the document or its legal validity whether it is called treaty, convention, charter, covenant, protocol, or by any other designation. What is essential is that there be "an international agreement concluded between States in written form [—undertakings may also be assumed orally and by way of unilateral declaration—] and governed by international law, whether embodied in a single instrument or in two or more related instruments", Vienna Convention on the Law of Treaties, 1969, Art. 2(1)(a), 8 I.L.M. 679. See §§299-315.

41.   There is as much debate in international law as there is in national jurisprudence over the use of the term 'source'. It has been suggested that it would be more correct to speak of treaties as 'law-creating processes' and the unwritten types of international law as 'law-determining agencies', Schwarzenberger, International Law, Vol. 1 (1957), ch. 2.

§8   In accordance with the Statute of the International Court of Justice,[42] "the Court, whose function is to decide in accordance with international law such disputes as are submitted to it, shall apply: (a) international conventions, whether general or particular,[43] establishing rules expressly recognized by the consenting states;[44] (b) international custom, as evidence of a general practice accepted as law;[45] (c) the general principles of law recognized by civilized nations;[46] (d) subject to the provisions of Article 59,[47] judicial decisions and the teachings of the most highly qualified publicists of the various nations, as subsidiary means for the determination of the rules of law."

42.   Art. 38.

43.   See §4.

44.   Provided that these rules do not run counter to any principles of jus cogens or the rights of a third power.

45.   It is not enough that the states appearing before the court have adopted a usage to a particular effect; the usage must have been followed in the belief that it was legally binding. See *Asylum Case* (Colombia/Peru), [1950] I.C.J. 266, 276; see note 62 under §11.

46.   This represents a concept going back to the nineteenth century and is based on the exclusion of colonial territories and 'backward' peoples, although it has been suggested that the I.C.J. should be asked for an advisory opinion as to the present meaning of the term, Schwarzenberger, International Law, Vol. 4 (1986), pp. 732-733.

47.   Since international law is a law based on consent, any decision of the court can only bind the parties thereto, and this excludes stare decisis as understood in national law.

§9   While Article 38 lays down the materials to which the Court is to have recourse, it also provides[48] that, with the agreement of the parties, principles ex aequo et bono[49] may be resorted to.

48.   Art. 38(2).

49.   This may be defined broadly as principles of fair-mindedness which may be applied regardless of the letter of the law.

§10   Every treaty, whether general or particular, bilateral or multi-lateral, lays down the law or defines the legal régime for its parties with regard to the subject-matter with which it deals. Nevertheless, treaties are sometimes subdivided into 'law-making treaties' and 'treaty-contracts'. The former title, sometimes even elevated to the level of 'international legislation', particularly when adopted under the auspices of an international organization,[50] is used to denote those treaties which are intended to be of general or universal application and which either codify existing law or develop it, in fields which may be described as being of special concern to more than two or three states alone. Among the treaties sometimes included in this category are those concerned with the law of armed conflict,[51] human rights,[52] terrorism,[53] diplomatic immunities and the diplomatic function as such,[54] the law of the sea[55] and the law concerning treaties.[56] However many parties there may be to such treaties, and however humanitarian or useful the subject-matter may be, such treaties do not affect non-parties.[57] The term contract-treaty tends to be used to denote bilateral treaties, or treaties between a very small number of states and dealing with only a limited subject-matter, e.g., extradition, although the Pan-American Convention on Extradition of Montevideo, 1933,[58] and the European Convention on Extradition, 1957,[59] were clearly intended to be 'law-making' for the members of the Pan-American Union and the Council of Europe, respectively. Perhaps the relationship between the two types of treaty may be seen if one looks to the relative ineffectiveness of the Hague Convention for Suppression of Unlawful Seizure of Aircraft, 1970,[60] and the 1973 agreement on the same issue between Canada and Cuba.[61]

50.   E.g., the United Nations General Assembly or International Law Commission or the International Civil Aviation Organisation. See Hudson, 1 Int. Leg. (1931), xiii-xiv.

51.   E.g., the Hague Conventions of 1907, the Red Cross Conventions of 1949 and the Geneva Protocols of 1977 (see Schindler and Toman, The Laws of Armed Conflicts (1982)). See §§329-382.

52.   The International Covenants on Economic, Social and Cultural Rights and on Civil and Political Rights, 1966, 993 U.N.T.S. 3, 999 U.N.T.S. 171. See §290.

53.   E.g., Convention on the Prevention and Punishment of Crimes against Internationally Protected Persons, including Diplomatic Agents, 1973, 1035 U.N.T.S. 167. See also §§189-213.

54.   Vienna Convention on Diplomatic Relations, 1961, 500 U.N.T.S. 95. See also §§150-157.

55.   1958 Conventions on Territorial Sea, 516 U.N.T.S. 205; High Seas, 450 U.N.T.S. 11; Fishing and Conservation of Living Resources, 559 U.N.T.S. 285; Continental Shelf, 499 U.N.T.S. 311; Convention on the Law of the Sea, 1982, 21 I.L.M. 1261. See also §§258-281.

56.   Vienna Convention on the Law of Treaties, 1969. See §§299-315.

57.   Save with the consent of such state, unless the treaty provision is declaratory of an existing rule of customary international law (Arts. 34-38).

58.   165 L.N.T.S. 45, see also, Draft Inter-American Convention on Extradition, 1973, 12 I.L.M. 537.

59.   359 U.N.T.S. 273.

60.   860 U.N.T.S. 105. In 1983, however, the Republic of [South] Korea returned a hijacked aircraft belonging to the Chinese People's Republic and sentenced the hijackers, despite the lack of diplomatic relations between the two states, because of their mutual acceptance of the Hague Convention.

61.   Williams, International Criminal Law, p. 650, renewed in 1979 and 1984.

§11   While treaties, at least those of a bilateral character, have been entered into since time immemorial, the majority of multilateral treaties date from the establishment of the League of Nations, although there are some of major significance, e.g., those of Westphalia, 1648, Vienna 1815, and The Hague, 1899 and 1907, which established rules of general or universal international law before its foundation. The number of such treaties was, however, relatively small and much of international law was to be found in unwritten customary law, as evidenced by the consistent practice of states. However, the fact that states have repeatedly behaved in a certain fashion does not necessarily mean that there is a legally binding custom obligating them to do so. It may be that this usage is based on courtesy towards each other or on convenience. To amount to a custom, the practice must be pursued in the belief that there is a legal obligation demanding such conduct. It has long been contended, for example, that there is a legal custom recognized in Latin America whereby ambassadors are entitled to afford asylum in their embassies to anybody seeking it, accompanied by the concomitant duty upon the territorial sovereign to observe such custom. In the *Asylum Case*[62] the International Court of Justice held that for a customary rule to be established as law it must be "in accordance with a constant and uniform usage practised by the States in question", although in the instant case there was in fact no "constant and uniform usage, accepted as law". This case turned on problems of American international law, but a custom may, of course, be applicable between two states alone, and "there is no reason why the number of States between which a local custom may be established on the basis of long practice must necessarily be larger than two. The Court sees no reason why long continued practice between two States accepted by them as regulating their relations should not form the basis of mutual rights and obligations between the two States".[63] There is no minimum period during which such a practice must be followed, but "a constant and uniform practice ... having continued over a period extending beyond a century and a quarter unaffected by the change of régime in respect of the intervening territory which occurred when India became independent, the Court is ... satisfied that that practice was accepted as law by the Parties and has given rise to a right and a correlative obligation".[64] When a rule of customary law is embodied or confirmed in a treaty, the fact that a particular state does not accept the treaty does not remove the obligation upon that state of recognizing the continued validity of the customary rule,[65] nor is a party able to exclude itself by way of a reservation[66] when ratifying the treaty.

62.   (Colombia/Peru), [1950] I.C.J. 266 at 276.

63.   *Right of Passage Over Indian Territory (Merits)* (India/Portugal), [1960] I.C.J. 6, 39.

64.   *Right of Passage Over Indian Territory, ante* at p. 40.

65.   See, e.g., *North Sea Continental Shelf Cases* (Germany/Denmark; Germany/Netherlands), [1969] I.C.J. 3 at 38: "speaking generally, it is a characteristic of purely conventional rules and obligations that, in regard to them, some faculty of making unilateral reservations may, within certain limits, be admitted; whereas this cannot be so in the case of general or customary law rules which, by their very nature, must have equal force for all members of the international community, and cannot therefore be the subject of any right of unilateral exclusion exercisable at will by any one of them in its favour. Consequently, it is to be expected that when, for whatever reason, rules or obligations of this order are embodied, or are intended to be reflected

in certain provisions of a convention, such provisions will figure among those in respect of which a right of unilateral reservation is not conferred, or is excluded."

66.   See note 65. Many treaties expressly make provision for ratifying parties to exclude the operation of particular articles as regards themselves. It is only when the treaty forbids the making of reservations or excludes specific articles from being reserved that such freedom of action is denied. If the treaty is silent, parties are free to make reservations. As to the Canadian attitude towards reservations, see Legal Bureau Memo, 9 Apr. 1984, (1985) 23 C.Y.B.I.L. 334-335. See §304.

§12   It has sometimes been contended that when principles of general or customary international law have been embodied in a convention, their future validity depends solely upon the convention, so that if the convention has been renounced or a provision therein subjected to reservation, the party renouncing or reserving is no longer bound. This argument has been expressly rejected by the International Court of Justice:[67] "The Court cannot dismiss claims [put forward] under principles of customary and general international law, simply because such principles have been enshrined in the texts of the conventions relied upon. . . . The fact that the above-mentioned principles, recognized as such, have been codified or embodied in multilateral conventions does not mean that they cease to exist and to apply as principles of customary law, even as regards countries that are parties to such conventions. Principles such as those of the non-use of force, non-intervention, respect for the independence and territorial integrity of States, and the freedom of navigation continue to be binding as part of customary international law, despite the operation of provisions of conventional law in which they have been incorporated."

67.   *Military and Paramilitary Activities in and against Nicaragua* (Nicaragua/U.S.), [1984] I.C.J. 392 at 424; [1986] I.C.J. 14 at 93-95. See also, Villiger, Customary International Law and Treaties, 1985.

§13   Since customary international law has grown over time and is unwritten, it is important to note how it is evidenced. The International Court has referred to the opinio juris sive necessitatis[68] "requisite for the formation of new rules of customary international law [passing] into the general corpus of international law, and now accepted as such by the opinio juris, so as to have become binding even for countries which have never, and do not, become parties to the Convention [which is alleged to embody such a rule]. There is no doubt that this process is a perfectly possible one and does from time to time occur: it constitutes indeed one of the recognized methods by which new rules of customary international law may be formed."[69] The court pointed out that other considerations would also be of significance, such as that the rule in question should be of a norm-creating character, should have been observed over a fairly considerable period of time and by a widespread and representative number of states,[70] including those whose particular interests might be specially affected, so that in connection with an alleged rule of customary law concerning the use of the high seas it would be necessary to note whether such practice was in fact followed by the majority of the most significant maritime powers. This latter fact may be illustrated by reference to the *The S.S. Lotus*[71] in which the Permanent Court of International Justice drew attention to the number of cases "in which . . . State[s] ha[ve] claimed a right to prosecute for an offence, committed on board a foreign vessel, which [they] regarded as punishable under [their] legislation." The opinio juris may also be determined by reference to state documents, doctrinal writings, consistent articles in bilateral treaties,[72] the decisions of international and national courts, and even the resolutions of international organizations, although it must be remembered that the majority of these are not legally binding. When assessing whether a particular usage does in fact amount to a statement of international customary law, reference must be made to both the behaviour of the state in question as well as the manner in which that state views its own conduct, that is to say whether there is evidence to show that it regards itself as obliged to act in that particular way.[73] It may even happen that the court will seek evidence of the existence of customary law in an unratified treaty if that treaty has been "adopted by an overwhelming majority of States."[74]

68.   This is sometimes described as the psychological element in the formation of custom, and may be defined as "the feeling on the part of the States that in acting as they act they are fulfilling a legal obligation" (Kopelmanas, "Custom as a Means of the Creation of International Law," (1937) 18 B.Y.I.L. 127 at 129).

69.   *North Sea Continental Shelf Cases, ante* at pp. 28, 41.

70.   "It is not to be expected that in the practice of States the application of the rules in question should have been perfect, in the sense that States should have refrained, with complete consistency, from [a particular line of conduct, in this case] the use of force or from intervention in each other's internal affairs. The Court does not consider that, for a rule to be established as customary, the corresponding practice must be in absolutely rigorous conformity with the rule. In order to deduce the existence of customary rules, the Court deems it sufficient that the conduct of States should, in general, be consistent with such rules, and that instances of State conduct inconsistent with a given rule should generally have been treated as breaches of that rule, not as indications of the recognition of a new rule. If a State acts in a way prima facie incompatible with a recognized rule, but defends its conduct by appealing to exceptions or justifications contained within the rule itself, then whether or not the State's conduct is in fact justifiable on that basis, the significance of that attitude is to confirm rather than to weaken the rule", *Military and Paramilitary Activities in and against Nicaragua* (Nicaragua/U.S.), [1986] I.C.J. 14 at 98.

71. See *The S.S. Lotus* (France/Turkey) (1937), 2 W.C.R. 20 at 41.

72. This is the case with, e.g., the development of the most-favoured-nation standard, see Schwarzenberger, International Law and Order (1971), ch. 8; see also, *Treatment of United States Nationals in Morocco,* [1952] I.C.J. 176, 187.

73. See, generally, D'Amato, The Concept of Custom in International Law (1971).

74. *Continental Shelf* (Libyan Arab Jamahariya/Malta), [1985] I.C.J. 13 at 29-30: "It is of course axiomatic that the material of customary international law is to be looked for primarily in the actual practice and opinio juris of States, even though multilateral conventions may have an important role to play in recording and defining rules deriving from custom, or indeed in developing them. There has in fact between much debate between the Parties in the present case as to the significance, for the delimitation of — and entitlement to — the continental shelf, of State practice in the matter . . . . Nevertheless, it cannot be denied that the 1982 Convention [on the Law of the Sea] is of major importance, having been adopted by an overwhelming majority of States; hence it is clearly the duty of the Court, even independently of references made to the Convention by the Parties, to consider in what degree any of its relevant provisions are binding upon the Parties as a rule of customary international law." See also, *Gulf of Maine Case* (Canada/U.S.), [1984] I.C.J. 246 at 299: "A body of rules is not to be looked for in customary international law which in fact comprises a limited set of norms for ensuring the co-existence and vital co-operation of the members of the international community together with a set of customary rules whose presence in the opinio juris of States can be tested by induction based on the analysis of a sufficiently extensive and convincing practice, and not by deduction from preconceived ideas. . .A. . .useful course is to seek a. . .formulation of the fundamental norm. . .whose existence in the legal convictions. . .of all States is apparent from an examination of the realities of international legal relations."

§14 General principles of law recognized by civilized nations, if they were readily ascertainable, would serve as a means of preventing lacunae when a court considering an international dispute had difficulty in ascertaining a relevant rule of international law. This means that it would be incumbent upon the court, having decided which countries are to be considered as 'civilized',[75] to seek for some relevant principle which was acceptable to them in their generality. Since no judge would ever concede that his own country was uncivilized, it means in practice that he would commence his search in the light of those principles which existed in his own system of law. Further, his search would be directed to those systems which had most in common with his own,[76] so that, in fact, the general principles of law recognized by civilized nations are probably no more than those principles which are recognized by one's own system and generally by those which are recognized by oneself as being civilized. It may be assumed that if one were able to find a general principle of law which was recognized by civilized nations, such a principle would almost certainly amount to a rule of customary international law,[77] so that the World Court has been somewhat unwilling to base itself upon such general principles,[78] although in the *Namibia*

Opinion[79] the Court came very close to regarding the condemnation of discrimination as a general principle and in the *Barcelona Traction* case[80] it treated "the basic rights of the human person" as being among the obligations of international law which are binding erga omnes. While the Court may be reluctant to apply general principles, individual judges in their separate or dissenting opinions frequently do so.[81]

75. See note 46, *ante*. See also, Butler, International Law in Comparative Perspective (1980), especially Green, "Comparative Law as a Source of International Law", pp. 139-152.

76. In *Petroleum Development Ltd.* v. *Sheikh of Abu Dhabi* (1951), 18 I.L.R. 144, when seeking the proper law of the contract, Lord Asquith of Bishopstone, Umpire, held: "If any municipal system of law were applicable, it would prima facie be that of Abu Dhabi. But no such law can reasonably be said to exist. . . . Nor can I see any basis on which the municipal law of England could apply. On the contrary, Clause 17 of the Agreement [between the parties] repels the notion that the municipal law of any country, as such, could be appropriate. The terms of that Clause invite, indeed prescribe, the application of principles rooted in the good sense and common practice of the generality of civilized nations — a sort of "modern law of nature". . . . But, albeit English Municipal Law is inapplicable *as such,* some of its rules are in my view so firmly grounded in reason, as to form part of this broad body of jurisprudence — this "modern law of nature," at 149 — and he applied them accordingly.

77. That reparation is due for a wrong suffered, *Chorzów Factory* (Indemnity) (Germany/Poland) (1928), 1 W.C.R. 646 at 677; see also, separate opinion by Judge Ammoun in *Barcelona Traction Case,* [1970] I.C.J. 3, 322.

78. *Chorzów Factory (Jurisdiction)* (1927), 1 W.C.R. 589 at 610.

79. *Namibia (South-West Africa) Opinion,* [1971] I.C.J. 16, 31-32.

80. *Barcelona Traction Case, ante.*

81. See, e.g., separate opinion by Judge Padilla Nervo and Judge Ammoun in *North Sea Continental Shelf Cases, ante* at 88-89 and 132-133, respectively.

§15 Article 38(1)(e) is based on recognition of the fact that states are independent and equal, and that submission to judicial determination of a problem depends upon their consent, and it is for this reason that it confirms that a judicial decision can only be binding as between the parties to a dispute.[82] Nevertheless, the draftsmen of the Statute were aware that problems relating to international law tend to be of more than particular interest and that expositions, interpretations and applications of a legal rule will be of interest to the world at large. Moreover, since problems are likely to recur, it is probable that tribunals will look to their predecessors in order to ascertain how their colleagues, particularly those among them who have received international recognition as outstanding international jurists,[83] dealt with similar problems. This means that when the International Court refers to an earlier decision and 'applies' it to the case before the Court, it is not accepting that earlier decision as a binding precedent which has to be followed, but, aware of the need to maintain certainty in the law, accepts that the exposition of the law to which it is referring is in accord with the Court's current view of the law, and considers that earlier exposition to be one upon which it could not improve. In addition, by accepting this earlier rendering, the judges are saved the need to develop and fully explain the basis for their own view.[84]

82.   Statute, Art. 59.

83.   E.g., Huber (Swiss), Anzilotti (Italian), Lauterpacht (British).

84.   *The S.S. Lotus, ante* at 33; *Corfu Channel Case* (Preliminary Objection) (G.B./ Albania), [1948] I.C.J. 15 at 28; *Nottebohm Case* (Preliminary Objection) (Guatemala/Liechtenstein), [1953] I.C.J. 111 at 119-120, and *Second Phase,* [1955] I.C.J. 4 at 23, when the Court expressly referred "to the practice of States, arbitral and judicial decisions and to the opinions of writers".

§16   It is not only to its own decisions that the World Court has had occasion to refer for guidance. It has also made use of the decisions of the Permanent Court of Arbitration[85] and even bilateral arbitral tribunals.[86] On occasion, the World Court has also referred to the decisions of national courts,[87] while the tribunal established to hear the *Trail Smelter* dispute[88] was expressly instructed to "apply the law and practice followed in dealing with cognate questions in the United States as well as international law and practice". While the tribunal said "there are, . . . as regards both air pollution and water pollution, certain decisions of the Supreme Court of the United States which may legitimately be taken as a guide in this field of international law, for it is reasonable to follow by analogy, in international cases, precedents established by that court in dealing with controversies between States of the Union or with other controversies concerning the quasi-sovereign rights of such States, where no contrary rule prevails in international law", it went on to give the impression that as a result of its analysis it found that the United States decisions concurred with the position as it existed in international law, rather than the contrary: "The Tribunal finds that the above decisions, taken as a whole, constitute an adequate basis for its conclusions, namely, that under the principles of international law, as well as of the law of the United States, no State has the right to permit the use of its territory in such a manner as to cause injury by fumes in or to the territory of another or the properties or persons therein . . . ."

85.   Established in accordance with Hague Convention I, 1899 and 1907. Despite its title, this tribunal is neither permanent nor a court stricto sensu. It consists of a panel of national appointees, from whom the parties to a dispute select the members of a tribunal which is established ad hoc to act as arbitrators for a particular dispute. The

award of this tribunal is advisory rather than obligatory, although it has normally been complied with. For an example of its awards being made use of, see *Status of Eastern Greenland* (Denmark/Norway) (1923), 3 W.C.R. 151 at 170. See Statement by Dept. of External Affairs; §401, note 6. For a survey and assessment of the Hague peace system, see Schwarzenberger, International Law, Vol. 4, 1986, ch. 6-12.

86. *Nottebohm Case, ante* at 119, "Since the *Alabama* case, it has been generally recognised, following the earlier precedents, that, in the absence of any agreement to the contrary, an international tribunal has the right to decide as to its own jurisdiction and has the power to interpret for this purpose the instruments which govern that jurisdiction."

87. *S.S. Lotus, ante* at 43-44.

88. (U.S./Canada) (1938/1941), 3 R.I.A.A. 1905 at 1964, 1965 (Arbitral Trib.).

§17 Although the primary function of an international tribunal is to decide in accordance with international law, it may in fact be called upon to interpret rules of national law. This is particularly the case if the issue before the tribunal raises problems of conflict of laws[89] or involves issues relating to the proper law of a contract. The approach of an international tribunal to this matter has been best stated by the World Court in the *Brazilian Loans Case:*[90] "Once the Court has arrived at the conclusion that it is necessary to apply the municipal law of a particular country, there seems no doubt that it must seek to apply it as it would be applied in that country. It would not be applying the municipal law of a country if it were to apply it in a manner different from that in which the law would be applied in the country in which it is in force. It follows that the Court must pay the utmost regard to the decisions of the municipal courts of a country, for it is with the aid of their jurisprudence that it will be enabled to decide what are the rules which, in actual fact, are applied in the country the law of which is recognized as applicable in a given case. If the Court were obliged to disregard the decisions of municipal courts, the result would be that it might in certain circumstances apply rules other than those actually applied; this would seem to be contrary to the whole theory on which the application of municipal law is based. Of course, the Court will endeavour to make a just appreciation of the jurisprudence of municipal courts. If this is uncertain or divided, it will rest with the Court to select the interpretation which it considers most in conformity with the law."

89. In the case governing the *Application of the Convention of 1902 governing the Guardianship of Infants,* [1958] I.C.J. 55 the court had to examine the law of both The Netherlands and Sweden. In 1983 Canada ratified the 1980 Convention on Civil Aspects of International Child Abduction.

90. (1929), 2 W.C.R. 344.

§18   Just as it is the primary task of an international tribunal to apply international law, so it is that of a national tribunal to apply municipal law. However, there are occasions, such as for the trial of pirates[91] or of war criminals[92] when a national court has to apply international law as if it were part of the national system. There are also numerous issues which raise problems of international law which do not normally get referred to international tribunals. Among such issues are those of state[93] or diplomatic immunity[94] from suit, which are themselves closely related to issues concerning the recognition of governments[95] or states,[96] the extent of territorial waters,[97] the interpretation of, for example, treaties concerning liability for damage arising from aerial travel,[98] claims to sovereignty over land[99] which raise issues of jurisdiction,[1] and the like.[2] In many of these instances, national courts will refer to the decisions of international tribunals[3] as well as to those of other countries.[4] On occasion a court will ask national governmental authorities for a statement as to the official view towards the issue of international law.[5]

91.   E.g., *The Le Louis* (1817), 2 Dods. 210 (H.C. of Admiralty); see also, *R. v. The 'North'* (1906), 37 S.C.R. 385 (S.C.C.). See §§189-213.

92.   *R. v. Brosig,* [1945] 2 D.L.R. 232 (Ont. C.A.); *R. v. Kaehler and Stolski,* [1945] 3 D.L.R. 272 (Alta. C.A.); *R. v. Guiseppe,* [1943] S.A.L.R. T.P.D. 139; *Stanislaus Krofan v. Public Prosecutor* (Singapore), [1967] 1 Malayan L.J. 133; *Public Prosecutor v. Koi,* [1968] A.C. 829 (P.C.); *Pius Nwaoga v. State,* [1972] 1 All Nigeria L.R. 149. As to the position in Canada, see War Crimes Act, S.C. 1946, c. 73, and, more importantly, an Act to amend the Criminal Code, the Immigration Act, 1976 and the Citizenship Act, S.C. 1987, c. 37. See §§359-382.

93.   *Congo (Republic) v. Venne,* [1971] S.C.R. 997 (S.C.C.). See §§158-162.

94.   *Rose v. R.,* [1947] 3 D.L.R. 618 (Que. K.B.); *R. v. Cossette-Trudel* (1979), 52 C.C.C. (2d) 352 (Que. C.S.P.); *Supreme People's Procuratorate v. Yang Kuo-Ching* (China) (1966), 40 I.L.R. 200; *R. v. Palacios* (1984), 7 D.L.R. (4th) 112 (Ont. C.A.). See also, Lee and Vechsler, "Sovereign, Diplomatic and Consular Immunities" in Macdonald *et al.,* Canadian Perspectives on International Law and Organization (1974), p. 184. See §§151-152.

95.   *Duff Development Co. v. Kelantan,* [1924] A.C. 797 (H.L.); *Sayce v. Ameer of Behawalpur,* [1952] 1 All E.R. 326 (K.B.); [1952] 2 All E.R. 64 (C.A.). See §§96-98.

96.   *Laane & Baltser v. Estonian State Cargo & Passenger S.S. Line* (The Elise), [1949] S.C.R. 530 (S.C.C.); and see Binavince, "Canadian Practice in Matters of Recognition", in Macdonald, Canadian Perspectives on International Law and Organization, p. 153. The leading cases are *The Arantzazu Mendi,* [1939] A.C. 256 (H.L.); and *The Cristina,* [1938] A.C. 485 (H.L.). See §§94-95.

97.   See *R. v. Keyn* (The Franconia) (1876), L.R. 2 Ex. D. 63; *R. v. The 'North',* ante; *Ref. Re Offshore Mineral Rights,* [1967] S.C.R. 792 (S.C.C.); *Ref. re Continental Shelf Offshore Nfld.,* [1984] 1 S.C.R. 86 (S.C.C.). See also Herman, "The Newfoundland Offshore Mineral Rights Reference", (1984) 22 C.Y.B.I.L. 194; Jewett, "The Evolution of the Legal Regime of the Continental Shelf " 22 C.Y.B.I.L. 153, 23 C.Y.B.I.L. 201. See §§258-281.

98. *Surprenant v. Air Can.* [1973] Que. C.A. 107 (Que. C.A.); *Day v. Trans-World Airlines Inc.* (1975), 393 F. Supp. 217 (U.S. Dist. Ct.); (1975), 528 F. 2d 31; *Fothergill v. Monarch Airlines*, [1980] 2 All E.R. 696 (H.L.). See §230.

99. *Re Labrador Boundary*, [1927] 2 D.L.R. 401 (P.C.). See §§237-257.

1. *R. v. Tootalik* E4-321 (1969), 71 W.W.R. 435 (N.W. Terr. Ct.); reversed on other grounds (1970), 74 W.W.R. 740 (N.W.T. C.A.).

2. For discussion of a number of these issues in Canada, see Macdonald, "The Relationship between International Law and Domestic Law in Canada", in Canadian Perspectives on International Law and Organization, p. 88.

3. See *Société Intercommunale Belge d'Electricité*, [1933] 1 Ch. 684 at 689-690 (C.A.); affirmed [1934] A.C. 161 at 173 (*sub nom. Feist v. Société Belge d'Electricité*) (H.L.); *R. v. International Trustee for the Protection of Bondholders Aktiengesellschaft*, [1937] A.C. 500 at 514 (H.L.); *Bank voor Handel en Scheepvart v. Slatford*, [1953] Q.B. 248 at 271 (Que. C.A.) in which Devlin J. found support for his view in the arbitration decision between the Reparation Commission and the United States — which he wrongly attributed to the Permanent Court — in the *Standard Oil Co. Tankers Claim*, (1926) 8 B.Y.I.L. 156. See also, Jenks, The Prospects of International Adjudication (1964), ch. 13; Schreuer, "The Authority of International Judicial Practice in Domestic Courts," (1974) 23 I.C.L.Q. 681; "The Implementation of International Judicial Decisions by Domestic Courts", (1975) 24 I.C.L.Q. 153, and "Concurrent Jurisdiction of National and International Tribunals," (1976) 13 Houston L.R. 508 as well as Decisions of International Institutions before Domestic Courts (1981). Courts of members of the European Community are being increasingly compelled to pay attention to the decisions of the European Court; see *Henn v. D.P.P.*, [1980] 2 W.L.R. 597 at 633 (H.L.) in which the House of Lords referred a preliminary issue to the European Court of Justice and then delivered judgment, in the light of that court's opinion and *Internationale Handels-gesellschaft mbH v. Einführ- und Vorratstelle für Getreide und Futtermittel*, [1974] 2 C.M.L.R. 540 (Federal Constitutional Ct. of Germany).

4. See *Congo (Republic) v. Venne*, [1971] S.C.R. 997 (S.C.C.); *Zodiack Int. Products Inc. v. Polish People's Republic* (1977), 4 B.L.R. 179 (Que. C.A.); *The Philippine Admiral*, [1976] 2 W.L.R. 216 (P.C.); *Trendtex Trading Corp. v. Central Bank of Nigeria*, [1977] 2 W.L.R. 356 (C.A.).

5. See memo by Legal Bureau of Dept. of External Affairs, 29 Apr. 1983, (1984) 22 C.Y.B.I.L. 331-3. See §51.

§19 When assessing the relative persuasive authority of international judicial decisions, those of permanent tribunals, and particularly of the International Court of Justice and its predecessor the Permanent Court of International Justice, take pride of place. Insofar as specialist courts are concerned, such as the European Communities Court, now known as the European Court of Justice, or the European Court of Human Rights, these may even supplant the World Court in their own field. The same is true of a tribunal established on a permanent basis by a bilateral treaty with the task of settling disputes arising under that treaty.[6] Insofar as other arbitral tribunals are concerned, their authority depends to a great extent upon the stature of individual arbitrators,[7] although the Permanent Court of Arbitration tends to receive higher respect since the arbitrators constitute a standing panel and the parties, generally speaking, have no control as to the procedure to be followed or the rules of law applied.[8] These comments apply more to the practice of international judicial tribunals than they do to that of national tribunals, for since these are, generally speaking, required to apply national law, there tends to be a hesitancy among them to refer to international decisions, although this is now changing and depends to a great extent upon the national courts involved, some countries paying more attention than others.[9]

6.   Such as the Iran-United States Claims Tribunal established under the Claims Settlement Declaration, 1981, 20 I.L.M. 230.

7.   This is clear from the respect accorded to Huber, sole arbitrator in the *Island of Palmas Case* (Netherlands/U.S.) (1928), 2 R.I.A.A. 829, former President and at the time of this arbitration Vice-President of the Permanent Court of International Justice.

8.   Unless specifically agreed otherwise by the parties, the P.C.A. operates in accordance with the terms of the Hague Convention for the Pacific Settlement of International Disputes, 1907, 100 B.F.S.P. 298.

9.   See literature cited in note 3. *Ref. re Continental Shelf Offshore Newfoundland,* [1984] 1 S.C.R. 86 (S.C.C.) the Supreme Court of Canada referred to the *North Sea Continental Shelf Cases,* [1969] I.C.J. 3, and the *Petroleum Development Ltd., v. Sheikh of Abu Dhabi* arbitration (1952), 18 I.L.R. 144.

§20   Since all states are sovereign equals it follows that, in strict law, the national courts of every country are entitled to equal respect, bearing in mind the internal hierarchy of each country, with the decisions of superior courts obviously prevailing over those of inferior tribunals. In practice, however, the courts of older countries, which have had long experience in international activity, and particularly those of the United Kingdom[10] and the United States,[11] tend to be referred to in preference to those of the newer countries. Similarly, where for geographic or political reasons a country may be considered as having specialist experience, such as the United Kingdom so far as the law of the sea is concerned,[12] the decisions of the courts of that country tend to be referred to. Occasionally, a particular judge has acquired sufficient status and general respect that foreign courts are prepared to treat his judgments as persuasive.[13]

10.   *Eichmann v. A.G. Israel* (1962), 36 I.L.R. 277; *Re Dom. Coal v. Cape Breton* (1963), 40 D.L.R. (2d) 593 (N.S. C.A.); *State v. Director of Prisons; Ex parte Schumann* (Ghana), [1966] G.L.R. 433 (C.A.); *Congo (Republic) v. Venne, ante.*

11. *Eichmann v. A.G. Israel, ante; Congo (Republic) v. Venne, ante; The Philippine Admiral, ante;* the Privy Council also referred to the *Venne* decision, as well as *Flota Maritima Browning de Cuba S.A. v. S.S. Can. Conqueror,* [1962] S.C.R. 598 (S.C.C.).

12. See *Rose v. Himely* (1808), 8 U.S. 241.

13. This is true of such persons as Lord Stowell (Sir William Scott), Chief Justice Marshall and Justice Story. See, e.g., Simmonds, Cases on the Law of the Sea, Vol. 1 (1976), Introduction.

§21 Although Article 38(1)(d) of the Statute of the World Court refers to the writings of the most highly qualified publicists of the various nations as a subsidiary source for determining the rules of law, the World Court has been reticent about citing any writers by name. The Court's attitude may be illustrated by its comments in *The S.S. Lotus* decision:[14] "as regards teachings of publicists, and apart from the question as to what their value may be from the point of view of establishing the existence of a rule of customary law, it is no doubt true that all or nearly all writers teach that ships on the high seas are subject exclusively to the jurisdiction of the State whose flag they fly. . . . On the other hand, there is no lack of writers who, upon a close study of the special question whether a State can prosecute for offences committed on board a foreign ship on the high seas, definitely come to the conclusion that such offences must be regarded as if they had been committed in the territory of the State whose flag the ship flies, and that consequently the general rules of each legal system in regard to offences committed abroad are applicable." Arbitral tribunals have been a little more tolerant towards writers, and in the *Tinoco Concessions* case[15] Chief Justice Taft as sole arbitrator seemed to hold writers in high estimation: "I have not been cited to text writers of authority or to decisions of significance indicating a general acquiescence of nations in such a rule. Without this, it cannot be applied here as a principle of international law." In the course of his award he did, however, quote Moore[16] and Borchard[17] and cited Kent, Wheaton, Hall and Woolsey. The German-Portuguese Special Tribunal in its opinion on the *Naulilaa* claim[18] made frequent reference to writers. Individual judges, when delivering separate or dissenting opinions, frequently have recourse to named writers,[19] many of whom tend to be somewhat obscure and hardly satisfying the definition embodied in Article 38.[20]

14. *Ante* at 41. The International Court of Justice has referred to the "tendency [which] prevails in the writings of publicists" and "the opinions of writers" (*Nottebohm Case* (Second Phase), [1955] 1 C.J. 4 at 22, 23).

15. (G.B./Costa Rica) (1973), 1 R.I.A.A. 369 at 384.

16. Digest of International Law, (1906).

17. Diplomatic Protection of Citizens Abroad (1928).

18.   (1928), 2 R.I.A.A. 1019 at 1025-1026, 1027, 1031. The Italian-U.S. Conciliation Commission in the *Mergé Claim* (1955), 14 R.I.A.A. 236, also cited writers (at 244-246), and said of the principle of dual nationality, which had its origin in private international law, that "decisions and legal writings . . . quickly transported it to the realm of public international law."

19.   This may be confirmed by consulting the list of authorities cited in each volume of Hambro/Rovine, The Case Law of the International Court. In the case concerning *Military and Paramilitary Activities in and against Nicaragua,* [1984] I.C.J. 392 at 468, Mosler J. cited both Briggs and Waldock.

20.   These have included student articles in law journals and unpublished theses.

§22   National courts are more prone to refer to individual writers by name than are international tribunals and tend, for the main part, to refer to the dead rather than the living, particularly making use of such classical writers as Grotius, Bynkershoek, Vattel and the like, with the same writers frequently being quoted to opposite effect by majority and minority judges.[21] In addition, it is noticeable that, regardless of the nationality of the tribunal, national judges appear to be equally aware as to the identity of those writers who are most universally recognized.[22] When a writer is cited, his status is the same as it is for a national tribunal faced with a problem of national law. He is cited as evidence of what the law may be and not as a dogmatic expression of the law.[23]

21.   *R. v. Keyn* (The Franconia), *ante*, is a good example of this.

22.   Perhaps the most commonly cited of modern writers is Oppenheim, International Law, particularly in the Lauterpacht editions. In *Rose v. R.,* [1947] 3 D.L.R. 618 (Que. K.B.) Bissonnette J. cited, among others, Fauchille, Bynkershoek, Vattel, Calvo, LeFur, Oppenheim, and Martens.

23.   In *Spinney's (1948) Ltd. v. Royal Insurance Co. Ltd.*, [1980] Ll. R. 406 at 429, Mustill J. said, "The statements of jurists are a useful source of insights, but they do not provide a direct solution."

§23   It is becoming more common nowadays, particularly in the case of international tribunals, to refer to state practice, rather than writers. "This refers to the practice adopted by States in their administrative and diplomatic actions, in their attitude towards the work of codification of the League of Nations and the United Nations and, where appropriate, in their domestic practice. If there is a consistent body of state practice and some international action in line with it, the result may be the genesis of a rule of customary law.[24] But if state practice is contradictory it may not be possible to adduce the existence of a general rule of law."[25] Once again, it must be borne in mind that the practice of some states may be of greater significance than that of others.[26]

24. *Nottebohm Case* (Second Phase), [1955] I.C.J. 4 at 21-23. See also, *Reservations to the Genocide Convention,* [1951] I.C.J. 15 at 22, 24; *North Sea Continental Shelf Cases* (Germany/Denmark; Germany/Netherlands), [1969] I.C.J. 3 at 44-45.

25. Rosenne, The Law and Practice of the International Court (1965), p. 616.

26. See §20.

§24 Increasingly, today, states have an opportunity to express their views as to the state of the law in a co-operative fashion by way of resolutions and declarations of international organizations. Strictly speaking, such resolutions and declarations lack any binding effect,[27] but "when they are concerned with general norms of international law", even when the organ itself or the resolution declares that it is a general norm, "then acceptance by a majority vote constitutes *evidence* of the opinions of governments in the world forum for the expression of such opinions. Even when they are framed as general principles, resolutions of this kind provide a basis for the progressive development of the law and the speedy consolidation of customary rules."[28] Constant reiteration in a series of resolutions, particularly if followed by state compliance, would constitute strong evidence of the development of a rule of customary law. The International Court has recognized the validity of resolutions of both the General Assembly and the Security Council in its *Namibia Opinion,*[29] and in the *Western Sahara* decision,[30] while individual judges have treated General Assembly resolutions in the field of human rights and the condemnation of apartheid as obligatory in every respect.[31] The Government of Canada has pointed out[32] that "while declarations are not per se legally binding instruments, they are widely referred to by some governments, NGO's and academics as indicators of standards to which states should aspire. In addition, Canadian courts have referred to U.N. declarations in interpreting Canadian law, despite the unresolved status of declarations under international law. For example, in the recent case of *McCann v. R.,*[33] the U.N. Standard Minimum Rules for the Treatment of Prisoners[34] were referred to in interpreting the meaning of 'cruel or unusual punishment' under the Canadian Bill of Rights. We therefore think such declarations should be examined rigorously both from the point of view of our ability to apply them domestically and their consistency with other principles or rules of international law. They should be as clear and precise in legal terms as possible and from a Canadian point of view should reflect standards: (1) with which Canada currently complies or (2) with which Canada intends to comply or (3) that Canada has an interest in other countries complying with."

27. See separate opinion by Lauterpacht J. *South-West Africa — Voting Procedure,* [1955] I.C.J. 67 at 115 *et seq.* See §417.

28. Brownlie, Principles of International Law (1979), p. 14 (italics in original). See *Military and Paramilitary Activities in and against Nicaragua* (Nicaragua/U.S.), [1986] I.C.J. 14, 99-100.

29. (South-West Africa), [1971] I.C.J. 16 at 46-57.

30. [1975] I.C.J. 4 at 30-37.

31. *Namibia Opinion, ante,* separate opinion by Vice-President Ammoun at 55.

32. Legal Bureau Memo, December 11, 1984, (1985), 23 C.Y.B.I.L. 347.

33. (1975), 68 D.L.R. (3d) 661 (Fed. T.D.).

34. Adopted by First U.N. Congress on the Prevention of Crime and the Treatment of Offenders, 1955, U.N., Human Rights: A Compilation of International Instruments, 1978, p. 65.

§25 Perhaps one of the clearest statements of the role of such resolutions today is to be found in Judge Tanaka's dissenting opinion in the *South West Africa Cases*:[35] "The appearance of organizations such as the League of Nations and the United Nations, with their agencies and affiliated institutions, replacing an important part of the traditional individualistic method of international negotiation by the method of 'parliamentary diplomacy', is bound to influence the mode of generation of customary international law. A State, instead of pronouncing its view to a few States directly concerned, has the opportunity, through the medium of an organization, to declare its position to all members of the organization and to know immediately their reaction on the same matter. In former days, practice, repetition and opinio juris sive necessitatis, which are the ingredients of customary law might be combined together in a very long and slow process extending over centuries. In the contemporary age of highly developed techniques of communication and information, the formation of a custom through the medium of international organizations is greatly facilitated and accelerated; the establishment of such a custom would require no more than one generation or even far less than that. This is one of the examples of the transformation of law inevitably produced by change in the social substratum."

35. (Second Phase), [1966] I.C.J. 6 at 291.

§26 While a resolution or declaration does not of itself possess obligatory force, it may contain elements which are expressive of the law, as was the case with the resolution affirming the Principles of International Law Recognized by the Charter and Judgment of the Nuremberg Tribunal.[36] The difference between a declaration and a resolution of the General Assembly of the United Nations has been explained by the Legal Department of the Secretariat:[37] "in view of the greater solemnity and significance of a declaration, it may be considered to import, on behalf of the organ adopting it, a strong expectation that Members of the international community will abide by it. Consequently, insofar as the expectation is gradually justified by State practice, a declaration may by custom become recognized as laying down rules binding upon States. In conclusion, it may be said that in United Nations practice, a declaration is a solemn instrument resorted to only in very rare cases relating to matters of major and lasting importance where maximum compliance is expected." In fact, the practice of issuing resolutions as declarations is becoming increasingly common, while it cannot be said that states are showing great willingness to abide by them or to regard their content as obligatory. Even when states comply with such declarations, it is by virtue of that state practice and not by way of the declaration that a rule of international law evolves. The Canadian view of the significance of United Nations resolutions is that "they are recommendations addressed to Member States and do not create legal obligations binding in international law. [However] to the extent that [they] are intended to be declaratory of international law, are adopted with the support of all or most Member States, and are observed in practice, resolutions such as the Universal Declaration of Human Rights may in time become evidence of the rules of customary international law on a particular subject."[38]

36. Res. 95 (I), Dec. 11, 1946, U.N.Y.B. 1946-47, 254.

37. U.N. Doc. E/CM.4/L 610, Apr. 2, 1962, cited in Schermers, International Institutional Law, (1972) p. 500.

38. Letter of the Legal Bureau, June 17, 1985, (1986), 24 C.Y.B.I.L. 396. For the Canadian view of the significance of declarations, see §24.

§27   When the International Court is called upon to examine the administrative practice of an international institution, it may rely on the practice of the United Nations as well as other specialized agencies in addition to that of the particular organization under discussion. This was in fact what the Court did in the course of its opinion on *Judgments of the Administrative Tribunal of the I.L.O. Upon Complaints Made Against UNESCO.*[39]

39. [1956] I.C.J. 77 at 91. See §§428-435.

§28   Although Article 38 of the Statute of the court indicates no particular hierarchy as among the law-creating processes and law-determining agencies, it is clear both in logic and in judicial practice that treaties, as the expression of the will of states, stand supreme and will prevail even over customary rules to the contrary.[40] Custom will prevail over general principles, although in practice the latter will probably amount to customary law. As to the hierarchy among the law-determining agencies, doctrinal writings come last, especially when there are judicial decisions or evidence of state practice[41] to the contrary.

40. See *The S.S. Wimbledon* (U.K., France, Italy, Japan/Germany) (1923), 1 W.C.R. 163 at 179.

41. More and more states are now making their state practice available, e.g., U.S.A.: Whiteman, Digest of International Law as supplemented by annual volumes of the Digest of U.S. Practice in International Law; France: Kiss, Répertoire Français de Droit International Public; Italy: La Prassi Italiana di Diritto Internazionale; Japan: Oda and Owada, The Practice of Japan in International Law, 1961-1970; U.K.: British Digest of International Law (only isolated volumes). In addition, most of the leading journals of international law contain supplements relating to local state practice, and individual writers are producing works expressing their national view, e.g. Castel, International Law Chiefly as Interpreted and Applied in Canada (1976/1987 ed. by Kindred, Castel and others), and the earlier Mackenzie and Laing, Canada and the Law of Nations (1938) and the collection of specialized essays in Macdonald *et al.*, Canadian Perspectives on International Law and Organization (1974); O'Connell, International Law in Australia (1965); T.M.C. Asser Institute, International Law in The Netherlands (1978-). See also, Cohen and Hungda, People's China and International Law, 1974; Oda and Owada, The Practice of Japan in International Law 1961-1970, 1982. For further references, see Green, "The Raw Materials of International Law", (1980), 29 I.C.L.Q. 187.

§29 It is possible that states, while willing to have their disputes adjudicated by a third party, even the International Court of Justice, are unwilling to have the decision rendered in accordance with the strict letter of the law. This possibility is recognized in Article 38(2) of the court's Statute which permits decisions ex aequo et bono at the express request of both parties to the dispute. Broadly speaking, it may be said that this enables the court to render a fair and equitable decision, especially when a decision according to the strict letter of the law might produce an injustice. In this, it represents English equity as originally understood. However, bearing in mind the rules and regulations that now attach to equity, care must be taken not to equate principles ex aequo et bono with Anglo-American conceptions of equity. Moreover, these principles differ from what is generally regarded as equity in juristic thinking, a point that is well illustrated by a comment of Judge Hudson in his individual opinion on the *Diversion of Waters from the Meuse*:[42] "The Court has not been expressly authorized by its Statute to apply equity as distinguished from law. .... Article 38 of the Statute expressly directs the application of 'general principles of law recognized by civilized nations', and in more than one nation principles of equity have an established place in the legal system. The Court's recognition of equity as a part of international law is in no way restricted by the special power conferred upon it 'to decide a case ex aequo et bono, if the parties agree thereto'. . . . It must be concluded, therefore, that under Article 38 of the Statute, if not independently of that Article, the Court has some freedom to consider principles of equity as part of the international law which it must apply."

42. (Netherlands/Belgium) (1937), 4 W.C.R. 178 at 232.

§30 To date, the court has never had occasion to decide a case in accordance with these principles, although by its declaration under Article 36 of the Statute[43] Guatemala expressly reserved 'the dispute between England and Guatemala concerning the restoration of the territory of Belize', unless the case were decided, as Guatemala had proposed during diplomatic discussions, ex aequo et bono. While Great Britain had already accepted the compulsory jurisdiction of the court, she considered it necessary to make a special declaration[44] accepting "the jurisdiction of the Court in all legal disputes concerning the interpretation, application or validity of any treaty relating to the boundaries of British Honduras [which meant the Belize dispute], and over any questions arising out of any conclusion which the Court may reach with regard to such treaty." Great Britain clearly thought that it had law on its side, while Guatemala considered only an extra-legal judgment might favour its view of the matter. Since the parties could not agree, the issue has never come to court.

43. Jan. 27, 1947; see Rosenne, Documents on the International Court of Justice (1979), p. 232. This declaration has now been withdrawn.
44. Feb. 13, 1946, Rosenne, *op. cit.*, p. 408 (now expired).

§31 Failure to authorize the court to decide ex aequo et bono may result in the court's inability to render an effective decision. Thus, the judgment in the *Haya de la Torre* case[45] concludes: "Having thus decided in accordance with the Havana Convention[46] the legal relations between the Parties with regard to the matters referred to it, the Court has completed its task. It is unable to give any practical advice as to the various courses which might be followed with a view to terminating the asylum, since, by doing so, it would depart from its judicial function. But it can be assumed that the Parties, now that their mutual legal relations have been made clear, will be able to find a practical and satisfactory solution by seeking guidance from these considerations of courtesy and good-neighbourliness which, in matters of asylum, have always held a prominent place in the relations between the Latin-American republics."[47]

45. [1951] I.C.J. 71 at 83 (Colombia/Peru).

46. Convention on Asylum, 1928, 132 L.N.T.S. 323: the court held that there was no legal right for the Colombian ambassador to provide asylum, and that the asylum should, therefore, be terminated.

47. The court considered the grant of diplomatic asylum in Latin America to be, in the absence of a treaty obligation, a mere usage and not a legal custom.

2. INTERNATIONAL AND NATIONAL LAW

§32 It is often debated among legal theorists whether national, or municipal as it is more commonly described by international lawyers, or international law holds supremacy the one over the other. For the main part, this discussion is theoretical and lacks practical significance. Prima facie, national courts will apply national law,[49] while international courts will decide in accordance with international law.[50] However, it may happen that an issue touching international law, such as the immunity of a foreign state[51] or diplomat,[52] may come before a national tribunal, while questions of national law, such as matters of contract[53] or the guardianship of infants,[54] may be in issue before an international tribunal. In such circumstances problems concerning the interrelationship of the two systems have to be examined.

49. For consideration of the interplay of national and international law by the Canadian court, see *Ref. re Continental Shelf Offshore Nfld.,* [1984] 1 S.C.R. 86 (S.C.C.); see also Herman, "The Newfoundland Offshore Mineral Rights Reference," (1984), 22 C.Y.B.I.L. 194.

50. Statute of the I.C.J., Art. 38: "The Court, whose function it is to decide in accordance with international law such disputes as are submitted to it, shall decide . . ."

51. *Congo (Republic) v. Venne,* [1971] S.C.R. 997 (S.C.C.).

52. *Ref. Re Power of Municipalities to Levy Rates on Foreign Legations & High Commrs. Residences,* [1943] S.C.R. 208 (S.C.C.); *Rose v. R.,* [1947] 3 D.L.R. 618 (Que. K.B.); *R. v. Palacios* (1984), 7. D.L.R. (4th) 112 (Ont. C.A.)

53. *Serbian and Brazilian Loans Cases* (1929), 1 W.C.R. 344.

54. *Application of the Convention of 1902 Governing the Guardianship of Infants,* [1958] I.C.J. 55.

§33 Some national constitutions make specific reference to international law as part of the law and may even go so far as to recognize the supremacy of international law. This is the case with the Basic Law of the German Federal Republic,[55] so that national laws which run counter to what the Basic Law describes as "general rules of public international law"[56] are, to that extent, null and void. Moreover, the Basic Law provides that such rules directly affect inhabitants of the Federal Republic, creating rights and imposing duties for them. On the other hand, violation of treaty obligations undertaken by the Federal Republic by reason of national law does not result in the invalidity of the legislation in question.[57]

55.   Art. 25: "The general rules of public international law are an integral part of federal law. They shall take precedence over the laws and shall directly create rights and duties for the inhabitants of the federal territory."

56.   The reference to international law does not include treaties unless they are declaratory of such general rules, nor rules of customary international law which do not amount to fundamental legal norms unalterable by treaty law (jus cogens, see §4 notes 14, 15). Any other rule of customary law will be revoked by later treaty provisions to which the Federal Republic is a party and do not become part of Germany's fundamental law, see *Assessment of Aliens for War Taxation Case* (1965), 43 I.L.R. 3.

57.   *Denominational Schools Case* (1967), 57 I.L.R. 1. See also *Internationale Handelsgesellschaft mbH v. Einführ- und Vorratsstelle für Getreide und Futtermittel*, [1974] 2 C.M.L.R. 540 (Fed. Constitutional Ct. of Germany).

§34   In other countries, for example the United States, the impact of international law upon national law is not so far-reaching. It is true that the Supreme Court operates on the basis that "International law is part of our law, and must be ascertained and administered by the courts of justice of appropriate jurisdiction, as often as rights depending upon it are duly presented for their determination. For this purpose, where there is no treaty, and no controlling executive or legislative act or judicial decision, resort must be had to the customs and usages of civilised nations."[58] Treaties, however, enjoy a special status under the Constitution.[59] This provides that all treaties[60] made by the United States constitute the supreme law of the land and override any state constitution or legislative act to the contrary. Since treaties are brought into effect by a two-thirds vote of the Senate,[61] as are all legislative measures, they override prior legislative measures inconsistent therewith.[62] However, later federal statutes will, from the point of view of United States national law, override earlier treaties with which such legislation is incompatible,[63] provided it appears to the courts that it was the intention of Congress to supersede the prior treaty by such legislation,[64] it being the presumption there as elsewhere that it is not the intention of the government to enact legislation incompatible with the country's international obligations.[65] Any international treaty obligation overridden by subsequent statute remains internationally binding upon the United States.[66]

58.   *The Paquete Habana* (1900), 175 U.S. 677 at 700, per Justice Gray; see also, *Filatiga v. Pena-Irala* (1980), 630 F. 2d 876.

59.   Art. VI, s. 2: "This Constitution and the Laws of the United States which shall be made in Pursuance thereof; and all Treaties made, or which shall be made under the Authority of the United States, shall be the supreme Law of the Land; and the Judges of every State shall be bound thereby, any Thing in the Constitution or Laws of Any State to the Contrary notwithstanding."

60.   The Constitution only refers to treaties, it does not include international arrangements resulting from executive agreements.

61.   Art. II, s. 2(2): the President "shall have power, by and with the advice of the Senate, to make treaties, provided two-thirds of the Senators present concur."

62.   *Cook v. United States* (1933), 288 U.S. 102. This only refers to self-executing treaties which do not require special legislation to make them effective internally. Whether a treaty is self-executing depends upon its interpretation (see American Law Institute's Second Restatement, Foreign Relations Law of the United States, (1965), ss. 147, 154); see also 1980 Tentative Draft No. 1 of Revised Restatement, ss. 131, 333, 334).

63.   *Chinese Exclusion Case* (1889), 130 U.S. 581.

64.   See *Cook v. United States, ante.*

65.   *Moser v. United States* (1951), 341 U.S. 41.

66.   Foreign Relations Law of the United States, s. 138. (For a later enunciation of the relationship between U.S. law and treaties, see 1980 Tentative Draft No. 1 of Revised Restatement, ss. 134-135).

§35 Problems will arise when states undertake treaty obligations which confer direct rights upon their nationals. If the national legislation has been amended to give effect to such provisions, there is no problem. This is the case with the United Kingdom's membership of the European Community in accordance with the Treaty of Rome.[67] In accordance with that Treaty the English Courts are obliged to refer issues concerning the application or interpretation of that Treaty to the European Court of Justice and must then apply such judgments as the court delivers.[68] The situation is different, however, when the treaty conferring such direct rights has not been embodied into legislation. By the European Convention on Human Rights,[69] the United Kingdom has acknowledged that its residents are entitled to the rights therein spelled out and by virtue of a declaration made under Article 25[70] such residents may lodge complaints to the Commission which, by Article 48,[71] may refer the matter to the European Court of Human Rights. Any judgment of the court is binding upon the party concerned.[72] The United Kingdom has not enacted the Convention into law and has been the defendant in a number of cases, many of which have been decided against her. In some cases, even in the absence of legislation, damages have been paid,[73] while in others the law has been amended to bring it into line with the decision.[74]

67. 1957, 298 U.N.T.S. 11, the U.K. acceded in 1972, Sweet & Maxwell's European Community Treaties, 1972, 244.

68. See *Henn v. D.P.P.*, [1980] 2 W.L.R. 597 (H.L.).

69. 1952, 213 U.N.T.S. 222.

70. "1. The Commission may receive petitions. . .from any person, non-governmental organization or group of individuals claiming to be the victim of a violation . . . , provided that the High Contracting Party against which the complaint has been lodged has declared that it recognizes the competence of the Commission to receive the complaint. . ."

71. "The following may bring a case before the Court, provided that the High Contracting Party concerned. . . [is] subject to the jurisdiction of the Court or, failing that, with the consent of the High Contracting Party concerned. . ."

72. Article 53.

73. See *Young, James and Webster Case* (1981/1982) 62 I.L.R. 359; 70 I.L.R. 334.

74. See *Dudgeon Case* (1981), 67 I.L.R. 395 — the law was changed by the Homosexual Offences (Northern Ireland) Order 1982.

§36   While Canada is not a party to any human rights treaty which, like the European Convention on Human Rights, confers enforceable rights upon its citizens, it is a party to the International Covenant on Civil and Political Rights.[75] The Covenant has no organ like the European Court, but Canada is a party to the Optional Protocol to the Covenant.[76] By Arlticle 1 "a State Party to the Covenant that becomes a party to the. . .Protocol recognizes the competence of the [Human Rights] Committee [established in accordance with Part IV of the Covenant] to receive and consider communications from individuals subject to its jurisdiction who claim to be victims of a violation by that State Party of any of the rights set forth in the Covenant."[77] While the Committee has only the power to make findings of fact or make recommendations, which may be ignored, such findings may lead to amendments in the national law to bring it into line with the obligations undertaken in accordance with the Covenant.[78]

75. 999 U.N.T.S. 171 — Canada acceded in 1976.

76. See note 75.

77. See *MacIsaac v. Canada* (1982), 71 I.L.R. 337 (U.N. Human Rights Committee) in which it was held that the non-retroactivity of sections of the 1977 Criminal Law Amendment Act vis-à-vis the 1970 Parole Act was not a breach of the Covenant.

78. See *Lovelace v. Canada* (1981), 68 I.L.R. 17 (U.N. Human Rights Committee) in which it was held that s. 12(1)(*b*) of the 1952 Indian Act was contrary to the non-discriminatory provisions of the Covenant. Canada accordingly amended the Indian Act; see also, Bayefsky, 'The Human Rights Committee and the Case of Sandra Lovelace', (1982), 20 C.Y.B.I.L. 244. See also *Koowarta v. Bjelke-Petersen* (1982), 68 I.L.R. 134 (Aust. H.C.)

§37 Generally speaking, insofar as customary international law is concerned, within Commonwealth countries this law, provided there is no statute to the contrary, tends to be applied as part of the law of the land.[79] This view that international law is part of the common law and thus part of the law of the land stems from Blackstone's statement[80] that in England "the law of nations is adopted in it's [sic] full extent by the common law, and is held to be part of the law of the land. And those acts of parliament, which have been made from time to time enforce this universal law, or to facilitate the execution of it's decisions, are not to be considered as introductive of any new rule, but merely as declaratory of the old fundamental constitutions of the kingdom,[81] without which it must cease to be part of the civilized world."

79. *R. v. The 'North'* (1906), 37 S.C.R. 385 (S.C.C.) at 394, per Davis J.; *Ref. Re Exemption of U.S. Forces from Proceedings in Cdn. Criminal Courts,* [1943] S.C.R. 483 (S.C.C.) at 516, per Taschereau J.

80. Commentaries on the Laws of England (1765), Vol. 4, ch. 5 (10th ed., 1787), 67.

81. *The Amazone,* [1940] P. 40 at 47 (C.A.), per Goddard L.J.

§38 The position in Canada is perhaps best expressed by the comment of Taschereau J. in the *Ref. Re. Exemption of U.S. Forces from Canadian Criminal Courts:*[82] ". . . I do not forget that international law has no application in Canada unless incorporated in our own domestic law. . . . The same principle has been held by this Court in the *Foreign Legations Reference,*[83] where my Lord the Chief Justice said: 'I think . . . that the proper conclusion from the legislation of the Imperial Parliament, particularly in the eighteenth century, in force, as some of the statutes were, when the common law was formally introduced into Upper Canada, . . . is that this rule, recognized by France, is also implicit in the principles of international law recognized by the law of England; and, consequently by the law of Ontario'. If not accepted in this country, international law would not be binding, but would merely be a code of unenforceable abstract rules of international morals. . . . I have come to the conclusion that there exists such a body of rules adopted by the nations of the world. These rules have been accepted by the highest courts of the United States, and some of them, applicable to the present case, have also been accepted by the Judicial Committee. I have to acknowledge their existence, and treat them as incorporated[84] in our domestic law. . . . And I see nothing in the laws of the land inconsistent with their application within our territory."[85]

82. [1943] S.C.R. 483 at 516 (S.C.C.).

83. *Ref. re Power of Municipalities to Levy Rates on Foreign Legations & High Commrs. Residences,* [1943] S.C.R. 208 at 230-231 (S.C.C.) per Sir Lyman Duff.

84. For discussion of the Canadian attitude to the doctrine of incorporation, see Herman, 'The Newfoundland Offshore Mineral Rights Reference: An Imperfect Mingling of International and Municipal Law', (1984), 22 C.Y.B.I.L. 194.

85. See Vanek, 'Is International Law Part of the Law of Canada?' (1949-50) 8 U. of T.L.J. 251; Macdonald, 'The Relationship Between International and Domestic Law in Canada,' in Macdonald et al., Canadian Perspectives on International Law and Organization, 1974, p. 88.

§39 Insofar as the United Kingdom is concerned, perhaps one of the clearest statements of the position is to be found in the comment of Lord Alverstone C.J. in *West Rand Gold Mining Co. Ltd. v. R.*[86] regarding "the proposition that international law forms part of the law of England. . . . It is quite true that whatever has received the common consent of civilized nations must have received the assent of our country, and that to which we have assented along with other nations in general may properly be called international law, and as such will be acknowledged and applied by our municipal tribunals when legitimate occasion arises for those tribunals to decide questions to which doctrines of international law may be relevant. But any doctrine so invoked must be one really accepted as binding between nations, and the international law sought to be applied must, like anything else, be proved by satisfactory evidence, which must show either that the particular proposition put forward has been recognized and acted upon by our own country, or that it is of such a nature, and has been so widely and generally accepted, that it can hardly be supposed that any civilized State would repudiate it."[87]

86. [1905] 2 K.B. 391 at 406 (D.C.).

87. Thus, in *Germany (Federal Republic) v. Rauca* (1982), 38 O.R. (2d) 705 at 708 (Ont. H.C.), Evans C.J. held that extradition treaties were within what s. 1 of the Canadian Charter of Rights and Freedoms (Constitution Act, 1982 [en. Canada Act, 1982 (U.K.) c. 11]) describes as "such reasonable limits prescribed by law as can be demonstrably justified in a free and democratic society." He was accepting "the well-recognized rule that courts apply a fair and liberal interpretation with a view to fulfilling Canada's international obligations in the community of nations." This decision was confirmed by the Court of Appeal which referred, also, to various international human rights instruments: (1983), 41 O.R. (2d) 225 (Ont. C.A.); *R. v. Ashford Remand Home (Governor); ex parte Postlethwaite,* [1987] 3 W.L.R. 1141, in which the House of Lords held that extradition treaties were to be interpreted liberally as contracts and not as statutes. See also *United States v. Smith* (1983), 42 O.R. (2d) 668 (Ont. H.C.).

§40 Despite the fact that Blackstone's statement appears to be dogmatic and Lord Alverstone appears to agree with him, more recent decisions of the English courts would indicate that it is only those rules of customary international law which have been clearly accepted and adopted by the English courts which will now be so respected. Thus, in

R. v. Secretary of State for the Home Department; Ex parte Thrakrar,[88] Lord Denning M.R. referred to earlier authorities to this effect, and opined that "they were speaking . . . only of that part of [international law] which was universally accepted and known for certain, such as the immunity of ambassadors. They were not speaking of rules which were not universally accepted or known for certain. In my opinion, the rules of international law only become part of our law insofar as they are accepted and adopted by us. I would follow the words of Lord Atkin in *Chung Chi Cheung v. R.*:[89] 'It must always be remembered that, so far, at any rate, as the courts of this country are concerned, international law has no validity save insofar as its principles are accepted and adopted by our own domestic law'." But this reference to acceptance by domestic law does not signify that a statute to this effect is required. It is sufficient that judicial practice has accepted the rule in issue.[90]

88. [1974] 1 Q.B. 684 at 701 (C.A.).

89. [1939] A.C. 160 at 167 (P.C.). This statement was also cited with approval by Duff C.J. in the *Foreign Legations Case*, [1943] S.C.R. 208 at 213 (S.C.C.).

90. See *Oppenheimer v. Cattermole*, [1976] A.C. 249 at 277 (H.L.), in which Lord Cross stated that the courts are obliged to enforce "clearly established rules of international law". For an example of the express rejection of an earlier and well recognized judicial view of international law by a United States tribunal, see *Filatiga v. Pena-Irala* (1980), 630 F. 2d 876 at 974, "the dictum in *Dreyfus v. von Finck* (1976), 534 F. 2d 24 at 31, to the effect that 'violations of international law do not occur when the aggrieved parties are nationals of the acting state,' is clearly out of tune with the current usage and practice of international law."

§41 On occasion, the English courts are called upon to apply international law simpliciter and virtually to the exclusion of any rules of national law. This occurs, for example, when the courts have to exercise jurisdiction in regard to an offence which is defined by international law, such as slave-trading. But if this is also declared to be criminal by statute,[91] and if the definition or terminology differs from that prescribed by international law, then no alien taken outside of the local jurisdiction may be tried for the statutory as distinct from the international offence.[92] Again, when proceeding against an accused for an offence defined by international law it may be necessary for a national court to ascertain whether the constituents of the alleged offence actually satisfy the requirements of international law, as was the case when the Hong Kong courts had to decide whether piracy had been committed although the act of robbery had not been completed. The Judicial Committee of the Privy Council held that international law did not posit such completion.[93] "It goes without saying, a State may expand or restrict the so vague and imprecise authority of international law. It may derogate from or amplify it through particular legislation, or even through a specific act."[94] However, in such a case the state in question can only apply its legislation to its own nationals or residents.

91. Slave Trade Act, 1811, 51 Geo. III, c. 23. Slave trading had been declared an offence at international law by the Treaty of Vienna, 1815, Additional Art., 65 C.T.S. 257, but the consequential legislation had not been enacted by France. See also §§189-213.

92. *The Le Louis* (1817), 2 Dods. 210 (H.C. of Admiralty). See, however, arrest warrant issued by the U.S. Dist. Ct. in *Re The Achille Lauro*, 1985, 24 I.L.M. 1509, at 1554-5.

93. *Re Piracy Jure Gentium*, [1934] A.C. 586 (P.C.).

94. *Rose v. R.*, [1947] 3 D.L.R. 618 (Que. Q.B.) at 645, per Bissonnette J.

§42 Similarly, if international law decrees that a particular national tribunal is to apply the rules of international law, then that court is bound and cannot deviate in the absence of statute. Thus, in *The Zamora*[95] the Judicial Committee pointed out that a prize court, though established by national law, is required to apply international law, subject to any statutory injunction to the contrary, but that an Order in Council extending the rights of the Crown, that is to say of the state, and reducing those of the enemy, will not be applied. However, a statute will prevail over a rule of international law, even one arising from an international treaty,[96] although there is a presumption that Parliament did not intend to legislate contrary to international law, and the only person entitled to complain against such breach of treaty is the other party, even though the breach may adversely affect the rights of a private individual.[97] These principles are, generally speaking, accepted by all Commonwealth countries.[98]

95. [1916] 2 A.C. 77 (P.C.).

96. *Collco Dealings Ltd. v. Inland Revenue Commrs.*, [1962] A.C. 1 at 19 (H.L.), per Lord Simonds.

97. *Collco Dealings Ltd. v. Inland Revenue Commrs., ante* at 22, per Lord Reid.

98. See, e.g., *R. v. Meikleham* (1905), 11 O.L.R. 366 (Ont. Div. Ct.); Vanek, "Is International Law Part of the Law of Canada?", (1949-50), 8 U.T.L.J. 251; Macdonald, "The Relationship between International Law and Domestic Law in Canada", in Macdonald *et al.*, Canadian Perspectives on International Law and Organization (1974), pp. 88, 99-111, 117-127; Castel, International Law Chiefly as Interpreted and Applied in Canada (1976), ch. 2, (1987), ch. 4.

§43 Problems frequently arise in connection with federal states relating to the extent to which constituent parts of the federation can enter into international commitments which would be binding upon the state,[99] as well as situations when the federal government undertakes commitments which it may not be able to fulfil internally due to constitutional limitations upon its competence.[1] As a result of this situation, federal states frequently find it difficult to ratify or accede to international treaties to which they have become parties, since the obligations accruing from such treaties can only be carried out by the authorities of constituent parts of the federation.[2] Consequently, treaties frequently include clauses that recognize the problems facing federal states.[3] On the other hand, states are unable to plead the deficiencies or technicalities of their national law as an excuse for failure to fulfil their obligations under international customary[4] or conventional[5] law. This problem has arisen in Canada with the adoption of the Charter of Rights and Freedoms[6] which raises the question whether the obligations under treaties infringe upon the constitutional rights guaranteed by the Charter. Thus it has been held that the obligation to extradite under treaty does not breach the Charter right to remain in Canada.[7]

99. Di Marzo, Component Units of Federal States and International Agreements (1980).

1. *A.G. Can. v. A.G. Ont.*, [1937] A.C. 325 (P.C.) re International Labour Organization Conventions.

2. Thus, Canada did not accede to the U.N. Conventions on Economic, Social and Cultural Rights and Civil and Political Rights of 1966 until May 1976. On the question of the Canadian position regarding treaties, see, e.g., Jacomy-Millette, "Treaty-Making Power and the Provinces", (1973) 4 Revue Générale de Droit, 131, Treaty Law in Canada, 1975, "L'Etat fédéré dans les relations internationales contemporaines," (1976) 14 C.Y.B.I.L. 3; Macdonald, "International Treaty Law and the Domestic Law of Canada", (1975) 2 Dalhousie Law J. 307; see also, Morris, "Canadian Federalism and International Law" in Macdonald *et al.*, Canadian Perspectives on International Law and Organization (1974), p. 55.

3. See, e.g., Art. 19(7) of the Amending Instrument of the Constitution of the International Labour Organization, 1946, 15 U.N.T.S. 35; see, also, Protocol I additional to the 1949 Geneva Conventions, 1977, Art. 83 re dissemination, 16 I.L.M. 1391 in Schindler and Toman, The Laws of Armed Conflicts (1982) pp. 551, 600: as the result of a Canadian amendment, while parties undertake to disseminate the Conventions and Protocol widely and include their study in military programmes, they are only obliged "to encourage the study thereof by the civilian population", thus recognizing that education is within provincial jurisdiction. The Canadian statement may be found in Levie, Protection of War Victims, vol. 4, 1981, at 170.

4. *The Alabama* (U.S./G.B.) (1872), 1 Moore, International Arbitrations 653, 656: "the government of Her Britannic Majesty cannot justify itself for a failure in due diligence on the plea of insufficiency of the legal means of action which it possessed." See also §325.

5. See, e.g., Art. 46 of Vienna Convention on the Law of Treaties, 1969, 8 I.L.M. 679, ratified by Canada 1970: "1. A State may not invoke the fact that its consent has been expressed in violation of a provision of its internal law regarding competence to conclude treaties as invalidating its consent unless that violation was manifest and

concerned a rule of internal law of fundamental importance. 2. A violation is manifest if it would be objectively evident to any State conducting itself in the matter in accordance with normal practice and in good faith." Normally, a state would be able to argue that it was entitled to assume that those speaking for another state were entitled to speak authoritatively so as to bind that state, while the latter would be able to contend that any enquiry as to the right of an authority to speak on its behalf was an infringement of its domestic jurisdiction. Now, however, there are so many published collections of constitutions that it may often be legitimately contended that the treaty-making processes of most states are easily ascertainable, see, e.g., U.N. Laws and Practices concerning the Conclusion of Treaties (1953). See §305.

6. Constitution Act, 1982 [en. by the Canada Act 1982 (U.K.), c. 11, Sched. B, Pt. I (Charter of Rights and Freedoms)]. See also Green, "The Canadian Charter of Rights and International Law", (1983), 20 C.Y.B.I.L. 3, and for a decision in which it was held that, in case of ambiguity, the Charter may be interpreted in the light of the International Covenant on Civil and Political Rights, see Re Mitchell and R. (1983), 42 O.R. (2d) 481 (Ont. H.C.).

7. Germany (Federal Republic) v. Rauca (1982), 38 O.R. (2d) 705 (Ont. H.C.); affirmed (1983), 41 O.R. (2d) 225 (Ont. C.A.).

§44 Occasionally problems arise because international commitments undertaken by a federal government in favour of a foreign state appear to be inconsistent with the law of a constituent part of the federation. To the extent that the federal power is solely responsible for the foreign relations of the state and the extent to which the judicial authorities apply the principle that they have no control over such foreign relations, the contradictory legal régime of the constituent authority will be disregarded.[8] To the greatest extent possible, such local legislation will be construed as not being inconsistent with the state's international obligations.[9] While it may happen that a part of a federal state enters into an arrangement with individuals which appears in the form of a treaty, but nevertheless because of its terms only binds that constituent and attaches no obligation to the federal state, perhaps the general principle is best expressed in the words of the Supreme Court of Canada in Ref. Re Offshore Mineral Rights (B.C.):[10] "it is Canada, not the Province of British Columbia, that will have to answer the claims of other members of the international community for breach of the obligations and responsibilities imposed by the Convention".

8. United States v. Pink (1942), 315 U.S. 203. See, for a comparative analysis of the position in Canada, the United States, Switzerland and the German Federal Republic, di Marzo, Component Units of Federal States and International Agreements (1980), ch. 3.

9. Arrow River and Tributaries Slide and Boom Co. v. Pigeon Timber Co., [1932] S.C.R. 495 (S.C.C.). See also, Ontario (A.G.) v. Scott, [1956] S.C.R. 137 (S.C.C.). See also Schneider v. R. (1979), 103 D.L.R. (3d) 29 (B.C. S.C.) in which it was held that a statute had to be applied extraterritorially according to its terms, and that no reliance

could be placed on international customary law re freedom of navigation; (affirmed [1981] 1 W.W.R. 511 (B.C. C.A.); affirmed (1982), 43 N.R. 91 (*sub nom. Schneider v. B.C.*) (S.C.C.).

10.   [1967] S.C.R. 792 at 821 (S.C.C.). See also *Ref. re Continental Shelf Offshore Nfld.*, [1984] 1 S.C.R. 86 (S.C.C.)

§45   While many states accept the view that international law is part of the law of the land,[11] as has been seen, this is not necessarily true with respect to treaties, many of which may require national legislation to give them legal effect within the territory of the party,[12] although failure to enact such legislation does not affect the party's liability towards other parties to the treaty.[13] In some cases, treaties are self-executing when they have effect within the territory of a party in the absence of any confirmatory legislation.[14] If the treaty does not affect private rights or seek to amend existing law, there is no need for any national legislation to give effect to it.[15] Non-self-executing treaties are usually those which affect private rights or seek to amend the law and these require legislation to become effective within the territory.[16] Occasionally, treaties may be partly self- and non-self-executing, as is the case with a treaty of peace which terminates the war automatically, but which would require national legislation when determining, for example, the vesting of enemy property and the situs of a debt.[17]

11.   See §§33-38 of this title and *Chung Chi Cheung v. R.*, [1939] A.C. 160 at 167 (P.C.) per Lord Atkin.

12.   This is particularly true if the treaty purports to confer rights upon individual nationals. Since only states are parties to a treaty, the rights so conferred require statutory confirmation to become effective; see *North Atlantic Coast Fisheries Case* (U.S./G.B.) (1910), 11 R.I.A.A. 167; *Civilian War Claimants Assn. v. R.*, [1932] A.C. 14 (H.L.). For Canadian practice, see *Khan v. Fredson Travel Inc.* (No. 2) (1982), 36 O.R. (2d) 17 (Ont. H.C.); *Vincent v. Min. of Employment & Immigration* (1983), 48 N.R. 214 at 221 (Fed. C.A.) per Cowan D.J.: "International conventions . . . are not as such, part of the law of Canada. Canada's obligations under those conventions are implemented, to the extent that Parliament so decides, by statutes of Canada"; see also §305.

13.   *Free Zones of Upper Savoy and Gex* (France/Switzerland) (1932), 2 W.C.R. 508; see also, American Law Institute, Restatement of the Law: Foreign Relations Law of the United States (Revised), Tentative Draft No. 1, s. 131, Comment h, Reporters' Notes, 7.

14.   See *Asakura v. Seattle (City)* (1924), 265 U.S. 332.

15.   The Geneva Conventions, 1929, were considered as effective in Canada even in the absence of any local legislation, see *R. v. Brosig*, [1945] 2 D.L.R. 232 (Ont. C.A.).

16.   Thus Canada signed the 1948 Genocide Convention, 78 U.N.T.S. 277, on Nov. 28, 1949, and ratified it on Sept. 3, 1952, giving effect to it in Canada by amendment of the Criminal Code, s. 281.1 [en. R.S.C. 1970, c. 11 (1st Supp.), s. 1].

17. *Bitter v. Secretary of State for Canada*, [1944] 3 D.L.R. 482, 497-8 (Ex. Ct.) per Thorsen J.

§46 The fact that a state has used terminology in its legislation that coincides with the terminology of international law does not mean that the courts of that state are bound by the international definition. In the *Le Louis*[18] Lord Stowell pointed out that the statutory description of slave trading as piracy was not sufficient to make this offence piracy jure gentium, while in *Kawasaki Kisen Kabushiki Kaisha of Kobe v. Bantham S.S. Co.*[19] the Court of Appeal took a similar view with regard to a charter party which contained a frustration clause in the event of Japan being involved in 'war', holding that in such an instrument the courts would apply the generally understood commercial meaning of that term even though it did not satisfy the prerequisites of international law.

18. (1817), 2 Dods. 210 (H.C. of Admiralty); see U.S. attitude in *Re The Achille Lauro*, 1985, 24 I.L.M. 1509 at 1556-9.

19. [1939] 2 K.B. 544 (C.A.). See §336.

§47 When national law as expressed in statute clearly opposes what is alleged to be customary international law, courts, at least in those countries which follow the English system, will apply the national law even at the risk of the decision resulting in international liability for the country concerned, although in such circumstances the government may indemnify the person affected by such a decision.[20] Similarly, if it is alleged by a defendant, as is common in extradition cases, that his presence within the jurisdiction is the result of a breach of international law by the local authorities, the courts will not allow such an allegation to inhibit the application of the local law.[21] Equally, courts will normally interpret legislation so as not to conflict with a state's international obligations.[22]

20. See *Mortensen v. Peters* (Scotland) (1906), 8 F. 93, in which the Danish master of a Norwegian fishing vessel was fined for illegal fishing in the Moray Firth contrary to certain Scottish regulatory acts, but at a point not within British territory. The fine imposed was remitted by the government, Oppenheim, International Law, Vol. 1, (1912) 264, (1955) 509, n. 1. Subsequent convictions were not sustained and offenders were released from jail, Fulton, Sovereignty of the Sea (1911), p. 727. See also *Schneider v. R.* (1979), 103 D.L.R. (3d) 29 (B.C. S.C.).

21. See, *R. v. O.C. Depot Battalion R.A.S.C. Colchester; Ex parte Elliott*, [1949] 1 All E.R. 373 (K.B.); *Eichmann v. A.G. Israel* (1962), 36 I.L.R. 277; *Ker v. Illinois* (1892), 119 U.S. 436; *U.S. v. Gengler* (1975), 510 F. 2d 62 — see, however, *U.S. v. Toscanino* (1974), 500 F. 2d 267 in which there were allegations of misconduct by U.S. government agents amounting to complicity in acts of torture sufficient to constitute a denial of due process. See e.g., dispute between Canada and U.S. concerning exercise of

jurisdiction by Florida courts over Jaffe illegally seized by U.S. bounty hunters, letter by Green in Edmonton Journal, Aug. 9, 1983.

22.   *A.U.P.E. v. R.* (1981), 130 D.L.R. (3d) 191 (Alta. C.A.); leave to appeal to S.C.C. refused (1981), 130 D.L.R. (3d) 191n (S.C.C.) holding that the Alberta Public Service Employee Relations Act, S.A. 1977, c. 40, denying the right to strike to most public employees was not contrary to International Labour Convention No. 87 concerning Freedom of Association and Protection of the Right to Organize 1948, C.T.S. 1974/14, nor any other customary or treaty rule of international law.

§48   On occasion, a state may enter into arrangements with its own subjects which are described as and drawn in the form of treaties. Such documents may appear so named as annexes to the statute which gives legal effect to the substance of the arrangement. Despite its nomenclature, such a document is not an instrument in international law even though the non-governmental party considers it to be such. This was the case, for instance, with the Anglo-Irish Treaty appended to the Irish Free State (Agreement) Act, 1922.[23]

23.   12 & 13 Geo. V, c. 4. This Treaty between the Government of the United Kingdom and the government of that part of British territory constituting Southern Ireland established the Irish Free State as a dominion. The Irish Free State government registered the 'treaty' in accordance with Article 18 of the Covenant of the League of Nations, leading to a British Note to the Secretary-General pointing out that the United Kingdom did not consider the Covenant in any way applicable to the "relations inter se of the various parts of the British Commonwealth", 27 L.N.T.S. 449. At that time none of the dominions possessed treaty-making powers, even though they were members of the League, and this was an attempt by some British subjects to secure international recognition for an agreement made with the Crown. The Lateran Treaty, 1929, (1929), 23 A.J.I.L., Supp. 187 between the King of Italy and Pope Pius XI, an Italian national, is somewhat different, since Italy thereby expressly acknowledged the sovereignty of the Holy See and recognized the State of the Vatican City under the sovereignty of the Supreme Pontiff.

§49   Somewhat related to the 'treaties' just referred to are the agreements made by a government or some agency that may be considered to be acting on behalf of a government with groups of individuals which purport to constitute 'peoples', and which agreements are frequently described as treaties. If such an agreement goes so far as to describe this group as a 'Nation', it becomes necessary to determine whether this constitutes recognition of a group that is entitled to international status or only enjoys legal personality in accordance with some system of national law.[24] The agreement made with such a group may have been made by a trading company, such as the Netherlands or British East India Co. or the Hudson Bay Co., with the native 'ruler' and may be of such a kind that suzerainty over the chief's lands passes to the company, which may be sufficiently identified with its home state to render that state sovereign over the lands thus acquired.[25] The general attitude towards the peoples affected by such agreements has been that they constitute wards of the state and do not possess any status of their own in international law.[26] It may happen that a particular state considers such a group as constituting an independent sovereign state[27] and its ruler an independent sovereign,[28] but such decisions are valid only for the recognizing state itself and have no effect insofar as a similar status on the international level is concerned. Even if hostilities between an established recognized state and such an aboriginal people have been terminated by a peace treaty, such a treaty is not a document in the eyes of international law and only enjoys such status as is conferred upon it by the law of the victorious state.[29] The situation may now be in the process of change, since the International Court of Justice has delivered judgments which recognize such peoples as possessing inchoate international personality with a right to self-determination.[30]

24. In the *Cayuga Indians Claim* (G.B./U.S.) (1926), 6 R.I.A.A. 173 it was held that the Cayuga Nation was "not a legal unit of international law. . . . So far as an Indian tribe exists as a legal unit, it is by virtue of the sovereign nation within whose territory the tribe occupies the land, and so far only as that law recognizes it" (176, 177).

25. *Island of Palmas Case* (Netherlands/U.S.) (1928), 2 R.I.A.A. 829.

26. See *Francis v. R.*, [1956] S.C.R. 618 (S.C.C.). In *Cherokee Nation v. Georgia* (1821), 5 Pet. 1 at 17, Marshall C.J. described Indian tribes as being "in a state of pupilage". See also, Green, "Legal Significance of Treaties affecting Canada's Indians", (1972) 1 Anglo-American Law Rev., 119; "Trusteeship and Canada's Indians", (1976) 3 Dalhousie Law J., 104. Vanderzwaay and Pharand, "Inuit and the Ice: Implications for Canadian Arctic Waters", (1983) 21 C.Y.B.I.L. 53.

27. *Duff Development Co. v. Kelantan (Govt.)*, [1924] A.C. 797 (H.L.).

28. *Mighell v. Sultan of Johore*, [1894] 1 Q.B. 149 (C.A.); *Sayce v. Ameer of Bahawalpur*, [1952] 1 All E.R. 326 (K.B.); [1952] 2 All E.R. 64 (C.A.).

29. *Hoani Te Heuheu Tukino v. Aotea District Maori Land Board*, [1941] A.C. 308 (P.C.) re the Treaty of Waitangi, 1840, terminating the Maori War.

30. E.g., *Namibia (South-West Africa) Opinion*, [1971] I.C.J. 16; *Western Sahara*, [1975] I.C.J. 4.

§50 For countries which have become members of the European Communities, rules of municipal law which conflict with the provisions of the Treaty of Rome[31] establishing the Communities and its Court are invalid.[32] Similarly, for those countries which have ratified the European Convention on Human Rights[33] any local laws inconsistent with that Convention are equally to be amended.[34]

31. 1957, 298 U.N.T.S. 11.

32. See *Application des Gaz S.A. v. Falks Veritas Ltd.*, [1974] 3 W.L.R. 235; *Henn v. D.P.P.*, [1980] 2 W.L.R. 597 (H.L.).

33. 1950, 213 U.N.T.S. 222.

34. See *Ireland v. U.K.* (1978), 58 I.L.R. 188; *Golder Case* (1975), 57 I.L.R. 200; *Engel Case* (1976), 58 I.L.R. 38.

§51 In common law countries courts, when faced with a problem concerning the national attitude to a problem of international law, refer to governmental authorities for a statement as to the national position. In Canada such statements are in the form of certificates by the Secretary of State for External Affairs and are accepted as conclusive by the courts.[35] Certificates are issued in relation to the recognition of states and governments, the existence of a state of war, the status of a monarch or diplomat, the extent of territorial limits,[36] or that an agreement has come into force on a certain date.[37] This enumeration is not exhaustive.

35. Memo by Legal Bureau, 29 Apr. 1983, (1984), 22 C.Y.B.I.L. 331-3, spells out the official view. See Act to amend the Criminal Code, the Immigration Act, 1976 and the Citizenship Act, S.C. 1987, c. 37.

36. Certificate by Sec. of State, 11 Apr. 1983, that "the waters of the Gulf of St. Lawrence are considered by the Government of Canada to be historic Canadian waters" is conclusive for the courts: (1984), 22 C.Y.B.I.L. 333.

37. Such a certificate was issued in *Re Chateau-Gai Wines Ltd. and Canada (A.G.)*, [1970] Ex. C.R. 366 (Ex. Ct.).

II International Personality

1. SUBJECTS OF INTERNATIONAL LAW

§52 According to the classical writers on international law, only states are recognized as possessing international legal personality and being subjects of international law. This view finds expression in the two editions of International Law edited by Oppenheim:[1] "Since the law of nations is based on the common consent of individual States,[2] and not of individual human beings,[3] States solely and exclusively are the subjects of International Law".[4] By the third edition, the first published after Oppenheim's death and the creation of the League of Nations, this is amended to indicate that the League too is to be considered a subject of international law.[5] By the time Lauterpacht brought out the fifth edition,[6] he found it necessary to add a new section in which it is said that "primarily States are subjects of International law ... and although States are the normal subjects of International Law they may treat individuals and other persons[7] as endowed directly with international rights and duties and constitute them to that extent subjects of International Law."[8]

1. 1905, 1912.

2. *West Rand Central Gold Mining Co. v. R.,* [1905] 2 K.B. 391 (D. C.); *The S.S. Lotus* (France/Turkey) (1927), 2 W.C.R. 20.

3. See §§282-293.

4. See §64.

5. A footnote indicates that "the Family of Nations being now organised as the League of Nations, the latter is, of course, the subject of rights as well as duties, and these rights and duties are international and not supranational." Insofar as the European Community is concerned, the extent to which by the Treaty of Rome, 1957, the law of the Community overrides or abrogates the municipal law of its members, such law may be considered as supra- rather than international; see *Application Des Gaz S.A. v. Falks Veritas Ltd.*, [1974] 3 W.L.R. 235; *Henn v. D.P.P.*, [1980] 2 W.L.R. 597 (H.L.)

6. 1937, 1947, 1948, 1955, s. 13a.

7. E.g., corporate persons like companies, as is the case with the European Community where, by the Treaty of Rome, such entities may appear before the European Court, see *Firma J. Nold v. European Communities Comm.*, [1974] 2 C.M.L.R. 338.

8. But such individuals or entities only enjoy international legal personality to the extent to, and the limits for which it has been endowed.

§53 In certain circumstances, entities which are not states may be recognized as possessing almost all the attributes and powers of states, so that their relations with other entities, including states, are conducted in accordance with international law. This is true of the United Nations which, by its Charter, is granted powers and competences which normally belong to states alone. Thus, it is able to enter into treaties, to conduct hostilities, to maintain armed forces, to administer territory and to exercise functional protection over its officials, akin to that exercised by states in respect of their diplomats.[9] Moreover, by Article 104 of the Charter "The Organization shall enjoy in the territory of each of its Members such legal capacity as may be necessary for the exercise of its functions and the fulfilment of its purposes."[10] It is also granted by Article 105 such immunities and privileges as may be necessary for this purpose, and this immunity extends to its officials even against the country of which an official may be a national.[11] However, the fact that the United Nations enjoys this international personality does not mean that it is a subject of international law in the same sense as is a state. In its advisory opinion on *Reparation for Injuries*[12] the International Court of Justice expressly stated that it had "come to the conclusion that the Organization is an international person. That is not the same thing as saying that it is a State, which it certainly is not, or that its legal personality and rights and duties are the same as those of a State. Still less is it the same thing as saying that it is a 'super-State'. . . . It is a subject of international law and capable of possessing international rights and duties, and it has capacity to maintain its rights by bringing international claims."

9. *Reparation for Injuries Suffered in the Service of the U.N.,* [1949] I.C.J. 174, 182-4. See also §§413-421.

10. *M. v. United Nations* (1966), 45 I.L.R. 446 (Civil Trib. of Brussels).

11. See Privileges and Immunities (International Organizations) Act, R.S.C. 1970, c. P-22; Dai, "The Headquarters Agreement between Canada and the International Civil Aviation Organization", (1964) 2 C.Y.B.I.L. 205; and letter of Bureau of Legal Affairs, Dept. of External Affairs, Jan. 5, 1971, (1972) 10 C.Y.B.I.L. 289. See also §§428-435.

12. *Reparation for Injuries Suffered in the Service of the U.N., ante,* at p. 179; see, also, *M. v. United Nations, ante;* and *A.G. v. Nissan,* [1970] A.C. 179 (H.L.).

§54 Most international institutions, apart from the United Nations, also enjoy international personality,[13] although in their case since the personality depends upon the constituent instrument it tends to be recognized only by the members of the institution in question, and it is only they which are bound, for example, to grant immunity to its officials, regardless of their nationality.[14] However, it is open to any state or other international organization to confer such personality on any particular international institution for any purpose that it chooses. Such personality exists, however, only for the limited purpose for which it is granted. This means that a non-member state or another institution is able to enter into an international agreement with such an organization within the limits of the latter's competence should the former so wish.

13. See *Re International Tin Council,* [1987] 1 All E.R. 890 (Ch.) in which the English Court of Chancery held that the International Tin Council was an international organization created by treaty, as "an international body corporate having a legal personality in international law, possessing international rights and duties and capable of maintaining its rights by bringing international claims." The English courts, therefore, were unable to issue a winding-up order. In *Maclaine Watson & Co. v. Department of Trade & Industry* (1987), *The Times,* 7 Sept., 1987, it was held that the International Tin Council was a legal entity distinct from its members, which were not liable for the liabilities of the Council. In *Shearson Lehman Bros. Inc. v. Maclaine Watson & Co.* the Court of Appeal upheld the confidentiality of the Council's official documents, "but the official archives must be limited to documents which were in the possession of the ITC. A copy which was no longer in the possession of the ITC could not itself be part of the official archives, even if some other copies, still retained by the ITC, were part of the official archives", *The Times,* 7 Sept. 1987, per Dillon L.J., and the House of Lords held that such documents cease to be privileged after disclosure to Council members, ([1988] 1 All E.R. 116 (C.A.)). See e.g., Schwarzenberger, International Law, Vol. 3, (1976) International Constitutional Law; Schermer, International Institutional Law (1972), esp. vol. II, ch. 11-13. See also §§413-426.

14. *Zoernsch v. Waldock,* [1964] 1 W.L.R. 675 (C.A.). See also *European Space Operations Centre (ESOC) Official Immunity Case* (1973), 73 I.L.R. 683 (German Fed. Labour Ct.).

§55 International personality also extends to a number of entities which, while not completely independent and even represented abroad by a third state, are considered to be states with sufficient personality to appear as a party before the International Court of Justice, although not a member of the United Nations. This is the case with Liechtenstein,[15] which is represented abroad by Switzerland. A similarly small state which enjoys even less international status is the Principality of Monaco, which is not a member of the United Nations or a party to the Statute of the World Court, although it does participate in some international conferences. By Article 1 of the 1962 Constitution "The Principality of Monaco is a sovereign and independent State within the framework of the general principles of international law and of particular conventions with France."[16] In addition to these two states, there is also another entity in Europe which is generally recognized as being a state, and has become a party to some international conventions.[17] However, it is under the suzerainty of the President of France and the Spanish Bishop of Urgel, and in 1951[18] the Court of First Instance at Perpignan, France, stated "Andorra is not a foreign State.... Andorra is a Principality, the co-ruler of which is . . . the President of the French Republic. In law and in fact it is under the protectorate[19] of France."

15. *Nottebohm Case* (Second Phase) (Liechtenstein/Guatemala), [1955] I.C.J. 4.

16. Until 1815 a French Protectorate, from 1815-1860 Protectorate of Sardinia, independence recognized 1861 under French protection, Constitution granted by Prince in 1911.

17. E.g., Universal Copyright Convention, 1952, 216 U.N.T.S. 134, Convention on Protection of Cultural Property, 1954, 249 U.N.T.S. 215, 240.

18. *Massip v. Cruzel* (France) (1951), 18 I.L.R. 52 (Ct. of First Instance).

19. On protectorates, see §68.

§56 Some measure of international status may be given to a city as distinct from a larger territory.[20] This has usually been done because of international rivalries[21] or because there has been some special international political reason for seeking to grant a special status, as was, for example, the case with Danzig[22] or Memel[23] after the First World War. After the second World War unsuccessful attempts were made to create a special status for Trieste[24] and Jerusalem,[25] although the four powers occupying Germany were able to establish Berlin as a corpus separatum enjoying a special legal status.[26] In each of these instances, the status was determined by treaty.

20. See Ydit, Internationalised Territories (1961).

21. E.g., the "International Zone of Tangier", 1 Whiteman 595-598.

22. See *Polish Postal Service in Danzig* (1925), 1 W.C.R. 440; *Polish Nationals in Danzig* (1932), 2 W.C.R. 789.

23. *Statute of the Memel Territory* (1932), 3 W.C.R. 35.

24. Treaty of Peace with Italy, 1947, 49 U.N.T.S. 126, art. 21, Annexes VI-X.

25. Gen. Ass. Res. 189 (II), 1947; see also, Lauterpacht, Jerusalem and the Holy Places (1968); Blum, The Juridical Status of Jerusalem (1944); Cattan, "The Status of Jerusalem", Journal of Palestine Studies (Spring 1981) p. 3.

26. See Green, "The Legal Status of Berlin" (1963), 10 Netherlands Int. Law Rev. 113; Zivier, The Legal Status of the Land Berlin (1977).

§57 The most important of the special entities enjoying international personality and recognized as such by all states, even though it is not a member of the United Nations nor a party to the Statute of the International Court of Justice, is the Holy See. Until their annexation by Italy in 1870 the Pope was the monarch of the Papal States and recognized as such. This was a status independent of any position he enjoyed as Head of the Catholic Church. After the annexation Italy enacted the Law of Guarantee recognizing the Pope's special status as Head of the Church and not as an Italian subject, a fact that has now been confirmed with the election of a Polish Pope. No foreign state recognized this Law, but nevertheless some, especially Catholic states, accredited diplomats to the Vatican in addition to Italy and signed agreements, described as concordats, with it. An increasing number of non-Catholic states have now accredited diplomatic representatives to the Holy See.[27] In 1929 Italy signed the Lateran Treaty with the Holy See,[28] acknowledging the Holy See's sovereignty in international matters in accordance with its traditions and the requirements of its world mission. The Vatican City was placed under the sovereignty of the Holy See and its right of legation recognized. By Article 24 of the Treaty "The Holy See, so far as concerns the sovereignty belonging to it in the international domain, declares that it wishes to remain and will remain removed from the temporal competitions among other states and from international meetings convoked with such a purpose, unless the parties to a dispute make a unanimous appeal to its mission of peace,[29] reserving to itself, however, the right to assert in every case its moral and spiritual power. In consequence, the City of the Vatican shall always and in every case be considered as neutral and inviolable territory." In accordance with its 'moral and spiritual' character, the Holy See frequently attends international conferences and may even become a party to an international agreement dealing with humanitarian law. Thus it signed the 1977 Geneva Protocols on Humanitarian Law in Armed Conflicts.

27.   In accordance with Art. 16 of the Vienna Convention on Diplomatic Relations, 1961, 500 U.N.T.S. 95, diplomats take precedence in accordance with the date of acceptance of credentials, although in Catholic countries it is traditional that the Papal Nuncio should always be the doyen. When Canada appointed its first ambassador to the Vatican in 1984 the government announced that the nuncio would always rank as doyen, but this accouncement was soon withdrawn. See Green, Letter to Globe and Mail, 21 Aug. 1984.

28.   (1929), 23 A.J.I.L., Supp. 187; see also, Kunz, 'The Status of the Holy See in International Law', (1952) 46 A.J.I.L. 308. For recent discussion of the legal relation between the Holy See and Italy, see Pergola and Duca, 'Community Law, International Law and the Italian Constitution,' (1985), 79 A.J.I.L. 598 at 607-608.

29.   This role tends to be reserved for disputes between Catholic states.

§58   The fact that a treaty has imposed a specific limitation upon the competence of a state in a limited sphere does not interfere with the international personality of the state or its status in international law. Thus, both Belgium and Switzerland were neutralized by treaty. This did not, however, prevent Belgium becoming a member of the League of Nations, although Switzerland maintained that this prevented her from joining that organization or the United Nations. The neutralization of Austria by agreement with the Great Powers[30] has not prevented it from joining the United Nations, while the constitutional limitation upon the maintenance of an armed force or the use of its defence forces outside of Japan has not prevented Japan from joining the United Nations or from becoming a member of the Security Council. In the same way, the reservation by the three Western Powers of their rights and responsibilities regarding Berlin and Germany as a whole embodied in the Convention on Relations between the Three Powers and the Federal Republic of Germany in no way restricts the personality or sovereignty of the Federal Republic.[31]

30. 1 Whiteman, 348-355; Kunz, 'Austria's Permanent Neutrality' (1956), 50 A.J.I.L. 418.

31. 1 Whiteman, 330-6. See, also, *United States v. Tiede* (1979), 19 I.L.M. 179, 193 (decision of U.S. Court of Berlin in which it was pointed out that even the prosecution conceded that the occupation of Berlin continued only to preserve democracy in the city).

§59 In recent years, a tendency has grown, with the emphasis in United Nations documents including the Charter and Resolutions relating to human rights, to refer to the right of self-determination for peoples. This tendency to some extent had already been envisaged by the Permanent Court of Justice in its advisory opinion on the *Greco-Bulgarian Communities*[32] when a 'community' was defined as "a group of persons living in a given country or locality, having a race, religion, language and traditions of their own and united by the identity of race, religion, language and traditions in a sentiment of solidarity, with a view to preserving their traditions, maintaining their form of worship, ensuring the instruction and upbringing of their children in accordance with the spirit and traditions of their race and rendering mutual assistance to each other." Since then, the World Court has found occasion to accord some international personality to a 'people' as what can only be described as an 'inchoate' subject of international law.[33] In addition, the United Nations has recognized national liberation movements as constituting subjects of international law and entitled to rights under international law. This trend has culminated in Article 1 of the 1977 Protocol I additional to the Geneva Conventions of 1949 concerning humanitarian law in international armed conflicts,[34] for it is now provided that "armed conflicts in which peoples are fighting against colonial domination and alien occupation and against racist régimes in the exercise of their right of self-determination, as enshrined in the Charter of the United Nations[35] and the Declaration on Principles of International Law concerning Friendly Relations and Co-operation among States in accordance with the Charter of the United Nations,"[36] constitute international conflicts. This means that the members of such a national liberation movement enjoy all the rights and obligations that international law imposes in respect of a belligerent engaged in an international armed conflict. Until 1977, only states were regarded as competent to wage such a conflict.

32. (1930), 2 W.C.R. 641.

33. *Western Sahara,* [1975] I.C.J. 4.

34. Art. 1(4). Schindler and Toman, The Laws of Armed Conflicts (1981), 551, (1977) 16 I.L.M. 1391, signed but not yet ratified by Canada. See §330.

35. Arts. 1(2), 55.

36. 1970, Res. 2625 (XXV).

§60 There is a growing tendency today, and this is reflected in statements made by individual members of the International Court of Justice, to suggest, since all states are personifications made up of individuals and in the light of increasing respect for human rights, that individuals too have become subjects of international law. It must not be overlooked, however, that one of the essential features of legal personality is the power to protect one's rights through the medium of judicial process. The Statute of the International Court of Justice expressly provides that only states may be parties to an action before the court,[37] so that the individual cannot defend any rights he may possess before that tribunal. When his rights are alleged to have been injured, it is his state which, in normal circumstances, decides whether or not those rights are to be pursued through the medium of international law.[38] Occasionally, states may by treaty confer direct rights upon their citizens, but even in the European Convention on Human Rights[39] the parties have not gone to the extent of permitting injured individuals to initiate proceedings before the European Court of Human Rights, although they may lodge complaints with the Commission.[40] The situation is different in the case of the European Community, for there individuals do possess a limited right of action.[41] It is sometimes claimed, since individuals may be subjected to criminal process on the basis of breaches of international law, for example as war criminals or pirates, that this constitutes recognition of their subjective personality. In fact, however, this merely confirms that individuals are nothing but objects[42] in the eyes of international law, for such persons are made amenable to trial by countries of which they are not nationals and which, in the absence of such authorization by international law, would lack the competence to try them.[43]

37. Statute, Art. 34(1). See §402.

38. *Barcelona Traction, Light & Power Co. (Second Phase)*, [1970] I.C.J. 3. See §321.

39. 1950, 213 U.N.T.S. 222.

40. See §293.

41. *Calleymeyn v. Belgium* (1974), 56 I.L.R. 533. See also §293.

42. See §282.

43. See §282.

§61 The state, which is the normal subject of international law, is considered to be supreme and independent of any higher authority and able to behave as it chooses, subject to any limitations that may be imposed upon it by virtue of rules of either customary or conventional international law. As a subject of international law enjoying international personality, the state is competent to hold territory, exercise rights and be subject to duties as regards other subjects of international law, exercise jurisdiction within its own territorial limits, enter into international agreements and by so doing accept limitations upon its own freedom of action, enjoy immunity from the jurisdiction of other subjects of international law, join international organizations in accordance with the conditions regulating membership, have recourse to the use of armed force to protect or assert its rights, to the extent that this is still permissible in accordance with the Charter of the United Nations,[44] and bring international claims.[45]

44. Even though, normally, treaties, and the Charter of the United Nations is a treaty, only impose obligations upon the parties, it may be argued that in view of the near universality of the United Nations the Charter may be binding even upon nonmembers. Moreover, by Article 2, paragraph 6 the parties to the Charter undertake "to ensure that states which are not Members ... act in accordance with [the] Principles [set out in Article 2] insofar as may be necessary for the maintenance of international peace and security."

45. By Article 34, paragraph 1, of the Statute of the International Court of Justice, only states may be parties to an action before the Court, although a non-state entity may have sufficient personality to appear before an ad hoc tribunal, e.g., *Petroleum Development Ltd. v. Sheikh of Abu Dhabi* (1951), 18 I.L.R. 144 by virtue of the agreement setting up the tribunal, or, in the case of certain international institutions to seek an advisory opinion from the World Court, Statute, Art. 65, paragraph 1, e.g., *Constitution of the Maritime Safety Ctee. of the Inter-Governmental Maritime Consultative Organization,* [1960] I.C.J. 150; *Nomination of the Netherland Wkrs. Delegate to the Third Session of the Int. Labour Conference* (1922), 1 W.C.R. 115. Equally, the parties to an instrument establishing an institution may create a special tribunal before which the institution may be able to appear, as is the case, e.g., with the European Comm. of Human Rights in accordance with Art. 48 of the European

Convention on Human Rights, 1950, 213 U.N.T.S. 222, and the European Communities under the Treaty of Rome, 1957, 298 U.N.T.S. 11, by Art. 173 of which actions may be brought by states, organs of the Community and even by individuals.

§62 In accordance with Article 4 of the Charter of the United Nations only states may be admitted as new members of the United Nations, but there is no definition of statehood in the Charter. In fact, this definition only applies to an entity seeking admission and has no application to any foundation member, that is to say, participant in the San Francisco Conference of 1945 at which the Charter was drafted. As a result, two constituent members of the Union of Soviet Socialist Republics, the Soviet Socialist Republics of Byelorussia and the Ukraine, are members of the United Nations, as was the Empire of India before it achieved independence in 1947. The same was true of the British Dominions insofar as membership of the League of Nations was concerned, for they were listed as original members in the Annex attached to the Covenant, which provided that "any fully self-governing State, Dominion or Colony" not so named might be admitted by decision of the League Assembly. Insofar as other international institutions are concerned, the test of membership depends upon the constituent instrument of the institution and this may enable non-states or entities not fully independent to become members. Thus, the "United Kingdom and United States Zones of Occupation of Germany" — Bizonia — signed the Convention for European Economic Cooperation[46] and became a member of the Organization with full and equal rights of membership. On the other hand, although the Constitution of the Organization of African Unity[47] provides that "each independent sovereign African State shall be entitled to become a Member", South Africa, which is a member of the United Nations and generally recognized as an independent African State, is excluded from membership.

46. 1948 (Pt. II), 151 B.F.S.P. 278.

47. 1963, 479 U.N.T.S. 39; Boutros Ghali, 'The Addis Ababa Charter', 546 International Conciliation (1964).

§63 Although there is no authoritative definition of a state, it is frequently said[48] that the conditions prescribed by Article 1 of the Montevideo Convention on the Rights and Duties of States, 1933 are of general application.[49] "The state as a person of international law should possess the following qualifications: a) a permanent population; b) a defined territory; c) government; and d) capacity to enter into relations with other states." Nevertheless, entities lacking one or more of these qualifications have been accepted as states enjoying international personality.[50] Similarly, the presence of such qualifications is no automatic guarantee that existing states will recognise the holder of such qualities as itself constituting a state.[51] However, it may happen that an entity which denies the statehood or existence of another may for particular reasons be compelled to concede certain of the rights of statehood, such as the competence to enter into a treaty or to engage in an armed conflict, as for example is the situation between Israel and its Arab neighbours, including Egypt prior to the signing of the Camp David Agreements in 1979. In order for international personalities to exist, the entity claiming such personality must be recognized by those existing subjects of international law against which it wishes to claim the rights pertaining to its personality,[52] and any additional requisite, such as a written constitution or the holding of democratic elections, may be imposed by a state from which recognition is requested, but this is a political and not a legal requirement.[53]

48. See, e.g., Lauterpacht, Recognition in International Law (1947), pp. 27-30; Chen, The International Law of Recognition (1951), pp. 54-60; Castel, International Law Chiefly as Applied and Interpreted in Canada (1976), pp. 47-8; 1987 ed. pp. 10-12.

49. 165 L.N.T.S. 19.

50. Thus, Poland was a party to the Treaty of Versailles, but only came into existence on the ratification of that Treaty, see, e.g., *German Interests in Polish Upper Silesia* (Merits) (Germany/Poland) (1926), 1 W.C.R. 510. The independence of Israel was recognized and its admission to the United Nations effected before its boundaries were defined.

51. This was the case with Bangladesh when it first broke away from Pakistan in 1972, and Rhodesia from its unilateral declaration of independence in 1965 until its replacement by Zimbabwe in 1980. For the Canadian refusal to recognize the unilateral declaration of independence of the Turkish Republic of Northern Cyprus, see statement by the Parliamentary Secretary of the Minister of Supplies and Services, House of Commons Debates, 28 Nov. 1983, at 29273-4, (1984), 22 C.Y.B.I.L. 341-342.

52. See §§91-109.

53. Chen, The International Law of Recognition (1951), pp. 60-2. By the Treaty of Berlin, 1878, 153 C.T.S. 172, special guarantees re minorities were imposed on the about-to-be-established Bulgaria, Montenegro, Roumania and Serbia.

§64 Since only 'states' can be admitted as members of the United Nations, membership in the organization is in fact confirmation of the international personality of the entity in question.[54] By Article 4 of the Charter, admission is effected by a two-thirds vote of the General Assembly in accordance with a positive, but not necessarily unanimous, decision of the Security Council.[55] Even though a particular member of

the United Nations may have voted against the admission of an applicant, or even expressed its belief that the applicant does not qualify as a
state, once the admission has been effected all opponents must accept, at
least for the purposes of the United Nations, that the member in question is a state entitled to all the rights that pertain to a member of the
United Nations, including eligibility for election to the Security Council.
This means that all members of the United Nations are obliged, in
accordance with Article 25 of the Charter, to carry out decisions of the
Council, even though such decisions may have been reached only by
reason of the vote of an entity alleged to be non-existent. Moreover,
since the competence of the United Nations extends to the making of
agreements even with its members, to compelling its members to participate in punitive measures, or calling upon its members to participate
in the administration of territory placed under its trusteeship, it becomes difficult to contend that an entity admitted to the United Nations
lacks any of the competences of any other state.

54.   In August 1949, Canada announced that it considered its vote in favour of
Israel's admission to the U.N. "as having implied full recognition by the Government
of Canada of the State of Israel", Israeli Foreign Office letter FO/I/(60), November
18, 1949.

55.   *Competence of the Gen. Assembly for the Admission of a State to the U.N.,* [1950]
I.C.J. 4. See also §414.

§65   However, this does not mean that admission to the organization is
tantamount to collective recognition sufficient to compel every member
to accept every other member as a state with which it must, for example,
enter into diplomatic or other relations. On the other hand, it may be
argued that refusal by one member of the United Nations to accept
another member as a state is incompatible with the obligation imposed
upon members by the Charter[56] to "fulfil in good faith the obligations
assumed by them in accordance with the present Charter", which involves acceptance of paragraph 1 of Article 2 postulating that one of the
principles of the United Nations is "to develop friendly relations among
nations".

56.   Art. 2.

§66   While membership of the United Nations is acknowledgement of
statehood, a Resolution of the United Nations General Assembly, such
as that of November 22, 1974[57] calling for the creation of a Palestinian
state and inviting the Palestine Liberation Organization as the representative of the Palestinian people to participate in the work of the General
Assembly and all international conferences convened under its auspices

in the capacity of an observer[58] does not create a subject of international law, even if it is granted all the rights of any other participant.[59] Similarly, the incorporation in the Mandate Treaty for Palestine[60] of references to a Jewish Agency, together with its right to advise and co-operate with the Mandatory Power in such matters "as may affect the establishment of the Jewish national home and the interests of the Jewish population in Palestine", did not confer any international personality upon that Agency,[61] although failure by the Mandatory to take account of its opinions might constitute a breach of the Mandate and criticism from the League's Permanent Mandates Commission. The fact that a non-governmental organization has rights conferred or obligations imposed upon it by treaty, similarly, does not mean that the organization is therefore possessed of international personality.[62]

57. Res. 3236 (XXIX); see also Res. 3375 (XXX) calling for acceptance of the P.L.O. "on an equal footing with all other parties" in all deliberations concerning the Middle East.

58. The P.L.O. and other national liberation movements which participated in the Diplomatic Conference on Humanitarian Law in Armed Conflicts did not sign the Protocols adopted in 1977, although they did sign the Final Act of the Conference, but separately from the states participating in the Conference.

59. As was the case with the U.N. Conference on Palestine, Geneva, 1983.

60. L.N. Doc. C. 529. M. 314. 1922. VI (1 Hudson, Int. Leg. 109), Art. 4.

61. On the status of the Jewish Agency, see Feinberg, "The Recognition of the Jewish People in International Law", (1948) J.Y.B.I.L. 1 at 19-24, reprinted in Studies in International Law (1979), pp. 229, 252-9.

62. See, e.g., the position of the International Committee of the Red Cross under the Geneva Conventions of 1949, Geneva Conventions Act, R.S.C. 1970, c. G-3, and under Protocol I additional to the Geneva Conventions of 1949.

§67 In the absence of any treaty imposing a particular constitutional form upon a state,[63] international law is not concerned with the internal constitutional arrangements or division of powers in a state. Insofar as international law is concerned, it is the state and not, for example, any constituent part of a federation that enjoys international personality and represents the state on the international level, although a particular treaty might recognize that it deals with matters which may render ratification difficult for a federal state and make provision accordingly.[64] On the other hand, third states may recognize constitutional arrangements and agree to enter into relations with a constituent part, granting the latter a limited personality enabling it to contract treaties, usually only those of a limited or specialist character. Thus, the Byelorussian and Ukrainian Soviet Socialist Republics are, in theory at least, as fully independent for the purposes of the United Nations as any other member and may bring actions before the World Court.[65] While Quebec enjoys a limited agreement-making competence, it does not enjoy international personality, nor is it regarded as a subject of international law. On the international level, other than in instances like the two Soviet Republics and even then only to a limited extent, it is the state itself, that is to say the Soviet Union, Canada, the United States or any other federal or composite state, which represents the entity on the international level entering treaties in the name of the state, even though by the constitution co-operation by a constituent part of the state may be necessary to give effect to treaty obligations,[66] and it is the state which becomes liable or entitled in respect of, for example, suits before an international tribunal.[67]

63. Such limitations if imposed are usually imposed upon a newly recognized government, e.g., the Polish Provisional Government by virtue of the Yalta Agreement, 1945, 1 Whiteman 130; see also, Chen, The International Law of Recognition (1951), ch. 17.

64. See, e.g., the revised 1946 Constitution of the International Labour Organization, 15 U.N.T.S. 35, Art. 19(7); see also, Vienna Convention on Treaties, 1969, 8 I.L.M. 679, Arts. 27, 46.

65. No judge of either nationality has ever been elected to the Court.

66. See Re Regulation and Control of Aeronautics in Canada, [1932] A.C. 54 (P.C.); Re Regulation and Control of Radio Communication in Canada, [1932] A.C. 304; Canada (A.G.) v. Ontario (A.G.) (Labour Conventions Case), [1937] A.C. 326; see also, Dufour, 'Fédéralisme canadien en droit international', in Macdonald, Canadian Perspectives on International Law and Organization (1974) p. 72; Morris, 'Canadian Federalism in International Law' (1975), 2 Dalhousie Law Journal 307. See also, DiMarzo, Component Units of Federal States and International Agreements (1980); and §§43, 44.

67. See Cayuga Indians Claim (G.B./U.S.) (1926), 6 R.I.A.A. 173.

§68 As has been indicated, there are some entities which enjoy a limited amount of international personality even though they are not states nor international institutions, whose status depends upon their constituent instruments. In the period before the establishment of the League of Nations, the most important of such entities were international protectorates. Most usually, a protectorate denotes a territory so completely under foreign supervision that the world regards that territory as being part of the sovereign possessions of the administering authority. However, from the point of view of the constitutional or imperial policy of that power the territory in question is not regarded, as are colonies, as forming part of the administrator's possessions, but is regarded as a separate sovereign power,[68] even though no other state recognizes it in the same way. On occasion, and frequently in order to settle international conflicts amicably, states have agreed to establish a protectorate by treaty so that the administering power is limited in its exercise of sovereignty, and the protected entity is regarded as being a separate international person with such powers of its own as the treaty establishing the protectorate leaves to it.[69] Unlike the colonial protectorate, international law recognizes the independent status of such protectorate,[70] even though on the international level it acts through the medium of the administering power, although officially, in so doing, the administrator is acting on behalf of the protectorate and not on behalf of itself. Today, with the emphasis on self-determination and independence, all protectorates have become or are in process of becoming independent states, so that the institution is largely of historic interest.

68.   Mighell v. Sultan of Johore, [1894] 1 Q.B. 149 (Que. C.A.); Duff Development Co. v. Kelantan Govt., [1924] A.C. 797 (H.L.); Sayce v. Ameer of Bahawalpur, [1952] 1 All E.R. 326 (K.B.); [1952] 2 All E.R. 64 (C.A.); Administration of the Territory of Papua New Guinea v. Guba (1973), 71 I.L.R. 39 (Aust. H.C.)

69.   Nationality Decrees in Tunis and Morocco (1923), 1 W.C.R. 145; Rights of U.S. Nationals in Morocco (France/U.S.), [1952] I.C.J. 176.

70.   Thus, in The Ionian Ships (1855), Spinks 193 (P.D.A.), it was held that a declaration of war by the protecting power was not sufficient to make the protectorate at war. A separate declaration to this effect would be necessary.

§69   The Covenant of the League of Nations introduced an international concept which, to some extent, appears to have been based on the international protectorate, in that an existing state was appointed as administrator of a non-self-governing entity but the extent of its rights of administration, falling short of sovereignty, was limited by international treaty, which also imposed some measure of international accountability. Instead of pursuing the traditional practice of allowing victors to seize territory from their defeated opponents, the Principal Allied and Associated Powers decided to introduce at the end of the first World War a new Mandates system based on the concept of an international trusteeship in favour of the local inhabitants. Broadly speaking, the essence of the Mandates system was that those territories taken from the defeated Central Powers and "inhabited by peoples not yet able to stand by themselves under the strenuous conditions of the modern world" should be administered by more advanced states committed to applying "the principle that the well-being and development of such peoples form a sacred trust of civilization".[71] The territories placed under Mandate were divided into three groups depending upon their state of development, the most advanced being those formerly belonging to the Turkish Empire, which had "reached a stage of development where their existence as independent nations can be provisionally recognized subject to the rendering of administrative advice and assistance by a Mandatory until such time as they are able to stand alone." Among these Class "A" Mandates was Palestine, placed under British Mandate with an obligation upon the Mandatory to place "the country under such political, administrative and economic conditions as will secure the establishment of the Jewish national home, . . . and the development of self-governing institutions, and also for safeguarding the civil and religious rights of all the inhabitants of Palestine, irrespective of race and religion."[72] Territories in Central Africa not yet so politically advanced were to be administered "under conditions which will guarantee freedom of conscience and religion, subject only to the maintenance of public order and morals, the prohibition of abuses such as the slave trade, the arms traffic and the liquor traffic, and the prevention of the establishment of fortifications or military and naval bases and of military training for the natives for other than police purposes and the defence of territory, and will also secure equal opportunities for the trade and commerce of other Members of the League", that is to say they were placed under the regime of the "open door".[73] Finally, "there are territories, such as South-West Africa and certain of the South Pacific Islands, which, owing to the sparseness of their population, or their small size, or their remoteness from the centres of civilization, or their geographical contiguity to the territory of the Mandatory, and other circumstances, can be best administered under the laws of the Mandatory as integral portions of its territory, subject to the safeguards above mentioned in the interests of the indigenous population."

71.   Covenant of the League of Nations, Art. 22.

72.   Art. 1, giving effect to the pledge in the Balfour Declaration, 1917, and repeated in the Preamble, "in favour of the establishment in Palestine of a national home for the Jewish people, it being clearly understood that nothing should be done which might prejudice the civil and religious rights of existing non-Jewish communities in Palestine, or the rights and political status enjoyed by Jews in any other country." For a discussion of the legal significance of the Balfour Declaration, see Feinberg, "The Recognition of the Jewish People in International Law", Studies in International Law (1979), pp. 239-242, 452-3, 527-8. For his comments on the Hussein-McMahon correspondence, 1915-16, concerning promises to the Arabs, see 451-4; see, also, Cattan, Palestine and International Law (1973).

73.   A principle intended to preclude undue economic exploitation by the Mandatory adversely to the interests of other League members. In practice, it tended to mean subjecting the territory to economic exploitation by all League members on equal terms.

§70   While sovereignty did not belong to the League, in no case, not even in that of South-West Africa or other Class "C" Mandates, did sovereignty pertain to the Mandatory. It was held in trust for the indigenous population until such time as that population would be able

to govern itself. The inhabitants of the territory did not become nationals of the Mandatory, so that unlike British colonial subjects they
could be deported from England back to, for example, Palestine.[74] At the
same time, at least in the case of the inhabitants of a Class "C" Mandate,
as for example South-West Africa, they could be tried and punished for
treason.[75] However, some protection was offered to the inhabitants by
reason of the supervision exercised under the authority of the League by
the Mandates Commission to which these inhabitants had the right to
present petitions.[76] The Commission also examined Reports from the
Mandatory and was empowered to comment thereon.

74. *R. v. Ketter*, [1940] 1 K.B. 787 (C.C.A.).

75. *R. v. Christian*, [1924] S.A.L.R. A.D. 101, in which it was held that the Union of
South Africa, as Mandatory, possessed 'internal sovereignty' over South-West
Africa.

76. *South-West Africa — Hearing of Petitioners,* [1956] I.C.J. 23.

§71   With the demise of the League and the adoption of the Charter of
the United Nations, the Mandates system was replaced by the International Trusteeship system.[77] By Article 77 of the Charter, three distinct
types of territory were envisaged as suitable for submission to the
system: (a) territories held under Mandate; (b) territories detached from
enemy states as a result of the Second World War; and (c) territories
voluntarily placed thereunder by states responsible for their administration. It was envisaged that the terms of the administration would be set
out in an agreement between the United Nations and the administering
power, and that the administration would be under the supervision of
the Trusteeship Council which would report to the General Assembly.
However, if any territory were declared to be a strategic area, supervision would be effected by the Security Council which would be responsible for approving the terms of the agreement.[78] In fact, the only trusteeship agreement relating to strategic areas was that exercised by the
United States in relation to the Pacific Islands formerly under Japanese
Mandate. As a result, by virtue of its right to exercise a veto under
Article 27 of the Charter, this meant that the United States would be able
to prevent any adverse decision by the United Nations relevant to its
administration of this territory.

77. Charter, Ch. XII.

78. Art. 83.

§72   By and large, the trusteeship system of the United Nations was
similar to the Mandates system of the League, its objectives being: "(a)

to further international peace and security; (b) to promote the political, economic, social, and educational advancement of the inhabitants of the trust territories, and their progressive development towards self-government or independence as may be appropriate to the particular circumstances of each territory and its peoples and the freely expressed wishes of the peoples concerned,[79] and as may be provided by the terms of each trusteeship agreement;[80] (c) to encourage respect for human rights and for fundamental freedoms for all without distinction as to race, sex, language, or religion, and to encourage recognition of the interdependence of the peoples of the world; and (d) to ensure equal treatment in social, economic and commercial matters for all Members of the United Nations and their nationals, and also equal treatment for the latter in the administration of justice, without prejudice to the attainment of the foregoing objectives . . . ."[81] The provisions of the Charter and those of the Covenant were not identical. It therefore became important in the case of South-West Africa, the only Mandated territory not placed under trusteeship, to examine the relationship between the two systems, and this was done by the International Court of Justice in its advisory opinion on the status of South-West Africa.[82] The court held that, despite the demise of the League, the Mandate was still in existence and that South Africa continued to be bound by the terms of Article 22 of the Covenant and to transmit petitions from the inhabitants, even though the voting procedure of the Trusteeship Council which had taken over the supervisory functions of the Permanent Mandates Commission of the League differed from that of the Commission.[83] It held that the provisions of Chapter XII of the Charter relating to the trusteeship system were applicable to South-West Africa, even though they did not impose any obligation upon South Africa to place the territory under trusteeship. Perhaps most importantly, the court was of opinion that South Africa could not terminate the Mandate unilaterally, but that "the competence to determine and modify the international status of the Territory rests with the Union of South Africa acting with the consent of the United Nations." Despite this finding, in 1966 the General Assembly of the United Nations terminated South Africa's Mandate,[84] in 1967 established a United Nations Council for South West Africa[85] and then changed the name of the territory to Namibia and adopted a number of proposals seeking South Africa's withdrawal.[86] The Security Council recognized the validity of these Resolutions, declared the continued administration to be illegal[87] and asked the court for an opinion on the legal consequences of South Africa's continuing administration despite these Resolutions. The court decided[88] that South Africa's continued presence was illegal and should terminate immediately, and that it was incumbent upon all members of the United Nations to recognize this illegality and incumbent upon non-members to assist the United Nations in its actions regarding Namibia. When Namibia acquires its independence, the only trust territory remaining will be that concerning the Pacific Islands,[89] although it was announced in 1987 that this would terminate shortly.

79. See *Northern Cameroons* (Preliminary Objections), [1963] I.C.J. 15.

80. The terms of the agreements were drawn up between the United Nations and the administering power, without any formal role for the territory or its inhabitants.

81. Charter of U.N., Art. 76.

82. *South-West Africa — International Status,* [1950] I.C.J. 128.

83. *South-West Africa — Voting Procedure,* [1955] I.C.J. 67.

84. Res. 2145 (XXI).

85. Res. 2248 (S-V).

86. Res. 2372 (XXII).

87. Security Council, Res. 276 (1970).

88. *Namibia (South-West Africa) Opinion,* [1971] I.C.J. 16. See, generally, Zacklin, "The Problem of Namibia in International Law", (1981) 171 Hague Recueil 233.

89. For comments on its status, see *Alig v. Trust Territory of the Pacific Islands* (1967), 61 I.L.R. 88 (Trust Territory H.C.). For comment re U.S. decision to terminate this status, see letter by R.S. Clark, 10 Jun., 1987, 81 A.J.I.L. 927.

§73 Occasionally there appears to be an international entity which in fact exists rather as a political concept than a legal reality. This is the case with the [British] Commonwealth.[90] When the United Kingdom declared war in August 1914 the Declaration was effective for the entire empire. By the time hostilities ceased, and as a result of the military contribution made by the individual Dominions and the Empire of India, the Treaty of Versailles was signed by the British Government representatives on behalf of the entire empire, followed by the representatives of Canada, Australia, South Africa, New Zealand and India, and each was an original member of the League of Nations.[91] Prior to that time, the United Kingdom signed treaties on behalf of the empire, unless territories were expressly excepted. Gradually, however, delegates from a Dominion were included in the United Kingdom delegation when the interests of that Dominion might be involved, and increasingly the Dominions were given the power to make their own treaties and to appoint their own diplomatic representatives, provided that the other negotiating party was agreeable. The Statute of Westminster, 1931,[92] was an internal British statute which gave municipal effect to what had become political reality, and opened the way to the acquisition of full sovereign power by the Dominions. Even though the Statute did not apply to the Empire of India, it was recognized that this territory could enter into treaties on its own and in its own name.[93] When war broke out in 1939, the United Kingdom declaration was effective only for itself, for India and the colonies. Each Dominion issued its own declaration and was at war only with effect from the date of such issuance, while the Irish Free State remained neutral throughout. This development together with the retention of India within the Commonwealth after becoming a Republic in 1949 illustrates effectively the divisibility of the Crown, although the Crown continues to be accepted as Head of the Commonwealth,[94] but remains the ruler only of those independent members which continue to recognize it as such. Although the individual members of the Commonwealth were members of the United Nations in their own right, the organization did, at the beginning, recognize that the Commonwealth was a unity and as a result, by virtue of the 'gentlemen's agreement' concerning the distribution of non-permanent seats on the Security Council,[95] reserved one such seat for the Commonwealth. This arrangement ended when in 1964, in order to break a voting deadlock, the seat formerly held by Ghana was divided between Czechoslovakia and Malaysia. With the expansion of non-permanent membership to meet the needs of the 'Third World,' the recognition of the Commonwealth as an entity entitled to a seat on the Council disappeared.[96] Today, the only semblances remaining of the unity of the Commonwealth are those relating to the formal title of the Crown and the periodic meetings that take place between Commonwealth heads of government or ministers.[97] The creation of a Commonwealth Secretariat[98] has not altered the legal status of the Commonwealth.

90. Neither the French Union nor the Netherlands-Indonesian Union ever really came into existence.

91. See §62. See, however, Gilmore, "Newfoundland and the League of Nations", (1980) 18 C.Y.B.I.L. 201.

92. 22 & 23 Geo. V., c. 4.

93. Thus, India was the only country to ratify the 1937 Convention for the Prevention and Punishment of Terrorism, 7 Hudson, Int. Leg. 862.

94. See R. v. Secretary of State for Foreign & Commonwealth Affairs; Ex parte the Indian Assn. of Alta., [1982] 2 All E.R. 118 (C.A.).

95. See, e.g., Green, "Gentlemen's Agreements and the Security Council", (1960) 13 Current Legal Problems 255; "Representation in the Security Council — A Survey", (1962) 11 Ind. Y.B.I.A. 48.

96. 1963, U.N. General Assembly Res. 1991 (XVIII).

97. See Papadopoulos, Multilateral Diplomacy within the Commonwealth (1982).

98. See note 97, ch. 3.

§74 It is not only on the international level that the developments relating to the Commonwealth have been acknowledged. On the municipal level, too, it is now accepted that the individual Dominions are in fact fully independent states and as such entitled in national courts to all the immunities of a foreign state.[99] In fact, an English court has gone so far as to accept that the authoritative statement as to the status and immunities of a constituent part of a federal Commonwealth country should come from the government of that country.[1] It is also accepted that, while Commonwealth countries are now completely sovereign with, since 1931, exclusive powers of statutory enactment,[2] statutes formerly enacted by the Imperial Parliament remain valid until abrogated, as do treaties entered into before that date.[3] Moreover, since the Statute of Westminster, it is clear that any documents, e.g., a statement referring to the 'British Colony or Dependency' "cannot be given effect to in such a way as to include" the Dominion.[4]

99. *Kahan v. Pakistan Federation,* [1951] 2 K.B. 1003 (C.A.); see also, Green, 'The Status of Pakistan', (1952) 6 Indian L.R. 65.

1. *Sayce v. Ameer of Bahawalpur,* [1952] 1 All E.R. 326 (K.B.); [1952] 2 All E.R. 64 (C.A.).

2. *R. v. Secretary of State for Foreign & Commonwealth Affairs, ante.*

3. *Ex parte O'Dell and Griffen,* [1953] O.R. 190 (Ont. H.C.).

4. *Re Brassey's Settlement: Barclay's Bank Ltd. v. Brassey,* [1955] 1 W.L.R. 192, 196 (Ch.) per Danckwerts J.

2. SOVEREIGNTY AND EQUALITY OF STATES

§75 Since there is no parliament able to legislate for all states, and since international law is recognized as being a law of consent to the rules of which the states agree to be bound, it is often said that, subject to clear rules of international law which are binding upon them, states are free to behave as they please. This is particularly true as regards matters occurring within the state's territorial limits, for "par in parem non habet imperium, no state can claim jurisdiction over another sovereign state".[5] This was expressed in far more symbolic language by Vattel in 1789:[6] "Since men are by nature equal, and their individual rights and obligations the same, as coming equally from nature, Nations, which are composed of men and may be regarded as many free persons living together in a state of nature, are by nature equal and hold from nature the same obligations and the same rights. Strength or weakness, in this case, counts for nothing. A dwarf is as much a man as a giant is; a small Republic is no less a sovereign State than the most powerful Kingdom."

5. *The Cristina,* [1938] A.C. 485 at 502, per Lord Wright.

6. Le Droit des Gens (1758) Introduction, s. 18 (Carnegie tr., p. 7).

§76 While the Covenant of the League of Nations made no express reference to the principle of sovereign equality, it nevertheless provided that "except where otherwise provided in this Covenant or by the terms of the present Treaty [of Versailles], decisions at any meeting of the Assembly or of the Council shall require the agreement of all of the Members of the League represented at the meeting".[7] There is, of course, nothing inconsistent with the concept of equality to provide in a treaty that certain measures may be taken in spite of the absence of unanimity, for by agreeing to such a voting procedure the parties are in fact exercising their sovereignty in a way that expresses their consent to such a procedure. It is, in fact, an exercise in consensual auto-limitation of sovereignty. In the case of the United Nations the situation is a little different. The first principle stated in the Charter is that "the Organization is based on the principle of the sovereign equality of all its Members",[8] but there is no instance when unanimity is required. By way of auto-limitation of their sovereignty, the members have agreed to accept in this organization, as in other international institutions, a variety of majority voting systems.

7. Art. 5(1). In fact, the unanimity rule, which in effect gives every member a power to veto, was not as destructive as might appear. In its advisory opinion in the *Mosul Case* (1925), 1 W.C.R. 722 at 742, the P.C.I.J. held that "In certain cases and more particularly in the case of the settlement of a dispute, the rule of unanimity is applicable, subject to the limitation that the votes cast by the representatives of the interested Parties do not affect the required unanimity", and may therefore be disregarded.

8. Art. 2(1). On equality of rights and voting, see §§417, 418.

§77 More serious, however, is the arrangement made with regard to membership and voting in the Security Council. Unlike the General Assembly in which each member of the United Nations is represented and has an equal vote, the Security Council consists of fifteen states of which five are permanent members, while the other ten are elected for two years from the general membership with each member, including the five permanent members, participating in the vote.[9] Moreover, by virtue of the amending Resolution the non-permanent seats are distributed in a fashion that hardly reflects the equal rights of the members.[10] In addition, the voting arrangements in the Security Council are similarly a denial of state equality. Decisions on substantive issue are taken by a majority of nine, "including the concurring votes of the permanent members".[11] This means that if a single permanent member refuses to concur, there is no binding decision,[12] even though that objecting member may be the sole dissenter,[13] and even if the General Assembly were to confirm the decision.[14] Although these provisions clearly run counter to the basic principle of the sovereign equality of all members, this equality is not in fact infringed since the members of the United Nations by accepting the Charter have agreed that some of them will be subjected to greater limitations upon their sovereignty than is the case with other members.

9. Charter of the U.N., Art. 23, as amended.

10. General Assembly Res. 1991 (XVIII), five from African and Asian States, one from East European States, two from Latin American States, and two from "Western European and other States".

11. Art. 27(3), as amended — in practice, if a permanent member abstains, this is not regarded as a failure to concur.

12. By Art. 25 the members undertake to carry out the decisions of the Council, regardless of their agreement with such decisions.

13. See Green, "The Security Council in Retreat", (1954) 8 Y.B.W.A. 95, 98-106.

14. See, however, the 'Uniting for Peace' Resolution, 1950, General Assembly Res. 377A (V).

§78 Perhaps the most authoritative statement on the meaning of sovereignty in international law was delivered by Max Huber as sole arbitrator in the *Island of Palmas Case* between the Netherlands and the United States:[15] "Sovereignty in the relations between States signifies independence. Independence in regard to a portion of the globe is the right to exercise therein, to the exclusion of any other State, the functions of a State. The development of the national organization of States during the last few centuries and, as a corollary, the development of international law have established the principle of the exclusive competence of the State in regard to its own territory in such a way as to make it the point of departure in settling most questions that concern international relations. . . . The fact that the functions of a State can be performed by any State within a given zone is . . . precisely the characteristic feature of the legal situation pertaining to those parts of the globe which, like the high seas[16] or lands without a master,[17] cannot or do not yet form the territory of a State. . . . Territorial sovereignty . . . involves the exclusive right to display the activities of a State. This right has as corollary a duty: the obligation to protect within the territory the rights of other States, in particular their right to integrity and inviolability in peace and in war, together with the rights which each State may claim for its nationals in foreign territory.[18] Without manifesting its territorial sovereignty in a manner corresponding to circumstances, the State cannot fulfil this duty. Territorial sovereignty cannot limit itself to its negative side, i.e., to excluding the activities of other States; for it serves to divide between nations the space upon which human activities are employed,[19] in order to assure them at all points the minimum of protection of which international law is the guardian. . . . International law, the structure of which is not based on any super-State organization,[20] cannot be presumed to reduce a right such as territorial sovereignty, with which almost all international relations are bound up, to the category of an abstract right, without concrete manifestations."

15. (1928), 2 R.I.A.A. 829, at 838 and 839.

16. Terra communis, the property of all, being part of the common heritage of humanity, open to user by all and not liable to be subjected to the sovereignty of any state. However, while before 1958 there was general agreement that a littoral state could claim sovereignty over the three miles of water bordering its territory, it is now generally asserted that claims to exclusive exploitation may extend to 200 miles. See §271.

17. Territorium nullius, territory belonging to no one, and therefore open to acquisition by any state able to assert title. It is probably true to say that today, with the exception of Antarctica, and there claims to sovereignty are forbidden by the Antarctica Treaty, 1959, 402 U.N.T.S. 71, there is no piece of land which is not claimed by an existing State, even if the claim of a particular state is challenged by some other state or by a 'people' claiming the right of self-determination in order to create a state. Similarly, according to the Moon Treaty (Agreement Governing the Activities of States on the Moon and Other Celestial Bodies), 1979, 18 I.L.M. 1434), which came into force in 1984 on receiving five ratifications, "The exploration and use of the moon shall be the province of all mankind and shall be carried out for the benefit and in the interests of all countries . . . . The moon and its natural resources are the common heritage of mankind. . . . The moon is not subject to national appropriation by any claim of sovereignty, by means of use or occupation, or by any other means", Arts. 4(1), 11(1), (2).

18. See §323. It is on this basis that Israel claimed its right to effect the Entebbe rescue in 1976 (Green, "Rescue at Entebbe — Legal Aspects", (1976) 6 I.Y.B.H.R. 311) and the U.S. attempted to rescue the Tehran hostages in 1980 (Green, "The Tehran Embassy Incident and International Law", 38 Behind the Headlines, No. 1 (1980) pp. 17-18; "The Tehran Embassy Incident — Legal Aspects", Archiv des Völkerrechts, (1980) 1, 21); Ronzitti, Rescuing Nationals Abroad, 1985.

19. See §§132-297.

20. See §§1-31.

§79 While Huber placed so much emphasis on territorial sovereignty, independence embraces more than the right of a state to enjoy its territory without interference. It is the essence of independence that there is no restriction upon the freedom of action of the state other than the restrictions that may be imposed upon it by customary or conventional international law. This means that sovereignty is wider than just the right to administer territory, it also entails independence from submission to the power of any other sovereign state.[21] Thus, when Austria undertook in the Treaty of St. Germain, 1919,[22] and again in 1922[23] not to alienate its independence in any way, this prevented the creation of a customs union between Austria and Germany which would have limited Austria's freedom in the economic sphere, for "irrespective of the definition of the independence of States which may be given by legal doctrine or may be adopted in particular instances in the practice of States, the independence of Austria, according to Article 88 of the Treaty of St. Germain, must be understood to mean the continued existence of Austria within her present frontiers as a separate State with the sole right of decision in all matters economic, political, financial or other with the result that that independence is violated, as soon as there is any violation thereof, either in the economic, political, or any other field, these different aspects of independence being in practice one and indivisible. . . . By 'alienation' . . . must be understood any voluntary act by the Austrian State which would cause it to lose its independence or which would modify its independence in that its sovereign will would be subordinated to the will of another Power or particular group of Powers, or would even be replaced by such will".[24]

21. See §68.
22. 112 B.F.S.P. 317.
23. Protocol to the Treaty of St. Germain of 1919, 12 L.N.T.S. 385.
24. *Austro-German Customs Union* (1931), 2 W.C.R. 713 at 718-9. It would seem that the Sri Lanka-India Agreement, 1987, 26 I.L.M. 1175, has this effect.

§80   While, as has been seen,[25] the United Nations "is based on the principle of the sovereign equality of all its Members," the Charter gives no indication of what is meant by sovereign equality. All it provides is that, "all Members, in order to ensure to all of them the rights and benefits resulting from membership shall fulfil in good faith the obligations assumed by them in accordance with the present Charter".[26] It goes on to provide that the Members will settle their disputes peacefully, will "refrain in their international relations from the threat or use of force against the territorial integrity or political independence of any state",[27] and guarantees that nothing in the Charter, other than Chapter VII relating to enforcement in connection with a threat to the peace, authorizes the United Nations "to intervene in matters which are essentially within the domestic jurisdiction of any State or shall require the Members to submit such matters to settlement under the present Charter".[28] Nevertheless, the organization claims the right to "ensure that states which are not Members of the United Nations act in accordance with [the] Principles [set out in Article 2] so far as may be necessary for the maintenance of international peace and security".[29] This would imply that the organization is claiming a right to limit the sovereignty of non-members in that it seeks to impose the principles embodied in the Charter upon states which have declined to become parties to that treaty. In fact, what it postulates is an obligation upon members to ensure such compliance.

25. See §76.
26. Charter of the U.N. Art. 2(2).
27. Art. 2(4).
28. Art. 2(7).
29. Art. 2(6).

§81 In what may be construed as an attempt to give further elaboration to the nature of sovereignty and the equal rights that stem from independence as embodied in the Charter of the United Nations, the General Assembly in 1970 adopted a Declaration on Principles of International Law concerning Friendly Relations among States in accordance with the Charter of the United Nations.[30] This Declaration lists seven principles which "constitute basic principles of international law ... [and] all States [are] to be guided by these principles in their international conduct and to develop their mutual relations on the basis of their strict observance": (a) the principle that States shall refrain in their international relations from the threat or use of force against the territorial integrity or political independence of any state, or in any other manner inconsistent with the purposes of the United Nations; (b) the principle that states shall settle their international disputes by peaceful means in such a manner that international peace and security and justice are not endangered; (c) the duty not to intervene in matters within the domestic jurisdiction of any state, in accordance with the Charter;[31] (d) the duty of states to cooperate with one another in accordance with the Charter; (e) the principle of equal rights and self-determination of peoples;[32] (f) the principle of sovereign equality of states; (g) the principle that states shall fulfil in good faith the obligations assumed by them in accordance with the Charter, so as to secure their more effective application within the international community, and so promote the realization of the purposes of the United Nations.

30. Res. 2625 (XXV), adopted without vote.

31. For the Canadian view of non-intervention, see Legal Bureau Memo, 1 Dec. 1983, (1984) 22 C.Y.B.I.L. 333-334.

32. The Canadian view on self-determination is to be found in a memorandum of the Legal Bureau, Dept. of External Affairs, 20 Aug. 1982, (1983) 21 C.Y.B.I.L. 318-9.

§82 Expanding upon these principles, the Declaration affirms that "All States enjoy sovereign equality. They have equal rights and duties and are equal members of the international community, notwithstanding differences of an economic, social, political or other nature. In particular, sovereign equality includes the following elements: (a) States are juridically equal; (b) each State enjoys the rights inherent in full sovereignty; (c) each State has the duty to respect the personality of other States; (d) the territorial integrity and political independence of the State are inviolable;[33] (e) each State has the right freely to choose and develop its political, social, economic and cultural systems; (f) each State has the duty to comply fully and in good faith with its international obligations and to live in peace with other States."

33.   It is arguable whether such actions as the Israeli rescue of hostages at Entebbe or the United States' attempt to do the same in Iran are compatible with this principle or not. See §78 note 18.

§83 Apart from threats to their territorial integrity and independence, states tend to regard acts which interfere with their domestic jurisdiction as blatant attempts to deny their sovereign equality. Article 15, paragraph 8, of the League Covenant provided that "if [a] dispute between the parties is claimed by one of them, and is found by the Council, to arise out of a matter which by international law is solely within the domestic jurisdiction of that party, the council shall so report, and make no recommendation as to its settlement." The use of the term 'solely' in conjunction with the measuring rod of international law necessitates assessment of the relative significance of international and domestic relevance, but denies subjective determination by the party putting forward the contention. This matter was analysed by the Permanent Court of International Justice in its advisory opinion on the *Nationality Decrees in Tunis and Morocco:*[34] "The question to be considered is not whether one of the parties to the dispute is or is not competent in law to take or to refrain from taking a particular action, but whether the jurisdiction claimed belongs *solely* to that party. From one point of view, it might well be said that the jurisdiction of a State is *exclusive* within the limits fixed by international law — using this expression in its wider sense, that is to say, embracing both customary law and general as well as particular treaty law. But a careful scrutiny of paragraph 8 of Article 15 shows that it is not in this sense that exclusive jurisdiction is referred to in that paragraph. The words 'solely within the domestic jurisdiction' seem rather to contemplate certain matters which, though they may very closely concern the interests of more than one State, are not, in principle, regulated by international law. As regards such matters, each State is sole judge. The question whether a certain matter is or is not solely within the jurisdiction of a State is an essentially relative question; it depends upon the development of international relations. Thus, in the present state of international law, questions of nationality are, in the opinion of the Court, in principle within this reserved domain.[35] ... [However,] it may well happen that, in a matter which, like that of nationality, is not, in principle, regulated by international law, the right of a State to use its discretion is nevertheless restricted by obligations which it may have undertaken towards other States. In such a case, jurisdiction which, in principle, belongs to the State, is limited by rules of international law. Article 15, paragraph 8, then ceases to apply as regards those States which are entitled to invoke such rules, and the dispute as to the question whether a State has or has not the right to take certain measures becomes in these circumstances a dispute of an international character and falls outside the scope of the exception. ... It must not, however, be forgotten that the provision contained in paragraph 8 ... is an exception to the principles [enunciated above] and does not therefore lend itself to an extensive interpretation. This consideration assumes especial importance in the case of a matter which, by international law, is, in principle, solely within the domestic jurisdiction of one Party, but in regard to which the other Party invokes international engagements which, in the opinion of that Party, are of a nature to preclude in the particular case such exclusive jurisdiction. ... It is certain ... that the mere fact that a State brings a dispute before the League of Nations does not suffice to give this dispute an international character [and] it is equally true that the mere fact that one of the parties appeals to engagements of an international character in order to contest the exclusive jurisdiction of the other is not enough to render the exception inapplicable."

34. (1923), 1 W.C.R. 145 at 155-7; see, however, §87 note 48.

35. In accordance with this 'development' and 'the present state of international law', there is a tendency in the U.N. to regard issues of human rights as they affect the treatment of nationals as not being within the exclusive domain, see §89.

§84 As a general statement of principle, the statement by the court in the *Nationality Decrees* case[36] opinion is still a valid definition of domestic jurisdiction according to international law. However, the language of the Charter[37] is wider than that of the Covenant. There is no longer a reference to the measuring rod of international law and the term 'solely' has been replaced by 'essentially,' thus introducing a far more liberal concept of relative significance and weight. Moreover, the omission of any reference to international law has enabled states when, for example, accepting the jurisdiction of the International Court of Justice in accordance with Article 36 of its Statute[38] to reserve to themselves the sole decision as to whether a matter falls 'essentially' within their domestic jurisdiction.[39] Despite the fact that this Article gives the court the sole authority to decide upon its jurisdiction, the court has held that a reservation to this effect is valid.[40] Moreover, insofar as discussion in organs of the United Nations is concerned, the contention that a matter is essentially within a member's domestic jurisdiction and thus within the exception of Article 2, paragraph 7, of the Charter or of the Declaration on Principles of International Law Concerning Friendly Relations among States, tends to be decided on political rather than legal grounds with a decision depending upon the question whether the country putting forward the exception can gather sufficient votes to create a majority friendly to its contention.

36.　*Nationality Decrees in Tunis and Morocco, ante.*

37.　Charter of the U.N., Art. 2(7).

38.　See §405.

39.　The United States was the first country to put forward this reservation which is known, generally, as the Connally amendment.

40.　See *Case of Certain Norwegian Loans* (France/Norway), [1957] I.C.J. 9 at 59 and *Interhandel Case* (Switzerland/U.S.), [1959] I.C.J. 6. In the former, Lauterpacht J. contended that, since such a reservation went to the root of the declaration accepting jurisdiction and was in breach of the court's exclusive jurisdiction under Article 36, the declaration was null and void and had the effect of negating the acceptance of jurisdiction by the state making the declaration. See §§407, 408.

§85　As is indicated by the limitation imposed by Article 2, paragraph 7, of the Charter on the power of the United Nations to encroach upon a state's domestic jurisdiction, it would seem that it is within the exclusive domestic jurisdiction of a state whether it becomes a member of an international institution and accepts the obligations of the constituent treaty, just as it is completely within the competence of a state whether, in the absence of a treaty obligation or a declaration under Article 36 of the Court's Statute, it accepts judicial settlement of disputes to which it is a party. This was made clear by the Permanent Court of International Justice in its advisory opinion on the *Status of Eastern Carelia*[41] when, in view of the Russian refusal to appear before either the League Council or the court, it declined to answer a request by the League Council whether certain articles in a Russo-Finnish treaty created international obligations binding Russia.

41. (1923), 1 W.C.R. 191 at 205: "It is with regret that the Court, the Russian Government having refused their concurrence, finds itself unable to pursue the investigations which . . . would require the consent and co-operation of both parties." See also *Buttes Gas & Oil Co. v. Hammer (No. 3); Occidental Petroleum Corp. v. Buttes Gas & Oil Co. (No. 2)*, [1980] 3 W.L.R. 668 at 678 (C.A.), per Lord Denning, M.R.

§86 On the other hand, the International Court of Justice did not hesitate in the *Reparation* opinion,[42] without even citing the *Eastern Carelia*[43] opinion, to hold that the United Nations possessed sufficient international personality to bring an action even against a non-member, while in its *Namibia Opinion*,[44] again without any reference to *Eastern Carelia*, it held that non-members were bound by the Security Council and General Assembly resolutions terminating South Africa's mandate over South West Africa.[45] Nevertheless, in its judgment in the *Monetary Gold* case[46] the court denied its jurisdiction in the absence of Albania, since "to adjudicate upon the international responsibility of Albania without her consent would run counter to a well-established rule of international law embodied in the Court's Statute, namely, that the Court can only exercise jurisdiction over a State with its consent."

42. *Reparation for Injuries Suffered in the Service of the U.N.*, [1949] I.C.J. 174 at 185.

43. *Status of Eastern Carelia, ante.*

44. [1971] I.C.J. 16 at 56.

45. See §§72, 420.

46. [1954] I.C.J. 19 at 32. This case had been brought by Italy against the U.K., France and the U.S., but Italy contended that the issue rested on a claim of its own against Albania, and that, since Albania would not appear before the court, the latter lacked jurisdiction to hear the case.

§87 It is generally accepted that among the issues which fall within the exclusive domain for determination by a state in exercise of its sovereignty are, as has been seen,[47] issues of nationality, although if the interests of another state are involved adversely this question may cease to be so reserved.[48] Another, and perhaps more significant issue concerns the state's territorial limits, although in this case if those limits are challenged by another state this is normally a question which would fall for international adjudication. However, in 1970 Canada announced that "disputes arising out of or concerning jurisdiction or rights claimed by Canada in respect of the conservation, management or exploitation of the living resources of the sea, or in respect of the prevention or control of pollution or contamination of the marine environment in marine areas adjacent to the coast of Canada" would not be considered as falling within those issues concerning which Canada was prepared to accept the 'compulsory'[49] jurisdiction of the World Court,[50] regardless of whether any other state, such as the United States, claimed jurisdiction in the same marine area. This reservation was withdrawn in 1985, although Canada reserved the right "at any time. . .either to add to, amend or withdraw any" reservation it might choose.[51] On the other hand, while in the absence of such a clear statement by a state, such issues would be suitable for international adjudication, courts in both the United Kingdom[52] and the United States[53] have made it clear that they would not be prepared to adjudicate in any fashion on issues affecting the territorial limits of foreign states.[54]

47.   *Nationality Decrees in Tunis and Morocco* (1923), 1 W.C.R. 145.

48.   *Nottebohm Case (Second Phase)* (Liechtenstein/Guatemala), [1955] I.C.J. 4.

49.   See §§420-424.

50.   Letter to U.N. Secretary General dated April 7, 1970, (1979-80) I.C.J. Y.B. 54, reproduced in Castel, International Law Chiefly as Interpreted and Applied in Canada (1976) p. 805.

51.   Declaration of 10 Oct. 1985, Y.B.I.C.J. 1985-1986, p. 64.

52.   *Buttes Gas & Oil Co. v. Hammer (No. 3); Occidental Petroleum Corp. v. Buttes Gas & Oil Co. (No. 2), ante,* at 678.

53.   *Occidental of Ummal Qaywayn v. A Certain Cargo of Petroleum Laden aboard the Tanker 'Dauntless Colocotronis'* (1978), 577 F. 2d 1196, and see, in particular, letter from State Dept. on role of court in disputes affecting foreign boundaries reproduced at n. 13 of decision.

54.   However, a court will rule on its own national boundaries, *Mortensen v. Peters* (1906), 8 F. 93; *The Fagernes,* [1927] P. 311 (C.A.); *Post Office v. Estuary Radio,* [1968] 2 Q.B. 740 (C.A.); *Dom. Coal Co. v. Cape Breton; N.S. Steel & Coal Co. v. Cape Breton* (1963), 48 M.P.R. 174 (N.S. C.A.); *Ref. re Offshore Mineral Rights (B.C.),* [1967] S.C.R. 792 (S.C.C.).

§88 Perhaps the field of sovereign authority that most affects the individual is that of criminal jurisdiction.[55] "A sovereign nation has exclusive jurisdiction to punish offences against its laws committed within its borders, unless it expressly or impliedly consents to surrender its jurisdiction.[56] The jurisdiction of the nation within its own territory, is necessarily exclusive and absolute; it is susceptible of no limitation, not imposed by itself. All exceptions . . . to the full and complete power of a nation within its own territories must be traced up to the consent of the nation itself. They can flow from no other legitimate source."[57] As a result of this power of consent, the state may agree to allow some other authority, for example, a foreign military authority, to exercise jurisdiction within its territory,[58] or may agree to a foreign state exercising jurisdiction over persons who may not normally be subject to such jurisdiction, such as members of a visiting military force.[59] In such circumstances the personnel affected will not be able to plead that the judicial process to which they have been thus subjected violates an "international standard of justice" or runs counter to their own constitutional rights,[60] or violates some principle of international law.[61] In the same way, it is not open to an accused to plead before a criminal tribunal that he has been brought within the jurisdiction by some irregular process, for example, as the result of having been kidnapped from foreign territory.[62] Finally, a court will not listen lightly to argument that the courts of a friendly sovereign state are likely to operate in a corrupt fashion.[63]

55. See §§136-140.

56. See §§145-163; *Wilson v. Girard* (1957), 354 U.S. 524.

57. *The Schooner Exchange v. M'Faddon* (1812), 7 Cranch 116 at 136 per Marshall C.J. See Castel, "Exemption from the Jurisdiction of Canadian Courts", (1971) 9 C.Y.B.I.L. 159.

58. *Amand v. Home Secretary and Min. of Defence of Royal Netherlands*, [1943] A.C. 147 (H.L.); *Ref. re Exemption of U.S. Forces from Proceedings in Can. Criminal Cts.*, [1943] S.C.R. 483 (S.C.C.).

59. See Visiting Forces Act, R.S.C. 1970, c. V-6, ss. 5, 6. See also *Re G.* (1988), The Times, 1 Mar. 1988 (Fam. D.).

60. *Holmes v. Laird* (1972), 459 F. 2d 1211 (Circuit Ct.).

61. *Tag v. Rogers* (1959), 267 F. 2d 664 at 666, as applied in *Holmes v. Laird, ante.*

62. See *Eichmann v. A.G. Israel* (1962), 36 I.L.R. 277 at 304-308, a fuller discussion is to be found in the judgment of the Dist. Ct., 36 I.L.R. 18, 257-70; *Ex parte Elliott*, [1949] 1 All E.R. 373 (K.B.); *State v. Heymann*, [1964] 4 S.A.L.R. 599; *Ker v. Illinois* (1886), 119 U.S. 436; *United States v. Marzano* (1975), 388 F. Supp. 906; *United States v. Toscanino* (1975), 398 F. Supp. 916; *United States v. Gengler* (1974), 510 F. 2d 62; *United States v. Deaton* (1978), 448 F. Supp. 533, "a court's manner of acquiring jurisdiction over a defendant is irrelevant as long as the accused receives due process of law in the trial of the merits of the indictment", per Lambros D.J.; for Can. jurisprudence in regard to wrongful arrest processes, see *R. v. Walton* (1905), 11 O.L.R. 94 (Ont. C.A.); and *Re Hartnett and R.; Re Hudson and R.*, [1974] 1 O.R. (2d) 206 (Ont. H.C.); see also, Williams, International Criminal Law Casebook (1978), pp. 214-217, 227-9, 261-268; Cole, "Extradition Treaties Abound But Unlawful Seizures Continue", 40 International Perspectives, Mar./Apr. 1975. The position in Canada may now have changed by virtue of the Charter of Rights and Freedoms.

63. *Re Arton (No. 1)*, [1896] 1 Q.B. 108 at 110 (Q.B.) per Lord Russell C.J.; *Re India and Mubarak Ali Ahmed*, [1952] 1 All E.R. 1060 at 1063 (Q.B.) per Lord Goddard C.J.

§89 Finally in respect of the sovereign state's rights to deal with matters within its domestic jurisdiction, it should be pointed out that traditionally and, generally speaking,[64] until the establishment of the United Nations, states claimed an absolute right to treat their own nationals in any manner they deemed fit, free of intervention by other states, other than criticism or protest based on moral or political grounds.[65] Since 1945, however, and particularly since the adoption of the Universal Declaration of Human Rights[66] and the International Covenant on Economic, Social and Cultural Rights and that on Civil and Political Rights,[67] it has become common to assert that all individuals, regardless of nationality, enjoy basic rights, even against their own state.[68] In fact, however, it is only as against parties to the European Convention on Human Rights[69] and the American Convention on Human Rights[70] that any effective means of protecting such rights exists.[71] Nevertheless, in 1980 a United States court held[72] that international law had now developed sufficiently to assert that the application of torture on behalf of a state "is now prohibited by the law of nations. This prohibition is clear and unambiguous, and admits of no distinction between treatment of aliens and citizens. . . . International law confers fundamental rights upon all people vis-à-vis their own governments." On the basis of this, the court was of opinion that a victim of such treatment could sue a representative of his own government under American law for injuries suffered from acts of torture inflicted in that government's territory.[73]

64. Subject to special treaties affecting, e.g., minorities, see §§214-222 below. Even Grotius, writing in 1625, recognized that in certain circumstances humanitarian considerations permitted a monarch to take action against another sovereign "for grievous violations of the Law of Nature or Nations" directed against the latter's subjects, De Jure Belli ac Pacis, Lib. II, Cap. 20, s. 40, 1 (Eng. tr. (1738) 436; Carnegie tr. (1925) 504). See Green, "The Role of Law in Establishing Norms of International Behavior," (1986) 17 I.Y.B.H.R. 189.

65. See Adler and Margalith, With Firmness in the Right: American Diplomatic Action Affecting Jews (1946).

66. 1948, res 217 (III) A.

67. 999 U.N.T.S. 171.

68. See, e.g., separate opinion of Ammoun V.P. in Namibia Opinion, [1971] I.C.J. 16 at 62, 72.

69. 1950, 213 U.N.T.S. 222.

70. 1969, 9 I.L.M. 673.

71. See §293.

72. Filatiga v. Pena-Irala (1980), 630 F. 2d 876 at 884, per Kaufman J.

73. The court expressly stated in Filatiga v. Pena-Irala, ante "that the dictum in Dreyfus v. von Finck (1976), 534 F. 2d 24 at 31, to the effect that 'violations of international law do not occur when the aggrieved parties are nationals of the acting state', is clearly out of tune with the current usage and practice of international law."

§90 Discussion of the sovereignty and equality of states may be closed by reiterating the principle that the right to independence is recognized by both international and municipal judicial tribunals as being the core of the matter. This means that even though the act of entering a treaty is an exercise of sovereignty and not an abandonment thereof[74]and while participation in a treaty may result in imposing limitations upon the exercise of sovereignty,[75] nevertheless such limitations will not be presumed[76] and will always be narrowly interpreted so that if more than one interpretation is possible the one imposing the minimum of obligations will be selected,[77] provided this does not result in defeating the purpose of the treaty.[78] As a result, the party putting forward a contention favouring a limitation of sovereignty will bear the burden of proving that contention,[79] or, in other words, when ambiguous instruments fall to be construed, construction is to be contra proferentem.[80]

74. *The S.S. Wimbledon* (France, G.B., Italy, Japan/Germany) (1923), 1 W.C.R. 163 at 168, 175.

75. Thus, the Pact of Paris, 1928, 94 L.N.T.S. 57, and the United Nations Charter impose restrictions on the sovereign right to resort to armed force.

76. *The S.S. Lotus* (France/Turkey) (1927), 2 W.C.R. 20 at 35.

77. *Mosul Case* (1925), 1 W.C.R. 722 at 737.

78. *Territorial Jurisdiction of the Order Comm.* (Czechoslovakia, France, Denmark, G.B., Germany, Sweden/Poland) (1925), 2 W.C.R. 611.

79. *North Atlantic Coast Fisheries* (G.B./U.S.) (1910), P.C.A. No. VII, 11 R.I.A.A. 167 at 180.

80. *Serbian and Brazilian Loans Case* (France/Brazil) (1929), 2 W.C.R. 344 at 404, 421.

3. RECOGNITION

§91 Since international law is a law based on consent,[81] it is clear that states are not bound by principles of law or the legal consequences arising from any factual situation to which they have not given their consent,[82] express or implied.

81. See §1.

82. See *Nottebohm Case* (Second Phase) (Liechtenstein/Guatemala), [1955] I.C.J. 4 at 19-20, where the question in issue was Guatemalan recognition of Liechtenstein naturalization law.

§92 While whenever there is a contention that a particular law or fact is *opposable*[83] to some entity the question of recognition by the latter is automatically put in issue, the concept of recognition is normally reserved to decide whether a particular government or state is recognized as having legal rights which prevail as regards the state against which the claim is put forward.[84]

83. That is to say, can be successfully put forward as authoritative as regards the state against which it is alleged. "A statement, act or situation which a subject of international law may not treat as res inter alios acta", Schwarzenberger, A Manual of International Law (1976), p. 563.

84. In municipal courts, such claims usually relate to immunity from jurisdiction; in international tribunals they frequently concern issues of liability, see *Tinoco Concessions* (G.B./Costa Rica) (1923), 1 R.I.A.A. 369.

§93 In the doctrine of international law there are two schools of thought concerning recognition. Firstly, it is argued that if the desiderata of statehood[85] exist as a fact, then there is an obligation upon other states to recognize this factual situation and accept the entity possessing such phenomena as a state and entitled to all the rights attaching to statehood.[86] This is known as the declaratory theory[87] and leaves no discretion to the states against which such rights are claimed. It has been contended, in fact, that "recognition is a right which other States are under an obligation to render",[88] even though there has never been an action brought by one state against another for injury suffered consequent upon delayed recognition.[89] Equally, an entity claiming to be a state has no option regarding its acceptance of the rules of international law, for by claiming the rights that attach to statehood it indicates its acceptance of the obligations that relate thereto: "the State newly arisen within the territorial domain of the family of nations becomes ipso facto and regardless of its consent a member of the international community and from that moment it becomes subject to all international rights and duties".[90] However, at the present time many newly created states contend that they are not bound by rules of international law alleged to exist at the time of the birth of such states, other than those to which they have expressly given their consent.[91]

85. See §63.

86. See §§75-90.

87. See Lauterpacht, Recognition in International Law (1947), pp. 41-51; Chen, The International Law of Recognition (1951), pp. 14-17, 51-53, 62-78, 90-93, 117-130; 2 Whiteman 17-26.

88. 2 Phillimore, Commentaries upon International Law (1882), 37.

89. On delayed recognition, see Lauterpacht *op. cit.*, pp. 74-75; Chen, *op. cit.*, pp. 51-54.

90. Kunz, Die Annerkennung von Staaten und Regierungen im Völkerrecht (1928), p. 88. (cited in Lauterpacht, *op. cit.*, p. 66); see also §§119-131 on continuity of personality; see also Hall, International Law (1924), pp. 19-20: "States being the persons governed by international law, communities are subjected to law . . . from the moment at which they acquire the marks of a state. So soon, therefore, as a society can point to the necessary marks, and indicates its intention of conforming to law, it

enters of right into the family of states, and must be treated in conformity with law."
See Snyder and Sathirathai, Third World Attitudes toward International Law, 1987.
91. See Green, "The Impact of the New States on International Law", in Law and
Society (1975), pp. 183, 223-225; see also Trudeau Press Conference, April 18, 1970, 9
I.L.M. 600 at 602-604; and letter to The Times (London), Aug. 14, 1978, by Shaupa
Kaukungun, Chief Representative for Western Europe of the South-West Africa
People's Organization re status of Walfish Bay under Treaty of Berlin, 1885, 165
C.T.S. 485.

§94 Secondly, and in contrast to the declaratory, is the constitutive
theory of recognition.[83] According to this theory, a state has no existence
in the eyes of international law, regardless of its factual existence, until it
has been recognized by states already in existence. In other words, it is
the act of recognition that creates the statehood. On the other hand, it is
generally accepted that even before recognition has taken place, the
embryo state does enjoy certain rights, for example, the right to territory,
so that no third state is able to argue that the territory in question is res
nullius and so open to occupation by any existing state.[93] Thus, the
Charter of the Organization of American States, Bogotá, 1948, states[94]:
"The political existence of the State is independent of recognition by
other States. Even before being recognized, the State has the right to
provide for its preservation and prosperity, and consequently to
organize itself as it sees fit, to legislate concerning its interests, to
administer its services, and to determine the jurisdiction and competence of its courts. The exercise of these rights is limited only by the
exercise of the rights of other States in accordance with international
law." All the rights herein mentioned may be regarded as falling within
the domestic competence of the entity in question. It is only when the
entity seeks to have relations with an existing State or vice versa that the
question of recognition and rights inter se arises. "Recognition implies
that the State granting it accepts the personality of the new State, with all
the rights and duties that international law prescribes for the two
States."[95] However, the fact that a limited form of relationship takes
place, as, for example, an armistice agreement to terminate hostilities,[96]
or co-signature of a multi-lateral treaty like the Pact of Paris, 1928,[97] or
the signing of a trade agreement[98] does not necessarily mean that the
signature of such an agreement constitutes recognition. In other words,
it is dangerous to imply recognition from conduct. Now, state practice
tends to rely upon direct and specific declarations of recognition, although an act by an existing state affecting the new entity might be of
such character that the actor regards it as involving recognition. Such a
situation arises when a member of the United Nations votes in favour of
the admission as a new member of an applicant not already recognized
by the voting State.[99]

92. Lauterpacht, Recognition in International Law (1947), pp. 38-41, 52-58; Chen, The International Law of Recognition (1951), pp. 17-18, 30-32, 39-51; 2 Whiteman 20-26.

93. See, e.g., attitude of U.S. towards newly proclaimed independence by Baltic States in 1919 and recognition of continued territorial integrity of Russia after destruction of Empire, 1 Hackworth 199-200. See also Oppenheim, who states: "There is no doubt that Statehood itself is independent of recognition. International Law does not say that a State is not in existence so long as it is not recognized, but it takes no notice of it before recognition", 1 International Law (1st ed., 1905), p. 110. This statement still appears in the 5th edition, the first edited by Lauterpacht, but has disappeared from those subsequently edited by him, although these retain the statement that "through recognition only and exclusively a State becomes an International Person and a subject of International Law", (8th ed., 1955), p. 126.

94. 119 U.N.T.S. 48. Supp. 43, Art. 9: this Article has become Art. 12 by the Protocol of Buenos Aires, 1967, 6 I.L.M. 310.

95. Art. 10, renumbered 13.

96. See the armistice Agreements between Israel and her Arab neighbours (1949, Egypt), 42 U.N.T.S. 251, Lebanon, p. 287, Jordan, p. 303, Syria, p. 327; see also Rosenne, Israel's Armistice Agreements with the Arab States (1951).

97. Kellogg-Briand Pact, 94 L.N.T.S. 57; see statement made by U.S. State Dept. re Soviet adherence to the Pact, 23 Oct. 1928, 1 Hackworth 353-4; see also U.S. statement in Protocol of Signature to International Sanitary Convention (1926), 78 L.N.T.S. 334. See also statement by Secretary of State for External Affairs re Test Ban Treaty 1963 (2 I.L.M. 883): "adherence to the Moscow Treaty, by régimes which are not already recognized by Canada in no way constituted extension of Canadian recognition to them", H.C. Deb. 1963, vol. 5, 5195. See Bot, Non-Recognition and Treaty Relations (1968). As to the effect of admission to the United Nations, see §64.

98. See Binavince, "Canadian Practice in Matters of Recognition" in Macdonald, Canadian Perspectives on International Law and Organization (1974), pp. 153, 181; Canada signed a trade agreement with East Germany in 1964, between 1970 and 1972 sought to put trade relations with the Democratic German Republic on a most-favoured-nation basis, but did not recognize the existence of the Republic until 1975.

99. This appears to have been the case as between Canada and Israel. In August 1949 Canada announced that she regarded her vote in favour of Israel's admission to the United Nations in May 1949 "as having implied fully recognition by the Government of Canada of the State of Israel", Israel Foreign Office letter, FO/I/60, Nov. 12, 1949; see Binavince, op. cit., p. 180. Prior to this, in December 1948 Canada had informed Israel that it "recognizes de facto the State of Israel in Palestine", ibid. 169; see also §98 note 37 re Republic of Korea; see, however, §96 note 30. De facto recognition tends to be used when it is not certain that the entity being recognized is likely to survive and is usually reserved as an interim process in the recognition of governments rather than of states: see §§97, 99, 102.

§95 In the light of state practice it may be said that recognition of a state is declaratory of a factual situation and constitutive of legal consequences, in the sense that the recognizing state acknowledges that the factual situation is such that the entity seeking recognition is entitled to all the rights and duties that attach to a subject of international law. The act of recognition is a political act by the recognizing state and depends on the exercise of discretion by that state. This may be seen in official statements made by the Secretary of State for External Affairs as to Canadian policy on this matter: "As far as recognition of states is concerned, the Canadian Government must first be satisfied that any entity claiming statehood meets the basic requirements of international law, that is, an independent government wielding effective authority over a definite territory. When these conditions appear to be fulfilled, the timing of recognition is determined in accordance with Canadian national interests, given the political and economic consequences of recognition. Once granted, state recognition survives changes in government,[1] unless it is explicitly withdrawn.[2] . . . Recognition of a foreign state is . . . an act of mixed character. It is legal inasmuch as the basic criteria which define a state are laid down by international law. It is political in the sense that an act of recognition expresses the attitude of one state towards another. When the question of recognition arises, the Government first examines whether the legal criteria for statehood are met — that is, whether the state in question has a definite territory, a stable population, and a viable independent government able to maintain public order.[3] Once these criteria are met, the Government examines, in the light of Canadian interests, whether an act of recognition is appropriate. There is no obligation on Canada to recognize another state.[4] Recognition can therefore be withheld, and has been withheld, in certain cases to indicate disapproval of policies especially repugnant to Canadians, such as those of the regime in Rhodesia.[5] Similarly, Canada refused to recognize the unilateral declaration of independence of the Turkish Republic of Northern Cyprus.[6] While recognition can be a purely political tool when it is used to give support to entities which do not yet meet the international legal criteria of statehood, this is not a practice that Canada follows."[7] The question of premature recognition, implied in this last comment, arises frequently in connection with attempts by parts of existing states to break away and form independent entities of their own, as happened, for example, with the dissolution of the Austro-Hungarian Empire. If the original state itself recognizes the new entity, there can be no question of premature recognition if recognition is extended by another state. Similarly, if the new entity is recognized in a treaty, for example, a peace treaty to which the original state is a party, there is again no question of premature recognition. If, however, the original state does not recognize the new entity which is still unable to satisfy the generally accepted criteria of statehood, a premature act of recognition would constitute a breach of the Charter of the United Nations which obligates members to respect the territorial integrity of states.[8] Moreover the United Nations Declaration on Friendly Relations, 1970[9] expressly states: "Nothing in the foregoing paragraphs [relating to non-self-governing territories] shall be construed as authorizing or encouraging any action which would dismember or impair, totally or in part, the territorial integrity or political unity of sovereign and independent States conducting themselves in compliance with the principle of equal rights and self-determination of peoples . . . possessed of a government representing the whole people belonging to the territory without distinction as to race, creed or colour. . . . Every State shall refrain from any action aimed at the partial or total disruption of the national unity and territorial integrity of any other State or country."

1. This illustrates the fact that the personality of the state is distinct from the identity of the government that represents it.

2. Letter by Mitchell Sharp (July 23, 1971), (1972) 10 C.Y.B.I.L. 308-309. The United Kingdom withdrew recognition of Abyssinia as an independent state when it extended de jure recognition to the King of Italy as Emperor of Ethiopia, *Haile Selassie v. Cable & Wireless (No. 2)*, [1939] Ch. 182 (C.A.). Similarly, when Canada recognized the People's Republic of China in 1969, this was tantamount to withdrawal of recognition from the Nationalist Republic of China: see Castel, International Law (1976), pp. 90-94; see also Green, "Representation versus Membership: The Chinese Precedent in the United Nations", (1972) 10 C.Y.B.I.L. 102, 128-129.

3. See §63.

4. Canada therefore rejects any idea that there is a duty to recognize as is inherent in Lauterpacht's view of the declaratory theory: "Although recognition is thus declaratory of an existing fact, such declaration, made in the *impartial fulfilment of a legal duty*, is constitutive as between the recognizing State and the community so recognized, of international rights and duties associated with full statehood", Lauterpacht, Recognition in International Law (1947), p. 6 (italics added).

5. Southern Rhodesia issued a unilateral declaration of independence as Rhodesia in 1965, but not a single state extended recognition (see Zacklin, The United Nations and Rhodesia (1974); Green "Rhodesian Independence — Legal or Illegal?", (1968) 6 Alta. L.R. 37 "Southern Rhodesian Independence", (1969) 14 Archiv des Völkerrechts 155). See *Re James*, [1977] 1 Ch. 41 (Ch.). When, however, Rhodesia was replaced by Zimbabwe in 1980, the latter received almost immediate recognition and admission to the United Nations.

6. Statement in House of Commons, 17 November 1983, at 28939, and 28 Nov. at 29273, (1984) 22 C.Y.B.I.L. pp. 340, 341.

7. Letter of Jan. 25, 1972, (1973) 11 C.Y.B.I.L. 308. See also, Binavince, "Canadian Practice in Matters of Recognition" in Macdonald, Canadian Perspectives on International Law and Organization (1974).

8. Art. 2(4). By para. 6 non-members, too, are required to recognize the principles embodied in Art. 2. The recognition by India of the independence of Bangladesh in Dec., 1971, largely as a result of Indian intervention in the civil war, was a clear breach of Art. 2(4) and was criticised by many members of the U.N. However, Bangladesh soon acquired recognition as an independent state from a number of states and was admitted to the United Nations in 1974.

9. General Assembly Res. 2625 (XXV).

§96 Since the state is the entity that constitutes the subject of international law, it is possible for this entity to be recognized even though its government does not receive the same treatment.[10] The effect of the recognition of a government is to enable official relations to be carried on between the recognizing state and the recognized entity. Normally, if the transition from the government of a state to another government is peaceful and in accordance with constitutional processes, no question of recognition of the new government arises.[11] Problems arise, however, when the entity claiming to be a government has assumed power with the birth of a new state or by seizing power as a result of some civil disturbance.[12] Broadly speaking, recognition is afforded to an authority which has clearly established itself as able to govern the territory in question and represent it on the international plane. This means that states enjoy a great amount of discretion in making this decision and occasionally specify broad outlines of policy which they assert will guide them in deciding this question. Thus, for some years the United States maintained that it would not recognize any government which had not come to power by constitutional processes and received the support of the population,[13] but this policy has not been consistently maintained.[14] Other countries have based their policy on effectiveness alone, maintaining that to act otherwise would amount to improper interference in the internal affairs of the country concerned.[15] Canadian practice tends to be based on the principle of effectiveness, and the issue of legitimacy or constitutionality and consent of the governed plays little or no part in the decision whether recognition should be extended. Similarly, the question whether the administration seeking recognition is prepared to fulfil existing international obligations[16] is not of major importance. Canadian policy in this regard may be seen in a memorandum issued by the Legal Bureau of the Department of External Affairs concerning the recognition of a government taking office after a coup d'état:[17] ". . . Il semble que ce nouveau régime remplisse les conditions juridiques pour qu'il soit reconnu: ainsi, il aurait déjà établi son autorité effective et ce, avec des perspectives raisonnables de permanence.[18] Il faudrait de plus que le nouveau régime endosse de façon tacite ou expresse les obligations internationales toutefois, cette condition doit être considérée comme secondaire par rapport à la question de l'autorité effective sur le pays. Même si les conditions dites juridiques sont remplies, il n'en reste pas moins que la décision du Canada doit être de nature 'politico-juridique'.[19] Il appartient donc au Ministre de prendre une décision au sujet de l'aspect politique du problème.[20] Si la décision prise est favorable à la reconnaissance, elle pourrait être exprimée de façon tacite par la

129

simple poursuite des relations diplomatiques normales[21]; toutefois, si le nouveau régime demandait de façon formelle, c'est-à-dire au moyen d'une Note diplomatique, à être reconnu, nous devrions faire part de notre décision de façon expresse et formelle au moyen d'une Note diplomatique".[22] As if to confirm the overriding significance of effectiveness and permanence, this memorandum continued "Selon la pratique canadienne en matière de reconnaissance, il serait, de plus, à propos d'attendre que la situation se soit stabilisée avant de poursuivre des relations diplomatiques normales avec ce pays." This statement of Canadian policy with regard to a government assuming power after a coup d'état is fully in accord with the general practice pursued by Canada:[23] "Canadian practice in the recognition of . . . changes in governments is to treat each situation on its own merits and an appropriate politico-legal decision is taken in due course. Some of the more relevant considerations governing Canadian practice are outlined.[24] . . . 'In general, Canadian practice in extending recognition follows that of other states with a Western legal heritage.[25] Thus Canada subscribes to the principle that the recognition of a government involves a decision as to whether an authority claiming to be the government of a state is entitled to be regarded as representing that state on the international plane. The essential question is whether the government in question is able to exercise effective control with a reasonable prospect of permanency in the area which it claims to govern;[26] the support it enjoys of the population and its expressed willingness to fulfil its international obligations may also be taken into account. While the act of recognition is essentially legal in character, the relevancy of political considerations is recognized in modern international practice.[27] Accordingly, there is scope for the exercise of a wide but not arbitrary[28] discretion in the determination of whether these considerations have been met. It may be worth noting that while previous acts of recognition are taken into consideration and may have some relevance as precedents, in point of fact each situation is considered on its own merits.[29] It is also perhaps worth noting here that Canada does not consider that an affirmative vote on the admission of a state to the United Nations, implies recognition of that state or its government.'[30] It seems to us that it would mark a significant departure in Canadian practice on recognition if Canada were to recognize the provisional government of a new state[31] before it met the standard criteria under international law for such recognition".[32]

10. Thus, while Canada recognized both the State of Vietnam and the Republic of Vietnam as successor states to the state of Vietnam recognized in 1952 while an associated state in the French Union, it only recognized the Government of the State of [South] Vietnam, Sharp letter (Oct. 4, 1971), (1972) 10 C.Y.B.I.L. 309.

11.   Sharp letter, §95 note 2 "Most of the time, when an orderly change of government or type of government occurs in a territorial entity recognized by Canada as a state, the question of recognition does not arise. In such cases, the recognition already granted to a previous government continues to apply to its successors."

12.   See text to note 17, *post*.

13.   The Wilsonian doctrine of legitimacy is discussed in 1 Hackworth 180-186, 2 Whiteman 69-71, Chen, The International Law of Recognition (1951), ch. 5. In 1917, the United States refused to recognize the régime of Tinoco who had seized power, and declared that "even if he is elected he will not be given recognition by the U.S.", which insisted that the only government it would recognize was one elected in accordance with the constitution as it existed before Tinoco seized power, 1 Hackworth 233-7. A number of other countries similarly refused to recognize the Tinoco government even after it had been confirmed by election, but nevertheless contended that, although unrecognized, it was sufficiently in authority and control to grant concessions to aliens which would be binding on the recognized successor government; *Tinoco Concessions* (G.B./Costa Rica) (1923), 1 R.I.A.A. 369. In *South Moluccus (Republic) v. Royal Packet Shipping Co.* (1951), 17 I.L.R. 143 at 147, the Amsterdam Court of Appeal held that, despite the absence of recognition, the Republic existed de facto. See, also, Galloway, Recognizing Foreign Governments: The Practice of the U.S., 1978. For an example of a successful government refusing to recognize the validity of acts of judges in an area under de facto control of rebels, see *Oguebie v. Odunwoke* (1979), 70 I.L.R. 17 (Nigeria S.C.).

14.   Thus, in May 1978, after a successful coup in Afghanistan establishing the Democratic Republic of Afghanistan, the United States announced its intention "to maintain diplomatic relations" on the assumption "that the Government of the Democratic Republic of Afghanistan will continue to honor and support the existing treaties and international agreements in force between our two States", (1978) U.S. Digest 64-65. In September 1969 the U.S. Senate had adopted a Resolution affirming its view "that when the U.S. recognizes a foreign government and exchanges diplomatic representatives with it, this does not of itself imply that the U.S. approves of the form, ideology, or policy of the foreign government," *ibid.* 65. On 1 Jan. 1979, the U.S. recognized the People's Republic of China despite the absence of any election indicating that the government enjoyed the support of the people, *ibid.* 70-75.

15.   This was the basis for U.K. recognition of the Soviet Government de facto in 1921 — "They may have as complete control over that vast territory as any Government could possibly have under present conditions, and therefore they have to be recognized as the de facto Government of that Empire" — although de jure recognition did not follow until 1924, Lauterpacht, Recognition in International Law (1947), pp. 338-339. In Jan. 1950, however, the U.K. recognized the People's Republic as the de jure government of China as "it is now in effective control of by far the greater part of the territory of China", Chen, The International Law of Recognition (1951), pp. 119-120; see also, *Civil Air Transport Inc. v. Central Air Transport Corp.*, [1953] A.C. 70 (P.C.). In March 1988 the U.S. continued to recognize as President of Panama an individual who had been replaced by the legislature under pressure from a military leader who had been dismissed by the former President and had been indicted in the U.S. on a variety of criminal charges.

16.   See *Tinoco Concessions, ante.*

17.   (1974) 12 C.Y.B.I.L. 300-301.

18.   If a 'government' appears to be administering an area, but there is doubt whether it will be able to remain in power, particularly during a civil war, the

tendency is to afford de facto recognition, *The Arantzazu Mendi*, [1939] A.C. 265 (H.L.). Similarly, if the 'government' describes itself as 'provisional' it will only receive de facto recognition: see Canada and Israel, 1948, Castel International Law (1976), pp. 87-88.

19. The varying attitudes to the grant of recognition to the People's Republic of China, with the U.K. recognizing in 1950, Canada in 1970 (Castel, *op. cit.*, p. 93) and the U.S. in 1979 illustrated this.

20. The members of the Organization of American States, and of the Pan-American Union, sought to forbid recognition of revolutionary régimes unless certain conditions were fulfilled, Thomas and Thomas, The Organization of American States (1963), ch. 11; see also Central American Treaty (1923), Art. 2 (2 Hudson, Int. Leg. 902).

21. Since diplomatic relations depend upon mutual acceptance and respect and since ambassadors are appointed by the head of state, the appointment of a diplomat, as distinct from a special agent, e.g., a trade representative (*Fenton Textile Association v. Krassin* (1921), 38 T.L.R. 260), confirms that the authority to which the diplomat is accredited is accepted as a government, even though there is no express statement to this effect.

22. On occasion, when a new government assumes power, or a new state comes into existence, a message of congratulation serves the same purpose, Memo. May 31, 1973, (1974) 12 C.Y.B.I.L. 299.

23. Memo. Sept. 30, 1973, 12 C.Y.B.I.L. 301-2. A somewhat more spelled-out statement is embodied in a memo of July 18, 1974, (1975) 13 C.Y.B.I.L. 355-6. See, however, §101.

24. This extract is taken from a memo of July 10, 1969.

25. This tends to refer to Commonwealth rather than U.S. practice.

26. It can happen that during a civil war two different administrations are recognized as effectively administering different areas of the same state, but only one of these will be recognized as the de jure government: see *The Arantzazu Mendi, ante.*

27. The recognition of the Chinese People's Republic, and its acceptance by the General Assembly as representing China as a member of the United Nations, is the clearest example of this, see §95 note 2 and §96 note 19.

28. In fact, there is no authority able to declare that the recognizing state has acted in an 'arbitrary' fashion, although its act might amount to premature recognition: see §98 note 5.

29. A similar situation prevails with regard to admissions to the U.N. Thus, the determination, when India divided into India and Pakistan, that India remained a foundation member while Pakistan, as a new state, had to apply for admission, as well as the policies adopted re the foundation and dissolution of the United Arab Republic and the withdrawal from and return to membership of Indonesia, confirm that none of these can be taken as a precedent for the future, see Green, "The Dissolution of States and Membership in the United Nations" (1967), 32 Sask. L.R. 93.

30. This statement is contrary to the attitude adopted by Canada towards Israel (see §94 note 99), and to the Republic of Korea (see §98 note 37). Moreover, since only a state can be admitted to the U.N. and since that state acts in the U.N. through its government, it is difficult to see how a member voting affirmatively for admission can deny that it has recognized both state and government.

31. See, however, U.K. recognition of the Lettish National Council and its Provisional Government in 1918, followed by recognition of Latvia in 1921: Lauterpacht, Recognition of International Law (1947), pp. 333-334; as to the Czech National Committee, *ibid.* 164.

32. Canada recognized the provisional government of Israel in December 1948, stating that "the recognition . . . is accorded in the knowledge that the boundaries of the new State have not as yet been precisely defined. . . ." (Castel, International Law (1976), p. 88; for short statements on Canadian, U.S. and British recognition practice, see 1987 ed., pp. 274-279).

§97 As may be seen from the Canadian statements of policy, in practice states frequently distinguish between de facto and de jure recognition. The former indicates that there is, in the view of the recognizing state, some doubt as to the permanence of the entity being recognized, so that the act of recognition is merely an acknowledgement that the latter does in fact exist and is regarded as being entitled to some of the legal consequences attaching to its status as a state or a government. De facto recognition is normally followed by recognition de jure, which constitutes an acknowledgement that the entity recognized is regarded as a state or government in the fullest sense of that term and entitled to all the rights and subject to all the obligations attaching to that status. Occasionally, the term de jure is used in a fashion that suggests that the state or government in question has come into existence in accordance with some legal or constitutional process,[33] but both terms should in fact not refer in any way to the mode of creation, or national legality, but merely to the nature of the recognition in the sense that different consequences flow from the type of recognition in question.

33. In the case of a state this may be, e.g., by way of agreement with a former colonial power or by creation through a peace treaty. In the case of a government, it implies that one which has come to power by revolution or civil war cannot be de jure or even perhaps de facto; see, however, *Tinoco Concessions, ante*: ". . . when recognition vel non of a government is . . . determined by inquiry, not into its de facto sovereignty and complete governmental control, but into its illegitimacy or irregularity of origin, [the] non-recognition loses something of evidential weight on the issue with which those applying the rules of international law are alone concerned. . . . To hold that a government which establishes itself and maintains a peaceful administration, with the acquiescence of the people for a substantial period of time, does not become a de facto government unless it conforms to a previous constitution would be to hold that within the rules of international law a revolution contrary to the fundamental law of the existing government cannot establish a new government. This cannot be, and is not, true. . . . To speak of a revolution creating a de facto government, which conforms to the limitations of the old constitution is to use a contradiction in terms" (per Taft, C.J., sole arbitrator, at p. 381). From this point of view the revolutionary government becomes de jure internally when a constitution is adopted to this effect, or when the local courts accept its legislation as legal.

§98　Generally speaking, the distinction between de jure and de facto recognition does not apply in the case of states, but only in regard to governments. This is particularly so nowadays as new entities invariably apply for admission to the United Nations immediately upon their establishment and, especially since the settlement of the conflict between east and west concerning multiple admissions in 1955,[34] the tendency is to admit the applicant as early as possible.[35] Since only states may be admitted to the United Nations,[36] countries voting in favour of the admission are construed as recognizing the applicant as a state in every sense of the word.[37] Insofar as those voting against admission may not yet have granted recognition, it is controversial whether joint membership of the United Nations implies recognition.[38]

34.　See Goodrich, The United Nations (1959), pp. 88-96.

35.　Seventeen new members, primarily former French African colonies, were admitted in 1960, and between 1961 and 1971 32 former colonies and protectorates became members; by 1959 membership had increased from the original 51 to 83, and by 1972 there were 132 members: see Goodrich, The United Nations in a Changing World (1974), pp. 47-48: "The expansion of membership since 1955 has taken place without extensive debate and with few objections being raised or critical questions asked. . . . Such discussions as have occurred on the admission of these states had not revealed any consistent attempt to judge whether these states met the requirements of Article 4, paragraph 1 of the Charter", ibid., p. 49. By 1983 there were 157 members.

36.　Charter of the United Nations, Art. 4, see §§62, 64, 414.

37.　See §64 note 54 re Canada and Israel; see, also, re request for recognition by Republic of Korea: "The Canadian Government . . . considers that the vote cast by the Canadian Delegation in the Security Council . . . in support of a resolution favouring the admission of the Republic of Korea to membership in the U.N. is to be regarded as full recognition by the Government of Canada of the Republic of Korea as an independent sovereign State . . .", (1949) External Affairs, No. 8, p. 19.

38.　See §64.

§99　On occasion, recognition has been granted to a state de facto to indicate that, while some of the conditions assumed necessary for statehood[39] are lacking, or it is not yet certain that independence is fully secured,[40] the recognizing state wishes to indicate its political approval of the new creation and its intention to deal with it as a state with the intention of extending de jure recognition when the defects have been remedied. This was the case with Canada's recognition of Israel.[41] It may be the case, however, that one of the factors normally considered essential for statehood, for example, fixed frontiers, takes so long to be determined that de jure recognition is afforded despite this lack. This is the case with Israel which has now been recognized de jure by the majority of states, even though its ultimate frontiers are still in dispute.[42]

39. See §63.

40. This is likely to be the case when the new entity breaks away from an existing state or is a colonial territory unilaterally declaring independence and it is not certain whether the colonial power will re-establish its authority, but, despite its unilateral declaration of independence, no state recognized Rhodesia de facto or de jure.

41. The Secretary of State for External Affairs announced on Dec. 24, 1948: "The Canadian Government has today informed the provisional government of Israel that the Canadian Government recognizes de facto the State of Israel in Palestine and that it also recognizes de facto the authority of the provisional government of Israel. The State of Israel was proclaimed on May 15, 1948. During the seven months that have elapsed, the State of Israel has, in the opinion of the Canadian Government, given satisfactory proof that it complies with the essential conditions of statehood. These essential conditions are generally recognized to be external independence and effective internal government within a reasonably well-defined territory. The provisional government of Israel has been informed that the recognition given by Canada is accorded in the knowledge that the boundaries of the new State have not as yet been precisely defined and in the hope that it may be possible to settle these and all other outstanding questions in the spirit of the resolution adopted by the General Assembly of the United Nations on December 11, 1948" (Res. 194 (III) calling for agreement and final settlement of all questions outstanding between Israel and the Arab states), 1 External Affairs, No. 1, 1949, 29, cited in Castel, pp. 87-88). See also the U.S. declaration of 14 May 1948, the day of Israel's declaration of independence: "The United States recognizes the provisional government as the de facto authority of the new State of Israel": 1 Whiteman 231, and statement by Jessup, Representative of the U.S., in the Security Council, Dec. 2, 1948, explaining Israel's qualification to become a member of the U.N. in accordance with the requirements of Art. 4 of the Charter: 1 Whiteman 230-231.

42. By the date of Israel's admission to the United Nations, May 11, 1949, 54 states, including 9 non-members, had recognized Israel as a state.

§100   The fact that a state has been recognized does not mean that this is also true of its government. This is especially the case when an existing government has been overthrown and other states have not yet decided that they wish to treat with the newly-established regime. Moreover, it must be borne in mind that the governmental structure is within the domestic jurisdiction of the state[43] and is no legal concern of any other state, nor, in the absence of any treaty regulation,[44] is it a matter affected by international law. Similarly, a change of government does not normally affect the personality of the state,[45] although it is sometimes contended that if a revolution substantially changes the entire structure of the state it may result in the replacement of the existing state, so that recognition of the new state entity becomes an issue.[46] Sometimes, a state may be absorbed by another state, either by annexation or by apparent agreement. When this occurs, third states may be unwilling for their own political reasons, or because they do not accept that the accession was voluntary, to recognize this de jure, while recognizing it as a fact. Such de facto recognition acknowledges that the absorbing state is the effective ruler of the former state.[47]

43. See §§78, 79, 83. See, however, the U.S. and Panama in 1988 at §96 note 15.

44. E.g., by the Treaty of Berlin, 1878 (153 C.T.S. 172), Bulgaria, for example, was required to accept religious freedom as part of its public law; similarly by the Peace Treaties, 1947 (Bulgaria, 41 U.N.T.S. 21; Hungary, 41 U.N.T.S. 135; Roumania, 42 U.N.T.S. 3; Finland, 48 U.N.T.S. 226; Italy, 49 U.N.T.S. 126), the former Axis powers were obliged to guarantee human rights to all within their jurisdiction and not to enact any discriminatory legislation; see also the Occupation Statute, 1949, (H.M.S.O., Cmd. 7677) whereby the Western Occupying Powers conferred self-government on the German Federal Republic; see Green, "The New Regime in Western Germany" (1949) 3 World Affairs 368.

45. See *Lehigh Valley Ry. v. Russia* (1927), 21 Fed. 396: "The granting or refusal of recognition has nothing to do with the recognition of the state itself. If a foreign state refuses the recognition of a change in the form of government of an old state, this latter does not thereby lose its recognition as an international person. . . . [T]he state is perpetual and survives the form of its government" (per Judge Manton at p. 400). See also *The Sapphire* (1871), 78 U.S. 164: "The actual person or party in power is but the agent and representative of the national sovereignty. A change in such representative works no change in the national sovereignty or its right" (per Bradley J. at p. 168). See also *Lazard Bros. & Co. v. Midland Bank*, [1933] A.C. 289 (H.L.): "The identity of the State remains the same for international purposes: the change from monarchy to republic does not, in general, abrogate treaties or conventions any more than loss or increase in territory" (per Lord Wright, at p. 307). Similarly, when the Shah of Iran was replaced by the Islamic Republic of Iran in 1979 this did not affect the state's membership in the United Nations.

46. Thus, in 1889, when Hayti was divided in two warring camps, with neither administration recognized by the U.S., it was held in *The Conserva* (1889), 38 Fed. 431, that there was no "prince, state, colony, district or people" within the terms of U.S. neutrality legislation. On this, Jaffe, Judicial Aspects of Foreign Relations (1933), p. 103 comments ". . . at that time there was no state of Hayti at all". In 1870 Bismarck refused to conclude peace with France on the ground that the French State had ceased to exist with the Revolution, Baty, "So-called De Facto Recognition", (1921-22) 31 Yale L.J. 470 at 472, note 5.

47. See *Laane & Baltser v. Estonian State Cargo & Passenger S.S. Line*, [1948] Ex. C.R. 435 (Ex. Ct.); affirmed, [1949] S.C.R. 530 (S.C.C.); the comments of Anglin D.J.A. (pp. 441, 442) in the New Brunswick Admiralty District are the more relevant re recognition. In the course of its comments to the court, the Dept. of External Affairs stated: "The Government of Canada recognizes that Estonia has de facto entered the U.S.S.R., but does not recognize this de jure. . . . The Government of Canada does not recognize de facto the Republic of Estonia as constituted prior to June 1940. The Republic of Estonia as constituted prior to June 1940 has ceased de facto to have any effective existence. . . . The Government of Canada recognizes that Estonia has de facto entered the U.S.S.R. but has not recognized this de jure. . . . The Government of Canada recognizes the Government of the Estonian Soviet Socialist Republic to be the de facto government of Estonia but does not recognize it as the de jure government of Estonia" (statement signed by Secretary of State for External Affairs).

§101   Canadian policy regarding the recognition of a government achieving power by revolution was, prior to 1973, one of "express recognition". More recently, however, it has been a policy of tacit recognition in the case of a change government in any state recognized by Canada.[48] In exceptional cases, as when competing authorities claim to be the effective government, "Canada would undertake a review of the legal criteria for recognition",[49] as happened in the case of China.

48.   When, however, President Marcos of the Philippines was overthrown in February, 1986, Canada extended express recognition to Mme Acquino as President.

49.   Statement supplied by Legal Bureau, Dept. of External Affairs, Feb. 1986; see, however, statement of 18 Jul. 1984, (1985) 13 C.Y.B.I.L. 354-6.

§102   Problems normally arise when there are two entities in a single state territory each claiming to be the government of that state. While there cannot be two de jure governments,[50] there can be one de jure recognized as sovereign over the entire state territory and one de facto recognized as actually exercising governmental authority and power over the territory under its administration.[51] Whether or not a particular entity is recognized as the government de jure or de facto is a decision made, at least in common law countries, by the executive,[52] with courts accepting this as authoritative,[53] but deciding for themselves the legal effect of the executive decision. Thus, in *The Arantzazu Mendi*[54] the court held that the British recognition of the Franco administration in that part of Spain under its control as exercising effective administrative control therein was tantamount to de facto recognition, while in *The Elise*[55] the Certificate from the Department of External Affairs stated that the effect of a Soviet decree applying to Estonia was for the court to decide. However, it may happen that the executive statement indicates that the court is precluded from giving effect to any particular legal consequence flowing from recognition of the entity as a government. In the *Civil Air Transport* case,[56] a Hong Kong Order in Council expressly forbade the court from denying itself jurisdiction on the ground that to exercise it would implead a foreign state. When de jure recognition has been extended it is usual for the courts, in the absence of a directive to the contrary or indicating a different date, to give the recognition retroactive effect to the date of establishment of the government.[57]

50.   However, it may happen, as it did with China after the Communist takeover in 1950, that different states recognize different authorities as the government de jure of the country. Insofar as China was concerned, this meant that some countries which had recognized the People's Republic as de jure government of China continued to accept the representative of the Nationalist Government in Taiwan as the proper authority to represent China in the United Nations: see Green, "Representation

versus Membership: The Chinese Precedent in the United Nations", (1972) 10 C.Y.B.I.L. 102.

51.   See *The Arantzazu Mendi*, [1939] A.C. 256 (H.L.); *Civil Air Transport Inc. v. Central Air Transport Corp.*, [1953] A.C. 70 (P.C.).

52.   *Civil Air Transport Inc. v. Central Air Transport Corp., ante*; see also *United States v. Pink* (1942), 315 U.S. 203 (S.C.); *Laane & Baltser v. Estonian State Cargo & Passenger S.S. Line, ante*; *Weinmann v. Republic of Latvia* (1959), 28 I.L.R. 385 (Fed. Rep. of Germany); *Re Oroli* (1942), 11 I.L.R. 13 (Australia); *United States v. Republic of China* (1950), 17 I.L.R. 168 (Australia); see also Jaffe, Judicial Aspects of Foreign Relations (1933); Lyons, "Conclusiveness of the Foreign Office Certificate", (1946) 23 Y.B.I.L. 240; "Conclusiveness of the Statements of the Executive: Continental and Latin American Practice", (1948) B.Y.B.I.L. 180; "Judicial Application of International Law and the 'Temporizing' Certificate of the Executive", (1952) 29 B.Y.B.I.L. 227; Hardy, "Certificats presentés en cour par le Ministère des Affaires extérieures: La pratique canadienne", (1977) 15 C.Y.B.I.L. 236. For an official Canadian view on the use of such certificates, see Legal Bureau memo, 29 April 1983, (1984) 22 C.Y.B.I.L. 331-3. See also *Sayce v. Ameer of Bahawalpur*, [1952] 2 All E.R. 64 (C.A.) in which the Court of Appeal accepted as binding a statement made by the Government of Pakistan to the Commonwealth Relations Office that the Ameer of Bahawalpur, despite the accession of his state to the Federation of Pakistan, at that time still a member of the Commonwealth, "continued to be a sovereign ruler and is entitled to immunity both within and outside Pakistan in civil cases". Normally, it is for the court before which a foreign state claims immunity to decide whether such immunity shall be granted. See §149.

53.   See the cases cited at notes 51, 52, and *Laane & Baltser v. Estonian State Cargo & Passenger S.S. Line, ante*. See also *Latvian Cargo & Passenger S.S. Line v. McGrath* (1951), 80 F. 2d 1000 at 1002 per Prettyman C.J.: ". . . when the executive branch of the Government has determined upon a foreign policy, which can be and is ascertained, and the non-recognition of specific foreign decrees is deliberate and shown to be part of that policy, such non-recognition must be given effect by the courts. The rule applicable in such circumstances is the same rule applicable to an act of recognition. Any other treatment of a deliberate policy and act of non-recognition would reduce the effective control over foreign affairs by the executive branch to a mere effectiveness [sic] of acts of recognition. The control of the executive branch over foreign affairs must necessarily be broader than that". See, however, *Wulfsohn v. Russian Federated Soviet Republic* (1923), 234 N.Y.S. 372.

54.   [1939] A.C. 256 at 265 (H.L.). Lord Atkin, with whom the other Law Lords agreed, said " 'By exercising de facto administrative control' or 'exercising effective administrative control', I understand exercising all the functions of a sovereign government. . . . [I]t seems to me that the recognition of a government as possessing all those attributes in a territory while not subordinate to any other government in that territory is to recognise it as sovereign, and for the purposes of international law as a foreign sovereign state. . . . I think that it was established by the Foreign Office letter that the Nationalist Government of Spain at the date of the writ was a foreign sovereign state and could not be impleaded": Lord Atkin has confused recognition of a government with that of a state. Lord Wright, at pp. 267-8, said: "The court is . . . bound without any qualification by the statement of the Foreign Office, which is the organ of H.M.G. for this purpose in a matter of this nature. Such a statement is a statement of fact, the contents of which are not open to be discussed by the court on grounds of law. . . . The question of law left to the court was what was the effect of

these facts on the issues before the court. For the purposes of this case the letter of the Foreign Office . . . stated sufficiently, and in substance, that the Nationalist Government of Spain had been recognized by H.M.G. as a de facto government, not subordinate to any other government in Spain, and ruling over the larger portion of Spain . . .". The Foreign Office statement also stated that "H.M.G. recognises the Government of the Spanish Republic [against which Franco's forces were in conflict] as the de jure government of Spain."

55. See note 47: the court held that, as a result of the statement that the Republic of Estonia had ceased to exist de facto, while the Government of the Estonian Soviet Socialist Republic was recognized de facto, and that this Republic had de facto entered the U.S.S.R., it was precluded from considering the constitutionality of the decree in question, while holding it to be within the constitutional competence of the de facto government.

56. *Civil Air Transport Inc. v. Central Air Transport Corp.*, [1953] A.C. 70 (P.C.). See notes 51 and 57 in fine.

57. See *Williams v. Bruffy* (1877), 96 U.S. 176; *Luther v. James Sagor & Co.*, [1921] 3 K.B. 532 at 549 (C.A.); *Gdynia Ameryka Linie Zeglugowe Spolka Akcyjna v. Boguslawski*, [1953] A.C. 11 (H.L.), in which it was held that insofar as the territory of Poland was concerned recognition was retroactive to one date, while another was operative in respect of control of the merchant fleet; *Civil Air Transport Inc. v. Central Air Transport Corp., ante*, at pp. 89, 93 per Viscount Simon, in which the Foreign Office certificate stated that de jure recognition of the Nationalist Government ceased at midnight on January 5/6, 1950 when de jure recognition of the People's Republic commenced, that the Nationalists "ceased to be the *de facto* government of different parts of the territories of the Republic of China as from the dates on which it ceased to be in effective control of those parts. . . . [I]n the period between October 1, 1949, and January 5/6, 1950, the Central People's Government was the de facto government of those parts of the territory of the Republic of China over which it had established effective control, and if control was established after October 1, 1949, as from dates when it established control." This was interpreted by the Privy Council to mean: ". . . the former Nationalist Government must be regarded as the sole de jure sovereign government of China up to midnight of January 5-6, 1950; that the present Communist Government was not the de jure government until that time; and that, while the Foreign Office . . . acknowledged that from October 1, 1949, onwards the de facto government of those parts of China in which the Nationalist Government had ceased to be in effective control was the Communist Government, H.M.G. had not announced or communicated their recognition of the Communist Government over any part of China before they recognized the Communist Government as the de jure government of China on January 5-6, 1950. . . . [R]etroactivity of recognition operates to validate acts of a de facto government which has subsequently become the new de jure government, and not to invalidate acts of the previous de jure government". In *Oetjen v. Central Leather Co.* (1918), 246 U.S. 297 at 302 per Clarke J. (S.C.), the U.S. Supreme Court stated: "It is also the result of interpretation by this Court of the principles of international law that when a Government which originates in revolution or revolt is recognized by the political department of our Government as the de jure Government of the country in which it is established, such recognition is retroactive in effect and validates all the actions and conduct of the Government so recognized from the commencement of its existence". In *Laane & Baltser v. Estonian State Cargo & Passenger S.S. Line, ante*, Anglin D.J.A. pointed out that "the Department of External Affairs . . . said that it was not possible to attach a date to the

recognition of the de facto government of Estonia. It was first settled by the Supreme Court of the United States in *Williams v. Bruffy* that the effect of such recognition is retroactive to the time of the original establishment of the government. That decision on that point was followed by the English Court of Appeal in *Luther v. Sagor* and by the House of Lords in *Lazard Bros. & Co. v. Midland Bank,* [ante]. As there are no Canadian decisions on this point I should follow those high authorities on a question of international law (*R. v. The 'North'* (1906), 37 S.C.R. 385 (S.C.C.)). The parties in their admissions assign June 17, 1940, as the date of the establishment of 'a new government' in Estonia, known as the E.S.S.R. No date is therein assigned to the entry of the E.S.S.R. as a constituent member of the U.S.S.R. In *A/S Tallina Laevauhisis v. Tallinna Shipping Co.* (1946), 79 L.L.R. 245 at 256, Atkinson J. says that this latter date was August 6, 1940. "In view of the nature of the de facto government already adopted for the purposes of this action that date would be appropriate, and the decrees and the statute which are material were all enacted in October 1940" (at p. 424). These decisions regarding Estonia should be compared with the decision of the U.S. Court of Claims in *Estonian State Cargo S.S. Line v. United States* (1953), 116 F. Supp. 447. Unlike the U.K. and Canada, the U.S. has refused — and still refuses ((1978) U.S. Digest 1359) to recognize the incorporation of the Baltic States into the U.S.S.R. even de facto: Judge Whitaker said, at p. 452: "The Executive Dept. of our Government has refused to recognize the incorporation of Estonia into the U.S.S.R. and has refused to recognize the validity of any decrees issued by the U.S.S.R., or of the Presidium of the Provisional Soviet Socialist Republic of Estonia relative to persons and property within the territory of Estonia. That action having been taken by the Executive Dept. of our Government, the courts have also uniformly refused to recognize the validity of such decrees."

§103 It was formerly considered that there were substantial differences in the legal effects of de facto and de jure recognition. Since it is the government de jure which represents the state and acts for it on the international level, it is this government which nominates representatives to the United Nations[58] and which appoints ambassadors to other states,[59] and it is this government which has title to the property of the state existing within the recognizing state,[60] although it is controversial whether it is only the legislation of a de jure government which is recognized as having extra-territorial effect.[61] Since de facto recognition is frequently granted because there is doubt as to the permanency of the government concerned, it is often maintained that it is only this form of recognition which is revocable.[62] In fact, however, when a new government of an existing state is recognized de jure, the former government's recognition de jure is withdrawn, although it is contended that the former government has ceased to exist.[63] Since the decision in *The Arantzazu Mendi*,[64] however, it seems to be accepted[65] that there are no longer any differences between de facto and de jure recognition, both forms granting immunity from jurisdiction in third states.[66]

58.　It is for the Committee on Credentials to decide on this issue, and as was shown in the case of China the representative may well be sent by an authority which was not even recognized de facto by a number of members: §102 note 50. See, however, rejection of credentials of South Africa since 1970 on ground that they were issued by a non-representation government. See text to §416 note 89.

59.   However, the U.S. appointed an ambassador to India before that country became formally independent: "It appears from a State Dept. communication which was before the lower Court that although our Government did not formally recognize India as an independent nation until August 15, 1947 [the date of the transfer of power from the U.K.], it took steps to recognize the Interim Government of India after its formation on September 2, 1946, by receiving in February 1947 India's first ambassador, whose credentials were signed by the British Crown, and accrediting the first United States ambassador to India in 1947"; *Murraka v. Bachrack Bros.* (1954), 215 F. 2d 547 at 551 per Harlan C.J. See, however, *Fenton Textile Assn. v. Krassin* (1922), 38 T.L.R. 260.

60.   *Haile Selassie v. Cable & Wireless Ltd. (No. 2)*, [1939] Ch. 182 (C.A.). As to effect of law within the state in question, the legislation of a de facto government receives as much respect as that of a de jure government; see *Luther v. James Sagor & Co., ante,* and *Oetjen v. Central Leather Co., ante.* See also *Union of Soviet Socialist Republics v. Balaiew* (1925), 42 T.L.R. 21, recognizing right of de jure government to state property in recognizing state.

61.   See, however, *Laane & Baltser v. Estonian State Cargo & Passenger S.S. Line, ante,* at p. 455: ". . . a de facto government has no less power than a de jure government to enact legislation with the intent that it apply extraterritorially."

62.   See Chen, The International Law of Recognition (1951), ch. 16. See, however, *Azazh Kebbeda Tesema v. Italian Govt.* (1940), 10 Ann. Dig. 93, in which the High Commissioner for Palestine informed Trusted C.J.: "I have been acquainted by the Secretary of State for the Colonies that the de jure recognition by H.M.G. of the Italian conquest of Ethiopia [recognized in *Haile Selassie v. Cable & Wireless Ltd. (No. 2), ante*], has been withdrawn".

63.   This was what happened in so far as the Nationalist Government of China was concerned: *Civil Air Transport Inc. v. Central Air Transport Corp., ante.*

64.   *The Arantzazu Mendi,* [1939] A.C. 256 at 264-5 per Lord Atkin: "By 'exercising de facto administrative control' . . . I understand exercising all the functions of a sovereign government, in maintaining law and order, instituting and maintaining courts of justice, adopting or imposing laws regulating the relations of the inhabitants of the territory to one another and to the government. It necessarily implies the ownership and control of property whether for military or civil purposes, including vessels whether warships or merchant ships. In those circumstances it seems to me that the recognition of a government as possessing all those attributes in a territory while not subordinate to any other government in that territory is to recognize it as sovereign. . . . There is ample authority for the proposition that there is no difference for the present purpose between recognition of a state de facto as opposed to de jure. All the reasons for immunity which are the basis of the doctrine in international law as incorporated into our law exist. There is the same necessity for reciprocal rights of immunity, the same feeling of injured pride if jurisdiction is sought to be exercised, the same risk of belligerent action if government property is seized or injured".

65.   *Estonian State Cargo & Passenger S.S. Line v. The Elise,* [1948] Ex. C.R. 435 at 454 (Ex. Ct.): "It is clear from those remarks of Lord Atkin that in the present case the legislative acts of the de facto government in question must be treated as if they emanated from a de jure government."

66. *The Gagara*, [1919] P. 95 (C.A.); *The Arantzazu Mendi, ante.*

§104 Problems arise when as a result of the occupation of its territory the government of the state has departed from that territory and set itself up as a government-in-exile in some friendly state, usually that of an ally during war. This occurred during the Second World War in the case of most of the countries occupied by Axis Powers, many of which established themselves in the United Kingdom. Problems arose over the ownership of property, claims regarding immunity from local jurisdiction, or the right to exercise jurisdiction over nationals alleged to be liable to military service. Thus, in *Re de Bruijn*,[67] when called upon to consider the application of the Foreign Forces Order[68] to a deserter from the Netherlands Forces in Canada, the Secretary of State for External Affairs informed the court: "The Government of Canada recognizes the Government of the Queen of the Netherlands, as now constituted in the United Kingdom, as the de jure Government of the Netherlands, including the whole of the Netherlands Empire whether in enemy occupation or otherwise. The Government of Canada recognizes the Government of the Netherlands as an ally in the present war. The Netherlands Force now present in Canada . . . is recognized by the Canadian Government as being a 'Foreign Force' within the meaning of the Foreign Forces Order 1941." This, of course, does not mean that the power actually in occupation of the territory is treated other than in de facto control with its legislation being accepted as effective within that territory.[69] When the government-in-exile is recognized by an ally in a common war, it is unlikely that the enemy occupying its territory will in fact have received any form of recognition, although the courts of that ally will recognize the occupation as a fact.[70]

67. (1942), 57 B.C.R. 281 (B.C. S.C.). See also *Re Amand*, [1941] 2 K.B. 239 (K.B.); *Haak v. Min. of External Affairs*, [1942] S.A.L.R. 318 (App. Div.); *Anderson v. N.V. Transandine Handelsmaatschappij* (1941), 28 N.Y.S. (2d) 547; 2 Whiteman 457-486, 6 Whiteman 354-378.

68. P.C. 2546, April 15, 1941.

69. *Bank of Ethiopia v. Nat. Bank of Egypt & Liguori*, [1937] 1 Ch. 513 (Ch.): in this case the Italian administration had been recognized de facto by the U.K. See also *Germany (Federal Republic) v. Rauca* (1982), 38 O.R. (2d) 705 (Ont. H.C.); affirmed (1983), 41 O.R. (2d) 225 (Ont. C.A.).

70. *Sovfracht (V/O) v. Van Udens Scheepvart en Agentuur Maatschappij (N.V. Gebr.)*, [1943] A.C. 203 (H.L.).

§105 It is not only states and governments that require recognition, but also any fact that is claimed to be opposable as regards the state against which it is put forward.[71] In certain circumstances, recognition is required of a situation that approaches that of the recognition of states and governments in that it gives the entity recognized certain rights against the recognizing authority, which rights normally operate only as between states. When a civil war takes place within a territory, it would be an unfriendly if not an illegal act for a third state to extend premature recognition[72] to the insurgents as a de facto government. However, the situation may be such that it is necessary for a third state to acknowledge that the insurgent authority is more than a band of brigands but enjoys some measure of respectability.[73] For example, nationals of the third state may be present in the territory controlled by the insurgents, and in order to protect their security the third state may extend recognition of the state of insurgency to enable such contact as may be necessary.[74] Recognition of insurgency does not mean that the insurgent or governmental authority is entitled to exercise any rights as a belligerent against the recognizing state, nor is that state obliged to behave as a neutral during an armed conflict.[75]

71. As to the effect of naturalization legislation, normally regarded as a matter of domestic jurisdiction (see §§96, 99), see *Nottebohm Case (Second Phase)* (Liechtenstein/Guatemala), [1955] I.C.J. 4.

72. See §95; see also §§383-396.

73. For some time it was considered that insurgents who had not been recognized as belligerents (see §§224-236) would be considered pirates if they seized vessels on the high seas: *The Ambrose Light* (1885), 25 Fed. 308; but this decision is now regarded as being too harsh: Fenwick, "Piracy" in the Caribbean", (1961) 55 A.J.I.L. 426 at 427; see also Green, "The Santa Maria: Rebels or Pirates", (1961) 37 B.Y.B.I.L. 495.

74. See Lauterpacht, Recognition of International Law (1947), ch. 16; Chen, The International Law of Recognition (1951), ch. 26; 2 Whiteman 486-523.

75. *The Three Friends* (1897), 166 U.S. 1, per Fuller C.J., at p. 52: "... the maintenance unbroken of peaceful relations between two powers when the domestic peace of one of them is disturbed is not neutrality in the sense in which the word is used when the disturbance has acquired such head as to have demanded the recognition of belligerency. And, as a mere fact of municipal administration, no nation can permit unauthorised acts of war within its territory in infraction of its sovereignty, while good faith towards friendly nations requires their prevention". See also Chen, *op. cit.*, pp. 401-403.

§106 When the civil strife has reached such a level of intensity that acts are being committed on a scale that, if the parties had been independent states, would warrant their describing the situation as one of war necessitating neutrality by third states, or if third states consider that their interests are so affected by the situation that their rights as neutrals should be respected, the situation may be recognized as one of belligerency. "The recognition of belligerency, while not conferring all the

rights of an independent state, concedes to the Government recognized
the rights, and imposes the obligations, of an independent state in
matters relating to the war being waged. . . . An insurgent [area] is the
same before as after the recognition of belligerency. . . . Belligerency is
recognized when a political struggle has attained a certain magnitude
and affects the interests of the recognizing power; and in the instance of
maritime operations, recognition may be compelled, or the vessels of
the insurgents, if molesting third parties,[76] may be pursued as pirates. . . .
But it belongs to the political department to determine when belligerency shall be recognized, and its action must be accepted according to
the terms and intention expressed. . . . The recognition of belligerency
involves the rights of blockade, visitation, search and seizure of contra-
band articles on the high seas, and abandonment of claims for reparation
on account of damages suffered by our citizens from the prevalence of
warfare".[77] In accordance with Protocol I, 1977, on Humanitarian Law
in International Armed Conflicts if the 'insurgents' are fighting for
national liberation the conflict is considered international with the
'insurgents' enjoying full belligerent rights.[78]

76. In neither *The Ambrose Light (ante)* nor The Santa Maria incident ("The Santa
Maria: Rebels or Pirates," (1961) 37 B.Y.B.I.L. 495), were foreign interests involved.

77. *The Three Friends, ante.* See also §384.

78. Schindler and Toman, The Laws of Armed Conflicts (1982), p. 551, Art. 1(4).

§107 It is not only during a civil conflict that the courts of third states
may be concerned with learning whether a 'war' exists, so that the rights
of the parties involved may be determined. Thus, a charterparty may be
terminated in the event of war existing in the area to which the vessel is
proceeding.[79] Equally, it may be necessary to know, for the purposes of
insurance policy frustration clauses, whether the accident has occurred
during a war[80] or after the war has ended.[81] In such circumstances there
is an increasing tendency to accept the ordinary and everyday meaning
of 'war' rather than any technical definition.[82]

79. See *Kawasaki Kisen Kabushiki Kaisha of Kobe v. Bantham S.S. Co.,* [1939] 2
K.B. 544 (C.A.).

80. See *Pan American Airways v. Aetna Casualty & Surety Co.* (1974), 505 F. 2d
989.

81. *Shneiderman v. Metro. Casualty Co. of N.Y.* (1961), 220 N.Y.S. 2d 947. These
issues are more correctly considered in connection with the use of force and its effects:
§§329-349.

82. In *Oppenheimer v. Cattermole,* [1976] A.C. 249 (H.L.), Lord Cross of Chelsea
stated: "I incline to think that 'During war time' for this purpose should be interpreted in a common sense way as 'until the end of fighting'. It appears to have been

assumed in the courts below that the relevant date would be not May 8, 1945, but July 9, 1951, when the government of this country declared that the state of war had ended. The man in the street would have been very surprised to be told in 1950 that we were still at war with Germany . . .", at 275-6.

§108 Just as it is within the political discretion of a state whether it will extend recognition to a state, government, insurgent or belligerent, so, in the absence of any treaty obligation,[83] there is no obligation, other than that relating to premature recognition,[84] forbidding the extension of recognition. Insofar as an act of recognition would result in the dismemberment of an existing state, this would, in the absence of similar action by that state itself, amount to a breach of the Charter of the United Nations.[85] There is, however, nothing to prevent a state or group of states from declaring that they will not as a matter of policy grant recognition to any changes brought about by the use of force or in any way contrary to treaty.[86] At the same time, if a territorial change has been brought about contrary to international law and the government of the state in question is still engaged in hostilities or peace has not yet been restored any act of recognition would be premature.[87]

83. See, e.g., Treaty of Washington (1907); see also §96 note 20.

84. See §95.

85. See §95.

86. See the so-called 'Stimson doctrine' promulgated by the U.S. in 1932 in relation to the Japanese attack on China, (1932) 26 A.J.I.L. 342, and the similar policy of the League of Nations, Walters, A History of the League of Nations (1952), p. 488; 1 Hackworth 344-8; see also Lauterpacht, Recognition of International Law (1947), ch. 21, Chen, The International Law of Recognition (1951), pp. 411-444. See also §96 note 20.

87. This was the case with the German occupation of Europe after 1938, although Austria was treated as 're-established' rather than 'liberated'. It is also true of Arab territories occupied by Israel. See also §§350-358.

§109 Normally, in the absence of an act of recognition, an entity will receive no rights or immunities from a judicial tribunal. Thus, prior to the recognition of the German Democratic Republic it was generally maintained that the only Government existing in Germany was the Federal Republic[88] and that the 'Democratic Republic' was an agent of the Soviet Union as occupying authority, even though the latter regarded that entity as an independent sovereign. The attitude of the western powers, at least prior to the admission of the Democratic Republic to the United Nations in 1973, is perhaps best expressed by Lord Reid in the House of Lords in *Carl-Zeiss-Stiftung v. Rayner & Keeler Ltd.*[89]: "The purpose of a certificate is to provide information about the status of foreign governments and states and therefore the statement [in the Foreign Office certificate] that since June, 1945, "Her Majesty's Government have recognised the state and Government of the Union of Soviet Socialist Republics as de jure entitled to exercise governing authority in respect of that zone" cannot merely mean that H.M.G. have granted this recognition so as to leave the courts of this country free to receive evidence as to whether the U.S.S.R. are still entitled to exercise governing authority there. The courts of this country are no more entitled to hold that sovereign, still recognized by our Government, has ceased in fact to be sovereign de jure than they are entitled to hold that a government not yet recognized has acquired sovereign status. So this certificate requires that we must take it as a fact that the U.S.S.R. have been since 1945 and still are de jure entitled to exercise that governing authority. The certificate makes no distinction between the period before and the period after the German Democratic Republic was set up. So we are bound to hold that the setting up of that Republic made no difference to the right of the U.S.S.R. to exercise governing authority in the zone. And it must follow that the U.S.S.R. could at any time lawfully bring to an end the German Democratic Republic and its Government and could then resume direct rule of the zone. But that is quite inconsistent with there having been any abdication by the U.S.S.R. of its rights when the German Democratic Republic was set up. . . . The U.S.S.R. may have purported to confer independence or sovereignty on the German Democratic Republic but . . . that certificate clearly requires us to hold that, whatever the U.S.S.R. may have purported to do, they did not in fact set up the German Democratic Republic as a sovereign or independent state. . . . [T]he only other possibility is that it was set up as a dependent or subordinate organisation through which the U.S.S.R. is entitled to exercise indirect rule."[90] Nevertheless, the House of Lords held that in accordance with the rules of the conflict of laws, the law applicable in this case was that prevailing in the Soviet zone which had been brought into force by the Democratic Republic. A somewhat similar decision was rendered in *Re Al-Fin Corporation's Patent,*[91] the Foreign Office having specifically said that it did not recognize any state in North Korea or any authority exercising control there, nevertheless conceded that the existence of authorities was a question of fact and that the government was aware that there were "certain authorities styling themselves 'The Government of the Democratic People's Republic of Korea' exercising control" there. The court held that on this basis, there was in fact a state in existence from the point of view of the application of the Patents Act 1949.[92] While the general practice is to deny procedural capacity to unrecognized authorities, practice is not consistent.[93] Moreover, the legislative and administrative acts of an unrecognized government[94] or state[95] are denied validity, even when there is no other effective authority which is recognized.

88. See *Kunstsammlungen zu Weimar v. Elicoforn* (1973), 478 F. 2d 231: the G.D.R. was recognized by the U.S. in 1974, and by others by 1974 and 1975.

89. [1967] A.C. 853 at 903-904 (H.L.). For an official Canadian view on the use of such certificates, see Legal Bureau memo, 29 April 1983, (1984) 22 C.Y.B.I.L. 331-333. Act to amend the Criminal Code, the Immigration Act, 1976 and the Citizenship Act, S.C. 1987, c. 37, amends s. 6(8) of the Criminal Code and provides that any certificate issued by authority of the Secretary of State, External Affairs, relating to existence of a state of war, or Canada's acceptance of a treaty is final.

90. See also judgment of Lord Wilberforce at pp. 950, 958-960.

91. [1970] Ch. 160 (Ch.).

92. 12, 13 & 14 Geo. 6, c. 62, s. 24.

93. In *Wulfsohn v. Russian Federated Soviet Republic* (1923), 234 N.Y.S. 372, this was acknowledged, while in *Russian Federated Soviet Republic v. Cibrario* (1923), 139 N.E. 259 it was denied. In *South Moluccas (Republic) v. Royal Packet Shipping Co.* (1951), 17 I.L.R. 143 at 147, it was held that, regardless of recognition by the Netherlands, the Republic existed de facto, and so "could be admitted as a party to legal proceedings in Holland". In *Billerbeck et Cie. v. Bergbau-Handel GmbH* (1967), 72 I.L.M. 59, the Swiss Federal Court held: "The fact that Switzerland has not recognized the German Democratic Republic as a State and has no diplomatic relations with it, does not prevent the application of the Convention [on Enforcement of Foreign Arbitral Awards, 1927, 92 L.N.T.S. 301]. The G.D.R. is, in any case, an independent territory from the legal point of view. If follows that it must be treated as a State in the sphere of private international law as well as with regard to international civil procedure."

94. *Madzimbamuto v. Lardner-Burke*, [1969] A.C. 645 (P.C.), denying legality of detention orders issued in Rhodesia after Unilateral Declaration of Independence (U.D.I.). In *Adams v. Adams*, [1970] 3 W.L.R. 934 (P.D.A.), a divorce granted by a judge appointed under the 1965 post-U.D.I. Constitution was refused recognition. In *Bilang v. Rigg*, [1972] N.Z.L.R. 954, the court resealed a grant of administration made after U.D.I. by an Assistant Master of the High Court of Rhodesia appointed after U.D.I., but this was refused by the Kenya High Court in *Re Maberley* (1976), 4 C.L.B. (1978) 94, despite the recognition of 'Rhodesia' as British in the Kenya Constitution, on the basis of a Foreign Office Certificate that the régime is "illegal and not a member of the Commonwealth. The Kenya Government has no dealings whatsoever with the illegal Rhodesian régime."

95. See *Morocco (A.G.) v. Toledano* (1963), 40 I.L.R. 40, for refusal to recognize an Israeli notarial certificate in view of Morocco's refusal to recognize Israel as a state.

4. INTERNATIONAL REPRESENTATION

§110 While states are recognized as subjects of international law possessing international personality,[96] they act through representatives nominated by their governments.[97] In the first instance, this representation is by the government itself, as is clearly indicated in the Preamble of the Charter of the United Nations, which opens by expressing the determination of "the peoples of the United Nations" to remove the scourge of war and goes on to declare that "*our respective Governments, through representatives assembled . . .* have agreed to the present Charter".[98] As between governments, the normal method of representation is through the medium of ministers possessing the power to act for their governments, or more usually today by way of diplomats[99] appointed as permanent representatives at each other's capital city. From the point of view of judicial practice, perhaps the clearest recognition of this dichotomy is to be found in the statement of the United States Supreme Court[1] that "the actual person or party in power is but the agent and representative of the national sovereignty. A change in such representative works no change in the national sovereignty or its rights." Nevertheless, even though it may be a state which has declared war, its government may not be regarded as its representative, so that the state would acquire no rights as a result of the declaration. Thus, in view of the fact that the Principal Allied and Associated Powers had refused to recognize the Tinoco régime in Costa Rica either as the de facto or de jure government[2] of that state, Costa Rica was not permitted to sign the Peace Treaty of Versailles despite its declaration of war against the Central Powers.[3] On the other hand, insofar as that unrecognized government undertook obligations that related to the welfare of Costa Rica, as distinct from the personal benefit of members of the administration, then the recognised successor government was held liable, for the Tinoco régime had for this purpose at least represented the state.[4]

96. See §§52-74.

97. *German Settlers in Poland* (1923), 1 W.C.R. 208; *Mosul Case* (1925), 1 W.C.R. 722 at 740: the League Council is "composed of representatives of Members, that is to say, of persons delegated by their respective Governments, from whom they receive instructions and whose responsibility they engage." See also §413.

98. Italics added.

99. *Russian Indemnity* (1912) (Russia/Turkey), (1916); Scott, Hague Court Reports 297, 317: "Diplomatic channels are the normal and regular means of communication between States in their relations governed by international law" (the authentic French text is in 11 R.I.A.A. 431, 443).

1. *The Sapphire* (1871), 78 U.S. 164 at 168, per Bradley J.; see also §100 note 45.

2. See §§100-103.

3. *Tinoco Concessions* (G.B./Costa Rica) (1923), 1 R.I.A.A. 369 at 381.

4. *Tinoco Concessions, ante*, at pp. 397-398.

§111 In former times, states acted directly through their sovereigns and it was understood that the state was bound by such acts. Even today, there may still be situations in which this may arise, although normally international relations are conducted through the medium of governmental representatives.[5] In the *Nuclear Tests Cases*[6] France was held to be bound by statements made by the President of the Republic, regardless of the circumstances and even at a press conference, which statements were considered to have been made on behalf of France: "There can be no doubt, in view of his functions, that his public communications or statements, oral or written, as Head of State,[7] are in international relations acts of the French state. His statements, and those of members of the French Government acting under his authority ... constitute a whole. Thus, in whatever form these statements were expressed, they must be held to constitute an engagement of the State, having regard to their intention and to the circumstances in which they were made." In some instances, a national constitution may authorize the head of state to represent the state for the purpose of entering into an international engagement, without any need for further governmental or parliamentary approval. Thus, in accordance with United States constitutional practice, an international agreement brought into effect other than by way of a treaty as defined in Article II of the United States Constitution is known as an executive agreement, and on occasion such agreements are made by the President acting alone.[8] However, while such an agreement might commit the United States on the international level, if it purported to usurp the powers of Congress or was inconsistent with an act of Congress, it would not be enforced by United States courts,[9] as would a treaty which is considered to be part of the law of the land.[10]

5.   In a memo Jan. 31, 1981, the Legal Bureau of the Dept. of External Affairs described "the diplomat [as] strictly the representative of the Head of State", (1981) 19 C.Y.B.I.L. 324 at 325.

6.   [1974] I.C.J. 253 at 269 (Australia/France); 457 at 474 (N.Z./France).

7.   For the Canadian view of status of head of state, see note 5 above.

8.   See American Law Institute, Restatement of the Law: Foreign Relations Law of the United States (Revised) Tentative Draft No. 1 (1980), s. 308: "Most sole executive agreements have involved the conduct of military operations or foreign relations matters that have no direct impact on private interests in the United States", Reporter's Notes, No. 2. See also agreement between the U.S. and Iran relative to release of U.S. hostages from Iran, signed by both states with Algeria rather than with each other, 20 I.L.M. 223.

9.   *United States v. Guy W. Copps Inc.* (1953), 204 F. 2d 655 (U.S. C.A.).

10.   See §34.

§112   Nowadays, the head of state does not normally enter into international negotiations or commitments, but acts either through a minister or a diplomat appointed for this purpose. In the case of the latter, his competence is limited by the credentials he carries, so that in some circumstances he may only represent his state for the purposes of signature of a document, while in others he may be authorized to enter a fully binding commitment. Little difficulty arises when these powers are spelled out in an instrument. Occasionally, however, a statement may be made orally. Problems may then arise whether in making that statement the spokesman is to be regarded as a representative of his state which thereby becomes bound by the statement. It is now well established that if a member of a government makes a statement on a matter normally regarded as falling within the competence of his department, in circumstances which suggest that he is so acting, and if a foreign state acts on the basis of that statement, the state of the minister concerned will be bound. Thus, in the *Eastern Greenland* case[11] the Permanent Court of International Justice "consider[ed] it beyond all dispute that a reply of this nature given by the Minister for Foreign Affairs on behalf of his Government in response to a request by the diplomatic representative of a foreign Power, in regard to a question falling within his province, is binding upon the country to which the Minister belongs", and it would appear that if he has gone beyond his constitutional powers this is a matter between him and his government and does not affect the rights of the government to whose representative the statement was made.[12] In the *Nuclear Tests*[13] cases, the International Court of Justice held that statements made by the Ministers of Defence and Foreign Affairs in their official capacity were binding upon France even when made to the world at large, that is to say erga omnes, and not directed to any particular foreign state.[14] It must be remembered, however, that in this instance the President of the Republic made similar public statements.[15]

11. *Legal Status of Eastern Greenland* (Denmark/Norway) (1933), 3 W.C.R. 151, 192 (P.C.I.J.).

12. Dissenting judgment by Anzilotti, at p. 207, who did not dissent on the binding character of the "Ihlen Declaration" as such.

13. *Nuclear Test Cases, ante.*

14. *Nuclear Test Cases, ante,* at pp. 267, 472.

15. *Nuclear Test Cases, ante,* at pp. 253, 457.

§113   The most common forum for making statements erga omnes that may bind the spokesman's state is the United Nations, where the spokesman is clearly representing his state.[16] Thus, in its advisory opinion on the *International Status of South-West Africa*[17] the court held that statements made by the delegate of the Union of South Africa with regard to continuation of the Mandate over South-West Africa were made by him as representative of his government and were binding thereon.

16. See §110 note 97 re League Council.

17. [1950] I.C.J. 128 at 134-136; see also *South-West Africa Cases* (Preliminary Objection) (Ethiopia/South Africa; Liberia/South Africa), [1962] I.C.J. 319 at 339.

§114 The question whether a particular official is acting in a representative capacity so as to bind his state is most important when treaty negotiations are undertaken. As has been pointed out,[18] normally the extent of the agent's powers will be spelled out in his credentials. However, there are occasions when no credentials are required or when the status of the person involved is such that it is clear that he is acting in a representative character and so binds his state. The Vienna Treaty on the Law of Treaties[19] provides: "1: A person is considered as representing a State for the purpose of adopting or authenticating the text of a treaty or for the purpose of expressing the consent of the State to be bound by a treaty if: (a) he produces appropriate full powers; or (b) it appears from the practice of the States concerned or from other circumstances that their intention was to consider that person as representing the State for such purposes and to dispense with full powers. 2: In virtue of their functions and without having to produce full powers, the following are considered as representing their State: (a) Heads of State, Heads of Government and Ministers for Foreign Affairs, for the purpose of all acts relating to the conclusion of a treaty; (b) heads of diplomatic missions, for the purpose of adopting the text of a treaty between the accrediting State and the State to which they are accredited; (c) representatives accredited by States to an international conference or to an international organization or one of its organs, for the purpose of adopting the text of a treaty in that conference, organization or organ." If an act relating to the conclusion of a treaty is performed by one not authorized to represent the state in accordance with the above-mentioned provision, his act lacks legal validity unless it is confirmed by the state concerned.[20]

18. See §112.

19. Art. 7, 1969, 8 I.L.M. 679, acceded to by Canada in 1970, in force 1980.

20. Art. 8.

§115 Circumstances may arise when the representative of one state is called upon to act on behalf of another state. This situation arises when hostilities have broken out between two states or when, for some other reason, there is no diplomatic representative of the one accredited to the other. In such a case, the representative acts as agent on behalf of the power protected and not of his own state. If, therefore, he commits some fault as regards the state on behalf of which he is acting, no liability falls upon the state of which he is the accredited representative.[21] Sometimes, when diplomatic relations are broken off a member of the withdrawing diplomatic staff may be attached to the 'protecting embassy' to look after the interests of nationals of the country whose staff has been withdrawn. On occasion, as the result of a treaty or an arbitral award the authorities of a foreign state may be authorized to act as if they had the powers of the officials of the authorizing state. Legislation[22] passed as a result of the *Behring Sea Arbitration*[23] authorized United States officers to exercise the like powers under the Act as enjoyed by British officers in relation to a British ship. Such powers of agency, however, will be narrowly interpreted, and only give "authority to act within the limits of [the] Act", and since the seizure was made for a reason not provided for by that Act, "it is impossible to say that . . . they were exercising that delegated authority",[24] and the United States was held liable.

21. *Chevreau Claim* (1931), 2 R.I.A.A. 1113 (no liability to France for injury suffered by French nationals because of carelessness of British consul acting as French consul at latter's request). See also *Case Concerning the Temple of Preah Vihear* (Merits) (Cambodia/Thailand), [1962] I.C.J. 6 at 26-27, in which Thailand was held bound by maps prepared by French cartographers to whom they had entrusted the task of preparation.

22. Behring Sea Award Act, 1894, 57 Vict., c. 2.

23. (1893), 1 Moore 755.

24. *The Wanderer* (G.B./U.S.) (1921), 6 R.I.A.A. 68 at 73-74.

§116 In rare circumstances, because of political difficulties, two states may agree that a single state shall represent both of them in a particular negotiation. Thus, in the negotiations and documents connected with the release of United States hostages by Iran, Algeria negotiated on behalf of the United States with Iran, and vice versa.[25]

25. See §111 note 8. The documents are reproduced in 20 I.L.M. 224-240.

§117 With the introduction of the mandates system of the League of Nations and its extension by way of the trusteeship system of the United Nations[26] a new concept of international representation was introduced. In accordance with the mandates system, the mandates were to be exercised "on behalf of the League of Nations" with the "well-being and development" of the territory forming "a sacred trust of civilization".[27] The World Court has interpreted this as creating a form of agency representative of the League,[28] and "the mandatories were to be the agents of, or trustees for the League" as a whole, but not for "each and every member of it individually".[29] Once it is conceded that a mandatory is an 'agent' of the League or its successor, exercising the mandate "on behalf of " the organization it is clear that the principal, that is to say the organization itself, is competent to terminate the mandate and declare the mandatory an illegal occupant.[30] If and when Namibia becomes independent, this concept of agency will terminate. It remains true, however, that the United Nations has the power to appoint representatives to act on its behalf, and if these representatives are injured in circumstances that would normally involve state responsibility, the United Nations is able to secure compensation not only in respect of the injury done to the individual agent, but also for the injury suffered by the United Nations itself.[31]

26. See §§69-72.

27. Covenant, Art. 22.

28. *Int. Status of South-West Africa, ante,* at pp. 130-131.

29. *South West Africa Cases* (Second Phase), [1966] I.C.J. 6 at 24.

30. *Namibia (South-West Africa) Opinion,* [1971] I.C.J. 16; see also §420.

31. *Reparation for Injuries Suffered in the Service of the U.N.,* [1949] I.C.J. 174 at 180-181, 187; see also §413.

§118   In view of the present attitude to the right of self-determination, now regarded as a right recognized by international law,[32] it may happen that the General Assembly of the United Nations may confirm the view of its credentials committee that the delegate of a member state is not properly appointed on the ground that the government of that member is not representative of the people,[33] although this does not affect the state's right as a member.[34]

32. See §59.

33. As has happened with South Africa since 1970.

34. See Opinion of U.N. Legal Division, Doc. A/8160, Nov. 11, 1970.

5. CONTINUITY OF INTERNATIONAL PERSONALITY

§119   The existence of a state is distinct from that of its government,[35] so that the disappearance of a government whether by constitutional or revolutionary means[36] has no effect upon the personality of the state.[37] Similarly, if a state increases or decreases in size, no change is effected in the state's legal personality. This is true when a state divides by consent into two,[38] or when part of a state breaks away as a result of revolution.[39] In both cases, the original state retains its personality even though the new entity needs to be recognized[40] in order to acquire legal personality.

The same is true if one state accedes to another to form an enlarged state, as was the case when Singapore joined Malaya to establish Malaysia[41] or when Zanzibar joined Tanganyika in Tanzania.[42] In both instances the tendency was to continue to regard the new entity as a continuation of one of the two partners, a situation which was followed when Syria joined Egypt to form the United Arab Republic, even to the extent of regarding Syria when it broke away as being the continuance of the state which had disappeared when the Republic has been established.[43] On occasion, it has even been considered that the development from non-self-governing status to statehood is only a change in form and does not affect the international obligations of the newly independent state.[44] On the other hand, it is generally agreed that, in accordance with the uti possidetis principle, when a dependent territory acquires independent statehood it succeeds to the territory within the frontiers established by the former ruler, although at times there is controversy as to whether the frontier in question was anything more than an administrative boundary.[45]

35. See §96; see also *Lehigh Valley Ry. v. Russia* (1927), 21 Fed. 396 at 400, per Manton J.: "The state is perpetual and survives the form of its government."

36. See *Tinoco Concessions* (G.B./Costa Rica) (1923), 1 R.I.A.A. 369, and Iran after the overthrow of the Shah and establishment of the Islamic Republic.

37. See §52.

38. As happened in the case of India in 1947.

39. As happened in the case of Pakistan in 1971.

40. Both Pakistan and Bangladesh had to be specifically recognized; on recognition generally see §§91-109.

41. See, e.g., Green, "Malaya, Singapore/Malaysia: Comments on State Competence, Succession and Continuity", (1966) 4 C.Y.B.I.L. 3.

42. See Green, "The Dissolution of States and Membership in the United Nations", (1967), 32 Sask. L.R. 93 at 110.

43. Green, *ibid.* at p. 106.

44. See *Shehadeh v. Commr. of Prisons* (1947), 14 Ann. Dig. 42, per FitzGerald C.J., Palestine.

45. See *Frontier Dispute* (Burkina Faso/Mali), [1986] I.C.J. 554 at 565-567.

§120   At one time it was contended that there was complete subrogation as to rights and duties under international law insofar as these may be considered as of a local character attaching to the particular piece of territory concerned.[46] However, the whole question as to the extent that succession ensues is controversial and it may now be said that at least insofar as treaties are concerned, the question of succession "is muddled. Yet, it seems generally agreed that some rights and duties do devolve on the new country, particularly those rights and duties locally connected to the area gaining independence. Particularly in reference to emerging nations, the weight of authority supports the view that new nations inherit the treaty obligations of the former colonies".[47] In fact, however, many new states were unwilling to accept that treaty obligations undertaken by a former imperial power continued as binding, but insisted instead that this would depend on a decision made by the successor on a case by case basis.[48] The situation is now regulated to some extent by the Vienna Convention on Succession of States in Respect of Treaties.[49] The Convention recognizes that an agreement between the predecessor and successor state does not of itself affect the situation as between the successor and other parties to the treaty in question, and the same is true of a unilateral declaration made by the successor state,[50] for such a situation depends upon the recognition by such parties that the successor state is entitled to the rights or bound by the obligations of such treaties.[51] Canada has not signed this Convention which requires fifteen ratifications to come into force.[52] Until it has become law, therefore, the traditional rules continue to apply.

46.   See, e.g., Hall, International Law (1924), pp. 114-115; O'Connell, 2 State Succession in Municipal Law and International Law (1967), p. 113.

47.   *Jhirad v. Ferrandina* (1973), 355 F. Supp. 1155 at 1157 per Duffy, D.J.; *Yangtze (London) Ltd. v. Barlas Bros. (Karachi) & Co.* (1961), 34 I.L.R. 27 (Pakistan).

48.   See statement by Uganda, 1963, and by Malawi, 1964, cited in International Law Association, The Effect of Independence on Treaties (1965), pp. 118, 388 (both are compared and cited with other examples in Green, Law and Society (1975), pp. 188-189). The 'clean slate' theory is discussed in *R. v. Commrs. of Correctional Services; ex parte FitzHenry* (1976), 72 I.L.R. 63 (Jamaica S.C.).

49.   1978, 17 I.L.M. 1488. See also Vienna Convention on Succession of States in Respect of State Property, Archives and Debts, 1983, 22 I.L.M. 306.

50.   Arts. 8, 9.

51.   See §§91, 92.

52.   By the end of 1986 it had received only seven, while that on State Property had not received a single ratification.

§121   Since every existing state is a member of the United Nations or some other international institution, problems arise concerning membership rights whenever a new state comes into existence. According to Article 4 of the United Nations Charter there are two types of membership, original and elected.[53] Insofar as a new state is concerned it is clear that such an entity must be admitted. Problems arose, however, in connection with the dissolution of the Empire of India, an original member of the United Nations, and the creation of India and Pakistan. It was decided by the United Nations that India would remain as an original member, but that Pakistan would have to be admitted.[54] Similar problems arise when an existing member joins with another member to form a new federation. When Zanzibar joined Tanganyika, the sole effect upon the United Nations was that the latter's membership continued under the name of Tanzania, while Zanzibar's membership disappeared with the disappearance of the state.[55] This appeared to be the case when Syria joined Egypt in the United Arab Republic, with a single membership continuing in the various organizations to which either belonged, such membership being under the name of the new Republic.[56] When this Republic broke down Syria was allowed to resume its former membership as an original member of the United Nations as if there had never been a hiatus.[57] Insofar as obligations resulting from membership of an international organization are concerned, the present practice appears to be that, so long as the new entity comes into existence by agreement, this is provided for in the devolution agreement entered between the predecessor and successor state.[58] However, such an agreement cannot provide that the new entity shall automatically be a member of any international organization of which the original state was a member.

53. See §414.

54. See Misra, 'Succession of States: Pakistan's Membership in the United Nations', (1965) 3 C.Y.B.I.L. 281. By Art. 4 of the 1978 Vienna Convention (see §120 note 49) it is made clear that none of the rules affecting succession to treaties affect the membership provisions of the constitutions of international institutions.

55. Green, "The Dissolution of States and Membership in The United Nations", (1967) 32 Sask. L.R. 93 at 110.

56. Green, *ante.*, at p. 106.

57. Green, *ante.*, at p. 108.

58. This occurred when Singapore left Malaysia; see Green, "Malaya, Singapore/ Malaysia: Comments on State Competence, Succession and Continuity", (1966) 4 C.Y.B.I.L. 3 at 41-42, it is also provided for in Art. 4 of the 1978 Vienna Convention.

§122   Questions arise not only in relation to the succession of a state to the treaty rights of its predecessor. They also arise in connection with rights that may have been granted to private individuals before the act of succession occurred. Normally speaking, the national law of the predecessor, other than concerning such matters as treason which depend upon allegiance, continues until such time as it is changed and rights which have arisen under that law continue.[59] If the rights in question belong to foreign nationals or stem from treaty, the successor state is obliged to give them full legal effect, so that rights which have become vested, but which may require some further action to give them full, legal validity are binding upon the successor.[60] Similarly, if aliens hold concessions which relate to the solum it is incumbent upon the successor to continue to recognize the validity of such concessions.[61] Likewise, if the successor state indicates that it adopts the conduct of its predecessor towards, for example, private contractors, the successor will be bound by such conduct.[62]Alternately, rights which residents may possess against a former sovereign are nowadays frequently only valid against the successor sovereign to the extent that the latter is prepared to recognize such liability.[63]

59. *Rajasthan v. Shyamlal* (India), 51 A.I.R. 1964 S.C. 1495.

60. See *German Settlers in Poland* (1923), 1 W.C.R. 208; *Lighthouses Arbitration* (France/Greece) (1956), 12 R.I.A.A. 155 (P.C.A.).

61. *Mavrommatis Jerusalem Concessions* (Merits) (Greece/G.B.) (1925), 1 W.C.R. 355; *Tinoco Concessions, ante*: in this case a government recognized de jure was held to have succeeded to certain obligations undertaken by an unrecognized predecessor.

62. *Lighthouses Arbitration, ante*, at p. 198.

63. *Pema Chibar v. Union of India*, 53 A.I.R. 1966 S.C. 442.

§123 From the point of view of the private individual, perhaps even more vital than questions relating to the continuance of his property or other rights, is the effect of state succession upon his legal status. Traditionally, the individual was treated as if he were the property of the sovereign of his territory and if the sovereign conveyed part of that territory, he also conveyed its inhabitants with the result that they acquired the nationality of the new sovereign to whom they owed allegiance.[64] However, nationality[65] is a matter which normally falls within the domestic jurisdiction of a state[66] which may legislate as to who is entitled to its nationality and may, therefore decide not to grant that nationality to those in the territory it takes over. Moreover, it may happen that the ceding state enters into an agreement with the successor whereby the nationals in the ceded territory may be entitled to retain their original nationality as a minority[67] or may be granted the right of option by way of a plebiscite.[68] In some cases, the persons who are nationals of a ceded territory retain their former nationality as well as acquiring the nationality of the new sovereign,[69] while in other cases a change in sovereignty may result in a loss of the former nationality without the persons concerned acquiring another in its place. By the Convention on the Reduction of Statelessness, 1961,[70] treaties providing for the transfer of territory are to include provisions to ensure that no persons shall become stateless as a result of such transfer.[71]

64. See *Calvin's Case* (1608), 2 State Tr. 559 (this was not a case of succession but of a personal union, i.e., a union of two independent states, England and Scotland, under a common sovereign).

65. See §283.

66. See §83.

67. See §§214-222.

68. See, e.g. Wambaugh, Plebiscites since the World War (1933).

69. See, e.g., Bar Yaacov, Dual Nationality (1961).

70. 989 U.N.T.S. 175. This Convention entered into force in December 1975, and Canada acceded in July 1978. By the end of Dec., 1986, only thirteen states had become parties thereto.

71. Art. 10.

§124 If a state, which is delictually liable to another,[72] ceases to exist, whether by annexation or voluntary cession, the successor state does not normally become liable for the wrongdoing of its predecessor.[73] If, however, the succeeding state condones the breach or accepts responsibility for it, succession ensues.[74] If the predecessor was burdened by a public debt, the successor does not automatically succeed to this obligation,[75] but if the succession follows from a treaty it is the latter which governs whether succession takes place or not and usually this will be confined to debts which may be described as for the benefit of or attaching to the territory which passes.[76] If the debt had been incurred for interests contrary to those of the successor state, for example to enable the extinguished state to conduct hostilities against the successor, succession does not occur. By the 1983 Vienna Convention on Succession of States in Respect of State Property, Archives and Debts, a successor state will normally succeed to the debts of the predecessor in accordance with agreements made between them, or, failing that, in accordance with equitable proportionality. In the case of a newly independent state there is no succession to debts unless there is an agreement with the former sovereign to this effect. Any such agreement, however, "shall not infringe the principle of the permanent sovereignty of every people over its wealth and natural resources, nor shall its implementation endanger the fundamental economic equilibria of the newly independent State".[77]

72. See §§316-328.

73. *Brown Claim* (G.B./U.S.) (1923), 6 R.I.A.A. 120; *Hawaiian Claims* (1925), 6 R.I.A.A. 157.

74. *Lighthouses Arbitration, ante; Re Bounoula* (1970), 72 I.L.R. 56 (France Conseil d'Etat).

75. See, however, *Tinoco Concessions, ante.*

76. *Ottoman Debt Arb.* (Bulgaria, Iraq, Palestine, Transjordan, Greece, Italy/Turkey) (1925), 1 R.I.A.A. 529 at 531.

77. See §120 note 49.

§125 Insofar as state-owned, that is to say, public, property is concerned the question of ownership depends upon whether the succession has been to the entire territory or only to part thereof. In the case of the former, all public property, wherever situated, at home or abroad, passes.[78] As to the latter, there is only succession to public property present in the part of the territory ceded.[79] By the 1983 Convention[80] this matter is generally regulated by treaty between the successor and the predecessor, or in accordance with Part II of the Convention.

78. *Haile Selassie v. Cable & Wireless Ltd. (No. 2)*, [1939] Ch. 182 (C.A.).

79. *Peter Pazmany University* (Czechoslovakia/Hungary) (1933), 3 W.C.R. 311, 340.

80. Vienna Convention on Succession of States in Respect of State Property, Archives and Debts, 1983.

§126 Insofar as Canada is concerned, it was laid down by the Supreme Court in *St. Catherine's Milling & Lumber Co. v. R.*[81] that when the King of France ceded all his sovereign rights in Canada to England by the Treaty of Paris, 1763[82] this included all the lands then occupied by the Indians. After the passage of the Statute of Westminster, 1931,[83] when Canada became fully independent acquiring full responsibility for the conduct of its own international affairs, both Canada and the foreign states, parties to thirty-five extradition treaties concluded by Great Britain and extended to Canada were accepted as having been succeeded to by Canada which thereby assumed all rights and duties thereunder.[84] The view of Canada generally may be seen in the light of a statement issued by the Department of External Affairs in 1967 concerning Newfoundland:[85] "... The view of the Government on the question of Newfoundland treaty succession has in the past been that Newfoundland became part of Canada by a form of cession and that consequently, in accordance with the appropriate rules of international law, agreements binding upon Newfoundland prior to Union lapsed, except for those obligations arising from agreements locally connected which had established proprietary or quasi-proprietary rights, and Newfoundland became bound by treaty obligations of general application to Canada. ..."

81. (1887), 13 S.C.R. 577 (S.C.C.).

82. 42 C.T.S. 279.

83. 22 & 23 Geo. V, c. 4. See also §131.

84. See Aide-Memoire of Dept. of External Affairs, Castel, International Law (1976), p. 135. See also *Ex parte O'Dell and Griffen*, [1953] O.R. 190 (Ont. H.C.).

85. 27 Nov. 1967, (1968) 6 C.Y.B.I.L. 276.

§127 The practice of the older countries of the Commonwealth has been that on achieving its international independence a dominion succeeds to all treaties that had been entered into by the United Kingdom and which had been extended to that dominion prior to its independence, for it has been "the traditional view amongst the older Commonwealth countries that the older British dominions had inherited all the treaty rights and obligations arising out of treaties concluded by the United Kingdom and applying to the dominions".[86] But "the continued unilateral listing by [a dominion] of imperial treaties is no guarantee that other parties acknowledge this devolution".[87] The newly-independent Commonwealth countries have varied in their approach to this problem. Some assumed all pre-existing treaty responsibilities; others accepted all existing treaties for a trial period, at the end of which they indicated those they were prepared to succeed to definitively; others left the matter to be determined by customary international law; while others made a general declaration as to policy.[88]

86. Aide-Memoire of Dept. of External Affairs, Castel, International Law (1976), p. 135.

87. O'Connell, International Law in Australia (1965), p. 24, where reference is made to a refusal by Venezuela to recognize the Australian listing in its Treaty Series of the 1825 Anglo-Venezuelan Treaty of Amity, Commerce and Navigation, 12 B.F.S.P. 661.

88. See Udokang, Succession of New States to International Treaties (1972); 2 O'Connell, State Succession in Municipal and International Law (1967); Report to Helsinki Conference of International Law Association (1966).

§128 This divergence of practice led the Canadian Department of External Affairs to state:[89] "The Canadian Government is aware that a great deal of uncertainty exists at present concerning the rules of customary international law applicable to state succession in respect of treaties. . . . The Canadian Government is of the view, however, that this uncertainty arises from state practice which has developed after 1945, particularly in respect of the accession to independence of the emerging nations of Africa and Asia. While many of the Commonwealth countries which attained independence after the Second World War have adopted different positions, the position which Canada has consistently taken since the 1920's, and which has never before been questioned, is that the older British Dominions, including Canada, inherited all the treaty rights and obligations of general application to the United Kingdom[90] and the Dominion in question at the time the Dominions acquired separate international status. In contrast to this pre-World War II practice, since the Second World War the independence agreements of the newer members of the Commonwealth have included express provisions dealing with the question of treaty succession. There is therefore a valid basis for suggesting that different rules apply to post-World War II succession than applied at the time Canada succeeded to treaties concluded on its behalf by the United Kingdom".[91]

89.   Aide-Memoire of Dept. of External Affairs, Castel, International Law (1976), p. 135.

90.   It would seem that when Pakistan separated from India in 1947, "she automatically became party to certain multilateral Conventions of universal application binding India": Tandon, Public International Law (1965), p. 174. This did not, however, extend to the U.N. Charter: see §121.

91.   See, e.g., *Molefi v. Principal Legal Adviser*, [1971] A.C. 182 (P.C.), in which it was held that Lesotho did not succeed to the Convention relating to the Status of Refugees, 1951 (189 U.N.T.S. 137), which had been extended by the U.K. to the colony of Basutoland: Lesotho had announced it would indicate its attitude to all prior treaties. In fact, Lesotho acceded in 1981.

§129   The attitude of Canada towards the succession to treaties by newly-independent states may be seen from a later External Affairs memorandum:[92] ". . . most newly-independent states in the postwar period have tended towards the succession to at least some of the treaties of the predecessor states unless consideration as to the manner in which the state came into being or as to the political nature of the subject matter render the treaty either impossible or invidious of performance by the new state. The Canadian approach with respect to the devolution of treaty rights and obligations to newly-independent states has been along essentially empirical lines. Where a newly-independent state has announced that it intends to be bound by all or certain categories of treaties which in the past were extended to it by the metropolitan country concerned, Canada has, as a rule, tacitly accepted such a declaration and has regarded that country as being a party to the treaties concerned. However, when a state has not made any such declaration or its declaration has appeared to Canada to be ambiguous, then, as the need arose, we have normally sought information from the government of that state as to whether it considered itself a party to the particular multilateral or bilateral treaty in connection with which we require such information."

95.   Nov. 26, 1970, (1971) 9 C.Y.B.I.L. 304.

§130   It is not only when a former colony becomes independent that problems arise concerning the continuity of treaty rights and obligations. The Mandate for South-West Africa[93] was conferred by the Council of the League of Nations upon "His Britannic Majesty for and on behalf of the Government of the Union of South Africa." By virtue of statements made by the representative of South Africa at the closing session of the League of Nations and the opening session of the United Nations, it was clear that South Africa considered the Mandate to continue despite the demise of the League, and this was the view of the International Court of Justice,[94] although it recognized that the United Nations was incapable of succeeding to all the functions of its predecessor insofar as supervision of mandates was concerned.[95] When the Union left the Commonwealth to become the Republic of South Africa in 1961, it did not alter the existence of the international personality[96] of the country, nor was it suggested that the Mandate had terminated or that the Republic did not continue to exercise the rights and carry the burdens of the Mandatory under the Mandate. In fact, it was only because this was so, that the World Court was called upon to consider whether the Republic was in breach of the Mandate,[97] and whether the United Nations had the power to terminate it.[98]

93. 1920, 1 Hudson, Int. Leg. 57.

94. *Int. Status of South-West Africa,* [1950] I.C.J. 128.

95. *South-West Africa — Voting Procedure,* [1955] I.C.J. 67; *Admissibility of Hearings of Petitioners by the Committee on South-West Africa,* [1956]I.C.J. 23. See §419.

96. See §63.

97. *Southwest Africa Cases* (Preliminary Objection) (Ethiopia/South Africa; Liberia/South Africa), [1962] I.C.J. 319; Second Phase, [1966] I.C.J. 6.

98. *Namibia (South-West Africa),* [1971] I.C.J. 16. See §420.

§131 The question of the continuity of Imperial obligations in respect of an independent Commonwealth country[99] came into issue during the drafting of Canada's new Constitution during 1981 and 1982. The Canadian Indians contended that their treaties had been made with the Crown,[1] that they bound the Crown in a personal obligation as the Queen of England and that their rights had not been affected by the creation of Canada and that, since they were still in relation to the Queen, their rights could not be affected in any way by the Government of Canada or its new legislation. In reply, the Government of Canada maintained that the Royal Proclamation of 1763, under which aboriginal rights were claimed, as well as the treaties, had been signed in right of Canada and that it was for the Government of Canada alone to decide whether these were to continue regardless of anything appearing in the Constitution. The views of the Government were supported by the Court of Appeal in *R. v. Secretary of State for Foreign and Commonwealth Affairs; Ex parte the Indian Assn. of Alta.:*[2] ". . . obligations which were previously binding upon Canada simpliciter are now to be treated as divided. They are to be applied to the dominion or province or territory to which they relate: and confined to it. Thus the obligations to which the Crown bound itself in the royal proclamation of 1763 are now to be confined to the territories to which they related and are binding only on the Crown in respect of those territories: and the treaties by which the Crown bound itself in 1875 are to be confined to those territories and binding on the Crown only in respect of those territories. None of them is any longer binding on the Crown in respect of the United Kingdom. . . . [N]ow that the Crown is separate and divisible, the obligations under the proclamation and the Treaties are obligations of the Crown in respect of Canada. They are not obligations of the Crown in respect of the United Kingdom. It is, therefore not permissible for the Indian peoples to bring an action in this country to enforce these obligations. Their only recourse is in the courts of Canada.[3] . . . It is settled law that, although Her Majesty is the personal Sovereign of the peoples inhabiting many of the territories within the Commonwealth, all rights and obligations of the Crown, other than those concerning the Queen in her personal capacity, can only arise in relation to a particular government within those territories. . . . [A]lthough the relevant agreements with the Indian peoples are known as 'treaties', they are not treaties in the sense of public international law.[4] They were not treaties between sovereign states, so no question of state succession arises. . . . [T]here may be a devolution of rights and obligations of the Crown in respect of the government of Great Britain to another government within the Commonwealth without any express statutory or other transfer, but merely by virtue of the creation of the new government and of the assignment to it of responsibilities which relate to the rights and obligations in question.[5] . . . Crown . . . obligations exist only in respect of that government within the realm of the Crown against which such obligations can be enforced. . . . [T]he effect of the [British North America] Act of 1867 and of its successors was to transfer to Canada, as between the governments of the Dominion and the Provinces, every aspect of legislative and executive power in relation to Canada's internal affairs.[6] . . . [A]ny treaty or other obligations which the Crown had entered into with the Indian peoples of Canada in right of the United Kingdom had become the responsibility of the government of Canada with the attainment of independence, at the latest with the Statute of Westminster, 1931. . . . [T]he cession of land by the Indians, in exchange for which the Crown granted certain rights and privileges, was to the government of the Dominion of Canada for Her Majesty the Queen. Next, when the Crown agreed to lay aside reserves for the Indians, they were to be administered and dealt with for them by Her Majesty's

Government of the Dominion of Canada. . . . [T]he rights granted . . . by the relevant Treaty were granted to [the Indians] by the Crown in right of Canada and not by the Crown in right of the United Kingdom. . . . [T]he Crown is a constitutional monarchy, acting only on the advice of its relevant ministers. Two hundred years ago, insofar as North America was concerned, these were clearly the ministers of the United Kingdom Government. Equally clearly, in 1982 . . . the relevant ministers upon whose advice the Crown acts in relation to Canada and its provinces are those of Her Government in the Dominion and those provinces. . . . [A]ny treaty or other obligations still owed by the Crown to the Indian peoples of Canada are owed by the Crown in the right of the Dominion of Canada and not in the right of the United Kingdom. If such obligations still exist . . . their extent is . . . not a matter for this court. It is a matter for the courts of Canada."[7] As pointed out this was not an issue of state succession. The decision is important as an illustration of the issues of continuity of sovereign power and of a government.

99. See Lawford, 'The Practice Concerning Treaty Succession in the Commonwealth; (1967) 5 C.Y.B.I.L. 3.

1. See, e.g., Green, "Legal Significance of Treaties Affecting Canada's Indians, (1972) 1 Anglo-Amer. Law Rev. 119.

2. [1982] 2 All E.R. 118 (C.A.).

3. *R. v. Secretary of State for Foreign & Commonwealth Affairs,* [1982] 2 All E.R. 118 (C.A.), at pp. 128-129 per Lord Denning M.R.

4. See §§299-315.

5. See *Federal Commr. of Taxation v. Official Liquidator of E.O. Farley Ltd.,* (1940) 63 Commonwealth Law Reports 278.

6. *R. v. Secretary of State for Foreign & Commonwealth Affairs, ante,* at pp. 131-134, per Kerr L.J.

7. *R. v. Secretary of State for Foreign & Commonwealth Affairs, ante,* at pp. 140-142 per May L.J.

III State Jurisdiction

1. FORMS OF STATE JURISDICTION

§132 State jurisdiction indicates the competence which a state possesses to exercise its sovereign authority and also the area of such competence, both territorial and personal. Since states enjoy sovereign equality[1] and are considered to have consented to the operation of the rules of international law,[2] their jurisdiction is considered to be exclusive and omnipotent save to the extent that it is limited by such rules of international law. In practice this means that limitations upon the exercise of a state's jurisdiction must be clearly expressed and will be narrowly interpreted.[3] If, therefore, a treaty is expressed as possessing more than one authoritative text and the languages used differ, the text that will be accepted is that which imposes the narrowest obligation upon the parties, for it will be presumed that they are at least agreed to this extent.[4] Equally, if an international instrument establishes an international organisation and no provision is made in that instrument either permitting or forbidding withdrawal from the organisation, it is clear that the member states have reserved to themselves the right of withdrawal.[5] In the same way, if a treaty is silent as to the permissibility or otherwise of reservations, it will be construed to permit the parties to attach reservations unless the reservation runs counter to the purpose of the treaty.[6]

1. See §§75-90.

2. See §1.

3. *The S.S. Lotus* (France/Turkey) (1927), 2 W.C.R. 20 at 35; *The S.S. Wimbledon* (France, G.B., Italy, Japan/Germany) (1923), 1 W.C.R. 163 at 175.

4. *Mosul Case* (1925), 1 W.C.R. 722: "If the wording of a treaty provision is not clear, in choosing between several admissible interpretations, the one which involves the minimum of obligations for the Parties should be adopted." See also, Nuremberg Charter as modified by the Protocol of Oct. 6, 1945, (1968) 2 Schwarzenberger, Int. Law 496-497; see also Vienna Convention on the Law of Treaties, 1969, Art. 33. See Tabory, Multilingualism in International Law and Institutions, 1980. See §310.

5. This is the position in respect of the U.N. Charter; see the withdrawal of Indonesia in 1965, 13 Whiteman, 223, and the legal position was in no way affected by the decision of the membership to acquiesce in 1966 in the Indonesian view that it had not 'withdrawn' but only 'ceased to cooperate' and was now resuming cooperation, 13 Whiteman at 227. See §§415,416.

6. See *Reservations to the Convention on Genocide*, [1951] I.C.J. 15. In accordance with this Opinion of the World Court, Art. 19(c) of the Vienna Convention on the Law

165

of Treaties provides that reservations "incompatible with the object and purpose of the treaty" are not valid. See §304.

§133   Subject to such limitations as may be imposed upon its exercise by international law,[7] territorial jurisdiction is coexistent with territorial sovereignty. In the *North Atlantic Coast Fisheries Case*[8] the Permanent Court of Arbitration stated that "one of the essential elements of sovereignty is that it is to be exercised within the territorial limits, and that, failing proof to the contrary, the territory is coterminous with the sovereignty". Normally speaking, therefore, no third state or other authority is able to exercise jurisdiction within the territory of a particular state.[9] On another occasion, the Permanent Court of Arbitration defined jurisdiction as consisting "in the actual display of state activities, such as belong to the territorial sovereign".[10] This jurisdictional competence is not only negative in the sense of competence to exclude any exercise of sovereign authority by another power, but also includes a positive duty. While "[t]erritorial sovereignty . . . involves the exclusive right to display the activities of a State[, t]his right has as corollary a duty: the obligation to protect within the territory the rights of other States, in particular the right to integrity and inviolability in peace and war, together with the rights which each State may claim for its nationals in foreign territory. Without manifesting its territorial sovereignty in a manner corresponding to circumstances, the State cannot fulfil this duty. Territorial sovereignty cannot limit itself to its negative side, i.e., to excluding the activities of other States; for it serves to divide between nations the space upon which human activities are employed, in order to assure them at all points the minimum of protection of which international law is the guardian".[11]

7. See §§145-163.
8. (1910), 11 R.I.A.A. 167 at 180.
9. See U.N. Charter, Art. 2(7); and §83.
10. *Island of Palmas Case* (Netherlands/U.S.) (1928), 2 R.I.A.A. 829 at 839.
11. *Island of Palmas Case, ante.*

§134   In practice, territorial jurisdiction implies the power of the state to exercise its authority over all events occurring within its territorial limits, although states may be limited in this exercise by the rules of customary international law[12] or by any limitation imposed by treaties to which the state is a party.[13] Since the state's jurisdiction is limited territorially, this means that any claim by the state to exercise its jurisdiction in connection with events occurring outside its territorial limits can only be exercised when the object of that exercise, be it a human being[14] or property, is physically present within the territory. This does not, however, prevent a state from attempting to exercise its jurisdiction by way of judicial process over a person who is abroad. For the exercise to have any practical value presence within the territory is necessary, although extradition[15] might be granted in respect of a fugitive offender who had been sentenced in absentia.[16] It should be pointed out that the International Military Tribunal at Nuremberg tried and sentenced Martin Bormann in his absence.[17]

12. See §§145-163.

13. See §§164-236.

14. Thus, the German Federal Republic claims the power to exercise jurisdiction over certain crimes wherever committed; see *Re Bunge* (1981) in which an East German border guard was sentenced to six years in jail for shooting dead a superior officer in order to escape to the West, The Times (London), Oct. 17, 1981. See also *The S.S. Lotus, ante*: ". . . jurisdiction is certainly territorial; it cannot be exercised by a State outside its territory except by virtue of a permissible rule derived from international custom or from a convention. It does not, however, follow that international law prohibits a State from exercising jurisdiction in its own territory, in respect of any case which relates to acts which have taken place abroad, and in which it cannot rely on some permissible rule of international law. . . . Far from laying down a general prohibition to the effect that States may not extend the application of their laws and the jurisdiction of their courts to persons, property and acts outside their territory, it leaves them in this respect a wide measure of discretion which is only limited in certain cases by prohibitive rules; as regards other cases, every State remains free to adopt the principles which it regards as best and most suitable. . . . [A]ll that can be required of a State is that it should not overstep the limits which international law places upon its jurisdiction; within these limits, its title to exercise jurisdiction rests in its sovereignty".

15. See §§202-208.

16. See *R. v. Brixton Prison (Governor); ex parte Caborn-Waterfield,* [1960] 2 Q.B. 498 (D.C.) See §140.

17. *Nuremberg Judgment* (1964) Cmd. 6964, (1947) 41 A.J.I.L. 172.

§135 Territorial jurisdiction manifests itself most clearly by the exercise of legislative,[18] administrative or judicial activity within the territory, and such manifestations of jurisdiction are often coterminous with evidence of ownership and therefore sovereignty over territory.[19]

18. *Legal Status of Eastern Greenland* (1933), 3 W.C.R. 151 at 173: "legislation is one of the most obvious forms of the exercise of sovereign power".

19. See §§237-257. See also *Minquiers and Ecrehos Case* (France/G.B.), [1953] I.C.J. 47.

§136 The judicial exercise of jurisdiction is most usually shown in relation to the criminal law. Criminal jurisdiction is territorial when the crime has been committed within the territory and when the criminal is present,[20] and this is so regardless of the nationality of the offender.[21] Jurisdiction will also be exercised if the crime takes effect within the national territory[22] or is directed against a national and the offender comes within the territory.[23]

20. *R. v. Tootalik E4-321* (1970), 71 W.W.R. 435 (N.W.T. Terr. Ct.). In *R. v. Brixton Prison (Governor); ex parte Minervini*, [1959] 1 Q.B. 155 (D.C.), it was held that the term 'territory' in an extradition treaty was equivalent to 'jurisdiction', so as to permit the return to Norway of an Italian seaman charged with murder on a Norwegian ship on the high seas. See Criminal Code, s. 5(2).

21. See, e.g., Territorial Waters Jurisdiction Act, 1878, 41 & 42 Vict. c. 73, s. 2: "An offence committed by a person, whether or not he is a subject of Her Majesty, on the open sea within the territorial waters of Her Majesty's dominions, is an offence within the jurisdiction of the Admiral, although it may have been committed on board or by means of a foreign ship . . ." This statute was enacted as a consequence of the decision in *R. v. Keyn* (The Franconia) (1876), L.R. 2 Ex. D. 63. See, however, §§145-163.

22. See *R. v. Godfrey*, [1923] 1 K.B. 24 (K.B.)(extradition to Switzerland of a person in England as accessory before the fact to an offence committed in Switzerland). See Immigration Act, S.C. 1976-77, c. 52, ss. 101-102.

23. See *The S.S. Lotus* (1927), 2 W.C.R. 20 at 35.

§137   In the exercise of its jurisdiction a tribunal is not normally concerned with the manner in which an accused has been brought before it, whether this results from the non-application of a treaty provision,[24] or whether it is the result of an illegal action abroad by state agents, whether with or without the complicity of local officials,[25] or whether it is the result of a criminal action committed abroad, especially if the court exercising jurisdiction is able to identify some link between the victims of the crime and the state of which the court is an organ.[26]

24. In *R. v. Corrigan*, [1931] 1 K.B. 527 (C.A.), the accused had appeared before an extradition tribunal in France on a charge of false pretences, but waived all the formalities and was handed to the British authorities. The court held that it had jurisdiction to try him for offences not included in the extradition request. See also *R. v. O.C., Depot Battalion, R.A.S.C., Colchester; Ex parte Elliott*, [1949] 1 All E.R. 373 (K.B.), in which the accused was arrested in Belgium by British military police accompanied by Belgian police officers. He was escorted to Germany and thence to England without any extradition or other proceedings. See also, *R. v. Walton* (1950), 10 C.C.C. 269 (Ont. C.A.). See La Forest, Extradition To and From Canada, 1977, 39-41.

25. See *Ker v. Illinois* (1886), 119 United States 436; *United States v. Toscanino* (1974), 500 F. 2d 267; (1975) 398 F. Supp. 916; and *United States v. Gengler* (1975), 510 F. 2d 62, in which U.S. courts refused to grant habeas corpus to applicants alleging abduction and ill-treatment by U.S. officials with the compliance of local officials, and their subsequent transportation to the U.S., in defiance of due process

and without extradition proceedings. See also *State v. Heymann*, [1966] 4 S.A.L.R. 599; and *Eichmann v. A.G. Israel* (1962), 36 I.L.R. 277.

26. In the *Eichmann* case, *ante*, one of the grounds for jurisdiction was the close link between Jewish victims of the holocaust and the State of Israel and with survivors of the holocaust resident there; see Green, "The Maxim Nullum Crimen Sine Lege and the Eichmann Trial", (1962) 38 B.Y.B.I.L. 457 at 464-465.

§138   On occasion, a state will exercise jurisdiction over an offender who has committed an offence abroad if that offence is directed against the security of the state in question regardless of the nationality of the offender.[27] In such circumstances the practice is to describe the jurisdiction as protective rather than territorial.[28]

27. *Joyce v. D.P.P.*, [1946] A.C. 347 (H.L.), although in this case, since the offence was committed in time of war and the offender claimed enemy nationality, the issue turned on the question of allegiance as evidenced by the securing of a passport. See also *Rocha v. United States* (1961), 288 F. 2d 545 (prosecution for false statements made to consular official abroad in obtaining immigrant visa).

28. See American Law Institute, Restatement of the Law: Foreign Relations Law of the United States (Revised), Tentative Draft No. 2, 1981, 402: ". . . a state may, under international law, exercise jurisdiction to prescribe and apply its law with respect to . . . (3) certain conduct outside its territory by persons not its nationals which is directed against the security of the state or certain state interests. . . . COMMENT (d) Subsection (3) restates the 'protective principle' of jurisdiction. International law has recognized the right of a state to punish certain limited offences committed outside its territory by persons who are not its nationals — offences directed against the security of the state or against important state interests or functions, e.g., espionage, counterfeiting of the state's seal or currency, the falsification of official documents, as well as perjury before consular officials or conspiracies to violate the immigration or customs laws, which are likely to be committed outside the territory by aliens. The protective principle may be seen as a special case of the exercise of jurisdiction based on the effect of the act upon or in a state's territory, but has been treated as an independent basis of jurisdiction." By the 1984 Act to Combat International Terrorism, 98 Stat. 2706, Public Law 98-533, 24 I.L.M. 1015, the United States extended this 'protective principle' to enable the trial of any terrorist, regardless of nationality or the place of the act of terrorism, if any U.S. citizen was a victim of this act. In September, 1987, an alleged terrorist was 'enticed' on to a U.S. vessel in the Mediterranean and transported to the U.S. to stand trial in connection with an aerial hijacking in which four of the passengers were U.S. citizens. See *Molvan v. A.G. Palestine* (The Aysa), [1948] A.C. 531 (P.C.) (jurisdiction exercised over vessel captured on high seas and intending to breach immigration regulations). As to treason committed by an offender outside of Canada, see Criminal Code, s. 46(3) [am. S.C. 1974-75-76, c. 105 s. 2].

§139   An example of Canadian exercise of the protective principle may be found in the Criminal Law Amendment Act, 1985, concerning fraud committed in relation to a passport by a person outside of Canada. Moreover, even though the person be outside of Canada, proceedings may be commenced against him in any territorial division in Canada.[29] Further, by the Deterrents and Detention Bill, 1987,[30] intended to deal with illegal immigration into Canada, it is made an offence to incite persons to become immigrants. In addition, authority is given to the Minister of Immigration to turn away vessels he reasonably suspects to be engaged in transporting persons to Canada contrary to this legislation, when such vessel is in the internal waters of Canada, the territorial sea of Canada or twelve nautical miles of the outer limit of the territorial sea of Canada.[31] Reasonable force may be used to give effect to this provision, which may result in seizure.

29. 1985, c. 19, s. 9.

30. An Act to amend the Immigration Act, 1976 and the Criminal Code in consequence thereof, Bill C-84, 1987.

31. See *Molvan v. A.G. Palestine, ante*

§140 In some circumstances a court will exercise its jurisdiction over a person present in its territory in order to give effect to a judgment of a foreign court delivered in absentia, but in respect of an offence committed in the territory over which that foreign court exercises jurisdiction.[32]

32. See *R. v. Brixton Prison (Governor); Ex parte Caborn-Waterfield*, [1960] 2 Q.B. 498 (D.C.)(in fact, extradition was denied on technical grounds).

§141 Although the territorial seas constitute part of the territory of a state,[33] the jurisdiction of the littoral state is limited. While a state is entitled to enact legislation regarding fishing, navigation, pollution and the like,[34] both warships[35] and merchant vessels[36] are entitled to a right of innocent passage[37] through the territorial sea. The criminal jurisdiction of the coastal state may be exercised in respect of a crime committed on board a ship passing through the territorial seas only if the consequences of the crime extend to the coastal state, or is of a kind to disturb the peace of that state or the good order of the territorial sea; or if local assistance is requested by the vessel's captain or the flag state's consul; or for the suppression of the traffic in narcotics; or to effect an arrest or an investigation of a ship passing through the territorial sea after leaving internal waters.[38] The coastal state cannot exercise its jurisdiction over a vessel passing through its territorial sea in respect of any offence committed before entry into that sea, so long as the ship in question is not passing through internal waters.[39] However, if the offence is continuing or the voyage is intended to promote an offence within the territorial sea, the littoral state may take steps to frustrate the offence or penalise the offender.[40]

33. Convention on the Territorial Sea, 1958, 516 U.N.T.S. 205, Art. 1; U.N. Convention on the Law of the Sea, 1982, 21 I.L.M. 1261, Art. 2. See §§258, 259.

34. See, e.g., Canadian Declaration, Apr. 7, 1970, accepting jurisdiction of the I.C.J. under Art. 36 of the Court's Statute, reserving "(d) disputes arising out of or concerning jurisdiction or rights claimed or exercised by Canada in respect of the conservation, management or exploitation of the living resources of the sea, or in respect of the prevention or control of pollution or contamination of the marine environment in marine areas adjacent to the coast of Canada", I.C.J.Y.B. 1981-1982, 62 (cancelled 1985).

35. See *Corfu Channel (Merits)* (G.B./Albania), [1949] I.C.J. 4; 1958, Arts. 14, 15, 23; 1982, Arts. 17, 20, 24, 29-32.

36. 1958, Arts. 14, 15, 18; 1982, Arts. 17, 24, 27, 28.

37. 1958, Art. 14; 1982, Arts. 17-19.

38. 1958, Art. 19(1), (2); 1982, Art. 27.

39. 1958, Art. 19(5). This would not prevent a repetition of the Eisler case, 1949, in which a fugitive wanted in the United States was removed from a Polish vessel lying in Cowes Roads, Southampton Harbour: see Green, "Recent Trends in the Law of Extradition", (1953) 6 Current Legal Problems, 274, 275-276; Jennings, (1949) 26 B.Y.B.I.L. 468; Finch, "The Eisler Extradition Case", (1949) 43 A.J.I.L. 487; 1982, Art. 27(5). See generally §§259-281.

40. See Canadian legislation with regard to the transport of illegal immigrants into Canada, §139.

§142 Apart from exercising jurisdiction on account of the territoriality of the offence, states also do so on a personal basis. This is to say because of the special link, usually nationality,[41] between itself and the offender.[42] It has been said[43] that "[t]he authority possessed by a state community over its members being the result of the personal relation existing between it and the individuals of which it is formed; its laws travel with them wherever they go, both to places within and without the jurisdiction of other powers. A state cannot enforce its laws within the territory of another state;[44] but its subjects remain under an obligation not to disregard them, their social relations for all purposes as within its territory are determined by them, and it preserves the power of compelling observance by punishment if a person who has broken them returns within its jurisdiction."[45] However, most states, and particularly those possessing a common law tradition, only claim to exercise jurisdiction over nationals for offences committed abroad if those offences are regarded as particularly heinous or contrary to public policy. The crimes commonly regarded as being so subject are treason,[46] counterfeiting, murder,[47] bigamy[48] and the like. In addition, if an alien is under the protection of the state, as when, for example, he is a sailor on a foreign ship,[49] or claims protection by virtue of a wrongly obtained passport,[50] he is subject to the criminal jurisdiction of the country concerned. The fact that jurisdiction of a personal character might be claimed by the offender's state of nationality does not prevent jurisdiction from being exercised on the basis of territoriality by the state in which the offence was committed.

41.   The principle of extra-territorial jurisdiction over nationals is recognised in *The S.S. Lotus*, (1927), 2 W.C.R. 20 at 36.

42.   In *Joyce v. D.P.P.*, [1946] A.C.l 347 (H.L.), this link was based on allegiance dependent upon a wrongfully obtained passport.

43.   Hall, International Law (1924), p. 56.

44.   This may be permitted by statute or treaty as in the case of visiting forces in time of war; see *Re Amand (No. 2)*, [1942] 1 K.B. 445 (K.B.) . See Visiting Forces Act, R.S.C. 1970, c. V-6, s. 6.

45.   This is true even for a person whose home state does not abandon its own claims on naturalization, or if a state claims as its own persons born abroad of parents possessing the claimant state's nationality.

46.   *R. v. Casement*, [1917] 1 K.B. 98 (C.A.). See Criminal Code, s. 46(3) [am. 1974-75-76, c. 105, s. 2].

47.   *R. v. Azzopardi*, [1843] 1 Car. & K. 203; see also *R. v. Dudley* (1884), 14 Q.B.D. 273 (Q.B.)(murder by 'necessity' on the high seas).

48.   *Trial of Earl Russell*, [1901] A.C. 446 (H.L.).

49.   *R. v. Sattler* (1858), Dears & Bell 525.

50.   *Joyce v. D.P.P., ante.*

§143   There are certain offences which are regarded by international law as being so heinous that those committing them are considered hostes humani generis and international law recognizes that it is within the competence of any state finding itself in possession of such an offender to exercise jurisdiction over him, regardless of his nationality, the locus of the offence or the nationality of the victim. The crime most generally recognized as being subject to universal jurisdiction is piracy.[51] However, this is only true to the extent that the offence satisfies the international law definition, namely "any illegal acts of violence or detention, or any act of depredation, committed for private ends by the crew or the passengers of a private ship or a private aircraft, and directed: (i) on the high seas, against another ship or aircraft, or against persons or property on board such ship or aircraft; (ii) against a ship, aircraft, persons or property in a place outside the jurisdiction of any State". If a statutory definition is wider than this, it may only be applied against national ships.[52] The only other offences which seem to be accepted as being subject to universal jurisdiction are war crimes, although it is controversial whether customary international law would authorize a neutral to prosecute a war criminal found in its territory. In the case of belligerents, however, there is no doubt that they possess jurisdiction over such crimes, regardless of the nationality of the offender or the victim or the place of commission.[53] It is also sometimes contended that universal jurisdiction exists in regard to crimes against humanity. Although there is no clearly acceptable definition of such crimes, a United States tribunal held in 1980 that torture had become a crime under international law and was justiciable by every country in the world.[54] It is doubtful, however, whether this decision would be acceptable as expressive of customary law. However, for parties to the European and American Conventions on Human Rights,[55] or of the United Nations Convention of 1984,[56] any use of torture would be a breach of treaty.

51. This is true only of piracy jure gentium, an offence of depredation committed for private purposes on or related to the high seas, see *Magellan Pirates* (1853), 1 Spinks 81, and *Re Piracy Jure Gentium*, [1934] A.C. 586 (P.C.). See now Convention on the High Seas, 1958, 450 U.N.T.S. 11, Art. 15; 1982, Art. 101. For an incident described by the U.S. as piracy by the law of nations, but not falling within the Convention definition, see *Re The Achille Lauro*, 1985, 24 I.L.M. 1509, at 1556-9.

52. See *The Le Louis* (1817) 2 Dods. 210 (H. C. of Admiralty).

53. See §199 where the present Canadian law is considered, and §§359-382.

54. *Filatiga v. Pena-Irala* (1980), 630 F. 2d 876.

55. (European) 1950, 213 U.N.T.S. 222, Art. 3; see, however, *Ireland v. U.K.* (1978), 58 I.L.R. 188; (American) 1969, 9 I.L.M. 99, Art. 5(2).

56. Convention Against Torture and Other Cruel, Inhuman or Degrading Treatment or Punishment, 1984, 23 I.L.M. 1027, ratified by Canada in June 1987; at the same time the Criminal Code was amended to make the use of torture an offence, S.C. 1987, c. 13.

§144 It is sometimes asserted that slave-trading is an offence subject to universal jurisdiction.[57] However, in view of the provisions in the Slavery Conventions[58] calling upon states to make slavery and the slave-trade criminal offences under their national legislation,[59] this would hardly seem to be the case, particularly as there have been only 75 ratifications to the revised League Convention of 1926 and 102 ratifications to the latest Convention of 1956. Canada is a party to both of these Conventions. At present there is a tendency for conventions dealing with such offences as aerial hijacking,[60] the taking of hostages,[61] the prevention of terrorism against internationally protected persons, including diplomats,[62] and the like, to include provisions requiring the parties to amend their national criminal codes when necessary and to undertake to observe the principle aut dedere, aut judicare, that is to say either to prosecute offenders found within their territory or to surrender them for trial to states whose interests have been affected.[63] A similar provision is to be found in the Convention Against Torture,[64] and

Canada has amended the Criminal Code to give effect to the relevant provisions of each of these Conventions.[65]

57. This was certainly not the case in 1817: see *The Le Louis, ante.*

58. See General Act of Berlin, 1885, 76 B.F.S.P. 4; General Act and Declaration of Brussels, 1890, 82 B.F.S.P. 55; Treaty of St.-Germain-en-Laye, 1919, 112 B.F.S.P. 901; Slavery Convention, 1926, 60 L.N.T.S. 253, as amended by the 1953 Protocol, 212 U.N.T.S. 17; Supplementary Convention on Slavery, 1956, 266 U.N.T.S. 3.

59. See, e.g., 1956 Convention, Art. 1.

60. Tokyo Convention Offences and Certain Other Acts Committed on Board Aircraft, 1970, Can. T.S. No. 5; Hague Convention for the Suppression of Unlawful Seizure of Aircraft, 1972, Can. T.S. No. 23; Montreal Convention for the Suppression of Unlawful Acts against the Safety of Civil Aviation, 1971, 974 U.N.T.S. 177. Canada is a party to each of these.

61. International Convention against the Taking of Hostages, 1979, 18 I.L.M. 1458.

62. 1973, in force, 1035 U.N.T.S. 167. Canada is a party. For the Canadian view as to who constitute internationally protected persons, see Legal Bureau memo., 4 Dec. 1985, (1986) 24 C.Y.B.I.L. 392-294, and for a statement concerning punishment of offenders, see statement in Sixth Committee of General Assembly, 2 Oct. 1985, (1986) 24 C.Y.B.I.L. 395-396.

63. As was illustrated by the incident affecting the U.S. embassy in Tehran, 1979-80, this Convention lacks 'teeth'; see *U.S. Diplomatic and Consular Staff in Tehran* (1979), I.C.J. Rep. 7; (1980) I.C.J. Rep. 3; see also, Green, "The Tehran Embassy Incident — Legal Aspects", (1980) 19 Archiv des Völkerrechts 1. On international criminal law, see §§189-213.

64. See §143 note 56.

65. See the Criminal Law Amendment Act, S.C. 1985, c. 19; see also, Williams, 'The Criminal Law Amendment Act 1985: Implications for International Criminal Law', (1985) 23 C.Y.B.I.L. 226.

2. CUSTOMARY LAW LIMITATIONS ON STATE JURISDICTION

§145 For the main part the limitations imposed by customary law upon the exercise of state jurisdiction are based on the principle of the sovereign equality of states,[66] as a result of which no state may be subjected to the jurisdiction of another state without its express consent.[67]

66. See §§75-90.

67. For Canadian view on Extraterritoriality, see Memo of Legal Bureau, Dept. of External Affairs, 27 Sept. 1982, (1983) 21 C.Y.B.I.L. 302-4.

§146 International customary law prescribes that certain parts of the earth's surface, e.g., the high seas,[68] are part of the common heritage of mankind and cannot be subjected to the jurisdiction of any state, so that in the absence of any special permissive rule of international law, whether by treaty or custom, as in the case of piracy jure gentium,[69] only a national state can exercise jurisdiction in respect of its nationals or vessels flying its flag.

68. See §§258-281.

69. *Re Piracy Jure Gentium*, [1934] A.C. 586 (P.C.); see also, *The Le Louis* (1817), 2 Dods. 210 (H.C. of Admiralty); *Magellan Pirates* (1853), 1 Spinks 81. See now, Geneva Convention on the High Seas, 1958, 450 U.N.T.S. 11, Art. 15; U.N. Convention on the Law of the Sea, 1982, 21 I.L.M. 1261, Art. 101.

§147 In some instances international customary law provides that even parts of the territorial sea[70] may be open to the shipping of all countries, including capital ships as in the case of an international waterway, part of which runs through the territorial sea,[71] or if a merchant ship is compelled to seek shelter because of stress or weather.[72] Moreover, all vessels are entitled to a right of innocent passage through a state's territorial sea without becoming subject to that state's jurisdiction,[73] so long as the vessel in question does not, in the absence of distress, put into harbour.

70. See §259.

71. See *Corfu Channel Case (Merits)* (G.B./Albania), [1949] I.C.J. 4; see also, Geneva Convention on the Territorial Sea, 1958, 516 U.N.T.S. 205, Art. 16(4); 1982, Arts. 38, 44, 45(2).

72. *The Eleanor* (1809), Edw. 135; *The Brig Concord* (1915), 9 Cranch 387; *The Carlo-Alberto* (France) (1832), Sirey part i. In *The New York* (1818), 16 U.S. 59 at 68, per Livingston J., it was stated that "The necessity must be urgent, and proceed from such a state of things as may be supposed to produce in the mind of a skilful mariner, a well-grounded apprehension of the loss of vessel and cargo, or the lives of the crew". See also *The May v. R.*, [1931] S.C.R. 374 (S.C.C.).

73. This right is recognized by Malloy, De Jure Maritimo et Navali (1682), Bk. II, ch. XVI. See now, 1958 Convention, *ante*, Arts. 14, 15; 1982 Convention, Arts. 17, 24(2). See also, §§258-281.

§148 As has been seen, states claim exclusive competence in the domestic sphere,[74] so that within their territorial limits their jurisdiction is only limited to the extent that customary law or treaty provision requires. Insofar as customary law is concerned, this means that no state enjoys competence over the affairs of another, so that jurisdictional immunity is enjoyed by states, their sovereigns,[75] their governments and their agents.[76] In fact, since states were traditionally regarded as the property of their monarchs, the immunity of the sovereign precedes that of the state.[77]

74. See §83.

75. In Jan. 1984, the teen-aged son of President Obote of Uganda was detained at Gatwick Airport, U.K., for possession of drugs, but was not charged because of immunity of heads of state and members of immediate family; The Times, Jan. 5, 1984.

76. For a Canadian view as to who constitute the 'agents' of a state and the type of immunity they receive, see Legal Bureau memo, 4 Dec. 1985, (1986) 24 C.Y.B.I.L. 392-394.

77. See Memo. of Legal Bureau, Dept. External Affairs, Jan. 31, 1981, re visiting heads of state, (1981) 19 C.Y.B.I.L. 324-5.

§149 The question whether a defendant is in fact a foreign sovereign depends on recognition,[78] and this is a matter for decision by the national authorities so that a person may be accepted as a sovereign and entitled to the relevant immunity even though he is not afforded such recognition by any other state, and even if the actual exercise of sovereignty is restricted.[79] If a foreign sovereign is the plaintiff in an action, his acceptance of the jurisdiction makes him amenable to a counterclaim and he is unable to plead immunity to such claim.[80] The immunity that is enjoyed by the sovereign also extends to his property.[81]

78. *Sayce v. Ameer of Bahawalpur*, [1952] 1 All E.R. 326 (Q.B.); [1952] 2 All E.R. 64 (C.A.). See §§91-109.

79. *Mighell v. Sultan of Johore*, [1894] 1 Q.B. 149 (C.A.); see also *Statham v. Statham*, [1912] P. 92 (P.D.A.).

80. This means that if, e.g., a sovereign has brought a claim and secured a judgment in a court in enemy-occupied territory, he is liable to an originating summons brought under post-liberation legislation to set aside such judgment, *Sultan of Johore v. Abubakar Tunku Aris Bendahara*, [1952] A.C. 318 (P.C.). See also, *Chinese Embassy (Immunities) Case* (Germany) (1925), 3 Ann. Dig. 321.

81. *De Haber v. Queen of Portugal* (Spain) (1851), 17 Q.B. 195 (Q.B.).

§150 The ultimate assertion of state authority is the exercise of criminal jurisdiction, and this normally extends to all persons within the territorial limits of the state.[82] However, if the alleged offender is a diplomat or some other agent of a foreign state the territorial state is unable to exercise its criminal jurisdiction in the absence of a waiver of immunity by the offender's own state authority.[83] At one time it was considered that an ambassador was able to waive the immunity of his junior staff,[84] but now by the Vienna Convention on Diplomatic Relations, 1961,[85] which "recalls that peoples of all nations from ancient times have recognized the status of diplomatic agents[86] . . . [and a]ffirms that the rules of customary law should continue to govern questions not expressly regulated by" its provisions,[87] "the immunity from jurisdiction of diplomatic agents and of persons enjoying immunity under [the

Convention] may be waived by the sending State [and] must always be express".[88]

82. See §136.

83. *R. v. Madan*, [1961] 2 Q.B. 1 (C.A.) (waiver by the accused himself is no waiver).

84. *R. v. A.B.*, [1941] 1 K.B. 454 at 457 (C.C.A.) per Lord Caldecote C.J.: "The first thing to be said is that the privilege claimed by the appellant is a privilege which is derived from, and in law is the privilege of, the ambassador and ultimately of the State which sends the ambassador. It was a privilege which was originally based on the comity of nations, before it was declared by 7 Anne, c. 12, 1708". See also *Dickinson v. Del Solar*, [1930] 1 K.B. 376 at 380, per Lord Hewart C.J.: "The privilege is the privilege of the Sovereign by whom the diplomatic agent is accredited, and it may be waived with the sanction of the sovereign or the official superior of the agent."

85. 500 U.N.T.S. 95, ratified by Canada in 1961. See Green, "Trends in the Law Concerning Diplomats", (1981) 19 C.Y.B.I.L. 132.

86. See *Case Concerning U.S. Diplomatic and Consular Staff in Tehran* (Provisional Measures), [1979] I.C.J. 7 at 19-20; (Judgment), [1980] I.C.J. 3 at 40: ". . . The institution of diplomacy, with its concomitant privileges and immunities, has withstood the test of centuries and proved to be an instrument essential for effective co-operation in the international community, and for enabling States, irrespective of their differing constitutional and social systems, to achieve mutual understanding and to resolve their differences by peaceful means . . . . [W]hile no State is under any obligation to maintain diplomatic or consular relations with another, yet it cannot fail to recognize the imperative obligations inherent therein, now codified in the Vienna Conventions. . . . The rules of diplomatic law . . . constitute a self-contained régime which, on the one hand, lays down the receiving State's obligations regarding the facilities, privileges and immunities to be accorded to diplomatic missions and, on the other, foresees their possible abuse by members of the missions and specifies the means at the disposal of the receiving State to counter any such abuse. These means are, by their nature, entirely efficacious, for unless the sending State recalls the member of the mission objected to forthwith, the prospect of the almost immediate loss of his privileges and immunities, because of the withdrawal by the receiving State of his recognition as a member of the mission, will in practice compel that person, in his own interest, to depart at once. But the principle of the inviolability of the persons of diplomatic agents and the premises of diplomatic missions is one of the very foundations of this long-established regime, to the evolution of which the traditions of Islam made a substantial contribution. . . . Even in the case of armed conflict or in the case of a breach of diplomatic relations . . . both the inviolability of the members of a diplomatic mission and of the premises, property and archives of the mission must be respected by the receiving State. Naturally, the observance of this principle does not mean . . . that a diplomatic agent caught in the act of committing an . . . offence may not, on occasion, be briefly arrested by the police of the receiving State in order to prevent the commission of the particular crime." See also, Green, "The Tehran Embassy Incident — Legal Aspects", (1980) 19 Archiv des Völkerrechts 1. Although the court made it clear that these immunities stem from customary law, Canada has indicated that they exist reciprocally, and "s'il lui apparaît 'que les privilèges et immunités accordés à la mission diplomatique ou au poste consulaire canadiens à l'étranger, ou à toute personne concernée par la mission ou par un tel poste, sont inférieurs à ceux que confère la présente Loi [State Immunity Act, S.C. 1980-81-82, c. 95, Art. 2(4)] à la mission diplomatique ou au poste consulaire de ce

pays, ou aux personnes concernées par la mission ou par un tel poste", Legal Bureau memo. Sept. 1985, (1986) 24 C.Y.B.I.L. 395.

87.   Preamble; see also, *The Amazone*, [1940] P. 40 (C.A.), in which it is pointed out that the 1708 Statute is only declaratory of the common law and not exhaustive on the immunities of diplomats.

88.   Art. 32. This is in accordance with *R. v. Madan, ante*, in which it was held that a waiver by the proper authority given after conviction was no waiver, although the courts left open whether a retrospective waiver would have been effective if it had been declared as being such. For Canadian statement that the immunity belongs to the state and not to the representative in a personal fashion, see statement to §144 note 62.

§151   The immunity enjoyed by diplomats applies to their missions, the members of their families and to their documents.[89] But the immunity of such documents cannot be pleaded by a non-diplomatic defendant charged with a criminal offence,[90] although such immunity might attach if the head of mission, from which the documents came, claimed immunity in respect thereof. By the Vienna Convention on Diplomatic Relations,[91] however, "the archives and documents of the mission shall be inviolable at any time and wherever they may be", so that it would appear that such documents could not be used in such a case. On the other hand, the Convention specifically defines the functions of a diplomatic mission[92] and provides that "it is the duty of all persons enjoying such privileges and immunities to respect the laws and regulations of the receiving State. They also have the duty not to interfere in the internal affairs of that State".[93]

89.   Arts. 22, 24, 37. Re documents, see *Fayed v. Al-Tajir*, [1987] 2 All E.R. 346 (C.A.). The Article extends immunity from dues and taxes to the non-local private servants of mission members. However, the national law of the receiving state may widen this; see *Private Servant of Diplomat Case* (1971), 71 I.L.R. 546 (Austria S.C.).

90.   See *Rose v. R.*, [1947] 3 D.L.R. 618 (Que. K.B.).

91.   Art. 24.

92.   Art. 3. In a statement in the House of Commons, 19 Jan. 1983, at 21979, the Parliamentary Secretary to the Ministry of Finance, stated "that diplomats are posted to Canada for valid and entirely legitimate reasons. They have important functions to fulfil representing their countries' interests here, just as our representatives have in their countries. We encourage normal diplomatic functions by any embassy and we expect the same treatment for our representatives abroad. . . . [T]he Government does not hesitate to demand the withdrawal of personnel from Canada who have abused their diplomatic status or have behaved in ways contrary to their responsibilities as representatives of their countries. . . . [S]ince 1978 a total of 18 foreign officials from four different countries have been declared persona non grata", (1984) 22 C.Y.B.I.L. 337.

93.   Art. 41.

§152   In addition to his immunity from criminal proceedings, a diplomat is immune from civil suit unless his immunity is waived,[94] and such waiver must be express and cannot be implied.[95] If the diplomat ceases to be accredited for any reason, whether because he has been recalled[96] or because the receiving state has declared him persona non grata, he enjoys a period of grace to clear up his affairs and his immunity continues during this period.[97] If, however, he is a junior diplomat and the ambassador has declared his appointment at an end and has also waived his immunity, he becomes liable to the local jurisdiction immediately.[98] If a diplomat has incurred some civil liability while enjoying immunity, he can be sued in connection therewith after the immunity ceases, but any action which has been so instituted will terminate if the defendant again acquires diplomatic status.[99]

94.   *Engelke v. Musmann*, [1928] A.C. 433 (H.L.); *The Amazone, ante*; Vienna Convention, 1961, Art. 31, but immunity will not apply "in the case of (a) a real action relative to private immovable property situated in the territory of the receiving State, unless he holds it on behalf of the sending State for the purposes of the mission; (b) an action relating to succession in which the diplomatic agent is involved as executor, administrator, heir or legatee as a private person and not on behalf of the sending State; (c) an action relating to any professional or commercial activity exercised by the diplomatic agent in the receiving State outside his official functions. A diplomatic agent is not obliged to give evidence as a witness".

95.   Art. 32(2). In this connection it should be pointed out that, since in Canada a coroner's inquest is a judicial process, the immunity extends to both a diplomatic corps and any member of the diplomatic corps who might be summoned as a witness; Memo by Legal Bureau, Dept. of External Affairs, 17 Dec., 1981, (1982) 20 C.Y.B.I.L. 258-8.

96.   In such a case, or if he otherwise ceases to be a diplomat, he becomes liable to extradition as any private individual, Memo of Legal Bureau, Dept. of External Affairs, 29 Sept., 1982, (1983) 21 C.Y.B.I.L. 307-8.

97.   *Musurus Bey v. Gadban*, [1894] 2 Q.B. 352 (C.A.); Art. 39(2).

98.   *R. v. A.B., ante. R. v. Palacios* (1984), 7 D.L.R. (4th) 112 (Ont. C.A.). In Aug. 1983, Palacios, a member of the Nicaraguan Embassy in Ottawa was arrested and denied bail on drug and weapon charges. In denying his claim to diplomatic immunity, the Department for External Affairs maintained that this ended when the embassy informed the Department that he had been reassigned. There was apparently no reference to days of grace, nor did the Department agree to the embassy's assertion that he had been temporarily reinstated in Ottawa. The Ont. C.A. upheld the immunity; and the former diplomat was ordered to leave Canada in Feb. 1984; Globe and Mail, Feb. 24, 1984.

99.   *Ghosh v. D'Rozario*, [1963] 1 Q.B. 106 (C.A.); leave to appeal to H.L. refused [1962] 1 W.L.R. 1083 (H.L.).

§153   Even though a diplomatic representative is immune from arrest, the Legal Bureau of the Department of External Affairs agrees "with the procedure of temporary detention of a foreign representative where it is necessary to prevent the commission of a serious offence which endangers his safety, that of the public, or the security of the state. It is generally recognized in international law and practice that the principle of inviolability of the diplomatic agent should not prevent the receiving state from taking measures as necessary for its own protection,[1] that of the public and the diplomat himself. Should such an incident occur, the Department would have a defensible position and would support police action taken for those reasons".[2] Further, if a diplomat carries arms without a permit, he may be disarmed by the police and declared persona non grata.[3]

1. See Green, "Trends in the Law Concerning Diplomats", (1981), 19 C.Y.B.I.L. 132.

2. 5 May, 1982 (1983), 21 C.Y.B.I.L. 309.

3. (1983) 21 C.Y.B.I.L. 310.

§154 Normally, diplomatic agents should possess the nationality of the sending state,[4] but the receiving state may agree to accept the appointment of one of its own nationals, in which case he, too, will enjoy immunity in respect of official acts.[5]

4. Vienna Convention, 1961, Art. 37.

5. Art. 38, which states that in such a case he "shall enjoy only immunity from jurisdiction, and inviolability, in respect of official acts performed in the exercise of his functions". See also *Macartney v. Garbutt* (1890), 24 Q.B.D. 368 (Q.B.). As to the posting as a diplomatic representative a person with double nationality, one of which is Canadian, see Memoire du 26 Mars 1962, par le bureau juridique, (1983) 21 C.Y.B.I.L. 310-1.

§155 Not only are diplomats immune from suit in the courts, they are also exempt from liability in respect of local taxes imposed upon the premises used for official purposes.[6] This immunity also extends to their personal property which cannot be seized for non-payment of local taxes.[7] The immunity from local taxation is enjoyed by consular officials as well as diplomatic personnel,[8] although the immunities normally granted to the former are not as wide as those enjoyed by diplomats and are more strictly confined to their official position.[9]

6. See *Ref. re Power of Municipalities to Levy Rates on Foreign Legations and High Commissioners' Residences*, [1943] S.C.R. 208 (S.C.C.); see also *United States v. Arlington (City)* (1982) 669 F. 2d 925 (C.A., 4th Circuit). See, generally, Dufour, "La protection des communités diplomatiques et consulaires au Canada", (1973) 11 C.Y.B.I.L. 123; (1974) 12 C.Y.B.I.L. 3.

7. *Macartney v. Garbutt, ante.*

8. *Yin-Tso Hsiung v. Toronto*, [1950] 4 D.L.R. 209 (Ont. H.C.).

9. See now, Vienna Convention on Consular Relations, 1963, 596 U.N.T.S. 261, to which Canada acceded in 1974; see also, *Re L.* (1977), (1978) 4 Commonwealth Law Bulletin, 51 (N.Z. S.C.). In *Re Rissmann* (1970/1972), 71 I.L.R. 577 (Italy Ct. of Cassation) it was held within a consul's functions to issue a German passport to a minor possessing German and Italian nationality to enable her to join her father in Germany who had been declared her guardian by a German court, even though an Italian judge had entrusted her to her mother in Italy.

§156 If a diplomat rents property and fails to pay the local taxes which are then levied against the landlord, the latter cannot recover from his tenant even though the lease may have had a covenant for payment by the tenants.[10] This inability to recover from a diplomatic tenant is not sufficient ground to exercise a landlord's right to refuse to approve a sublease on the ground that the subtenant is a diplomat,[11] nor are they liable, for example, under a covenant for repairs in a lease.[12] Even when the diplomat submits to the jurisdiction, this submission relates only to the process and not to execution.[13]

10. *Parkinson v. Potter* (1885), 16 Q.B.D. 152 (D.C.).
11. *Parker v. Boggan*, [1947] K.B. 346 (K.B.).
12. *Intpro Properties (U.K.) Ltd. v. Sauvel*, [1983] 1 All E.R. 658 (Q.B.).
13. *Re Suarez*, [1918] 1 Ch. 176 (C.A.); *Dickinson v. Del Solar,* [1930] 1 K.B. 376 (K.B.).

§157 The immunity enjoyed by a diplomat only relates to the local jurisdiction. It does not affect the diplomat's legal liability, as is clear from the fact that the immunity may be waived.[14] Moreover, once he has ceased to be a diplomat, his immunity ceases and he may be sued even in respect of matters which arose while he was a diplomat.[15]

14. *Dickinson v. Del Solar, ante.*
15. *Ghosh v. D'Rozario, ante.*

§158 Diplomats are merely agents of the state which has sent them and the immunity they enjoy is granted to them in this capacity.[16] The general rule with regard to the immunity of state agencies and organs is considered to have been enunciated by Chief Justice Marshall of the United States Supreme Court in *The Schooner Exchange v. M'Faddon*[17] when dealing with the immunity of an armed public ship. This immunity has been extended to armed forces passing through or present in the territory of a friendly state,[18] organs of government[19] and to state trading enterprises, although there is now a tendency to deny immunity to the latter.[20]

16. For Canadian statement to this effect see Statement cited §144 note 62.

17. (1812) 7 Cranch 116 at 118: ". . . One sovereign being in no respect amenable to another; and being bound by obligations of the highest character not to degrade the dignity of his nation, by placing himself or its sovereign rights within the jurisdiction of another, can be supposed to enter a foreign territory only under an express license, or in the confidence that the immunities belonging to his independent sovereign station, though not expressly stipulated, are reserved by implication, and will be extended to him. This perfect equality and absolute independence of sovereigns, and this common interest compelling them to mutual intercourse, and an interchange of good offices with each other, have given rise to a class of cases in which every sovereign is understood to wave [sic] the exercise of a part of that complete territorial jurisdiction, which has been stated to be the attribute of every nation."

18. See *Amand v. Home Secretary*, [1943] A.C. 147 (H.L.). The status of such forces is now frequently regulated by agreement between the state of the visiting force and the host country and in accordance with the terms of the latter's legislation, see, e.g., *Ref. Re Exemption of U.S. Forces from Canadian Criminal Law*, [1943] S.C.R. 483 (S.C.C.);and Visiting Forces Act, R.S.C. 1970, c. V-6; *Wilson v. Girard* (1957), 354 U.S. 524.

19. See *Krajina v. Tass Agency*, [1949] 2 All E.R. 274 (C.A.); in *Re Burodine* (1987) the London correspondent ot Tass was fined and banned from driving after admitting driving with excess alcohol, *The Times* (London) 14 Mar. 1987. In *Mellenger v. N.B. Development Corp.*, [1971] 1 W.L.R. 604 at 609, it was held that "the Crown is sovereign in New Brunswick for provincial powers . . . [and] that the Province of New Brunswick is a sovereign state in its own right, and entitled . . . to claim sovereignty. . . . [Since the Corporation] has never pursued any ordinary trade or commerce [it] is in the same position as a government department, and is entitled to plead sovereign immunity," per Lord Denning, M.R. In *Ferranti-Packard Ltd. v. Cushman Rentals Ltd.* (1980), 30 O.R. (2d) 194 (Ont. H.C.); affirmed (1981), 31 O.R. (2d) 799 (Ont. C.A.) it was held that the fact that the New York statute creating the N.Y. State Thruway Authority gave the Authority a "governmental function" was not enough to create it a state organ entitled to immunity.

20. See §§160-162.

§159   The law with regard to state trading agencies is normally considered to stem from the decision in *The Parlement Belge*,[21] in which it was held that a mail packet belonging to the King of the Belgians was entitled to absolute immunity, even though it might be contended that the carrying of packages was a commercial and not a state function falling within the jus imperii. With the increase in state trading resulting from the number of states applying socialist economic and trading principles, it became clear that such commercial enterprises were enjoying an unfair advantage when compared with non-state enterprises and that states were receiving immunity from legal liability in circumstances where it could not be considered that their dignity as states warranted such immunity.

21. (1880), 5 P.D. 197.

§160   The United States was the first country to indicate that it was no longer prepared to concede absolute immunity to a state trading agency. In 1952 the State Department issued the Tate Letter[22] intimating its intention in the future to apply the 'restrictive' theory of sovereign immunity, whereby "the immunity of the sovereign is recognised with regard to sovereign or public acts (jure imperii) of a state, but not with respect to private acts (jure gestionis)."

22.   6 Whiteman 569-571; see also *Alfred Dunhill of London Inc. v. Cuba (Republic)* (1976), 425 U.S. 682 (S.C.); *Jackson v. People's Republic of China* (1986) 794 Fed. Rep. 2d 1490 (C.A.) (refused to give the Tate Letter retroactive effect pre-1952 events, since to do so "would interfere with antecedent rights of other sovereigns and also with antedecent principles of law that the United States followed until 1952").

§161   The United States was not alone in adopting the restrictive theory. While the United Kingdom and the members of the Commonwealth, Czechoslovakia, Estonia, Poland and, prior to the Tate Letter, the United States, all applied the absolute theory, and the same appeared to be the case with Brazil, Chile, China, Hungary, Japan, Luxembourg, Norway and Portugal, the Netherlands, Sweden and Argentina appeared to apply both theories, but the restrictive theory has always been applied by Belgium, and Italy, followed by Egypt, Switzerland, France, Austria, Greece, Germany and increasingly the Netherlands. Moreover, a large number of countries, including some which had habitually applied the absolute theory, became parties to the 1926 Brussels Convention for the Unification of Certain Rules relating to the Immunity of State-owned Vessels[23] by which immunity was denied to such vessels, and although not a party to the Convention, the United States adhered to this policy. Today, most countries have abandoned the restrictive theory insofar as state trading enterprises are concerned.[24]

23.   176 L.N.T.S. 199.

24.   *The Philippine Admiral*, [1977] A.C. 373 (P.C.) (appeal to the Privy Council from Hong Kong, in which reference was made to the Tate Letter and in which it was held that *The Parlement Belge, ante,* had been misconstrued); but in *Trendtex Trading Corp. v. Central Bank of Nigeria*, [1977] 2 W.L.R. 356 (C.A.), the Court of Appeal held that the absolute rule prevailed until overruled by the House of Lords, and this occurred in *I Congresso del Partido*, [1981] 3 W.L.R. 328. The situation in England is now governed by the State Immunity Act, 1978, c. 33. See also, decision of French Cour de Cassation in *Sonatrach v. Migeon* (1985) 26 I.L.M. 998. The restrictive principle was applied in the Federal Republic of Germany in *Y.M.N. Establishment (sub nom. Nonresident Petitioner) v. Central Bank of Nigeria* (1975), (1977) 16 I.L.M. 501. Se Emanuelli, 'L'immunité souveraine et la coutume internationale; de l'immunité absolue à l'immunité relative', (1984) 22 C.Y.B.I.l. 26.

§162 The situation in Canada has been somewhat confused. In *Smith v. Cdn. Javelin Ltd.*[25] it was held that the restrictive doctrine was applicable in Ontario, although in *Khan v. Fredson Travel Inc.* (No. 2)[26] it was suggested that this was, in fact, not certain. Quebec has also applied the restrictive theory,[27] but when it did so in *Congo (Republic) v. Venne*,[28] the majority of the Supreme Court declined to express itself as it held that the Congolese act in question was a public act and so immune.[29] By the State Immunity Act, 1982,[30] the restrictive policy has been adopted:[31] "a foreign state is not immune from the jurisdiction of a court in any proceedings that relate to any commercial activity of the foreign state . . . [or] any death or personal injury, or any damage or loss of property that occurs in Canada . . . [or] an action in rem against a ship owned or operated by the state, or an action in personam for enforcing a claim in connection with such a ship, if, at the time the claim arose or the proceedings were commenced, the ship was being used or was intended for use in a commercial activity . . . [or] an action in rem against any cargo owned by the state if, at the time the claim arose or the proceedings were commenced, the cargo and the ship carrying the cargo were being used or intended for use in a commercial activity, or an action in personam for enforcing a claim in connection with such cargo if, at the time the claim arose or proceedings were commenced, the ship carrying the cargo was being used or was intended for use in a commercial activity . . . [and] a ship or cargo owned by a foreign state includes any ship or cargo in the possession or control of the state[32] and any ship or cargo in which the state claims an interest[33] . . . [or] any proceedings that relate to an interest of the state in property that arises by way of succession, gift or bona vacantia."

25. (1976), 12 O.R. (2d) 244 (Ont. H.C.).

26. (1982), 36 O.R. (2d) 17 (Ont. H.C.).

27. *Allan Construction Ltd. v. Venezuela*, [1968] Que. P.R. 145 (Que. S.C.); *Zodiack Int. Products Inc. v. Polish People's Republic* (1977), 81 D.L.R. (3d) 656 (Que. C.A.); see also Vincke, "Certain aspects de l'évolution récente du problème de l'immunité de juridiction des états", (1969) 7 C.Y.B.I.L. 224: Castel, "Exemption from the Jurisdiction of Canadian Courts", (1971) 9 C.Y.B.I.L. 154.

28. (1968), 5 D.L.R. (3d) 128 (Que. C.A.); reversed [1971] S.C.R. 997 (S.C.C).

29. *Congo (Republic) v. Venne, ante.*

30. S.C. 1980-81-82, c. 95. As to the operation of the Act and the fiscal immunity of a foreign state trading bank, see Memo of Legal Bureau, Dept. of External Affairs, Jan. 1982, (1983), 21 C.Y.B.I.L. 306-7. See also, Legal Bureau memo, Sept. 1985, (1986) 24 C.Y.B.I.L. 394. See also, Molot and Jewett, "The State Immunity Act of Canada", (1982) 20 C.Y.B.I.L. 79; Castel, 1987 ed., 307-312.

31. Ss. 5-8.

32. In *Juan Ysmael v. Indonesian Govt.*, [1955] A.C. 72 (P.C.), the Privy Council had held that a foreign state could be called upon to prove the validity of its claim to possess an interest. In *Royal Bank v. Corriveau* (1980), 30 O.R. (2d) 653 (Ont. H.C.) a claim was brought for damage to property leased to the government of Cuba and it was sought to recover against funds held by the Bank. It was held "that the leased premises were for governmental use and the moneys in the bank were in the 'possession' of the foreign Sovereign State. . . . Cuba is entitled to claim sovereign immunity" at 659.

33. This raises a possibility that a Canadian court would no longer continue to apply the principles laid down in *The Arantzazu Mendi*, [1939] A.C. 256 (H.L.) or *The Cristina*, [1938] A.C. 485 (H.L.), which formed the basis for many of the absolute immunity judgments. Emanuelli, "L'immunité souveraine et la coutume internationale: de l'immunité aboluë à l'immunité relative" (1984) C.Y.B.I.L. 26.

§163 The adoption of the restrictive concept of state immunity does not impinge upon the rule forbidding the direct impleading of a foreign state or government, whether that government is de facto[34] or de jure.[35] Equally, if a foreign state becomes impleaded in an action brought against a private individual or company, immunity will be granted to the extent that the foreign state's interests are involved.[36] Similarly, the courts of one country will not adjudicate upon the transaction of a foreign government should this be raised in an action before these courts.[37]

34. *The Arantzazu Mendi, ante.*

35. *The Cristina, ante.*

36. *United States v. Dollfus Mieg et Cie S.A.*, [1952] A.C. 582 (H.L.).

37. *Buttes Gas and Oil Co. v. Hammer*, [1981] 3 W.L.R. 787 (H.L.). See also *Empresa Exportadora De Azucar v. Industria Azucarera Nacional SA*, [1983] Lloyd's Rep. 171 (C.A.).

3. ENVIRONMENT AND POLLUTION CONTROL

§164 Sic utere tuo ut alienum non laedas[38] is a fundamental principle of the common law, but it also finds some expression in international law.

38. "Every man must use his own property as not to harm that of another," 9 Co. Rep. 59; 1 Blackstone, Commentaries, 306. See Beesley, "The Canadian Approach to International Environmental Protection Law," (1973), 11 C.Y.B.I.L. 3; Johnston, "International Environmental Law: Recent Developments and Canadian Contributions", Macdonald *et al.*, Canadian Perspectives on International Law and Organization (1974), p. 555; Castel, 1987 ed., 834-853.

§165 There is, however, no expressly recognized rule of customary international law with regard to pollution causing damage in the territory of a neighbouring state, nor is there any generally applicable universal treaty dealing with this matter.[39] Nevertheless, in its draft on state responsibility of 1979 the International Law Commission stated that "...on the basis of the rules of international law in force, an international crime may result...from...(d) a serious breach of an international obligation of essential importance for the safeguarding and preservation of the human environment, such as those prohibiting massive pollution of the atmosphere or of the sea".[40] A number of treaties do, however, attack this issue in order to ensure full observance of the purpose for which the treaty has been drawn up.[41] In addition, some treaties of a multi-lateral character are directed solely to the prevention of a particular type of pollution.[42] However, many of the treaties which are important in this field tend to be bilateral[43] or regional.[44]

39. See, e.g., Barros and Johnston, The International Law of Pollution (1973). Springer, The International Law of Pollution, 1983.

40. (1979-II) Y.B.I.L.C. 91-93, Art. 19; see Green, 'New Trends in International Criminal Law", (1981) 11 I.Y.B.H.R. 9, at 28 et seqq.; Springer,op. cit, at 127.

41. E.g., Geneva Convention on the High Seas, 1958, 450 U.N.T.S. 11, Arts. 24, 25, not ratified by Canada. See also, 1982 U.N. Convention on the Law of the Sea, 21 I.L.M. 1261, Part XII, Arts. 192-237. See also, Geneva Convention on Long-Range Transboundary Air Pollution, 1979, 18 I.L.M. 1442, which was ratified by Canada in 1981. For statements in the House of Commons regarding acid rain and similar problems with the United States, see Commons Debates, 18 Mar. 1985 at 3108, 24 Sept. 1985 at 6920, 25 Nov. 1985 at 8797-98 and Oct. 24 at 7996-97, (1986) 24 C.Y.B.I.L. 431-434.

42. E.g., International Convention for Prevention of Pollution of the Sea by Oil, 1954/1971, 327 U.N.T.S. 3, 600 U.N.T.S. 332. See also Canada Shipping Act, R.S.C. 1970, c. S-9; for unilateral Canadian action, Arctic Waters Pollution Act, R.S.C. 1970, c. 2 (1st Supp.), and Canada Shipping Act, Part XX [en. R.S.C. 1970, c. 27 (2nd Supp.) s. 3(2)]; Green, "Canada and Arctic Sovereignty", (1970) 48 C.B.R. 740, "International Law and Canada's Anti-Pollution Legislation", (1971) 50 Oregon Law Review 463; also Pharand, The Law of the Sea of the Arctic (1973) Part VI; Bankes "Environmental Protection in Antarctica: A Comment on the Convention on the Conservation of Antarctic Marine Living Resources," (1980, 19 I.L.M. 841), (1981) 19 C.Y.B.I.L. 303. See also §263.

43. See Canada-U.S. Memo. re Transboundary Air Pollution 1980, 20 I.L.M. 690. See the position between Canada and the U.S. re the Great Lakes and the St. Lawrence Seaway, e.g. Castel, International Law (1976), pp. 807-832, 1987 ed., 860-872; Bédard, "La Régime juridique des Grands Lacs", Macdonald et al., Canadian Perspectives on International Law and Organization (1974) p. 500; Jordan, "The International Joint Commission and Canada-United States Boundary Relations", ibid. p. 522; Agreement on Great Lakes Water Quality, 1972, Can. T.S. No. 12; Cohen, The Regime of Boundary Waters — The Canadian-United States Experience (1977); Piper, The International Law of the Great Lakes (1967), pp. 84-87. See also, U.S.-Mexican Treaty on Utilization of Waters of Colorado and Tijuana Rivers and of Rio Grande, 1944, 3 U.N.T.S. 313. See Cooper, 'The Management of International

Environmental Disputes in the Context of Canada-United States Relations: A Survey and Evaluation of Techniques and Mechanisms', (1986) 24 C.Y.B.I.L. 247.

44. Nordic Convention on Protection of the Environment, 1970, 13 I.L.M. 591. See also 1982 U.N. Convention on the Law of the Sea, Arts. 197-201.

§166 Major problems have arisen in connection with oil pollution, particularly in the case of discharge from or destruction of giant tankers, as exemplified by the loss of the *Torrey Canyon* in 1977. Now the issue of marine pollution is Part XII of the United Nations Law of the Sea Convention of 1982,[45] although this Convention was not signed by Japan, Saudi Arabia or the United States and does not come into force until it has been ratified or acceded to by sixty states. Problems have also arisen as a result of pollution of international rivers, especially the Rhine, often by way of industrial waste.[46]

45. 21 I.L.M. 1261, esp. Arts. 207-233. See *Re Sedco Inc.* (1982) 543 F. Supp. 561 (U.S. Dist. Ct.); Green, 'International Law and Canada's Anti-Pollution Legislation', (1971), 50 Oregon L.R. 462.

46. See generally, Lammers, Pollution of International Watercourses, 1984.

§167 Occasionally, states will enter into an agreement to submit a specific pollution issue to arbitration. This occurred between the United States and Canada in relation to damage suffered in the United States as a result of fumes produced by a smelter at Trail, British Columbia.[47] In this case the Arbitral Tribunal pointed out that it was not concerned with the question whether the sovereignty of the United States had in any way been infringed or violated by these fumes, since its sole task was to interpret the bilateral Convention and determine the existence of damage and the indemnity to be paid by Canada. The Tribunal based much of its reasoning on decisions by the United States Supreme Court[48] and based its award of damages on proximity of injury. In this particular case, the court was authorized by the parties to indicate a régime for the future which might be expected to prevent a future recurrence. As a result of the *Trail Smelter Arbitration* award it is now generally agreed that "under the principles of international law . . . no State has the right to use or permit the use of its territory in such a manner as to cause injury by fumes in or to the territory of another or the properties or persons therein, when the case is of serious consequence and the injury is established by clear and convincing evidence."[49]

47. *Trail Smelter Arbitration* (U.S./Can.) (1938/1941), 3 R.I.A.A. 1905 (Arbitral Trib.).

48. *Georgia v. Tennessee Copper Co.* (1907), 206 U.S. 230; *Georgia v. Ducktown Sulphur, Copper & Iron Co.* (1915), 237 U.S. 474 (re air pollution); *Missouri v. Illinois*

(1906), 200 U.S. 496; *New Jersey v. City of New York* (1931), 283 U.S. 473 (re water pollution).

49. *Trail Smelter Arbitration, ante* at p. 1965.

§168 The proliferation of nuclear testing has made the problem of air and environmental pollution one of major significance. The First Geneva Conference on the Law of the Sea, 1958 adopted a resolution "recognizing the need for international action in the field of disposal of radioactive wastes in the sea" and called upon the International Atomic Energy Agency to "pursue whatever studies and take whatever action is necessary to assist States in controlling the discharge of radioactive materials to the sea, in promulgating standards, and in drawing up internationally acceptable regulations to prevent pollution of the sea by radioactive materials in amounts which would adversely affect man and his marine resources".[50] In 1963 the Treaty Banning Nuclear Weapons Tests in Outer Space and Under Water[51] was adopted. This forbade[52] testing "in any . . . environment if such explosion causes radioactive debris to be present outside the territorial limits of the state under whose jurisdiction or control such explosion is conducted."

50. U.K., Cmnd. 594 (1958), p. 48. See also Convention on Dumping of Wastes at Sea, 1972, 11 I.L.M. 1294.

51. 1964, Can. T.S. No. 1; (1963) 480 U.N.T.S. 43.

52. Art. 1(1)(b).

§169 Not all states have become parties to the Nuclear Tests Ban Treaty and France and China, among others, have continued testing. In 1973, both Australia and New Zealand, fearing the effects of radioactive fallout from announced forthcoming French tests in the Pacific, sought a ruling from the International Court of Justice that such tests were illegal.[53] After the initiation of the proceedings, France issued a number of statements intimating that no further tests would occur and the Court decided by a majority that it was therefore not called upon to give a decision. Not even the dissenting judges were prepared to assert that nuclear testing was contrary to international law, and one of the concurring judges pointed out that the Treaty could be denounced while state practice indicated that customary law did not make such testing illegal.[54]

53. *Nuclear Tests Cases,* [1974] I.C.J. 253, 457.

54. Judge Petren, at p. 305.

§170 While not expressly concerned with environmental pollution, the Treaty on Principles Governing the Activities of States in the Exploration and Use of Outer Space, including the Moon and Other Celestial

Bodies, 1967,[55] imposes a liability upon a launching state "for damage to another State Party to the Treaty or to its natural or juridical persons by such object or its component parts on the Earth, in air space or in outer space, including the moon and other celestial bodies". Related thereto are the Conventions on the Rescue and Return of Astronauts and the Return of Objects Launched into Outer Space, 1967,[56] and on International Liability for Damage Caused by Space Objects, 1972.[57] The effect of these Conventions is to impose an obligation upon a state in whose territory an 'object' lands to return it, while a launching state is absolutely liable to pay compensation for damage. Problems connected with the falling to earth in the Northwest Territories, Alberta and Saskatchewan of the nuclear reactor of a Soviet satellite in 1978 indicated that the relevant treaties did not adequately deal with the manner in which such objects are to be gathered or the extent of the recovery expenses involved, for by way of final settlement the Soviet Union agreed to pay approximately half of the Canadian claim.[58]

55. Art. 7, (1967) Can. T.S. No. 19.

56. (1975) Can. T.S. No. 6.

57. (1975) Can. T.S. No. 7.

58. See Exchange of Notes between Canada and the U.S.S.R. re Soviet Cosmos 954, (1979) 18 I.L.M. 899-930; Protocol of Settlement, 1981, 20 I.L.M. 689.

§171 There are no established rules of international law for the protection of the environment as such.[59] In 1968 the General Assembly of the United Nations adopted a Resolution[60] to convene a Conference on the Human Environment. General Guidelines for the Preservation of the Marine Environment, based on a Canadian Working Paper, were drawn up at the 1971 Ottawa meeting of an Intergovernmental Working Group[61] and these were approved at the Stockholm Conference on Human Environment convened by the United Nations in 1972. The Declaration adopted by this Conference[62] is not a treaty, but a number of its principles may be regarded as declaratory of customary law. These are to be found in 26 Principles of which Principle 21, reflecting the view of the *Trail Smelter Arbitration* Tribunal,[63] is perhaps the most important: "States have, in accordance with the Charter of the United Nations and the principles of international law, the sovereign right to exploit their own resources pursuant to their own environmental policies, and the responsibility to ensure that activities within their jurisdiction or control do not cause damage to the environment of other States or of areas beyond the limits of national jurisdiction."

59. See, however, draft of I.L.C. in §165 note 40.

60.　Res. 2398 (XXIII).

61.　Barros and Johnston, "International Environmental Law: Recent Developments and Canadian Contributions", Macdonald *et al.*, Canadian Perspectives on International Law and Organization (1974), p. 323. McRae and Goundrey, "Environmental Jurisdiction in Arctic Waters", (1982) 16 U.B.C.L.R. 197; see also, Handl, "International Liability of States for Marine Pollution", (1983) 21 C.Y.B.I.L. 85.

62.　11 I.L.M. 1972, 1416.

63.　(1938/1941), 3 R.I.A.A. 1905 (Arbitral Trib.).

§172 Even before the Stockholm Conference on the Human Environment, some countries had adopted legislation for the protection of the national environment. This was done in the United States in 1969[64] and ever since environmental groups have sought injunctions when they have considered particular projects as likely to affect the environment adversely, while in Canada various provinces have enacted legislation regulating the amount of pollution emission and imposed penalties for exceeding such limits.[65]

64.　National Environment Policy Act, 42 U.S. Code Annotated, s. 4321, see *Sierra Club v. Coleman* (1976), 421 F. Supp. 63 (U.S. Dist. Ct.).

65.　E.g. Clean Air Act, R.S.A. 1980, c. C-12; Clean Water Act, R.S.A. 1980, c. C-13; also Canada-U.S. Memo concerning Transboundary Air Pollution 1980, 20 I.L.M. 690, and the Convention on Long-Range Transboundary Air Pollution, 1979, 8 I.L.M. 1442, ratified by Canada in 1981. Protocol to the convention 1984, 24 I.L.M. 484. See FitzGerald, "The Proposed Canada-U.S. Transboundary Air Pollution Agreement", (1982) 20 C.Y.B.I.L. 219.

§173 The environment must be protected in time of peace, but also during armed conflict. While there is no treaty forbidding the use of nuclear weapons during armed conflict,[66] Article 55 of Protocol I additional to the Geneva Conventions of 1949 relating to humanitarian law in international armed conflict[67] provides: "Care shall be taken in warfare to protect the natural environment against widespread, long-term and severe damage. This protection includes a prohibition of the use of methods or means of warfare which are intended or may be expected to cause such damage to the natural environment and thereby to prejudice the health or survival of the population. Attacks against the natural environment by way of reprisals are prohibited." There is also a United Nations Convention on the Prohibition of Military or any other Hostile Use of Environmental Modification Techniques.[68] While Canada has not ratified the Protocol, it ratified the Convention in 1981.

66.　See Green, 'Nuclear Weapons and the Law of Armed Conflict', in Records of 1987 Canadian Conference on Nuclear Weapons and The Law, 1988.

67.   1977, (1977) 16 I.L.M. 1391; Schindler/Toman, The Laws of Armed Conflicts (1981) p. 551.

68.   1976, (1977) 16 I.L.M. 88; Schindler/Toman, *op cit.,* p. 131.

4. FISHERIES, CANALS AND WATER USE

§174   The right to use the water within a state's territorial limits as well as the resources to be found therein is inherent in the possession of such waters.[69] However, the exclusive use of such waters may be limited by customary law or by agreement, so that non-nationals may enjoy rights within the waters in question.

69.   See §§258-281 below on maritime frontiers.

§175   Perhaps the oldest of such rights relates to fishing. A state has complete control over fisheries lying within its territorial sea,[70] although problems may arise as to the limits of that sea[71] or the state may by treaty allow non-nationals to fish within those waters. When such a treaty right has been conferred it does not mean that any servitude has been created on behalf of the beneficiary, nor does it deny the right of the grantor to regulate the fishery in question — for this is one of the rights of sovereignty and is preserved unless expressly limited by the treaty. As a result, the regulatory function may be exercised by the coastal state alone, unless the contrary is clearly provided by the treaty conferring the fishery rights. The right to regulate, however, must be exercised in good faith so as not to detract from the rights granted by the treaty, and in the absence of clear provision to the contrary a fishery grant includes the right of the nationals of the grantee to employ non-nationals, so long as such non-nationals derive no direct benefit from the treaty itself. The right of the fishing vessels to enter coastal bays or harbours for shelter, repairs, wood and water is not part of the fishery right as such, but is inherent "in the duties of hospitality and humanity which all civilized nations impose upon themselves".[72]

70.   See *La Bretagne Arbitration* (1986), 17 Revue Général de Droit 813 (Canada/ France Arb. Trib.) discussed by Arbour, 'L'Affaire du chalutier-usine "La Bretagne" ou les droits de l'Etat côtier dans sa zone économique exclusive', (1986) 24 C.Y.B.I.L. 61.

71.   In the past it was generally accepted that the maximum limit of the territorial sea was three miles, with Norway habitually claiming four miles. There were, however, problems as to the method of drawing the baselines from which the waters should be measured. In the *Anglo-Norwegian Fisheries Case,* [1951] I.C.J. 116, the court held that, in the case of a heavily indented coast, the baseline might consist of a series of straight-lines joining headlands, so long as they followed the general direction of the coast. This has now been confirmed by Art. 4 of the Geneva Convention on the

Territorial Sea, 1958, 516 U.N.T.S. 205, but the Convention did not specify the width of the territorial sea. Instead, it provided that a contiguous zone seaward of the territorial sea might be claimed, so long as the outer limit of that zone was not more than 12 miles from the baseline; see also Art. 3 of the 1982 U.N. Convention on the Law of the Sea (21 I.L.M. 1261). Since 1958 most states have claimed a territorial sea of 12 miles, although a new belt of 200 miles is now being generally accepted as an exclusive economic zone. Canada's territorial sea extends 12 miles, with such fishing zones adjacent thereto as may be prescribed by the Governor in Council, Territorial Sea and Fishing Zones Act, R.S.C. 1970, c. T-7, s. 3 [subs. (1) re-en. R.S.C. 1970, c. 45 (1st Supp.), s. 1], s. 5 [subss. (1), (2) re-en. R.S.C. 1970, c. 45 (1st Supp.), s. 3(1)]. While Canada has proclaimed an exclusive 200-mile fishing zone, she has not, as yet, proclaimed an exclusive economic zone, but will probably do so now that the 1982 Convention on the Law of the Sea provides in Art. 55 for state jurisdiction over the exclusive economic zone, while by Art. 57 its breadth is not to exceed 200 miles from the baseline from which the territorial sea is measured. See §271. Braen, "La contrôle par le Canada des pêches étrangères dans sa zone de pêche", (1983), 21 C.Y.B.I.L. 3.

72.　　These principles were laid down by Permanent Ct. of Arbitration in the *North Atlantic Coast Fisheries Case* (G.B./U.S.) (1910), 11 R.I.A.A. 167.

§176 By the Geneva Convention on the Continental Shelf, 1958,[73] coastal states exercise sovereign rights over the shelf for the purpose of exploiting its natural resources, although such rights do not affect the legal status of the superjacent waters or the airspace above those waters. Insofar as fisheries are concerned, it has been accepted in state practice that, regardless of any rights appurtenant to the continental shelf, a coastal state has fishery rights within 12 miles of its baseline, with a preferential right in adjacent waters when there is a special dependence by the coastal state on its coastal fisheries.[74] The existence of such preferential rights, however, does not authorize the coastal state to disregard the pre-existing rights of other states in the adjacent waters affected, and the reasonable rights of other states must be considered.[75] In determining the relative rights in such circumstances an effort should be made to bring about an equitable apportionment of the fishing resources in accordance with the particular situation, and bearing in mind the rights of all states which have fishing interests in the area. By the 1982 Convention on the Law of the Sea,[76] the coastal state enjoys full sovereign rights over the living resources on the seabed, subsoil and in the superjacent waters of the exclusive economic zone[77] and shall determine the allowable catch in the light of conservation needs,[78] and it is only when the coastal state is unable itself to exploit fully the allowable catch that it need make arrangements permitting other states to enjoy the surplus, bearing in mind "[t]he requirements of developing states in the subregion or region in harvesting part of the surplus and the need to minimize economic dislocation in states whose nationals have habitually fished in the zone or which have made substantial efforts in research and identification of stocks".[79]

73. 499 U.N.T.S. 311, Arts. 2, 3, ratified by Canada in 1970; Convention on the Law of the Sea, 1982, 21 I.L.M. 1261, Arts. 77, 78. See §249.

74. *Fisheries Jurisdiction Cases* (U.K./Iceland; Germany/Iceland), [1974] I.C.J. 3, 175 at 23. See also, Yogis, "Canadian Fisheries and International Law", Macdonald *et al.,* Canadian Perspectives on International Law and Organization (1974) p. 398. For comments on over-fishing in the 200-mile zone see statements in House of Commons, 2 May, 9 May, 6 Jun. 1985 (Debates, at 4336-38, 4571-72, 5512-13) (1976) 24 C.Y.B.I.L. 425-8.

75. Geneva Convention on Fishing and Conservation of the Living Resources of the High Seas, 1958, 559 U.N.T.S. 285, not ratified by Canada. See Art. 6.

76. See §175 note 71.

77. Art. 56. See §271.

78. Convention on the Law of the Sea, 1982, Art. 61.

79. Art. 62.

§177 If a canal crosses the territory of a state to join two portions of the high seas, the status of that canal is regulated by treaty made by the coastal state and seagoing states.[80] There is no right under customary international law requiring the coastal state to allow passage through the canal. However, if such a canal has been constructed and placed under a treaty régime, even though it does not give direct access from one part of the high seas to another, but was intended to facilitate the passage across territory for national ships, that canal, too, if later opened to international shipping, will be construed as being within the régime of canals as indicated by treaties governing international canals which join parts of the high seas.[81] Whether a particular canal has been opened to the use of all nations, or only to those party to the regulatory treaties, depends upon the terms of the treaties and the intentions of the parties, as modified by practice.[82] In fact, practice with regard to the Suez and Panama Canals would indicate that universal usage has become part of the canal régime. It also depends on the terms of the treaty governing each treaty, whether the territorial state has the competence to close the Canal in time of armed conflict.[83]

80. The Suez Canal was, prior to the Egyptian nationalization, regulated in accordance with the régime established by the Convention of Constantinople, 1884 (79 B.F.S.P. 18), which declared the Canal to be "always free and open, in time of war as in time of peace, to every vessel of commerce or war without distinction of flag." This freedom of navigation was extended to states which were not parties to the Convention. After the Egyptian nationalization, 1956, Egypt announced its intention to continue to keep the Canal open to all, but, despite its armistice agreement with Israel, even neutral ships proceeding to or from Israel via the Canal were seized as prize, *The Inge Toft* (1960), 31 I.L.R. 509. By Art. 5 of the Peace Treaty of 1979, (1979) 18 I.L.M. 362, Egypt undertook that Israel would enjoy equal rights in the Canal with all other states. Unlike the Suez Canal, which was regulated by a single multilateral treaty, the Panama Canal régime was established by two bilateral

treaties. The Hay-Varilla Treaty between the U.S. and Panama, 1903, 2 Malloy's Treaties 1349, and the Hay-Pauncefote Treaty, 1903, between the U.S. and the U.K., 94 B.F.S.P. 46, and neither of these provided for free navigation on a universal basis. The Canal was, however, placed under the virtual sovereignty of the U.S. which allowed passage to all, although after the U.S. entry into World War I in 1917 passage was denied to the shipping of an enemy or the allies of an enemy. The Panama Canal Treaty, 1977, (1977) 16 I.L.M. 1021, repeals the Hay-Varilla Treaty and restores full sovereignty to Panama. By Art. 1(2) the U.S. is granted, "for the duration of the Treaty, the rights necessary to regulate the transit of ships through the Panama Canal, and to manage, operate, maintain, improve, protect and defend the Canal." The Canal remains open to world shipping. The Kiel Canal which is solely within German territory joins the Baltic and North Sea and, by the Treaty of Versailles, 1919, 112 B.F.S.P. 1, was declared "free and open to the vessels of commerce and war of all nations at peace with Germany on terms of entire equality". The Treaty of Versailles was denounced by Germany in 1936, and in the *Kiel Canal Collision Case* (1950), 17 I.L.R. 133, the Supreme Ct. in the British Zone was of opinion that the Canal's international status had been terminated by this denunciation. However, in 1952 the U.S. State Dept. considered the Versailles articles on the Canal to be "again fully operative", 3 Whiteman 260. At the present moment, all three Canals are open to international shipping.

81. *The S.S. Wimbledon* (France, G.B., Italy, Japan/Germany) (1923), 1 W.C.R. 163.

82. See note 80 *ante*, re Panama.

83. In *The Wimbledon, ante*, the Permanent Ct. held that Germany's obligations under the Treaty overrode her obligations as a neutral in accordance with customary law.

§178 While the rights of a littoral state concerning a canal are governed by treaty, if there is a natural waterway lying within a state's territorial sea but joining two parts of the high seas the strait in question, provided it constitutes a necessary means of international navigation,[84] is considered in accordance with customary law to be open to the shipping of all by way of innocent passage, and this right even extends to warships.[85]

84. *Corfu Channel (Merits)* (G.B./Albania), [1949] I.C.J. 4. Canada does not consider any of the straits lying in Can. waters as being customarily used for international navigation, and are thus considered not to be international waterways.

85. The right of warships to enjoy innocent passage through the territorial sea was confirmed by the Geneva Convention on the Territorial Sea, 1958, Art. 14. By Part III of the 1982 Convention on the Law of the Sea a new régime will be established for straits "which are used for international navigation between one area of the high seas or an exclusive economic zone and another area of the high seas or an exclusive economic zone" (Art. 37), and ships shall be entitled to a "right of transit passage, which shall not be impeded" (Art. 38). See §272.

§179 If a navigable river runs through more than one state, it does not follow, in the absence of treaty, that there is freedom of navigation for riparian states,[86] and still less for non-riparian states. There are many such rivers in Europe and the status of each is regulated by treaty. In a series of judgments and advisory opinions[87]the World Court intimated that the provisions in these treaties were sufficiently similar to be considered to constitute an international river régime. As a result, freedom of navigation[88] is construed as extending to all navigable parts of the river system on a basis of perfect equality, with artificial waterways connecting naturally navigable sections being regarded as part of the system. Whether non-riparian states would be entitled to the right of navigation would depend on the treaty governing a particular river. As between Canada and the United States, the St. Lawrence is governed in accordance with the terms of the St. Lawrence Seaway Agreement, 1952.[89] In addition, by Article 5(2) of the General Agreement on Tariffs and Trade,[90] "There shall be freedom of transit through the territory of each contracting party, via the routes most convenient for international transit, for traffic in transit to and from the territory of other contracting parties. No distinction shall be made which is based on the flag of vessels, the place of origin, departure, entry, exit or destination, or on any circumstances relating to the ownership of goods, of vessels, or of other means of transport."

86. See *Faber Case* (Germany/Venezuela) (1903), 10 R.I.A.A. 438 at 466. *Frigerio v. Federal Department of Transport* (1968), 72 I.L.R. 679 (Switz. Fed. Trib.)

87. The rivers involved are the Danube, the Elbe, the Oder, the Scheld, the Rhine and the Meuse, see (1957) 1 Schwarzenberger, Int. Law ch. 13 for an analysis of these rulings.

88. See, e.g., Vitány, The International Régime of River Navigation (1979); Zacklin and Caflisch, The Legal Régime of International Rivers and Lakes (1981).

89. 1952, Can. T.S. No. 30; see Baxter, Documents on the St. Lawrence Seaway (1960); Lawford, "Treaties and Rights of Transit on the St. Lawrence", (1961) 39 C.B.R. 577; also, Bourne, "Canada and the Law of International Drainage Basins" Macdonald, *et al.*, Canadian Perspectives on International Law and Organization (1974), p. 468. Wex, "The Legal Status of the International Joint Commission under International and Municipal Law", (1978) 16 C.Y.B.I.L. 276. Rigaldies, 'Le statut du golfe de Saint-Laurent en droit international public', (1985) 23 C.Y.B.I.L. 80, and for government statement that the waters of the Gulf of St. Lawrence are considered by the Government of Canada to be "historic Canadian waters", (1984) 22 C.Y.B.I.L. 333. As to the meaning of "free and open" navigation under the Webster-Ashburton Treaty 1842 (93 C.T.S. 416) and the Treaty of Washington 1871 (61 B.F.S.P. 40), see *Arrow River & Tributaries Slide & Boom Co. v. Pigeon Timber Co.,* [1932] S.C.R. 459 (S.C.C.); see Memo of Legal Bureau, Dept. of External Affairs 9 Oct. 1981, (1982) 20 C.Y.B.I.L. 292-6.

90. 1947, 55 U.N.T.S. 187; for amendments, see GATT, Basic Instruments and Selected Documents.

§180 When a river[91] or a lake[92] is shared by two or more states, problems will arise in connection with the use of the waters by one to the disadvantage of the other. Regarding the St. Lawrence, its uses are supervised by the International Joint Commission between Canada and the United States.[93] Lake Lanoux, the waters of which are shared by France and Spain, is similarly regulated by a mixed commission.[94] While the controlling treaty might seek to limit damage affecting one riparian as a result of the activities of another, it has been held that there is not, "in international common law, any rule forbidding one State, acting to safeguard its legitimate interests, to put itself in a position which would permit it, in effect, seriously to injure a neighbouring State in violation of its international pledges."[95] At the same time, if there is reference to the need for prior agreement between the parties before one or other may institute any undertaking affecting the interests of the other, this does not give the latter a right of veto, save when the treaty makes clear provision to this effect, although both states must exercise good faith. At present, "International practice reflects the conviction that States ought to strive to conclude such agreements: there would thus appear to be an obligation to accept in good faith all communications and contracts which could, by a broad comparison of interests and by reciprocal good will, provide States with the best conditions for concluding agreements. . . . The rule that States may utilize the hydraulic power of international watercourses only on condition of a prior agreement between the interested States cannot be established as a custom, even less as a general principle of law".[96] The existence of a rule requiring prior agreement can only exist if so provided by treaty.[97]

91. E.g., St. Lawrence; see note 89, *ante*.

92. The Great Lakes, see Agreement on Great Lakes Water Quality, 1972, Can. T.S. No. 12; Lake Lanoux; see note 94.

93. See §165 note 43.

94. Treaty of Bayonne, and Additional Act, 1866, 132 C.T.S. 359.

95. *Lake Lanoux Arb.* (France/Spain) (1957), 12 R.I.A.A. 281 (French original) at 305, 24 I.L.R. 101 at 126 (Arbitral Trib.).

96. *Lake Lanoux Arb., ante,* at pp. 308 and 130 respectively.

97. On the use of the waters of international drainage basins, see Bourne, *op. cit.*; Chauhan, Settlement of International Water Law Disputes on International Drainage Basins (1982).

5. INTERNATIONAL ECONOMIC LAW

§181 Problems of international economic law traditionally tended to be issues concerning the trading activities of states and were regarded as being beyond the competence of national tribunals[98] until the recent developments which have drawn a distinction between matters falling within normal trading activities as distinct from those jure imperii.[99]

However, with the rise of organizations like the European Economic Community numerous economic issues have fallen for consideration by international tribunals, in this case the European Court, while national courts have had to take judicial note of the Treaty of Rome[1] and of the decisions of the European Court.[2] In addition, participation in organizations like GATT (General Agreement for Tariffs and Trade) has affected the commercial practices and policies of member countries.[3]

98. See §159.

99. See §§160-162.

1. 1957, 298 U.N.T.S. 11. In *Trendtex Trading Corp. v. Central Bank of Nigeria*, [1977] 2 W.L.R. 356 (C.A.), Lord Denning M.R. pointed out that "the Treaty of Rome is part of the law of England. One of the objectives contained in Article 3(h) [of that Treaty] is to ensure 'the approximation of the laws of member states to the extent required for the proper functioning of the common market'."

2. See *Internationale Handelsgesellschaft mbH v. Einfuhr-und Vorratsstelle für Getreide und Futtermittel*, [1974] 2 C.M.L.R. 540 (Fed. Constitutional Ct. of Germany).

3. See, e.g., Bernier, "La Règlementation canadienne en matière de commerce et de douanes", Macdonald *et al.*, Canadian Perspectives on International Law and Organization (1974), p. 726.

§182 In the absence of treaty restrictions, states have complete freedom in their economic activities. Economic independence is, therefore, an essential part of sovereignty and any threat to such economic independence is tantamount to a threat to sovereignty as such.[4] In the face of such a threat, a state is entitled to take protective measures of an economic character by way of legitimate measures in self-defence.[5]

4. By the Treaty of St. Germain, 1919, 112 B.F.S.P. 317, Austria was forbidden to do anything which might compromise its independence. In 1931 it proposed to enter into a customs union with Germany and the League of Nations sought an advisory opinion from the World Court on the legality of this proposal. In its opinion on the *Austro-German Customs Union* (1931), 2 W.C.R. 713 at 719, 720, the court said: "The independence of Austria ... must be understood to mean the continued existence of Austria within her present frontiers as a separate State *with sole right of decision in all matters economic*, political, *financial* or other, with the result that independence is violated, as soon as there is any violation thereof, either in the economic, political, or any other field, *these different aspects of independence being in practice one and indivisible. . . . [A] violation of [its] 'economic independence' would be a violation of 'the independence of Austria'* " (italics added).

5. This is significant in considering the legitimacy of Canada's anti-pollution legislation, see Green, "International Law and Canada's Anti-Pollution Legislation", (1971) 50 Oregon Law Review 469. See also Canada's Foreign Investment Review Act, S.C. 1973-74, c. 46 [am. S.C. 1976-77, c. 52; 1980-81-82-83, c. 107; 1984, c. 31; rep. and sub. Investment Canada Act, S.C. 1985, c. 20]. Albrecht, "Canadian Foreign

Investment Policy and the International Politico-Legal Process", (1983), 21 C.Y.B.I.L. 149.

§183 Since States were free to conduct their economic activities as they pleased, there was no obligation in customary law that they should trade with one another. Nor was their any rule to prevent their taking economic sanctions against a state if the latter were considered to have broken its international obligations or offended in some other way. Under Article 2, paragraph 4, of the Charter of the United Nations, however, "Members [are to] refrain in their international relations from the threat or use of force against the territorial integrity or political independence of any state, or act in any manner inconsistent with the purposes of the United Nations". It has been suggested, therefore, that any attempt to impose economic sanctions, other than in accordance with a decision of the Security Council, would constitute a breach of this obligation.[6] The United Nations Declaration on Friendly Relations[7] expressly condemns "the use of economic, political or any other type of measures to coerce another State in order to obtain from it the subordination of the exercise of its sovereign rights and to secure from it advantages of any kind." In the view of Canada,[8] customary international law accords states a wide degree of latitude in implementing measures of an economic nature in retaliation against objectionable conduct by other states, provided such measures do not violate specific international legal obligations undertaken by way of treaty, for example. Thus, even measures of reprisal that would otherwise constitute an illegal act, such as the breach of a treaty, are exceptionally permitted in retaliation against an internationally illegal act perpetrated by the state against which the measures are directed. It may be suggested, however, that the sanctions violate customary norms of international law reflected in certain United Nations Declarations... Accepting for the purposes of argument that the United Nations Declaration [on Friendly Relations] is a proper statement of international law, it is clear that it is the purpose behind certain economic measures that serves as the essential criterion to separate legally permissible conduct from illicit conduct." Canada, therefore, supports the application of economic sanctions against South Africa,[9] as it had done against Rhodesia[10] and Iran."[11]

6. See Mosler, The International Society as a Legal Community, 1980, at 279-280.

7. Res. 2625 (XXV), 1970, 3rd Principle.

8. Legal Bureau memo 3 Jun. 1985 (1986) 24 C.Y.B.I.L. 387-388.

9. Legal Bureau memo. 9 Apr. 1984 (1985) 23 C.Y.B.I.L. 336. See Statement by Sec. State Ext. Aff., House of Commons 13 Sept. 1985, Debates 6587-89 (1986) 24

C.Y.B.I.L. 407-411, and statement by Prime Minister, 28 Oct. 1985, Debates 8066-67 C.Y.B.I.L. 411-413. See §422.

10. See Letter by Sec. State Ext. Aff., 31 Oct. 1974, (1975) 13 C.Y.B.I.L. 371-372. See §422.

11. Statement by Secretary of State for External Affairs, 16 Jul. 1980, House of Commons Debates at 2981, (1981) 19 C.Y.B.I.L. 372-374. See, generally, Macdonald, 'Economic Sanctions in the International System', (1969) 7 C.Y.B.I.L. 61.

§184 One of the oldest economic treaty relationships to have developed relates to most-favoured-nation treatment. In order to protect the economic interests of their merchants against adverse discrimination states, since feudal times,[12] often included in their bilateral agreements a provision whereby such merchants were granted treatment no less favourable than that granted to merchants of third states. Often the third states were specifically indicated,[13] as was the field in which the concession was granted.[14] In course of time, by reason of repetition of such clauses in treaties between a variety of states there developed a most-favoured-nation standard,[15] whereby it became unnecessary to indicate the nature of the concession granted[16] or to name any country as the tertium comparationis.[17] If most-favoured-nation treatment is granted but no third state is in fact enjoying the privilege, the concession has only a potential value acquiring substance when there is some third state enjoying a privilege. The reason for this is that use of the most-favoured-nation clause involves treaty-making by reference and not by incorporation.[18] In other words, the clause enables the parties to a treaty to effect amendments to that treaty without the need of renegotiating, by indicating that the treaty is to be interpreted to extend to the parties all concessions that may be granted by either of them for so long as such concessions are granted. If treaty-making by incorporation were involved, once a concession had been granted to a third party and extended to the beneficiary of the clause, the latter would continue to enjoy the concession even though this was no longer true of the tertium comparationis,[19] but it is the most-favoured-nation treaty which governs the situation not that with any third party.[20]

12. See, e.g., Schwarzenberger, "The Most-Favoured-Nation Standard in British State Practice", (1945) 22 B.Y.I.L. 96.

13. The Anglo-Danish Treaty of Peace and Commerce, 1661, 6 C.T.S. 233, expressly mentioned privileges enjoyed by "the Dutch or any other nation", Art. 24.

14. See, e.g., Anglo-Persian Treaty of Peace, 1857, 116 C.T.S. 329, Art. 9: "The high contracting parties engage that, in the establishment and recognition of consuls-general, consuls, vice-consuls, and consular agents, each shall be placed in the dominions of the other on the footing of the most favoured nation; and that the treatment of their respective subjects, and their trade, shall also, in every respect, be

placed on the footing of the treatment of the subjects and commerce of the most favoured nation."

15. Schwarzenberger, *op. cit.* at pp. 102-8.

16. By the Anglo-Persian Commercial Convention, 1903, 19 C.T.S. 375, Art. 2, "It is formally stipulated that British subjects and imports into Persia, as well as Persian subjects and Persian imports into the British Empire, shall continue to enjoy under all conditions most-favoured-nation treatment."

17. However, occasionally, for historic or other special reasons, a particular country is named as being outside the purview of those to be treated as tertia comparationes. This used to be the position with regard to imperial preference as among parts of the Commonwealth. In its trade treaty with the Soviet Union, 1956, Canada agreed that its charges for wheat would be those charged to its major customers at the times of the Soviet purchases, while Art. 7 excluded from the most-favoured-nation (m-f-n) treatment accorded to the Soviet Union any advantages accorded to members of the Commonwealth or their dependencies: Can. T.S. 1956, No. 1. See also Soviet-Danish Agreement, 1923, Art. 2 of which denies to Denmark any special privileges given to a third country recognizing the Soviet Union de jure, prior to Denmark doing the same, Taracouzio, The Soviet Union and International Law (1935), pp. 260-1.

18. See discussion by International Court of Justice in *Rights of U.S. Nationals in Morocco* (France/U.S.), [1952] I.C.J. 176 at 191-2.

19. "When provisions granting fiscal immunity in treaties between Morocco and third States have been abrogated or renounced, these provisions can no longer be relied upon by virtue of a most-favoured-nation clause": [1952] I.C.J. at 204. The court also pointed out that if the third party had given a 'temporary undertaking' not to exercise its privileges, the beneficiary of m-f-n treatment would equally not be entitled to the privileges so long as this undertaking persisted, [1952] I.C.J. at 194. In other words, the benefits of m-f-n treatment are only enjoyed so long as there is in fact a third party actually enjoying privileges which may serve as a standard of comparison.

20. *Anglo-Iranian Oil Co. Case (Jurisdiction)* (G.B./Iran), [1952] I.C.J. 93 at 109.

§185   The purpose of most-favoured-treatment is "to establish and maintain at all times fundamental quality without discrimination among all the countries concerned".[21] In the case of a federation this would mean that legislative action taken against a particular group of aliens despite the existence of a treaty binding the federal government to grant most-favoured-nation treatment would either be invalid as unconstitutional,[22] or would involve the international responsibility of the federal government on account of a breach of that treaty.[23] While it is the purpose of the most-favoured-nation standard to achieve equality without discrimination, most-favoured-nation clauses must be interpreted ejusdem generis so that a grant of most-favoured-nation treatment in one field does not mean that the beneficiary will thereby enjoy all privileges granted to third states.[24]

21. *U.S. Nationals in Morocco, ante* at 192.

22. *Re Oriental Orders in Council Variation Act, B.C.* (Employment of Aliens) (1922), 63 S.C.R. 293, which held that the British Columbia Act, c. 49 of 1921, excluding Chinese and Japanese from certain forms of employment was contrary to British North America Act, 1867, s. 91, and the Japanese Treaty Act, 1913, 3 & 4 Geo. V. c. 27, whereby the High Contracting Parties "shall in all that relates to the pursuit of their industries, callings, professions, and educational studies be placed in all respects on the same footing as the subjects or citizens of the most favoured nation."

23. In *Re Oriental Orders in Council Variation Act, B.C., ante* Davies C.J. said: "The Crown was undoubtedly bound by the force of the 'Japanese Treaty Act' of 1913 to perform within Canada its treaty obligations, and, if so, I cannot understand how it can be successfully contended that the Crown by force of enactments of a provincial legislature directly or indirectly breaks its treaty obligations".

24. *Ambatielos Claim* (Greece/G.B.) (1956), 12 R.I.A.A. 83 at 107: ". . . the Commission holds that the most-favoured-nation clause can only attract matters belonging to the same category of subject as that to which the clause itself relates". See also Note from Secretary of State Kellogg to Japanese Ambassador, Oct. 8, 1926, denying that m-f-n in a commercial treaty extends to international air navigation: 5 Hackworth 291.

§186 It is generally accepted that most-favoured-nation clauses are to be applied on a basis of reciprocity, so that "each signatory grants to the other the broadest rights and privileges which it accords to any other nation in other treaties it has made or will make."[25] However, the significance of the most-favoured-nation clause in bilateral freedom of commerce and navigation treaties has lost some of its impact with the introduction of a general most-favoured-nation clause in the General Agreement on Tariffs and Trade,[26] so that parties to the Agreement, including Canada, now only sign such bilateral treaties with non-members of the GATT.

25. *Kolovrat v. Oregon* (1961), 366 U.S. 187 at 193.

26. 1947, 55 U.N.T.S. 187. See Bernier, "La Règlementation canadienne en matière de commerce et de douanes", Macdonald *et al.*, Canadian Perspectives on International Law and Organization (1974), p. 726.

§187 Under pressure from the Third World and developing countries generally, the General Assembly in 1974 adopted a Charter of Economic rights and Duties of States,[27] intended to give effect to the Declaration on the Establishment of a New International Economic Order.[28] The Charter confirms permanent sovereignty over the possession, use and disposal of the state's wealth, natural resources and economic activities, as well as the right to regulate foreign investment and multilateral corporations, including the right "to nationalise, expropriate or transfer ownership of foreign property [against compensation], taking into account its relevant laws and regulations and all circumstances that the State considers pertinent". Disputes are to be settled in accordance with the local law,[29] unless other means are decided upon "on the basis of the sovereignty of States and in accordance with the principle of freedom of choice".[30] Of more importance, perhaps, for the future are the obligations to promote the development of international trade to facilitate "more rational and equitable economic relations. . .[and] have the responsibility to co-operate in the economic, social, cultural, scientific and technological fields for the promotion of economic and social progress throughout the world, especially that of the developing countries".[31] There are a number of other provisions in favour of the developing world, with developed countries[32] called upon to "grant generalized preferential, non-reciprocal and non-discriminatoy treatment to developing countries [and to take account of] the close interrelationship between the well-being of the developed countries and the growth and development of the developing countries, and the fact that the prosperity of the international community as a whole depends upon the prosperity of its constituent parts".[33]

27. Res. 3281(XXIX) 14 I.L.M. 251; Canada abstained from voting.

28. Res. 3201 (S-VI) 13 I.L.M. 715; adopted without vote.

29. See §322 re Calvo Clause.

30. Art 2.

31. Arts. 6, 8

32. See Wigdor, "Canada and the New International Economic Order", (1982) 20 C.Y.B.I.L. 161; statement by Canadian delegate in 6th committee debate on Principles and Norms of International Economic Law relating to the New International Economic Order, 29 Nov. 1982 (1983), 21 C.Y.B.I.L. 315-6.

33. Arts. 19,31.

§188　Economic problems frequently arise in connection with the infringement of trade names and often these names are protected by virtue of registration in accordance with statutes giving effect to bilateral agreements. Respecting Canada, "so soon as one concludes that the effect of the agreement approved by the Act[34] is to require that appellations of origin registered be protected in Canada, no administrative authority may validly direct otherwise. It is difficult to see how a government official can claim to act contrary to undertakings of the Canadian government which the latter has decided to maintain in force".[35] For members of the European Common Market the situation has been changed somewhat since the Treaty of Rome[36] has introduced such new torts as "undue restriction of competition within the common market" and "abuse of dominant position within the common market". As a result the English Court of Appeal has greatly restricted the scope of copyright.[37]

34. Canada-France Trade Agreement Act, S.C. 1932-33, c. 31, denounced by Canada, 1977.

35. *Chateau-Gai Wines Ltd. v. Institut Nat. des Appellations d'Origine des Vins et Eaux-de-Vie*, [1975] 1 S.C.R. 190 (S.C.C.); *J. Bollinger v. Costa Brava Wine Co.*, [1961] R.P.C. 116 (Ch.).

36. 1957, 298 U.N.T.S. 11.

37. *Application des Gaz SA v. Falks Veritas Ltd.*, [1974] 3 W.L.R. 235. See on competition generally, Henry, "International Aspects of Competition Policy", Macdonald *et al., op. cit.*, p. 756.

6. INTERNATIONAL CRIMINAL LAW

§189 International law lacks any criminal code or criminal court. However, efforts have been made during the last fifty years to draw up such a code[38] or to establish a court.[39] After the assassination of Alexander of Yugoslavia in 1934, the League of Nations sponsored the drafting of a convention directed against terrorism,[40] but this was ratified by only one state, while the accompanying statute for an international criminal court[41] has not received a single ratification. However, the International Law Commission of the United Nations has spent a great deal of effort in preparing a draft code of offences against the peace and security of mankind,[42] which is primarily based on the principles propounded by the Nuremberg Tribunal which tried the principal Nazi war criminals in 1946.[43] Since then, the Commission has directed its attention to issues of state responsibility and has approved a series of provisions which concern international criminal law, with the majority of the offences being committed by states or at their initiative.[44] In addition, a variety of bodies has been concerned with attempting to draft an international criminal code[45] or to enunciate a statute for an international criminal court.[46]

38. See Mueller and Wise, International Criminal Law (1965); Bassiouni and Nanda, A Treatise on International Criminal Law (1973); Bassiouni, International Criminal Law — A Draft International Criminal Code (1980); Bassiouni, ed., International Criminal Law, vol. 1, Crimes (1986); Green, 'An International Criminal Code — Now?' (1976) 3 Dal. L.J. 560; "Is There An International Criminal Law?', (1983) 21 Alta. L.R. 251.

39. See, e.g., Ferencz, An International Criminal Court — A Documentary History and Analysis (1980). Bassiouni, ed., International Criminal Law, vol. 2, Procedure, 1986, vol. 3, Enforcement, 1987.

40. Convention for the Prevention and Punishment of Terrorism, 1937, 7 Hudson, Int. Leg. 862.

41. Convention for the Creation of an International Criminal Court, 1937, 7 Hudson, Int. Leg. 878.

42. 1954, 9 U.N. GAOR, 11-2, Doc. a/2693; see Johnson, "The Draft Code of Offences against the Peace and Security of Mankind", (1955), 4 I.C.L.Q. 445.

43.　G.A. Res. affirming the Nuremberg Principles, 1946, Res. 95(I). See also, *Nuremberg Judgment* (1946), Cmd. 6964, (1947) A.J.I.L. 172.

44.　These are based on a Report prepared by Professor Ago. For a critical analysis, see Green, 'New Trends in International Criminal Law', (1981) 11 I.Y.B.H.R. 9. See §213.

45.　E.g., International Association for Penal Law.

46.　Eg., Foundation for the Establishment of an International Criminal Court.

§190　Apart from these unsuccessful efforts to create an international criminal code or establish an international criminal court, some steps towards declaring certain acts criminal in accordance with international law have been the consequence of a variety of treaties. By virtue of such treaties, particular acts have been declared as crimes and the parties to the treaties have undertaken either to amend their criminal law so as to make such acts punishable within the national system, or else to hand over those accused of such offences to stand trial in countries able to show a prima facie interest in instituting such proceedings. The most important of such treaties is the Genocide Convention,[47] which was ratified by Canada in 1952.[48] The parties to this Convention "confirm that genocide, whether committed in time of peace or in time of war, is a crime under international law which they undertake to prevent and punish."

47.　1948, 78 U.N.T.S. 277.

48.　See Canadian Criminal Code s. 281.1 [en. R.S.C. 1970, c. 11 (1st Supp.), s. 1].

§191　By article 2, genocide "means any of the following acts committed with intent to destroy, in whole or in part, a national, ethical, racial or religious group, as such: (a) killing members of the group; (b) causing serious bodily or mental harm to members of the group; (c) deliberately inflicting on the group conditions of life calculated to bring about its physical destruction in whole or in part; (d) imposing measures intended to prevent births within the group; (e) forcibly transferring children of the group to another group." The Convention provides that the status of an accused, as head of state or government, for example, shall not constitute any bar to trial[49] and envisages the possibility of the establishment of an international criminal tribunal to try those charged with genocide. Pending the establishment of such a tribunal proceedings are to take place before "a competent tribunal of the State in the territory of which the act was committed",[50] and if the latter seeks the extradition of the alleged offender,[51] it is provided that genocide cannot be considered a political offence,[52] which normally constitutes a ground for denying extradition.[53]

49. Genocide Convention, 1948, Art. 4.

50. Art. 6.

51. See §202.

52. Art. 7.

53. See §204.

§192 Another treaty-created offence is torture.[54] Torture is defined[55] as "any act by which severe pain or suffering, whether physical or mental, is intentionally inflicted on a person for such purposes as obtaining from him or a third person information or a confession, punishing him for an act he or a third person has committed or is suspected of having committed, or intimidating or coercing him or a third person, or for any reason based on discrimination of any kind, when such pain or suffering is inflicted by or at the instigation of or with the consent or acquiescence of a public official or other person acting in an official capacity.[56] It does not include pain or suffering arising only from, inherent in or incidental to lawful sanctions". Parties are obliged to amend their law to prevent and punish torture occurring within their jurisdiction.[57] As with the European Convention on Human Rights,[58] torture is not permitted even in time of armed conflict.[59] Parties are obliged to try any person within their territory charged with torture or to hand him over for trial to another party claiming jurisdiction.[60] However, the principle of non-refoulement[61] is to be respected. The Convention also provides for the establishment of a Supervisory Committee[62] which may set up an ad hoc Conciliation Commission when considered necessary. The Committee's jurisdiction only extends to those parties which expressly opt therefor.

54. Convention Against Torture and Other Cruel, Inhuman or Degrading Treatment of punishment 1984, 23 I.L.M. 1027. Canada ratified this convention in June 1987, when Canada amended the Criminal Code (S.C. 1987, c. 13) to make torture an offence. See also, Declaration unilaterale du Canada contre la torture, 17 Dec. 1982, (1983) 21 C.Y.B.I.L. 316-7.

55. Art. 1

56. Arts. 2, 4. By S.C. 1987, c. 13, superior orders do not constitute a defence.

57. 1950, 213 U.N.T.S. 222.

58. For a discussion of the difference between torture and inhuman or degrading treatment, and for comments on official and unofficial acts of violence under the European Convention, see *Ireland v. United Kingdom* (1978), 58 I.L.R. 188 (European Ct. of Human Rights).

59. Art. 2(2). See also, Protocol I Additional to Geneva Conventions of 1949, 1977, 16 I.L.M. 1391, Art. 75(2)(a), §334. As to the general problem of human rights in wartime, see Green, "Human Rights and the Law of Armed Conflict", ch. 5, Essays on the Modern Law of War (1985).

60. Arts. 5-8.

61. Art. 3: "No State Party shall expel, return (refouler) or extradite a person to another state where there are substantial grounds for believing that he would be in danger of being subjected to torture".

62. Art. 21.

§193 A number of treaties dealing with various aspects of terrorism have also introduced the aut dedere aut judicare principle,[63] and this is especially so since terrorism has become a major international problem. Thus, under the auspices of the International Civil Aviation Organization, and in response to a variety of offences against aircraft and aerial transport, including hijacking,[64] three conventions were drawn up[65] each of which makes it obligatory for the contracting states to make the specific offences dealt with criminal under their national law.[66] Similar provisions are to be found in some treaties drawn up under the auspices of the United Nations, such as, the Convention on the Prevention and Punishment of Crimes against Internationally Protected Persons, including Diplomatic Agents,[67] the International Convention on the Suppression and Punishment of the Crime of Apartheid,[68] the International Convention against the Taking of Hostages,[69] or the Convention on the Physical Protection of Nuclear Material.[70] By virtue of these conventions, the offences which they condemn as international crimes are not to be treated as political and if not already included in extradition treaties affecting the parties will be deemed to be so included. However, criminality does not attach to such acts if committed in the name of self-determination by a national movement seeking liberation from alien, colonialist or racist régimes.[71] It must be borne in mind that these treaties are only effective for those countries which have ratified them.

63. This principle was recognized by Grotius, De Jure Belli ac Pacis (1625), Bk. II, Ch. XXI, S. 4: ". . . it seems reasonable, that the State where the convicted Offender lives or has taken Shelter, should, upon Application being made to it, either punish the demanded Person according to his Demerits, or else deliver him up to be treated at the Discretion of the Injured Party" (Eng. tr., London (1728) p. 457, Carnegie tr. p. 527).

64. Hijacking is the unlawful seizure or deviation of an aircraft, see McWhinney, The Illegal Diversion of Aircraft and International Law (1987); McWhinney, Aerial Piracy and International Law (1987); Joyner, Aerial Hijacking as an International Crime (1974).

65. Tokyo Convention on Offences and Certain Other Acts Committed on Board Aircraft, 1963, 704 U.N.T.S. 219; Hague Convention for the Suppression of Unlawful Seizure of Aircraft, 1970, 860 U.N.T.S. 105; Montreal Convention for the Suppression of Unlawful Acts Against the Safety of Civil Aviation, 1971, 974 U.N.T.S. 177. Canada is a party to each of these Conventions and has also entered

into a bilateral pact with Cuba on the hijacking of aircraft and vessels, 1973 Can. T.S. No. 11, renewed 1984 with effect from 15 Feb. 1983.

66. Arts. 3, 2, 5, resp. See Criminal Code Amendment S.C. 1972, c. 13, ss. 6, 76.1, 76.2, 76.3. See also Green, "Terrorism — The Canadian Perspective", in Alexander, International Terrorism — National, Regional and Global Perspectives (1976), p. 3.

67. 1973, 1035 U.N.T.S. 167, Arts. 3, 5, 6, ratified by Canada 1976, made criminal by Criminal Law Amendment Act, S.C. 1985, c. 19, ss. 56, 57. For a statement defining those considered by Canada as internationally protected persons, see Legal Bureau memo. 4 Dec. 1985, (1986) 24 C.Y.B.I.L. 392-394. See *Case Concerning U.S. Diplomatic and Consular Staff in Tehran* (Provisional Measures), [1979] I.C.J. 7; (Judgment), [1980] I.C.J. 3.

68. 1973, 13 I.L.M. 50, Arts. 1(2), 4, 5 — Canada has not signed this Convention. See §§210, 211.

69. 1979, 18 I.L.M. 1456, Arts. 2, 5, 6, 8, 9. Canada ratified this Convention in Dec. 1985 and made hostage-taking criminal by s. 41 of the 1985 Act.

70. 1979, 18 I.L.M. 1422, Art. 11; see also Arts. 8-10, signed by Canada 1980. This Convention is given effect to by s. 6 of the Criminal Code, as amended by the 1985 Act. See, generally, on the hostage-taking and nuclear protection conventions and Canadian law, Williams, 'The Criminal Law Amendment Act 1985: Implications for International Criminal Law', (1985) 23 C.Y.B.I.L. 226.

71. In accordance with Art. 1(4) of Protocol 1 additional to the Geneva Convention of 1949, 16 I.L.M. 1391; Schindler and Toman, The Laws of Armed Conflicts (1982), p. 551, acts of violence committed by such a movement during an armed struggle aimed at achieving its self-determination are to be regarded as legitimate acts of international armed conflict. Canada has signed but not ratified this Protocol.

§194 Perhaps the most serious difficulty confronting efforts to secure effective United Nations action against terrorism lies in the fact that many third world countries, which now control the majority in the General Assembly, are ideologically sympathetic to terrorist movements, especially when they act in the name of national liberation or self-determination. Often this sympathy is disguised by language which indicates the necessity of dealing with the causes of terrorism.[72] Sometimes, there is even a direct statement that acts done in the name of self-determination do not fall within the condemnation of terrorism contained in the Resolution.[73] After the *Achille Lauro* incident both the Security Council[74] and the General Assembly[75] issued what appeared to be blanket condemnations of every kind of terrorist act. The General Assembly Resolution confirmed earlier resolutions with regard to terrorism, thus indirectly preserving its approval in the cause of national liberation.

72. See Res. 3034 (XXVII) 1972.

73. The Resolution (Res. 3166 - XXVIII) to which the Convention on Internationally Protected Persons is an Annex, provides that the "Convention could not in any way prejudice the exercise of the legitimate right to self-determination and

independence. . ." Although there is no provision to this effect in the Convention, the Resolution stipulates that it shall always be published together with the Convention, for the provisions of the two are 'related'.

74. Statement by President on behalf of Council 9 Oct. 1985, 24 I.L.M. 1565.

75. Res. 40/61, 9 Dec., 1985.

§195 In addition to these agreements directed against acts of terrorism, there are some older conventions which oblige the parties thereto to make specific acts criminal. Thus, the Universal Postal Convention[76] forbids the counterfeiting of stamps as well as the sending through the mails of certain named drugs as well as explosive or inflammable substances. Similar provisions appear in the Conventions on the Traffic of Women and Children, now replaced by the 1949 Convention for the Suppression of the Traffic in Persons and of the Exploitation of the Prostitution of Others,[77] for the Suppression of the Circulation of and Traffic in Obscene Publications,[78] on Narcotic Drugs,[79] for the Suppression of Counterfeiting Currency,[80] and on the Means of Prohibiting and Preventing the Illicit Import, Export and Transfer of Ownership of Cultural Property.[81]

76. 1957, 364 U.N.T.S. 3, Art. 47 — Canada is a party.

77. 96 U.N.T.S. 271. Canada is not a party to this Convention but is a party to earlier Conventions directed to the suppression of the white slave traffic.

78. First adopted 1910 [am. 1947, 1949], 47 U.N.T.S. 159 — Canada is a party.

79. Single Convention on Narcotic Drugs, 1961, 570 U.N.T.S. 557, Art. 36 — Canada is a party.

80. 1929, 112 U.N.T.S. 371 — Canada is not a party.

81. 1970, 10 I.L.M. 289. Canada is a party, see Cultural Property Export and Import Act, S.C. 1974-75, c. 50. See also Williams, International and National Protection of Movable Cultural Property (1978).

§196 Apart from acts which have been declared international crimes by treaty, certain acts have been regarded as international crimes in accordance with customary international law.[82] Perhaps the oldest of such crimes is piracy, although care must be taken to distinguish between piracy jure gentium[83] and piracy by national law, and to the extent that the national definition is wider than the international the former will only apply to nationals and not to aliens.[84] As early as 1615,[85] Chief Justice Coke described a pirate as hostis humani generis, and it is now recognized that a pirate, regardless of his nationality, may be tried by any state within whose jurisdiction he may find himself.[86] The customary definition of a pirate may be found in Molloy:[87] "A Pirate is a Sea-Thief, or Hostis humani generis, who for to enrich himself, either by surprise or open force, sets upon Merchants and others trading by Sea, ever spoiling their Lading, if by any possibility they can get the mastery, sometimes bereaving them of their lives, and sinking of their Ships. . . . By the Laws of Nature Princes and States are responsible for their neglect, if they do not provide Ships of War, and other remedies for the restraining of these sort of Robbers. . . ." It is clear, however, that the act of robbery need not be completed,[88] nor need every act of depredation take place upon the sea.[89] When Palestinian terrorists, who were already on board, seized the italian liner *Achille Lauro* on the high seas in 1985, taking hostage the crew and a number of passengers, some of whom were American, one of whom they murdered, the United States issued warrants of arrest charging them with piracy against the law of nations, even though the act did not appear to fall within the Convention[90] definition, since the terrorists did not come from another vessel, nor was there any act of private depredation.[91]

82. See §§11-13.

83. See *Re Piracy Jure Gentium*, [1934] A.C. 586 (P.C.). See Criminal Code, s. 75.

84. See *The Le Louis* (1817), 2 Dods. 210 (H.C. of Admiralty). See Criminal Code, s. 76.

85. *R. v. Marsh* (1615), 3 Bulstr. 27.

86. *The S.S. Lotus* (France/Turkey) (1927), 2 W.C.R. 20, dissenting opinions by Lord Finlay: ". . . pirates have been regarded as hostes humani generis and might be tried in the courts of any country" (at 58), and Moore: "Piracy by law of nations, in its jurisdictional aspects, is sui generis. Though statutes may provide for its punishment, it is an offence against the law of nations; and as the scene of the pirate's operations is the high seas [see, however, n. 89 below], which it is not the right or duty of any nation to police, he is denied the protection of the flag which he may carry, and is treated as an outlaw, as the enemy of all mankind — hostis humani generis — whom any nation may in the interest of all capture and punish" (at 69).

87. De Jure Maritimo et Navali (1682) Bk. I, Ch. IV, Ss. I, II.

88. *Re Piracy Jure Gentium, ante.*

89. See *Magellan Pirates* (1853), 1 Spinks 81: "I am not disposed to hold that the doctrine that the port, forming a part of the dominions of the State to which it belongs, ought in all cases divest robbery and murder done in such port of the character of piracy" (at. p. 86, per Dr. Lushington).

90. See §143.

91. 24 I.L.M. 1509; see Green, "Terrorism and the Law of the Sea", (1987) Festschrift for Shabtai Rosenne; see also Green, "The Santa Maria: Rebels or Pirates", (1961) 37 B.Y.I.L. 495.

§197 The customary law definition of piracy has now been replaced by the Geneva Convention on the High Seas, 1958.[92] Article 15 defines piracy as "any illegal acts of violence, detention or any act of depredation, committed for private ends[93] by the crew or the passengers of a private ship or a private aircraft, and directed: (a) on the high seas, against another ship or aircraft, or against persons or property on board such ship or aircraft; (b) against a ship, aircraft, persons or property in a place outside the jurisdiction of any state. . . ." The Convention also imposes an obligation upon all states to "cooperate to the fullest possible extent in the repression of piracy on the high seas or in any other place outside the jurisdiction of any State."[94]

92. 450 U.N.T.S. 82. Canada has not ratified this Convention, but since s. 75(1) of the Criminal Code provides that "every one commits piracy who does an act that, by the law of nations, is piracy", and since the majority of maritime states now accept this definition and it appears in Art. 101 of the 1982 Convention on the Law of the Sea, 21 I.L.M. 1261, for which Canada voted in 1982, and has since signed, it would seem that Canada accepts this definition.

93. This raises questions as to the nature of acts of seizure committed on the high seas by rebels, see, e.g., Green, "The Santa Maria: Rebels or Pirates", (1961) 37 B.Y.I.L. 495; Fenwick, "The Santa Maria, "Piracy" in the Caribbean", (1961) 55 A.J.I.L. 426. See Green, 'Terrorism and the Law of the Sea', note 91.

94. Once the pirate vessel enters the territorial sea of any state only that state has the right to exercise jurisdiction. Art. 14; Art. 100 of the 1982 Convention on the Law of the Sea.

§198 Customary international law also recognizes that persons accused of war crimes[95] may be tried, and if guilty punished, by any belligerent into whose hands they fall, regardless of the nationality of the offender[96] or of the victim or of the locus of the offence. In the absence of treaty, it is controversial whether neutrals may try such offenders. The Regulations attached to Hague Convention IV on the Laws and Customs of Warfare on Land, 1907,[97] lay down a number of rules concerning conduct during hostilities. The Convention only provides, however, for payment of compensation by a belligerent violating the Regulations and makes the belligerent liable for all breaches committed by its personnel.[98] The Nuremberg Tribunal, in its *Judgment*,[99] stated that "violations of [its] provisions constituted crimes for which the guilty individuals were punishable . . . [and] by 1939 these rules laid down in the Convention were recognized by all civilized nations, and were regarded as being declaratory of the laws and customs of war".[1] Some of the Conventions on the law of armed conflict[2] define particular acts as war crimes or grave breaches of the law of armed conflict and recognize the rights of parties to those Conventions to try offenders.[3]

95. See §§359-382. See also, War Crimes Act, S.C. 1946, c. 73, and Green, "Canadian Law and the Punishment of War Crimes", (1980) 28 Chitty's L.J. 249; The Law of Armed Conflict and the Enforcement of International Criminal Law (1984) 22 C.Y.B.I.L. 3.

96. Members of one's own forces committing offences which, if committed by an alien would amount to war crimes, are tried in accordance with the national criminal or military law; see *United States v. Calley* (1969/71/73) 46 C.M.R. 1131, 48 C.M.R. 19, 1 M.L.R. 2488.

97. Schindler and Toman, The Laws of Armed Conflict (1982), p. 57.

98. Art. 3.

99. *Nuremberg Judgement* (1946), Cmd. 6964; (1947) 41 A.J.I.L. 172.

1. *Nuremberg Judgment, ante* at pp. 64-5 (Cmd.), pp. 248-9 (A.J.I.L.).

2. See §§359-382.

3. See, e.g., Geneva Protocol I, Additional to Geneva Conventions of 1949, 1977, 16 I.L.M. 1391, Arts. 86, 88; Schindler and Toman, *op cit.,* p. 551.

§199 Despite the various agreements during the Second World War to seek out and try war criminals, there was evidence to suggest that a number of such persons had taken refuge in Canada, where many of them had acquired Canadian nationality by naturalization or immigrant status. As a result of agitation that such persons should be brought to trial, the Government established the Deschênes Commission of Inquiry on War Criminals, which made a number of recommendations for the amendment of Canadian criminal law so as to create jurisdiction over persons in Canada accused of war crimes or crimes against humanity.[4] By amendment to s. 6 of the Criminal Code (am. S.C. 1987, c. 37), it is provided that "every person who, either before or after the coming into force of this subsection,[5] commits an act or omission outside Canada that constitutes a war crime[6] or a crime against humanity[7] and that, if committed in Canada, would constitute an offence against the laws of Canada in force at the time of the act or omission (i) that person is a Canadian citizen or is employed by Canada in a civilian or military capacity, (ii) that person is a citizen of, or is employed in a civilian or military capacity by, a state that is engaged in an armed conflict against Canada, or (iii) the victim of the act or omission is a Canadian citizen or a citizen of a state that is allied with Canada in an armed conflict; or (b) at the time of the act or omission, Canada could, in conformity with international law,[8] exercise jurisdiction over the person with respect to the act or omission on the basis of the person's presence in Canada and subsequent to the time of the act or omission the person is present in Canada." The accused may "rely on any justification, excuse or defence available under the laws of Canada or under international law at that time or at the time of proceedings." In accordance with the Nuremberg Principles[9] and general principles of customary international law[10] it is no defence that the act in question was committed "[i]n obedience to or in conformity with the law in force at the time and in the place of its commission."

4. Commission of Inquiry on War Criminals, Report, Part I, Public (1986).

5. Criminal Code, s. 6 (1.91). See Green, 'Canadian Law, War Crimes and Crimes against Humanity', (1987) 58 B.Y.I.L.

6. "...an act or omission that is committed during an international armed conflict, whether or not it constituted a contravention of the law in force at the time and in the place of its commission, and that, at the time and in that place, constitutes a contravention of the customary international law or conventional international law applicable in international armed conflicts."

7. "...means murder, extermination, enslavement, deportation, persecution or any other inhumane act or omission that is committed against any civilian population or any identifiable group of persons, whether or not it constitutes a contravention of the law in force at the time and in the place of its commission, and that, at that time and in that place, constitutes a contravention of customary international law or conventional international law or is criminal according to the general principles of law recognized by the community of nations."

8. This would imply that, although the measure is silent on this issue, proceedings could be launched against a member of an allied force.

9. General Assembly, Res. 95 (I).

10. See §325.

§200 It is often claimed that slavery and the slave trade are forbidden by international law and that slave traders are guilty of an international crime. During the eighteenth and nineteenth centuries, the Royal Navy tried to suppress the trade regardless of the nationality of the trader or the flag of his ship[11] and, to this end, relied largely on legislation which declared slave-trading to be piracy.[12] However, it was only after the Treaty of Paris, 1814,[13] that France agreed to co-operate in the suppression of the trade, and even then traders could not be prosecuted by a third state in the absence of treaty obligations undertaken by their own country recognizing this liability.[14] At the Congress of Vienna, 1815,[15] the powers agreed to the condemnation of the slave trade in principle. Today, the situation is governed by the Slavery Convention, 1926,[16] whereby states undertook to take steps to prevent and suppress the embarkation, disembarkation and transport of slaves in their territorial sea and on all vessels flying their flags. This Convention has been amended by the Supplementary Convention on the Abolition of Slavery, the Slave Trade, and Institutions and Practices Similar to Slavery, 1956.[17] Moreover, the 1958 Geneva Convention on the High Seas[18] provides "Every State shall adopt effective measures to prevent and punish the transport of slaves in ships authorized to fly its flag, and to prevent the unlawful use of its flag[19] for that purpose. Any slave taking refuge on board any ship, whatever its flag, shall ipso facto be free." Canada has not ratified the 1958 Convention, but is a party to the two Slavery Conventions.

11. See Ward, The Royal Navy and the Slavers (1969). See also, 2 Hackworth 660-2, for discussion of Anglo-U.S. differences in this regard.

12. Slave Trade Act, 1811, 51 Geo. III, c. 23.

13. 63 C.T.S. 193.

14. *The Le Louis* (1817), 2 Dods. 210 (H.C. of Admiralty).

15. Additional Article to the Treaty of Vienna, 1815, 65 C.T.S. 257.

16. 182 L.N.T.S. 271.

17. 266 U.N.T.S. 3.

18. Geneva Convention on the High Seas, 1958, Art. 13; Convention on the Law of the Sea, 1982, Art. 99.

19. For the status of a vessel flying an unauthorized or non-existent flag, see *Molvan v. A.G. Palestine (The Asya)*, [1948] A.C. 351 (P.C.).

§201 Apart from offences which are described as crimes in accordance with international law, international law is also concerned with securing the trial and punishment of offenders who have committed a crime in one country and have escaped to another in the hope of avoiding trial. On occasion, offenders have sought to evade the local jurisdiction by taking refuge in a diplomatic embassy. Diplomatic asylum is not generally recognized, except when the fugitive is in immediate danger for his life or physical safety,[20] although many Latin American countries do grant asylum to fugitive politicians and some are parties to treaties recognizing this as a legal right.[21] The Canadian view[22] is that ". . . the right to grant extraterritorial asylum[23] is exceptional since it constitutes an infringement on the sovereignty of the territorial State. There is no general right of diplomatic asylum recognized in international law at this time. . . . [H]owever, international law does recognize that in certain circumstances or on extraordinary humanitarian grounds diplomatic asylum can be granted. . . . Asylum and temporary safe haven will never be granted to an ordinary criminal attempting to escape from normal process of law. . . ." Difficulties arise in classifying whether the asylum seeker is in fact an ordinary criminal or a true fugitive, and whether the embassy granting the refuge is authorized to make a unilateral qualification of the alleged offences to this effect.[24]

20. Occasionally, however, an embassy will grant extended asylum even when any such danger has ceased, e.g., the U.S. embassy in Budapest and Cardinal Mindszenty from 1956-1971. See Green, "Trends in the Law Concerning Diplomats", (1981) 19 C.Y.B.I.L. 132, 141-6.

21. See *Asylum Case* (Colombia/Peru), [1950] I.C.J. 266; *Haya de la Torre Case*, [1951] I.C.J. 71.

22. Memorandum of Dept. of External Affairs, 1980, (1980) 18 C.Y.B.I.L. 304-5, concerning asylum for U.S. diplomats in Iran.

23. Asylum granted in embassy, legations, consulate, etc.

24. See *Asylum Case, ante.*

§202 When a fugitive is present in any state there is no obligation under customary international law requiring that state either to grant him refuge or to transfer him to any state seeking to exercise jurisdiction over him. However, since the middle of the nineteenth century, states have entered into treaties, normally bilateral in character, whereby they undertake to extradite any fugitive offender required for trial by a treaty partner. In most cases extradition will only be granted in respect of offences specified in the particular treaty[25] and in accordance with procedures laid down in national legislation. In the case of Canada, this legislation is spelled out in the Extradition Act,[26] which allows for extradition even to a country with which no treaty has been signed if a proclamation to this effect has been issued by the Governor General.[27] If an offender is extradited, he may only be tried for the offence for which extradition has been granted[28] and normally extradition will only be granted if the alleged offence is a similar crime by the law of the requested as well as that of the requesting state, provided a prima facie case exists.[29] It is not for the extradition judge to decide whether the evidence is credible. This is a matter for the jury before which the criminal will eventually appear.[30]

25. However, there is now a growing trend not to include such lists, but to stipulate instead that extradition shall be granted in respect of all offences punishable by, e.g., twelve months' imprisonment in both states; see U.S.-Italy Extradition Treaty 1983, 24 I.L.M. 1527.

26. R.S.C. 1970, c. E-21.

27. S. 35. Such an order has been issued extending the operation of the Act to India, 119 Canada Gazette, 2 Nov. 1985. On the Canadian practice, generally, see LaForest, Extradition To and From Canada (1977); see also Green, "Immigration, Extradition and Asylum in Canadian Law and Practice", in Macdonald, Canadian Perspectives on International Law and Practice (1974), p. 244.

28. *Royal Govt. of Greece v. Gov. Brixton Prison; Ex parte Kotronis*, [1971] A.C. 250 (H.L.). See also *United States v. Rauscher* (1886), 119 U.S. 407; *Buck v. R.* (1917), 55 S.C.R. 133 (S.C.C.); *R. v. MacDonald* (1982), 40 O.R. (2d) 39 (Ont. H.C.).

29. *Jennings v. United States*, [1982] 3 All E.R. 104 (H.L.) — U.S. applied for extradition for manslaughter as result of death ensuing from drunken driving. English Ct. of Appeal held that death caused by a motor driver no longer amounted to manslaughter, and even if it did no English jury would have convicted on the evidence. Overruled by House of Lords, which held (at p. 111) offence of causing death by reckless driving still manslaughter by law of England, though made a distinct statutory offence in 1977. Therefore, request for extradition of person charged in California with manslaughter in circumstances which would justify commital in England on charge of causing death by reckless driving, where other requirements of Extradition Treaty with U.S. satisfied, should be granted.

30. *United States v. Sheppard* (1977), 70 D.L.R. (3d) 136 (S.C.C.).

§203 If an offender has been brought back to the country seeking to exercise criminal jurisdiction without the extradition process having been pursued, this does not exempt him from trial,[31] even though it may provide a claim for breach of sovereignty by the state from which he has been abducted,[32] but that state may demand his return and the extradition of his abductors,[33] and the accused may have a claim against his abductors.[34] If the offender has waived his right to an extradition hearing and agreed to return, then none of the limitations attaching to extradition apply.[35] Similarly, a returned offender has no right to claim that his return was in breach of the extradition treaty, since the treaty only grants rights to its parties.[36]

31. This can be seen from the case of Barbie deported from Bolivia to France in 1983 to stand trial for war crimes.

32. *Eichmann v. A.G. Israel* (1962), 36 I.L.R. 277; see also *Ker v. Illinois* (1886), 119 U.S. 436; *R. v. O.C. Depot Battalion. R.A.S.C., Colchester; Ex parte Elliott*, [1949] 1 All E.R. 373 (K.B.); *United States v. Toscanino* (1974), 500 F. 2d 267; *United States v. Gengler* (1974), 510 F. 2d 62. See Cole, "Extradition Treaties Abound but Unlawful Seizures Continue", (1975), International Perspectives, p. 40.

33. As happened in the case of Jaffe seized in Canada by U.S. bounty hunters, see Green letter, Edmonton Journal, Aug. 9, 1983, and Bassiouni, International Extradition: U.S. Law and Practice (1983), V S. 4-18. By the 1988 Protocol Amending the Extradition Treaty between Canada and the U.S., and an Exchange of Letters dated 11 Jan. 1988, seizure by bounty hunters was recognized as extraditable.

34. *R. v. Walton* (1905), 10 C.C.C. 269 (Ont. C.A.).

35. *R. v. Corrigan*, [1931] 1 K.B. 527 (C.A.). See also, *R. v. Flannery* (1923), 40 C.C.C. 263 (Alta. C.A.); *R. v. Gagnon* (1956), 117 C.C.C. 61 (Que. C.S.P.).

36. *Germany v. Pohle* (Germany) (1977) (Fed. Constitutional Ct.), Green, International Law through the Cases (1978), p. 383.

§204 Most extradition treaties, and numerous extradition acts, expressly exclude from extradition those guilty of a political offence.[37] Yet, there is no universally accepted definition of what constitutes a political offence. Canada[38] and most other common law countries[39] apply the definition enunciated by Denman J. in 1891:[40] ". . . to exclude extradition for such an act as murder, which is one of the extradition offences, it must at least be shown that the act is done in furtherance of, done with the intention of assistance, as a sort of overt act in the course of acting in a political matter, a political rising, or a dispute between two parties in the State as to which is to have the Government[41] in its hands. . . ." If the political situation in a country is such that there can be no organized political movement on whose behalf such an offence might be committed, the definition may be interpreted liberally to cover an offender who has acted against state interests or who might be proceeded against for political reasons rather than for common crimes.[42] However, the fact that the offender has some political motive for his act is not sufficient to make the act a political offence and give him immunity from extradition,[43] although some countries will refuse extradition if the offender committed his act while escaping from a dictatorial regime.[44]

37. Extradition Act, R.S.C. 1970, c. E-21, s. 21: No fugitive is liable to surrender under this Part if it appears (a) that the offence in respect of which proceedings are taken under this Act is one of a political character, or (b) that such proceedings are being taken with a view to prosecute or punish him for an offence of a political character. S. 22: Where the Minister of Justice at any time determines (a) that the offence in respect of which proceedings are being taken under this Part is one of a political character, (b) that the proceedings are, in fact, being taken with a view to try or punish the fugitive for an offence of a political character . . . he may refuse to make an order for surrender, and may . . . cancel . . . any warrant issued by a judge under this Part, and order the fugitive to be discharged out of custody on any committal made under this Part . . . ."

38. *Re Fedorenko* (1910), 17 C.C.C. 268 (Man. K.B.); *Re Commonwealth of Puerto Rico and Hernandez* (1972), 30 D.L.R. (3d) 260 (Ont. Co. Ct.); *Re State of Wisconsin and Armstrong* (1972), 28 D.L.R. (3d) 513 (Ont. Co. Ct.); jurisdiction to review affirmed (1972), 30 D.L.R. (3d) 727 (Ont. C.A.); application to review dismissed (1973), 32 D.L.R. (3d) 265 (Ont. C.A.); leave to appeal to S.C.C. dismissed without reasons (1973), 32 D.L.R. (3d) 265n (S.C.C.); see also, Castel and Edwards, "Political Offences: Extradition and Deportation", (1975) 13 Osgoode Hall L.J. 89, 118-20.

39. *Karadzole v. Artukovic* (1957), 247 F. 2d 198. Artukovic was ultimately deported to Yugoslavia, where he was sentenced to death for war crimes.

40. *Re Castioni*, [1891] 1 Q.B. 149 at 156 (C.A.). See Green, "The Nature of Political Offences", (1965) 7 Journal of Indian Law Institute 1.

41. *Re Meunier*, [1894] 2 Q.B. 415 (D.C.), (denied that an anarchist could ever be a political offender).

42. *R. v. of Brixton Prison (Governor); Ex parte Kolczynski*, [1955] 1 Q.B. 540 (D.C.). This immunity from extradition may also follow from application of the principle of "non-refoulement", described by the U.N. Conference on Statelessness, 1954, unanimously, "as an expression of the generally accepted principle that no State should expel or return a person in any manner whatsoever to the frontiers of territories where his life or freedom would be threatened on account of his race, religion, nationality, membership of a particular social group or political opinion." This statement appears as Part IV of the Final Act, The Convention Relating to the Status of Stateless Persons, 360 U.N.T.S. 117. This Convention has not been signed or ratified by Canada, although Canada is a party to the Refugees Convention, 1951, 189 U.N.T.S. 137 in which the same provision appears as Art. 33.

43. *Schtraks v. Israel*, [1964] A.C. 556 (H.L.).

44. *Re Kavic, Bjelanovic and Arsenijevic* (Switzerland) (1952), 19 I.L.R. 371.

§205 Some countries are not prepared to accept the defence of political offence if the crime alleged is one warranting severe moral condemnation in that the common crime far outweighed the political characteristics.[45] This moral condemnation also extends to fugitives charged with war crimes, who have contended that their acts were political since they were committed at the instruction of the offender's government,[46] although judges have also pointed out that such acts would not fall within the requirement that at the time of the offence the accused was acting in opposition to the requesting state or government.[47]

45. See *Re Campora* (Chile) (1957), 24 I.L.R. 518.

46. See *State v. Director of Prisons; Ex parte Schumann* (Ghana) (1966), 39 I.L.R. 433: ". . . Merely carrying out wicked orders [euthanasia and mass sterilization] or plans of a governing political party by State agents against the persons or properties of individuals or groups of individuals who manifestly do not demonstrate any organized violent resistance to the execution of those plans would not stamp the offences committed in such a situation with political character so as to afford the perpetrators an excuse from due prosecution. It is absolutely absurd to me to hold that what is clearly murder in one territory in response to the superior orders of a ruling political party against helpless victims in a lunatic asylum should not lie and the offender [should not be] extradited because it was done in obedience to superior orders of a governing political party" (per Lassey J.A., at pp. 451-2). See also, comments of Akufo-Addo C.J.: "The offence of murder with which [S] is charged is . . . no more of a political character than the offence of, say, robbery with violence or burglary committed by a political party activist in a desperate bid to seek means of replenishing the dwindling coffers of his political party" (at p. 439).

47. See *Re Extradition Act 1870*, [1969] 1 W.L.R. 12 (Q.B.). A witness in England was ordered to give evidence under s. 70 of the Act re a charge against a Nazi on trial in Germany for war-time atrocities. It was held that the fact the Fed. Rep. might gain political advantage from the trial did not render it of a 'political character'.

§206 While war crimes might not be political offences providing immunity from extradition, some acts connected with an armed conflict may be non-extraditable, so that a fugitive extradited for some offence committed in relation to that conflict might not be triable in respect of some other offence so committed.[48]

48. *Ktir v. Fed. Public Prosecutor* (1961), 34 I.L.R. 143 (Switz. S. Fed. Ct.) — member of Algerian National Liberation Front extradited to France for killing Algerian 'traitor', but Swiss Federal Court made extradition conditional on his not being tried for any offence relating to organization of the Front. See Green, "Political Offences, War Crimes and Extradition", (1962) 11 I.C.L.Q. 329.

§207 A complex problem has arisen in Canada concerning the impact of the Charter of Rights and Freedoms[49] upon requests for extradition. In accordance with s. 6(1) of the Charter "every citizen of Canada has the right to enter, remain in and leave Canada." It has been contended[50] that to extradite a Canadian is to infringe this constitutional right. However, it has been held[51] that the provision in s. 1 of the Charter subjecting the rights postulated in the Charter "to such reasonable limits prescribed by law as can be demonstrably justified in a free and democratic society" clearly covers the obligation to extradite. "The court must decide what is a reasonable limit demonstrably justified in a free and democratic society by reference to Canadian society and by the application of principles of political science. Criteria by which these issues are to be assessed are to be found within the Charter itself, which means that the courts are entitled to look at those societies in which as a matter of common law freedoms and democratic rights similar to those referred to in the Charter are enjoyed."[52]

49. Constitution Act, 1982, Part I.

50. See, e.g., *Germany v. Rauca* (1982), 38 O.R. (2d) 705 (Ont. H.C.).

51. *Germany v. Rauca, ante;* see also, *U.S. v. Smith* (1983), 42 O.R. (2d) 668 (Ont. H.C.).

52. *Germany v. Rauca, ante* at p. 716, per Evans C.J.H.C. See Green, "The Canadian Charter of Rights and International Law", (1982), 20 C.Y.B.I.L. 3.

§208 Frequently fugitives charged by requesting countries with acts of terrorism, whether so defined by treaty[53] or by common language,[54] maintain that their acts were politically motivated[55] or that they were committed as part and parcel of an 'armed conflict' directed against a government of which they disapproved. Occasionally, they have even claimed a right to be treated as prisoners of war.[56] In most cases, at least when the offender's return is requested from a western state, the courts have held that the offender, not being a member of a regular armed force or acting on behalf of a recognized authority,[57] is a common criminal and liable to extradition.[58] It has also been held that, whereas insurance is not payable in respect of war risks, this is not the case where this type of offence is concerned.[59]

53. See §193.

54. E.g., acts of violence directed against the civilian population or as defined by national legislation, e.g. U.K. Prevention of Terrorism (Temporary Provisions) Act, 1974, c. 55, 1976, c. 8.

55. See Bassiouni, International Terrorism and Political Crimes (1975).

56. See *Folkerts Case* (Netherlands) (1977), Rolno 3853/77, Green, "Terrorism and the Courts", (1981) 11 Man. L.J. 333 at 348; see also *United States v. Morales* (1979), 78 C.R. 414 (E. Dist. N.Y.).

57. See *Eain v. Wilkes* (1981), 641 F. 2d 504.

58. In *McGlinchey v. Wren,* [1983] 3 Irish Law Rep. Monthly 169 (Eire S.C.) concerning plea by member of I.R.A., O'Higgins C.J., at pp. 171-172, questioned whether murder of a civilian could ever be political and said "The judicial authorities on the scope of [political] offences have in many respects been rendered obsolete by the fact that modern terrorist violence, whether undertaken by military or paramilitary organizations, or by individuals or groups of individuals, is often the antithesis of what could reasonably be regarded as political, either in itself or in its connections."

59. *Pan American World Airways Inc. v. Aetna Casualty & Surety Co.* (1974), 505 F.
2d 989.

§209 In an attempt to prevent terrorists from evading extradition by
pleading the political offence defence, the majority of international
agreements seeking to define crimes by international law,[60] impose an
obligation upon the parties tomake the various offences extraditable or
to treat them as falling within the terms of their extradition legislation.
In addition, there is a tendency now, in order to deal with terrorist acts,
to amend the definition of political offence to an extent to make it
impossible for any terrorist or other accused to plead the political
defence to evade extradition.[61]

60. §§191, 193.

61. See the 1985 Supplementary Treaty to the U.K./U.S. Extradition Treaty of
1972, 24 I.L.M. 1105. 'Art. 1. . . .none of the following offences shall be regarded as an
offence of a political character: [a - d, offenses against the conventions on hijacking,
internationally protected persons or hostage-taking]; (e) murder; (f) manslaughter; (g)
maliciously wounding or inflicting grievous bodily harm; (h) kidnapping, abduction,
false imprisonment or unlawful detention, including the taking of a hostage; (i) the
following offences relating to explosives: (1) the causing of an explosion likely to
endanger the life or cause serious damage to property; or (2) conspiracy to cause such
an explosion; or (3) the making or possession of an explosive substance by a person
who intends either himself or through another person to endanger the life or cause
serious damage to property; (j) the following offenses relating to firearms or ammunition: (1) the possession of a firearm or ammunition by a person who intends either
himself or through another person to endanger life; or (2) the use of a firearm by a
person with intent to resist or prevent the arrest or detention of himself or another
person; (k) damaging property with intent to endanger life or with reckless disregard
as to whether the life of another would thereby be endangered; (l) an attempt to
commit any of the foregoing offences." Similar limitations on the political offence
defence were made in 1988 to the extradition treaty between Canada and the U.S.,
Dept. External Affairs, News Release, No. 009, 11 Jan. 1988. See, on Irish Republican
Army 'fugitives', *Re Doherty* (1984) 599 F. Supp. 270; *Quinn v. Robinson* (1986) 783
Fed. Rep. 2d 776 (C.A.).

§210 In addition to the attempts to create new international crimes
such as terrorism or aerial hijacking, the United Nations has sought by
treaty to create a new offence which it describes as a crime against
humanity. The crime of apartheid, which clearly reflects the political
ideologies of the current majority in the United Nations, has been
condemned as such by the International Convention on the Suppression
and Punishment of the Crime of Apartheid:[62] "Article I: 1. The States
Parties to the present Convention declare that apartheid is a crime
against humanity and that inhuman acts resulting from the policies and

practices of apartheid and similar policies and practices of racial segregation and discrimination . . . are crimes violating the principles of international law, in particular the purposes and principles of the Charter of the United Nations, and constituting a serious threat to international peace and security.[63] 2. The States Parties to the present Convention declare criminal those organizations, institutions and individuals committing the crime of apartheid; Article II: For the purpose of the present Convention, the term 'the crime of apartheid' which shall include similar policies and practices of racial segregation and discrimination as practised in southern Africa, shall apply to the following inhuman acts committed for the purpose of establishing and maintaining domination by one racial group of persons over any other racial group of persons and systematically oppressing them: (a) Denial to a member or members of a racial group or groups of the right to life and liberty of person: (i) by murder of members of a racial group or groups; (ii) by the infliction upon the members of a racial group or groups of serious bodily or mental harm by the infringement of their freedom or dignity, or by subjecting them to torture or to cruel, inhuman or degrading treatment or punishment; (iii) by arbitrary arrest and illegal imprisonment of the members of a racial group or groups; (b) Deliberate imposition on a racial group or groups of living conditions calculated to cause its or their physical destruction in whole or in part; (c) Any legislative measures and other measures calculated to prevent a racial group or groups from participation in the political, social, economic and cultural life of the country and the deliberate creation of conditions preventing the full development of such a group or groups, in particular by denying to members of a racial group or groups basic human rights and freedoms, including the right to work, the right to form recognized trade unions, the right to education, the right to leave and to return to their own country, the right to a nationality, the right to freedom of movement and residence, the right to freedom of opinion and expression, and the right to freedom of peaceful assembly and association; (d) Any measures, including legislative measures, designed to divide the population along racial lines by the creation of separate reserves and ghettos for the members of a racial group or groups, the prohibition of mixed marriages among members of various racial groups, the expropriation of landed property belonging to a racial group or groups or to members thereof; (e) Exploitation of the labour of the members of a racial group or groups, in particular by submitting them to forced labour; (f) Persecution of organizations and persons, by depriving them of fundamental rights and freedoms, because they oppose apartheid."[64]

62. 1973, G.A. Res. 3068 (XXVIII), 13 I.L.M. 50. This Convention has not been acceded to by Canada or any other western democratic state. However, to the extent

that any of these acts amount to genocide, it should be remembered that Canada is a party to the Genocide Convention, see §190.

63.   As such, the Security Council, in accordance with Chapter VII of the Charter, would be able to order members to take coercive military measures against a state practising or tolerating apartheid.

64.   The definition, especially (1)(iii) and (c)-(f) reflect conditions in South Africa.

§211   The Convention does not envisage the creation of any international tribunal, but leaves jurisdiction to the "competent tribunal of any State Party to the Convention which may acquire jurisdiction over the person of the accused or by an international penal tribunal having jurisdiction with respect to those State Parties which shall have accepted its jurisdiction"[65] and such jurisdiction will extend "to individuals, members of organizations and institutions and representatives of the State, whether residing in the territory of the State in which the acts are perpetrated or in some other State".[66] It should be noted that apartheid is also condemned as a grave breach of the humanitarian rules relating to armed conflict.[67]

65.   Art. VI.

66.   Art. III.

67.   See §§364-368.

§212   In recent years some states, including Canada,[68] have entered into bilateral treaties providing for the Transfer of Prisoners. Under such treaties, the nationals of one party sentenced by a court of the other party may request a transfer to his home state to serve his sentence. His transfer renders him entitled to all the rights of his national penal system, including parole and the like.

68.   Canada has signed such treaties with the U.S.A., 1977; Mexico, 1974; Bolivia, 1980; France, 1979; Thailand, 1983. Canada is also a party to the multilateral Convention on the Transfer of Sentenced Persons drawn up by the Council of Europe, 1983, 22 I.L.M. 530. Legislative effect was given to this arrangement by the Transfer of Offenders Act, S.C. 1977-78, c. 21. See, Bassiouni, "Perspectives on the Transfer of Prisoners Between the U.S. and Mexico and the U.S. and Canada", (1978) 11 Vanderbilt Journal of Transnational Law, 249; National Council for Welfare of Prisoners Abroad (U.K.), *Transfer Prisoner Treaties: The How and Why*, (1980); the Canada-U.S. Treaty is considered at 13-14.

§213   Attempts have also been made to create international criminal responsibility in the case of offences which might be attributable to the state as such. In 1947, the General Assembly instructed the International Law Commission to draft a Code of Offences against the Peace and Security of Mankind.[69] In 1979, in the light of the General Assembly's decision not to proceed in this matter,[70] the Commission decided to draft a General Code on State Responsibility.[71] By Article 19, any "act of a State which constitutes a breach of an international obligation is an international wrongful act",[72] and "2. An international wrongful act which results from the breach by a State of an international obligation so essential for the protection of fundamental interests of the international community that its breach is recognized as a crime by that community as a whole, constitutes an international crime. 3. Subject to paragraph 2, and on the basis of the rules of international law in force, an international crime may result, inter alia, from: (a) a serious breach of an international obligation of essential importance for the maintenance of international peace and security, such as that prohibiting aggression; (b) a serious breach of an international obligation for safeguarding the right of self-determination of peoples, such as that prohibiting the establishment or maintenance by force of colonial domination; (c) a serious breach on a widespread scale of an international obligation of essential importance for safeguarding the human being, such as those prohibiting slavery, genocide and apartheid; (d) a serious breach of an international obligation of essential importance for the safeguarding and preservation of the human environment, such as those prohibiting massive pollution of the atmosphere or of the seas".[73] Even should these proposals ultimately be accepted by states, there still remains the question of the proper tribunal for exercising jurisdiction and the method by which states may be subjected to that jurisdiction. The Draft recognized that if a state consents to an act that would otherwise be forbidden, no wrongfulness on the part of the actor arises. However, this is not the case if the act in question is contrary to a 'peremptory norm of international law', defined as "a norm accepted and recognized by the international community of States, as a whole, as a norm from which no derogation is permitted and which can be modified only by a subsequent norm of general international law having the same character".[74]

69.   Res. 177 (II). See (1951) 2 Y.B. Int. Law Comm. 43-69.

70.   Res. 898 (IX).

71.   18 I.L.M. 1568.

72.   See §§316-328.

73.   See Green "New Trends in International Criminal Law", (1981) 11 I.Y.B.H.R. 11 at 24-40.

74.   Art. 29. Unfortunately, there is no indication in the draft as to how such a 'preremptory norm' is to be found.

7. PROTECTION OF MINORITIES

§214 There is no rule in international customary law relating to the protection of minorities. Minorities possess the nationality of the country in which they reside and are entitled to no privileges or rights other than those enjoyed by other nationals. According to customary law it is solely within the domestic jurisdiction[75] of the state to decide on the treatment of its nationals, including any decision to discriminate against any particular group.

75. See §83.

§215 Problems relating to minorities frequently arise when a state is made up of more than one national, ethnic or religious group.[76] In such cases, states interested in the welfare of such groups often enter into treaties binding the state in whose territory the group appears to treat that group on a basis of equality with the majority of the population.[77] However, equality does not mean simply the absence of discrimination. What is required is real and not formal equality,[78] so that in some circumstances the minority might require what appears to be preferential treatment as compared with the rest of the population.[79] Real equality has been defined by the Permanent Court of International Justice: "Equality in law precludes discrimination of any kind; whereas equality in fact may involve the necessity of different treatment in order to attain a result which establishes an equilibrium between different situations. . . . The equality between members of the majority and of the minority must be an effective, genuine equality . . . ."[80]

76. This was particularly the case with some of the states, e.g. Bulgaria, Romania, established towards the end of the nineteenth century, and the successor states of the Austro-Hungarian Empire established after World War I, e.g. Czechoslovakia, Yugoslavia. See Green "Protection of Minorities in the League of Nations and the United Nations," Gotlieb, Human Rights Federalism and Minorities (1970), p. 180. This is made clear in a Legal Bureau memo., 9 Sept. 1985, which deals with the problem of individual and collective human rights: "The collective aspect of human rights relates to those human rights which are enjoyed by individuals by virtue of belonging to a collectivity or group. These collective human rights are generally exercised in concert with others. In the Canadian context this would refer to matters such as rights of minorities" (1986) 24 C.Y.B.I.L. 389.

77. E.g., Treaties between the Principal Allied and Associated Powers and Poland, 1919, 1 Hudson Int. Leg. 283, Czechoslovakia, 1919, 1 Hudson, Int. Leg. 298; Yugoslavia, 1919, 1 Hudson, Int. Leg. 312; Romania, 1919, 1 Hudson, Int. Leg. 426; Greece, 1920 (re Albania, Bulgarian and Turkish citizens, 1 Hudson, Int. Leg. 489) — the British Empire ratified each of these treaties.

78.   See *German Settlers in Poland* (1923), 1 W.C.R. 208 at 218; "There must be equality in fact as well as ostensible legal equality in the sense of the absence of discrimination in the words of the law".

79.   See Convention on the Elimination of All Forms of Racial Discrimination, 1966, 660 U.N.T.S. 195: Art. 1(4) "Special measures taken for the sole purpose of securing adequate advancement of certain racial or ethnic groups or individuals requiring such protection as may be necessary in order to ensure such groups or individuals equal enjoyment or exercise of human rights and fundamental freedoms shall not be deemed racial discrimination, provided, however, that such measures do not, as a consequence, lead to the maintenance of separate rights for different racial groups and that they shall not be continued after the objectives for which they were taken have been achieved." Art. 2(4) "States Parties shall, when the circumstances so warrant, take in the social, economic, cultural and other fields, special and concrete measures to ensure the adequate development and protection of certain racial groups or individuals belonging to them, for the purpose of guaranteeing them the full and equal enjoyment of human rights and fundamental freedoms. These measures shall in no case entail as a consequence the maintenance of unequal or separate rights for different racial groups after the objectives for which they were taken have been achieved." Canada ratified this Convention in 1970.

80.   *Minority Schools in Albania* (1935), 3 W.C.R. 485 at 498; see also *Brown v. Bd. of Education of Topeka* (1955), 349 U.S. 296, though this concerned equality under the U.S. Constitution.

§216   The minorities treaties signed after the First World War were consistent in their provisions, and by 1921 it was possible to speak of a minorities régime enabling states to undertake obligations towards their minorities by way of a unilateral declaration,[81] as distinct from a formal treaty.[13]

81.   See §300.

82.   Declaration re Minorities Made by Albania on Admission to League of Nations, 1921, 1 Hudson, Int. Leg. 733.

§217   Minorities have never been defined as such, but the term has never been understood to apply to any and every group of aliens.[83] There must be a recognizably large group differing in a variety of ethnic, social and cultural characteristics from the majority population. The nearest to a judicial definition was provided by the Permanent Court of International Justice,[84] although the definition was of a 'community' rather than of a minority as such: ". . . a group of persons living in a given country or locality, having a race, religion, language and traditions of their own and united by the identity of race, religion, language and traditions in a sentiment of solidarity, with a view to preserving their traditions, maintaining their form of worship, ensuring the instruction and upbringing of their children in accordance with the spirit and traditions of their race and rendering mutual assistance to each other."

83. See Resolution XX of the Third Meeting of Foreign Ministers of the American Republics, 1942, 8 Whiteman 376 "In accordance with its historical, racial, political, and judicial tradition, there is and can be no room in America for the so-called racial, linguistic or religious 'minorities'; and . . . reiterates the principle of American Public Law, according to which aliens residing in an American State are subject to the jurisdiction of that State, and the Governments and agencies of the countries of which such aliens are nationals cannot lawfully interfere, directly or indirectly, in domestic affairs for the purpose of controlling the status or activities of such aliens."

84. *Greco-Bulgarian Communities* (1930), 2 W.C.R. 641 at 653-4. For Canadian comment on the difficulty of defining 'people', see Legal Bureau memo., §215 note 76.

§218 The purpose of minorities protection as indicated by the Minorities Treaties and construed as fundamental to the minorities régime ". . . is to secure for certain elements incorporated in a State, the population of which differs from them in race, language or religion, the possibility of living peaceably alongside that population and cooperating amicably with it, while at the same time preserving the characteristics which distinguish them from the majority, and satisfying the ensuing special needs. In order to attain this object, two things were regarded as particularly necessary . . . The first is to ensure that nationals belonging to racial, religious or linguistic minorities shall be placed in every respect on a footing of perfect equality with the other nationals of that State. The second is to ensure for the minority elements suitable means for the preservation of their racial peculiarities, their traditions and their national characteristics.[85] These two requirements are indeed closely interlocked, for there would be no true equality between a majority[86] and a minority if the latter were deprived of its own institutions, and were consequently compelled to renounce that which constitutes the very essence of its being as a minority".[87]

85. Thus, the Legal Bureau has pointed out that "the right to profess and practice religious beliefs is in practical terms (at least in the way most religions function) only meaningful in a collective setting. The same is true, to a great extent, of the right to education. Therefore, the aggregate enjoyment of certain (perhaps most) rights provides the necessary context for the enjoyment and protection of individual human rights", §215 note 76.

86. See *State of Bombay v. Bombay Education Soc.* (1954), A.I.R.S.C. 561 in which the Supreme Court of India held that education rights guaranteed to minorities by the Indian Constitution extended equally to the majority. In this case, Bombay State had passed legislation restricting the right to attend English language schools to certain minorities while requiring the majority to be educated in the vernacular. This was held to be a denial of the rights of the majority.

87. *Minority Schools in Albania, ante,* at 496.

§219 During the existence of the League of Nations the minorities régime was supervised by a Permanent Minorities Commission with the possibility of reference to the Permanent Court of International Justice. With the demise of the League the Commission ceased to exist, and the role of the International Court of Justice became dependent on specific treaties regulating the treatment of minorities, or potential requests from the United Nations for advisory opinions within this field. No such opinion has been requested, although the Peace Treaties of 1947 entered into by Bulgaria, Hungary and Romania[88] guaranteed equal treatment to all and provided for determination of disputes by the court. However, when such a dispute did arise, the reference to the court by the General Assembly did not deal with matters of substance, but was confined to problems of interpretation of the particular treaties.[89] No treaty dealing with minorities entered into since 1945[90] has been referred for judicial settlement.[91] Moreover, it would appear that even though the United Nations has no organ equivalent to the Permanent Minorities Commission, the overall supervisory responsibilities of the League in relation to minorities still exist,[92] and may be exercised by way of the organs concerned with human rights or by a request for an advisory opinion from the World Court.

88.   41 U.N.T.S. 21; 41 U.N.T.S. 135; 42 U.N.T.S. 3 respectively.

89.   *Interpretation of Peace Treaties,* [1950] I.C.J. 65, 221.

90.   E.g., Indo-Pakistan Agreement on Minorities Affairs, (1950) U.N.Y.B.H.R. for 1950, p. 436.

91.   However, in *Re Young, James and Webster (The Closed Shop Case)* (1981), 62 I.L.R. 359 at 381-382 (European Ct. of Human Rights) the court said: ". . . pluralism, tolerance and broadmindedness are hallmarks of a 'democratic society'. Although individual interests must on occasion be subordinated to those of a group, democracy does not simply mean that the views of a majority must always prevail: a balance must be achieved which ensures the fair and proper treatment of minorities and avoids any abuse of a dominant position."

92.   Memo. of U.N. Secretariat to UNESCO stated that the Second World War "in itself has not caused the extinction of the obligations relating to minorities", Doc. E/CN.4/367/1950, p. 3.

§220   For the majority of states, including Canada,[93] the only obligation relating to the protection of minorities, outside of the provisions of national law, are to be found in multilateral treaties concerning human rights, and the provisions therein tend to be general in character, forbidding any form of discrimination, rather than providing specific rights for minorities. The Convention on the Elimination of All Forms of Racial Discrimination[94] does, however, recognize that certain groups in the state may require special privileges if they are to enjoy equal rights with the rest of the population. But such privileges must terminate once equality has been achieved.

93. See, e.g., Humphrey, "The Role of Canada in the United Nations Program for the Promotion of Human Rights", in Macdonald, Canadian Perspectives on International Law and Organization (1974), p. 612; Macdonald and Humphrey, The Practice of Freedom: Canadian Essays on Human Rights and Freedoms (1979).

94. 1966, 660 U.N.T.S. 195, ratified by Canada in 1970. The U.N. Declaration on Elimination of All Forms of Intolerance and of Discrimination Based on Religion or Belief, 1981 (Res. 36/55) seeks to guarantee equality to religious minorities, but makes no provision for any special treatment.

§221 The document which is regarded as being the basis of enjoyment of equal rights for all is the Universal Declaration of Human Rights.[95] This is a Resolution of the General Assembly of the United Nations, and, as such, lacks any legal obligatory force.[96] However, it is invariably referred to in other United Nations documents on human rights and in the Preambles of international covenants in this field, and is generally looked upon as the standard of measurement of human rights instruments and the behaviour of states. The Declaration makes no reference to minorities or their rights. It simply states: "Everyone is entitled to all the rights and freedoms set forth in this Declaration without distinction of any kind, such as race, colour, sex, language, religion, political or other opinion, national or social origin, property, birth or other status."[97] This right of enjoyment without discrimination is elevated into an obligation upon the parties to the International Covenant on Civil and Political Rights[98] and the only reference to minority rights is to be found in Article 27: "In those States in which ethnic, religious or linguistic minorities exist, persons belonging to such minorities shall not be denied the right, in community with the other members of their group, to enjoy their own culture, to profess their own religion, or to use their own language."[99]

95. 1948, Res. 217 (III) A.

96. See §417.

97. Art. 2(1).

98. 1966, 999 U.N.T.S. 171, Art. 2(1). Canada became a party in 1976.

99. See Legal Bureau memo, §215 note 76.

§222 Despite the reference to the minority group's right to enjoy its own culture and use its own language, the Covenant makes no reference to the group's right maintain its own schools to teach that language and preserve its culture.[1] However, states which are parties to the UNESCO Convention against Discrimination in Education[2] have agreed that "It is essential to recognize the right of members of national minorities to carry on their own educational activities, including the maintenance of schools and, depending on the educational policy of each State, the use or the teaching of their own language,[3] provided however: (i) That this right is not exercised in a manner which prevents the members of these minorities from understanding the culture and language of the community as a whole and from participating in its activities, or which prejudices national sovereignty. . . ." The extent of a minority's right to be educated in its own language was examined by the European Court of Human Rights in the *Belgian Linguistics Case*[4] which concerned discriminatory treatment as between Flemish and French speaking schools, contrary to the European Convention on Human Rights[5] and its First Protocol.[6] Legislation had been enacted which provided state-aided education in unilinguistic schools in unilinguistic areas, and "the Court finds [the] purpose [of the legislation] is to achieve linguistic unity within the two large regions of Belgium in which a large majority of the population speaks only one of the two national languages. This legislation makes scarcely viable schools in which teaching is conducted solely in the national language that is not that of the majority of the inhabitants of the region. . . . [I]t tends to prevent in the Dutch [Flemish] unilingual region, the establishment or the maintenance of schools which teach only in French. Such a measure cannot be considered arbitrary. . . . [I]t is based on the objective element which the region constitutes . . . [and] on a public interest, namely, to ensure that all schools dependent on the State and existing in a unilingual region, conduct their teaching in a language which is essentially that of the region. . . . [T]he legislature, in adopting the system in issue, has pursued an objective concerned with the public interest: to favour linguistic unity within the unilingual regions and, in particular, to promote among pupils a knowledge in depth of the usual language of the region. This objective concerned with the public interest does not, in itself, involve any element of discrimination." While this decision is strictly only relevant to its own circumstances, the reasoning may be of general application in interpreting linguistic and educational rights where minorities are concerned.[7]

1. It was the right of the Greek minority to maintain such schools that was in issue in the *Minority Schools in Albania* case, §215 note 80.

2. 1960, U.N. Y.B. H.R. for 1961, p. 437, Art. 5(1)(c).

3. Although Canada is not a party to this Convention, it would seem that these terms are wide enough to allow for such legislation as the Quebec Language Charter, S.Q. 1977, c. 5; see Beaudoin, 'Linguistic Rights in Canada' in Macdonald and Humphrey, The Practice of Freedom: Canadian Essays on Human Rights and Freedoms (1979), p. 197. See, also, McRae, "The Constitutional Protection of Linguistic Rights in Bilingual and Multilingual States" Gotlieb, Human Rights Federalism and Minorities (1970), p. 211. See Legal Bureau memo., §215 note 76.

4. (Merits) (1968), 45 I.L.R. 114, 174, 216 (European Ct. of Human Rights).

5. 1950, 213 U.N.T.S. 222.

6. 1952, 213 U.N.T.S. 262. See also Head "Regional Developments Respecting Human Rights: The Implications for Canada," Gotlieb, *op. cit.*, p. 228.

7. In addition to the Quebec Language Charter (Bill 101), reference might be made to the Belgian Decree of 1973 whereby Dutch became the sole language of communication between management and labour in firms in the Flemish regions: ". . . The language to use for social relations between employers and workers, as well as for all business acts prescribed by the law, is Dutch." Officials of the Permanent Commission of Linguistic Control may "penetrate freely, at any moment of the day or night, without prior warning" into premises to ascertain that the law is being observed.

§223 The relationship between the rights of a minority and the principle of self-determination at least as understood by Canada, is expressed as follows:[7.1] "Self-determination is a legal principle, the scope of which is still unclear in international law. Like other international legal principles, it has political implications and may be open to subjective interpretations . . . The Friendly Relations Declaration[7.2] indicates that the principle of self-determination will operate in states where the government does not represent all the people. It is not to be construed, however, as authorizing the territorial dismemberment of an independent state possessed of a government representing the whole people belonging to the territory without distinction as to race, creed or colour. Moreover the exercise of the right of self-determination is not limited to the creation of an independent state, but can be expressed through local autonomy, association or integration with another state, self-government or other political status freely determined by a people. The Canadian view is that the principle of self-determination is applicable in colonial situations and not to the case of ethnic, religious or linguistic minorities in non-colonial states. Minority rights are protected by provisions of international human rights instruments of customary international law. Canada has generally favoured a broad interpretation of the principle of self-determination in internatonal form, with the exception of its application to the metropolitan territory of a democratic state".

7.1 Memo of Legal Bureau, Dept. of External Affairs, 20 Aug. 1982, (1983) 21 C.Y.B.I.L. 318-9.

7.2. Res. 2625 (XXV). In a further memo, 9 Sept. 1985, the Legal Bureau said: "The most controversial collective right is the right of self-determination. It is true that states do not, in the western legal system, have human rights . . . . The rights of states in international law (by virtue of treaty or customary international law) are well-established. But these are rights vis-à-vis other states, in accordance with the traditional doctrine that only states can be subjects of international law (this doctrine has become somewhat eroded by the growth of international human rights law . . .) . . . A state therefore would not be said to have a right of self-determination although the people in that state would if they were ruled by what could be described as an alien or oppressive authority. We should therefore be careful not to confuse the rights of a people (whatever they are) with those of a state" (1986) 24 C.Y.B.I.L. pp. 389-390.

8. AIR LAW

§224 In international customary law, each state is sovereign over the air space above its territory.[8] This is confirmed in Article 1 of the Paris Convention on the Regulation of Aerial Navigation, 1919,[9] and the Chicago Convention on International Civil Aviation, 1944,[10] although there is little agreement as to the height to which sovereignty extends.[11] It is only as a result of international agreements that states enjoy a right to fly over another's territory or pick up passengers therein.

8. Cujus est solum ejus est usque ad coelum, Coke on Littleton 4a. See *Public Prosecutor v. Janos V.* (1972), 71 I.L.R. 229, at 231 (Austria S.C.); *Re Capital Cities Communications Inc. and C.R.T.C.* (1975), 52 D.L.R. (3d) 415 (Fed. C.A.) in which it was held that radio frequencies in air space are public property and not subject to private ownership.

9. 11 L.N.T.S. 173.

10. 15 U.N.T.S. 295.

11. See, e.g. Cooper, Exploration in Aerospace Law (1968), p. 8.

§225 Most countries, including Canada, are parties to the Chicago Convention which regulates international civil air traffic and supervises its operation through the International Civil Aviation Organization.[12] The Convention has been supplemented by two further agreements[13] introducing what are generally known as the 'five freedoms' of the air:[14] "1. The privilege to fly across its territory without landing; 2. The privilege to land for non-traffic purposes; 3. The privilege to put down passengers, mail and cargo taken on in the territory of the State whose nationality the aircraft possesses; 4. The privilege to take on passengers, mail and cargo destined for the territory of the State whose nationality the aircraft possesses; 5. The privilege to take on passengers, mail and cargo destined for the territory of any other contracting State and the privilege to put down passengers, mail and cargo coming from any such territory." The last two freedoms above-mentioned have not been widely conceded and for the main part where they do exist it is by reason of bilaterial agreements. The 'five freedoms' are only relevant to scheduled flights.

12. The Organization has its seat in Montreal.

13. The International Air Services Transit Agreement, 1944, 84 U.N.T.S. 389, and the International Air Transport Agreement, 1944, 171 U.N.T.S. 387. The former, known as the 'two freedoms' agreement, is widely accepted, while the latter, known as

the 'five freedoms' agreement, has only been accepted by a small number of states. Canada is a party to only the 'two freedoms' agreement.

14. McWhinney and Bradley, The Freedom of the Air (1969).

§226 In accordance with Article 6 of the Chicago Convention, scheduled international air services may only operate into or over the territory[15] of a contracting state with the special permission or other authorization of the state and in accordance with the terms of such authorization. Normally, this is determined by the bilateral agreement made between the territorial and the flag states concerned. By Article 9, a state "may, for reasons of military necessity or public safety, restrict or prohibit uniformly the aircraft of other States from flying over certain areas of its territory [, but s]uch prohibited areas shall be of reasonable extent and location so as not to interfere unnecessarily with air navigation. Descriptions of such prohibited areas . . . shall be communicated as soon as possible to the other contracting States and to the International Civil Aviation Organization." In addition, a state is permitted, "in exceptional circumstances or during a period of emergency, or in the interest of public safety, and with immediate effect, temporarily to restrict or prohibit flying over the whole or any part of its territory," and it may require any aircraft entering the areas indicated as closed "to effect a landing as soon as possible . . . at some designated airport within its territory." The Convention does not specify the means that are to be employed by the territorial state to effect such a landing, but it is generally accepted that recourse should be had to ground-to-air contact, air-to-air radio and visual communication, and the use of warning shots fired parallel to the line of flight.[16] There are also no enforcement or punitive provisions in the Convention and, in the event of a breach by any contracting state, other states will be obliged to take such retaliatory or reprisal[17] measures as they deem pertinent,[18] while the Council of the International Civil Aviation Organization "shall" report to contracting states and the Organization's Assembly any infraction of the Convention.[19] It "may" also conduct research into all aspects of air transport and navigation which are of international importance and study any matters affecting the organization and operation of international air transport.[20]

15. By Art. 2 the "territory of a State shall be deemed to be the land areas and territorial waters adjacent thereto under the sovereignty, suzerainty, protection or mandate of such State."

16. This is an adaptation of the rules pertaining to the stopping of vessels at sea. The method of visual contact is by 'wing waggling'. There was much dispute in 1983 whether the Soviet Union had followed these practices prior to shooting down a Korean civil aircraft which had flown off course and was overflying Soviet closed

security areas. In fact, "the International Air Transport Association said 'You can never say that anyone is entitled to kill 269 human beings, but the Soviet Union has followed standard recognized procedure and, leaving aside the humanitarian and moral case, they have a pretty sound case in law'. This is because it issued advanced warning to all airliners that it reserved the right to protect the integrity of its air-space around Sakhalin island 'by any means', which included shooting down even civil aircraft", The Times, Sept. 13, 1983. FitzGerald, "The Use of Force against Civil Aircraft: The Aftermath of the KAL 007 Incident", (1984) 22 C.Y.B.I.L. 291. As a result of the KAL 007 indicent the Chicago Convention was amended in 1984. By Art 3 bis "The Contracting States recognize that every State must refrain from resorting to the use of weapons against civil aircraft in flight and that, in case of interception, the lives of persons on board and the safety of aircraft must not be endangered . . .", (1984) 22 C.Y.B.I.L. 291 at 309. The Article requires aircraft to comply with any instruction to land, but there is not indication of the action to be taken if this order is ignored.

17.   A reprisal is an illegal measure resorted to with the intent of compelling cessation of a prior illegal measure; see §337 note 34.

18.   Thus, after the Soviet destruction of a Korean aircraft in 1983 a number of countries, including Canada, temporarily refused landing rights to the Soviet airline Aeroflot and cancelled flight by their own aircraft to the Soviet Union.

19.   Art. 54.

20.   Art. 55.

§227   Since territorial states when enforcing restrictions on the right to overfly are obliged "not to interfere unnecessarily with air navigation",[21] it is clear that they must do nothing to endanger overflying aircraft. To this end, "each contracting State undertakes to collaborate in securing the highest practicable degree of uniformity in regulations, standards, procedures and organization in relation to aircraft, personnel, airways and auxiliary services in all matters in which such uniformity will facilitate and improve air navigation [and] to this end the International Civil Aviation Organization (ICAO) shall adopt and amend from time to time, as may be necessary, international standards and recommended practices and procedures".[22] If any state is unable to comply with such standards it must inform the Organization of such differences.[23] In accordance with the obligation to secure safety in air navigation, "each contracting State undertakes to provide such measures of assistance to aircraft in distress[24] in its territory as it may find practicable, and to permit, subject to control by its own authorities, the owners of the aircraft or the authorities of the State in which the aircraft is registered to provide such measures of assistance as may be necessitated in the circumstances. Each contracting State, when undertaking search for missing aircraft, will collaborate in coordinated measures which may be recommended from time to time pursuant to this Convention".[25]

21. Art. 9.

22. Art. 37.

23. Art. 38.

24. Mere deviation from a scheduled route or overflight of closed areas is not ipso facto evidence that an aircraft is in distress.

25. The Soviet Union refused to allow Korean or other vessels to enter its territorial sea to assist in the search for the wreckage of the downed Korean aircraft or the corpses of its passengers, and opposed measures proposed by the Security Council of the U.N. and the I.C.A.O. directed at setting up an international inquiry into the circumstances of the downing of the Korean aircraft, vetoing the former and refusing to cooperate with the latter and in March 1984, condemned the report issued by the I.C.A.O. although it did not oppose the adoption of Art. 3 bis, which was agreed by acclamation.

§228 The Chicago Convention is only applicable to civil aircraft and has no application in the case of state aircraft,[26] which may overfly another state or land therein only when so authorized by special agreement or otherwise, and only in accordance with the terms of such authorization.[27] In order to preserve the rights of civil aircraft under the Convention, "each contracting State agrees not to use civil aviation for any purpose inconsistent with the aims of the Convention".[28] To use a civil aircraft for espionage purposes would clearly be in contravention of this provision, but there is nothing in the Convention to indicate the manner in which a territorial state is to determine whether a civil aircraft is engaged in unlawful activities.[29] This leaves open the question of how extreme may be the measures which an overflown state may take against a civil aircraft when that aircraft is overflying the territory of such a state with or without permission and has ignored orders to depart or land.[30]

26. State aircraft are those "used in military, customs and police services."

27. Art. 3.

28. Art. 4.

29. The Soviet Union maintained that the Korean aircraft which it shot down in 1983 not only failed to respond to instructions to identify itself or land, but was also engaged in espionage although it provided no substantial evidence to support this allegation.

30. See FitzGerald, "The Use and Force against Civil Aircraft", (1984) 22 C.Y.B.I.L. 291.

§229 The I.C.A.O. Council has a general supervisory function and its jurisdictional capacity may be seen from the judgment of the International Court of Justice in a dispute between India and Pakistan arising from the conditions laid down by India concerning the resumption of overflights after their suspension.[31] The Council has also been responsible for drafting the various Conventions which are directed at dealing with offences concerning aircraft, including aerial hijacking.[32]

> 31. *Jurisdiction of the ICAO Council*, [1972] I.C.J. 46. See FitzGerald: "The Judgement of the I.C.J. on the Appeal Relating to the Jurisdiction of the ICAO Council", (1974) 12 C.Y.B.I.L. 153.
>
> 32. See §193.

§230 Many of the issues concerning international air law which have been submitted for judicial settlement concern claims arising from injury or loss suffered during flight. These matters are regulated by the Warsaw Convention on International Carriage by Air, 1929,[33] as amended by the Hague Protocol, 1955,[34] which have the force of law in Canada by the Carriage by Air Act.[35] The Warsaw Convention is concerned with liability arising from 'international carriage', which is defined as ". . . any carriage in which, according to the contract made by the parties, the place of departure and the place of destination, whether or not there be a break in the carriage or a transhipment,[36] are situated either within the territories of two High Contracting Parties, or within the territory of a single High Contracting Party, if there is an agreed stopping place within a territory subject to the sovereignty, suzerainty, mandate or authority of another Power, even though that Power is not a party to this Convention. A carriage without such an agreed stopping place between territories subject to the sovereignty, suzerainty, mandate or authority of the same High Contracting Party is not deemed to be international for the purposes of this Convention."

> 33. 137 U.N.T.S. 11.
>
> 34. 478 U.N.T.S. 371.
>
> 35. R.S.C. 1970, c. C-14.
>
> 36. This break may occur in the country of departure, *Grein c. Imperial Airways Ltd.*, [1936] 2 All E.R. 1258 (K.B.). In *Surprenant v. Air Can.*, [1973] Que. C.A. 107 (Que. C.A.), the contract was for a flight from Montreal to Los Angeles with a stopover at Toronto, and it was after this stop-over that the crash occurred at Malton, Ont.

§231 Once it is decided that the flight was an international carriage, the Warsaw Convention is relevant in deciding whether damage has occurred and the extent of the liability. Insofar as Canada is concerned, even though the English and French texts of statutes are equally authentic,[37] it is the French text of the Warsaw Convention, which is reproduced as Schedule I of the Carriage by Air Act, which is authoritative,[38] for in accordance with Article 36 of the Convention it was "drawn up in French in a single copy." It has been held in England, too, that the French text being authentic must be given precedence over the English translation which appears as an annex to the English Carriage by Air Acts,[39] so that the term 'avarie' translated as 'damage' requires actual loss and not simply damage.[40] When luggage has been lost, the liability of the carrier is strictly limited and depends on the terms of the ticket, which consists of a combined passage ticket and a baggage check. Liability relates to 'registered baggage', although the term 'registered' is not defined in the Convention. However, by Article 4 the number and weight of packages must be recorded on the baggage check. If there is any irregularity in registration, such as the omission of this detail, the baggage check remains a 'baggage check' and if the carrier indicates on the ticket the Convention's limitations he is protected by the Convention despite the irregularity.[41]

37. Constitution Act, 1867 (U.K.), c. 3 [title am. Constitution Act, 1982, s. 53(1)].

38. *Surprenant v. Air Can., ante.*

39. Carriage by Air Act, 1932, 22 & 23 Geo. V, c. 36; Carriage by Air Act, 1961, 9 & 10 Eliz. II, c. 27.

40. Warsaw Convention, Art. 26(2). In Art. 18, both 'avarie' and 'dommage' are translated as damage.

41. *Fothergill v. Monarch Airlines,* [1981] A.C. 251 (H.L.)(Green, International Law Through the Cases (1978) p. 602 reproduces the Queen's Bench judgment which was affirmed on appeal but reversed by the House of Lords).

§232 If the injury or loss suffered by the passenger is the result of the carelessness or recklessness of the carrier or his servants or agents, the limitations of the Convention do not apply and full compensation becomes available.[42]

42. Art. 35 as amended: "The limits of liability specified in Art. 22 shall not apply if it is proved that the damage resulted from an act or omission of the carrier, his servants or agents, done with intent to cause damage or recklessly and with knowledge that damage would probably result . . .". See *Goldman v. Thai Airways Int. Ltd.* (1981), 125 Solicitor's Journal 413 (pilot failed to follow precautions laid down in his manual respecting clear air turbulence and did not instruct passengers to fasten seatbelts. The notice on the seat back was only a recommendation and failure to follow it did not amount to contributory negligence. Reversed on appeal, holding pilot's failure did not amount to 'recklessness,' [1983] 1 W.L.R. 1186 *(sub nom. Goldman v. Thai International)*(C.A.); *Swiss Bank Corp. v. Air Can.* (1981), 129 D.L.R. (3d) 85 (Fed. T.D.). In *Khan v. Fredson Travel Inc.* (No. 2)(1982), 36 O.R. 17 (Ont. H.C.) an action was brought arising from the hijack of a Pakistan International Airlines plane, it being alleged that there was negligence in the security arrangements at Karachi Airport. Steele J. held that liability under the Warsaw Convention 1924 (137 L.N.T.S. 11) in respect of a government's breach within its own territory could not be charged by a private individual, but only by another party to the Convention.

Magdelénat, "La réclamation canadienne pour les victimes du vol KAL 007", (1984) 22 C.Y.B.I.L. 312.

§233 In recent years a number of passengers have suffered injury as a result of terrorist activities directed against aircraft. Some of these attacks have occurred while the aircraft was still on the ground and insurance companies have alleged that at the time in question the passengers were not embarking or disembarking as required by the Convention.[43] If the passengers are attacked while awaiting processing they are understood to be in the course of embarkation and the carrier is liable.[44]

43. Art. 17: "The carrier is liable for damage sustained in the event of the death or wounding of a passenger or any other bodily injury suffered by a passenger, if the accident which caused the damage so sustained took place on board the aircraft or in the course of any of the operations of embarking or disembarking." By Art. 18 liability with respect to damage to baggage lasts so long as the baggage is in the care of the carrier.

44. *Day v. Trans World Airlines Inc.* (1975), 393 F. Supp. 217 (U.S. Dist. Ct.); affirmed (1975), 528 F. 2d 31.

§234 When terrorist acts directed against aircraft have occurred, insurance companies have frequently contended that there is no liability on the basis that the act fell within the war exception clause. It has been held, however, that if the group responsible for the damage has not been recognised by the government of the forum as a state or a belligerent, or acting on behalf of an authority so recognized, the act in question would be a criminal act and outside the scope of the exception.[45] Similarly if it is a state organ which is responsible for the destruction of an aircraft, the act will only fall within the war exception clause if it results "from systematic armed aggression accomplished by the aggressor with the intent to wage war."[46]

45. *Pan American World Airways Inc. v. Aetna Casualty & Surety Co.* (1974), 505 F. 2d 989.

46. *Borysoglebski v. Continental Insurance Co.* (1974), (1975) 14 I.L.M. 78 (U.S. Dist. Ct.) (Lybian passenger aircraft shot down over Israel-occupied air space east of Cairo at a time when no active hostilities were in operation between Israel and Egypt, while none had ever taken place between Israel and Lybia).

§235 In addition to problems relating to international air traffic, developments concerning outer space have also given rise to legal problems. While it is recognised that the territorial state enjoys sovereignty over its air space[47] which can only be traversed with its consent, a principle of customary law seems to have developed whereby states do not protest at the passage of orbiting satellites above their territory. They are, however, entitled to object if the satellite is used for espionage.[48]

47. See §224.

48. In 1962 the Soviet Union shot down an American U-2 aircraft engaged in espionage over its territory.

§236 According to the Treaty on Principles Governing the Activities of States in the Exploration and Use of Outer Space including the Moon and Other Celestial Bodies,[49] outer space, the moon and other celestial bodies cannot be subjected to any state's sovereignty and any activities relating to outer space must be conducted in the interest of the maintenance of international peace and security and used only for peaceful purposes. Moreover,[50] "The exploration and use of outer space, including the moon and other celestial bodies, shall be carried out for the benefit and in the interests of all countries, irrespective of their degree of economic or scientific development, and shall be the province of all mankind. There shall be freedom of scientific investigation in outer space, including the moon and other celestial bodies, and States shall facilitate and encourage international cooperation in such investigation." Further, states which are parties to the Treaty "bear international responsibility for national activities in outer space"[51] and by the Convention on International Liability for Damage caused by Space Objects[52] "a launching State shall be absolutely liable to pay compensation for damage caused by its space object on the surface of the earth or to aircraft in flight."[53]

49. 1967, 610 U.N.T.S. 205 — ratified by Canada 1967.

50. Art. 1.

51. Art. 6.

52. 1972, 10 I.L.M. 965, Art. 2 — this is the text of the Draft which was adopted by the General Assembly in 1971, Res. 2777 (XXVI). Canada abstained from voting on this Resolution, but ratified the Treaty in 1975.

53. The Convention provides for diplomatic settlement of a claim, suit in the courts of the launching state or by way of a Claims Commission. In 1978 debris from Soviet Cosmos 954 fell on Canada and the Canadian claim for the consequential damage was pursued through diplomatic channels (the relevant diplomatic documents are reproduced in 18 I.L.M. 899-930), with a final settlement in accordance with the terms of a Protocol between the two countries signed in Moscow in April 1981 (20 I.L.M. 689). The original Canadian claim was for $6,041,174.70, but the settlement was for $3 million. See §170.

IV Objects of International Law

1. TERRITORY AND LAND FRONTIERS

§237 Sovereignty and the rights attaching thereto stem from the possession of territory, which may be either land or water.[1]

1. See §§258-281 re maritime frontiers.

§238 Territory may be acquired either by original or derivative title. Original title arises when the state claiming the title acquires territory which has not formerly been under the sovereignty of any other recognized entity. In earlier times the most obvious method of acquiring original title was by discovery and it was contended that territory was unoccupied, and so terra nullius,[2] so long as no existing recognized state exercised authority over it.[3] It did not matter that the territory in question was already inhabited by an aboriginal people, unless the native inhabitants enjoyed a sufficiently organized form of administration to contend that they in fact possessed a government whose rights had to be recognized.[4]

2. Land belonging to no one.

3. In practice this was understood to mean recognized Christian states. In his Bull inter caetera, 1493 (1 Davenport, European Treaties bearing on the History of the United States and its Dependencies (1917), p. 75), Pope Alexander VI divided the 'undiscovered' western world between Spain and Portugal. This grant was not recognized by such states as England and France, but it formed part of the basis for Spanish claims in Latin America, and has occasionally been put forward by Latin American countries, including Argentina in respect of both the Falklands and Antarctica.

4. See, e.g., *Western Sahara,* [1975] I.C.J. 4 at 39: ". . . the State practice of the [late nineteenth century] indicates that territories inhabited by tribes or peoples having a social and political organization were not regarded as terrae nullius. It shows that in the case of such territories the acquisition of sovereignty was not generally considered as effected unilaterally through 'occupation' of terra nullius by original title but through agreements concluded with local rulers. . . . [S]uch agreements with local rulers, whether or not considered as an actual 'cession' of territory, were regarded as derivative roots of title, and not original titles obtained by occupation of terrae nullius." England did not assume sovereignty over the territory of the native princes of India, chieftains in Africa or sultans in Malaya. Instead, England entered into treaties with these rulers establishing protectorates (see §68) and continuing to treat the rulers as independent sovereigns: see *Mighell v. Sultan of Johore*, [1894] 1 Q.B. 149 (C.A.). See Lindley, The Acquisition and Government of Backward Territory in International Law (1926). See also, Green and Dickason, The Law of Nations and the Old World, 1988.

239

§239 Once sovereignty has been established in this way it can only be destroyed by another recognized sovereign or if the occupant abandons it with intent to give up that sovereignty.[5] If the power exercising sovereignty is overthrown or expelled by indigenous inhabitants who are not themselves recognized as possessing statehood, such overthrow does not effect extinction of the sovereignty in question.[6]

5. See, e.g., *Legal Status of Eastern Greenland* (Denmark/Norway) (1933), 3 W.C.R. 151 at 172: "As regards voluntary abandonment, there is nothing to show any definite renunciation on the part of the kings of Norway or Denmark." As to Argentina's allegations of 'voluntary abandonment' of the Falklands by Great Britain, see Green, "The Falklands, the War and the Law", (1984) 38 Y.B.W.A. 89.

6. *Legal Status of Eastern Greenland, ante,* at pp. 171-2: "The word 'conquest' is not an appropriate phrase, even if it is assumed that it was fighting with the Eskimos which led to the downfall of the settlements. Conquest only operates as a cause of loss of sovereignty when there is a war between two States and by reason of the defeat of one of them sovereignty over territory passes from the loser to the victorious State. The principle does not apply where a settlement has been established in a distant country and its inhabitants are massacred by the aboriginal population".

§240 Discovery alone is not a ground for title, even though the discoverers may have left some sign behind, such as a plaque or a flag,[7] unless there is also some continuing evidence of subjection of the territory in question to the authority of the discoverer. Such evidence may be in the form of constant assertions and advertisement of the title, accompanied by protests when aliens have attempted to settle or visit without permission, or similar manifestations even though there be no actual settlement.[8] Discovery is, in fact, an inchoate title until it is perfected by some evidence of effective administration, but it is good against any state putting forward a later title based on an alleged discovery or some other contention such as propinquity, proximity[9] or necessary hinterland.[10]

7. See Keller *et al.*: Creation of Rights of Sovereignty through Symbolic Acts, 1400-1800 (1967).

8. *Clipperton Island* (France/Mexico) (1931), 2 R.I.A.A. 1105. See also Green, "The Falklands, the War and the Law," *ante.*

9. See, *Island of Palmas Case* (Netherlands/U.S.) (1928), 2 R.I.A.A. 829 at 869: "The title of contiguity, understood as a basis of territorial sovereignty has no foundation in international law."

10. *Island of Palmas Case, ante,* at p. 840: ". . . neighbouring states may by convention fix limits to their own sovereignty, even in regions such as the interior of sparsely explored continents where such sovereignty is scarcely manifested, and in this way each may prevent the other from any penetration of its territory. The delimitation of Hinterland may also be mentioned in this connection." In the *Walfish Bay* arbitration between Britain and Germany (1911), 11 R.I.A.A. 265 at 306-7, it was pointed

out that the hinterland doctrine "requires for its application the existence or assertion of political influence over certain territory, or a treaty in which it is concretely formulated".

§241   Occupation in regard to the acquisition of territory does not mean physical presence, although this is, of course, not precluded. What is required is clear manifestation of the intention to administer the area to the exclusion of any other state doing the same. Nor does it require that any settlement should be completely uninterrupted and continuous or even extensive in character, for the "intermittance and discontinuity compatible with the maintenance of the right necessarily differ according as inhabited or uninhabited regions are involved, or regions enclosed within territories in which sovereignty is incontestably displayed or again regions accessible from, for instance, the high seas."[11] Thus, the evidence of the acquisition of sovereignty over, for example, arctic or tundra-covered territory is weaker than that which would be required in a temperate region, and this is even more true if part of the territory consists of sea-ice. In such circumstances it is the reality of the exercise of jurisdiction and the intention so to do that become decisive.[12]

11.   *Island of Palmas Case, ante*, at p. 840.

12.   *R. v. Tootalik E4-321* (1970), 71 W.W.R. 435 at 454 (N.W.T. Terr. Ct.); reversed on other grounds (1970), 74 W.W.R. 740 (N.W.T. C.A.). See also Head, "Canadian Claims to Territorial Sovereignty in the Arctic Regions", (1962-3) 9 McGill L.J. 200; Green, "Canada and Arctic Sovereignty", (1970) 48 Can. Bar Review 740. Smedal, Acquisition of Sovereignty over Polar Areas (1931); Smith, "Sovereignty in the North: The Canadian Aspect of an International Problem", Macdonald, The Arctic Frontier (1966), p. 194. Vanderzwaag and Pharand, "Inuit and the Ice", (1983) 21 C.Y.B.I.L. 53; Boyd, "The Legal Status of the Arctic Sea Ice", (1984) 22 C.Y.B.I.L. 98.

§242   Where the territory in question constitutes a series of islands, whether these constitute an archipelago[13] or not, the evidence of the exercise of sovereignty sufficient to acquire title to the territory will depend on local circumstances,[14] "while the occupation of the principal islands of an archipelago must also be deemed to include the occupation of islets and rocks in the same archipelago, which have not been actually occupied by another State."[15]

13.   See Herman, 'The Modern Concept of the Off-Lying Archipelago in International Law', (1985) 23 C.Y.B.I.L. 172.

14.   In the *Minquiers and Ecrehos* case (France/G.B.), [1953] I.C.J. 47, such facts as the holding of inquests, levying of rates, and building of huts for use by fishermen are held sufficient. In the same case, Judge Basdevant, in an individual opinion, referred to the treaty of 1360 which related to these islands and pointed out the importance of military authority for acquiring title in those days: ". . . this idea involves the

establishment of English military authority in these islands, the possibility of action taken by the King's agents in respect of the inhabitants and, by the same token, the prevention of foreign action in the islands thus occupied. But none of these elements are to be looked for in the case of the Ecrehos and the Minquiers, islets and rocks which are practically uninhabited and most of which are uninhabitable. From a military point of view, for the King of England to hold them, it is not necessary that he should maintain a garrison there; it is sufficient that by reason of his military and naval power he should be in a position to intervene there when he considers it appropriate without being prevented from doing so by the forces of the King of France and that, by the same token, he should be in a position to prevent intervention by these forces. It would seem probable that the King of England, who had established himself in the principal Channel Islands and who remained there by virtue of the naval power available to him, was thus in a position to take such action in respect of the Ecrehos and the Minquiers. . . . [T]he propinquity of these islets in relation to Jersey tends to confirm this probability" (p. 78). See also *Rann of Kutch Arb.* (India/Pakistan) (1968), 50 I.L.R. 2 at 329-87.

15. Individual opinion of Levi Carneiro J., *Minquiers and Ecrehos, ante,* at p. 99.

§243 For sovereignty to result from occupation, the occupation must not be secret,[16] but must be open, peaceful and continuous. In such circumstances title will accrue by acquisitive prescription, even though international law does not prescribe any minimum period for this to occur, and is an application of the maxim quieta non movere.[17] It is clear, however, that jurisdiction must have been displayed "long enough to enable any Power who might have considered herself as possessing sovereignty over the island, or having a claim to sovereignty, to have, according to local conditions, a reasonable possibility for ascertaining the existence of a state of things contrary to her real or alleged rights."[18]

16. A "clandestine exercise of state sovereignty over an inhabited territory during a considerable length of time would seem to be impossible", *Island of Palmas Case, ante,* at p. 868.

17. "It is a well established principle in the law of nations that every effort should be made to avoid modifying a state of affairs which has existed over a long period of time," *Grisbadarna* (Norway/Sweden) (1909), P.C.A. 11 R.I.A.A. 147 at 161.

18. *Island of Palmas Case, ante,* at p. 867 and 868.

§244 In the event of a dispute based on a title depending on the display of state authority and one based on discovery, the issue would be resolved in accordance with the comment of Judge Huber in the *Island of Palmas Case*:[19] An "inchoate title based on display of State authority, would ... prevail over an inchoate title derived from discovery, especially if this latter title had been left for a very long time without completion by occupation; and it would equally prevail over any claim which, in equity, might be deduced from the notion of contiguity. International law, like law in general, has the object of assuring the

coexistence of different interests which are worthy of legal protection. If
... only one of two conflicting interests is to prevail, because sovereignty
can be attributed to but one of the Parties,[20] the interest which involves
the maintenance of a state of things having offered at the critical time to
the inhabitants of the disputed territory and to other States a certain
guarantee for the respect of their rights ought, in doubt, to prevail over
an interest which — supposing it to be recognized in international law —
has not yet received any concrete form of development".

19. *Island of Palmas Case, ante*, at p. 870.

20. It is possible that two states may agree to share sovereignty by way of a
condominium, as was the case with the Anglo-Egyptian Sudan or the New Hebrides
jointly ruled by England and France.

§245 While attempts have been made by individual discoverers to
occupy terra nullius and assert sovereignty over it, this has not been
generally recognized by existing states, at least so long as the de facto
'sovereign' remains a subject of his national state.[21] However, if the
individual or corporation claiming sovereignty renounces his or its
original loyalty and is recognized as a separate state by others, then
sovereignty may be acquired in this way. Normally, however, it is only
when the individual or corporation acts in the name or on behalf of the
national state that sovereignty is acquired in this way, and it is then
acquired for the state. This, in fact, is the manner in which title was
acquired through the treaties or other activities of such trading companies as the Hudson Bay Company[22] or the Dutch[23] or British East
India Companies.[24]

21. It was only in the case of Sir James Brooke, to whom the Sultan of Borneo
granted the government of Sarawak in 1842, that anything approaching this situation
occurred, and Sarawak became a British protectorate in 1888; see 2 Smith, Great
Britain and the Law of Nations, (1935), pp. 83-96.

22. See Lindley, The Acquisition and Government of Backward Territory in International Law (1926), pp. 95-6; Castel, International Law Chiefly as Interpreted and
Applied in Canada (1976), p. 46n.

23. *Island of Palmas Case, ante*, at pp. 858-9: "The acts of the East India Co., in
view of occupying or colonizing the regions in issue in the present affair must, in
international law, be entirely assimilated to acts of the Netherlands State itself. From
the end of the 16th till the 19th century, companies formed by individuals and
engaged in economic pursuits (Chartered Companies), were invested by the State to
whom they were subject with public powers for the acquisition and administration of
colonies. The Dutch East India Co. is one of the best known. Article V of the Treaty of
Münster [1648, 1 C.T.S. 70] and consequently also the Treaty of Utrecht [1714, 29
C.T.S. 99] clearly show that the East and West India Companies were entitled to
create situations recognized by international law; ... The conclusion of conventions,
even of a political nature, was by Article XXXV of the Charter of 1602, within the

powers of the Company. It is a question for decision in each individual case whether a contract concluded by the Company falls within the range of simple economic transactions or is of a political and public administrative nature. As regards *contracts between a State* or a Company such as the Dutch East India Company and *native princes or chiefs of peoples* not recognized as members of the community of nations, they are not, in the international law sense, treaties or conventions capable of creating rights and obligations such as may, in international law, arise out of treaties. But, on the other hand, contracts of this nature are not wholly void of indirect effects on situations governed by international law; if they do not constitute titles in international law, they are none the less facts of which the law must in certain circumstances take account. From the time of the discoveries until recent times, colonial territory has very often been acquired, especially in the East Indies, by means of contracts with the native authorities, which contracts leave the existing organization more or less intact as regards the native population, whilst granting to the colonizing Power, besides economic advantages such as monopolies or navigation and commercial privileges, also the exclusive direction of relations with other Powers [see *Mighell v. Sultan of Johore*, [1894] 1 Q.B. 149 (C.A.), and *Duff Development Co. v. Kelantan*, [1924] A.C. 797 (H.L.)] and the right to exercise public authority in regard to their own nationals and to foreigners. The form of the legal relations created by such contracts is most generally that of suzerain and vassal, or of the so-called colonial protectorate [see §68]. In substance, it is not an agreement between equals; it is rather a form of internal organization of a colonial territory, on the basis of autonomy for the natives. In order to regularize the situation as regards other States, this organization requires to be completed by the establishment of powers to ensure the fulfilment of the obligations imposed by international law on every State in regard to its own territory. And thus suzerainty over the native State becomes the basis of territorial sovereignty as towards other members of the community of nations. It is the sum-total of functions allotted either to the native authorities or to those of the colonial Power which decides the question whether at any certain period the conditions required for the existence of sovereignty are fulfilled. It is a question to be decided in each case whether such a régime is to be considered as effective or whether it is essentially fictitious, either for the whole or a part of the territory. There always remains reserved the question whether the establishment of such a system is not forbidden by the pre-existing rights of other States" (italics in original). See Green, "Legal Significance of Treaties Affecting Canada's Indians", (1972) 1 Anglo-Amer. L.R. 119.

24. See *Rann of Kutch Arb., ante.*

§246 New problems have arisen in recent times due to the development of the concept of self-determination as a legal principle. On occasion proposals for decolonization and consequential independence have been challenged by neighbouring states contending that at the time of the original colonization the territory in question was not terra nullius amenable to colonization, but part of the territory of a neighbouring state, or part of a people sufficiently organized for none of the territory in question to be regarded as terra nullius.[25] Each case must be decided on its own merits, in the light of its own history paying proper attention to ethical and social considerations. Thus, in the *Western Sahara* case, the

World Court pointed out[26] that while there may exist "many ties of a racial, linguistic, religious, cultural and economic nature between varying tribes . . . whose peoples dwelt in the . . . region [one cannot ignore] the independence of . . . many of the tribes in relation to one another and, despite some forms of common activity, the absence among them of any common institutions or organs, even of a quite minimal character. Accordingly, the court is unable to find that the information before it provides any basis for considering the . . . tribes which existed in the region to have constituted . . . 'an entity capable of availing itself of obligations incumbent upon [the] Members [of the United Nations]'.[27] . . . The difficulty [is] that [the entity] did not have the character of a personality or corporate entity distinct from the several . . . tribes which composed it." As a result the court was of the opinion that there were insufficient 'legal ties' between the tribes in the territory in question and the neighbouring nation to constitute a single sovereign entity, and this is unaffected by similarities of customs or 'geographic overlappings' of nomadic movement. Such statements are of significance in assessing, for example, the legal status of the Inuit or Indian groups in Canada.

25. *Western Sahara*, [1975] I.C.J. 4.
26. *Western Sahara, ante*, at p. 63.
27. *Reparation for Injuries Suffered in the Service of the U.N.*, [1949] I.C.J. 174.

§247 Despite the modern pressure for self-determination, it is generally agreed that this right does not involve the dismemberment of an existing state.[28] When non-self-governing territories acquire their independence, they do so within the territorial limits of the former ruler, in accordance with the uti possidetis principle. This matter was considered by the International Court of Justice in the *Frontier Dispute* between Burkina Faso and the Republic of Mali:[29] "The territorial boundaries which have to be respected may derive from international frontiers which previously divided a colony of one State from a colony of another, or indeed a colonial territory from the territory of an independent State, or one which was under protectorate, but has retained its international personality. There is no doubt that the obligation to respect pre-existing international frontiers in the event of a State succession derives from a general rule of international law, whether or not the rule is expressed in the formula uti possidetis. Hence the numerous solemn affirmations of the intangibility of the frontiers existing at the time of the independence of African States, whether made by senior African statesmen or by organs of the Organization of African Unity itself, are declaratory rather than constitutive: they recognize and confirm an existing principle, and do not seek to consecrate a new principle or the extension to Africa of a rule previously applied only in another continent.[30] However, it may be wondered how the time-hallowed principle has been able to withstand the new approaches of international law as expressed in Africa, where the successive attainment of independence and the emergence of new States has been accompanied by a certain questioning of traditional international law. At first sight this principle conflicts outright with . . . the right of peoples to self-determination. In fact, however, the maintenance of the territorial status quo in Africa is often seen as the wisest course, to preserve what has been achieved by peoples who have struggled for their independence, and to avoid a disruption which would deprive the continent of the gains achieved by much sacrifice. The essential requirement of stability in order to survive, to develop and gradually to consolidate their independence in all fields, has induced African States judiciously to consent to the respecting of colonial frontiers, and to take account of it in the interpretation of the principle of self-determination of peoples. Thus the principle of uti possidetis has kept its place among the most important legal principles, despite the apparent contradiction which explained its coexistence alongside the new norms."

28. See §223.

29. *Frontier Dispute* (Burkina Faso/Mali), [1986] I.C.J. 554 at 566-567.

30. The principle is usually considered to be peculiar to Latin America, see Cukwurah, The Settlement of Boundary Disputes in International Law, 1967, 112-116, 190-199.

§248 Apart from discovery accompanied by occupation, or occupation alone, original title to territory may also be acquired by natural causes. This occurs, for example, when the sea deposits subsoil on the coastal region extending the territory which is already under sovereignty. In such a case there is unlikely to be any problem as to sovereignty over the territory. Problems may, however, arise when the accretion results from the movements of a boundary river[31] shifting soil from one bank to the other,[32] with the international boundary following the new *thalweg*, that is to say the centre of the main channel of the river. When, however, avulsion occurs, that is to say the river leaves its former bed and seeks a new channel, the old boundary remains.[33]

31. A river forming the frontier between two states.

32. See *The Anna* (1805), 5 C. Rob. 373, 385c, re 'islands' and mud flats formed by debris brought down by the river; *Clarke v. Edmonton*, [1930] S.C.R. 137 (S.C.C.), per Lamont J.: ". . . The term 'accretion' denotes the increase which land bordering on a river or on the sea undergoes through the silting up of soil, sand or other substance, or the permanent retiral of the waters. This increase must be formed by a process so slow

and gradual as to be, in a practical sense, imperceptible, by which is meant that the addition cannot be observed in its actual progress from moment to moment or from hour to hour, although, after a certain period, it can be observed that there has been a fresh addition to the shore line. The increase must also result from the action of the water in the ordinary course of the operations of nature and not from some unusual or unnatural action by which a considerable quantity of soil is suddenly swept from the land of one man and deposited on, or annexed to, the land of another. . . . The test . . . is . . . whether, taking into consideration all the incidents contributing to the addition, it properly comes within what is known to the Roman law as 'alluvion' [Inst. 1, 2, t. 1, s. 20], which implies a gradual increment imperceptibly deposited, as distinguished from 'avulsion', which implies a sudden and visible removal of a quantity of soil from one man's land to that of another, which may be followed and identified, or of the sudden alteration of the river's channel."

33. See Vattel, Le Droit des Gens (1758), Liv. II, ch. XXII, ss. 267-9 (Carnegie tr., 1916, 104-5);*Nebraska v. Iowa* (1892), 143 U.S. 359 at 368: "It is settled law that when grants of land border on running water, and the banks are changed by that gradual process known as 'accretion', the riparian owner's boundary line still remains the stream, although, during the years, by this accretion, the actual area of his possession may vary. . . . It is equally settled that where a stream, which is a boundary, from any cause suddenly abandons its old and seeks a new bed, such change of channel works no change of boundary; and that the boundary remains as it was, in the center of the old channel, although no water may be flowing therein. This sudden and rapid change of channel is termed, in the law, 'avulsion'." In the *Chamizal Arbitration* (1911), 11 R.I.A.A. 316 at 320, which depended on the interpretation of treaties between the U.S. and Mexico, the tribunal pointed out that "[i]t is conceded on both sides that . . . according to well-known principles of international law this fluvial boundary would continue, notwithstanding modification of the course of the river caused by gradual accretion on the one bank or degradation on the other bank; whereas if the river deserted its original bed and forced for itself a new channel in another direction the boundary would remain in the middle of the deserted river bed".

§249 Territory may be acquired by derivative as well as original title. That is to say, the territory in question has already been subjected to the sovereignty of another state. Perhaps the oldest form of derivative title was that based on conquest. However, it is now well established that conquest requires the sanctification of recognition[34] if it is to be creative of title, and it is also now accepted that conquest cannot form the basis of title so long as hostilities continue.[35] Moreover, since the adoption of the Charter of the United Nations with its obligation to renounce force[36] and to settle disputes pacifically,[37] it is no longer possible to claim title through occupatio bellica.[38] However, if as a result of hostilities one of the belligerents ceases to exist as a state, its title to territory is extinguished by debellatio,[39] but it is not acquired by the victor unless other states recognize the latter's claim. Insofar as title derived from conquest, this was only true so long as the conqueror was itself a recognized state, so that 'conquest' by aboriginal inhabitants of a territory would not destroy the recognized sovereign's title over that territory or confer any rights in the aboriginal conquerors.[40]

34. See §§91-109.

35. This was the case with the German 'annexation' of such occupied territories as Poland during World War II.

36. Art. 2(4); see also Pact of Paris (Kellogg-Briand), 1928, 94 L.N.T.S. 57.

37. Art. 2(3).

38. Thus Israel is not able to claim legal title to Jerusalem or any of the territories 'occupied' as a result of its various wars, regardless of Israeli claims to have annexed any of these.

39. Extinction by act of war, as was the case with Germany after its unconditional surrender (1 Schwarzenberger, International Law (1957), pp. 297-8), although the victors expressly refused to acquire title to German territory, see *R. v. Bottrill; Ex parte Kuechenmeister*, [1947] K.B. 41 (C.A.).

40. *Legal Status of Eastern Greenland* (Denmark/Norway) (1933), 3 W.C.R. 151. See text to §239 note 6.

§250 The most common form of acquiring derivative title to territory is by cession, when one sovereign concedes title to all or part of its territory to another. This may be effected in a variety of ways. It may result from a peace treaty when the defeated state is required to surrender part of its formerly held territory, as was the case with Germany[41] and the Austro-Hungarian Empire[42] after the First World War, or Japan[43] or Italy[44] after the Second. It may also be the consequence of a grant of independence by a ruler to a formerly non-self-governing territory, as happened with, for example, the British colonies after 1947.[45] Or it may be the consequence of a treaty recognizing the right of a minority population to join a neighbouring territory whose inhabitants possess the same ethnic background.[46] In some cases, where the two states concerned are in dispute, the title may be settled by arbitration.[47] Occasionally, states may agree to the cession of a territory which is in dispute without any need to resort to arbitration.[48]

41. Treaty of Versailles, 1919, 112 B.F.S.P. 1.

42. Treaty of St. Germain, 1919, 112 B.F.S.P. 514; Treaty of Trianon, 1920, 113 B.F.S.P. 486.

43. Treaty of Peace with Japan, 1951, 136 U.N.T.S. 45.

44. Treaty of Peace with Italy, 1947, 49 U.N.T.S. 3, Art. 2; see also *Frontier (Local Authorities) Award* (France/Italy) (1953), 20 I.L.R. 63.

45. In the case of the partition of the Empire of India problems arose re territorial divisions between India and Pakistan; see, *Rann of Kutch Arb., ante*.

46. See, e.g., Treaty of Versailles, Art. 34 re Saar Territory.

47. See *Alaska Boundary* (G.B./U.S.) (1903), 15 R.I.A.A. 481; *Sovereignty over Certain Frontier Land* (Belgium/Netherlands), [1959] I.C.J. 209.

48. This seems to have been the purpose of negotiations between the U.K. and Spain re Gibraltar, and prior to the armed conflict of 1982, between the U.K. and Argentina re the Falklands.

§251 One of the most complex issues relating to title to territory concerns the location of boundaries. In many cases, frontier lines have grown up by custom and long usage and are often based on geographic features, such as a watercourse[49] or the summit of a mountain ridge,[50] although frequently this will itself give rise to disputes as to where the exact geographic line runs,[51] or because a state maintains that its proper frontier should be what it describes as the natural or geographic frontier[52] which coincides with its conception of defence needs.[53]

49. See *Island of Timor Case* (Netherlands/Portugal) (1914), 11 R.I.A.A. 481 at 508.

50. This was the case with the McMahon Line demarcating the Indo-Tibetan frontier.

51. See the Indo-Chinese border dispute: Green, "Legal Aspects of the Sino-Indian Border Dispute", (1960) 1 The China Quarterly 42.

52. In the *Gulf of Maine Case* (Canada/U.S.), [1984] I.C.J. 246 the court said (at 277): "It must be emphasized that a delimitation, whether of a maritime or of a land boundary, is a legal-political operation, and that it is not the case that where a natural boundary is discernible, the political delimitation necessarily has to follow the same line."

53. This is one of the arguments put forward by Israel re the Golan Heights and the West Bank of the Jordan.

§252 States will often put forward maps to indicate where the boundary they claim is alleged to run. In such cases, maps prepared by neutral cartographers or those presented by the party contesting the claim are of greater validity than those prepared on behalf of the claimant.[54] However, maps are only evidence and "do not constitute a sufficiently important contribution to enable a decision to be based on them."[55] For this reason, errors in the names of places are not binding if it is clear that the parties had some other name or place in mind.[56] By and large, more important than maps or any other symbol of a frontier, including marker posts, is the attitude of the states concerned as evidenced by their activities. Thus, acknowledgement of the national flag[57] or request for permission to enter, especially if persisted in over a period of time,[58] will be taken as evidence of acquiescence in the existence of a border.

54. *Case Concerning the Temple of Preah Vihear (Merits)* (Cambodia/Thailand), [1962] I.C.J. 6 at 22-4, 26-7, 29; *Frontier Dispute* (Burkina Faso/Mali), [1986] I.C.J. 554 at 582-583; *Re Labrador Boundary*, [1927] 2 D.L.R. 401 at 428 (P.C.).

55. *Minquiers and Ecrehos Case* (France/G.B.), [1953] I.C.J. 47: see opinion of Judge Levy Carneiro at p. 105.

56. *Island of Palmas Case, ante,* at pp. 844-845, 853, 854; *Island of Timor Case, ante,* at p. 507: *falsa demonstratio non nocet.*

57. *Temple of Preah Vihear, ante,* at p. 30.

58. In the *Case Concerning the Arbitral Award by the King of Spain in 1906,* [1960] I.C.J. 192 at 213, it was held that Nicaragua's recognition of the award in favour of Honduras "by express declaration and by conduct" amounted to recognition of the validity of the award and could not be retracted from.

§253 States often attempt to settle their boundaries by treaty using specific geographic reference points or descriptive remarks concerning, for example, the main course of a river[59] or its mouth. In many cases disputes arise as to the exact geographic meaning of such references and these differences have to be settled by arbitration.[60]

59. *Argentine-Chile Frontier Case* (1966), 38 I.L.R. 10 at 93, complicated since the same name was given by each country to a different channel. The court stated that it is a "general principle that where an instrument (for example, a treaty or an award) has laid down that a boundary must follow a river, and that river divides into two or more channels, and nothing is specified in that instrument as to which channel the boundary shall follow, the boundary must normally follow the major channel. The question which is the major channel is a geographic question . . .", and in deciding which was the 'major channel' the court referred to both historical and scientific facts.

60. See, e.g., *St. Croix River Arbitration* between the U.S. and Canada (1798), 1 & 2 Moore, International Adjudications (Modern Series). For a general discussion of Canada's land frontiers see Castel, International Law, pp. 217-31; 1987, pp. 374-388.

§254 In a federal state, disputes over boundaries frequently arise and these are often settled in accordance with the rules which would apply in international cases and this was the basis on which the Privy Council relied in determining the meaning of the 'coast' in the *Labrador Boundary* case.[61]

61. *Re Labrador Boundary, ante.*

§255 Sometimes it is important from the point of view of a private individual to know exactly where a land frontier runs for his claims to, for example, compensation for nationalization may depend thereon. Here again, the issue will ultimately depend upon judicial interpretation of the factual situation.[62]

62. See, e.g., *Silberg and Mogilanski Claims* (U.S.) (1961), 3 Whitemann 278-283 (Foreign Claims Settlement Comm.), which referred to the changes in the Polish-Russian frontier consequent upon the acceptance at the Yalta Conference, 1945, of the Curzon Line, so that Poland no longer enjoyed sovereignty over territory east of the Line and could not nationalize it or be held liable for compensation.

§256   Title to territory is lost by cession, conquest[63] or abandonment, so long as it is clear that it was the intention of the reputed sovereign to abandon title.[64] However, it may happen that though a treaty purports to cede territory a judicial body holds that by the constitution, whether written or unwritten, such a treaty cannot be ratified without prior legislative approval or amendment of the constitution.[65]

> 63.   See §239 note 6. Peace Treaties also frequently involve abandonment of title; see Japanese Peace Treaty, 1951, 136 U.N.T.S. 45, Art. 2, for Japan's abandonment of title over Formosa (Taiwan), although sovereignty over the island was not transferred to any other authority: see Green, "Representation versus Membership: The Chinese Precedent in the United Nations" (1972), 10 C.Y.B.I.L. 102, at 128-30, where the Canadian attitude is discussed.
>
> 64.   See §239 note 5.
>
> 65.   *Kazi Mukhlesur Rahman v. Bangladesh* (1974), 70 I.L.R. 36 (Bangladesh C.A.) in which the court held that, at least in Commonwealth countries, this is now generally accepted, as it is in the Vienna Convention on Treaties, 1969, 8 I.L.M. 679, Art. 46.

§257   There is now a new development in international law. By treaty the acquisition of title to some territories at present regarded as terrae nullius has been forbidden, at least for the parties to the treaty. This is the position with regard to Antarctica, where existing claims have been frozen.[66]

> 66.   Antarctica Treaty, 1959, 402 U.N.T.S. 71, Art. 4. A similar ban on the acquisition of title applies to the moon and other celestial bodies in outer space: Treaty on Principles Governing the Activities of States in the Exploration and Use of Outer Space, Including the Moon and Other Celestial Bodies, 1967, 6 I.L.M. 386, Art. 2.

2. MARITIME FRONTIERS AND THE HIGH SEAS

§258   It is accepted in international law that a state bordering the sea is entitled to exercise its sovereignty over a limited area of the sea which is regarded as part of the littoral state's territory.[67] In classical times[68] the extent of this sea was measured by the range of coastal guns,[69] which in state practice came to be fixed at three miles.[70] However, a number of states have claimed up to twelve miles, which is the distance claimed by Canada under the Territorial Sea and Fishing Zones Act.[71] By the 1982 United Nations Convention on the Law of the Sea[72] this is the maximum permitted.

> 67.   *Anglo-Norwegian Fisheries Case,* [1951] I.C.J. 116 at 133: "It is the land which confers upon the coastal State a right to the waters off its coasts." In his dissent (at p. 160) Judge McNair said: "To every State whose land territory is at any place washed by the sea, international law attaches a corresponding portion of maritime territory

consisting of what the law calls territorial waters. . . . No State can refuse them. . . . The possession of this territory is not dependent upon the will of the State, but compulsory."

68. This signifies the 'classical' writers of international law, particularly those of the seventeenth and eighteenth centuries.

69. Potestatem terrae finitur ubi finitur armorum vis, Bynkershoek, De Dominio Maris (1702), ch. 2, (Carnegie tr. 44). In The Sovereignty of the Sea (1911), Fulton quotes (at p. 156) a Dutch diplomatic note addressed to English Commissioners dated 1610: "For that it is by the lawe of nacions, no prince can Challenge further into the Sea than he can comñand with a Cannon except Gulfes within their Land from one point to an other."

70. See Walker, "Territorial Waters: The Cannon Shot Rule", (1945) 22 B.Y.B.I.L. 210. See also *The Grace* (1894), 4 Ex. C.R. 283 at 289 (Ex. Ct.) per McDougall L.J.: "Upon the ocean the law of nations recognizes the limit of three marine miles from the shore as the only portion of the ocean in respect of which a state can claim to exercise territorial rights." The decision whether a particular piece of water lies within the territorial sea depends upon national claims: see *Mortensen v. Peters* (Scotland) (1906), 8 F. 93; *The Fagernes*, [1927] P. 311 (C.A.); *Ref. Re Offshore Mineral Rights (B.C.)*, [1967] S.C.R. 792 (S.C.C.). See Warbrick, "The Boundary Between England and Scotland in the Solway Firth", (1980) 51 B.Y.B.I.L. 163. *Ref. re Continental Shelf Offshore Nfld.*, [1984] 1 S.C.R. 86 (S.C.C.). In *R. v. Farnquist* (1980), 54 C.C.C. (2d) 417 (Ont. Prov. Ct.) the Provincial Court of Ontario, Criminal Division, held that the Canadian portion of the Great Lakes were inland waters of Canada. In its memo of 29 Apr. 1983 the Legal Bureau stated that "the waters of the Gulf of St. Lawrence are considered by the Government of Canada to be historic Canadian waters", (1984) 22 C.Y.B.I.L. 333; Rigaldies, 'Le statut du golfe du Saint-Laurent en droit international public', (1985) 23 C.Y.B.I.L. 80.

71. R.S.C. 1970, c. T-7. The U.S. recognizes only a three-mile limit.

72. 21 I.L.M. 1261, Art. 3. This Treaty, which Canada signed, but the U.K. and U.S. did not, represents the maximum of international agreement. The U.S. is opposed to many of the provisions relating to exploitation of the resources of the seabed and subsoil. G.B. has expressed the same opposition. See Alexandrowicz, "Canadian Approaches to the Seabed Régime", Macdonald *et al.*, Canadian Perspectives on International Law and Organization (1974), p. 410. In the *Jan Mayen Continental Shelf Case* (Iceland/Norway) (1981), 62 I.L.R. 108, the Conciliation Commission held that the 1980 Draft represents current customary law, and recognized Jan Mayen island as possessing a territorial sea, continental shelf and economic zone. See also *Continental Shelf Case* (Tunisia/Libya), [1982] I.C.J. 18 at 38; and the *Gulf of Maine Case* (Canada/U.S.), [1984] I.C.J. 246 at 294.

§259 Although it was accepted that states could exercise their sovereignty and their jurisdiction within the territorial sea, it was understood that this jurisdiction did not apply to warships which may only be present with the consent of the territorial state,[73] nor will it extend to other state-owned vessels,[74] although there is now a tendency to deny such immunity if the state-owned ship is engaged in normal commercial activities.[75] Similarly, a ship driven to take refuge in a foreign port or territorial waters by stress of weather or overriding necessity is also outside local jurisdiction.[76]

73.   *The Schooner Exchange v. M'Faddon* (1812), 7 Cranch 116.

74.   *The Parlement Belge* (1880), L.R. 5 P.D. 197.

75.   See §§159-162. See also State Immunity Act, S.C. 1980-81, c. 95.

76.   *The Eleanor* (1809), Edw. 135. See also, *The May v. R.*, [1931] S.C.R. 374 at 382 (S.C.C.) per Lamont J.: ". . . an entry by a foreign vessel into Canadian waters cannot be justified on the ground of 'stress of weather' unless the weather is such as to produce in the mind of a reasonably competent and skilful master, possessing courage and firmness, a well grounded bona fide apprehension that if he remains outside the territorial waters he will put in jeopardy his vessel and cargo".

§260   In addition to the immunity just referred to, it is a principle of international law that foreign ships enjoy a right of innocent passage through a state's territorial waters. This principle of customary law[77] is confirmed by the 1958 Geneva Convention on the Territorial Sea and Contiguous Zone.[78] "Passage means navigation through the territorial sea for the purpose of either traversing that sea without entering internal waters,[79] or of proceeding to internal waters, or of making for the high seas from internal waters. [It] includes stopping and anchoring, but only insofar as the same are incidental to ordinary navigation or are rendered necessary by force majeure or by distress."[80] Passage is innocent so long as it is not prejudicial to the peace, good order or security of the coastal state, and in the case of a fishing vessel its passage is only innocent so long as it observes any laws made by the coastal state to prevent its fishing within territorial waters.[81] Ships exercising the right of innocent passage must comply with the coastal state's regulations relating to transport and navigation,[82] while the coastal state must give publicity to any danger to navigation of which it has knowledge.[83]

77.   *The D.C. Whitney v. St. Clair Navigation Co.* (1907), 38 S.C.R. 303 at 311 (S.C.C.) per Davies J.: ". . . jurisdiction does not exist against a ship passing along the coast in the exercise of innocent passage or through channels or arms of the sea which, by international law or special convention, are declared free and open to the ships of her nationality, unless expressly given by statute".

78.   516 U.N.T.S. 205, Art. 14(1): ". . . ships of all States, whether coastal or not, shall enjoy the right of innocent passage through the territorial sea": Canada is not a party to this Convention. See also Convention on the Law of the Sea, 1982, Art. 17. See *Military and Paramilitary Activities in and against Nicaragua* (Nicaragua/U.S.), [1986] I.C.J. 14, 111-112, in which the I.C.J. treated the clauses on innocent passage in the 1982 Convention as declaratory of customary law.

79.   The waters of ports, harbours and roadsteads, as well as internal gulfs and bays — including those regarded as internal by historic title (e.g. Conception Bay: *Direct U.S. Cable Co. v. Anglo-American Telegraph Co.* (1877), 2 App. Cas. 394 (P.C.); *Mowat v. McFee* (1880), 5 S.C.R. 66 (S.C.C.)) — straits, lakes, rivers and internal

canals are all within the territorial sovereignty of the state and under its jurisdiction in the same way as any other territory, although the Kiel Canal has been opened to the shipping of all nations: see *The S.S. Wimbledon* (France, G.B., Italy, Japan/Germany) (1923), 1 W.C.R. 163. By Art. 8 of the 1982 Convention, waters landward of the baseline of the territorial sea form part of the state's inland waters. As to the territorial character of non-historic bays, see 1958 Geneva Convention, Art. 7; 1982 Convention, Art. 10.

80. See *The May, ante.* 1958 Geneva Convention, Art. 14(2), (3); 1982 Convention, Art. 18.

81. 1958 Geneva Convention, Art. 14(4), (5); 1982 Convention, Art. 19 is more detailed in its specification and includes "any activity not having a direct bearing on passage."

82. 1958 Geneva Convention, Art. 17; 1982 Convention, Art. 21(4).

83. 1958 Geneva Convention, Art. 15(2); 1982 Convention, Art. 24(2). See also *Corfu Channel Case* (Merits) (G.B./Albania), [1949] I.C.J. 4.

§261   Traditionally, coastal states have been permitted to exercise a limited jurisdiction for customs purposes and the control of smuggling in an area of the sea contiguous to their territorial waters.[84] In accordance with the 1958 Convention states are authorized to exercise such control within this contiguous zone as may be necessary to prevent infringement of their customs, fiscal, immigration[85] or sanitary regulations and punish any infringements.[86] The contiguous zone may not extend more than twelve miles[87] seaward from the baseline[88] from which the territorial sea itself is measured.

84.   *Fudge v. R.*, [1940] Ex. C.R. 187 (Ex. Ct.). See Fenrick, "Legal Limits on the Use of Force by Canadian Warships Engaged in Law Enforcement", (1980) 18 C.Y.B.I.L. 113. See also re boarding of Danish trawler in British fishing grounds, The Times, Apr. 1, 1983. See also Report of Commission of Enquiry re *The Red Crusader* (U.K./Denmark)(1962), 35 I.L.R. 485.

85.   By Bill C-84, 1987, to deter the smuggling of illegal immigrants Canada seeks power to stop and order the departure from its internal waters, its territorial sea or twelve nautical miles therefrom of any vessel carrying such immigrants, "and any such direction may be enforced by such force as is reasonable in the circumstances", s. 8.

86.   Art. 24; Art. 33(1) of the 1982 Convention.

87.   1982 Convention, Art. 33(2), the contiguous zone may extend to 24 miles from the baseline.

88.   Methods of measuring the baseline vary. If the coast is fairly regular the practice is to make use of the low water mark of the spring tides, and this is the method advocated by Art. 3 of the 1958 Geneva Convention; 1982 Convention, Art. 5. Sometimes a trace parallèle is drawn on navigational charts reproducing the outline of the coast. Occasionally arcs of circles are drawn from the most prominent headlands. When there is a severely indented coast, straight lines may be drawn joining such headlands, so that all waters landward of them become internal. In the *Anglo-Norwegian Fisheries Case*, *ante*, the World Court approved such a method for the

Norwegian coast, approving some very lengthy lines, holding that it was only necessary that they follow the general direction of the coast. See now 1958 Convention, Art. 4; 1982 Convention, Art. 7.

§262   While ships sailing through the territorial sea are immune from local jurisdiction while exercising the right of innocent passage, they become so liable if they disturb the local peace. Thus, the coastal state will exercise jurisdiction in the event of an injury consequential upon a collision within this area,[89] but this jurisdiction does not normally extend to offences committed on board the ship itself.[90] However, states do frequently enact legislation subjecting vessels passing through their territorial waters to any anti-pollution or fishing regulations that may exist.[91]

89.   See *R. v. Keyn (The Franconia)* (1876), L.R. 2 Ex. D. 63; and Territorial Waters Jurisdiction Act 1878, 41 & 42 Vict., c. 73.

90.   By Art. 27 of the 1982 Convention: "(1) The criminal jurisdiction of the coastal State should not be exercised on board a foreign ship passing through the territorial sea to arrest any person or to conduct any investigation in connection with any crime committed on board the ship during its voyage, save only in the following cases: (a) If the consequences of the crime extend to the coastal State; (b) If the crime is of a kind to disturb the peace of the country or the good order of the territorial sea; (c) If the assistance of the local authorities has been requested by the captain of the ship or by a diplomatic agent or consular officer of the flag State; or (d) If such measures are necessary for the suppression of illicit traffic in narcotic drugs or psychotropic substances. (2) The above provisions do not affect the right of the coastal State to take any steps authorised by its laws for the purpose of an arrest or investigation on board a foreign ship passing through the territorial sea after leaving internal waters. . . . (5) Except as provided in Part XII [Protection and Preservation of the Marine Environment] or with respect to violations of laws and regulations adopted in accordance with Part V [Exclusive Economic Zone (see §271)], the coastal State may not take any steps on board a foreign ship passing through the territorial sea to arrest any person or to conduct any investigation in connection with any crime committed before the ship entered the territorial sea, if the ship, proceeding from a foreign port, is only passing through the territorial sea without entering internal waters."

91.   See *The Grace,* (1984), 4 Ex. C.R. 283 (Ex. Ct.).

§263   Canada has enacted a variety of legislative measures concerning its jurisdiction over foreign vessels while in the Canadian territorial sea. Thus by the Criminal Code:[92] "where an offence is committed by a person, whether or not he is a Canadian citizen, on the territorial sea of Canada . . ., whether or not it was committed on board or by means of a Canadian ship, the offence is within the competence of and shall be tried by the court having jurisdiction in respect of similar offences in the territorial division nearest to the place where the offence was committed, and shall be tried in the same manner as if the offence has been committed within that territorial division." By the Oil and Gas Act,[93] the Act and Regulations made thereunder apply to: "those submarine areas not within a province,[94] adjacent to the coast of Canada and extending throughout the natural prolongation of the land territory of Canada to the outer edge of the continental margin or to a distance of 200 nautical miles from the baselines from which the breadth of the territorial sea of Canada is measured,[95] whichever is the greater."

92. R.S.C. 1970, c. C-34, s. 433; *R. v. Farnquist* (1980), 54 C.C.C. (2d) 417 (Ont. Prov. Ct.). See Bill C-84, 1987, §261 note 85.

93. S.C. 1980-81, c. 81, s. 76(*b*).

94. See *Ref. re Offshore Mineral Rights (B.C.)*, [1967] S.C.R. 792 (S.C.C.), in which the Supreme Court upheld Canada's title as against British Columbia's claim to ownership of the territorial sea and continental shelf. In 1984, problems arose when the Newfoundland government forbade offshore winter drilling operations in the absence of what it regarded as adequate safety facilities, while the federal government maintained that such drilling should continue until forbidden by Ottawa on the ground that offshore drilling was solely within federal jurisdiction. The Supreme Court upheld the claims of the federal government, *Ref. re Continental Shelf Offshore Nfld.,* [1984] 1 S.C.R. 86 (S.C.C.); see Herman, "The Newfoundland Offshore Mineral Rights References", (1984) 22 C.Y.B.I.L. 194; see also, Marston, 'The Strait of Georgia Reference', (1985) 23 C.Y.B.I.L. 34.

95. The former Act, Oil and Gas Production and Conservation Act, R.S.C. 1970, c. O-4, s. 3, used as its outer limit the continental shelf, as defined in the Geneva Convention on the Continental Shelf, 1958, 499 U.N.T.S. 311, to which Canada is a party. For a fuller account of the continental shelf, see §§266-270. See Alexandrowicz, "Canadian Approaches to the Seabed Régime", Macdonald *et al.*, Canadian Perspectives on International Law and Organization (1974).

§264 By the Arctic Waters Pollution Prevention Act[96] and the Canada Shipping Act[97] regulations may be promulgated for the prevention of pollution which apply to all shipping in Canadian waters, and it is even provided that "[w]here the Minister has reasonable cause to believe that a ship is in distress, stranded, wrecked, sunk or abandoned is discharging or is likely to discharge a pollutant into any waters to which this Part [XX of the amending Act which is concerned with pollution] applies, he may, or he may authorize any person to, destroy, if necessary, or remove, if possible, and sell or otherwise dispose of the ship, its cargo or other material on board the ship."[98] Similarly, any ship navigating in Canadian waters without being fitted with a proper radio station and not complying with the relevant regulations is guilty of an offence. Regulations of general application may also be made under the Fisheries Act[99] with regard to the method of fishing and amounts of fish that may be taken in Canadian waters.

96. R.S.C. 1970, c. 2 (1st Supp.). See Morin, "Le progrès technique, la pollution et l'evolution récente du droit de la mer au Canada, particulièrement à l'égard de l'Arctique", (1970) 8 C.Y.B.I.L. 158; Pharand, The Law of the Sea of the Arctic (1973).

97. R.S.C. 1970, c. S-9.

98. R.S.C. 1970, c. 27 (2nd Supp.), s. 729(1). See also, Green, "International Law and Canada's Anti-Pollution Legislation", (1971) 50 Oregon Law Review 463. See §§164-173.

99. R.S.C. 1970, c. F-14. See Coastal Fisheries Protection Act, R.S.C. 1970, c. C-21. See also Legault, "Maritime Claims", Macdonald et al., Canadian Perspectives on International Law and Organization (1974).

§265 A coastal state has no jurisdiction over a foreign capital ship in its territorial sea.[1] However, while "the ports of a friendly nation are considered as open to the public ships of all Powers with whom it is at peace, and they are supposed to enter such ports and to remain in them while allowed to remain, under the protection of the Government of the place,"[2] "if any warship does not comply with the regulations of the coastal State concerning passage through the territorial sea and disregards any request for compliance which is made to it, the coastal State may require the warship to leave the territorial sea."[3] In accordance with the 1982 Convention, the flag state will bear responsibility for any damage caused by a warship or other non-commercial government-owned ship due to non-compliance with the coastal state's regulations concerning passage through its territorial sea.[4] Even submarines enjoy a right of innocent passage through the territorial sea, so long as they navigate on the surface and show their flag.[5]

1. The Schooner Exchange v. M'Faddon (1812), 7 Cranch 116; 1982 Convention on the Law of the Sea, Art. 32.

2. The Schooner Exchange v. M'Faddon, ante, at p. 141, per Marshall C.J.

3. Geneva Convention on the Territorial Sea, Art. 23; 1982 Convention, Art. 30.

4. Art. 31.

5. 1958 Geneva Convention, Art. 14(6); 1982 Convention, Art. 20.

§266 Since the end of the Second World War an increasing number of states have claimed sovereignty over the continental shelf adjoining their coast, while some, like Argentina, which lacked a continental shelf, have claimed an area of sea extending 200 miles from the coast. Most maritime states have rejected this latter claim, but the 1958 Geneva Convention on the Continental Shelf[6] recognizes that the coastal state "exercises over the continental shelf sovereign rights for the purpose of exploring it and exploiting its natural resources". Such rights are exclusive so that, even though the coastal state does not itself exercise those rights, no foreign state may do so without the consent of the coastal state. Moreover, the rights of the coastal state exist ipso jure and do not depend upon occupation,[7] proclamation or any overt act by the coastal state. While Canada has made no formal declaration of sovereignty over its continental shelf, the Oil and Gas Production and Conservation Act[8] makes it clear that Canada in fact does exercise its sovereign rights in connection therewith.

6.   499 U.N.T.S. 311, Art. 2(1), (2).

7.   Art. 2(3).

8.   R.S.C. 1970, c. O-4. See also, Alexandrowicz, "Canadian Approaches to the Seabed Régime", Macdonald *et al.*, Canadian Perspectives on International Law and Organization (1974). Jewett, "The Evolution of the Legal Regime of the Continental Shelf", (1984) 24 C.Y.B.I.L. 153.

§267   The 1958 Convention defines the continental shelf[9] as "the seabed and subsoil of the submarine areas adjacent to the coast but outside the area of the territorial sea, to a depth of 200 metres or, beyond that limit, to where the depth of the superjacent waters admits of the exploitation of the natural resources of the said areas [and] the seabed and subsoil of similar submarine areas adjacent to the coasts of islands." The right of exploitation relates to[10] "mineral and other non-living resources of the seabed and subsoil together with living organisms belonging to sedentary species, that is to say, organisms which, at the harvestable stage, either are immobile on or under the seabed or are unable to move except in constant physical contact with the seabed or the subsoil."

9.   Art. 1. For the 1982 definition, see §270. It should be noted that only 55 states are parties to the 1958 Convention, while the 1982 Convention is not yet in force: "the current state of customary law on the question of the outer limit is, therefore, of great legal significance: it governs both the mutual relations of States not parties to the Geneva Convention, and the relations between States not parties and those States which are parties to the Convention. It is also a matter of increasing practical importance as, with technological and economic developments, the search for off-shore oil and gas moves into ever deeper waters", Hutchinson, 'The Seaward Limit to Continental Shelf Jurisdiction in Customary International Law', (1985) 56 B.Y.B.I.L. 111.

10.   Art. 2(4).

§268   The legal status of the superjacent waters over the continental shelf and of the airspace above it is not affected by the coastal state's rights,[11] and in exercising its rights the coastal state must not cause "any unjustifiable interference with navigation, fishing or the conservation of the living resources of the sea, nor . . . with fundamental oceanographic or other scientific research carried out with the intention of open publication."[12] While the continental shelf belongs as of right to the coastal state and the International Court has described it as a "natural prolongation of its land territory into and under the sea,"[13] "where the same continental shelf is adjacent to the territories of two or more States, whose coasts are opposite each other, the boundary of the continental shelf appertaining to such States shall be determined by agreement between them. In the absence of agreement, and unless another boundary line is justified by special circumstances, the boundary is the median line, every point of which is equidistant from the nearest points of the baselines from which the breadth of the territorial sea of each State is measured. Where the same continental shelf is adjacent to the territories of two adjacent States, the boundary of the continental shelf shall be determined by agreement between them. In the absence of agreement, and unless another boundary line is justified by special circumstances,[14] the boundary shall be determined by application of the principle of equidistance from the nearest points of the baselines from which the breadth of the territorial sea of each State is measured."[15] However, the principle of equidistance is not a rule of customary law[16] and when Canada ratified the Convention it issued a declaration to the effect that "the presence of an accidental feature such as a depression or a channel in a submerged area should not be regarded as constituting an interruption in the natural prolongation of the land territory of the coastal state into and under the sea."[17]

11.   Art. 3.

12.   Art. 5(1).

13.   *North Sea Continental Shelf Cases* (Germany/Denmark; Germany/ Netherlands), [1969] I.C.J. 3 at 22.

14.   For a discussion of the 'special circumstances' rule see dissent of Oda J. in *Continental Shelf* (Libyan Arab Jamaharya/Malta), [1985] I.C.J. 123 at 141-163.

15.   Art. 6(1), (2).

16.   *North Sea Continental Shelf Cases, ante*, at pp. 25-27, 41-44. See also Rigaldes "La délimitation du plateau continental entre états voisins," (1976) 14 C.Y.B.I.L. 116; McRae, "Proportionality and the Gulf of Maine Maritime Boundary Dispute", (1981) 19 C.Y.B.I.L. 287. *Gulf of Maine Case* (Canada/U.S.), [1984] I.C.J. 246 at 334-337, and Judge Schwebel's dissent, 354-358. Legault and McRae, "The Gulf of Maine Case", (1984) 22 C.Y.B.I.L. 267. See also, *Continental Shelf* (Libyan Arab Jamaharya/Malta), [1985] I.C.J. 13 at 37-38.

17.   See, U.N., Multilateral Treaties Deposited with the Secretary-General — Status as at 31 Dec. 1982, 25.

§269   The dispute between Canada and the United States over the maritime boundary dividing the continental shelf and fisheries zones of the two countries was referred to the International Court of Justice by way of a special agreement providing for decision by a chamber of five judges.[18] In contrast to this agreement to accept judicial settlement of this dispute, it should be noted that Canada in 1970 added a reservation to its declaration accepting the compulsory jurisdiction of the International Court of Justice in accordance with Article 36 of the Court's Statute,[19] denying jurisdiction in respect of "disputes arising out of or concerning jurisdiction or rights claimed or exercised by Canada in respect of the conservation, management of exploitation of the living resources or control of pollution or contamination of the marine environment in marine areas adjacent to the coast of Canada".[20] This particular reservation was withdrawn in November 1984.[21]

18. Compromise to Submit to Chamber of I.C.J., notified to Court 25 Nov. 1981, General List No. 67. The Order establishing the Special Chamber was issued on 30 Jan. 1982, [1982] I.C.J. 3. The decision in the case is reported at [1984] I.C.J. 246.

19. See §405.

20. I.C.J. Rep. Yearbook 1980-1981, 58. See also Legault, "Maritime Claims", Macdonald et al., Canadian Perspectives on International Law and Organization (1974).

21. See §411.

§270   The definition of the continental shelf has been widened by the 1982 Convention:[22] "The continental shelf of a coastal State comprises the sea-bed and subsoil of the submarine areas that extend beyond its territorial sea throughout the natural prolongation of its land territory to the outer edge of the continental margin, or to a distance of 200 nautical miles from the baselines from which the breadth of the territorial sea is measured where the outer edge of the continental margin does not extend to that distance. . . . The continental margin comprises the submerged prolongation of the land mass of the coastal State, and consists of the sea-bed and subsoil of the shelf, the slope and the rise. It does not include the deep ocean floor with its oceanic ridges or the ridges thereof." The Convention then specifies the method of delimitation when the margin extends beyond 200 nautical miles and requires the coastal state to inform the Commission on the Limits of the Continental Shelf to be established in accordance with the Convention of the limits of its continental shelf beyond the 200-mile exclusive economic zone.

22.   Convention on the Law of the Sea, Art. 76(1), (3). See also Jan Mayen Continental Shelf Case (Iceland/Norway) (1981), 62 I.L.R. 108; Continental Shelf Case (Tunisia/Libya), [1982] I.C.J. 18 at 47-49.

§271 Of recent years a variety of states, including Canada, claimed a 200-mile exclusive fishing zone,[23] and it was in connection with the lines thus drawn that the dispute with the United States over the Gulf of Maine maritime boundary was referred to the World Court which based its decision on "equitable criteria", having regard to agreement of the parties and the concept of equidistance.[24] This exclusive fishing zone has now given place to demands for an exclusive economic zone extending for 200 miles measured from the baseline of the territorial sea, and this claim is given legal recognition by the 1982 Convention.[25] Within this zone the coastal state has[26] "(a) sovereign rights for the purpose of exploring and exploiting, conserving and managing the natural resources, whether living or non-living, of the sea-bed and subsoil and the superjacent waters, and with regard to other activities for the economic exploitation and exploration of the zone, such as the production of energy from the water, currents and winds; (b) jurisdiction . . . with regard to (i) the establishment and use of artificial islands, installations and structures; (ii) marine scientific research; (iii) the protection and preservation of the marine environment. . . ."

23. Order in Council, Canada Gazette, Nov. 1, 1976; see also (1977) 15 C.Y.B.I.L. 326-330. See Legault, "Maritime Claims," Macdonald *et al.*, Canadian Perspectives on International Law and Organization (1974).

24. See §269 note 18. The court expressed the "fundamental norm" of maritime frontier delimitation as follows: "(1) No maritime delimitation between States with opposite or adjacent coast may be effected unilaterally by one of those States. Such delimitation must be sought and effected by means of an agreement, following negotiations conducted in good faith and with the genuine intention of achieving a positive result. Where, however, such agreement cannot be achieved, delimitation should be effected by recourse to a third party possessing the necessary competence. (2) In either case, delimitation is to be effected by the application of equitable criteria and by the use of practical methods capable of ensuring, with regard to the geographic configuration of the area and other relevant circumstances, an equitable result", [1984] I.C.J. 246 at 299-300. See also, Willis, 'From Precedent to Precedent: The Triumph of Pragmatism in the Law of Maritime Boundaries', (1986) 24 C.Y.B.I.l. 3.

25. Arts. 55, 57. See Lefebvre, "Le concept de la zone économique exclusive et la Conférence Diplomatique de L'Organisation maritime internationale de 1984', (1984) 24 C.Y.B.I.L. 225.

26. Art. 56. See Arbour, 'L'Affaire du chalutier-usine "La Bretagne" ou les droits de l'Etat côtier dans sa zone économique exclusive', (1986) 24 C.Y.B.I.L. 61.

§272 The right of all states to navigate and overfly the exclusive economic zone is preserved, as is the right "of laying submarine cables and pipelines, and other internationally lawful uses of the sea related to these freedoms such as those associated with the operation of ships, aircraft and submarine cables and pipelines . . . [and] in exercising their rights and performing their duties . . . in the exclusive economic zone, States shall have due regard to the rights and duties of the coastal State and shall comply with the laws and regulations adopted by the coastal State. . . ."[27]

27. Art. 58. For judicial examination of significance of the zone, see *Jan Mayen Continental Shelf Case, ante.* In the *Continental Shelf* (Libya/Malta) *ante*, the I.C.J. stated, at 33: ". . . As the 1982 Convention demonstrates, the two institutions — continental shelf and exclusive economic zone — are linked together in modern law. Since the rights enjoyed by a State over its continental shelf would also be possessed by it over the sea-bed and subsoil of any exclusive economic zone which it might proclaim, one of the relevant circumstances to be taken into account for the delimitation of the continental shelf of a State is the legally permissible extent of the exclusive economic zone pertaining to that same State. This does not mean that the concept of the continental shelf has been absorbed by that of the exclusive economic zone; it does however signify that greater importance must be attributed to elements, such as distance from the coast, which are common to both concepts."

§273   The Convention also spells out the rights and duties with regard to the operation of artificial islands, installations and structures and grants the coastal state the right to regulate the size of allowable catches of the living resources of the area, while providing for the conservation and exploitation of migratory species, andromous stocks, catadromous and sedentary species, and the like.[28] While the Convention has not yet been adopted and Canada has not yet passed any legislation claiming an exclusive economic zone, it has proclaimed a 200-mile exclusive fishing zone and enjoys by virtue of its regulations concerning the continental shelf, fisheries, pollution and the like, most of the rights which are provided for under the Convention.

28. Arts. 60, 61, 64, 66-68. See Yogis, "Canadian Fisheries and International Law," Macdonald *et al.*, Canadian Perspectives on International Law and Organization (1974), p. 398.

§274   On occasion a natural strait joining two parts of the high seas lies within the territorial sea of two neighbouring states. According to the International Court of Justice[29] it is "generally recognized and in accordance with international custom that States in time of peace have a right to send [even] their warships through straits used for international navigation[30] between two parts of the high seas without the previous authorization of a coastal State, provided that the passage is *innocent*. Unless otherwise prescribed in an international convention, there is no right for a coastal State to prohibit such passage through straits in time of peace."

29. *Corfu Channel Case (Merits)* (G.B./Albania), [1949] I.C.J. 4 at 28.

30. According to the court, this does not depend on "the volume of traffic passing through the Strait or in its greater or lesser importance for international navigation. But . . . the decisive criterion is rather its geographical situation as connecting two parts of the high seas and the fact of its being used for international navigation. Nor can it be decisive that this Strait is not a necessary route between two parts of the high seas, but only an alternative passage. . . . It has nevertheless been a useful route for international maritime traffic": *Corfu Channel Case, ante.*

§275 While the 1958 Geneva Convention on the Territorial Sea and Contiguous Zone permitted a coastal state to suspend temporarily the right of innocent passage through specified areas of the territorial sea if this was essential for the protection of its security, it nevertheless provided that "there shall be no suspension of the innocent passage of foreign ships through straits which are used for international navigation between one part of the high seas and another part of the high seas or the territorial sea of a foreign State".[31]

31. Art. 16(3), (4).

§276 The 1982 Convention is more complex in its provisions than was the 1958 Convention. Instead of a right of innocent passage through "straits which are used for international navigation between one area of the high seas or an exclusive economic zone and another area of the high seas or an exclusive economic zone."[32] it provides for a right of transit passage which must not be hampered or suspended by the coastal state.[33] The right of transit passage comprises[34] "the exercise . . . of the freedom of navigation and overflight solely for the purpose of continuous and expeditious transit of the strait between one area of the high seas or an exclusive economic zone and another area of the high seas or an exclusive economic zone. However, the requirement of continuous and expeditious transit does not preclude passage through the strait for the purpose of entering, leaving or returning from a State bordering the strait, subject to the conditions of entry to that State."

32. Art. 37.
33. Art. 44.
34. Art. 38.

§277 Generally speaking, except for such matters as may be controlled when occurring in the contiguous zone[35] or the exclusive economic zone,[36] or specially provided for by international customary law, such as the control of piracy[37] or the slave trade,[38] the rights of a coastal state over foreign shipping on the high seas are strictly limited. However, international law does recognize a right of hot pursuit from the territorial sea into the high seas when the vessel concerned or a person on board has committed a violation of a coastal state's laws while in that state's territorial sea. Such a pursuit must be continuous having commenced within the territorial sea,[39] and the pursuer "seizes at his peril. If he establishes the forfeiture, he is justified. If he fails, he must make full compensation in damages."[40] In certain cases, if the pursued vessel fails to obey an order to stop, the pursuer may resort to force, even though this results in the sinking of the vessel.[41] By the 1958 Geneva Convention on the High Seas[42] the hot pursuit may continue into the contiguous zone, but it must cease once the pursued vessel enters the territorial sea of its national or a third state. By the 1982 Convention,[43] the right of hot pursuit applies in the case of violations of the coastal state's regulations relating to the exclusive economic zone or the continental shelf, including safety zones around continental shelf installations.

35. See §261.

36. See §271.

37. See *Re Piracy Jure Gentium*, [1934] A.C. 586 (P.C.). See also Geneva Convention on the High Seas, 1958, 450 U.N.T.S. 511, Arts. 14-21; 1982 Convention on the Law of the Sea, Arts. 100-107: for the first time, it is provided that "acts of piracy . . . committed by a warship, government ship or government aircraft whose crew has mutinied and taken control of the ship or aircraft are assimilated to acts committed by a private ship": Art. 102. On the issue of rebels as pirates, see *The Magellan Pirates* (1853), 1 Spinks 81, and Green, "The Santa Maria: Rebels or Pirates", (1961) 37 B.Y.B.I.L. 496.

38. 1958 Convention, Art. 13; 1982 Convention, Art. 99. In *The Le Louis* (1817), 2 Dods. 210 (H.C. of Admiralty), Sir William Scott held that a state could not by national law treat slave-trading by foreigners as piracy.

39. *R. v. The 'North'* (1905) 11 Ex. C.R. 141 (Ex. Ct.).

40. *The Marianna Flora* (1826), 11 Wheaton 1 at 42, per Story J.

41. *The I'm Alone* (1933/1935), 3 R.I.A.A. 1609 (Can.-U.S.: Special Joint Comm.). In this case, however, it was held that the international sinking was unjustified within the terms of the Anglo-U.S. Convention on the Prevention of Smuggling of Intoxicating Liquors, 1924, 27 L.N.T.S. 182. Nevertheless, the U.S. was held not liable to pay compensation in respect of the loss of the ship or cargo, but should acknowledge the illegality of the sinking and pay compensation in respect thereof and in respect of the members of the crew. See also *The Red Crusader* (1962), 35 I.L.R. 485 (Denmark/U.K. Comm. of Enquiry).

42. Art. 73.

43. Art. 111(2).

§278 To a great extent, the 1982 Convention largely confirms international customary law with regard to the high seas, which are open to all states both coastal and land-locked. Among the rights enjoyed by states are freedom of navigation, overflight, to lay submarine cables and pipelines, to construct artificial islands and other installations, of fishing[44] and of scientific research. Most of these rights are, however, subject to conditions laid down in relevant portions of the Convention, and may only be exercised "with due regard for the interests of other States in their exercise of the freedom of the high seas".[45] In addition, the high seas are to be reserved for peaceful purposes,[46] nor may any part of the high seas be subjected by any state to its sovereignty,[47] while there is an obligation upon all states to require their ships to assist all persons and vessels in distress on the high seas,[48] and to co-operate in the repression of piracy.[49] States are also required to forbid the transport of slaves and to provide that any slave taking refuge on its ships automatically acquires his freedom.[50]

44. This right is subject to a duty to take measures for conservation of the living resources of the seas, Arts. 117-119.

45. Art. 87.

46. Art. 88, but this does not interfere with the maritime rights of a belligerent during war.

47. Art. 89. There are limited historical exceptions, e.g., pearl and chank fisheries off Sri Lanka; coral off Australia; sponges off Greece.

48. Art. 98.

49. Art. 100

50. Art. 99. *Smith v. Brown* (1705) 20 Howell's St. Tr. 666; *Somerset's Case* (1772) 20 Howell's St. Tr. 1; Blackstone, Commentaries on the Law of England, 1787, vol. 1, pp. 127, 244.

§279   Technological advances have made it possible to exploit the resources of the seabed and its subsoil at great depths, far beyond the continental margin. The Convention describes "the sea-bed and ocean floor and subsoil thereof, beyond the limits of national jurisdiction" as "the Area",[51] and this Area and its resources constitute "the common heritage of mankind."[52] This means that "no state shall claim or exercise sovereignty or sovereign rights over any part of the Area or its resources, nor shall any State or natural or juridical person appropriate any part thereof. No such claim or exercise of sovereignty or sovereign rights nor such appropriation shall be recognized. All rights in the resources of the Area are vested in mankind as a whole on whose behalf the Authority shall act. These resources are not subject to alienation . . . . Activities in the Area shall . . . be carried out for the benefit of mankind as a whole, irrespective of the geographical location of States, whether coastal or landlocked, and taking into particular consideration the interests and needs of developing States and of peoples who have not attained full independence or other self-governing status recognized by the United Nations . . ."[53] The Area is to be "open to use exclusively for peaceful purposes by all States, whether coastal or land-locked, without discrimination",[54] while the resources are to be administered in accordance with regulations laid down by an International Seabed Authority.[55] The Authority is also to "provide for the equitable sharing of financial and other economic benefits",[56] bearing in mind the special position of developing States, whose "effective participation . . . in activities in the Area shall be promoted . . . having due regard to their special interests and needs,[57] and in particular the special needs of the land-locked and geographically disadvantaged among them to overcome difficulties arising from their disadvantaged location, including remoteness from the Area and difficulty of access to and from it".[58]

51. Art. 1,1(1).

52. Art. 136.

53. Arts. 137, 140.

54. Art. 141.

55. Arts. 156-191.

56. Art. 140(1).

57. It is this emphasis on the needs of the developing and land-locked that is partly responsible for U.S. refusal to sign the Convention.

58. Art. 148.

§280   States have become increasingly concerned about radio broadcasting stations operating from off-shore. By the 1982 Convention[59] "any person engaged in unauthorized broadcasting from the high seas may be prosecuted before the court of the flag State of the vessel, the place of registry of the installation, the State of which the person is a national, any place where the transmission can be received or any State where authorized radio communication is suffering interference [and such a State may] arrest any person or ship engaged in unauthorized broadcasting and seize the broadcasting apparatus."

59. Art. 109(2), (3). See also *Post Office v. Estuary Radio*, [1968] 2 Q.B. 740 (C.A.). See Dalfen, "Telecommunications", Macdonald *et al.*, Canadian Perspectives on International Law and Organization (1974), p. 337.

§281   While a number of states have passed legislation for the conservation of the marine resources off their coasts, the 1958 Geneva Convention on Fishing and Conservation of the Living Resources[60] seeks to impose obligations on all states to regulate the activities of their nationals when engaged in fishing on the high seas and these provisions are consolidated in the 1982 Convention on the Law of the Sea.[61]

60. 559 U.N.T.S. 285 — Canada is not a party to this Convention. See Yogis, "Canadian Fisheries and International Law", Macdonald *et al.*, Canadian Perspectives on International Law and Organization (1974); Castel, 1987 ed., pp. 789-803.

61. Arts. 116-120. These articles are additional to those concerning conservation of resources in the exclusive economic zone: see §271.

3. INDIVIDUALS, CORPORATIONS AND SHIPS

§282 Since international law was traditionally regarded as a law between states, the individual tended to be looked upon as an object devoid of legal personality. While he might be the object of a rule of international law and liable to trial and punishment by a state for any breach thereof, as in the case of piracy[62] or war crimes,[63] this merely meant that the state into whose hands he might fall would be entitled to try him for that offence, even though there was no other basis on which it could rest its claim to exercise criminal jurisdiction.[64] Insofar as it would appear that a treaty has conferred rights upon an individual, he has no direct means of seeking their enforcement.[65] His enjoyment of the rights in question will depend upon the actions of the obligated state, and if that state fails to carry out its obligations the individual will depend upon the actions of some other party to the treaty. Normally, the only party that will be able to take such action is the state of which the individual is a national, and in the absence of any rule of national law to the contrary, the advantages of the treaty pertain only to the state and are extended to the individual ex gratia.[66]

62. See §143.

63. See §§359-382.

64. See §§135-138.

65. See *Khan v. Fredson Travel Inc.* (No.2)(1982), 36 O.R. (2d) 17 (Ont. H.C.).

66.   *Civilian War Claimants Assn. v. R.*, [1932] A.C. 14 (H.L.); *Ritcher v. R.*, [1943] Ex. C.R. 64 (Ex. Ct.)(where property held by the custodian of alien property was to be distributed at the end of the war among "the several nationals of the German Reich entitled thereto" and "Canada must regulate this question of unliquidated property belonging to Germans with the German Reich and not with the German subjects").

§283 The link between a state and an individual, on which will depend the right of a state to act on behalf of that individual, is nationality.[67] In most instances, nationality is acquired at birth and it will depend on the law of the place of birth whether this is to be decided in accordance with the jus soli, that is to say by the locus of birth regardless of any other consideration, or by the jus sanguinis, when it is governed by inheritance, usually through the father,[68] although in the case of an illegitimate child it is through the mother. By the Canadian Citizenship Act[69] nationality stems from birth in Canada, or birth abroad if either parent was a Canadian at the time of birth. Nationality may also be acquired by naturalization, when an alien is granted the nationality of some state other than that of the nationality with which he was born. By a somewhat unique action, and as had been done in the United States, the House of Commons resolved[70] to confer Canadian nationality upon Raoul Wallenberg, Secretary of the Swedish Legation in Hungary during the Second World War, for his efforts on behalf of Hungarian Jews, and who was believed to a prisoner in Soviet custody since 1945.

67. *Reparation for Injuries Suffered in the Service of the U.N.,* [1949] I.C.J. 174 at 181-2; *Barcelona Traction, Light & Power Co. (Second Phase)* (Belgium/Spain), [1970] I.C.J. 3 at 32-33.

68. See *Pinson Claim* (France/Mexico) (1928), 5 R.I.A.A. 327, although in this case there was a conflict and the tribunal ruled in favour of the jus sanguinis, which was French, particularly as the individual in question had exercised his civil rights and obligations in France rather than in Mexico, the place of his birth.

69. S.C. 1974-75-76, c. 108, s. 3.

70. House of Commons Debates, 9 Dec. 1985, at 9308, (1986) 24 C.Y.B.I.L. 404.

§284 Nationality being a matter which essentially falls within the domestic jurisdiction,[71] questions relating to it are decided in accordance with the law of the state the nationality of which is being claimed.[72] However, this law must comply with any existing rules of international law,[73] and in the case of nationality based on naturalization it is open to the state adversely affected by such claim to refuse to recognize it, being entitled to investigate whether there was a genuine link between the individual and the naturalizing state or whether the naturalization was based on some ulterior motive to the disadvantage of the contesting state.[74]

71. *Nationality Decrees in Tunis and Morocco* (1923), 1 W.C.R. 145 at 156: ". . . in the present state of international law, questions of nationality are . . . in principle within this reserved domain [see §§83-85]. . . . [I]t may well happen that, in a matter which, like that of nationality, is not, in principle, regulated by international law, the right of a State to use its discretion is nevertheless restricted by obligations which it may have undertaken towards other States. In such a case, jurisdiction which, in principle, belongs solely to the State, is limited by rules of international law."

72. *Nottebohm Case (Second Phase)* (Liechtenstein/Guatemala), [1955] I.C.J. 4 at 20: "It is for Liechtenstein, as it is for every sovereign State, to settle by its own legislation the rules relating to the acquisition of its nationality, and to confer that nationality by naturalization granted by its own organs in accordance with that legislation. . . . Nationality has its most immediate, its most far-reaching and, for most people, its only effects within the legal system of the State conferring it. Nationality serves above all to determine that the person upon whom it is conferred enjoys the rights and is bound by the obligations which the law of the State in question

grants to or imposes on its nationals. This is implied in the wider concept that nationality is within the domestic jurisdiction of the State."

73. "To exercise protection, to apply to the Court, is to place oneself on the plane of international law. It is international law which determines whether a State is entitled to exercise protection and to seise the Court": *Nottebohm Case* (Second Phase), *ante*, at p. 21. See also *Pinson Claim, ante*, at p. 371: "An international tribunal ought to determine the nationality of claimants, . . . in principle independently of the prescriptions of the claimant's municipal law. National regulations are not without importance, but they are not binding on such a tribunal. . . . It is more logical not to bind the tribunal to any municipal system of proof, but to leave it with entire liberty to assess the proofs tendered in accordance with the circumstances of the case"; e.g., birth certificate, certificate of consular registration, military service, voting records, etc.

74. *Nottebohm Case* (Second Phase), *ante*, at p. 26: ". . . [The] facts clearly establish, on the one hand, the absence of any bond of attachment between N and Liechtenstein and, on the other hand, the existence of a long-standing and close connection between him and Guatemala, a link which his naturalization in no way weakened. That naturalization was not based on any real prior connection with Liechtenstein, nor did it in any way alter the manner of life of the person upon whom it was conferred in exceptional circumstances [most of the requirements of Liechtenstein law were waived] of speed and accommodation. In both respects, it was lacking in the genuineness requisite to an act of such importance, if it is entitled to be respected by a State in the position of Guatemala. It was granted without regard to the concept of nationality adopted in international relations. Naturalization was asked for not so much for the purpose of obtaining a legal recognition of N's membership in fact in the population of Liechtenstein, as it was to enable him to substitute for his status as a national of a belligerent State that of a national of a neutral State [N was a German national resident in Guatemala, which seized his property as enemy; Liechtenstein was neutral], with the sole aim of thus coming within the protection of Liechtenstein but not of becoming wedded to its traditions, its interests, its way of life or of assuming the obligations — other than fiscal obligations [in consideration of which the naturalization was granted] — and exercising the rights pertaining to the status thus acquired. Guatemala is under no obligation to recognize a nationality granted in such circumstances."

§285 Since an individual may find himself as a result of the operation of the jus soli and the jus sanguinis possessed of dual nationality, problems arise in the event of there being a conflict between the two nations concerned, even though an attempt was made by the League of Nations in 1930 to reduce some of the complications[75] and particularly those relating to military obligations.[76] While an individual may seek to discard one of these nationalities by naturalization, whether he has been successful or not depends upon the law of the country whose nationality is in question.[77] If an individual possessing dual nationality finds himself in one of the countries concerned, he is unable to invoke the protection of his other nationality against that country.[78] Moreover, such a person may find himself liable to the obligation of military service in both countries.[79] The current Canadian passport carries a statement to the effect: "Canadians may have dual nationality through birth, descent, marriage[80] or naturalization. They are advised that while in the country of their other nationality they may be subject to all its laws and obligations, including military service."[81] If the issue of dual nationality arises before a third state, the latter "is not entitled to contest the claim of one of the two Powers whose national is interested in the case by referring to the nationality of the other Power."[82]

75. Convention on Certain Questions Relating to Nationality Laws, 1930, 179 L.N.T.S. 89. Canada is a party to this Convention.

76. Protocol re Military Obligations in Certain Cases of Double Nationality, 1930, 178 L.N.T.S. 227. Canada is not a party to this Protocol.

77. See statement of Dept. of External Affairs, March 1967 (1968), 16 C.Y.B.I.L. 272: "Many countries do not recognize the acquisition of another nationality by their citizens as affecting in any way the citizenship they already possess and are not prepared to relieve such persons of the responsibilities and obligations which devolve upon their citizens. Since this practice has the sanction of international law the authorities of the countries concerned are entitled in their own territory to require all their citizens, whether dual nationals or otherwise, to comply with the stipulations of their laws, just as Canada insists that Canadian citizens who are also nationals of another country must be treated in Canada as having the same rights, privileges and responsibilities as all other citizens." By English law, a dual national cannot make a declaration of alienage so as to lose his British nationality if the U.K. is at war: *R. v. Lynch*, [1903] 1 K.B. 444; see also *R. v. C.O., 30 Battalion Middlesex Regiment; Ex parte Freyberger*, [1917] 2 K.B. 129 at 139, per Swinfen Eady L.J. See *Oppenheimer v. Cattermole*, [1976] A.C. 249 (H.L.).

78. See, however, *Re Rissmann* (1970/1972), 71 I.L.R. 577 (Italy Ct. of Cassation) at §155 note 9. In the *Pinson Claim, ante*, the Tribunal looked at the facts in order to ascertain the effective and overriding nationality. By Art. 3 of the Statute of the World Court if a dual national is elected a judge, he "shall be deemed to be a national of the one in which he ordinarily exercises civil and political rights." Thus, Judges Read (Canada), McNair (U.K.), Benegal Rao (India), and Zafrulla Khan (Pakistan), have overlapped in their terms of service, although all held British nationality as citizens of Commonwealth countries. For a judicial decision on 'overriding nationality', see *Espahanian v. Bank Tejarat* (1983), 72 I.L.R. 478 at 484-489 (Iran-U.S. Claims Trib.).

79. See *Murray v. Parkes*, [1942] 2 K.B. 124 (K.B.). By U.S. law if a dual national voluntarily does military service in the country of his non-American nationality he loses his U.S. nationality: *Nishikawa v. Dulles* (1958), 356 U.S. 129.

80. More and more countries are now giving a wife an option to retain her original nationality if this differs from that of her husband.

81. For a statement on Canadian policy concerning Canadian citizens of East European origin visiting East European countries, see House of Commons Debates 13 Dec. 1983, 160-61 (1984) C.Y.B.I.L. 343.

82. *Salem Case* (U.S. v. Egypt) (1932), 2 R.I.A.A. 1161 at 1188.

§286 It is a generally accepted principle of international law that a state must receive back those individuals who possess its nationality if they should be expelled by or denied admission to another state.[83] However, on occasion states have argued that this is only true when the person possessing its nationality really has some intimate link with the state and is not a national by mere formality of law, as is the case when he has been born in a colonial territory to which the nationality of the ruling country has been extended.[84] If this view of the duties of the state of nationality becomes generally accepted, it might well reduce the status of those enjoying a particular nationality by virtue of the jus sanguinis.[85]

83. See Memo. of Legal Bureau, Dept. of External Affairs, Nov. 14, 1974, (1975) 13 C.Y.B.I.L. 352-4: "We believe ... that a government has an obligation toward Canada and toward their own nationals to re-admit those who are currently illegally in this country, should they be deported back to their country of nationality. Our research has turned up no instances where the issuing state has added a requirement for re-entry visas for their nationals. Even if it were a bona fide requirement under foreign municipal law, it cannot fetter this country's right to expel or avoid the obligation to accept pursuant to the customary rules of international law. . . . To hold otherwise, would contradict the basic principle of the readmissibility of nationals to their own country, and undermine the integrity of the passport as an international travel document . . . ." On the nature of the passport, see *R. v. Brailsford*, [1905] 2 K.B. 730 (D.C.), and *Joyce v. D.P.P.*, [1946] A.C. 347 (H.L.). Arkelian, "The Right to a Passport in Canadian Law", (1983) 21 C.Y.B.I.L. 284.

84. See *R. v. Secretary of State for the Home Dept.; Ex parte Thrakrar*, [1974] 2 W.L.R. 593 (C.A.).

85. See British Nationality Act, 1981, c. 61. The Act also affects the status of some individuals claiming British nationality in accordance with the jus soli.

§287 There is one instance where dual nationality takes on a special significance and the fact of its existence does not preclude an action against one of the states, the nationality of which is possessed by the individual claimant. In accordance with the Peace Treaties signed with the minor Axis Powers in 1947, the latter undertook to restore to 'United Nations nationals' all property taken from them. 'United Nations nationals' were defined as "individuals who are nationals of any of the United Nations,[86] or corporations or associations organised under the laws of any of the United Nations, at the coming into force of the present Treaty, provided that the said individuals, corporations or associations also had that status [at a named date]", and it was irrelevant that they might also possess or have possessed the nationality of the particular Axis power concerned.[87] Perhaps even more important was the provision that "the term 'United Nations nationals' also includes individuals, corporations or associations which, under the laws in force in [Italy/Romania/Bulgaria/Hungary/Finland] during the war, have been treated as enemy".[88]

86. This was the name of the alliance against the Axis Powers.

87. *Mergé Claim* (1955), 14 R.I.A.A. 236 at 238 (Italian-U.S. Conciliation Comm.).

88. In the *Flegenheimer Case* (1958), 14 R.I.A.A. 327, 'U.N. national' status was denied to a person acquiring both U.S. and German nationality at birth, but losing former by parental naturalization, and who had been rendered stateless by German anti-Semitic legislation, but who could not prove he had been treated as an enemy by Italy when in Canada or the U.S., which were at war with Italy. It was claimed that while in the U.S. and before U.S. entered war he had, as a result of Italian anti-Semitic legislation, sold property in Italy at a disadvantageous rate. After the U.S. entered war, he reacquired U.S. nationality.

§288 Problems involving nationality also arise if a state deprives individuals of their nationality or if, for various reasons, as for example when a new state comes into existence and introduces restrictive nationality legislation, individuals never acquire a nationality, although normally the inhabitants will acquire as they do in the case of cession of territory[89] the nationality of the new sovereign. While Canada is not a party to the Convention Relating to the Status of Stateless Persons,[90] it has ratified the Convention on the Reduction of Statelessness,[91] which, among other things, seeks to ensure that if the local law provides for loss of nationality, for whatever reason, this shall only ensue provided another nationality is acquired. It also forbids a state from depriving individuals of their nationality on account of racial, ethnic, religious or political grounds.[92] Despite these treaties, it has become common for various states to expel groups of individual residents for these or similar reasons,[93] while many individuals have left their home state because of political differences with the local government.[94] In an attempt to give such persons some measure of protection, the United Nations, following the example of the League of Nations, has established a United Nations High Commissioner for Refugees, and a number of states, including Canada, have become parties to the Convention Relating to the Status of Refugees, 1951, and the related Protocol of 1967.[95]

89. *Russian Nobleman Nationality Case* (1971), 72 I.L.R. 435, 438-442 (German Fed. Rep. Bavaria S.C.).

90. 1954, 360 U.N.T.S. 117.

91. 1961, 989 U.N.T.S. 195.

92. Art. 9. This was largely a consequence of Nazi German legislation against Jews.

93. Thus, both Kenya and Uganda have expelled their Asian populations.

94. *Russian Nobleman Nationality Case, ante* at 438: "In principle the flight of an emigrant does not signify the permanent abandonment of his home country so that it does not normally correspond with either his intention or his interests for his emigration to be regarded as a basis for the loss of his nationality and its associated rights. However, particularly in those cases where emigrants later no longer wish to return to their country of origin, and renounce the rights arising from that nationality

[see, however, *Joyce v. D.P.P.*, [1946] A.C. 347 (H.L.)], it may be very difficult to determine at what stage they have finally abandoned any desire to return. This would create an unacceptable level of legal uncertainty with regard to the question of when loss of nationality occurred. This can only be remedied by the enactment of a law governing the rules for loss of nationality, which is the common practice internationally."

95.   189 U.N.T.S. 137, 606 U.N.T.S. 267, respectively. See Green, "Refugees and Refugee Status—Causes and Treatment in Historico-Legal Perspective", 13 Thesaurus Acroasium (Thessaloniki) (1987), pp. 537-616.

§289   Partly to give effect to its obligations under the Refugees Convention, Canada's Immigration Act, 1976,[96] provides that "Canadian immigration policy and the rules and regulations made under this Act shall be designed and administered in such a manner as to promote the domestic and international interests of Canada recognizing the need . . . (g) to fulfil Canada's legal obligations with respect to refugees and to uphold its humanitarian tradition with respect to the displaced and the persecuted."[97] A convention 'refugee' is one who, "owing to well-founded fear of being persecuted for reasons of race, religion, nationality, membership of a particular social group or political opinion, is outside the country of his nationality and is unable or, owing to such fear, is unwilling to avail himself of the protection of that country; or who, not having a nationality and being outside the country of his former habitual residence, is unable or, owing to such fear, is unwilling to return to it".[98] While there is no obligation to grant refugee status to a person who is illegally present in a territory,[99] he may not be returned to "the frontiers of territories where his life or freedom would be threatened on account of his race, religion, nationality, membership of a particular social group or political opinion" — non-refoulement[1].

96.   S.C. 1976-77, c. 52. See also *Haitian Refugee Centre v. Smith* (1982), 21 I.L.M. 603 (U.S.). In *Secretary of State for the Home Dept. v. Two Citizens of Chile,* [1977] Imm. A.R. 36 at 42, it was held that in considering political asylum applications the provisions of the U.K. Immigration Act, 1971, and the rules made thereunder must be applied, although "the United Nations Convention and the Universal Declaration of Human Rights . . . may well be of assistance in indicating the way in which the Act and Rules should be interpreted". See Gotlieb, "Canada and the Refugee Question in International Law", (1975) 13 C.Y.B.I.L. 3. See also Green, "Immigration, Extradition and Asylum in Canadian Law and Practice", Macdonald *et al.*, Canadian Perspectives on International Law and Organization, (1974), p. 244. See *Hurt v. Min. of Manpower & Immigration,* [1978] 2 F.C. 340 (Fed. C.A.); *Darwich v. Min. of Manpower & Immigration,* [1979] 1 F.C. 365 (Fed. C.A.); *Quezada v. Min. of Employment & Immigration* (1979), 30 N.R. 603 (Fed. C.A.); *Astudillo v. Min. of Employment & Immigration* (1979), 31 N.R. 121 (Fed. C.A.); *Re Petersen* (1968), 7 I.A.C. 222; *Min. of Employment & Immigration v. Hudnick,* [1980] 1 F.C. 180 (Fed. C.A.); and especially *Vincent v. Min. of Employment & Immigration* (1983), 48 N.R. 214 (Fed. C.A.).

97. For a general statement re refugee determination and immigrant status, see Legal Bureau memo. 18 Apr. 1985, (1986) 24 C.Y.B.I.L. 390. However, by Bills C-55 and C-84 of 1987, Canada's policy with regard to the admission of persons claiming refugee status is to be radically changed in view of the suspicion that numerous 'illegal' immigrants were seeking such status wrongly. While Canada intended to return some applicants to the country of first refuge it undertook to continue to recognize the principle on non-refoulement (§192). Canada also pursued a policy of granting refugee status to those coming from 'Communist' countries as well as those in which internal disturbance or civil war was taking place.

98. 189 U.N.T.S. 137, Art. 1,A(2). See *Rajudeen v. Minister of Employment & Immigration* (1984), 55 N.R. 129 (Fed. C.A.).

99. Art. 31. See *R. v. Secretary of State for Home Department; ex parte Singh* (1987), The Times, 8 June 1987 (D.C.).

1. Art. 32. In *Boun-Leua v. Min. of Employment & Immigration* (1981), 113 D.L.R. (3d) 414 (Fed. C.A.) it was held that a ministerial certificate of 'Convention refugee' status was not a statement that the person was 'lawfully present' in Canada, but merely a guarantee against refoulement.

§290   Under the auspices of the United Nations a number of attempts have been made to confer positive rights upon individuals to prevent discrimination on the basis of 'race, sex, language or religion'.[2] The first major step to this end was the adoption of the Universal Declaration of Human Rights, 1948,[3] but since this was a Resolution of the General Assembly[4] it imposes no obligation on any state and confers no legally enforceable rights. This has been followed by the International Covenants on Economic, Social and Cultural Rights, and on Civil and Political Rights adopted in 1966[5] and ratified by Canada in 1976. While these Covenants have created legally binding obligations for their parties, they provide no enforcement procedure. However, the Covenant on Civil and Political Rights provides for a Committee on Human Rights[6] to which the parties have undertaken to submit reports.[7] Moreover, by Article 41 of the Covenant "A State Party to the present Covenant may at any time declare . . . that it recognizes the competence of the Committee to receive and consider communications to the effect that a State Party claims that another State Party is not fulfilling its obligations under the present Covenant. Communications under this Article may be received and considered only if submitted by a State Party which has made a declaration recognizing in regard to itself the competence of the Committee. . . ." However, before an individual is competent to refer a complaint to the Committee, that individual must have exhausted all available domestic remedies.[8]

2. Charter of the U.N., Art. 1(3). See also, International Convention on the Elimination of All Forms of Racial Discrimination 1965, 660 U.N.T.S. 295, ratified by

Canada in 1970, and U.N. Declaration on the Elimination of All Forms of Intolerance and of Discrimination Based on Religion or Belief 1981, General Assembly Res. 36/55, 21 I.L.M. 205.

3.   Res. 217 (III)A.

4.   See §417. This does not mean that the Declaration is not regularly invoked by States when seeking to condemn violations of human rights by other states.

5.   993 U.N.T.S. 3; 999 U.N.T.S. 171, respectively.

6.   For Canada's view of the working of the Human Rights Committee, see statement to U.N. Third Committee, 25 Nov. 1983, (1984) 22 C.Y.B.I.L. 329.

7.   See Turp, 'La préparation et la présentation de rapports périodiques du Canada en application des traités relatifs aux droits et libertés', (1986) 24 C.Y.B.I.L. 161.

8.   Optional Protocol, 1966, 999 U.N.T.S. 171, Art. 2. A similar provision is to be found in the European Convention on Human Rights, 1950, 213 U.N.T.S. 222. For a decision dealing with 'effective' domestic remedies, see *Silver Case* (1983), 72 I.L.R. 374, 373-376 (European Ct. of Human Rights); and for another on exhaustion of local remedies, *Pakelli Case* (1983), 72 I.L.R. 414, 424 (European Ct. of Human Rights). See §322.

§291   Canada has made such a declaration,[9] and has also acceded to the Optional Protocol of the Covenant recognizing "the competence of the Committee to receive and consider communications from individuals subject to its jurisdiction who claim to be victims of a violation by that State Party of any of the rights set forth in the Covenant." As a result of this undertaking the Committee has held Canada to be in breach of the Covenant in respect of the position of Indian women under the Indian Act.[10]

9.   Text is reproduced in U.N., Multilateral Treaties Deposited with the Secretary-General — Status as at 31 Dec. 1986, p. 138.

10.   R.S.C. 1970, C. I-6, s. 12; *Lovelace Case* (1981), 171 I.L.R. 337 (Human Rights Comm.). The Act was accordingly amended in 1985.

§292   In addition to its obligations under the International Covenant on Civil and Political Rights, which forbids any discrimination on the ground of sex,[11] Canada is also a party to the Convention on the Political Rights of Women, 1953[12] and the Convention on the Elimination of All Forms of Discrimination against Women, 1981.[13] While both seek to remove any form of discrimination as between men and women and call for legislation to this end, it is only the 1981 convention that contains any supervisory machinery by way of a Committee to which annual reports are to be submitted and which may make suggestions and recommendations thereon.[14] Disputes between parties as to the interpretation or application of the convention which are not settled by negotiation are to be submitted to arbitration.[15]

11. Art. 2(1).

12. 193 U.N.T.S. 135. *See Canada (A.G.) v. Stuart,* [1983] 1 F.C. 651 (Fed. C.A.); leave to appeal to S.C.C. refused (1982), 45 N.R. 531 (S.C.C.) (held the Convention could not be used to construe and interpret the Unemployment Insurance Act, S.C. 1970-71-72, c. 48, which had been given a prior statutory definition by the Supreme Court).

13. 19 I.L.M. 33. In connection with this Convention, a Legal Bureau memo, 23 Oct. 1985, pointed out that it contained no article forbidding reservations, which were therefore permissible provided they were not incompatible with its objects and purposes. However, "as a general principle we believe Canada should discourage reservations to human rights conventions. At the same time, we believe that this principle must be balanced with the important goal of universal acceptance of these human rights conventions. We consider that it is important to encourage ratifications so that states become part of the international system of scrutiny through the reporting requirement in most human rights conventions" (1986) 24 C.Y.B.I.L. 402.

14. Arts. 17, 18, 21.

15. Art. 29.

§293 In addition to their obligations as parties to the International Covenants some states, members of regional organizations, have entered into treaty obligations giving individuals effective protection insofar as human rights are concerned. The two most important of these are the European Convention on Human Rights[16] and the American Convention on Human Rights.[17] The method of enforcement provided by both Conventions is by way of a Commission to which complaints may be directed by any party to the Convention even though this complaint is made on behalf of an individual who is not a national of the complainant. In addition, complaints may be lodged by an individual even against his own state. Failing settlement of the dispute through the medium of the Commission, the Commission or any party to the Convention, but not an individual complainant, may refer the issue for adjudication to the relevant regional Court of Human Rights.[18] There is also the Court of the European Communities established under the Treaty of Rome setting up the European Economic Community.[19] This court, too, frequently deals with the rights of individuals in such matters as immigration,[20] nondiscrimination in employment,[21] and the like, but in this case both companies and individuals have a right to sue.

16. 1950, 213 U.N.T.S. 222.

17. 1969, 9 I.L.M. 673.

18. The Statute of the Inter-American Court of Human Rights was not drawn up until 1980. On the other hand, the European Court of Human Rights has been most active. Perhaps its most important judgment resulted from the British declaration of emergency in Northern Ireland, leading to Irish complaints alleging torture, denial of fair trial and the like by the U.K. against Northern Irish detainees, all of whom

enjoyed British nationality. The judgment also dealt with the problem of derogation of rights in time of emergency: *Ireland v. United Kingdom* (1978), 58 I.L.R. 188 (European Ct. of Human Rights); see also Green, "Derogation of Human Rights in Emergency Situations", (1978), 16 C.Y.B.I.L. 92. The court has also dealt with such matters as minority linguistic rights: *Belgian Linguistics Case* (Merits) (1968), 45 I.L.R. 114; (judicial birching) *Tyrer Case* (1978), 58 I.L.R. 339; (freedom of the press and contempt of court) *Sunday Times (Thalidomide) Case* (1979), 58 I.L.R. 490; and 61 I.L.R. 341; (the rights of male homosexuals in Northern Ireland) *Dudgeon Case* (1981/1983), 67 I.L.R. 395; *Young and Others* (1981), 62 I.L.R. 359; 70 I.L.R. 334 (the right not to join a trade union); (disciplinary proceedings and the right to a fair trial); *Le Compte v. Belgium* (1981), 62 I.L.R. 318; *Campbell and Cosans Case* (1982), 67 I.L.R. 480 (European Ct. of Human Rights)(corporal punishment in Scottish schools).

19. 1957, 298 U.N.T.S. 11.

20. *Van Duyn v. Home Office*, [1975] 2 W.L.R. 760, [1975] 1 C.M.L.R. 1 (European Ct. of Justice).

21. *Prais v. Council of the European Communities*, [1976] 2 C.M.L.R. 708 (Ct. of Justice of the European Communities). See also *Ostreicher v. Secretary of State for the Environment*, [1978] 3 All E.R. 82 (C.A.).

§294 Aliens abroad, whether as residents or temporary visitors, are subject to the criminal law on the principle of territoriality. However, many countries are critical of the conditions in which their convicted nationals are housed and they have therfore entered into agreements whereby such nationals may be returned home to serve their sentence in national prisons.[22] Canada is a party to such treaties[23] and enacted the Transfer of Offenders Act, 1978, to enable Canadian prisoners to be returned to Canada.[24] Canada has also become a party to the 1983 Council of Europe Convention on the Transfer of Sentenced Persons.[25]

22. See 1980 Report of the U.K. National Council for the Welfare of Prisoners Abroad, Prison Transfer Treaties: The How and Why.

23. Canada and U.S., 1977; Canada and Mexico, 1977; Canada and France, 1979; see Bassiouni, 'Perspectives on the Transfer of Prisoners Between the U.S. and Mexico and the U.S. and Canada, (1978) 11 Vanderbilt J. Int'l L. 249.

24. 26-27 Eliz. II, 1977-78, C-21.

25. 1983, 22 I.L.M. 530. This was superseded by the European Communities Convention on the Transfer of Convicts 1987, The Times 26 May 1987.

§295 As with individuals, so in the case of corporations any rights they may claim under international law depend on the link of nationality. While, prima facie, this may depend on the place of incorporation,[26] this presumption may be rebutted by 'piercing the veil of corporate personality' and seeking the true place from which the corporation is controlled.[27] This was the approach adopted by the World Court when examining expropriation of state-owned German property. It pointed out that the rules regarding nationality were applicable by analogy to corporations.[28] It emphasized, however, that every case must be decided on its own facts.[29] As a result, it may easily happen that a variety of states are entitled to act on behalf of a specific corporation, because of the distribution of subsidiary companies, their registration in different states and the mixed nationalities of their shareholders or boards of directors.[30]

26.   *Cdn. Pacific Railway v. Western Union Telegraph Co.* (1889), 17 S.C.R. 151 (S.C.C.). See also *Agency of Can. Car & Foundry Co. (U.S.) v. Germany* (1939), 8 R.I.A.A. 460 at 466: "It is a settled general rule in America that regardless of the place of residence or citizenship of the incorporators or shareholders, the sovereignty by which a corporation was created, or under whose laws it was organized, determines its national character": Supplemental Opinion of American Commissioner; *Standard Oil Co. Tankers* (U.S./Reparation Comm.) (1926), 2 R.I.A.A. 777 at 787-793. See also *Sumitomo Shoji Amer. Inc. v. Avagliano* (1982), 21 I.L.M. 791 (U.S. S.C.).

27.   *Daimler Co. v. Continental Tyre & Rubber Co.*, [1916] 2 A.C. 307 (H.L.). See, however, *Sovfracht (V/O) v. Van Udens Scheepvaart en Argentuur Maatschappij (N.V. Gebr.)*, [1943] A.C. 203 (H.L.); *Alcan Aluminum Ltd. v. Ircable Corp.* (1983), 72 I.L.R. 725 (Iran/U.S. Claims Trib.)

28.   *German Interests in Polish Upper Silesia* (Merits) (Germany/Poland) (1926), 1 W.C.R. 510 at 565: "It is not possible to apply the conception of a 'controlled company' [i.e., one controlled by German nationals] to every kind of juristic person; it would rather appear, in the light of wartime legislation to which the régime of liquidation belongs, that this conception refers more particularly to associations with an economic purpose, there being, moreover, no necessity to draw a distinction in this connection between associations which merely constitute a contractual relation and those which possess a distinct legal personality. On the other hand, the conception of a 'national' also covers . . . communes such as the City of Ratibor. . . . A Prussian commune is a corporation on a territorial basis, formed by the national inhabitants, upon whom municipal law confers the capacity of members of the commune. Generally speaking, only nationals will take part in the administration of the commune. Again, communes, outside their own sphere of activity, also exercise functions as organs of the State itself; they are subject to the control of the State authorities as regards both the activities which are directly incumbent upon them and those which they undertake in virtue of powers delegated by the State. An essential and necessary bond therefore unites the commune and the State of which it forms part; consequently, it is natural, from the standpoint of the régime of liquidation, to assimilate such communities of nationals of a State to individuals who, precisely by reason of their nationality, are, in so far as their property is concerned, subject to the régime established for nationals of this State. It follows . . . that the commune of Ratibor falls within the category of 'German nationals'. . . ."

29.   *German Interest in Polish Upper Silesia* (Merits), *ante*, at p. 560: "The Geneva Convention does not, any more than the Treaty of Versailles [the two instruments under which the liquidations were taking place], define the factors which constitute control and the existence of which may involve the liquidation of a company's property. . . . [T]he conception of control, in the Geneva Convention, is an essentially economic one and it contemplates a preponderant influence over the general policy. Criteria of an external nature, such as the situation of the registered offices, the place

of foundation, the legislation under which the Company has been formed, etc., which have long been applied, without any relation to the question of liquidation, by the legislation and jurisprudence of the different countries, seem to have been replaced in the Geneva Convention, and in so far as concerns the liquidation régime, by a more elastic criterion which enables, in spite of appearances, physical persons of a particular nationality to be reached. The régime is therefore based on the nationality of the citizens of the State subject to liquidation, who are owners or beneficiaries of the property, rights and interests liable to liquidations. Seeing that the conception of 'control' is an essentially economic conception, decisive importance must not be attached to the functions which, by law or under their Statutes, are performed by certain organs, such as, for instance, the Boards of Control of Limited Companies; such functions must not be taken as a rigid legal criterion. On the contrary, each case must be considered on its individual merits. There is, however, in the conception of control adopted in the Geneva Convention, one rigid juridical factor, namely, the nationality of the physical persons who exercise control. . . ."

30. *Barcelona Traction, Light & Power Co.* (Second Phase) (Belgium/Spain), [1970] I.C.J. 4. See also, for interpretation of a treaty discriminating between a parent company and its subsidiaries, *Sumitomo Shoji Amer. Inc. v. Avagliano, ante.*

§296   Ships, too, have a nationality,[31] and it is on the existence of this nationality that their rights depend. Thus, though it is accepted that ships are immune from foreign jurisdiction when upon the high seas,[32] this right does not belong to the ship as such, nor to its master. The right to protest at any interference with this freedom belongs to the state of nationality, that is to say the flag state,[33] and in the absence of any such state the ship is liable to seizure and condemnation.[34] This would also be the case with any ship, even one flying a national flag to which it was entitled, turned away or seized by Canada in accordance with the 1987 legislative proposals for the control of immigrants.[35]

31. The rules regarding the nationality of aircraft are embodied in the Chicago Convention, 1944 (Arts. 17-21), and are similar to those for ships.

32. See §277.

33. Geneva Convention on the High Seas, 1958, 450 U.N.T.S. 11, Art. 5(1): "Each State shall fix the conditions for the grant of its nationality to ships, for the registration of ships in its territory, and for the right to fly its flag. Ships have the nationality of the State whose flag they are entitled to fly. There must exist a genuine link between the State and the ship, in particular, the State must effectively exercise its jurisdiction and control in administrative, technical and social matters over ships flying its flag." Art. 6: "Ships sail under the flag of one State only and . . . [a] ship which sails under the flags of two or more States, using them according to convenience, may not claim any of the nationalities in question with respect to any other State, and may be assimilated to a ship without nationality. . . . A ship may not change its flag during a voyage or while in a port of call, save in the case of a real transfer of ownership or change of registry." See now Convention on the Law of the Sea, 1982, 21 I.L.M. 1261, Arts. 91, 92, 94. For the Canadian law concerning the nationality of ships, see Maritime Code Act, S.C. 1977-78, c. 41, s. 6.

34. *Molvan v. A.G. Palestine (The Asya)*, [1948] A.C. 351 (P.C.).

35. Bill C-84, s. 11.

§297 While the port of registry is significant in determining the nationality of a ship, there is no law of the port of registry as such. The law to which the ship is normally subject is the law of the nation in which the port of registry is situated.[36] Although the national law governs administrative and social matters within the ship,[37] a foreign state cannot claim that its labour legislation shall apply to the crew of a ship registered abroad, even though the ship belongs to a company controlled by that state and is part of a shipping line the bulk of the trade of which is with the state seeking to apply its law.[38] On the other hand, in the event of an accident injuring a member of the crew while the ship is in foreign territorial waters, or a port or roadstead, it is the law of the latter which will govern the case as the lex delicti.[39]

36. *MacKinnon v. Iberia Shipping Co.* (1955), S.C. 20 (Scotland Ct. of Sessions).

37. See note 33 ante. See also *United States v. Reagan* (1971), 453 F. 2d 165.

38. *McCulloch v. Sociedad Nacional de Marineros de Honduras* (1963), 372 U.S. 10 (S.C.).

39. *MacKinnon v. Iberia Shipping Co.* (1955), S.C. 20 (Scotland Ct. of Sessions). See, however, *Romero v. International Terminal Operating Co.* (1956), 358 U.S. 354, in which it was held that some significant contact with the local state beyond mere presence was required.

§298 In 1987, during the conflict between Iraq and Iran, problems arose with regard to the safety of oil tankers in the Persian Gulf.[40] Most of these tankers belonged to small states or states which were too far away to provide naval protection. The United States declared that it would be prepared to allow such vessels, particularly those belonging to Kuwait, to fly the United States flag and sail under convoy of United States war vessels.[41] There was apparently no indication that the ships had changed their nationality. Similar proposals were made in respect of the United Kingdom, but the Department of Transport indicated[42] that "the owners would have to set up a United Kingdom registered company, the skipper and certain officers would have to be British or hold British or Commonwealth qualifications, and certain manning and safety regulations would have to be met. [Mere R]eflagging would not automatically entitle the vessels to protection by British warships". This would only follow if the ships were properly registered, described as a commercial or procedural act not related to nationality.[43]

40. It would appear that at no time was any reference made to the right of a belligerent to inhibit neutral traffic with its enemy.

41. In time of war neutral vessels will often sail in a convoy provided by a belligerent, but this is not the case in this instance.

42. The Times, 22 July, 1987.

43. The regulations with regard to registration of a ship as Canadian will be found in the Canada Shipping Act, R.S.C. 1970, c. S-9, 1st Supp., c. 38 and 2nd Supp., c. 27, while by the Canadian Citizenship Act, S.C. 1974-75-76, c. 108, no alien can be owner of a Canadian ship.

V International Transactions

1. TREATIES AND OTHER INTERNATIONAL AGREEMENTS

§299 In accordance with the Vienna Convention on the Law of Treaties[1] a treaty is "an international agreement concluded between States in written form and governed by international law, whether embodied in a single instrument or in two or more related instruments[2] and whatever its particular designation."[3] However, a Final Act is only a record of what has been agreed to at an international conference. It "is not a legally binding instrument; it does not impose binding obligations on its signatories . . .[i.e.]is in the nature of a declaration of intent . . . Although [a] Final Act does not of itself have the status of binding international law, it is in many instances declaratory of existing international law".[4]

1. 1969, 8 I.L.M. 679, Art. 2(1)(a). Canada is a party to this Convention.

2. Such as an exchange of letters, or the series of declarations made under Art. 36 (the 'Optional Clause': see §301 and §§405, 406) of the Statute of the International Court of Justice. See also *Ambatielos Case (Jurisdiction)* (Greece/G.B.), [1952] I.C.J. 28, in which the relationship between two Treaties and a Declaration was examined.

3. It makes no difference whether the agreement is called a treaty, convention, charter, covenant, statute, or any other name so long as it is clear that the intention is to effect an agreement. The term 'protocol' is usually reserved for an instrument that is added to an agreement either by way of annex or as a supplement, and it is not always entered into at the same time as the principal document. In *R. v. Ashford Remand Centre (Governor); ex parte Postlethwaite,* [1987] 3 W.L.R. 1141 (H.L.), the House of Lords held that treaties are to be construed as contracts and not as statutes, and should therefore be given a liberal interpretation.

4. Statement 7 Jan. 1982 by Legal Bureau, Dept. of External Affairs re Helsinki Final Act 1983, (14 I.L.M. 1291), (1983) 21 C.Y.B.I.L. 317-8. In fact the Act expressly stated that it was not to be registered with the U.N. Secretariat under Art. 102 of the Charter which requires all treaties to be so registered.

§300 Despite this definition, it is still possible for a state to commit itself to another by a unilateral declaration,[5] or even to the world at large by a general declaration.[6] Such a declaration may be oral or written in form, but it must be made by an official representative of the state[7] within the sphere of his activities and in circumstances which would lead the recipient to assume that it was made with the intent of binding the declarant state.[8]

5. See *Legal Status of Eastern Greenland* (Denmark/Norway) (1933), 3 W.C.R. 151. In the *Frontier Dispute* judgment (Burkina Faso/Mali), [1986] I.C.J. 554, the I.C.J.

pointed out (573-4) that "the statement of Mali's Head of State . . . was not made during negotiations or talks between the two Parties; at most, it took the form of a unilateral act by the Government of Mali. Such declarations 'concerning legal or factual situations' may indeed 'have the effect of creating legal obligations' for the State on whose behalf they are made . . . But . . . it all depends on the intention of the State in question. . . . The Chamber considers that it has a duty to show even greater caution when it is a question of a unilateral declaration not directed to any particular recipient. In order to assess the intentions of the author of a unilateral act, account must be taken of all the factual circumstances in which the act occurred. . . . [T]here are no grounds to interpret the declaration made by Mali's Head of State . . . as a unilateral act with legal implications in regard to the present case." See also note 8.

6.   *Nuclear Tests Cases* (Australia/France; N.Z./France), [1974] I.C.J. 251, 457.

7.   In the *Legal Status of Eastern Greenland* case the statement was made by the foreign minister in reply to a question posed by an ambassador, while in the *Nuclear Tests Cases* there were in addition statements made by the President in public pronouncements.

8.   See *Nuclear Tests Cases, ante,* at p. 267: "It is well recognized that declarations made by way of unilateral acts, concerning legal or factual situations, may have the effect of creating legal obligations. Declarations of this kind may be, and often are, very specific. When it is the intention of the State making the declaration that it should become bound according to its terms, that intention confers on the declaration the character of a legal undertaking, the State being thenceforth legally required to follow a course of conduct consistent with the declaration. An undertaking of this kind, if given publicly, and with an intent to be bound, even though not made within the context of international negotiations, is binding. In these circumstances, nothing in the nature of a quid pro quo nor any subsequent acceptance of the declaration, nor even a reply or reaction from other States, is required for the declaration to take effect, since such a requirement would be inconsistent with the strictly unilateral nature of the juridical act by which the pronouncement by the State was made. Of course, not all unilateral acts imply obligation; but a State may choose to take up a certain position in relation to a particular matter with the intention of being bound — the intention to be ascertained by interpretation of the act." See also in this connection the court's interpretation of statements made by the delegate of South Africa in the League of Nations and the United Nations with regard to the continuance of the South-West Africa Mandate after the demise of the League of Nations: *Int. Status of South-West Africa,* [1950] I.C.J. 128 at 135-6, 142.

§301 On occasion, a unilateral statement may be made when similar statements have already been made or are subsequently made by other states relating to a similar matter. In such a case, the unilateral statements taken together constitute a series of binding treaties. The principal instance of this is the series of declarations made under the 'Optional Clause' of the Statute of the World Court.[9] Even in the absence of such a declaration a state may obligate itself by a declaration which ignores another state's irregularity of conduct, such as acquiescing in a wrong approach to the court by a declaration which estops it from contesting the court's jurisdiction.[10]

9. See *Right of Passage over Indian Territory* (Preliminary Objections) (Portugal/India), [1957] I.C.J. 125 at 146: "... by the deposit of its Declaration of Acceptance with the Secretary-General [of the United Nations], the accepting State becomes a Party to the system of the Optional Clause in relation to the other declarant States, with all the rights and obligations deriving from Article 36. The contractual relation between the Parties and the compulsory jurisdiction of the Court resulting therefrom are established, 'ipso facto and without special agreement', by the fact of the making of the Declaration. Accordingly, every State which makes a Declaration of Acceptance must be deemed to take into account the possibility that, under the Statute, it may at any time find itself subjected to the obligations of the Optional Clause in relation to a new Signatory as a result of the deposit by that Signatory of a Declaration of Acceptance. A State accepting the jurisdiction of the Court must expect that an Application may be filed against it on the same day on which that State deposits with the Secretary-General its Declaration of Acceptance. For it is on that very day that the consensual bond, which is the basis of the Optional Clause, comes into being between the States concerned", even though the 'defendant' state has not yet been informed of the deposit of the declaration. See dissenting opinion of Armand-Ugon J. *Barcelona Traction Light & Power Co.* (Prelim. Objections) (Belgium/Spain), [1964] I.C.J. 6 at 135: "It is true that the declarations were unilateral undertakings. But as those declarations were addressed to other States, which had accepted the same obligation, they gave rise to agreements of a treaty character concerning jurisdiction which were legally equivalent to the jurisdictional clause embodied in a treaty or convention.... These declarations... had the same force and the same legal content as a provision in a treaty." Canada's current declaration under the Optional Clause was made in 1985. See §411. See also, *Military and Paramilitary Activities in and against Nicaragua*, [1984] I.C.J. 392, 411-420.

10. *The Corfu Channel Case (Preliminary Objection)* (G.B./Albania), [1948] I.C.J. 15 at 27-29.

§302 Although treaties have traditionally been made between states, and this is the situation envisaged by the Vienna Convention on the Law of Treaties, an internationally binding agreement can be entered into by the United Nations[11] or some other international institution possessing the necessary competence.[12] Moreover, in some instances the international agreement in question may be made between international organizations themselves.[13]

11. *Reparation for Injuries Suffered in the Service of the U.N.*, [1949] I.C.J. 174 at 178-9: "The Charter ... has given [the Organization] special tasks ... providing for the conclusion of agreements between the Organization and its Members." See, e.g., Headquarters Agreement between the United Nations and the United States, 1947, 11 U.N.T.S. 11; and Agreement by way of Exchange of Letters between Egypt and United Nations concerning U.N. Emergency Force in Egypt, Doc. A/3526, 1957, Higgins, 1 United Nations Peacekeeping 1946-1967 (1969), p. 373.

12. See, e.g., Headquarters Agreement between Canada and the International Civil Aviation Organization, 1951, 96 U.N.T.S. 155, and Exchange of Notes constituting a Supplementary H.Q. Premises Agreement, T.S. 1971/17.

13. See, e.g., Agreement between League of Nations and United Nations, 1946, 1 U.N.T.S. 110.

§303 Treaties are entered into after preparation by representatives of the parties in accordance with the powers conferred upon them in their credentials. In most cases, especially when the document has been drawn up by a multi-lateral conference the representatives will only have the power to sign. Signatures may be of the actual treaty or of a Final Act which constitutes a record of the conference and what has been agreed.[14] In such cases, the draft is then referred back to governments for signature. With the rise of democratic government, most treaties require ratification, often in accordance with the procedures of domestic law,[15] before they come into effect.[16] When a treaty has been signed and prior to ratification, even though the treaty is not yet in force, there is an obligation upon a party to refrain from any action which would be inconsistent with its objects or purposes, and this has been made a legal obligation by the Vienna Convention on the Law of Treaties.[17]

14.   As a record of proceedings this may be signed by a non-state organization which has participated in the drafting conference, even though as a non-state it cannot sign the treaty that has been drafted: see, e.g., Final Act of Geneva Conference on Humanitarian Law in Armed Conflicts, Schindler and Toman, The Laws of Armed Conflicts (1982), p. 549.

15.   U.N. Charter, Art. 110(1): "The present Charter shall be ratified by the signatory states in accordance with their respective constitutional processes."

16.   *Ambatielos Case* (Jurisdiction), *ante*, at pp. 42-3. For a discussion of the U.K. ratification practice, see dissenting opinion by McNair J. at pp. 59-62.

17.   Art. 18: "A State is obliged to refrain from acts which would defeat the object and purpose of a treaty when (a) it has signed or has exchanged instruments constituting the treaty subject to ratification, acceptance or approval, until it shall have made its intention clear not to become a party to the treaty; or (b) it has expressed its consent to be bound by the treaty, pending the entry into force of the treaty and provided that such entry into force is not unduly delayed."

§304 Since treaties limit the freedom of action of a party to the extent provided in the text, a party is free, so long as this is not forbidden by the treaty, when signing or ratifying the treaty, to add any reservation it chooses.[18] However, such a reservation should not be contrary to the purpose of the treaty or of such a character as to render it nugatory.[19] If the treaty expressly permits a particular reservation there is no need for it to be accepted by other parties, unless the treaty provides otherwise.[20] Since a reservation not expressly permitted amounts to a unilateral attempt to amend the treaty it must be accepted by the other parties, and if "it appears from the limited number of the negotiating States and the object and purpose of a treaty that the application of the treaty in its entirety between all the parties is an essential condition of the consent of each one to be bound by the treaty, a reservation requires acceptance by all the parties".[21] On the other hand, when consent of all the parties is not necessary, the presence of reservations may mean that a treaty is in force as between some of the ratifying powers and not as between others.[22] In addition to reservations, a state may issue a statement of understanding or interpretation when voting on a particular clause to a treaty or on signature.[23] According to the Vienna Convention on the Law of Treaties, if it is intended that such an interpretation shall amount to a reservation this fact must be confirmed on ratification, although any acceptance of that interpretation does not require confirmation.[24] A reservation is considered to have been accepted by a party to the treaty if there has been no objection made to it.[25] If a state which objects to a reservation has not at the same time objected to the coming into force of the treaty as between itself and the reserving state, the remaining provisions of the treaty are considered to be in force.[26]

18.   Vienna Convention on the Law of Treaties, Art. 19: "A State may, when signing, ratifying, accepting, approving or acceding to a treaty, formulate a reservation unless . . ."

19.   Art. 19(c): ". . . unless the reservation is incompatible with the object and purpose of the treaty." For a Canadian comment on reservations, particularly with regard to the Geneva Gas Protocol, 1925, 94 L.N.T.S. 65, and the proposed chemical weapons convention, see Legal Bureau memo. 9 Apr. 1984, (1985) 23 C.Y.B.I.L. 333.

20.   Art. 20(1).

21.   Art. 20(2).

22.   *Reservations to the Convention on Genocide,* [1951] I.C.J. 15 at 29-30: ". . . if a party to the Convention objects to a reservation which it considers to be incompatible with the object and purpose of the Convention, it can in fact consider that the reserving State is not a party to the Convention; if, on the other hand, a party accepts the reservation as being compatible with the object and purpose of the Convention, it can in fact consider that the reserving State is a party to the Convention." See also Vienna Convention, Art. 20(4).

23.   When signing Additional Protocol I, 1977, to the Geneva Conventions of 12 August 1949, Canada made a Declaration: "Some provisions are formulated in such a way that they give rise to different, even contradictory, interpretations. My Government does not wish at this juncture to raise these problems, but it reserves the right to do so before it ratifies the Protocol", Schindler and Toman, The Laws of Armed Conflict (1982), p. 633. The U.K. and U.S. 'understandings' were much more detailed and specific: Schindler and Toman, *op. cit.,* pp. 634-636. In a memo of 23 Oct. 1985, the Legal Bureau stated that "a declaration [of intervention] explains or clarifies the meaning of the provisions of the treaty but does not exclude or vary its legal effect", (1986) 24 C.Y.B.I.L. 396, at 402.

24.   Art. 23(2), (3).

25.   Art. 20(5) requires the objection to be made within twelve months of notification of the reservation or of acceptance of the treaty, whichever is the later.

26.   Art. 21(1): "A reservation established with regard to another party . . . (a) modifies for the reserving State in its relations with that other party the provisions of

the treaty to which the reservation relates to the extent of the reservation; and (b) modifies the provisions to the same extent for that other party in its relations with the reserving State." (3): "When a State objecting to a reservation has not opposed the entry into force of the treaty between itself and the reserving State, the provisions to which the reservation relates do not apply as between the two States to the extent of the reservation."

§305   The procedures for entering treaties and whether a treaty or other international agreement requires approval by the national legislature depend upon the requirements of municipal law.[27] Insofar as Canada is concerned: "International agreements may be brought directly to the attention of Parliament and the approval of both houses may be sought by Joint Resolution before Canada commits itself to treaties which involve military or economic sanctions, political or military commitments of a far-reaching character, or the large expenditure of public funds. The decision on whether Parliamentary approval should be sought is made, in each instance, by the Government of the day. Recent practice seems to have been to seek Parliamentary approval by resolution for only the most important treaties. The last agreement to have been submitted to Parliament for approval by resolution was the Canada-United States Automotive Products Agreement, which was approved by a joint resolution of the House of Commons and the Senate in 1966. The Charter of the United Nations and the North Atlantic Treaty were approved by resolution of both Houses of Parliament.[28] . . . While the Auto Pact was the last agreement submitted to Parliament for approval by joint resolution, Parliamentary approval has been expressly sought and obtained in the implementing legislation giving effect to [a number of] double taxation agreements. . . . All treaties of any significance are tabled in the House of Commons and the Senate after they enter into force. This is done by a routine tabling exercise, normally once or twice a year. The most recent occasion on which a group of agreements were tabled in Parliament was July 17, 1980, when the Secretary of State for External Affairs tabled 46 bilateral agreements and 9 multilateral agreements. On occasion, governments may wish to bring a proposed agreement to the attention of their national legislatures before it has been signed. This was the case with the Transit Pipeline Agreement between Canada and the United States. . . . In the case of extradition treaties there is a legislative requirement for them to be tabled. Section 7 of the Extradition Act[29] reads in part: '. . . any extradition arrangement shall be, as soon as possible, published in the Canada Gazette and laid before both Houses of Parliament'. . . . The practice has grown up in recent years of tabling in Parliament bilateral nuclear cooperation and fisheries agreements. . . . In Canada treaties are not self-executing and do not constitute part of the law of the land merely by virtue of their conclusion. Treaties require implementing legislation in order to change domestic law.[30] Many international agreements require legislation to make them effective in Canadian domestic law. The legislation may be either federal or provincial or a combination of both in fields of shared jurisdiction.[31] Canada will not normally become a party to an international agreement which requires implementing legislation until the necessary legislation has been enacted.[32] If the legislation falls within federal jurisdiction, the implementing legislation will often include a section stating that Parliament approves the agreement[33]. . . . Part III of the Canada Gazette, in its periodical Table of Public Statutes, under the heading 'Agreements', lists Acts of Parliament which deal with or relate to international treaties".[34] The fact that a treaty has been signed and ratified but not yet enacted into national law does not preclude the international liability of the signatory under the treaty.

27. See Gotlieb, Canadian Treaty-Making (1968); Gotlieb, "Canadian Treaty-Making, Informal Agreements and Interdepartmental Agreements", in Macdonald *et al.*, Canadian Perspectives on International Law and Organization (1974), p. 229; Jacomy-Millette, Treaty Law in Canada (1975); Plouffe, "Les arrangements internationaux des agences et ministères du Canada", (1983) 21 C.Y.B.I.L. 176. Canada's view on the means of giving consent to being bound by a treaty are expressed in a reply sent by the Legal Bureau to a Council of Europe questionnaire, Feb. 1, 1985, (1986) 24 C.Y.B.I.L. 397-402.

28. Other agreements so approved include the trade agreements with Bulgaria, 1963, and Hungary, both approved in 1965, and the Columbia River Treaty approved in 1964. In the answer of Feb. 1985 the Legal Bureau stated "It is Canadian practice to secure the enactment by Parliament of any necessary implementing legislation before the Government expresses its consent to be bound by a treaty".

29. R.S.C. 1970, c. E-21.

30. *Canada v. (A.G.) v. Ontario (A.G.)(Labour Conventions Case)*, [1937] A.C. 326 at 347 (P.C.) per Lord Atkin: "Within the British Empire there is a well-established rule that the making of a treaty is an executive act, while the performance of its obligations, if they entail alteration of the existing domestic law, requires legislative action." See also *Arrow River & Tributaries Slide & Boom Co. v. Pigeon Timber Co.*, [1932] S.C.R. 495 at 510 (S.C.C.) per Lamont J.: "The treaty in itself is not equivalent to an Imperial Act and, without the sanction of Parliament, the Crown cannot alter existing law by entering into a contract with a foreign power"; *Vincent v. Min. of Employment & Immigration* (1983), 48 N.R. 214 at 221 (Fed. C.A.) per Cowan D.J.: "International conventions . . . are not, as such, part of the law of Canada. Canada's obligations under those conventions are implemented, to the extent Parliament so decides, by statutes of Canada"; see also Macdonald, "The Relationship between International Law and Domestic Law in Canada", in Macdonald, *op. cit.*, pp. 88, 117-130, and "International Law and the Domestic Law of Canada", (1975) 2 Dal. Law J. 307.

31. See Morris, "Canadian Federalism and International Law", in Macdonald, *op. cit.*, p. 55; Dufour, "Fédéralisme Canadien et droit international", Macdonald, *op.*

cit., p. 72; LaForest, "The Labour Conventions Case Revisited", (1974) 12 C.Y.B.I.L. 137; Jacomy-Millette, "L'Etat fédéré dans les relations internationales contemporaines: le cas de Canada", (1976) 14 C.Y.B.I.L. 3; di Marzo, "The Legal Status of Agreements Concluded by Competent Units of Federal States with Foreign Entities", (1978) C.Y.B.I.L. 197 at 206 *et seq.*, and Component Units of Federal States and International Agreements (1980). For the view of Canada on the use of federal state clauses in treaties, see letter of Legal Bureau, 17 Mar. 1982, (1983) 21 C.Y.B.I.L. 319-23.

32.   This often accounts for the delay between Canadian signature or accession to multilateral treaties — Canada signed the Genocide Convention on Nov. 28, 1949, and did not ratify it until Sept. 3, 1952; Canada never signed the 1966 International Covenants on Economic and Social Rights and Political and Civil Rights, and did not accede to them until May 19, 1976.

33.   The text of the agreement is often printed as a schedule to the legislation: see, e.g., Japanese Treaty Act 1913, 3 & 4 Geo. V, c. 27, considered in *Re Oriental Orders in Council Variation Act, B.C. (Employment of Aliens)*, (1922), 63 S.C.R. 293 (S.C.C.); see also Carriage by Air Act, R.S.C. 1970, c. C-14, Schedule I, the Warsaw Convention, 1929, Schedule III, Hague Protocol 1955; *Surprenant v. Air Can.*, [1973] Que. C.A. 107 (Que. C.A.).

34.   Statement of Dept. of External Affairs, May 21, 1981.

§306   The preamble of a treaty does not constitute a substantive part of the treaty, nor does it by itself create legal obligations. "Increasingly, preambles are more of ideological rather than legal significance. They are intended to set the background for the substantive obligations in the operative part of the convention. In becoming party to the CEDAW[35] Canada undertook to report on the measures taken to implement the operative articles of the convention, and not the preamble".[36] Nevertheless, the Vienna Convention on Treaties[37] makes it clear that "the context for the purpose of the interpretation of a treaty" includes the preamble in addition to the text.[38]

35.   Convention on the Elimination of All Forms of Discrimination against Women, 1981, 19 I.L.M. 33 — the Preamble comprises 15 paragraphs, including condemnations of apartheid and poverty, and approval of the new economic order.

36.   Legal Bureau memo, 11 Dec. 1984, (1985) 23 C.Y.B.I.L. 347.

37.   1969, 8 I.L.M. 679.

38.   Art. 31(2). The memo states "... the normative, or operative, parts of the convention may be interpreted in the light of the preamble, but this does not in our opinion justify questions on matters covered by the preamble alone."

§307   Since treaties are agreements between entities possessed of international personality,[39] they do not confer rights upon objects of international law, such as individuals[40] or ships.[41] However, these might be the indirect beneficiaries of a treaty.[42] Whether individuals are able to rely upon a treaty before the courts of their own country depends on national legislation. In most cases, the treaty in question must have been enacted into national law for this to be possible.[43] Contrarily, treaties may have the effect of imposing obligations upon[44] or reducing the rights of individuals.[45]

39. See §§52-74 and §§299-300.

40. See *Arrow River & Tributaries Slide & Boom Co. v. Pigeon Timber Co., ante*, at p. 510 (S.C.C.) per Lamont J.: "Where, as here, a treaty provides that certain rights or privileges are to be enjoyed by the subjects of both contracting parties, these rights and privileges are, under our [Canadian] law, enforceable by the courts only where the treaty has been implemented or sanctioned by legislation rendering it binding upon the subject. Upon this point I agree with the view expressed by both courts below; 'that, in British countries, treaties to which Great Britain is a party are not as such binding upon the individual subjects, but are only contracts binding in honour upon the contracting States' [e.g., *Arrow River & Tributaries Slide & Boom Co. v. Pidgeon Timber Co.* (1930), 65 O.L.R. 575 at 581-2 (Ont. H.C.)]. In this respect our law would seem to differ from that of the United States where, by an express provision of the Constitution [Art. 6, c. 1, 2], treaties duly made are 'the supreme law of the land' equally with Acts of Congress duly passed. They are thus cognizable in both the federal and state courts. In the case before us it is not suggested that any legislation, Imperial or Canadian, was ever passed implementing or sanctioning the provision [in issue]. That provision, therefore, has only the force of a contract between Great Britain and the United States which is ineffectual to impose any limitation upon the legislative power exclusively bestowed by the Imperial Parliament upon the legislature of a province. In the absence of affirming legislation this provision of the treaty cannot be enforced by any of our courts whose authority is derived from municipal law." See also *Civilian War Claimants Assn. v. R.*, [1932] A.C. 14 (H.L.); *Ritcher v. R.*, [1943] Ex. C.R. 64 (Ex. Ct.); *Khan v. Fredson Travel Inc.* (No. 2)(1982), 36 O.R. (2d) 17 (Ont. H.C.). See also §§282-297.

41. *The Ships Taken at Genoa* (1803), 4 C. Rob. 388 (H.C. of Admiralty) re exemption of shipping from seizure in connection with the signature of a capitulation.

42. See European Convention on Human Rights, 213 U.N.T.S. 222, Art. 1: "The High Contracting Parties shall secure to everyone within their jurisdiction the rights and freedoms defined in Section I of this Convention." By Section II, Art. 19: "to ensure the observance of the engagements undertaken by the High Contracting Parties in the present Convention, there shall be set up (1) a European Commission of Human Rights . . . ; and (2) a European Court of Human Rights. . . ." By Art. 25 individuals enjoy the right of petition to the Commission, but by Art. 48 the jurisdiction of the court may only be invoked by the Commission or a High Contracting Party.

43. See *Silver Case* (1983), 72 I.L.R. 334, 376 (European Ct. of Human Rights) concerning European Convention and English Law.

44. See Genocide Convention, 1948, 78 U.N.T.S. 277, Art. 4: "Persons committing genocide . . . shall be punished, whether they are constitutionally responsible rulers, public officials or private individuals." Canada is a party to this Convention, and the Criminal Code has been amended to render genocide a crime under Canadian law: s. 281.1.

45. The authority granted to any captor to try, e.g., a war criminal or a pirate has this effect, for it enables jurisdiction to be exercised even though there is no direct link

between the offender and the state seeking to try him, neither because of the locus of the offence, nor the nationality of the offender or his victim. See §§189-213, §§359-382.

§308 On the basis of the principle res inter alios acta and the maxim pacta tertiis nec nocent nec prosunt,[46] non-parties to an agreement are normally unable to bear the burdens[47] or enjoy the benefits of the agreement.[48] Yet, it cannot be ignored that the United Nations purports to have the power to impose burdens upon non-members,[49] and the World Court has upheld this view,[50] although individual judges have expressed strong reservations.[51] Moreover, contracting parties may create rights and duties for nationals of third states which are subject to the jurisdiction of a contracting party to the convention, even though the state of which they are nationals is not a party to that convention.[52]

46. Agreements shall neither burden nor benefit third parties. See McNair, Law of Treaties (1961), Ch. 16. See *North Sea Continental Shelf Cases* (Germany/Denmark; Germany/Netherlands), [1969] I.C.J. 3, at 26; *Vernicos Shipping Co. v. U.S.* (1965), 349 F. 2d 468. See also Vienna Convention on the Law of Treaties, Art. 34.

47. See, e.g., *Status of Eastern Carelia* (1923), 1 W.C.R. 191 at 204: "As concerns States not Members of the League, . . . the submission of a dispute between them and a Member of the League for solution according to the methods provided for in the Covenant, could take place only by virtue of their consent."

48. See *Chorzów Factory (Indemnity)* (Germany/Poland) (1928), 1 W.C.R. 646 at 676, denying Poland's right to invoke the Armistice Convention, 1918, to which it was not a party; *Free Zones of Upper Savoy and the District of Gex* (France/ Switzerland) (1932), 2 W.C.R. 508 at 547: "It cannot be lightly presumed that stipulations favourable to a third State have been adopted with the object of creating an actual right in its favour. There is however nothing to prevent the will of sovereign States from having this object and this effect. The question of the existence of a right acquired under an instrument drawn between other States is therefore one to be decided in each particular case: it must be ascertained whether the States which have stipulated in favour of a third State meant to create for that State an actual right which the latter has accepted as such." See Vienna Convention on the Law of Treaties, Arts. 35, 36.

49. Charter of the United Nations, Art. 2(6): "The Organization shall ensure that states which are not Members of the United Nations act in accordance with these Principles so far as may be necessary for the maintenance of international peace and security."

50. *Reparation for Injuries Suffered in the Service of the U.N.,* [1949] I.C.J. 174 at 185: ". . . fifty States, representing the vast majority of the members of the international community, had the power, in conformity with international law, to bring into being an entity possessing objective international personality, and not merely personality recognized by them alone, together with capacity to bring international claims". Art. 38 of the Convention recognizes that a treaty provision may become a rule of customary law and, as such, binding on third states.

51. See dissenting opinion of Krylov J. at p. 219: ". . . we must found the right of the Organization to bring an international claim . . . on the express consent of the States,

either by the preparation and conclusion of a general convention, or by agreements concluded between the Organization and the respective State in each individual case." See also separate opinion of Read J. in *Int. Status of South-West Africa*, [1950] I.C.J. 128 at 165: "It is a principle of international law that the parties of a multilateral treaty, regardless of their number or importance, cannot prejudice the legal rights of other States." And for a decision in which the court adopted the more traditional view of the rights of a third party, see *Monetary Gold* (Italy/France, G.B., U.S.), [1954] I.C.J. 19.

52.   *Velleman en Tas N.V. v. Leonidas* (1971), 70 I.L.R. 435 (Netherlands D.C.). This is the case with the European Convention on Human Rights. See§§35, 36.

§309   A basic exception to the rule that third parties cannot benefit from treaties to which they are not a party lies in treaties concerning most-favoured-nation treatment.[53] By virtue of the most-favoured-nation standard, a beneficiary is not to be treated in any discriminatory fashion[54] as compared with any other state[55] enjoying a benefit within the same field as the original grant.[56] The benefit enjoyed under a most-favoured-nation treaty will continue so long as the original treaty subsists or a third party actually enjoys a privilege.[57] In some ways it may be considered that most-favoured-nation treaties do not constitute an exception to the general rule regarding the position of third parties to treaties. The most-favoured-nation system represents a form of treaty-making by reference and incorporation,[58] that is to say, the most-favoured-nations clause opens the way to incorporate into the original treaty of the beneficiary of most-favoured-nation treatment benefits granted in a treaty to any third party, so long as there is some third-party privilege to which reference may be made and such privilege is in fact being enjoyed.

53.   *Anglo-Iranian Oil Co. Case (Jurisdiction)* (G.B./Iran), [1952] I.C.J. 93 at 109: "[I]n order that the United Kingdom may enjoy the benefit of any treaty concluded by Iran with a third party by virtue of a most-favoured-nation clause contained in a treaty concluded by the United Kingdom with Iran, the United Kingdom must be in a position to invoke the latter treaty. The treaty containing the most-favoured-nation clause is the basic treaty upon which the United Kingdom must rely. It is this treaty which establishes the juridical link between the United Kingdom and a third-party treaty and confers upon that State the rights enjoyed by the third party. A third-party treaty, independent of and isolated from the basic treaty, cannot produce any legal effect as between the United Kingdom and Iran: it is res inter alios acta." See also §§184, 185.

54.   See *Re Oriental Orders in Council Variation Act, B.C.* (Employment of Aliens), *ante,* per Davies C.J.: "[T]he province attempts to discriminate and to put the Japanese on a footing less favourable than that of the subjects of the most favoured nation. This is contrary to the obligations of the treaty and in direct conflict with the Dominion statute which must prevail under the powers conferred by s. 132 of the B.N.A. Act".

55. *Rights of U.S. Nationals in Morocco* (France/U.S.), [1952] I.C.J. 176 at 192: ". . . the intention of the most-favoured-nation clauses was to establish and maintain at all times fundamental equality without discrimination among all the countries concerned."

56. *Anglo-Iranian Oil Co. Case, ante,* at p. 106: "[The U.K. objected] that the Government of Iran, at or about the time it signed the Declaration [under Art. 36 of the Court's Statute], concluded with a number of other States bilateral treaties which provide for arbitration of disputes relating to treaties already concluded or to be concluded. This attitude is said to be contrary to the view that the Government of Iran desired to exclude from the jurisdiction of the Court treaties accepted by it before the ratification of the Declaration. The objection loses all weight when it is viewed in the light of the special reasons which prompted the formulation by the Iranian Government of its Declaration on the one hand, and the arbitration clauses inserted in certain treaties on the other. That Government was dealing with two different situations. . . . It is quite understandable that it was disposed to accept the arbitration clause as it is expressed in the treaties concluded with certain States which were willing to give up capitulatory rights. But the Government of Iran was confronted with an entirely different problem when it was preparing a Declaration . . . binding itself to submit to the jurisdiction of the Court in relation to all States which had signed similar Declarations or which might do so in the future, whether such States had concluded with Iran treaties replacing the regime of capitulations or not", and the British contention was rejected. See also *Ambatielos Claim* (Greece/G.B.) (1956), 12 R.I.A.A. 83 at 107: "The Commission holds that the most-favoured-nation clause can only attract matters belonging to the same category of subject as that to which the clause relates."

57. *Rights of U.S. Nationals in Morocco, ante,* at p. 204: "It is submitted on behalf of the United States that the most-favoured-nation clauses in treaties with countries like Morocco were not intended to create merely temporary or dependent rights, but were intended to incorporate permanently these rights and render them independent of the treaties by which they were originally accorded. It is consequently contended that the right to fiscal immunity accorded by the [British and Spanish Treaties] was incorporated in the treaties which guaranteed to the United States most-favoured-nation treatment, with the result that this right would continue even if the rights and privileges granted by [those] Treaties should come to an end. . . . [T]he Court is unable to accept this contention, it is not established that most-favoured-nation clauses in treaties with Morocco have a meaning and effect other than such clauses in other treaties or are governed by different rules of law. When provisions granting fiscal immunity in treaties between Morocco and third States have been abrogated or renounced, these provisions can no longer be relied upon by virtue of a most-favoured-nation clause." Similarly, "the failure by a Power, to which a favour has been granted to exercise that favour does affect or prejudice the right of any other Power entitled to that favour by virtue of a most-favoured-nation clause. For all useful purposes, suspending the exercise of a favour is equivalent to failure to exercise it." (Dissenting opinion at p. 226).

58. *Rights of U.S. Nationals in Morocco, ante,* p. 191: "[The U.S. contention] was based on the view that the most-favoured-nation clauses in treaties made with countries like Morocco should be regarded as a form of drafting by reference rather than as a method for the establishment and maintenance of equality of treatment without discrimination amongst the various countries concerned. According to this view, rights and privileges which a country was entitled to invoke by virtue of a most-

favoured-nation clause, and which were in existence at the date of its coming into force, would be incorporated permanently by reference and enjoyed and exercised even after the abrogation of the treaty provisions from which they had been deprived. . . . [T]his contention is inconsistent with the intentions of the parties now in question . . . [and] would run contrary to the principle of equality and it would perpetuate discrimination."

§310 Problems frequently arise in connection with the interpretation of treaties. The essential purpose of interpretation is to ascertain the intention of the parties and, to the extent that this is possible, words are to be read in their ordinary and everyday meaning so long as such an interpretation in no way frustrates the purposes for which the treaty has been created.[59] In some cases the treaty will itself contain an interpretation clause. When this occurs care must be taken to ensure that the treaty is interpreted in accordance with such clause and that a dispute as to the meaning of the clause is not confused with a dispute as to the application or meaning of the treaty itself.[60] When the treaty is written in two or more languages of equal authenticity it will often require that reference be made to the text in which it was drafted.[61] When the language is ambiguous or the parties differ as to the meaning of a clause it is a general principle that the meaning which imposes least restrictions on the sovereignty of the parties is the one that will be chosen.[62] It is also possible to ascertain the true meaning of a clause by reference to another treaty between the same parties,[63] just as treaties may be used to interpret national legislation.[64]

59.   *The J.H. Nickerson* (Can.) (1871), Young Adm. 96 at 100: "The first article of the Convention of 1818 must be construed, as all other instruments are, with a view to the surrounding circumstances and according to the plain meaning of the words employed"; *Competence of Gen. Assembly for the Admission of a State to the United Nations,* [1950] I.C.J. 4 at 8; and *Certain Expenses of the United Nations,* [1962] I.C.J. 151 but see especially separate opinion by Sir Percy Spender at pp. 185-6 ". . . In a written instrument [the] meaning [of words] primarily is to be ascertained from the context, the setting, in which they are found. The cardinal rule of interpretation . . . is that words are to be read . . . in their natural and ordinary sense. If so read they make sense, that is the end of the matter. If, however, so read they are ambiguous or lead to an unreasonable result, then and then only must the Court, by resort to other methods of interpretation, seek to ascertain what the words really meant when they used the words under consideration. . . . [In so far as the United Nations Charter is concerned, since i]t was intended to apply to varying conditions in a changing and evolving world community and to a multiplicity of unpredictable situations and events [, i]ts provisions were intended to adjust themselves to the ever changing pattern of international existence. . . . [I]ts particular provisions should receive a broad and liberal interpretation unless the context of any particular provision requires, or there is to be found elsewhere in the Charter, something to compel a narrower and restricted interpretation. The stated purposes of the Charter should be the prime consideration. . . . Interpretation of the Charter should be directed to giving effect to that purpose, not to

frustrate it. If two interpretations are possible in relation to any particular provision of it, that which is favourable to the accomplishment of purpose and not restrictive of it must be preferred. A general rule is that words used in a treaty should be read as having the meaning they bore therein when it came into existence. But this meaning must be consistent with the purposes sought to be achieved." See also Convention, Art. 31 which provides that a treaty must be interpreted in good faith and for the purpose of interpretation shall include its preamble and annexes; as to the status of annexes and the legal effect of, e.g., a memorandum of understanding, see comment by Legal Bureau, Dept. of External Affairs, 19 Nov. 1981, (1982) 20 C.Y.B.I.L. 297-8 — . . . "the effect of simply annexing a MOU does not elevate that MOU to the level of an international obligation governed by international law".

60. *Interpretation of Peace Treaties,* [1950] I.C.J. 65 at 221.

61. See *Surprenant v. Air Can.,* [1973] Que. C.A. 107 (Que. C.A.) per Deschenes J.: The Warsaw Convention on Carriage by Air, 1929 (137 L.N.T.S. 11) was drawn up in French in a single copy, while the 1955 Hague Protocol thereto (478 U.N.T.S. 371) had authentic texts in French, English and Spanish, with the French prevailing in the event of discrepancy. "It is clear that on the international language, the French text is official for both conventions. However, it is not necessarily the same in Canadian law where an English translation of the Warsaw Convention and the English version of the Hague Protocol have both been incorporated into Canadian law with the same authority as the official French text. . . . Here, where the language of the Convention and the Protocol has the status of an official language, it is essential that we avoid difficulties in interpretation which may result from differences or weaknesses in translation. Our English versions faithfully reproduce the provisions which enjoy precedence in the original French text. It seems clear to me, therefore, that one does not have to afford these English texts the same authority as is accorded ordinary Canadian legislation, especially in the case of the Convention, where one finds a simple domestic translation which does not enjoy the same authenticity which the contracting parties have given to the English text of the Protocol. . . . If one follows the requirements of procedure, it is to be noted that the Convention does not contain any rule of interpretation in respect of its own text; it follows therefore that each national tribunal must apply its own norms of interpretation . . .". See also *Fothergill v. Monarch Airlines,* [1981] A.C. 251 (H.L.). See Vienna Convention on the Law of Treaties, Art. 33.

62. *The S.S. Lotus* (France/Turkey) (1927), 2 W.C.R. 20 at 35: ("Restrictions upon the independence of States cannot be presumed."); *Mavrommatis Palestine Concessions* (Greece/G.B.) (1924), 1 W.C.R. 293 at 307 ("[W]here two versions possessing equal authority exist one of which appears to have a wider bearing than the other, it is bound to adopt the more limited interpretation which can be made to harmonise with both versions and which, as far as it goes, is doubtless in accordance with the common intention of the Parties.")

63. *Greek National Residence Permit Case* (1971), 72 I.L.R. 570 (German Fed. Rep. S. Admin. Ct.).

64. *R. v. Videoflicks Ltd.* (1984), 14 D.L.R. (4th) 10 (Ont. C.A.); *Ref. re Public Service Employee Relations Act,* [1985] 2 W.W.R. 289 (Alta. C.A.); *Ford v. Quebec (P.G.),* [1985] C.S. 147 (Que. S.C.).

§311 States are free to enter into such agreements as they please, provided that the agreement does not purport to affect adversely the rights of a third state or a peremptory norm of international law.[65] Parties are presumed to have entered into a treaty in good faith[66] and any breach of the treaty results in international responsibility rendering the party causing the breach liable to make reparation.[67] However, a party which has suffered no actual injury as a result of the breach, while it may have a right to institute proceedings,[68] is unable to recover any concrete reparations, such as damages, in respect of that breach if it appears that the obligation is owed not to them individually, but in their corporate capacity, for example, as members of the League of Nations.[69] If the breach is material, the treaty may be denounced by the other party or parties,[70] provided that the breach in question does not relate to a provision "relating to the protection of the human person contained in treaties of a humanitarian character".[71]

65. Jus cogens: Vienna Convention on the Law of Treaties, Art. 53: ". . . a peremptory norm of general international law is a norm accepted and recognized by the international community of States as a whole as a norm from which no derogation is permitted and which can be modified only by a subsequent norm of general international law having the same character." By Art. 64: "If a new peremptory norm of general international law emerges, any existing treaty which is in conflict with the norm becomes void and terminates."

66. See *North Atlantic Coast Fisheries Case* (G.B./U.S.) (1910), R.I.A.A. 167 at 186: "Every State has to execute the obligations incurred by Treaty bona fide, and is urged thereto by the ordinary sanctions of International Law in regard to Treaty obligations." See, also Vienna Convention, Art. 26.

67. See *Interpretation of Peace Treaties, ante*, at p. 228: ". . . refusal to fulfil a treaty obligation involves international responsibility"; *Chorzów Factory (Indemnity), ante*, at p. 662: ". . . reparation [is] the corollary of the violation of obligations resulting from an engagement between States". See §§316-328.

68. *South-West Africa Cases (Preliminary Objection)* (Ethiopia/South Africa; Liberia/South Africa), [1962] I.C.J. 319.

69. *South-West Africa Cases (Second Phase)* (Ethiopia/South Africa; Liberia/South Africa), [1966] I.C.J. 6.

70. Vienna Convention, Art. 60. See also, *Chorzów Factory (Jurisdiction)* (Germany/Poland) (1927), 1 W.C.R. 589 at 610: "It is a principle generally accepted in the jurisprudence of international arbitration, as well as by municipal courts, that one Party cannot avail himself of the fact that the other has not fulfilled some obligation or has not had recourse to some means of redress, if the former party has, by some illegal act, prevented the latter from fulfilling the obligation in question, or from having recourse to the tribunal which would have been open to him." See *Pablo Nájera (France) v. United Mexican States* (1928), 5 R.I.A.A. 466, in which it was held that Mexico could not defend its failure to carry out a treaty with France on the ground that the latter as a member of the League of Nations had failed to register the treaty with the League Secretariat in accordance with its obligations under the Covenant, when Mexico was itself not a member of the League.

71. Vienna Convention, Art. 60(5).

§312　Parties to a treaty are free to suspend, terminate or abrogate their engagement by common consent.[72] However, a party may only denounce a treaty unilaterally if that is expressly provided for, or if it is established that the parties intended to admit such a possibility, or such a right may be deduced from the nature of the treaty,[73] or in the case of material breach by another party.[74] If the treaty is multi-lateral in character, some of the parties may, provided this is not forbidden by the treaty and their action does not adversely affect the interests of third parties, agree to suspend the operation of some of the provisions of the treaty as between themselves.[75] If the parties to a treaty enter into a later engagement dealing with the same matter there is a presumption that the later treaty is intended to replace the earlier one.[76] Normally, too, treaties are suspended,[77] but not necessarily abrogated,[78] if an armed conflict occurs between the parties. This does not apply to treaties specially entered into relating to the conduct of armed conflict.[79]

72.　See *Smith v. Ont. & Minn. Power Co.* (1918), 44 O.L.R. 43 at 49 (Ont. C.A.) per Riddell J.: "I have no shadow of doubt of the power of the United States and Canada, acting together, to abrogate this provision [of the Ashburton Treaty, 1842, Art. 2 (93 C.T.S. 416)], at least so far as it affects the citizens or subjects of the two countries". See also Vienna Convention, Arts. 54, 57.

73.　Convention, Art. 56.

74.　Convention, Art. 60. See §311.

75.　Convention, Art. 58.

76.　*Ambatielos Case (Jurisdiction)* (Greece/G.B.), [1952] I.C.J. 28 at 43. See also Convention, Art. 59.

77.　See, e.g., *Re Extradition of D'Amico* (1959), F. Supp. 648 at 653 (Dist. Ct.): ". . . while the [Extradition] Treaty of 1868 [between the U.S. and Italy (137 C.T.S. 155)] may be considered to have been suspended during World War II until the treaty of peace between the two Governments, it is in that class of treaty which is revived by a formal cessation of hostilities."

78.　See *Francis v. R.*, [1956] S.C.R. 618 (S.C.C.); and *Karnuth v. United States* (1928), 279 U.S. 231, for illustrations of the fact that some of the clauses of a treaty are suspended while others are abrogated by the outbreak of war. See *Lanificio Branditex v. Società Azais e Vidal* (1971), 71 I.L.R. 595 (Italy Ct. of Cassation).

79.　See Schindler and Toman, The Laws of Armed Conflicts (1982); see also §§329-349.

§313　In exceptional circumstances a right of unilateral denunciation of a treaty may arise. This is so when performance of obligations under the treaty become impossible, as, for example, if one of the parties to the treaty ceases to exist, although in such cases a successor state may be liable.[80] Impossibility as a ground for denunciation also occurs if the method of performance becomes impossible, as is the case if the currency in which treaty payments are to be made ceases to exist as legal tender.[81] Impossibility cannot be pleaded by a state which has itself been responsible for rendering performance impossible.[82]

80. See §120. See also *Ottoman Debt Arb.* (Bulgaria, Iraq, Palestine, Transjordan, Greece, Italy/Turkey) (1925), 1 R.I.A.A. 529.

81. *Serbian and Brazilian Loans* (France/Yugoslavia; France/Brazil) (1929), 2 W.C.R. 344 (when a 'gold clause' was interpreted as a gold value as distinct from a gold specie clause); *Right of Passage over Indian Territory* (Merits) (Portugal/India), [1960] I.C.J. 6 at 53, 87, 88, per Spiropoulos, Armand-Ugon, Moreno Quintana JJ.

82. Convention, Art. 61(2).

§314 Denunciation is also possible in accordance with the doctrine rebus sic stantibus,[83] on the basis of the implied inclusion in a treaty of a clause authorizing denunciation if the circumstances prevailing at the time of contracting the treaty have changed so radically that it may be presumed the parties would have provided for denunciation or termination had they envisaged the change in circumstances.[84] It has been generally accepted in the past that for such a denunciation to be effective the other party or parties to the treaty must acquiesce.[85] What this really means is that if the denunciation is contested it may lead to the allegation of a breach of the treaty requiring settlement by diplomacy or judicial process. It would appear, however, that the Vienna Convention on the Law of Treaties, while narrowing the operation of the doctrine, restores the unilateral right to denounce for changed circumstances.[86]

83. See McNair, Law of Treaties (1961), Ch. 42. See also *Kergall v. Common Assembly of the European Coal & Steel Community* (1955), 23 I.L.R. 628 at 652-658 (European Communities Ct.).

84. See, e.g., U.S. denunciation of International Load Line Convention, 1930 (135 L.N.T.S. 303) in 1941 on grounds that peace was an essential requirement for its operation, 5 Hackworth 355-356.

85. See *Nationality Decrees in Tunis and Morocco* (1923), 1 W.C.R. 145 at 159; and *Free Zones of Upper Savoy and the District of Gex* (France/Switzerland) (1932), 2 W.C.R. 448 at 470-471, separate opinion of Negulesco J.

86. Art. 62: "1. A fundamental change of circumstances which has occurred with regard to those existing at the time of the conclusion of a treaty, and which was not foreseen by the parties, may not be invoked as a ground for terminating or withdrawing from the treaty unless: (a) the existence of those circumstances constituted an essential basis of the consent of the parties to be bound by the treaty; and (b) the effect of the change is radically to transform the extent of obligations still to be performed under the treaty. 2. A fundamental change of circumstances may not be invoked as a ground for terminating or withdrawing from a treaty: (a) if the treaty establishes a boundary; or (b) if the fundamental change is the result of a breach by the party invoking it either of an obligation under the treaty or of any other international obligation owed to any other party to the treaty. 3. If, under the foregoing paragraphs, a party may invoke a fundamental change of circumstances as a ground for terminating or withdrawing from a treaty it may also invoke the change as a ground for

suspending the operation of the treaty." See dissenting judgment of Schwebel J. in *Military and Paramilitary Activities in and against Nicaragua*, [1984] I.C.J. 392, 619-621.

§315 Apart from change of circumstances as a ground for denunciation, states often maintain that if performance of a treaty would be likely to endanger their existence or welfare, they are entitled to denounce the treaty.[87] Similarly, many newly independent states contend that treaties entered into under duress may be denounced,[88] and this same contention is frequently put forward by a state which considers that it had earlier accepted a treaty only because it was too weak in comparison with the other party to avoid such acceptance.[89] However, a mere change in status of a party does not suffice to terminate a treaty.[90]

87.   See *Lucerne v. Aargau* (1882) (Switzerland), cited by McNair in Law of Treaties (1961), p. 690, n. 4: "There is no doubt that treaties may be denounced unilaterally by the party under obligation, if their continuance is incompatible with its vital interests as an independent commonwealth or with its fundamental purposes . . ." See also, *Bremen, Free Hansa (City) v. Prussia* (Germany) (1925), 3 Ann. Dig. 352.

88.   If this were conceded in so far as the state itself is concerned, few peace treaties would be carried out. However, if duress is applied against the representative of the state, the treaty would be invalid: Convention, Art. 51. Moreover, if a treaty is obtained by the threat or use of force in violation of the principles of international law embodied in the U.N. Charter that treaty is void: Art. 52.

89.   This contention was put forward by China in October 1982 when giving notice that it did not regard the treaties with U.K. relating to Hong Kong as binding. The view that unequal treaties do not constitute binding obligations is supported by Communist writers: see Haraszti, Some Fundamental Problems of the Law of Treaties (1973), pp. 157-158. A number of allegedly unequal treaties were repudiated by the Soviet Union after the Revolution: see Tunkin, Theory of International Law (1974), pp. 11-14. See also Sinha, New Nations and the Law of Nations (1967), p. 85. See also §113.

90.   See *Ex parte O'Dell and Griffen*, [1953] O.R. 190 (Ont. H.C.). On termination generally, see David, The Strategy of Treaty Termination (1975).

2. INTERNATIONAL RESPONSIBILITY

§316 International law recognizes that individuals may be guilty of certain offences which are described as international crimes.[91] As yet, there is no way in which a state can be considered to have committed an international crime in the strict sense of the law, though the International Law Commission in its Draft Rules on International Responsibility,[92] envisages the possibility that certain acts when committed by states will constitute international crimes.[93] All other illegal acts committed by states are described as international delicts,[94] and this includes breaches of treaty obligations.[95]

91.   See §§189-213.

92.   Arts. 1-32, (1979) 18 I.L.M. 1568, Arts. 33-35, (1980) 74 A.J.I.L. 962.

93.   Art. 19(3). See §213.

94.   Art. 19(4): "Any internationally wrongful act which is not an international crime in accordance with paragraph 2 constitutes an international delict."

95.   Art. 17: "1. An act of a State which constitutes a breach of an international obligation is an internationally wrongful act regardless of the origin, whether customary, conventional or other, of that obligation. 2. The origin of the international obligation breached by a State does not affect the international responsibility arising from the internationally wrongful act of that State." On state responsibility, generally, see Brownlie, System of the Law of Nations: State Responsibility (Part I), 1983.

§317   While every breach of an international obligation prima facie gives rise to international responsibility,[96] regardless of whether the state act in question is in conformity with international law,[97] the act or omission ceases to be a breach "if, subsequently, such an act has become compulsory by virtue of a peremptory norm of general international law".[98]

96.   Art. 1: "Every internationally wrongful act of a State entails the international responsibility of that State." See also Art. 17: note 95, *ante*.

97.   Art. 4: "An act of a State may only be characterized as internationally wrongful by international law. Such characterization cannot be affected by the characterization of the same act as lawful by internal law."

98.   Art. 29(2): ". . . a peremptory norm of general international law is a norm accepted and recognized by the international community of States as a whole as a norm from which no derogation is permitted and which can be modified only by a subsequent norm of general international law having the same character."

§318   While no state is able on its own authority to declare that an act is contrary to international law, it must be borne in mind that often the only means to ascertain that an obligation does in fact exist at international law, or that an act is contrary to international law, is by virtue of the attitude of third states frequently expressed through the medium of judicial decisions.[99] In such a case, it may well be that a particular state condemns an act as contrary to international law in the light of its own interpretation of United Nations resolutions, national declarations of policy, and the like.[1]

99.   See §§15-20.

1.   See *Filatiga v. Pena-Irala* (1980), 630 F. 2d 876, in which a United States court held that torture was a crime by international law and awarded damages against the Paraguayan Inspector General of Police. No other court has applied the same reasoning.

§319 It is a general principle of law recognized by civilized nations, and as such a principle of international law,[2] that every breach of an obligation carries the duty to make reparation,[3] the aim being to wipe out all the consequences of the wrongful act and re-establish the situation as it would have been had the act not taken place.[4] Actual restoration of the status quo ante[5] is frequently impossible and the most common basis for measuring reparation is monetary.[6] It may well be that the injured state is content with some other form of satisfaction, which may even be an apology by the wrongdoer, or a mere statement of guilt by an international tribunal.[7]

2. See §14.

3. See, e.g., *Lusitania Cases* (U.S./Germany) (1923), 7 R.I.A.A. 32 at 35: "It is a general rule of both the civil and the common law that every invasion of private right imports an injury and that for every such injury the law gives a remedy. Speaking generally, that remedy must be commensurate with the injury received.... [Thus] in death cases the right of action is for the loss sustained by the *claimants*, not by the estate. The basis of damages is not the physical or mental suffering of deceased or his loss or the loss to his estate, but the losses resulting to claimants from his death" (italics in original). Gray, 'Is There an International Law of Remedies?', (195) 56 B.Y.B.I.L. 25.

4. See *Chorzów Factory (Indemnity)* (Germany/Poland) (1928), 1 W.C.R. 646 at 677-678: "The essential principle contained in the notion of an illegal act — a principle which seems to be established by international practice and in particular by the decisions of arbitral tribunals — is that reparation must, as far as possible, wipe out all the consequences of the illegal act and reestablish the situation which would, in all probability, have existed if that act had not been committed."

5. *Chorzów Factory (Indemnity), ante,* at p. 678: "Restitution in kind, or, if this is not possible, payment of a sum corresponding to the value which a restitution in kind would bear; the award, if need be, of damages for loss sustained which would not be covered by restitution in kind or payment in place of it — such are the principles which should serve to determine the amount of compensation due for an act contrary to international law.... The dispossession of an industrial undertaking [in this case contrary to treaty] involves the obligation to restore the undertaking and, if this is not possible, to pay its value at the time of the indemnification, which value is designed to take the place of restitution which has become impossible. To this obligation, in virtue of the general principles of international law, must be added that of compensating loss sustained as the result of the seizure." See also *Norwegian Shipowners' Claims* (Norway/U.S.) (1922), 1 R.I.A.A. 309 at 338 (P.C.A.): "Just compensation implies a complete restoration of the status quo ante, based ... upon the loss of profits of the owners as compared with other owners of similar property."

6. See Grotius, De Jure Belli ac Pacis (1625), Lib. II, cap. XVII, s. 22: "pecunia communis est rerum utilium mensura", cited in *Lusitania Cases, ante,* at p. 35. Thus, countries, including Canada, whose nationals were killed when the Soviet Union shot down a Korean aircraft in 1983 put in claims for monetary compensation.

7. See *Corfu Channel Case (Merits)* (G.B./Albania), [1949] I.C.J. 4 at 35: "[T]o ensure respect for international law of which it is the organ, the Court must declare that the action of the British Navy constituted a violation of Albanian sovereignty.

This declaration is in accordance with the request made by Albania through her Counsel, and is in itself appropriate satisfaction." See also *The Carthage* (France/ Italy) (1913), 11 R.I.A.A. 456 at 460 (P.C.A.); *The Manouba* (1913), 11 R.I.A.A. 471 at 475: "Where one Power has failed to carry out its obligations, whether general or particular, towards another Power, the very statement of this fact, especially in an arbitral award, amounts to a serious sanction." See also Bissonnette, La Satisfaction comme Mode de Réparation en Droit International (1952).

§320 While reparation has to be made for a wrongful act, this is only the case if the claimant has a legal interest,[8] for international law does not recognize anything in the nature of an actio popularis.[9] Moreover, there must be an existing conflict between the claimant and the defendant concerning a right of the claimant,[10] even though in exceptional cases a declaratory judgment may be delivered by the World Court when there is no longer an issue in dispute.[11] "There is no inherent reason precluding . . . any international tribunal from providing for representative or class claims, despite difficulties they present. In recent years procedures have been developed to deal with a multitude of cases having common issues of fact and law, large numbers of parties similarly situated or other cases presenting unusual problems which require extraordinary treatment. Procedures for international adjudications can and should keep pace with present-day commercial realities and litigation techniques".[12]

8. See *South-West Africa Cases (Second Phase)* (Ethiopia/South Africa; Liberia/ South Africa), [1966] I.C.J. 6 at 32: "Such [legal] rights or interests, in order to exist, must be clearly vested in those who claim, by some text or instrument, or rule of law . . ." In this case, the Court held that it was only the League of Nations as such, not individual members, which possessed such an interest. It did state, however, "[I]t may be said that a legal right or interest need not necessarily relate to anything material or 'tangible', and can be infringed even though no prejudice of a material kind has been suffered. In this connection, the provisions of certain treaties and other international instruments of a humanitarian character [see, for example, the rights of parties to the European Convention on Human Rights, 1950, 213 U.N.T.S. 222: see §293], and the terms of various arbitral and judicial decisions, are cited as indicating that, for instance, States may be entitled to uphold some general principle even though the particular contravention of it alleged has not affected their own material interests; — that again, States may have a legal interest in vindicating a principle of international law, even though they have, in the given case, suffered no material prejudice, or ask only for token damages": *ibid*. See note 7, *ante*.

9. ". . . the argument [that the applicants may bring the action] amounts to a plea that the Court should allow the equivalent of an 'actio popularis', or right resident in any member of a community to take legal action in vindication of a public interest. But although a right of this kind may be known to certain municipal systems of law, it is not known to international law as it stands at present", *South-West Africa Cases (Second Phase), ante*, at p. 47. This does not mean that the majority of members of an

international organization, like the United Nations or the International Civil Aviation Organization, cannot condemn the actions of a member or recommend sanctions against it, as happened in the case of the Soviet Union after the shooting down of a Korean aircraft in 1983.

10. See *Northern Cameroons Case (Preliminary Objections)* (Cameroon/G.B.), [1963] I.C.J. 15 at 33-34: "The function of the Court is to state the law, but it may pronounce judgment only in connection with concrete cases where there exists at the time of the adjudication an actual controversy involving a conflict of legal interests between the parties. The Court's judgment must have some practical consequence in the sense that it can affect existing legal rights or obligations of the parties, thus removing uncertainty from their legal relations."

11. See *Northern Cameroons Case (Preliminary Objections), ante*, at p. 37: "That the Court may, in an appropriate case, make a declaratory judgment is indisputable. . . . [E]ven if the Court finds that it has jurisdiction, it is not obliged to exercise it in all cases. . . . Moreover the Court observes that if in a declaratory judgment it expounds a rule of customary law or interprets a treaty which remains in force, its judgment has a continuing applicability. But in this case there is a dispute about the interpretation and application of a treaty . . . which has now been terminated, is no longer in force, and there can be no opportunity for a future act of interpretation or application of that treaty in accordance with any judgment the Court might render." See also dissenting judgment of Jessup J. in the *South-West Africa Cases* (Second Phase), *ante*, at p. 328: "The Applicants have not asked for an award of damages or for any other material amend for their own individual benefit. They have in effect, and in part, asked for a declaratory judgment interpreting certain parts of the Mandate for South West Africa. The Court having decided in 1962 [I.C.J. 319] that they had standing (locus standi) to bring the action, they are now entitled to a declaratory judgment without any further showing of interest."

12. *Alcan Aluminum Ltd. v. Ircable Corp.* (1983), 72 I.L.R. 725, 732-733 (Iran/U.S. Claims Trib.).

§321 Most international tortious claims arise from injuries suffered by individuals either to their person[13] or their property,[14] but the damage suffered must not be too remote.[15] Normally, too, a state can only bring a claim on behalf of its nationals.[16] However, in accordance with the 1947 Peace Treaties claims may be made on behalf of 'United Nations nationals', defined as "individuals who are nationals of any of the United Nations, or corporations or associations organized under the laws of any of the United Nations, at the coming into force of the present Treaty, provided that the said individuals, corporations or associations also had this status on . . . the date of the Armistice [with the country in question]. The term 'United Nations nationals' also includes all individuals, corporations or associations which, under the laws in force in [that country] during the war, have been treated as enemy."[17] Similarly, in exceptional instances a state may be able to bring a claim on behalf of a non-national, provided there is some evidence of a link between the individual and the state indicating some measure of protection being exercised by the latter.[18]

13. See, e.g., *Lusitania Cases, ante; Corfu Channel Case (Merits), ante; Caire Claim* (France/Mexico) (1929), 5 R.I.A.A. 516.

14. *Pinson Claim* (France/Mexico) (1928), 5 R.I.A.A. 327. *Currie Claim* (G.B./Italy) (1954), 14 R.I.A.A. 21.

15. See *Trail Smelter Arbitration* (U.S./Canada) (1938/1941), 3 R.I.A.A. 1905 at 1931: "With regard to 'damages in respect of business enterprises', counsel . . . stated: 'The business men unquestionably have suffered loss of business and impairment of the value of good will because of the reduced economic status of the residents of the damaged area.' The Tribunal is of opinion that damage of this nature 'due to reduced economic status' of residents in the area is too indirect, remote, and uncertain to be appraised and not such for which an indemnity can be awarded." In *Chorzów Factory (Indemnity), ante*, at pp. 681-682, the Court discussed the issue of lucrum cessans and deducted costs of upkeep, improvement and normal development.

16. See *Dickson Car Wheel Co. Claim* (U.S./Mexico) (1931), 4 R.I.A.A. 669 at 678: "The injury inflicted upon an individual, a national of the claimant State, which implies a violation of the obligations imposed by international law upon each member of the Community of Nations, constitutes an act internationally unlawful, because it signifies an offence against the State to which the individual is united by the bond of nationality. The only juridical relation, therefore, which authorizes a State to exact from another the performance of conduct prescribed by international law with respect to individuals is the bond of nationality [see *Nottebohm Case* (Second Phase) (Liechtenstein/Guatemala), [1955] I.C.J. 4]. This is the link existing between the law and individuals and through it alone are individuals enabled to invoke the protection of a State and the latter empowered to intervene on their behalf. A State, for example, does not commit an international delinquency in inflicting an injury upon an individual lacking nationality, and consequently, no State is empowered to intervene or complain on his behalf either before or after the injury." See also *Barcelona Traction, Light & Power Co. (Second Phase)* (Belgium/Spain), [1970] I.C.J. 3 at 42: "In allocating corporate entities to States for the purpose of diplomatic protection, international law is based, but only to a limited extent, on an analogy with the rules governing the nationality of individuals. The traditional rule attributes the right of diplomatic protection of a corporate entity to the State under the laws of which it is incorporated and in whose territory it has its registered office. These two criteria have been confirmed by long practice and by numerous international instruments. . . . [I]t is not disputed that the company was incorporated in Canada and has its registered office in that country. The incorporation of the company under the law of Canada was an act of free choice. Not only did the founders of the company seek its incorporation under Canadian law but it has remained under that law for a period of over 50 years. It has maintained in Canada its registered office, its accounts and its share registers. Board meetings were held there for many years; it has been listed in the records of the Canadian tax authorities. Thus a close and permanent connection has been established, fortified by the passage of over half a century." See Copithorne, "State Responsibility and International Claims", Macdonald et al., *Canadian Perspectives on International Law and Organization* (1974), p. 207.

17. *Fubini Claim* (Italy/U.S.) (1959), 14 R.I.A.A. 420; *Mergé Claim* (U.S./Italy) (1955), 14 R.I.A.A. 236 (Italian-U.S. Conciliation Comm.).

18. *Barcelona Traction, Light & Power Co.* (Second Phase), *ante*, at p. 42: ". . . further or different links are at times said to be required in order that a right of diplomatic protection should exist. Indeed, it has been the practice of some States to give a company incorporated under their law diplomatic protection solely when it has

its seat (siège social) or management or centre of control in their territory, or when a majority or a substantial portion of the shares has been owned by nationals of the State concerned. Only then, it has been held, does there exist between the corporation and the State in question a genuine connection of the kind familiar from other branches of international law. However, in the particular field of the diplomatic protection of corporate entities, no absolute test of the 'genuine connection' has found general acceptance. Such tests as have been applied are of a relative nature, and sometimes links with one State have had to be weighed against those with another." See *Reparation for Injuries Suffered in the Service of the U.N.*, [1949] I.C.J. 174 at 184: "Upon examination of the character of the functions entrusted to the [United Nations] Organization and of the nature of the missions of its agents, it becomes clear that the capacity of the Organization to exercise a measure of functional protection of its agents arises by necessary intendment out of the Charter. . . . In claiming reparation based on the injury suffered by its agent, the Organization does not represent the agent, but is asserting its own right, the right to ensure respect for undertakings entered into towards the Organization." A contrario, see *Eichmann v. Israel* (1962), 36 I.L.R. 277, in which the Israeli courts upheld their jurisdiction on the basis of Israel's special relation to the victims of his crimes. See Green, "The Maxim Nullum Crimen Sine Lege and the Eichmann Trial", (1962) 38 B.Y.B.I.L. 457, 463-8.

§322 Since the link between an individual claimant and the state bringing his claim is nationality[19] and the claim in fact belongs to the state,[20] even though it may be based on the injury suffered by the individual, the latter is unable, by his own action, to interfere with the state's right to protect him. Equally, the state of nationality has every right to cancel by agreement any claims belonging to its nationals because of the illegal acts of another state.[21] Often, in order to secure some commercial advantage, an alien individual when entering into contractual relations abroad may agree that his activities will be subject to the local law and that he will forego any right to call upon his state to intervene on his behalf. This Calvo Clause[22] embodied in his contract can only affect his own rights. It cannot in any way impinge upon the discretionary right enjoyed by his state to intervene diplomatically in the event that its right to have its nationals treated properly is not observed.[23] Whether the Calvo doctrine is invoked or not, there cannot be any exercise of diplomatic intervention or recourse to international arbitration or judicial process in respect of the alleged wrongdoing until the individual alleging the wrong has exhausted local remedies[24] — provided there are such remedies to exhaust.[25]

19.　*Alcan Aluminum Ltd. v. Ircable Corp.* (1983), 72 I.L.R. 75 (Iran/U.S. Claims Trib.). See Amersinghe, State Responsibility for Injuries to Aliens, 1967; Lillich, The Human Rights of Aliens in Contemporary International Law, 1984.

20.　"It is an elementary principle of international law that a State is entitled to protect its subjects, when injured by acts contrary to international law committed by another State, from whom they have been unable to obtain satisfaction through the ordinary channels. By taking up the case of one of its subjects and by resorting to diplomatic action or international judicial proceedings on his behalf, a State is in reality asserting its own rights — its right to ensure, in the person of its subjects, respect fot the rules of international law. . . . Once a State has taken up a case on behalf of one of its subjects before an international tribunal, in the eyes of the latter the State is sole claimant", *Mavrommatis Palestine Concessions* (Greece/G.B.)(1924), 1 W.C.R. 293 at 302.

21. See *Dames v. Regan* (1981), 453 U.S. 654 (U.S. S.C.).

22. So-called after the Argentine foreign minister, first enunciated in his Derecho International (1868), SS. 185-186, and elaborated in his Le droit international théorique et pratique (5th ed. 1896), tr. Shea, The Calvo Clause (1955), p. 18: "It is certain that aliens who establish themselves in a country have the same right to protection as nationals, but they ought not to lay claim to a protection more extended. If they suffer any wrong, they ought to count on the government of the country prosecuting the delinquents, and not claim from the state to which the authors of the violence belong any pecuniary indemnity." *Reavis v. Exxon Corp.* (1977), 577 F. 2d 1196 (N.Y. S.C.).

23. See *North American Dredging Co. Claim* (U.S./Mexico) (1926), 4 R.I.A.A. 26 at 29 et seq.: ". . . an alien [may] lawfully make such a promise . . . but . . . he cannot deprive the government of his nation of its undoubted right of applying international remedies to violations of international law committed to his damage. Such government frequently has a larger interest in maintaining the principles of international law than in recovering damage for one of its citizens in a particular case, and manifestly such citizen cannot by contract tie in this respect the hands of his Government. . . . The purpose of such a contract is to draw a reasonable and practical line between Mexico's sovereign right of jurisdiction within its own territory, on the one hand, and the sovereign right of protection of the Government of an alien whose person or property is within such territory, on the other hand. . . . [The purpose of the clause in the contract] was to bind the claimant to be governed by the laws of Mexico and to use the remedies existing under such laws. . . . But this provision did not, and could not, deprive the claimant of his American citizenship and all that that implies. It did not take from him his undoubted right to apply to his own Government for protection if the resort to the Mexican tribunals or other authorities available to him resulted in a denial or delay of justice as that term is used in international law. . . . The basis of his appeal would be not a construction of his contract . . . but rather an intentionally illegal act. . . . He did not and could not affect the right of his Government to extend to him its protection in general or to extend to him its protection against breaches of international law."

24. See *The Ambatielos Claim* (Greece/G.B.) (1956), 12 R.I.A.A. 83 at 118-123: "The rule . . . means that the State against which an international action is brought for injuries suffered by private individuals has the right to resist such an action if the persons alleged to have been injured have not first exhausted all the remedies available to them under the municipal law of that State. The defendant State has the right to demand that full advantage shall be taken of all local remedies before the matters in dispute are taken up on the international level by the State of which the persons alleged to be injured are nationals. . . . These 'local remedies' include not only reference to the courts and tribunals, but also the use of the procedural facilities which municipal law makes available to litigants before such courts and tribunals. It is the whole system of legal protection, as provided by municipal law, which must have been put to the test before a State, as the protector of its nationals, can prosecute the claim on the international plane . . ." For the official Canadian view on this issue, see Letter of Under-Secretary of State for External Affairs, 18 Oct. 1967: ". . . Under well-

established principles of international law, certain prerequisites must have been fulfilled to justify the espousal of a claim by diplomatic intervention by one State on behalf of its nationals against another State. Among the requirements, generally speaking, are that all legal remedies (in the country concerned) must have been exhausted and that a denial of justice has resulted. Such a denial of justice might take the form of an unwarranted delay or obstruction of access to the courts, a manifestly unfair hearing or judgment, or discrimination. Furthermore, the failure . . . if property should be expropriated to pay any compensation, or to pay adequate compensation, could constitute a denial of justice . . ."; (1968) 6 C.Y.B.I.L. 263. See §290.

25.　*Ambatielos Claim, ante,* at p. 119: "The ineffectiveness of local remedies may result clearly from the municipal law itself. That is the case, for example, when a Court of Appeal is not competent to reconsider the judgement given by a Court of first instance on matters of fact, and when, failing such reconsideration, no redress can be obtained." See also *Mexican Union Ry. Claim* (U.S./Mexico) (1930), 5 R.I.I.A. 115 at 122, in which a Calvo Clause was held to be subject to the local remedies rule, but "the claimant never sought redress by application to the local courts or to the National Claims Commission. . . . If . . . the claimant would have been unable to obtain justice, no international tribunal would have denied it access, on the ground of the engagement subscribed to by it. But the claimant omitted to pursue its right by taking that course, and acted as if said course had never been indicated by the State and accepted by it, and as there can be no question of denial of justice or delay of justice, as long as justice has not been appealed to, the [tribunal] cannot regard the claimant as a victim of international delinquency." See Head, "A Fresh Look at the Local Remedies Rule," (1967) 5 C.Y.B.I.L. 142. See §290.

§323　It is not only when there is no local tribunal or other authority to which an applicant can apply that a denial of justice may ensue.[26] In the first place, national judicial standards must amount to what is broadly known as the minimum standards of international law in regard to the treatment of foreigners.[27] While it may not be easy to define what such standards are, the situation is now a little clearer than it was before World War II since the International Covenant on Civil and Political Rights,[28] to which Canada is a party, clearly stipulates: "1. All persons shall be equal before the courts and tribunals. In the determination of any criminal charge against him, or of his rights and obligations in a suit at law, everyone shall be entitled to a fair and public hearing by a competent, independent and impartial tribunal[29] established by law. . . . 2. Everyone charged with a criminal offence shall have the right to be presumed innocent until proved guilty according to law. 3. In the determination of any criminal charge against him, everyone shall be entitled to the following minimum guarantees, in full equality: (a) to be informed promptly and in detail in a language which he understands of the nature and cause of the charge against him;[30] (b) to have adequate time and facilities for the preparation of his defence and to communicate with counsel of his own choosing; (c) to be tried without undue delay;[31] (d) to be tried in his presence, and to defend himself in person or through legal assistance of his own choosing; ... and to have legal assistance assigned to him, in any case where the interests of justice so require, and without payment by him in such case if he does not have sufficient means to pay for it; (e) to examine, or have examined,[32] the witnesses against him and to have the attendance and examination of witnesses on his behalf under the same conditions as witnesses against him;[33] (f) to have the free assistance of an interpreter if he cannot understand or speak the language used in court;[34] (g) not to be compelled to testify against himself or to confess guilt. . . . 5. Everyone convicted of a crime shall have the right to his conviction and sentence being reviewed by a higher tribunal according to law. . . . 7. No one shall be tried or punished again for an offence for which he has already been finally convicted or acquitted in accordance with the law and penal procedure of each country."[35] It is also clearly established in international law that the criminal law must be applied without discrimination as between nationals and aliens.[36] On occasion, however, international law may postulate discrimination in favour of aliens, when the treatment of nationals falls below that of civilised standards.[37] By analogy, these standards may be interpreted to inquire whether a civil tribunal measures up to minimum standards. With the adoption of the International Covenant on Civil and Political Rights, the requirements relating to a fair trial for aliens are equally applicable to nationals. As a result, for those states bound by the Covenant, state responsibility may arise because of the improper treatment of nationals.[38] However, there is no effective sanction that can be applied against the offending state in such a case. For those parties to the European Convention on Human Rights which have accepted the jurisdiction of the court, responsibility arises in regard to nationals and resident aliens alike, and in such cases damages may be awarded.[39]

26. For a discussion of the various meanings of this term, see, e.g., *Chattin Claim* (U.S./Mexico) (1927), 4 R.I.A.A. 282 at 286 *et seq.* See Adede, "A Fresh Look at the Doctrine of Denial of Justice under International Law", (1976) 14 C.Y.B.I.L. 73.

27. See, e.g., *Neer Claim* (U.S./Mexico) (1926), 4 R.I.A.A. 60 at 61-62: ". . . the propriety of governmental acts should be put to the test of international standards, and the treatment of an alien, in order to constitute an international delinquency, should amount to an outrage, to bad faith, to wilful neglect of duty, or to an insufficiency of governmental act [e.g., failure to seek after assassins] so far short of international standards that every reasonable and impartial man would readily recognize its insufficiency. Whether the insufficiency proceeds from deficient execution of an intelligent law or from the fact that the laws of the country do not empower the authorities to measure up to international standards is immaterial." See also Roth, The Minimum Standard of International Law Applied to Aliens, 1949. In exceptional circumstances, a state may even be entitled to intervene by force to protect its nationals, see §78, note 18.

28. 1966, 99 U.N.T.S. 171, Art. 14. See also European Convention on Human Rights, 1950, 213 U.N.T.S. 222, Art. 6.

20. *Le Compte Case* (1981) 62 I.L.R. 319 at 342 (European Ct. of Human Rights): "The presence of judges making up half the membership, including the Chairman with a casting vote, provides a definite assurance of impartiality and the method of election of the medical members cannot suffice to bear out a charge of bias. . . . Again, the personal impartiality of each member must be presumed until there is proof to the contrary . . . ." The difficulty of proving such an allegation is perhaps illustrated by *Re India and Mubarak Ali Ahmed*, [1952] 1 All E.R. 1060 at 1063 (D.C.), per Lord Goddard C.J.: ". . . we are now asked to refuse to send him back to India because, it is said, he will not get a fair trial. I think it would be an impossible position for this court to take up to say that they would not return a person for trial to a country which is a member of the Commonwealth and where it is known that courts of justice have been presided over by Indian judges for very many years because we thought the court would not give him a fair trial. That would be an insult to the courts of India." For a judicial riposte to an allegation of partiality on the part of judges of the I.C.J., see *Military and Paramilitary Activities in and against Nicaragua* (Nicaragua/U.S.), [1986] I.C.J. Rep. 14, Sep. Op. of Lachs J., 158-160.

30. See *Faulkner Claim* (U.S./Mexico) (1926), 4 R.I.A.A. 67.

31. *König Case* (1978), 58 I.L.R. 370 at 399-412 (European Ct. of Human Rights), which concerned 'undue delay' re disciplinary hearing alleging unprofessional conduct against a German doctor; European Convention, Art. 6(1).

32. *Ireland v. United Kingdom* (1978), 58 I.L.R. 188 at 280 (European Ct. of Human Rights).

33. See, e.g., *Engel Case* (1976), 58 I.L.R. 38 at 86 (European Ct. of Human Rights), confirming the right of the national (in this case, military) authorities to decide upon the relevance of proposed evidence.

34. *Luedicke Case* (1978), 58 I.L.R. 463 at 479-484 (European Ct. of Human Rights).

35. These rights are even guaranteed in time of armed conflict, see §§347, 357, 368 note 3, §396 note 97.

36. *Salem Case* (U.S./Egypt) (1933), 2 R.I.A.A. 1165 at 1202: ". . . international law has from the beginning conceived under the notion of 'denial of justice' forming base of political claims only exorbitant cases of judicial injustice. Absolute denial of justice; inexcusable delay of proceedings; obvious discrimination of foreigners against natives . . ." See also *Chattin Claim, ante*, in which this allegation was rejected.

37. See note 27 *ante. Roberts Claim* (U.S./Mexico) (1926), 4 R.I.A.A. 77 at 80: "Facts with respect to equality of treatment of aliens and nationals may be important in determining the merits of a complaint of mistreatment of an alien. But such equality is not the ultimate test of the propriety of the acts of authorities in the light of international law. That test is, broadly speaking, whether aliens are treated in accordance with ordinary standards of civilization. . . ."

38. *Camargo v. Colombia* (1982) 71 I.L.R. 317 (U.N. Human Rights Ctee.).

39. *Young, James and Webster Case* (1981/82), 62 I.L.R. 359; 70 I.L.R. 334 (European Ct. of Human Rights).

§324 Not all acts which cause injury to aliens or their property give rise to international responsibility and a right in their state to afford diplomatic intervention. Insofar as acts of the judiciary are concerned, so long as these amount to a denial or delay of justice, there can be no doubt as to the responsibility of the state.[40]

40. See Freeman, Denial of Justice, 1938. See §§322, 323.

§325 On occasion, acts of the legislature may also result in international responsibility. A state is unable to plead that its municipal law does not meet the requirements of international law.[41] Nor can it plead that, according to its constitution, statutes override earlier treaties as is the case in the United States.[42] Equally, it cannot plead that as a result of its federal constitution it is not liable for the acts of a non-federal authority.[43] If, as a result of such a federal constitution, there is a sequence of competences, the federal government cannot plead on the international level that it is unable to fulfil its treaty obligations, since this requires legislation by a lesser organ than the central government,[44] although in Canada provincial legislation running counter to treaty obligations is treated as invalid.[45]

41. See, e.g., *The Alabama* (U.S./G.B.) (1872), 1 Moore, Int. Arbs. 653 at 656: "The government of Her Britannic Majesty cannot justify itself for a failure in due diligence on the plea of insufficiency of the legal means of action which it possesses." See also *Polish Nationals in Danzig* (1932), 2 W.C.R. 789 at 804: "[W]hile on the one hand, according to generally accepted principles, a State cannot rely, as against another State on the provisions of the latter's Constitution, but only on international law and international obligations duly accepted, on the other hand and conversely, a State cannot adduce as against another State its own Constitution with a view to evading obligations incumbent upon it under international law or treaties in force."

42. Art. VI. See *Tinoco Concessions* (G.B./Costa Rica) (1923), 1 R.I.A.A. 369 at 386 per Taft C.J.: "The Constitution of the United States makes the Constitution, laws passed in pursuance thereof, and treaties of the United States the supreme law of the land. Under that provision a treaty may repeal a statute, and a statute may repeal a treaty. The Supreme Court cannot under the Constitution recognize and enforce rights accruing to aliens under a treaty which Congress has repealed by statute. In an international tribunal, however, the unilateral repeal of a treaty by statute would not affect the rights arising under it and its judgment would necessarily give effect to the treaty and hold the statute repealing it of no effect." See also *Greco-Bulgarian Communities* (1930), 2 W.C.R. 641 at 661: "[I]t is a generally accepted principle of international law that in the relations between Powers who are contracting Parties to a treaty, the provisions of municipal law cannot prevail over those of a treaty."

43. See *Amelia de Brissot Case* (U.S./Venezuela) (1885), 3 Moore, International Arbitrations, 2949 at 2971 per Findlay, Commr.: "Whatever may be the relations inter sese between the constituent parts of a federative body, admitted as such into the family of nations, they can play no part in determining the liability of the body by its

own distinctive name to other nations for wrongs inflicted by any of the parts or within the domestic jurisdiction of the same."

44.　*Canada (A.G.) v. Ontario (A.G.)(Labour Conventions Case)*, [1937] A.C. 326 at 348, per Lord Atkin: "Once [treaty obligations are created], while they bind the State as against the other contracting Parties, Parliament may refuse to perform them and so leave the State in default. In a unitary State whose Legislature possesses unlimited powers the problem is simple. Parliament will either fulfil, or not, treaty obligations imposed upon the State by its executive. The nature of the obligation does not affect the authority of the Legislature to make them law if it so chooses. But in a State where the Legislature does not possess absolute authority, in a federal State where legislative authority is limited by a constitutional document, or is divided up between different Legislatures in accordance with classes of subject-matter submitted for legislation, the problem is complex. The obligation imposed by treaty may have to be performed, if at all, by several Legislatures; and the executive have the task of obtaining the legislative assent not of one Parliament to whom they may be responsible, but possibly of several Parliaments to whom they stand in no direct relation."

45.　*Re Oriental Orders in Council Variation Act, B.C. (Employment of Aliens)*, [1924] A.C. 203 (P.C.); *R. v. Stuart*, [1924] 3 W.W.R. 648 (Man. C.A.).

§326　Insofar as lesser organs of the state are concerned, such as military personnel[46] or police officers,[47] the responsibility of the state depends on whether the personnel in question were acting in that capacity or may be considered to have been acting as private individuals who happened to hold a particular status.[48] If the tortfeasor is a public official acting in that capacity,[49] his rank has no effect upon the international responsibility of the state:[50] "In considering the question of a nation's responsibility for acts of persons in its service, whether they be acts of commission or omission, . . . it is pertinent to bear in mind a distinction between wrongful conduct resulting in a direct injury to an alien . . . and conduct resulting in the failure of a government to live up to its obligations under international law. . . . [I]t is undoubtedly a sound general principle that, whenever misconduct on the part of any such persons,[51] whatever may be their particular status or rank under domestic law, results in the failure of a nation to perform its obligations under international law, the nation must bear the responsibility for the acts of its servants."

46.　*Stephens Claim* (U.S./Mexico) (1927), 4 R.I.A.A. 265 at 267 (soldiers firing recklessly when ordered to stop a car). See Freeman, Responsibility of States for Unlawful Acts of Their Armed Forces, 1957.

47.　*Pugh Claim* (G.B./Panama) (1933), 3 R.I.A.A. 1439 at 1448-1449 (which examines when a constable may use force by way of his club); *Suarez de Guerrero v. Colombia* (1982), 70 I.L.R. 267 (U.N. Human Rights Ctee.). State responsibility clearly arises when the police action is part of a consistent practice indicating orders to this effect, see *Ireland v. United Kingdom* (1978), 58 I.L.R. 188 (European Ct. of Human Rights); *Vadivel Mahenthiran v. A.G.* (1980), 71 I.L.R. 294, 300-303 (Sri Lanka S.C.), following *Ireland v. United Kingdom* (Art. 11 of Sri Lanka Constitution reproduces Art. 5 of Universal Declaration of Human Rights and Art. 3 of European Convention).

48.   *Mallén Claim* (U.S./Mexico) (1927), 4 R.I.A.A. 173 at 174: "The evidence ... clearly indicates a malevolent and unlawful act of a private individual who happened to be an official"; *Gordon Claim*, (U.S./Mexico) (1930), 4 R.I.A.A. 586 at 588: "Everything then leads to the belief that the act in question was outside the line of service and the performance of the duty of a military officer, and was a private act and under those conditions the Mexican Government is not responsible for the injury suffered by Gordon"; *Morton Claim* (U.S./Mexico) (1929), 4 R.I.A.A. 428. See also this case of municipal law, *Velmurugu v. A.G. and Chundra Perera* (1981), (1983) Commonwealth Law Bulletin 860 (Sri Lanka S.C.).

49.   See *The Jessie* (G.B./U.S.) (1926), 6 R.I.A.A. 57 at 59, re wrongful seizure of Canadian schooners by U.S. naval authorities who "acted bona fide, but though their bona fides might be invoked ... to their own Government, its effect is merely to show that their conduct constituted an error in judgment, and any Government is responsible to other Governments for errors in judgment of its officials purporting to act within the scope of their duties and vested with power to enforce their demands."

50.   *Massey Claim* (U.S./Mexico) (1927), 4 R.I.A.A. 155 at 159.

51.   *Way Claim* (U.S./Mexico) (1928), 4 R.I.A.A. 391 at 400: "... persons concerned with the discharge of governmental functions. ... [T]he delinquency on the part of such persons is a misfortune for which the nation must bear the responsibility."

§327   Normally, a government is not responsible for wrongful acts committed by an individual against an alien, and it is not enough that such an act could have been prevented had there been sufficient officials present at the time. "There must be shown special circumstances from which the responsibility of the authorities arises; either their behaviour in connection with the particular occurrence, or a general failure to comply with their duty to maintain order, to prevent crimes or to prosecute and punish criminals".[52] The individual offender carries no international liability, but remains liable to prosecution under the local law, while "the government is liable for not having measured up to its duty of diligently prosecuting and properly punishing" him.[53] For a state to carry responsibility for the acts of individuals there must be some evidence of fault on the part of that state, usually but not always arising after the wrongful act has taken place. However, this does not mean that a state is necessarily liable for having failed to prevent a wrongful act.[54] Thus, in the *Corfu Channel Case*, although Albania claimed that it was unaware of the source of the mines in the Channel, the court held, on the basis of the Albanian contention that the Channel was under surveillance, that Albania was liable, regardless of the unknown individuals responsible for the mine-laying, because this could not have occurred without the knowledge of the Albanian authorities.[55]

52. *Noyes Claim* (U.S./Panama) (1933), 6 R.I.A.A. 308 at 311. See Forde, 'Non-Governmental Interferences with Human Rights', (1985) 56 B.Y.B.I.L. 253, 266-271.

53. *Janes Claim* (U.S./Mexico) (1926), 4 R.I.A.A. 82 at 87, 89: "The present case . . . is one of nonrepression. . . . The State . . . has transgressed a provision of international law as to State duties. . . . The Government can be sentenced once the nonperformance of its judicial duty is proven to amount to an international delinquency. . . . The damage caused by the Government's negligence is the damage resulting from the nonpunishment of the murderer. . . . If the Government had not committed its delinquency — if it had apprehended and punished C - J's family would have been spared indignant neglect and would have had an opportunity of subjecting the murderer to a civil suit. Even if the non-punishment were conceived as some kind of approval . . . still approving a crime has never been deemed identical with being an accomplice to that crime; and even if nonpunishment of a murderer really amounted to complicity in the murder, still it is not permissible to treat this derivative and remote liability not as an attenuate form of responsibility, but as just as serious as if the Government had perpetrated the killing with its own hands. . . . The indignity done the relatives of J by nonpunishment . . . is . . . a damage directly caused to an individual by a Government. If this damage is different from the damage caused by the killing, it is quite as different from the wounding of the national honour and national feeling of the State to which the victim was a national. . . . [The concept of] claims for losses or damages suffered by persons or their properties, is sufficiently broad to cover not only reparation (compensation) for material losses in the narrow sense, but also satisfaction for damages of the stamp of indignity, grief and other similar wrongs. . . . As to the measure of such a damage caused by the delinquency of a Government, . . . computation . . . is not more difficult than computation in other cases of denial of justice such as illegal encroachment of one's liberty, harsh treatment in jail, insults and menaces of prisoners, or even nonpunishment of the perpetrator of a crime which is not an attack on one's property or one's earning capacity, for instance an attack on one's reputation and honour. Not only the individual grief of the claimants should be taken into account, but a reasonable and substantial redress should be made for the mistrust and lack of safety, resulting from the Government's attitude. If the nonprosecution and nonpunishment of crimes (or of specific crimes) in a certain period and place occurs with regularity such nonrepression may even assume the character of a nonprevention and be treated as such."

54. See *U.S. Diplomatic and Consular Staff in Tehran,* [1980] I.C.J. 3 at 29-30.

55. *Corfu Channel Case* (Merits) (G.B./Albania), [1949] I.C.J. 4 at 18, 22: "It is clear that knowledge of the minelaying cannot be imputed to the Albanian Government by reason merely of the fact that a minefield discovered in Albanian territorial waters caused the explosions of which the British warships were the victims. It is true . . . that a State on whose territory or in whose waters an act contrary to international law has occurred, may be called upon to give an explanation. It is also true that a State cannot evade such a request by limiting itself to a reply that it is ignorant of the circumstances of the act and of its authors. . . . [I]t cannot be concluded from the mere fact of the control exercised by a State over its territory and waters that that State necessarily knew, or ought to have known, of any unlawful act perpetrated therein, nor yet that it necessarily knew, or should have known, the authors. . . . From all the facts . . . the Court draws the conclusion that the laying of the minefield which caused the explosions . . . could not have been accomplished without the knowledge of the Albanian Government. . . . [Albania shares] every State's obligation not to allow knowingly its

territory to be used for acts contrary to the rights of others. . . . [N]othing was attempted by the Albanian authorities to prevent the disaster. These grave omissions involve the international responsibility of Albania." For a discussion of culpa and state responsibility, see the dissenting opinion of Krylov J.at pp. 68, 71. See *Janes Claim, ante*, at p. 87: "A reasoning based on presumed complicity may have some sound foundation in cases of nonprevention where a Government knows of an *intended* injurious crime, might have averted it, but for some reason constituting its liability did not do so" (italics in original). Compare *U.S. Diplomatic and Consular Staff in Tehran, ante.*

§328 When an insurrection occurs in a country aliens are often the victims of acts of unlawful violence committed by the insurrectionists. If the latter are successful and subsequently form the government, they are responsible for the wrongful acts committed during their struggle to secure power,[56] and also become liable for the acts of the legitimate government which they have replaced.[57] If, however, they are unsuccessful, the legitimate government may not be liable.[58] However, acts of a routine administrative nature, such as the issue of postal orders, will become the responsibility of the legitimate government.[59] Moreover, a successful government may enter into a treaty undertaking to compensate aliens for injuries caused during the insurrection, even though they were the result of insurgent agencies.[60] Insofar as aliens are injured as a result of mob violence, the local government is responsible only if it has failed to take reasonable preventive or precautionary measures[61] or if there has been official indifference or connivance.[62] As with insurrections, a government may agree by treaty to meet the claims for damage arising from such mob violence.[63]

56. See *Hopkins Claim* (U.S./Mexico) (1926), 4 R.I.A.A. 41 at 45: "How far can an administration which seizes the reins of government by force and is illegal in its inception bind the nation? . . . The acts of [such an authority] become binding on the nation as of the date territory comes under its domination and control *conditioned* upon its ultimate success" (italics in original); *Bolivar Ry. Claim* (G.B./Venezuela) (1904), 9 R.I.A.A. 445 at 453: "The nation is responsible for the debts contracted by its titular government, and that responsibility continues through all the changing forms of government until the obligation is discharged. The nation is responsible for the obligations of a successful revolution from its beginning, because in theory, it represented ab initio a changing national will, crystallizing in the finally successful result. . . . Success demonstrates that from the beginning it was registering the national will." See also *Williams v. Bruffy* (1877), 96 U.S. 176 at 186.

57. See *Pinson Claim* (France/Mexico) (1928), 5 R.I.A.A. 327 at 430 citing with approval Borchard, Diplomatic Protection of Citizens Abroad (1928), p. 241: "The government created [through a successful revolution] is liable for the acts of the revolutionists as well as for those of the titular government it has replaced. Its acts are considered as at least those of a general de facto government, for which the state is liable from the beginning of the revolution. . . . Thus the government created through a successful revolution becomes liable for all services rendered to the revolutionists.

The unlawful acts of successful revolutionists render the government equally liable. The successful revolutionists appear to be bound from the beginning of the revolution by the stipulations of national treaties, for the violation of which they will be held liable as successors to the titular government."

58.   See *Home Missionary Society Claim* (U.S./G.B.) (1920), 6 R.I.A.A. 42 at 44: "It is a well-established principle of international law that no government can be held responsible for the act of rebellious bodies of men committed in violation of its authority, where it is itself guilty of no breach of good faith, or of no negligence in suppressing insurrection. . . . [T]here is no evidence . . . that [the defendant British Government] failed in its duty to afford adequate protection for life and property."

59.   *Hopkins Claim, ante,* at pp. 44-45.

60.   This was the policy pursued by Mexico with the United States, France, Germany and Great Britain. By contrast, in 1981, after the release of the U.S. hostage in Iran, the U.S. agreed that no U.S. citizen could bring a claim against Iran for injury suffered during the Islamic Revolution, during which the seizure of the embassy had occurred, see *Persinger v. Islamic Republic of Iran* (1983), 690 F. 2d 1010 (U.S. D.C.); affirmed 729 F. 2d 835 (U.S. C.A.)(there is a note to the report that it will not appear in the bound volume, a full text is printed in 72 I.L.R. 132).

61.   *Ziat, Ben Kiram Claim* (G.B./Spain) (1924), 2 R.I.A.A. 729 at 730-731, dismissing charges of non-prevention, non-suppression, tardiness and failure to prosecute.

62.   See *Youmans Claim* (U.S./Mexico) (1926), 4 R.I.I.A. 110. See, however, *Case Concerning U.S. Diplomatic and Consular Staff in Tehran* (U.S./Iran), [1980] I.C.J. 3.

63.   See *Panama Riot Claims* (U.S./Colombia) (1866), 2 Moore, International Arbitrations, 1361. After Algeria achieved independence in 1962, it was agreed with France that Algeria would pay compensation for damage suffered by French judges staying on, and if this was not forthcoming compensation was to be paid by France, see *Benejam Case* (1968), 72 I.L.R. 267 (France Conseil d'Etat).

VI The Law of Armed Conflict

1. THE NATURE OF WAR AND
THE LAW OF ARMED CONFLICT

§329 According to the classicists, "war is the situation of those who dispute by force of arms,[1] it is a just and public contest of arms,[2] a condition of lawful hostile offence existing for just cause[3] between royal or quasi-royal powers, declared[4] by public authority.[5]" According to more modern authorities, "public war is a state of armed hostility between sovereign nations or governments,[6] a contention between two or more States through their armed forces, for the purpose of overpowering each other and imposing such conditions of peace as the victor pleases.[7]"

1. Grotius, De Jure Belli ac Pacis (1625) Lib. I, Cap. I, S. 2, Eng. tr. (1738) 2, Carnegie tr. p. 33.

2. Gentili, De Jure Belli (1612) Cap. II, Carnegie tr., p. 12.

3. The concept of a 'just war' has disappeared as a matter of law, even though a party to a conflict may, for political or ideological reasons, describe its cause in the conflict as just, as was the case with the Archbishop of Canterbury concerning the British cause during the Falklands conflict, 1982.

4. According to Hague Convention III, 1907 (British Manual of Military Law, Part III, Law of Land Warfare (1958) p. 201), "hostilities must not commence without a previous and unequivocal warning, which shall take the form either of a declaration of war, giving reasons, or of an ultimatum with a conditional declaration of war." In recent times, hostilities have commenced without a declaration, and the declaration has come either from the victim of an attack or of an ally coming to its assistance. According to the Geneva Conventions of 1949, relative to the wounded and sick, the shipwrecked, prisoners of war and civilians (Schindler and Toman, The Laws of Armed Conflicts (1981), p. 305), Art. 2 of each applies "to all cases of declared war *or of any other armed conflict* which may arise between two or more of the High Contracting Parties, even if the state of war is not recognized by one of them." See *The Brig Dart* (1812), Stewart 301; *The Eliza Ann* (1813), 1 Dods. 244. At the outbreak of the Falklands War, the Prime Minister of Great Britain stated that Geneva Convention III (Prisoners of War) did not apply to captured Argentine personnel since there was no declared war, but she soon changed this opinion; for discussion of some of the legal problems relating to that conflict, see Green, "The Falklands, the Law and the War," 38 Y.B. World Affairs 1984 p. 89.

5. Textor, Synopsis Juris Gentium (1680) Cap. XVI, s. 6, Carnegie tr. p. 160.

6. Lieber Instructions for the Government of Armies of the United States in the Field, General Orders No. 100, 1863 (Schindler and Toman, *op. cit.,* p. 3), Art. 20.

7. 2 Oppenheim, International Law, 1st ed. (1906) p. 56, 7th ed. (1952) p. 202.

317

§330 It is an essential characteristic of these definitions that a war is fought between states through the agency of their armed forces. However, many of the armed conflicts which have occurred since the end of World War II have arisen from independence struggles or other operations in which one of the contestants has not been a state. In accordance with Protocol I additional to the Geneva Conventions of 1949 relating to the Protection of Victims of International Armed Conflicts, 1977,[8] the definition has been extended to "include armed conflicts in which peoples are fighting against colonial domination and alien occupation and against racist régimes in the exercise of their right of self-determination, as enshrined in the Charter of the United Nations[9] and the Declaration on Principles of International Law concerning Friendly Relations and Co-operation among States in accordance with the Charter of the United Nations".[10]

8. Schindler and Toman, *op. cit.* p. 551; 16 I.L.M. 1391, Art. 1(4). While the Protocol is in force, having received the requisite 2 ratifications, Canada has not become a party, nor has any leading western Power, nor the Soviet Union.

9. Art. 1: "The Purposes of the United Nations are . . . 2. To develop friendly relations among nations based on respect for the principle of equal rights and self-determination of peoples. . . ."

10. 1970, Res. 2625 (XXV): "The principle of equal rights and self-determination of peoples — . . . all peoples have the right freely to determine, without external interference, their political status. . . . Every State has the duty to promote . . . realization of the principle of equal rights and self-determination of peoples . . . bearing in mind that subjection of peoples to alien subjugation, domination and exploitation constitutes a violation of the principle, . . . and is contrary to the Charter."

§331 In accordance with the Charter of the United Nations war is illegal,[11] although a war in self-defence is still allowed.[12] Moreover, aggressive war is a crime.[13] Nevertheless, the purpose of the law of war is to regulate behaviour when armed conflict occurs, with the object of reducing its adverse effects by agreeing to fix "the technical limits at which the necessities of war ought to yield to the requirements of humanity [and since] the only legitimate object which States shall endeavour to accomplish during war is to weaken the military forces of the enemy . . . this object would be exceeded by the employment of arms which uselessly aggravate the sufferings of disabled men,[14] or render their death inevitable [,] the employment of such arms would, therefore, be contrary to the laws of humanity."[15]

11. Charter, Art 2(4): "All Members shall refrain in their international relations from the threat or use of force against the territorial integrity or political independence of any state. . . ." In *Dalmia Cement Ltd. v. Naltional Bank of Pakistan* (1976),

67 I.L.R. 611 (Int. Chamber of Commerce Arb. Trib.). Lalive, sole arbitrator, interpreted the clauses of the Charter relating to resort to force, as follows, at 619: "in *case of doubt* as to the answer to be given that question [whether 'a state of war' exists], the answer should be negative rather than affirmative, for the existence of a state of war can certainly not be *presumed* between members of the UNO. On the contrary, it must be presumed, *in dubio,* that each Member State, if and when it is using force, intends to use it in a manner consistent with its obligations under the Charter (especially under Article 2(4))."

12.   Charter, Art. 51: "Nothing in the present Charter shall impair the inherent right of individual or collective self-defence if an armed attack occurs against a Member of the United Nations, until the Security Council has taken the necessary measures to maintain international peace and security.... " See Green, "Armed Conflict, War and Self Defence", (1957) 6 Archiv des Völkerrechts 387. For the Canadian view of the legality of a defensive "first strike", see Memo by Legal Bureau, Dept. of External Affairs, 27 Nov. 1981, (1982) 20 C.Y.B.I.L. 303-4. In the case concerning *Military and Paramilitary Activities in and against Nicaragua* (Nicaragua/U.S.) [1986] I.C.J. 14 at 102-103, the I.C.J. said: " ... in the language of Art. 51 ..., the inherent right (or 'droit naturel') which any State possesses in the event of an armed attack, covers both collective and individual self-defence. Thus, the Charter itself testifies to the existence of the right of collective self-defence in customary international law. Moreover, just as the wording of certain General Assembly declarations adopted by States demonstrates their recognition of the principle of the prohibition of force as definitely a matter of customary international law, some of the wording in those declarations operates similarly in respect of the right of self-defence (both collective and individual). ... [See the Friendly Relations Declaration, which] demonstrates that the States represented in the General Assembly regard the exception to the prohibition of force constituted by the right of individual or collective self-defence as already a matter of collective self-defence. ... In the case of individual self-defence, the exercise of this right is subject to the State concerned having been the victim of an armed attack. Reliance on collective self-defence of course does not remove the need for this." For the view of the court on the use of force under the Charter and international customary law, see pp. 104-109.

13.   The Pact of Paris (Kellogg-Briand Treaty), 1928, 94 L.N.T.S. 57, as interpreted by the Nuremberg Tribunal, *Nuremberg Judgment* (1946) Cmd. 6964, 13, (1947) 41 A.J.I.L. 172 at 186; "To initiate a war of aggression is not only an international crime; it is the supreme international crime. ... " See also, the U.N. Definition of Agression, General Assembly Res. 3314, 1974 (XXIX) Art. 5(2): "A war of aggression is a crime against international peace. Agression gives rise to international responsibility." However, the Resolution expressly states, Art. 7, that "nothing in this definition ... could in any way prejudice the right to self-determination, freedom and independence. ... "

14.   The proviso is now expressed so as to forbid the use of weapons which cause 'unnecessary suffering', see Regulations respecting the Laws and Customs of War on Land, Art. 22, 23(3), annexed to Hague Convention IV, 1907 (Schindler and Toman, *op. cit.* p. 57): "The right of belligerents to adopt means of injuring the enemy is not unlimited. ... it is especially forbidden ... to employ arms, projectiles, or material calculated to cause unnecessary suffering"; see, also, Protocol I, Art. 35. This limitation is understood in an objective and not a subjective sense, and relates to suffering over and above that necessary to achieve the desired military objective.

15.   Declaration of St. Petersburg, 1868 (Schindler and Toman, *op. cit.* p. 95).

§332 The laws relating to warfare are not modern and trace their origin back to feudal times and the age of chivalry, and are based on the usages of chivalry, the laws of humanity and civilization, and the dictates of conscience. These principles are still recognized and formulated in what is known as the de Martens Clause, and find expression in the Preamble to Hague Convention IV:[16] "It has not been found possible at present to concert regulations covering all the circumstances which arise in practice. On the other hand, the High Contracting Parties clearly do not intend that unforeseen cases should, in the absence of a written undertaking, be left to the arbitrary judgment of military commanders. Until a more complete code of the laws of war has been issued,[17] the High Contracting Parties deem it expedient to declare that, in cases not included in the Regulations[18] adopted by them, the inhabitants and the belligerents remain under the protection and the rule of the principles of the law of nations, as they result from the usages established among civilized peoples, from the laws of humanity, and the dictates of the public conscience."

16. Schindler and Toman, The Laws of Armed Conflict (1973), p. 64; drafted by de Martens, Russian delegate to the Hague Peace Conference, 1899.

17. No such code has been issued.

18. I.e., those annexed to the Convention.

§333 The laws of war may be divided into two branches. The Hague Law[19] relates primarily to the actual conduct of hostilities and the rights and obligations borne by belligerents and neutrals alike, while the Geneva Law[20] seeks to introduce humanitarian principles on behalf of those hors de combat.[21]

19. This is to be found in a series of Conventions drawn up at the two Hague Peace Conferences of 1899 and 1907, with most of the texts reproduced in Schindler and Toman, op. cit.. See also Convention on Prohibitions or Restrictions on the Use of Certain Conventional Weapons Which May Be Deemed to be Excessively Injurious or to Have Indiscriminate Effect, (1981) 19 I.L.M. 1523, which Canada has signed; Fenrick, "New Developments in the Law Concerning the Use of Conventional Weapons in Armed Conflict", (1981) 19 C.Y.B.I.l. 229.

20. There are four Geneva Conventions adopted in 1949 dealing with the wounded and sick both in land and sea warfare, with prisoners of war and with civilians in the hands of an 'adverse party', the term now generally employed in the place of 'enemy'. The texts are reproduced in Schindler and Toman op. cit. In addition, there are the two Additional Protocols of 1977, the one relating to international armed conflicts, and the other to non-international armed conflict. See §§383-396. Schindler and Toman, op. cit.; 16 I.L.M. 1391, 1442 respectively. For Canadian proposals see Wolfe, "War and Military Operations", Macdonald et al., Canadian Perspectives on International Law and Organization (1974), p. 620.

21.   This term applies to those, like the wounded and prisoners of war, who were engaged in combat and have become placed out of it, as well as to those, like the clergy and Red Cross and medical personnel, as well as civilians, who have never been so engaged.

§334   Although the larger part of the law of war is to be found in these Conventions, there is still a great deal of this law which rests on custom.[22] Much of what is embodied in the Conventions is actually codification of that custom and it is generally accepted that, unlike the normal rule of treaty law whereby a treaty does not affect third parties,[23] non-parties are in fact bound by the Conventions or those parts of them which are regarded as having become part of customary law. This is particularly true of the Regulations relating to the Laws and Customs of War on Land annexed to Hague Convention IV.[24] Some of the Conventions contain an all-participation clause, purporting to be applicable only when all the belligerents in a conflict are parties to the relevant Convention. In practice, however, a more realistic approach has been adopted so as to allow a Convention, for example, relating to maritime warfare to apply as between maritime belligerents.[25]

22.   This is clear, particularly as regards maritime warfare, from a number of nineteenth century Canadian decisions, see Green, "Canada's Role in the Development of the Law of Armed Conflict", (1980) 17 C.Y.B.I.L. p. 91 or Essays on the Modern Law of War (1985), ch. 13.

23.   See §§307-309.

24.   *Nuremberg Judgment, ante*, at 65, at 248-249: "The rules of land warfare expressed in the Convention undoubtedly represented an advance over existing international law at the time of their adoption. But the Convention expressly stated that it was an attempt 'to revise the general laws and customs of war,' which it thus recognized to be then existing, but by 1939 these rules laid down in the Convention were recognized by all civilized nations, and were regarded as being declaratory of the laws and customs of war. . . ."

25.   See e.g. *The Blonde*, [1922] 1 A.C. 313 (P.C.). See, with regard to Hague Convention XIII, 1907 (Schindler and Toman, *op. cit.* (1981), p. 855), *Attilio Regolo and Other Ships* (U.S., G.B., Italy/Spain) (1945), 12 R.I.A.A. 7, 8.

§335   Until comparatively recently the tendency was to divide international law into a law of peace and a law of war, with no intermediate stage.[26] Gradually, it became clear that there could be an armed conflict between states which neither was prepared to regard as an actual war,[27] with all the legal concomitants, such as breach of relations, trading with the enemy legislation, observance of their duties by neutrals and the like. In such circumstances there could be simultaneous observance of parts of both the law of peace and the law of war.[28]

26. Grotius, De Jure Belli ac Pacis (1625), Lib. III, Cap. XXI, s. 1, p. 715, "there is no middle between war and peace", citing Cicero, Philippic VIII, Cap. I, "inter bellum ac pacem medium nihil fit." See *Janson v. Driefontein Consolidated Mines*, [1902] A.C. 484 at 497 (H.L.): "the law recognizes a state of peace and a state of war, but . . . it knows nothing of an intermediate state which is neither the one thing nor the other — neither peace nor war", per Lord Macnaghten. See, also, Schwarzenberger, 'Jus Pacis ac Belli?' (1943) 37 A.J.I.L. 460, and Green, "Armed Conflict, War and Self Defence", (1957) 6 Archiv des Völkerrechts 387 at 388-391.

27. Thus, on Nov. 1, 1956, the British Prime Minister stated that, as a result of the military operations between the U.K. and Egypt without any declaration of war, the two countries were "in a state of armed conflict", Hansard, Commons, Col. 1645 p. 558. See, also, relations between China and Japan between 1931 and 1941, discussed in *Kawasaki Kisen Kabushiki Kaisha of Kobe v. Bantham S.S. Co.*, [1939] 2 K.B. 544 (C.A.). See also *Navios Corp. v. The Ulysses II* (1958), 161 F. Supp. 952; *Dalmia Cement Ltd. v. National Bank of Pakistan*, ante at 616, 622. For the Canadian view as to the existence of "a state of war", see comments by Legal Bureau, Dept. of External Affairs, 27 Apr. 1982, 21 C.Y.B.I.L. 316. These views were expressed in relation to the Falklands conflict between Argentina and the U.K.; see also, Green, "The Falklands, The Law and the War", (1984) 38 Y.B.W.A. 89.

28. Thus, while captured personnel may be treated as prisoners of war, trading between nationals on both sides may continue. See *Lee v. Madigan* (1958), 358 U.S. 228 at 231: "Congress in drafting laws may decide that the Nation may be 'at war' for one purpose, and 'at peace' for another. It may use the same words broadly in one context, narrowly in another", per Douglas J. Re Falklands war, see Green, "The Falklands, the Law and the War," *ante*.

§336 In order that states become bound by the full rigours of the law of war, a war must be recognized[29] to exist. However, what comprises war for the purposes of international law may not be the same as what constitutes a war for the purposes of the law of contract[30] or of insurance.[31] For these purposes, the factual realities are of more importance than any theoretical legal conceptions.[32] Similarly, the courts may decide that for the purposes of the criminal law 'a war' may exist because of the factual situation regardless of legal niceties.[33]

29. See §§91, 92. In 1987, although third states referred to the hostilities between Iran and Iraq as "war", they were not prepared to concede to either belligerent the right to interfere with neutral vessels trading in oil with either party, nor to tolerate the use of mines in the Persian Gulf. The two parties did not consider themselves as legally at 'war' until eight years after hostilities began.

30. See *Kawasaki Kisen Kabushiki Kaisha of Kobe v. Bantham S.S. Co.*, ante, at pp. 558-559: "[I]n the particular context in which the word 'war' is found in this charterparty, that word must be construed, having regard to the general tenor and purpose of the document, in what may be called a common sense way. . . . [T]o suggest that, within the meaning of this charterparty, war had not broken out involving Japan on the relevant date is to attribute to the parties to it a desire to import into their contract some obscure and uncertain technicalities of international law rather than the common-sense of business men", per Sir Wilfrid Greene M.R.

See, however, *Spanish Govt. v. North of England S.S. Co.* (1938), 54 T.L.R. 852, in which the word 'blockade' was construed in its strict legal sense. See also *Navios Corp. v. The Ulyssess II, ante*, at 940-941: ". . . the clause . . . included in the charterparties permitted owners to take advantage of an increase [in freight rates] only 'if war is declared'. On the other hand, the closing of the [Suez] Canal and the increase in freight and charter rates lend support to the argument that the clause should not be given a highly legalistic construction to defeat Owners' right to cancel. The charterparties are commercial contracts and not international agreements such as treaties. The nature of the agreements and their context indicate that the phrase 'if war is declared' should be interpreted as it would be understood by business men engaged in the shipping business." In the case of an insurance policy referring to 'civil war', there is apparently no need to secure an executive statement, *Spinney's (1948) Ltd. v. Royal Ins. Co.*, [1980] Ll. 406 at 429, "The words under consideration are to be given their ordinary business meaning, which is not necessarily the same as the one they bear in Public International Law. The statements of jurists are a useful source of insights, but they do not provide a direct solution", per Mustill J., re civil war in Lebanon.

31.   *Shneiderman v. Metro. Casualty Co. of N.Y.* (1961), 220 N.Y.S. 2d 947 at 950-952: ". . . The words used [in the exclusion clause, 'caused by war or any act of war'] are to be taken and read in their plain and ordinary sense. . . . [A]n insurance policy is generally a contract with the average man who presumably is unfamiliar with the existence of a state of war from the strictly political, military and/or legal standpoint. Such a man would read the term war in a policy exclusory clause in the sense that term is commonly used and understood in the every day expression rather than as used and understood in international relations and military affairs. . . . [T]he term war when used in an exclusory clause of an insurance policy is generally construed as referring to the period of actual hostilities, that is, in the absence of context plainly having the effect of broadening the term beyond such limits. . . . Here, the company used ambiguous terms. In generally excluding from coverage death 'caused by war or any act of war', it used terms which are incapable of exact definition and wording which is susceptible to different meanings. . . ." See *Jackson v. North American Ins. Co. of Virginia* (1971), 183 S.E. 2d 160-162, in which it was held that in the absence of a declaration by Congress there was no 'war in the legal sense' against North Vietnam, but "our use of armed forces there does constitute war in the material sense . . . [as] evidenced by the use of armed forces by the parties. . . . [W]e believe it reasonable to conclude that the parties intended to bargain against coverage only in case of an announced and definite state of war – war in its legal sense."

32.   *New York Ins. Co. v. Durham* (1948), 166 F. 2d 874 at 876: "War, in the practical and realistic sense in which it is commonly used, refers to the period of hostilities and not to a technical state of war. . . ." See *Oppenheimer v. Cattermole*, [1976] A.C. 249 (H.L.) per Lord Cross at 275-276: "I incline to think that 'during war time' for this purpose should be interpreted in a commonsense way as 'until the end of the fighting'. It appears to have been assumed in the courts below that the relevant date would be not May 8, 1945, but July 9, 1951, when the government of this country declared that the state of war had ended. The man in the street would have been very surprised to be told in 1950 that we were still at war with Germany; and . . . I can see no reason why the suspension of recognition of changes in nationality should be artificially extended in this way."

33.   See *Burns v. R.* (1950/1951), 20 I.L.R. 596 (N.S.W. C.A.) discussed in Green, "The Nature of the "War" in Korea", (1951) 4 I.L.Q. 462; and, re desertion during the Vietnam war, *Broussard v. Patton* (1972), 566 F. 2d 816.

§337 On the international level, too, military operations may take place between states without any intention that they should develop into a war. This is the case, for example, when a state responds to an illegal act by way of another illegal act intending to bring the former act to an end. Such a reprisal must be proportionate, though it need not be of the same kind as the original illegality.[34] Whether this reprisal will constitute a causa belli will be decided by the state against which it has been exercised. Again, a state may resort to measures which would normally only be regarded as legal in time of war and the terminology of war and the law of armed conflict may be employed,[35] but in the absence of an animus belligerendi war will not be considered to have taken place.[36]

34. *The Naulilaa Incident* (Portugal/Germany) (1928), 2 R.I.A.A. 1012 at 1019, 1026, 1028: "Reprisals [are] . . . acts of self-help by the injured State, acts in retaliation for acts contrary to international law on the part of the offending State, which have remained unredressed after a demand for amends. In consequence of such measures, the observance of this or that rule of international law is temporarily suspended in the relations between the two States. They are limited by considerations of humanity and the rules of good faith applicable in the relations between States. They seek to impose on the offending State reparation for the offence, the return to legality and the avoidance of new offences. The definition does not require that the reprisals should be proportionate to the offence. . . . [However, i]n so far as international law in the making as a result of the experiences of [World War I] is concerned, it certainly tends to restrict the notion of legitimate reprisals and to prohibit any excess. . . . Germany [the defendant state] admitted the need for proportion between the reprisals and the offence. Even if it is admitted that international law only requires relative approxima- tion of the reprisals to the offence, reprisals out of all proportion to the act that inspired them ought certainly to be considered as excessive and illegal." See Fenrick, "The Rule of Proportionality and Protocol I in Conventional Warfare", (1982) 98 M.L.R. 91.

35. See *Venezuelan Preferential Claims* (Germany, G.B., Italy/Venezuela) (1904), 9 R.I.A.A. 107 (P.C.A.) in which the difficulty of classification is clear: ". . . the Tribunal considers itself absolutely incompetent to give a decision as to the character of the military operations undertaken . . . against Venezuela; the Tribunal . . . was not called upon to decide whether the three Blockading Powers had exhausted all pacific methods in their dispute with Venezuela in order to prevent the employment of force; . . . after the war between Germany, Great Britain and Italy on the one hand and Venezuela on the other hand no formal treaty of peace was concluded between the belligerent Powers" (at 109-110). The Award continued with references to 'bellig- erents', 'allied Powers', 'neutral Powers' and 'warlike operations'. It was this resort to armed force to ensure the payment of contract debts that led to the adoption of the 'Porter Convention', Hague Convention II, 1907, regarding the Recovery of Contract Debts, Scott, Hague Conventions and Declarations of 1899 and 1907, p. 89.

36. In 1982 during the Israeli invasion of Lebanon, there was no 'war' between Israel and Lebanon since the operations were directed against Palestinian 'terrorists'. Nevertheless, in its Report into the events in Shatila and Sabra camps, the Kahan Commission (22 I.L.M. 473) used language which clearly reflected the language of war and suggested the existence of an animus belligerendi; see Green, Essays on the

Modern Law of War (1985), ch. 10, 'War Crimes Extradition and Command Responsibility', at 228 et seq. See *Al Nawar v. Minister of Defence* (1982), 16 I.Y.B.H.R. 321 (Israel S.C.).

§338   Problems also arise when considering whether a war has ceased or not. If peace has been restored by a treaty it brings all the effects and implications of the law of war to an end,[37] subject to any clauses that may appear in the treaty. However, a mere cessation of hostilities brought about by an armistice does not have the same effect.[38] With respect to prisoners of war, the Geneva Convention provides for their release and repatriation without delay upon the cessation of hostilities,[39] and since prisoners cannot agree to derogate from any of their rights under the Convention[40] this prevents them from staying voluntarily or otherwise in the territory of their captor.[41] The Civilians Convention, terminates "on the general close of military operations", although it continues to operate in occupied territory[42] for one year longer.[43]

37.   *The Schooner Sophie* (1805), 6 C. Rob. 138 (H.C. of Admiralty).

38.   *The S.S. Wimbledon* (France, G.B., Italy, Japan/Germany) (1923), 1 W.C.R. 163 at 182, dissenting opinion of Anzilotti and Huber JJ. See also *Attilió Regolo and Other Ships, ante*: "Since an armistice was a cessation of hostilities and not peace, the general principles, rights and duties of neutrality still hold good for neutrals." See also *The Lea Lott* (U.A.R.) (1959), 28 I.L.R. 652. The cessation of hostilities during the Falklands conflict without an Argentine statement that peace had been restored created difficulties between U.K. and Argentina.

39.   Geneva Convention III (Prisoners of War), 75 U.N.T.S. 135, Schindler and Toman, The Laws of Armed Conflict (1981), p. 355, Art. 118.

40.   Art. 7. See §349.

41.   See Baxter, "Asylum to Prisoners of War", (1953) 30 B.Y.I.L. 489; Levie, Prisoners of War in International Armed Conflicts (1978), pp. 419-421.

42.   See §§350-358.

43.   Geneva Convention IV (Civilians), 74 U.N.T.S. 287, Art. 6, Schindler and Toman, *op. cit.,* p. 427.

§339   As with the commencement of war, so from the point of view of municipal courts the termination of war does not depend on the concepts of international law. In the absence of a treaty of peace, a number of countries will issue governmental orders[44] or pass specific legislation bringing the war to an end and restoring peace.[45] In the absence of such an executive or legislative act, the courts tend to construe the relationship that actually exists between the belligerents.[46] An international tribunal, the task of which is, unless instructed otherwise, to apply international law, is not bound by the views of the parties on this issue as expressed in executive statements.[47]

44. See *Mansur Ali v. Arodhendu Shekhar Chattarjee* (1968), 71 I.L.R. 708 (Pakistan S.C.) in which it was held that, despite the cessation of hostilities in accordance with a Security Council resolution and a joint declaration by India and Pakistan 'acknowledging the end of belligerency', whether the war had terminated was a question for the executive and, quoting Halsbury's *Laws of England*, 'The correct procedure therefore, for the Courts to follow, whenever a question of this nature crops up is to obtain the views of the Government . . . and to follow them", at 711.

45. See *Bordier v. Lorilleux* (France) (1960), 40 I.L.R. 434 (Ct. of Cassation), in which it was held that the French Law of 1946 fixing the date of the cessation of hostilities would give effect to a conveyance referring to "the signing of the peace treaty between France and Germany", which has still not been signed.

46. *R. v. Bottrill; Ex parte Kuechenmeister*, [1947] K.B. 41 at 50: "If the King says by an Act of State that the Commonwealth of countries over which he reigns is at war with a particular foreign State, it is at war with that State, and the certificate of the Secretary of State is conclusive. . . . When the King makes peace with any enemy State, the war comes to an end, but it does not come to an end before that peace is made. Whether international law has a different rule is irrelevant. . . . It follows, therefore, that the certificate of the Secretary of State for Foreign Affairs, which says in terms that we are still at war with Germany, is binding at least in our municipal law. . . . In our municipal law, whether it differs from international law or not, a state of war can continue, and the war with Germany is continuing, in spite of the fact that Germany then ceased to have any independent central government", per Scott L.J. In fact, not only had hostilities ceased, but Germany was under inter-Allied occupation. See also *Re Hourigan*, [1946] N.Z.L.R. 1; *Yudsin v. Estate of Shanti* (Israel) (1953), 19 I.L.R. 555; *Lee v. Madigan, ante; Shneiderman v. Metro. Casualty Co. of N.Y., ante; Oppenheimer v. Cattermole, ante.*

47. See *Dalmia Cement Ltd. v. National Bank of Pakistan* (1976), 67 I.L.R. 611 at 623-629 (Int. Chamber of Commerce Arb. Trib.).

§340 Modern war has demonstrated that the law with regard to maritime warfare[48] and the rights of neutrals[49] has become relatively unimportant, while there has never been any clearly acknowledged law concerning aerial warfare.[50] It is the law concerning land warfare which is important, and to some extent its rules have been extended to the other theatres of operations by analogy.[51] Thus the restrictions regarding the use of weapons based as they are on humanitarian principles,[52] on the nature of military objectives,[53] or the issue of combatant status,[54] are of general application.

48. This is not true regarding war crimes arising from disregard of rules concerning submarine warfare, see *Peleus Trial* (G.B.) (1945), Cameron, The Peleus Trial (1948). See, however, *Nuremberg Judgment* (1946), Cmd. 6964, (1947) 41 A.J.I.L. 172 in which, because of the orders and activities of the Allied Powers regarding maritime warfare, the Tribunal was "not prepared to hold Doenitz liable for his conduct of submarine warfare against British armed merchant ships . . . [and] the sentence of Doenitz is not assessed on the ground of his breaches of the international law of

submarine warfare", (at 108-109, 304-305, respectively). On war crimes generally, see §§359-382.

49.   See *Attilió Regolo and Other Ships*, (1945) 12 R.I.A.A. 7, concerning the duties of a neutral in naval warfare under Hague Convention XIII, 1907 (Schindler and Toman, *op. cit.* (1981), at p. 855) and after the signing of an armistice. In 1987, during the Iran-Iraq war, the neutral naval powers refused to recognise the exercise of belligerent rights againt oil tankers trading to or from belligerent ports.

50.   See Green, "Aerial Considerations in the Law of Armed Conflict", in Essays on the Modern Law of War (1985), ch. 8.

51.   *Coenca Bros. v. Germany* (1927), 7 M.A.T. 683, at 687: ". . . There is no reason why the rules adopted for bombardment in war on land should not apply equally to aerial bombardment." For a judicial discussion of the legality of atomic warfare, see *Shimoda v. Japan* (1963), 32 I.L.R. 626 (Japan D.C.); see Green, 'Nuclear Weapons and the Law of Armed Conflict', in Report of 1987 Canadian Conference on Nuclear Weapons and The Law (1988).

52.   See §331 notes 14, 15.

53.   See Protocol I Additional to Geneva Conventions (1949) Relating to the Protection of Victims of Int. Armed Conflicts, 1977, 16 I.L.M. 1391, Arts. 48, 49(3): "The provisions of this Section [Part IV, Section I — General Protection against Effects of Hostilities] apply to land, air or sea warfare which may affect the civilian population, individual civilians or civilian objects on land. They further apply to all attacks from the sea or from the air against objectives on land. . . ."

54.   *Ibid.*, Arts. 43, 44.

§341   The Hague Regulations, 1907, define those who are to be regarded as belligerents and to whom the laws of war apply: "The laws, rights and duties of war apply not only to armies, but also to militia and volunteer corps fullfilling the following conditions: 1. To be commanded by a person responsible for his subordinates; 2. To have a fixed distinctive emblem recognizable at a distance; 3. To carry arms openly; and 4. To conduct their operations in, accordance with the laws of war.[55] . . . The inhabitants of a territory which has not been occupied, who, on the approach of the enemy, spontaneously take up arms [as a levée en masse] to resist the invading troops without having had time to organize themselves in accordance with Article 1, shall be regarded as belligerents if they carry arms openly and if they respect the laws and customs of war.[56] The armed forces of the belligerent parties may consist of combatants and non-combatants.[57] In the case of capture by the enemy, both have a right to be treated as prisoners of war."[58]

55.   Hague Regulations respecting the Laws and Customs of War on Land, Annex to Hague Convention IV, 1907, Art. 1.

56.   Art. 2.

57.   E.g., war correspondents, medical personnel, camp followers, etc., see Geneva Convention III (Prisoners of War) 1949, Art. 4.

58.   Hague Relations respecting the Laws and Customs of War on Land, Art. 3.

§342   In order to broaden the protection of the humanitarian principles which apply in armed conflict, the definition has been widened somewhat by Article 43 of Protocol I, at least insofar as the characterization of armed forces is concerned: "1. The armed forces of a Party to a conflict consist of all organized armed forces, groups and units which are under a command responsible to that Party for the conduct of its subordinates,[59] even if that Party is represented by a government or an authority not recognized by an adverse Party. Such armed forces shall be subject to an internal disciplinary system which, inter alia, shall enforce compliance with the rules of international law applicable in armed conflict. 2. Members of the armed forces of a Party to a conflict (other than medical personnel and chaplains covered by Article 33 of the Third Convention)[60] are combatants, that is to say, they have the right to participate directly in hostilities. . . ." This widened definition is partly a recognition of the extended definition of an international armed conflict to include conflicts in the name of self determination.[61]

59.   Protocol I, Additional to Geneva Conventions (1949) Relating to the Protection of Victims of International Armed Conflicts, 1977, 16 I.L.M. 1391, Art. 86 imposes a duty upon superiors to prevent illegal acts by subordinates "if they knew, or had information which should have enabled them to conclude in the circumstances at the time, that [they were] committing or [were] going to commit such a breach if they did not take all feasible measures within their power to prevent or repress that breach." Failure by a commander to take such measures makes him amenable to penal or disciplinary proceedings. This provision is confirmatory of existing customary law, see *Re Yamashita* (1945), 4 L.R.T.W.C. 1 at 34-35, (1946) 327 U.S. 1 at 11-12: ". . . the gist of the charge is an unlawful breach of duty by the petitioner as an army commander to control the operations of the members of his command by 'permitting them to commit' the extensive and widespread atrocities specified. The question is then whether the law of war imposes on an army commander a duty to take such appropriate measures as are within his power to control the troops under his command for the prevention of the specified acts which are violations of the law . . . and whether he may be charged with personal responsibility for his failure to take such measures when violations result. . . ." The Supreme Court confirmed the finding of guilt. See also *Milch Trial* (U.S.) (1947), 7 L.R.T.W.C. 27 at 62. See also Israel, Final Report of Commission of Inquiry into the Events at the Refugee Camps in Beirut, (Kahan Report), 1983, 22 I.L.M. 473; Essays on the Modern Law of War, 1985, ch. 10.
60.   Geneva Convention III (Prisoners of War), 1949, Schindler and Toman, *op. cit.,* p. 355, "Members of the medical personnel and chaplains while retained by the Detaining Power with a view to assisting prisoners of war, shall not be considered as prisoners of war. They shall, receive as a minimum the benefits and protection of the present Convention, and shall also be granted all facilities necessary to provide for the medical care of, and religious ministration to prisoners of war." See, Essays on the Modern Law of War, 1985, ch. 6.
61.   See §330.

§343   By Article 44 of the Protocol, any combatant as so defined who falls into the power of an adverse party shall be a prisoner of war.

However the Protocol acknowledges that in, for example, a war of national liberation some of the combatants may not wear uniforms or other distinguishing marks, therefore[62] while "combatants are obliged to distinguish themselves from the civilian population while they are engaged in an attack or in a military operation preparatory to an attack[63] ... there are situations in armed conflicts where, owing to the nature of the hostilities an armed combatant cannot so distinguish himself, [in which case] he shall retain his status as a combatant, provided that, in such situations, he carries his arms openly: (a) during each military engagement, and (b) during such time as he is visible to the adversary while he is engaged in a military deployment preceding the launching of an attack in which he is to participate. ... This Article is not intended to change the generally accepted practice of States, with respect to the wearing of the uniform by combatants assigned to the regular, uniformed armed units of a Party to the conflict."

62. Protocol I to Geneva Conventions (1949), 1977, 16 I.L.M. 1391, Art. 44(3).

63. Art. 49(1): " 'Attacks' means acts of violence against the adversary, whether in offence or in defence."

§344   Prisoners of war are to be treated in accordance with the terms of the Prisoners of War Convention,[64] as amended by Protocol I.[65] If any problem arises as to the captive's entitlement to be treated as such, he is to be so treated until such time as his status has been determined by a competent tribunal.[66] Moreover, by Protocol I a combatant who fails to meet the provisions laid down in Article 44, paragraph 3,[67] while forfeiting his right to be a prisoner of war is nevertheless to "be given protections equivalent in all respects to those accorded to prisoners of war" by the Convention and the Protocol. It would seem that members of the regular armed forces who operate in acts of sabotage while not wearing uniform lose their prisoner of war status.[68] Alternatively, mercenaries[69] are denied the right to be combatants or prisoners of war. In the same way, captured personnel who change their allegiance and join the forces of their captor are not entitled to be treated as prisoners of war if they are recaptured.[70]

64. Geneva Convention III (Prisoners of War) 1949, *ante.*

65. Protocol I to the Geneva Conventions (1949), 1977, 16 I.L.M. 1391.

66. Geneva Convention III, Art. 5. See *Public Prosecutor v. Koi*, [1968] A.C. 829 (P.C.).

67. See note 62 ante.

68. See *Osman Bin Haji Mohamed Ali v. Public Prosecutor*, [1969] 1 A.C. 430 at 454 (P.C.): "[I]f they were members of the Indonesian armed forces ... they forfeited their right under the Convention by engaging in sabotage in civilian clothes. ... Having

forfeited their rights, there was . . . no room for the application of article 5 of the Convention. . . ."

69.   Protocol I, Art. 47, which defines a mercenary as "any person who (a) is specially recruited locally or abroad in order to fight in an armed conflict; (b) does, in fact, take a direct part in the hostilities; (c) is motivated to take part in the hostilities essentially for the desire of private gain and, in fact, is promised, by or on behalf of a Party to the conflict, material compensation substantially in excess of that promised or paid to combatants of similar ranks and functions in the armed forces of that Party; (d) is neither a national of a Party to the conflict nor a resident of territory controlled by a Party to the conflict; (e) is not a member of the armed forces of a Party to the conflict; and (f) has not been sent by a State which is not a Party to the conflict on official duty as a member of its armed forces." Since these requirements are cumulative it is relatively easy for a person to avoid falling within the definition. See Lockwood, "Report on the Trial of Mercenaries", (1977) 7 Man. L.J. 183; Green, "The Status of Mercenaries in International Law", Essays on the Modern Law of War, 1985, ch. 9. The U.N. General Assembly has under consideration the adoption of a convention on mercenaries.

70.   Geneva Convention III, Art. 130 makes it a 'grave breach' to compel "a prisoner of war to serve in the forces of the hostile Power," while Art. 7 forbids a prisoner from renouncing any of the privileges granted him by the Convention, which such enlistment would do. See *Public Prosecutor, v. Koi, ante,* at p. 856: "The position of the accused was covered prima facie by customary International Law as stated in . . . Oppenheim's Int. Law, 7th ed. (1952), vol. 2, p. 268 . . . 'The privileges of members of armed forces cannot be claimed by members of the armed forces of a belligerent who go over to the forces of the enemy and are afterwards captured by the former. They may be, and always are, treated as criminals. The same applies to traitorous subjects of a belligerent who, without having been members of his armed forces, fight in the armed forces of the enemy. Even if they appear under the protection of a flag of truce, deserters and traitors may be seized and punished", per Lord Hodson. See also, *Jabir v. Military Commander of the Judea and Sumeria Region* (1982), 13 I.Y.B.H.R. 371 (Israel Military Ct.). See National Defence Act, R.S.C. 1970, c. N-4, s. 64(*b*). See *Gozawa Trial* (G.B.) (1945), Sleeman, The Gozawa Trial (1948); and Green, "The Indian National Army Trials", (1947) 11 Mod. L.R. 47.

§345   Prisoners of war are a valuable source of military information, though they are only bound to give their name, rank, date of birth and army personal number.[71] Unless a prisoner has given his parole[72] he is entitled to attempt to escape. If this is frustrated, he may only be subjected to disciplinary as distinct from penal sanction and this is so even if he is a recidivist.[73] If the escape has succeeded, but the individual concerned is recaptured, he is not liable to any punishment in respect of the escape.[74] "Offences committed by prisoners of war with the sole intention of facilitating their escape and which do not entail any violence against life or limb, such as offences against public property, theft without intention of self-enrichment, the drawing up or use of false papers, the wearing of civilian clothing, shall occasion disciplinary punishment only."[75] Offences not directed to facilitating the escape are treated as ordinary crimes.[76] A representative of the Protecting Power[77] must be notified of any trial against a prisoner and is entitled to be present.[78]

71. Geneva Convention III (Prisoners of War) 1949, 75 U.N.T.S. 135, Art. 17. An unsuccessful attempt was made during the Falklands campaign to get Argentina Commander Astiz to provide information of his activities in Argentina before outbreak of hostilities, *The Times* (London), May 13, 14, 1982; see also Draper letter, *The Times*, May 19, 1982.

72. Art. 21. It would seem that the National Defence Act, s. 66 forbids Canadian personnel from giving their parole: "Every person who . . . (*b*) having been made a prisoner of war, fails to rejoin Her Majesty's service when able to do so . . . is guilty of an offence. . . ."

73. Geneva Convention III, 1949, Art. 92.

74. Art. 91.

75. Art. 93. See *R. v. Krebs*, [1943] 4 D.L.R. 553 (Ont. Mag. Ct.) in which it was held that everything stolen by K would be extremely useful in an endeavour to escape from Canada.

76. See *R. v. Brosig*, [1945] 2 D.L.R. 232 (Ont. C.A.); *R. v. Kaehler*, [1945] 3 D.L.R. 272 (Alta. C.A.); *R. v. Shindler* (1944), 82 C.C.C. 206 (Alta. Police Ct.).

77. Art. 8; see also, Protocol I to Geneva Conventions (1949), 1977, Art. 5.

78. Geneva Convention III, Arts. 104, 105. *R. v. Giuseppe*, [1942] S.A.L.R. T.P.D. 139.

§346 Prisoners of war may only be tried by military courts, unless the law of the Detaining Power permits civil courts to try its own personnel for similar offences,[79] and prisoners who are tried for offences, such as war crimes, committed before capture retain their privileges under the Convention.[80] By Article 102, they must be tried by the same courts as are members of the forces of the Detaining Power. This means that no trial conducted by the prisoners of their own personnel, even if authorized by the Detaining Power,[81] is valid, and if any execution is carried out as a result thereof, those responsible are liable to trial for murder.[82] In fact, the Geneva Conventions Act[83] makes prisoners of war in Canadian hands subject to the Code of Service Discipline.[84]

79. Geneva Convention III, 1949, 75 U.N.T.S. 135, Art. 84.

80. Art. 85. The Soviet Union and its socialist allies made reservations (see §304) to this provision.

81. Thus, the trial and execution of a German deserter by a German court martial held by the commander of German troops who had surrendered to Canadian forces in Europe, using rifles supplied by the Canadians, on the ground that, as they had surrendered and been made responsible for their own discipline, they were no longer prisoners, is a breach of international law, Commons Debates, Oct. 11, 1966, col. 8511, Dec. 21, 1966, col. 11445.

82. See *R. v. Perzenowski; R. v. Wolf; R. v. Busch; R. v. Mueller*, [1947] 1 D.L.R. 705 (Alta. C.A.); *R. v. Werner*, [1947] 2 S.A.L.R. 828.

83. R.S.C. 1970, c. G-3, s. 7(1).

84. National Defence Act, ss. 55-211 [as amended].

§347 Prisoners of war may not be charged with any act not forbidden by the law of the Detaining Power or by international law at the time of that act and no pressure may be applied on them to induce them to plead guilty. At trial, they are also entitled to present their defence[85] and receive professional assistance.[86] The trial must offer "the essential guarantees of independence and impartiality as generally recognized".[87] Moreover, prisoners of war may not be subjected to reprisals,[88] whether in retaliation for acts by their national state or by fellow prisoners.

85. See *Re Rohde* (G.B.) (1946) 13 Ann. Dig. 294; Webb, The Natzweiler Trial (1949).

86. Geneva Convention III, Art. 99; also, Protocol I to Geneva Conventions (1949), 1977, Art. 75.

87. Geneva Convention III, Arts. 84, 105.

88. Geneva Convention III, Art. 13.

§348 In accordance with Article 121 of Geneva Convention III, 1949, every death or injury suffered by a prisoner of war, whether caused by a sentry or any other person, must form the subject of an official enquiry by the Detaining Power and the Protecting Power[89] must be informed. If the enquiry indicates guilt those responsible must be prosecuted.[90]

89. A Protecting Power is a country appointed to represent the interests of a party to the conflict and accepted by the adverse party. See also §352.

90. See, for incidents arising in connection with the Falklands conflict, *The Times*, Apr. 29, May 13, Jul. 2, 1982.

§349 Finally, it should be noted that, in order to ensure that prisoners are properly treated at all times, the Geneva Prisoners of War Convention III[91] expressly provides that while the parties to a conflict may enter into agreements outside the scope of or limiting the Convention, "no special agreement shall adversely affect the situation of prisoners of war ... nor restrict rights which [the Convention] confers upon them." Further, "prisoners of war may in no circumstances renounce in part or in entirety the rights secured to them by the present Convention, and by the special agreements ..., if such there be." They cannot agree, therefore, not to be repatriated, even though they may fear the actions their own government may take against them if repatriated.[92]

91. 1949, Arts. 6, 7.

92. At the end of World War II the Western Allies forcibly returned to the Soviet authorities Soviet prisoners freed from German captivity, as well as Soviet and other ex-Russian personnel who had served with the Axis forces. Many of these committed suicide rather than be repatriated, see, Bethell, The Last Secret (1974).

2. MILITARY OCCUPATION

§350 When a belligerent enters the territory of an adverse party there is no change in the title of the latter,[93] and the belligerent's rights and duties as an occupant are spelled out by international law. According to the Hague Regulations,[94] for territory to be occupied it must be under the actual authority of the hostile force and the law relating to occupation only extends as far as such authority has been established and can be exercised. This does not mean that there is no occupation in this sense if there are sporadic acts of violence by remnants of the sovereign's forces left behind, by incursions by elements of the national forces, or by civilian residents, although insofar as the latter are concerned such acts are not the acts of combatants and will be treated as having been carried out by unprotected personnel, unlike the members of a levée en masse who are protected as combatants.[95]

93. See *Compensation (Germany) Case* (1959), 28 I.L.R. 648 at 651 (Fed. German S.C.): "The military occupation of Poland resulted in only temporary control over the occupied parts of the country. The occupied territory remains the State territory of the occupied State, whose sovereignty is not extinguished. The nationality of the inhabitants of the territory remains unaffected. Any measures taken by the Occupying Power which are designed to alter this legal position are contrary to international law and invalid. The legal position certainly cannot change while the war is still in progress and being continued by the Allies of the occupied State, which leaves open the possibility that the occupied territory may become free again. . . . [T]he view that the Polish State ceased to exist and that former Polish citizens lost their Polish nationality [when Germany proclaimed its incorporation of Poland] is based solely on the attitude adopted by the German Reich, which is not recognized in international law. . . ." See also *Lighthouses Arbitration* (France/Greece) (1956), 12 R.I.A.A. 155 (P.C.A.). Israel's annexation of Jerusalem, the Golan Heights and the West Bank has not been recognized.

94. Hague Regulations respecting the Laws and Customs of War on Land, Annex to Hague Convention IV, 1907, Art. 42; see Schindler and Toman, The Laws of Armed Conflicts (1981), p. 57.

95. See §341.

§351 The first duty of the occupant is to secure the maintenance of order and safety and, since sovereignty has not passed into his hands,[96] to respect to the greatest extent possible the laws already in force,[97] respecting individual lives and property, as well as religious convictions and liberty.[98] To this end, local courts should be maintained to the greatest extent possible and in accordance with their normal procedure. If local judges or advocates refuse to co-operate, the occupant may install his own judges or authorize the appearance of advocates who would not otherwise be eligible.[99] However, in accordance with the Civilians Convention, 1949,[1] while local tribunals should continue to function, the occupant may take such penal action as may be necessary to preserve the security of his forces and his occupation,[2] but the inhabitants may not be punished in any way for acts committed or opinions expressed before the occupation or during any temporary interruption thereof.[3] In all cases, the occupant must bear in mind that the citizens of the occupied territory do not owe any allegiance to him,[4] nor may they be forced to swear this to him.[5] Consequently, they cannot be made to take part in military operations against their own sovereign.[6]

96.   See *Compensation (Germany) Case, ante.* See also *Christian Soc. for the Holy Places v. Min. of Defence* (Israel) (1972), 52 I.L.R. 512.

97.   Hague Regulations, Annex to Hague Convention IV, 1907, art. 43. See *Haezni v. Min. of Defence* (Israel) (1980), (1981), 11 I.Y.B.H.R. 358. See Kuttner, 'Israel and the West Bank', (1977) 7 I.Y.B.H.R. 166; Singer, 'The Establishment of a Civil Administration in the Areas Administered by Israel,' (1982) 12 I.Y.B.H.R. 259.

98.   Art. 46.

99.   See *Mohd Amin al-Ja'bar v. Ahmad Ya'qub 'Abd al-Karim al-Awiwi* (Israel) (1968), 42 I.L.R. 484.

1.   Geneva Convention IV (Civilians) 1949, 74 U.N.T.S. 287, (Schindler and Toman, *op. cit.* p. 427).

2.   Art. 64. The Convention states that any military courts established for this purpose must comply with general principles of law, and it lays down the procedures and minimum norms to be followed: see *Military Prosecutor v. Mohd Samikh Amin Ibrahim al Nassar* (Israel) (1969), 48 I.L.R. 486.

3.   Convention, Art. 70. This Article also provides immunity from prosecution of nationals of the occupant who had sought refuge in the occupied territory, "except for offences committed after the outbreak of hostilities or for offences under common law committed before the outbreak of hostilities which, according to the law of the occupied state, would have justified extradition in time of peace." Further protection of refugees is provided in accordance with Protocol I Additional to the Geneva Conventions (1949), 1977, 16 I.L.M. 1391, Art. 73 (Schindler and Toman, *op. cit.*, p. 551).

4.   This is the combined effect of Arts. 44 and 45 of the Hague Regulations, while Art. 31 of the Geneva Convention IV forbids coercion to secure information.

5.   Regulations, Art. 45.

6.   Convention, Art. 51.

§352   The occupying power is not allowed to indulge in individual or mass deportations from the occupied territory, though this is permitted if the safety of the population or military reasons demand.[7] In the same way, and in recognition of the continuing sovereignty of the displaced national authorities, the occupant must not transfer parts of its own civilian population into the occupied territory.[8] To ensure that the occupant carries out its obligations towards the civilian population in proper form, the Convention provides for the appointment of a Protecting Power[9] and confers a variety of duties and rights upon it. In an attempt to ensure better operation of the Protecting Power system, Protocol I to the Geneva Conventions lays down more specific and detailed regulations concerning the appointment of such a Power and the training of those intended to carry out its activities.[10]

7.   Geneva Convention IV, 1949, Art. 49. See *Abu Awad Case* (Israel) (1979), 9 I.Y.B.H.R. 343; *Kawasme v. Min. of Defence* (Israel), (1981) 11 I.Y.B.H.R. 349.

8.   Art. 49. Problems have arisen in connection with the Israeli establishment of settlements in the occupied West Bank areas, although it has been argued that there was no former sovereign of these areas.

9.   Art. 9.

10.   Protocol I Additional to the Geneva Conventions (1949), 1977, 16 I.L.M. 1391, Arts. 5, 6.

§353   While pillage[11] and the seizure of private property[12] are forbidden, an occupant is entitled to levy such taxes and dues as are imposed for the benefit of the state, and so far as possible this shall be in accordance with the existing system.[13] Further taxes may only be imposed if required for army needs or the administration of the territory.[14] The occupant is, however, permitted to seize state funds and securities, arms depots, means of transport and of communication,[15] but must not interfere with submarine cables connecting the occupied with neutral territory except in case of absolute necessity.[16] The property of municipalities, as well as of religious, charitable, educational, scientific and artistic institutions, even when owned by the state, are to be treated as private property and if seized, destroyed or wilfully damaged, the offender is liable to suit.[17]

11.   Hague Regulations, Annex to Hague Convention IV, 1907, Art. 47; Geneva Convention IV, 1949, Art. 33. If pillaged property can subsequently be identified, in accordance with the principle of postliminium (Justinian, Institutes, 1, 12, 5), it will be restored to the original owner, see *Re Nat. Bank of Albania's Gold* (U.S./France/Italy/U.K.) (1953) 12 R.I.A.A. 13, *(sub nom. Gold Looted by Germany)* 20 I.L.R. 441.

12.   Regulations, Art. 46; Convention, Art. 53 forbids destruction of real or personal property, whether owned privately or publicly or by social or cooperative organizations, unless this is rendered absolutely necessary by military operations. See also, Convention, Art. 97 re property of detainees.

13.   Regulations, Art. 48. See *Abu Aita v. Commander, Judea and Sumeria Region* (1981), 13 I.Y.B.H.R. 348 (Israel H.C.).

14. Art. 49.

15. Arts. 53, 54. See also, *N.V. de Bataafsche Petroleum Maatschappij v. War Damage Comm.* (Singapore Oil Stocks Case) (Singapore) (1956), 23 I.L.R. 810 (C.A.).

16. Regulations, Art. 54; see *Eastern Extension, Australasia & China Telegraph Co. (G.B.) v. United States* (1923), 6 R.I.A.A. 112.

17. Regulations, Art. 56. See also, Hague Convention on Cultural Property, 1954, Schindler and Toman, *op. cit.*, p. 661.

§354 Although the Hague Regulations[18] laid down a code of conduct for an occupying power, they did not provide a sufficiently detailed statement as to the rights of the civilian population in occupied territory. As a result of atrocities committed against such populations during World War II[19] the Convention relative to the Protection of Civilian Persons in Time of War was adopted in 1949.[20] This attempted to fill the lacuna. Perhaps the most important provision is that which confirms that the Convention covers "the whole of the populations of the countries in conflict, without any adverse distinction based, in particular, on race, nationality, religion or political opinion, and [is] intended to alleviate the sufferings caused by war".[21]

18. Hague Regulations, Annex to the Hague Convention IV, 1907.

19. See §§359-382.

20. Geneva Convention IV (Civilians), 1949, 74 U.N.T.S. 287, Schindler and Toman, *op. cit.*, p. 427.

21. Art. 13.

§355 To some extent it may be said that, making allowances for the difference in circumstances, the Convention[22] seeks to provide civilians with the care and protection that the Conventions on Prisoners of War and the Sick and Wounded[23] provide for those who are rendered hors de combat by war action. Thus, it contains provisions concerning the care of the sick[24] and forbids coercion[25] against protected persons,[26] while at the same time ensuring that such special concerns as the care of families and children are adequately provided for. In view of the medical experiments that were conducted against civilians in occupied territories during World War II,[27] the Convention stipulates:[28] "The High Contracting Parties specifically agree that each of them is prohibited from taking any measure of such a character as to cause the physical extermination of protected persons in their hands. This prohibition applies not only to murder, torture, corporal punishment, mutilation and medical or scientific experiments not necessitated by the medical treatment of a protected person, but also to any other measures of brutality whether applied by civilian or military agents." Equally reflecting the

War experience, "No protected person may be punished for an offence he or she has not personally committed. Collective penalties[29] and likewise all measures of intimidation or of terrorism are prohibited. Pillage is prohibited [and] reprisals[30] against protected persons and their property[31] [and t]he taking of hostages [are] prohibited".[32]

22. Geneva Convention IV (Civilians), 1949, 74 U.N.T.S. 287.

23. Geneva Convention I (Wounded and Sick); Geneva Convention II (Wounded, Sick and Shipwrecked) (Maritime); Geneva Convention III (Prisoners of War), 1949.

24. Geneva Convention IV, 1949, Art. 16.

25. Art. 31.

26. Art. 4: "Persons protected by the Convention are those who, at a given moment and in any manner whatsoever, find themselves, in case of a conflict or occupation, in the hands of a Party to the conflict or Occupying Power of which they are not nationals. Nationals of a State which is not bound by the Convention are not protected by it. Nationals of a neutral State who find themselves in the territory of a belligerent State, shall not be regarded as protected persons while the State of which they are nationals has normal diplomatic representation with the State in whose hands they are." Part II of the Convention concerning General Protection of Populations against Certain Consequences of War is of general application to "the whole of the populations of the countries in conflict." Persons protected by the Conventions on the sick, wounded, shipwrecked and prisoners of war are not 'protected persons' under Convention IV.

27. See §360 note 61.

28. Art. 32; see also Protocol I, Additional to the Geneva Conventions (1949), 1977, 16 I.L.M. 1391, Art. 75.

29. Problems have arisen because of the use of collective punishment by Israel in the occupied territories.

30. This term is probably not used in its strict legal connotation (see §337), but is intended to forbid making civilians the victims of any type of retaliatory action. The intent of the prohibition is to protect those most readily available for retailiatory action by a belligerent. A similar ban on reprisals exists in respect of prisoners of war, see text to §347 note 88.

31. Convention, Art. 33.

32. Art. 34; Protocol I, Art. 75(2)(c). For a discussion of the hostage issue in customary law, see *List Trial* (Hostages Trial) (U.S.) (1948), 15 Ann. Dig. 632 at 641-647.

§356 It is incumbent upon the occupying power to ensure that adequate food and medical[33] supplies are maintained for the civilian population, and may only requisition such supplies, against payment, for the occupation forces and administration personnel, but "only if the requirements of the civilian population have been taken into account",[34] and if any part of the occupied territory is inadequately supplied relief schemes shall be permitted and facilitated.[35] Moreover, the activities of such organizations as the Red Cross and similar relief societies are to be permitted to continue their humanitarian activities,[36] and steps shall be taken to look after the welfare of children and of their education,[37] and efforts shall be made to maintain families as units.[38]

33. See *Re Gerike* (G.B.) (1946), 14 Ann. Dig. 304; Brand, The Velpke Baby Home Trial (1950).

34. Geneva Convention IV, 1949, Art. 55, Protocol I, 1977, Art. 69.

35. Convention, Arts. 59-62.

36. Convention, Art. 63; Protocol I, Art. 70.

37. Convention, Arts. 24, 50; Protocol I, Arts. 77, 78.

38. Convention, Art. 26, see also Art. 25 re family correspondence; Protocol I, Arts. 74, 75(5), 77, 78.

§357 To ensure that persons in the power of a party to the conflict receive at least minimal treatment of a humanitarian character, Protocol I provides a statement of fundamental guarantees:[39] "1. Insofar as they are affected by [an international armed conflict] persons who are in the power of a Party to the conflict and who do not benefit from more favourable treatment under the Conventions or this Protocol shall be treated humanely in all circumstances and shall enjoy, as a minimum, the protection provided by this Article without any adverse distinction based upon race, colour,[40] sex,[41] language, religion or belief, political or other opinion, national or social origin, wealth, birth or other status, or on any other similar criteria. Each Party shall respect the person, honour, convictions and religious practices[42] of all such persons. 2. The following acts are and shall remain prohibited at any time and in any place whatsoever, whether committed by civilian or by military agents: (a) violence to the life, health or physical or mental well-being of persons, in particular: (i) murder; (ii) torture of all kinds, whether physical or mental; (iii) corporal punishment; and (iv) mutilation; (b) outrages upon personal dignity, in particular humiliating and degrading treatment, enforced prostitution and any form of indecent assault;[43] (c) the taking of hostages; (d) collective punishments; and (e) threats to commit any of the foregoing acts. 3. Any person arrested, detained or interned for actions related to the armed conflict shall be informed promptly, in a language he understands, of the reasons why these measures have been taken. Except in cases of arrest or detention for penal offences, such persons shall be released with the minimum delay possible and in any event as soon as the circumstances justifying the arrest, detention or internment have ceased to exist. 4. No sentence may be passed and no penalty may be executed on a person found guilty of a penal offence related to the armed conflict except pursuant to a conviction pronounced by an impartial and regularly constituted court respecting the generally recognized principles of regular judicial procedure, which include the following: (a) the procedure shall provide for an accused to be informed without delay of the particulars of the offence alleged against him and shall afford the accused before and during his trial all necessary rights and means of defence; (b) no one shall be convicted of an offence except on the basis of individual penal responsibility; (c) no one shall be accused or convicted of a criminal offence on account of any act or omission which did not constitute a criminal offence under the national or international law to which he was subject at the time when it was committed; nor shall a heavier penalty be imposed than that which was applicable at the time when the criminal offence was committed; if, after the commission of the offence, provision is made by law for the imposition of a lighter penalty, the offender shall benefit thereby; (d) anyone charged with an offence is presumed innocent until proved guilty according to law; (e) anyone charged with an offence shall have the right to be tried in his presence; (f) no one shall be compelled to testify against himself or to confess guilt; (g) anyone charged with an offence shall have the right to examine, or have examined, the witnesses against him and to obtain the attendance and examination of witnesses on his behalf under the same conditions as witnesses against him; (h) no one shall be prosecuted or punished by the same Party for an offence in respect of which a final judgment acquitting or convicting that person has been previously announced under the same law and judicial procedure;[44] (i) anyone prosecuted for an offence shall have the right to have the judgment pronounced publicly; and (j) a convicted person shall be advised on conviction of his judicial and other remedies and of the time limits within which they may be exercised. 5. Women whose liberty has been restricted for reasons related to the armed conflict shall be held in quarters separate from men's quarters. They shall be under the immediate supervision of women.[45] Nevertheless, in cases where families are detained or interned, they shall, whenever possible, be held in the same place and accommodated as family units. 6. Persons who are arrested, detained or interned for reasons related to the armed conflict shall enjoy the protection provided by this Article until their final release, repatriation or re-establishment, after the end of the armed conflict. 7. In order to avoid any doubt concerning the prosecution and trial of persons accused of war crimes or crimes against humanity,[46] the following principles shall apply: (a) persons who are accused of such crimes should be submitted for the purpose of prosecution and trial in accordance with the applicable rules of international law; (b) any such persons who do not benefit from more favourable treatment under the Conventions or this Protocol shall be accorded the treatment provided by this Article, whether or not the crimes of which they are accused constitute grave breaches of the Conventions or of this Protocol.[47] 8. No provisions of this Article may be construed as limiting or infringing any other more favourable provision granting greater protection, under any applicable rules of international law,[48] to persons covered by paragraph 1."

39. Protocol I Additional to Geneva Conventions of 1949, 1977 16 I.L.M. 1391 Art. 75.

40. Art. 85(4)(c) makes apartheid and other 'outrages' based on racial discrimination 'grave breaches'. See §§367, 368.

41. However, Art. 76 provides that "women shall be the object of special respect and shall be protected in particular against rape, forced prostitution and any other form of indecent assault."

42. Geneva Convention IV (Civilians), 1949, 74 U.N.T.S. 287, Art. 58 provides: "The Occupying Power shall permit ministers of religion to give spiritual assistance to the members of their religious communities. The Occupying Power shall accept consignments of books and articles required for religious needs and shall facilitate their distribution in occupied territory." Art. 15(5) of Protocol I provides that "civilian religious personnel shall be respected and protected."

43. Despite this provision, Art. 76(1) of Protocol I specifically protects women against rape, forced prostitution and any other form of indecent assault.

44. Thus, there is nothing to prevent a person prosecuted and punished for war crimes by an occupying power from being tried and punished subsequently by his home state for the same offence if contrary to national criminal law.

45. Despite para. 1, there is no similar provision for male custodians of male detainees.

46. See §§359-382.

47. The Soviet Union made a statement when this paragraph was adopted to the effect that "its effects do not extend to war criminals or spies. National legislation should apply to this category of persons, and they should not enjoy international protection", 4 Levie, Protection of War Victims (1981), p. 82; see also §346 note 80.

48. This preserves all the protections guaranteed by customary or conventional law.

§358 If a state occupies territory the title to which is in dispute or, as in the case of the West Bank now occupied by Israel, alleged to have never been under the sovereignty of any particular state, or occupies the territory of a state with which it is not in a state of armed conflict or war, but does so for purposes of security or to suppress alleged terrorist activities, it is open to the occupant to declare its intention to apply the principles of the Civilians Convention to the extent it considers it practicable.

3. WAR CRIMES

§359 War crimes may be defined as breaches of the laws of war, whether those laws be customary or conventional. While the Hague

Regulations[49] contain no provision for the trial of those guilty of such crimes, Convention IV[50] provides:[51] "A belligerent party which violates the provisions of the . . . Regulations shall, if the case demands, be liable to pay compensation. It shall be responsible for all acts committed by persons forming part of its armed forces." Even though the Hague Convention refers to offences committed by members of the armed forces, war crimes can in fact be committed by civilians too.[52] War crimes are committed against the international law of war, so that any legislative attempt to define, for example, espionage as a war crime is only relevant from the municipal point of view.[53]

49. Hague Regulations respecting the Laws and Customs of War on Land, Annex to Hague Convention IV, 1907.

50. Hague Convention IV, 1907.

51. Schindler and Toman, The Laws of Armed Conflicts, (1981) p. 57, Art. 3.

52. *Re Klein* (U.S.) (1945), 13 Ann. Dig. 253; Kindred, The Hadamar Trial (1949).

53. By Art. 46 of Protocol I, 1977, 16 I.L.M. 1391 (Schindler and Toman, *op. cit.*, p. 551) captured spies, unless they are members of the armed forces captured in uniform, are not entitled to be treated as prisoners of war. This Protocol has not yet been ratified by Canada.

§360   While no person may be tried for a war crime unless the act in question was an offence against the laws of war at the time of its commission,[54] the specification of acts amounting to war crimes derives from customary international law and includes such offences as "murder, ill-treatment or deportation to slave labour or for any other purposes of civilian population of or in occupied territory, murder or ill-treatment of prisoners of war or persons on the seas, killing of hostages, plunder of public or private property, wanton destruction of cities, towns or villages, or devastation not justified by military necessity".[55] This list is not exclusive, for the definition extends to every breach of the laws and customs of war and includes, for example, resorting to warlike acts after an armistice,[56] failing to protect prisoners from violence,[57] denial of quarter,[58] breaches of the requirement of fair trial of accused persons,[59] abuse of a white flag or any protected sign,[60] medical experimentation[61] and the like.

54. Geneva Convention III (Prisoners of War), 1949, 75 U.N.T.S. 135, Art. 99 (Schindler and Toman, *op. cit.*, p. 345), which is law for Canada by the Geneva Conventions Act, R.S.C. 1970, c. G-3. While the crimes alleged against Eichmann (see *Eichmann v. A.G. Israel* (Israel) (1962), 36 I.L.R. 277) amounted to genocide (see Genocide Convention, 1948, 78 U.N.T.S. 277, Art. 1), he was not charged with this offence per se since it was not defined as a specific offence until the Convention in 1948, while the offences charged had all occurred between 1939 and 1945.

55. This is the list given in the London Agreement for the Prosecution and Punishment of the Major War Criminals of the European Axis (the London Charter), 1945, 82 U.N.T.S. 279, Art. 6(b) (Schindler and Toman, *op. cit.*, p. 823).

56. See *Re Grumpelt* (Scuttled U-Boats Case) (G.B.) (1946), 1 L.R.T.W.C. 55.

57. See *Re Heyer* (Essen Lynching Case) (G.B.) (1945), 1 L.R.T.W.C. 88.

58. See *Re Meyer (Kurt)* (1945), 4 L.R.T.W.C. 97; a trial by a Cdn. Military Ct. sitting in Germany.

59. See *Re Altstötter* (The Justice Trial) (U.S.) (1947), 6 L.R.T.W.C. 1; *Re Rohde* (G.B.) (1946), 13 Ann. Dig. 294; Webb, The Natzweiler Trial (1949).

60. Hague Regulations, Annex to Hague Convention IV, 1907 Art. 23(f). Such abuses, if intended to mislead the adverse party into giving protection, are described as acts of perfidy. By Protocol I to the Geneva Conventions of 1949, 1977, 16 I.L.M. 1391, Art. 37, "1. It is prohibited to kill, injure or capture an adversary by resort to perfidy. Acts inviting the confidence of an adversary to lead him to believe that he is entitled to, or is obliged to accord, protection under the rules of international law applicable to armed conflict, with intent to betray that confidence, shall constitute perfidy. The following acts are examples of perfidy: (a) the feigning of an intent to negotiate under a flag of truce or of a surrender; (b) the feigning of an incapacitation by wounds or sickness; (c) the feigning of civilian, non-combatant status; and (d) the feigning of protected status by the use of signs, emblems or uniforms of the United Nations or of neutrals or other States not Parties to the conflict. 2. Ruses of war are not prohibited...." By Art. 38 it is forbidden wrongly to use such protected emblems as the Red Cross, the Red Crescent or the Red Lion and Sun, and by Art. 39 "it is prohibited to make use of the flags or military emblems, insignia or uniforms of adverse Parties while engaging in attacks or in order to shield, favour, protect or impede military operations...." The Red Shield of David used by Israel is not a protected emblem, but its use appears to be respected.

61. *Re Brandt* (The Doctors' Trial) (U.S.) (1947), cited in *Milch Trial* (U.S.) (1947), 7 L.R.T.W.C. at 49-52 — the minimum requirements for a legal medical experiment are spelled out at 49-50; see Green, Essays on the Modern Law of War (1985), ch. 6 at 122-125.

§361 The British Manual of Military Law,[62] which is in use by the Canadian Forces, provides the following additional list: "(a) treacherous request for quarter; (b) maltreatment of dead bodies;[63] (c) firing on undefended localities and non-military objectives; (d) abuse of or firing on a flag of truce;[64] (e) misuse of the Red Cross or equivalent emblem; (f) use of civilian clothing or enemy uniform by troops engaged in a battle;[65] (g) using expanding bullets or poisoned or otherwise forbidden arms or ammunition; (h) improper use of a privileged building for military purposes; (i) poisoning of wells, streams, and other sources of water supply; (j) pillage; (k) compelling prisoners of war to perform prohibited work;[66] (l) killing without trial of spies, saboteurs, partisans[67] and others who have committed hostile acts; (m) using and, in particular, deporting civilians for forced labour; (n) violation of surrender terms; (o) bombardment of hospitals and other privileged buildings;[68] (p) participation in hostilities by civilians [other than as a levée en masse];[69] (q) killing of hostages;[70] (r) using asphyxiating, poisonous or other gases, and all analogous liquids, materials or devices;[71] (s) using bacteriological methods of warfare;[72] and (t) genocide."[73]

62. Part III — The Law of Land Warfare, para. 626.

63. Thus, the collection of ears in order to facilitate a body count is forbidden.

64. See Protocol I Additional to Geneva Conventions 1949, 1977 16 I.L.M. 1391, Arts. 38, 37(d).

65. Art. 39(2).

66. The Geneva Convention III (Prisoners of War), 1949, 75 U.N.T.S. 135, Art. 52, only permits the employment of prisoners of war on unhealthy or dangerous work if they volunteer, and the removal of mines and similar devices is considered dangerous work. See also *Flick Trial* (U.S.) (1947), 9 L.R.T.W.C. 1, in which accused were found guilty of employing prisoners of war in work directly related to war operations. See also *Milch Trial* (U.S.) (1947), 14 Ann. Dig. 299 at 300-302 (the report cited in §360 note 61 is not so detailed on this point). There were reports, that the U.K. used Argentine prisoners in the Falklands to clear minefields and munitions dumps, some of which had been booby-trapped, *The Times*, June 3, 1982; *Ottawa Citizen*, June 3, 1982.

67. During World War II the Allied High Command announced that partisan units were regarded as embodied in the regular forces and were to be treated as such.

68. If privileged buildings are used for warlike purposes, e.g., military personnel are given accommodation, they lose their privileged position.

69. See §§341-343, citing Hague Regs., Annex to Hague Convention IV, 1907, Art. 2.

70. Protocol I, 1977, Art. 75(2)(c) prohibits the taking of hostages.

71. See Geneva Protocol for the Prohibition of the Use of Asphyxiating, Poisonous or Other Gases, and of Bacteriological Methods of Warfare, 1925, 94 L.N.T.S. 65. When acceding in 1930, Canada made a reservation: "The said Protocol is only binding on His Britannic Majesty as regards those Powers and States which have both signed and ratified the Protocol or have finally acceded thereto. The said Protocol shall cease to be binding on H.B.M. toward any Power at enmity with him whose armed forces, or the armed forces of whose allies, fail to respect the prohibition laid down in the Protocol." For Canadian comment to the effect that the ban on chemical weapons in the Geneva Gas Protocol has "entered into customary international law", see Legal Bureau memo. 9 Apr. 1984 (1985) 23 C.Y.B.I.L. 333 at 334.

72. See Convention on Prohibition of Development, Production and Stockpiling of Bacteriological (Biological) and Toxic Weapons and on Their Destruction, 1972, 11 I.L.M. 309. This Convention was ratified by Canada in 1972.

73. The list in the U.S. Army Field Manual, The Law of Land Warfare, FM27-10, para. 504 is somewhat shorter.

§362 The Charter establishing the Nuremberg Tribunal[74] widened the nature of war crimes by introducing new classifications: "Crimes against peace: namely, planning, preparation, initiation or waging of a war of aggression,[75] or a war in violation of international treaties,[76] agreements or assurances,[77] or participation in a common plan or conspiracy for the accomplishment of any of the foregoing; . . . Crimes against humanity: namely, murder, extermination, enslavement, deportation, and other inhumane acts committed against any civilian population,[78] before or during the war, or persecution on political, racial or religious grounds in execution of or in connection with any crime within the jurisdiction of the Tribunal,[79] whether or not in violation of the domestic law of the country where perpetrated".[80]

74. London Agreement for the Prosecution and Punishment of the Major War Criminals of the European Axis (The London Charter), 1945, 82 U.N.T.S. 279, Arts. 6(a), (c).

75. See *Nuremberg Judgment* (1946), Cmd. 6964, p. 13; (1947) 41 A.J.I.L. 172 at 186 (Int. Mil. Trib.): "To initiate a war of aggression is not only an international crime; it is the supreme international crime. . . ." See, also, the U.N. Definition of Aggression, G.A. Res. 3314 (XXIX), Art. 5(2): "A war of aggression is a crime against international peace. Aggression gives rise to international responsibility." However, the Resolution states, Art. 7: "nothing in this definition . . . could in any way prejudice the right to self-determination, freedom and independence. . . ." Art. 2 states that the "first use of armed force . . . shall constitute prima facie evidence of an act of aggression". See, however, Memo by Legal Bureau, Dept. of External Affairs on legality of a 'defensive first strike', 27 Nov. 1981 (1982) 20 C.Y.B.I.L. 303-4; also, *Military and Paramilitary Activities in and against Nicaragua* (Nicaragua/U.S.), [1986] I.C.J. 14 at 103-104.

76. It was thus unnecessary for the Tribunal to hold that "the solemn renunciation of war as an instrument of national policy necessarily involves the proposition that such a war is illegal in international law; and that those who plan and wage such a war . . . are committing a crime in so doing. . . . [T]he construction which the Tribunal place[s] upon the Pact of Paris [is] resort to a war of aggression is not merely illegal, but is criminal", (1946) Cmd. 6964, 39, 41; (1947) 41 A.J.I.L. 218, 220.

77. In the view of the Tribunal it was unnecessary "to discuss in any detail" the various treaties of mutual guarantee, arbitration and conciliation, and non-aggression entered into by Germany, (1946) Cmd. 6964, at 37; (1947) 41 A.J.I.L. at 215, 216.

78. It was this 'offence' that led directly to the adoption of Geneva Convention IV (Civilians), 1949, 75 U.N.T.S. 287, relative to the treatment of civilians in occupied territory, (Schindler and Toman, *op. cit.*, p. 427); see §§350-358.

79. It was only because of this wording that the Tribunal was able to consider persecution of German Jews and other citizens before the outbreak of war, see comments re Seyss-Inquart, (1946) Cmd. 6964, at 121; (1947) 41 A.J.I.L. at 319. As to crimes against humanity, generally: ". . . there is no doubt whatever that political opponents were murdered in Germany before the war, and that many of them were kept in concentration camps in circumstances of great horror and cruelty. The policy of terror was certainly carried out on a vast scale, and in many cases was organized and systematic. The policy of persecution, repression and murder of civilians in Germany before the war of 1939, who were likely to be hostile to the Government, was most ruthlessly carried out. The persecution of Jews during the same period is established beyond all doubt. To constitute crimes against humanity, the acts relied on before the outbreak of war must have been in execution of, or in connection with,

any crime within the jurisdiction of the Tribunal [— including the planning to wage aggressive war]. The Tribunal is of the opinion that revolting and horrible as many of these crimes were, it has not been satisfactorily proved that they were done in execution of, or in connection with, any such crime. The Tribunal therefore cannot make a general declaration that the acts before 1939 were crimes against humanity within the meaning of the Charter, but from the beginning of the war in 1939 war crimes were committed on a vast scale, which were also crimes against humanity; and insofar as the inhumane acts charged in the Indictment, and committed after the beginning of the war, did not constitute war crimes, they were all committed in execution of, or in connection with, the aggressive war, and therefore constituted crimes against humanity" (1946) Cmd. 6964, at 65; (1947) 41 A.J.I.L. at 249.

80. See text §373 note 21 and §382 note 51.

§363 While it would appear that the introduction of the crime against peace was the creation of retroactive criminality, it should be noted that the General Assembly of the United Nations in 1946 unanimously adopted a Resolution[81] expressing Affirmation of the Principles of International Law Recognized by the Charter of the Nuremberg Tribunal, and the International Law Commission in 1950 adopted a statement of Principles of International Law Recognized in the Charter of the Nuremberg Tribunal and in the Judgment of the Tribunal[82] reaffirming as crimes those listed in the Charter, and affirming that complicity "in the commission of a crime against peace, a war crime, or a crime against humanity . . . is a crime under international law."[83]

81. Res. 95(I), Schindler and Toman, The Laws of Armed Conflict (1981), p. 833.
82. *Ibid.*, p. 835.
83. See Green, 'The Law of Armed Conflict and the Enforcement of International Criminal Law', Essays on the Modern Law of War, 1985, ch. 11.

§364 Further elaboration of the concept of crimes against the law of armed conflict is to be found in the four Geneva Conventions of 1949, only on this occasion the nomenclature is different, with the offences being described as "grave breaches". For the purposes of the Conventions, acts are 'grave breaches' when committed against:[84] "(a) all persons protected by those Conventions: wilful killing, torture or inhuman treatment, including bacteriological experiments, and wilfully causing great suffering or serious injury to body or health; (b) prisoners of war: compelling a prisoner of war to serve in the forces of the hostile power and wilfully depriving a prisoner of war of the rights of fair trial and regular trial required in the P.O.W. Convention; (c) persons and property protected under the Civilian Convention: unlawful deportation or transfer or unlawful confinement, compelling a person to serve in the forces of a hostile power, or wilfully depriving him of the rights of fair and regular trial required in that Convention, the taking of hostages and the extensive destruction and appropriation of property not justified by military necessity and carried out unlawfully and wantonly; and (d) property protected by the Civilian, the Wounded and the Maritime Conventions: extensive destruction and appropriation of property not justified by military necessity and carried out unlawfully and wantonly."[85]

84. British "Manual of Military Law", para. 625.

85. Geneva Convention I (Wounded and Sick), 1949, 75 U.N.T.S. 31; Geneva Convention II (Maritime) (Wounded, Sick and Shipwrecked), 1949, 75 U.N.T.S. 851; Geneva Convention III (Prisoners of War), 1949, Art. 130; Geneva Convention IV (Civilians), 1949, 75 U.N.T.S. 287.

§365 In order to give effect to its obligations as a party to the Geneva Conventions, Canada's Geneva Conventions Act provides:[86] "(1) Any grave breach of any of the Geneva Conventions of 1949 . . . that would, if committed in Canada, be an offence under any provision of the Criminal Code or other Act of the Parliament of Canada, is an offence under such provision of the Criminal Code or other Act if committed outside Canada. (2) Where a person has committed an act or omission that is an offence by virtue of this section, the offence is within the competence of and may be tried and punished by the court having jurisdiction in respect of similar offences in the place in Canada where that person is found in the same manner as if the offence had been committed in that place, or by any other court to which jurisdiction has been lawfully transferred. (3) No proceedings . . . shall be instituted without the consent in writing of the Attorney General of Canada."

86. R.S.C. 1970, c. G-3, s. 3.

§366 In its commentary on this provision, the Canadian Defence Department's Manual of the Geneva Conventions[87] states: "Accordingly, Canadian civil courts have jurisdiction to try persons in Canada for grave breach offences committed outside Canada.[88] There is no question as to their having jurisdiction in respect of such offences committed in Canada." The Manual also points out[89] that: "These particular offences are already made crimes punishable under the Canadian Criminal Code; for instance, 'wilful killing' would constitute culpable homicide dealt with under ss. 194 to 211[90] thereof. Persons committing grave breach offences tried by Canadian courts would be charged under an appropriate section of the Canadian Criminal Code."[91]

87. Cdn. Forces Papers 122, para. 1949(3).

88. In *Germany (Federal Republic) v. Rauca* (1982), 38 O.R. (2d) 705 (Ont. H.C.) it was held that since the accused was found to be extraditable under the treaty with the Federal Republic, 1977, there was no need to consider the application of the Geneva Conventions Act and his possible amenability to trial in Canada. Moreover, Evans C.J.H.C. held that "The submission that legislation be enacted to apply retroactively is foreign to our concept of justice", (at p. 717).

89. Cdn. Forces Papers 122, para. 1050(3).

90. Now ss. 205-211.

91. For the present Canadian law with regard to the trial and punishment of war crimes and crimes against humanity see §199 *ante.*

§367 The category of grave breaches has been widened by the terms of Protocol I.[92] The Protocol expressly declares that the physical and mental health of all persons in the power of an adverse party or in any way deprived of their liberty in connection with an armed conflict is not to be endangered.[93] Accordingly, it is prohibited to subject such persons "to any medical procedure which is not indicated by the state of health of the person concerned and which is not consistent with generally accepted medical standards which would be applied under similar medical circumstances to persons who are nationals of the Party conducting the procedure and who are in no way deprived of liberty. 2. It is, in particular, prohibited to carry out on such persons, even with their consent: (a) physical mutilations; (b) medical or scientific experiments; (c) removal of tissue or organs for transplantation, except where these acts are justified in conformity with the conditions provided for in paragraph 1. 3. Exceptions to the prohibition in paragraph 2(c) may be made only in the case of donations of blood for transfusion or of skin for grafting,[94] provided that they are given voluntarily and without any coercion or inducement, under conditions consistent with generally accepted medical standards and controls designed for the benefit of both the donor and the recipient. 4. Any wilful act or omission which seriously endangers the physical or mental health or integrity of any person who is in the power of a Party other than the one on which he depends and which either violates any of the prohibitions in paragraphs 1 and 2 or fails to comply with the requirements of paragraph 3 shall be a grave breach of this Protocol."

92. Protocol I, Additional to Geneva Conventions of 1949, 1977, 16 I.L.M. 1391.

93. Art. 11.

94. This would suggest that, e.g., a prisoner of war could not offer a lung or kidney for a fellow prisoner, even if the latter were his brother.

§368 In addition,[95] "3. . . . the following acts shall be regarded as grave breaches of this Protocol, when committed wilfully, in violation of the relevant provisions of this Protocol, and causing death or serious injury to body or health: (a) making the civilian population or individual civilians the object of attack; (b) launching an indiscriminate attack affecting the civilian population or civilian objects in the knowledge that such attack will cause excessive loss of life, injury to civilians or damage to civilian objects [in relation to the concrete and direct military advantage anticipated];[96] (c) launching an attack against works or installations containing dangerous forces[97] in the knowledge that such attack will cause excessive loss of life, injury to civilians or damage to civilian objects . . .; (d) making non-defended localities and demilitarized zones the object of attack; (e) making a person the object of attack in the knowledge that he is hors de combat; (f) the perfidious use . . . of the distinctive emblem of the red cross, red crescent or red lion and sun or of other protective signs recognized by the Conventions or this Protocol.[98] 4. In addition . . . the following shall be regarded as grave breaches of this Protocol, when committed wilfully and in violation of the Conventions or the Protocol: (a) the transfer by the occupying Power of parts of its own civilian population into the territory it occupies, or the deportation or transfer of all or parts of the population of the occupied territory within or outside this territory, in violation of Article 49 of the Convention IV;[99] (b) unjustifiable delay in the repatriation of prisoners of war or civilians; (c) practices of apartheid[1] and other inhuman and degrading practices involving outrages upon person dignity, based on racial discrimination; (d) making the clearly-recognized historic monuments, works of art or places of worship which constitute the cultural or spiritual heritage of peoples and to which special protection has been given by special arrangement . . . the object of attack, causing as a result extensive destruction thereof, where there is no evidence of the violation by the adverse Party of Article 53, subparagraph (b),[2] and when such historic monuments, works of art and places of worship are not located in the immediate proximity of military objectives: (e) depriving a [protected] person . . . of rights of fair and regular trial.[3] 5. Without prejudice to the application of the Conventions and this Protocol, grave breaches of these instruments shall be regarded as war crimes."

---

95. Art. 85.

96. Art. 57(2)(a)(iii). This sub-paragraph requires an attack to be cancelled or suspended if such 'excessive incidental loss' may be expected.

97. Defined in Art. 56(1) as dams, dykes and nuclear electrical generating stations.

98. Those used, e.g., to mark cultural monuments, civil defence installations, and the like. The Red Shield used by Israel is not a 'protected' emblem.

99. See text to §351 note 6 and §352 note 7.

1. According to the International Convention on Suppression and Punishment of the Crime of Apartheid, 1973, 13 I.L.M. 50 (G.A. Res. 3068 (XXVIII), apartheid as defined in Art. 2 is a crime against humanity; see §210.

2. "... it is prohibited ... to use such objects in support of the military effort."

3. If a trial by military tribunal takes place, it must be in accordance with the requirements of justice and the rule of law.

§369 War crimes and grave breaches may be committed by any military personnel, whether in one's own forces or in those of the adverse party, or of an ally of either, as well as by civilians regardless of nationality.[4] Normally, if the offender is a member of the trying authority's forces, he will be tried in accordance with his own military law and not under international law, even though the crimes committed may be described as war crimes.[5]

4. See e.g., *Re Kramer* (G.B.) (1945), 2 L.R.T.W.C. 1; Phillips, The Belsen Trial (1949). Allied nationals were among the accused, while one of the named victims was an Italian, at the time of the offence an enemy national. The new Canadian law on the trial of war criminals, S.C. 1987, c. 37, omits allied personnel from its ambit. See §199.

5. See *United States v. Calley* (1969/71/73), 46 C.M.R. 1131, 48 C.M.R. 19, 1 M.L.R. 2488. See also, *Chief Military Prosecutor v. Melinki* (The Hafr Qassem Massacre)(1958), 2 Palestine Y.B.I.L. 69 (Israel Military C.A.); see also Israeli court martial of Sgt. Major Salah-Salah and others, Globe and Mail, Feb. 18, 1983.

§370 According to customary international law, heads of state are immune from suit in a foreign country,[6] and this immunity extends to criminal charges. However, by the Treaty of Versailles[7] an attempt was made to indict the ex-Emperor of Germany in respect of sovereign acts committed while head of state. When the London Charter establishing the Nuremberg Tribunal was adopted, it was stated that "the official position of defendants, whether as Heads of State or responsible officials in Government Departments, shall not be considered as freeing them from responsibility or mitigating punishment."[8] The non-immunity of Heads of State was confirmed by the International Law Commission in its statement of Principles.[9]

6. See §148 note 75, §149.

7. (1919), 112 B.F.S.P. 1, (1919) 13 A.J.I.L., Supp., Art. 227: "The Allied and Associate Powers publicly arraign William II of Hohenzollern, formerly German Emperor, for a supreme offence against international morality and the sanctity of treaties. A special tribunal will be constituted to try the accused.... In its decision the tribunal will be guided by the highest motives of international policy, with a view to vindicating the solemn obligations of international undertakings and the validity of international morality. ..." Napoleon, on the other hand, was never tried but banished by executive decision.

8. Charter of the Nuremberg Int. Military Trib., 1945, Art. 7. In the Charter establishing the Tokyo Tribunal (1946, U.S. Dept. of State, Occupation of Japan: Policy and Progress (1946) p. 146), the official position of the accused could be considered in mitigation of punishment, Art. 6. Oshima, former Japanese Ambassador to Germany, pleaded his diplomatic immunity, but the Tribunal held: "Diplomatic privilege does not import immunity from legal liability, but only exemption from trial by the courts of the State to which an ambassador is accredited. In any event this immunity has no relation to crimes under international law charged before a tribunal having jurisdiction", *Tokyo Judgment* (1948), 15 Ann. Dig. 356 at 372.

9. Principle III, Principles of International Law Recognised in the Charter of the Nuremberg Tribunal and in the Judgment of the Tribunal, 1946, U.N. G.A. Res. 95(I).

§371 Commanders at any level are not only liable for war crimes they may themselves have committed, or ordered to be committed,[10] but also for any crimes committed by their subordinates due to the failure of the commander to use his authority to prevent their commission or continued perpetration.[11] If an officer or N.C.O. of the commander's unit is present when a war crime is committed by members of that unit, the court may accept this as prima facie evidence of the commander's responsibility for that crime.[12] The liability of a commander is now clearly established "if [he] knew or had information which should have enabled [him] to conclude in the circumstances at the time, that [a subordinate] was committing or was going to commit a breach [of the Geneva Conventions, 1949 or Protocol I to the Conventions of 1949, 1977] and if [he] did not take all feasible measures within [his] power to prevent or repress the breach."[13]

10. *Re Dostler* (U.S.) (1945), 1 L.R.T.W.C. 22; *Re Kesselring* (G.B.) (1947), 8 L.R.T.W.C. 9; *Re Meyer (Kurt)* (1945), 4 L.R.T.W.C. 97 "There is no evidence that anyone heard any particular words uttered by the accused which would constitute an order, but it is not essential that such evidence be adduced. The giving of the order may be proved circumstantially . . . [but] before the Court finds an accused person guilty on circumstantial evidence, it must be satisfied not only that the circumstances are consistent with the accused having [given the order] but that they are inconsistent with any other rational conclusion . . ." (at 108) per Lt. Col. Bredin, Canadian J.A.G. Overseas, citing British Manual of Military Law (1929 ed.) Ch. VI, para. 42.

11. *Re Yamashita* (U.S.) (1946), 4 L.R.T.W.C. 1 at 34, 35: ". . . the crimes were so extensive and widespread . . . that they must either have been wilfully permitted . . . or secretly ordered by the accused. . . . [D]uring the period in question you failed to provide effective control of your troops as was required by the circumstances." See Parks, "Command Responsibility for War Crimes", (1973) 62 Military Law Review 1. See also Israel, Final Report of the Commission of Inquiry into the Events at the Refugee Camps in Beirut, 1983, 22 I.L.M. 473; see also Green Essays on the Modern Law of War, 1985, ch. 10.

12. *Re Meyer (Kurt), ante.*

13. Protocol I, Additional to the Geneva Conventions of 1949, 1977, 16 I.L.M. 1391, Art. 86.

§372 While commanders are liable for any criminal order they may give, a subordinate who carries out an order which involves the commission of a war crime is unable to plead compliance with orders as a defence.[14] The Nuremberg Charter provided[15] "The fact that the Defendant acted pursuant to order of his Government or of a superior shall not free him from responsibility, but may be considered in mitigation of punishment if the Tribunal determines that justice so requires". In assessing what justice requires, the Nuremberg Tribunal said[16] "That a soldier was ordered to kill or torture in violation of the international law of war has never been recognized as defence to such acts of brutality,[17] though . . . the order may be urged in mitigation of the punishment. The true test, which is found in varying degrees in the criminal law of most nations,[18] is not the existence of the order, but whether moral choice was in fact possible."

14. See Green, "Superior Orders and the Reasonable Man", (1970) 8 C.Y.B.I.L. 61; Superior Orders in National and International Law (1976); Dinstein, The Defence of 'Obedience to Superior Orders' in International Law (1965).

15. Charter of the Nuremberg International Military Tribunal, Art. 8.

16. *Nuremberg Judgment* (1946), Cmd. 6964, at 42, (1947) 41 A.J.I.L. 172 at 221.

17. See, e.g., *Llandovery Castle* (1921), Cmd. 450 decided by a German tribunal; Cameron, The Peleus Trial (1948), App. IX (and in a much abbreviated form 2 Ann. Dig. 429), which referred to the unlawful sinking of a hospital ship and subsequent firing upon survivors: ". . . According to para. 2 [of the German Military Penal Code, s. 47] the subordinate obeying an order is liable to punishment, if it was known to him that the order of the superior involved the infringement of civil or military law. . . . It is certainly to be urged in favour of the military subordinates that they are under no obligation to question the order of their superior officer [— whether this is so in any particular force depends on national law —], and they can count upon its legality. But no such confidence can be held to exist if such order is known universally to everybody, including the accused, to be without any doubt whatever against the law. This happens in only rare and exceptional cases. But this case was precisely one of them. . . . [The accused] had acquired the habit of obedience to military authority and could not rid themselves of it. This justifies the recognition of mitigating circumstances in determining the punishment. . . ." See also, *R. v. Smith* (Cape of Good Hope) (1900), 17 S.C. 561 at 567-568: "It is monstrous to suppose that a soldier would be protected where the order is grossly illegal. [But that he] is responsible if he obeys an order that is not strictly legal is an extreme proposition which the Court cannot accept. . . . Especially in time of war immediate obedience is required. . . . I think it is a safe rule to lay down that if a soldier honestly believes that he is doing his duty in obeying the commands of his superior, and if the orders are not so manifestly illegal that he must or ought to have known that they were unlawful, the private soldier would be protected by the orders of his superior officer", per Solomon J.P.

18.   See *R. v. Laroche*, [1964] S.C.R. 667 (S.C.C.); *State v. Shepard* (1967), 4 S.A.L.R. 170 at 178.

§373   The Statement of Principles enunciated by the International Law Commission adopts the language of the Judgment rather than that of the Charter:[19] "The fact that a person acted pursuant to order of his Government does not relieve him from responsibility under international law, provided a moral choice was in fact possible to him." As if to confirm the invalidity of a defence based on superior orders, the Commission also stated:[20] "The fact that internal law does not impose a penalty for an act which constitutes a crime under international law does not relieve the person who committed the act from responsibility under international law", and the fact that the act might have been consistent with national law will not excuse the accused if that law is clearly opposed to international law.[21]

19.   U.N.G.A. Resolution 95(I), 1946, Principles of International Law Recognised in the Charter of the Nuremberg Tribunal and in the Judgment of the Tribunal, Principle IV.

20.   Principle II.

21.   See, e.g., *State v. Director of Prisons; Ex parte Schumann* (Ghana), [1966] G.L.R. 703 (C.A.). In accordance with the new Canadian law, S.C. 1987, c. 37, "a person may be convicted of an offence . . . even if the act or omission is committed in obedience or to in conformity with the law in force at the time and in the place of its commission", s. 1 (1.94).

§374   The issue of 'moral choice' is inextricably bound up with knowledge of the lawfulness or otherwise of the order given. According to the Canadian Criminal Code:[22] "Every one who is bound by military law to obey the command of his superior officer is justified in obeying any command given by his superior officer for the suppression of a riot unless the order is manifestly unlawful . . . [and] the question whether an order is manifestly unlawful or not is a question of law."

22.   R.S.C. 1970, c. C-34, s. 32(2), (5).

§375   The National Defence Act[23] merely states that "every person who disobeys a lawful command of a superior officer is guilty of an offence. . . ." A contrario it would seem that an order to commit an act which was 'manifestly unlawful'[24] may be disobeyed, and this is confirmed by Queen's Regulations which provide[25] that "where the subordinate does not know the law or is uncertain of it he shall, even though he doubts the lawfulness of the command, obey unless the command is manifestly unlawful. . . . A manifestly unlawful order is one that would appear to a person of ordinary sense and understanding to be clearly illegal."

23. R.S.C. 1970, c. N-4, s. 73.

24. This is the language of the Criminal Code, s. 32(3) which allows non-compliance with a peace officer's order to use force to assist in suppressing a riot when that order is 'manifestly unlawful'.

25. Queen's Regulations and Orders for Canadian Armed Forces 1968 Revision, Vol. I (Administrative), Art. 19.015.

§376 If Canada adopts the proposal in Protocol I and appoints to commanders legal advisers qualified in the law of armed conflict[26] some of the difficulties in deciding upon the lawfulness of an order may be removed, especially if these officers or others similarly trained instruct the forces in the law of armed conflict.[27] Insofar as Canadian trials of war criminals are concerned, Canadian military tribunals applied the law as it was stated in the British Manual of Military Law.[28] ". . . the order must be obviously unlawful. While the three accused have stated in evidence that they felt obliged to obey the orders . . . nevertheless they all said that they thought the order to have been wrong, and, in any event, their lack of knowledge would afford them no defence because ignorance of the law is no excuse,[29] and . . . members of the armed forces are supposed to be aware of the law and usages of war and to endeavour to follow them. . . . It is for the Court to say if it was an obviously unlawful order, in which event obedience to such an order would not be an absolute defence, but any act to aid a known unlawful purpose would be aiding and abetting that purpose. . . ."[30]

26. Protocol I, Additional to the Geneva Conventions of 1949, 1977, 16 I.L.M. 1391, Art. 82; see Green, "The Role of Legal Advisers in the Armed Forces", Essays on the Modern Law of War, 1985, ch. 2.

27. Art. 82; see also, Green, "Scientia Juris and the Soldier", (1978) 9 Id Dritt (Univ. Malta Law Rev.) 37.

28. (1929 ed.), para. 443 [am. April 1944, Amendment 34]. This is based on 2 Oppenheim, International Law, 6th ed. (1940), s. 253, which is discussed in Green, "Superior Orders and the Reasonable Man", Essays on the Modern Law of War, 1985, ch. 3, at 57-58. Para. 443 reads "The fact that a rule of warfare has been violated in pursuance of an order of the belligerent Government or of an individual belligerent commander does not deprive the act in question of its character as a war crime, neither does it, in principle, confer upon the perpetrator immunity from punishment by the injured belligerent. Undoubtedly, a court confronted with the plea of superior orders adduced in justification of a war crime is bound to take into consideration the fact that the obedience to military orders, not obviously unlawful, is the duty of every member of the armed forces, and that the latter cannot, in conditions of war discipline, be expected to weigh scrupulously the legal merits of the order received. The question, however, is governed by the major principle that members of the armed

forces are bound to obey lawful orders only and that they therefore cannot escape liability if, in obedience to a command, they commit acts which both violate un-challenged rules of warfare and outrage the general sentiment of humanity."

29. See Green, "The Man in the Field and the Maxim Ignorantia Juris Non Excusat", Essays on the Modern Law of War, 1985, ch. 4.

30. *Re Holzer* (1946), Public Archives of Can., Record Group 25 F-3, vol. 1000, 345 at 349; see *Re Jung and Schumacher* (1946), cited Green, "Superior Orders and the Reasonable Man," (1980) 8 C.Y.B.I.L. 16 at 289-290.

§377   The military tribunals established by Canada for the trial of war criminals were set up in accordance with the War Crimes Regulations of 1945,[31] and these were themselves based on the English Royal Warrant of 1945.[32] The Regulations were given statutory force by the War Crimes Act of 1946.[33] The Statute is unlimited in duration[34] and applies to any war in which Canada is a belligerent.[35] Its intent, however, was to enable Canadian forces occupying enemy territory in Europe or the Far East to establish the necessary tribunals and to regulate their composition and procedure. The Regulations appended to the Act provide:[36] "Any Cana-dian flag, general or air officer commanding any Canadian forces, wher-ever such forces may be serving, whether in the field or in occupation of enemy territory or otherwise,[37] and any officer acting for such officer commanding in his absence, and any officer not below the rank of colonel, or its relative rank, whom such officer commanding, or officer acting for him in his absence, may authorize in writing in that behalf, shall have power to convene military courts for the trial of persons charged with having committed war crimes and to confirm the findings and sentences of such courts: Provided that no military court shall be convened for the trial of any person for a war crime unless the case has been certified by the Judge Advocate General, or any representative of his appointed by him for that purpose, as approved for trial."

31. P.C. 5831, 30 Aug. 1945.

32. Army Order 81/1945.

33. S.C. 1946, c. 73 (this Act is not reprinted in the 1970 edition of the Revised Statutes of Canada).

34. The Act is left unamended by S.C. 1987, c. 37.

35. See Schedule, Reg. 2(*f*): " 'war crime' means a violation of the laws and usages of war committed during any war in which Canada has been or may be engaged at any time after the ninth day of September, 1939." See, however, definition in S.C. 1987, c. 37 at §199.

36. Reg. 4(1).

37. Attempts have been made to suggest that the Act can operate to permit the arrest and trial of civilians, including Canadian nationals alleged to have committed war crimes, and who are now resident in Canada. In *Germany (Federal Republic) v. Rauca* (1982), 38 O.R. (2d) 705 (Ont. H.C.) this contention was raised by the defence,

but was avoided by Evans C.J. It was to correct this lacuna, that S.C. 1987, c. 37 was enacted. See Green, "Canadian Law and the Punishment of War Crimes", Essays on the Modern Law of War, 1985, ch. 12, and "Canadian Law, War Crimes and Crimes against Humanity," 59 B.Y.B.I.L. 1988.

§378 Moreover, "If it appears to a convening officer that a person then within the limits of his command or otherwise under his control has at any place committed a war crime he may direct that such person if not already in custody shall be taken into and kept in custody pending trial in such manner and in such charge as he may direct."[38]

    38. Reg. 6(1).

§379 The Act clearly indicates that while the court is established under Canadian law it is to apply the rules of international law. Thus, "the court shall take judicial notice of the laws and usages of war,"[39] and, reflecting the practice of war crimes tribunals,[40] "where there is evidence that more than one war crime has been committed by members of a formation, unit, body, or group while under the command of a single commander, the court may receive that evidence as prima facie evidence of the responsibility of the commander for those crimes. Where there is evidence that a war crime has been committed by members of a formation, unit, body or group that an officer or non-commissioned officer was present at or immediately before the time when such offence was committed, the court may receive that evidence as prima facie evidence of the responsibility of such officer or non-commissioned officer, and of the commander of such formation, unit, body, or group, for that crime."[41]

    39. Reg. 10(6).
    40. See §371 notes 10-12.
    41. Reg. 10(4), (5).

§380 With regard to penalties, the tribunal is authorized to sentence the accused to death, to life or lesser term of imprisonment, confiscation or fine,[42] and if the offence relates to money or other property it may order restitution or, if this is impossible, compensation.[43] In all cases, it must be remembered that in accordance with the Geneva Conventions of 1949, enemy prisoners are to be tried by the same courts and are amenable to the same sentences for the same offences as are the troops of the detaining power. By the Geneva Conventions Act,[44] "prisoners of war held by Canada are made subject to the Code of Service Discipline contained in the National Defence Act.[45] Accordingly, General, Disciplinary, and Standing Courts Martial (see s. 4 of the Geneva Conventions Act) have jurisdiction to try prisoners of war outside Canada for committing grave breach offences no matter where. The only notable limitation on the jurisdiction of these courts martial to try prisoners of war for grave breach offences is that, if a prisoner of war is held in Canada, he will have to be tried by a Canadian civil court for grave breach offences amounting to murder, rape or manslaughter if committed in Canada.[46] In the case of such offences committed outside Canada by a prisoner of war, both Canadian civil courts and the above-noted courts martial would have jurisdiction to try the offender in Canada."[47] Since this provision relates to the trial of grave breaches, it would appear that, for ordinary war crimes not amounting to grave breaches, the War Crimes Act, as affected by any provisions concerning trial in the Prisoners of War Convention (Geneva Convention III, 1949), would govern the trials of those accused of the lesser offences. The Canadian law with regard to the trial of those accused of war crimes or crimes against humanity was amended in 1987 in order to ensure that accused persons who might have become landed immigrants or Canadian citizens by naturalization should not be able to avoid trial by contending that the victim was not a Canadian, that the crime was committed outside of Canada, and by a person not a Canadian national.[48]

42. Reg. 11(1).

43. Reg. 11(2).

44. R.S.C. 1970, c. G-3, s. 7.

45. R.S.C. 1970, c. N-4, ss. 55-211 [as amended].

46. S. 61.

47. Cdn. Defence Dept.'s Manual of the Geneva Conventions, Cdn. Forces Papers 122, para. 1049(4).

48. S.C. 1987, c. 37. While this amends the Criminal Code, it apparently leaves the War Crimes Act unamended. See §§199 ante, 381 post. See Green, "Canadian Law, War Crimes and Crimes against Humanity," 59 B.Y.B.I.L. 1988.

§381 It is clear from the amendment to the Criminal Code, S.C. 1987, c. 37, that a Canadian court when seised of a charge of war crimes or crimes against humanity will apply both international and national law. War crimes are defined as constituting contraventions "of the customary international law or conventional international law applicable in international armed conflicts", while crimes against humanity are defined as contraventions "of customary international law or conventional international law or [are] criminal according to the general principles of law recognized by the community of nations".[49] In addition, the

Act defines what is meant by 'conventional international law'[50] and also provides that the accused may "rely on any justification, excuse or defence available under the laws of Canada or under international law at [the time of the act or omission] or at the time of the proceedings."

49. See §199 notes 6 and 7.

50. "(a) any convention, treaty or other international agreement that is in force and to which Canada is a party, of (b) any convention, treaty or other international agreement that is in force and the provisions of which Canada has agreed to accept and apply in an armed conflict in which it is involved." See Green, "Canadian Law, War Crimes and Crimes against Humanity," 59 B.Y.B.I.L. 1988.

§382 If an alleged war criminal is present in a country other than that which wishes to try him, the latter may seek his extradition. Even if the acts with which he has been charged have been committed in accordance with governmental orders or are claimed to have been legal in accordance with national law at the time of their commission, the defence of political offence[51] is not available to him.[52] Moreover, if his offences are common crimes under criminal law, the ordinary law of extradition will apply.[53]

51. See §204.

52. See *State v. Director of Prisons; Ex parte Schumann* (Ghana), [1966] G.L.R. 703 (C.A.). This decision is in line with that of *Kroeger v. Swiss Federal Prosecutor's Office* (1966), 72 I.L.R. 606 (Switz. Fed. Trib.)

53. See *Germany (Federal Republic) v. Rauca, ante.*

4. NON-INTERNATIONAL ARMED CONFLICT

§383 In accordance with international customary law incidents occurring within the territory of a sovereign state and affecting only that state and its citizens constitute a matter of domestic jurisdiction[54] and, as such, are beyond the consideration of international law.[55] As a result, a non-international conflict fought within the territory of a state and between citizens and their government was of no concern to international law. By the Geneva Conventions of 1949, however, an attempt was made to introduce some measure of international legal control by introducing minimum rules of humanitarian behaviour. By common Article 3:[56] "In the case of armed conflict not of an international character occurring in the territory of one of the High Contracting Parties, each Party to the conflict shall be bound to apply, as a minimum, the following provisions: (1) Persons taking no active part in the hostilities, including members of the armed forces who have laid down their arms and those placed hors de combat by sickness, wounds, detention, or any other cause, shall in all circumstances be treated humanely, without any adverse distinction founded on race, colour, religion or faith, sex, birth or wealth, or any other similar criteria. To this end the following acts are and shall remain prohibited at any time and in any place whatsoever with respect to the above-mentioned persons: (a) violence to life and person, in particular murder of all kinds, mutilation, cruel treatment and torture; (b) taking of hostages; (c) outrages upon personal dignity, in particular, humiliating and degrading treatment; (d) the passing of sentences and the carrying out of executions without previous judgment pronounced by a regularly constituted court affording all the judicial guarantees which are recognized as indispensable by civilized peoples. (2) The wounded and sick shall be collected and cared for. An impartial humanitarian body, such as the International Committee of the Red Cross, may offer its services to the Parties to the conflict. The Parties to the conflict shall further endeavour to bring into force, by means of special agreements, all or part of the other provisions of the present Convention. The application of the preceding provisions shall not affect the legal status of the Parties to the conflict." This last proviso allows the State authorities to continue to treat those engaged in conflict against them as traitors and to try them in accordance with national law, so long as their treatment pending and during trial does not fall below that postulated by the Article.[57] The Conventions do not treat breaches of Article 3 as grave breaches[58] and there is no method of supervision or punishment for infractions.

54. See §83.

55. Even the Covenant of the League of Nations, Art. 15(8) and the Charter of the United Nations, Art. 2(7) preclude these institutions from intervening in such matters unless, in the case of the latter, international peace and security are endangered.

56. See Schindler and Toman, The Laws of Armed Conflicts, (1981), Convention I (Wounded and Sick), p. 308; II (Wounded, Sick and Shipwrecked), p. 336; III (Ps. W.), p. 362; IV (Civilians), pp. 433-434.

57. See Green, 'The Indian National Army Trials', (1948), 11 Mod. L.R. 47; 'Le statut des Forces rebelles en droit international public', (1962) R.G.D.I.P. No. 1, 5.

58. See §§364-368.

§384 While international law might not regulate the conduct of a non-international conflict, some of the rules of the law of armed conflict may become relevant. This occurs when, for example, third states declare their neutrality,[59] or when a state of belligerency has been recognized by such a state[60] or proclaimed by the head of government involved.[61] In such circumstances third states are bound to recognize the consequences of the situation and become liable, for example, to observe a blockade declared by one of the parties.[62]

59. See, e.g., British declaration during American Civil War, May 13, 1861, 51 B.F.S.P. 165: ". . . We, being at Peace with the Government of the United States have declared our Royal determination to maintain a strict and impartial neutrality in the contest. . . ."

60. See, e.g., dispatch by Canning during the Greek revolution, Dec. 31, 1824: "We have openly and uniformly, from the time when the Greek struggle assumed the shape of a regular contest on the sea, professed an impartial neutrality between the two belligerent Parties, having allowed to each the free exercise of belligerent rights, such as the Law of Nations warrants — and specifically we have expressed our determination to respect the blockades of either party, when instituted and maintained according to practice of civilized War," 1 Smith, Great Britain and the Law of Nations (1932), p. 295.

61. President Lincoln issued a proclamation declaring a blockade of the Southern coasts, Apr. 19, 1861: ". . . deemed it advisable to set on foot a blockade of the ports within the states aforesaid in pursuance of the Laws of the United States and of the Law of Nations. . . . If, therefore, with a view to violate such blockade, a vessel shall approach, or shall attempt to leave any of the said ports she will be duly warned by the commander of one of the blockading vessels . . . and if the same vessel shall again attempt to enter or leave the blockaded port, she will be captured and sent to the nearest convenient port, for such proceedings against her and her cargo as prize as may be deemed advisable.": cited in Higgins, Hall's International Law (1928), p. 45, n. 1.

62. See The Prize Cases (1862), 2 Black 635 (U.S. S.C.) at pp. 639-640 per Grier J.: "After such an official recognition by the [foreign] sovereign, a citizen of a foreign State is estopped to deny the existence of a war with all its consequences as regards neutrals. They cannot ask a Court to affect a technical ignorance of the existence of a war, which all the world knows to be the greatest civil war known in the history of the human race, and thus cripple the arm of the Government and paralyze its power by subtle definition and ingenious sophisms."

§385 Problems may arise in connection with nomenclature. From the point of view of a municipal court, there may be use of words like war and insurrection intermixed, as well as such terms as enemies and traitors.[63] Even an international tribunal considering the liabilities of a government may be similarly confronted:[64] "The term 'revolution' has no precise meaning in international law. In the Franco-Mexican Convention [which had established the tribunal] it is not to be contrasted with the term 'insurrection' which indicates a more general idea, of which the 'revolution' is only a species. The question whether, within the terms of the Convention, an insurrectionary movement or a civil war is or is not a 'revolution' or a 'revolutionary movement' does not depend on its final seizure of power, nor on the more or less moral integrity of its originators or the lofty political and social ideals which inspired them, nor on the general or local character of the movement, nor on the recognition of the insurgents as belligerents by either the home government or third states. . . . [A]ll the forces who have participated in a revolutionary movement should be considered as 'revolutionary forces', that is to say, an armed movement, more or less organised, which, inspired by a political or social programme, or influenced by one or more determined personalities, or springing solely from general discontent with the dominant political régime in the country, has for its object the overthrow of a particular government or changes in the system of government."

63. *The Prize Cases, ante*, at pp. 636, 637: "Insurrection against a government may or may not culminate in an organized rebellion, but a civil war always begins by insurrection against the lawful authority of the Government. A civil war is never solemnly declared; it becomes such by its accidents — the number, power, and organization of the persons who originate and carry it on. When the party in rebellion occupy and hold in a hostile manner a certain portion of territory; have declared their independence; have cast off their allegiance; have organized armies; have commenced hostilities against their former sovereign, the world acknowledges them as belligerents, and the contest a *war. They* claim to be in arms to establish their liberty and independence, in order to become a sovereign State, while the sovereign treats them as insurgents and rebels who owe allegiance, and who should be punished with death for their treason." For discussion of the term 'enemy', see pp. 642-644.

64. *Pinson Claim* (France/Mexico) (1928), 5 R.I.A.A. 327 at 424. See also *Pan American World Airways Inc. v. Aetna Casualty & Surety Co.* (1974), 505 F. 2d 989, for discussion of insurrection and war in relation to acts of terrorism.

§386 These complexities are even more serious as the rebel movement becomes more organized and begins to take on the appearance of a de facto government:[65] "The exact distinction between a government de facto and the leaders of a revolutionary movement is very difficult to draw, the leaders of a seditious movement evolve gradually into a government de facto with the development and strengthening of their revolutionary movement. . . ." This fact has become of greater importance with the adoption of Protocol I concerning the application of humanitarian law in international armed conflict.[66] By Article 1 an armed conflict "in which peoples are fighting against colonial domination and alien occupation and against racist régimes in the exercise of their right of self-determination" is considered an international armed conflict and is regulated by the law relevant thereto. Difficulty lies in the fact that the Protocol nowhere defines such a struggle for self-determination, while any colonial or imperial power faced with such a struggle is likely to contend that it is, at most, engaged in suppressing a rebellion or conducting some other form of non-international conflict.[67]

65. *Pinson Claim, ante*, at p. 425.

66. 1977, Schindler and Toman, p. 551; see also §330.

67. This is the case with South Africa in relation to the activities of the African National Congress in the Republic and to the South West African People's Organization in Namibia.

§387 While those opposed to government forces may be regarded as traitors by the authorities and tried for treason,[68] a government may also decide to charge those committing acts which in an international armed conflict would constitute war crimes in the same way, and the defence of superior orders will be no more available in a non-international conflict than it is in an international one.[69] In assessing the nature of any such offence, care must be taken to ensure that the ideological nature of the conflict is not allowed to affect the legal realities.[70]

68. See §383 note 57.

69. See, e.g., *Pius Nwaoga v. State* (1972), 52 I.L.R. 494 (Nigeria).

70. *Pius Nwaoga v. State, ante,* at p. 497: "To our mind, deliberate and intentional killing of an unarmed person living peacefully inside the Federal Territory . . . is a crime against humanity, and even if committed during a civil war is in violation of the domestic law of the country, and must be punished."

§388 Civil war need not affect all the territories of the government against which the conflict is being fought. This is particularly true in the case of a state which has overseas territories and when part of the latter is seeking its independence.[71] Similarly, if a resident of a territory seeking independence joins the forces of another state equally engaged in an attempt to overthrow or destroy the state of which he is a resident, political considerations may affect the legal characterization of the hostilities and protect the resident from a charge of promoting civil war, while remaining liable for treason.[72]

71. *Société Purfina Française v. Cie. d'Assurances la Nationale* (1962), 44 I.L.R. 439 (France Ct. of Cassation) (holding that a civil war existed in Algeria, even though not in France); *Quinn v. Robinson* (1986) 783 F. 2d 776 at 813 (C.A.) (holding Irish Republican Army 'uprising' in Northern Ireland did not extend to England).

72. *Diab v. Israel (A.G.)* (Israel) (1952), 19 I.L.R. 550 (S.C.): "[The accused, an inhabitant of Israel, joined the Arab Liberation Army, and on his return was charged with promoting civil war under s. 53 of the Criminal Code Ordinance, 1936] . . . the war between the Arab States and Israel [while the former did not recognize Israel] was not a civil war within the meaning of . . . the Ordinance. Therefore, a person who took part in it against Israel, even though a resident of Israel, cannot be charged under the section. . . . [I]f a person resident in Israel, who owes a duty of allegiance towards Israel, takes part in a war against the State of Israel, that person can be charged with treason."

§389 The emotions evoked during a civil war frequently result in violence and atrocities exceeding those committed during an international armed conflict. In an attempt to subject non-international conflicts to some restraints in accordance with the principles of international humanitarian law, Protocol II additional to the Geneva Conventions of 1949 was adopted in 1977.[73] The purpose of the Protocol may be seen in a statement issued by Canada, which played a major part in its drafting:[74] "(1) The provisions of Protocol II must, individually and overall, be agreeable to all parties to the conflict, whether governmental or non-governmental. There should, therefore, be an obvious, practical benefit to be derived by each party in the observance of these provisions. (2) These provisions must be well within the perceived capacity of each party to apply them. They should, therefore, be kept as precise and simple as possible so as to be readily understood, and honoured by even a rudimentary organized group under responsible command, etc. (3) The Protocol should not be invoked as affecting the sovereignty of any State Party or the responsibility of its government to maintain law or order and to defend national unity and territorial integrity by legitimate means; nor should it be invoked to justify any outside intervention. (4) Nothing in the Protocol should suggest that dissidents must be treated legally other than as rebels. To move in the direction of recognizing the military activities of the rebels as having some degree of legitimacy, is to invite the expectation or even demand for Prisoner-of-War status on capture." Despite the role played in its drafting, Canada has not ratified Protocol II.

74. Schindler and Toman, *op. cit.*, p. 619.

75. Cited in Green, "Canada's Role in the Development of the Law of Armed Conflict". Essays on the Modern Law of War, (1985) ch. 13 at 274-275. The Canadian attitude to the Protocol is discussed at pp. 273-275. See also Wolfe, "War and Military Operations", Macdonald *et al.*, Canadian Perspectives on International Law and Organization (1974), pp. 620, 624-630.

§390 In its original proposal,[76] Canada suggested that the Protocol should "apply to all cases of armed conflict occurring in the territory of one of the High Contracting Parties, involving government forces on one side and armed forces whether regular or irregular on the other side and to which common Article 2[77] of the [Geneva] Conventions is not applicable." The Protocol, however, adopts a somewhat higher threshold. The nearest it comes to defining a non-international conflict is to provide:[78] "This Protocol which supplements Article 3 common to the Geneva Conventions[79] . . . shall apply to all armed conflicts which are not covered by Article 1 of . . ., Protocol I[80] and which take place in the territory of a High Contracting Party between its armed forces and dissident armed forces or other organized armed groups which, under responsible command, exercise such control over a part of its territory[81] as to enable them to carry out sustained and concerted military operations and to implement this Protocol."

76. See 1 Canadian Defence Quarterly (1971), 64-67.

77. ". . . shall apply to all cases of declared war or of any other armed conflict which may arise between two or more of the High Contracting Parties, even if the state of war is not recognized by one of them."

78. Protocol II, 16 I.L.M. 1442, Art. 1(1).

79. See §383 note 56.

80. See §330.

81. No such requirement is necessary in the case of a national liberation movement waging a conflict for self-determination under Art. 1 of Protocol I.

§391   These requirements appear to ensure that the Protocol shall only apply to a situation which has virtually hardened into a regular civil war. This is emphasized by the fact that the Protocol "shall not apply to situations of internal disturbances and tensions, such as riots, isolated and sporadic acts of violence and other acts of a similar nature, as not being armed conflicts".[82]

82. Art. 1(2). The Protocol does not apply to such events as the activities of terrorist groups, urban disturbances even if these are met by the organized armed forces of the state, the situation in Northern Ireland, or the 1970 Quebec crisis. Equally, terrorist groups cannot claim prisoner of war status under Protocol I: see *Folkerts Case* (Netherlands) (1977), Rolno 3853/73, cited in Green, "Terrorism and the Courts", (1981) 11 Man. L.J. 333 at 348 (see also §208 note 56).

§392   The Protocol provides that it in no way serves as a justification for any intervention "in the armed conflict or in the internal or external affairs of the High Contracting Party in which the conflict occurs," nor does it affect "the sovereignty of a State or the responsibility of the government, by all legitimate means, to maintain or re-establish law and order in the State or to defend the national unity and territorial integrity of the State",[83] nevertheless it seeks to apply[84] "without any adverse distinction founded on race, colour, sex, language, religion or belief, political or other opinion, national or social origin, wealth, birth or other status, or on any other similar criteria." Moreover, it prescribes the humane treatment that is to be afforded to all those not taking part in the conflict or who have ceased to do so, and seeks to ensure that such treatment shall be afforded to those who might be detained beyond the end of the conflict until such time as the detention ceases.[85]

83. Art. 3(1), (2).
84. Art. 2(1).
85. Art. 2(2).

§393 There is no provision in the Protocol for punishment in the event of a breach nor for any Protecting Power as there is in an international armed conflict.[86] However, "Relief societies located in the territory . . ., such as Red Cross . . . organizations, may offer their services for the performance of their traditional functions in relation to the victims of the armed conflict. The civilian population may, even on its own initiative, offer to collect and care for the wounded, sick and ship-wrecked[87] [, and] subject to national law,[88] no person engaged in medical activities may be penalized in any way for refusing or failing to give information concerning the wounded and sick who are, or who have been under his care".[89]

86. See §§351, 359-382.
87. Art. 18(1).
88. Which may be to the exact contrary.
89. Art. 10(4).

§394 While all the wounded and sick are to be humanely treated and receive medical attention without any adverse distinction,[90] and medical personnel are to be permitted to carry out their functions on behalf of both sides,[91] "the professional obligations of persons engaged in medical activities regarding information which they may acquire concerning the wounded and sick under their care shall, subject to national law, be respected."[92] As a result there is nothing in the Protocol to prevent the government from treating a medical officer as committing a criminal act if he were to refuse to give information as to the whereabouts of members of the opposing side whom he may have treated.

90. Art. 7.
91. Art. 10(1), (2).
92. Art. 10(3).

§395 As to the treatment to be afforded to those not participating in the conflict, including those who have been captured or are wounded and have ceased to participate, this is based on the similar provisions that apply to international armed conflicts. Thus, they "are entitled to respect for their person, honour and convictions and religious practices.

They shall in all circumstances be treated humanely, without any adverse distinction. It is prohibited to order that there shall be no survivors.[93] . . . [T]he following acts are and shall remain prohibited at any time and in any place whatsoever: (a) violence to the life, health and physical or mental well-being of persons, in particular murder as well as cruel treatment such as torture, mutilation or any form of corporal punishment; (b) collective punishments; (c) taking of hostages; (d) acts of terrorism; (e) outrages upon personal dignity, in particular humiliating and degrading treatment, rape, enforced prostitution and any form of indecent assault; (f) slavery and the slave trade in all their forms; (g) pillage; (h) threats to commit any of the foregoing acts."[94]

93. Art. 4(1).
94. Art. 4(2).

§396 Equally, special provision is made for the care of children[95] and of those who might be detained or whose liberty is restricted "for reasons related to the armed conflict".[96] With respect to prosecutions for acts connected with the conflict, the basic principles of the rule of law and impartial justice are postulated,[97] with the hope expressed[98] that "at the end of hostilities, the authorities in power shall endeavour to grant the broadest possible amnesty to persons who have participated in the armed conflict, or those deprived of their liberty for reasons related to the armed conflict, whether they are interned or detained." The Canadian attempt to ensure the postponement of all death sentences imposed in connection with the conflict until its termination, in the hope that those so sentenced might also benefit from the amnesty, was unsuccessful.

95. Art. 4(3).
96. Art. 5.
97. Art. 6(2)-(4): these subparagraphs largely flesh out common Art. 3; see §383.
98. Art. 6(5).

§397 During the nineteenth and early twentieth centuries, the European Powers and the United States considered themselves free to intervene in foreign non-international armed conflicts. They did so in two differing situations: (1) when the population revolted against a sovereign whose conduct was regarded by the Power concerned as tyrannical, or (2) when the government against which the conflict was being waged was an ally or a friend. However, by the 1930's, such action on either side in the conflict was becoming regarded as unlawful intervention and during the Spanish Civil War an official policy of non-intervention was pursued. After 1945, with the adoption of Article 2(7) of the Charter any such intervention was regarded as illegal and contrary to the principle of self determination, and was clearly condemned in the United Nations Declaration onFriendly Relations.[99] Moreover, since Protocol I, 1977[1] Article 1(4) makes wars for self-determination international conflicts, intervention on behalf of the government would be a breach of neutrality, while intervention on behalf of a national liberation movement is considered praiseworthy,[2] although by Protocol II,[3] intervention on either side is forbidden. The Canadian view[4] seems to be that aid to the government "is justifiable when the government in question is substantially in control of the territory and its existence is not seriously threatened by an insurgent movement. In such case, no judgment has to be made about the government's legitimacy. However, when two rival factions are competing over control, neither of which has established effective control over the territory or over a substantial part of it, the problem is much more difficult because . . . there is in international law no definition of legitimate government. In such circumstances acceptance of a request to intervene by one of the factions might well constitute an intervention in the domestic affairs of the state, and in some cases be inconsistent with the principle of self-determination. Thus, the legality of intervention in this situation is, to say the least, doubtful".

99. 1970, Res 2625 (XXV) Principle concerning the duty not to intervene in matters within the domestic jurisdiction of any State, in accordance with the Charter. See §81.

1. See §330.

2. Declaration on Friendly Relations — "In pursuit of the exercise of their right to self-determination, peoples are entitled to seek and to receive support. . . ."

3. Art. 3(2).

4. Memo by Legal Bureau, Dept. of External Affairs, 1 Dec. 1983, (1984) 22 C.Y.B.I.L. 333-4.

§398 As distinct from intervention during a civil war, a head of government may request a friendly state to intervene when a group of 'terrorists' overthrow the government in power and seek to set up a government of their own.[5] It may also happen that a group of states within the region where such an incident occurs may, claiming to be acting in the name of collective self-defence,[6] call upon an outside power to come to their aid on the plea that the group seizing power threatens the security of the entire regional group.[7]

5. In 1983 this was the situation in Grenada, when the "government", overthrown in a palace coup, was itself an administration that had taken office by way of a coup.

6. In its judgment concerning *Military and Paramilitary Activities in and against Nicaragua* (Nicaragua/U.S.) [1986] I.C.J. 14 at 103 (see §331 note 12) the I.C.J. stated that collective self-defence, like individual self-defence, was dependent upon an armed attack and "the question remains whether the lawfulness of the use of collective self-defence by the third State for the benefit of the attacked State also depends on a request addressed by that State to the third State ... [T]he Court finds that in customary international law ... there is no rule permitting the exercise of collective self-defence in the absence of a request by the State which is the victim of an armed attack. The Court concludes that the requirement of a request by the State which is the victim of the alleged attack is additional to the requirement that such a State should have declared itself to have been attacked. ... [I]f self-defence is advanced as a justification for measures which would otherwise be in breach both of the principle of customary international law and of that contained in [Article 51 of] the Charter, it is to be expected that the conditions contained in the Charter should be respected. Thus for the purpose of enquiry into the customary law position, the absence of a report to the Security Council in accordance with that Article may be one of the factors indicating whether the State in question was itself convinced that it was acting in self-defence", at 104-105.

7. See Green, 'The Rule of Law and the Use of Force — Falklands and Grenada', (1984) Can. Council on Int. Law, The Peaceful Settlement of Disputes 253, or (1986) 14 Archiv des Völkerrechts 173; American Bar Assn., 'Report of the Committee on Grenada', 1984, and comment thereon by Legal Advisor, Dept. of State, (1984) 78 A.J.I.L. 661; Moore, Law and the Grenada Invasion, 1984. For the Canadian view on the "legality of intervention in support of an existing government against a rebel or insurgent movement", see Legal Bureau memo 1 Dec. 1983, (1984) 22 C.Y.B.I.L. 333. See also, Doswald-Beck, 'The Legal Validity of Military Intervention by Invitation of the Government', (1985) 56 B.Y.I.L. 189.

§399 Regardless of any principle of international law purporting to prohibit intervention,[8] a state may claim that it has a right to intervene when it considers that the ideology of another state threatens the independence or political integrity of its neighbours or a region by threatening to export its ideas or to subvert its neighbours by assisting dissidents within those states. In such a case, claiming to be exercising its right to individual or collective self-defence,[9] the protesting state may resort to measures of force, such as blockading the ports of the 'offending' state by the use of mines,[10] by supporting[11] or instigating[12] dissident activities within the territory. All such acts were alleged by Nicaragua against the United States, and the International Court of Justice held such measures to be incompatible with international law as it applied between states members of the United Nations, particularly as they were ostensibly at peace and not at war. The court called for the termination of these acts.[13]

8. See the Declaration on Friendly Relations, 1970, General Assembly Res. 2625 (XXV). See §§397, 398.

9. See §§331, 398.

10. *Military and Paramilitary Activities in and against Nicaragua, ante* at pp. 111-112, 128-129.

11. *Ante* at pp. 103-104.

12. *Ante* at pp. 48-51.

13. The court's comments on the law concerning the use of force are to be found at p. 98 et seqq. (see §331). It is held that the war between the Nicaraguan Government and its opponents amounted to a non-international confict, while the acts of the United States fell "under the rules relating to international conflicts", at 114, even though there was no breach of diplomatic relations, let alone any declaration of war or belligerency, (see §§384, 385), though there may have been an animus belligerendi, (see §337). At pp. 112-115, the court considered the relevance of the rules of international humanitarian law.

VII The Law of
International Organizations

1. INTERNATIONAL JUDICIAL INSTITUTIONS

§400 International judicial settlement is conducted by way of arbitration tribunals, conciliation commissions and courts. They may be either ad hoc established to deal with a particular issue or a series of issues arising from a specific incident like a civil war or in relation to a particular treaty, or they may be permanent, similar in some respects to the judicial system within the state. Since international law is based on the consent of states,[1] submission to jurisdiction similarly requires consent, although a treaty may provide that any disputes in relation thereto shall be submitted to arbitration[2] or judicial settlement,[3] while parties to the Statute of the International Court of Justice are able in accordance with Article 36[4] to agree in advance to accept the jurisdiction of the Court, and all parties appear before the Court on a basis of equality.[5]

1. See text to note 4 under §1.

2. See Anglo-Greek Treaty of Commerce and Navigation, 1926, 61 L.N.T.S. 16, which was the basis for the *Ambatielos Claim* (1956), 12 R.I.A.A. 83.

3. See Optional Protocol to Vienna Convention on Diplomatic Relations, 1961, 500 U.N.T.S. 95, and Convention on Prevention and Punishment of Crimes against Internationally Protected Persons, including Diplomatic Agents, 1973, 1035 U.N.T.S. 167, Art. 13(1), both of which were considered by the World Court in the *Case concerning U.S. Diplomatic and Consular Staff in Tehran* (U.S./Iran), [1979] I.C.J. 7; [1980] I.C.J. 3; Green, "The Tehran Embassy Incident — Legal Aspects", (1980) 19 Archiv des Völkerrechts 1.

4. Commonly known as the 'Optional Clause': see §§405-411, and Merrills, 'The Optional Clause Today,' (1979) 50 B.Y.B.I.L. 87.

5. Statute of the International Court of Justice, Art. 35(2). On international judicial law generally, see Schwarzenberger, International Law, vol. 4, International Judicial Law, 1986, and on the I.C.J. in particular, Rosenne, The International Court of Justice, 1957, The Law and Practice of the International Court, 1965. See also, Gruss, The Future of the International Court of Justice, 1976 (2 vols.).

§401 Ad hoc tribunals may consist of a single arbitrator or a panel chosen by the parties, which may or may not include nationals of the parties in dispute, or the presiding member may, in accordance with the treaty establishing the tribunal, be selected by the President of the International Court. In the case of the Permanent Court of Arbitration the members are chosen by the parties from a pre-existing panel.[6] Where the International Court of Justice is concerned, the judges are chosen for a fixed term, subject to reappointment, by election by the General Assembly and the Security Council of the United Nations.[7] Normally, the parties have no part in the selection of those who will hear their case since a full court of fifteen judges usually sits, although a bench of nine will constitute a quorum.[8] The court may also sit in chambers appointed to hear special categories of cases or to deal with a particular case.[9] On occasion the parties may indicate the judges they wish to comprise such a chamber, as was done by Canada and the United States when submitting to the court the *Delimitation of the Maritime Boundary in the Gulf of Maine Area*.[10] Normally, international judicial tribunals comprise an odd number on the bench. In the event of the votes of the national representatives on an arbitral tribunal being equal, the neutral chairman has a deciding vote although the constituent instrument setting up the tribunal usually expresses this competence by referring to a majority vote,[11] while in the case of the International Court of Justice the President of the Court has a casting vote in addition to his ordinary vote.[12]

6. Hague Convention I for the Pacific Settlement of International Disputes, 1899 and 1907, 100 B.F.S.P. 298, 1 Scott, The Hague Court Reports (1916), p. xxxiii, Art. 23 in 1899, 44 in 1907. Canada is a party to this Convention and the Dept. of External Affairs has pointed out: "Strictly speaking, the Permanent Court of Arbitration has no continuing sphere of jurisdiction. Each tribunal created within its framework has only the competence conferred upon it by the agreement to submit to arbitration concluded by the parties to a dispute. The arbitrators are freely chosen by the parties from a list comprising the names of members of all the national groups of parties to the Court", (1960) 12 External Affairs 774. If the parties do not specify the rules of law or procedure to be applied, the tribunal will apply the Convention simpliciter.

7. Statute of the International Court of Justice, Art. 4: judges are nominated by the national groups in the P.C.A., and by Art. 6 "before making these nominations, each national group is recommended to consult its highest court of justice, its legal faculties and schools of law, and its national academies and national sections of international academies devoted to the study of law." In the event of there being no judge of the nationality of a party to a case, a national judge ad hoc may be appointed: Art. 31(2), (3).

8. Art. 25.

9. Art. 26.

10. [1982] I.C.J. 3 at 10: see statement by Oda J. concurring; "it should in my view have been made known that the Court, for reasons best known to itself, has approved the composition of the Chamber entirely in accordance with the latest wishes of the parties. . . ." It was on this ground that both Morozov and El-Khani JJ. dissented. For the *Frontier Dispute* (Burkina Faso/Mali), [1985] I.C.J. 6, the chamber consisted of two judges ad hoc appointed by the parties and three were elected by the Court itself in accordance with Art. 26 of the Statute.

11. See, e.g., the relevant provisions in the 1947 Peace Treaties as discussed in the *Interpretation of Peace Treaties,* [1950] I.C.J. 65 at 221.

12. Art. 55(2); the decision in *South-West Africa Cases (Second Phase)* (Ethiopia/ South Africa; Liberia/South Africa), [1966] I.C.J. 6 was reached in this way.

§402 Only states may be parties to an action before the International Court of Justice[13] and the decision rendered is only binding upon the parties and in respect of the particular case in issue.[14] However, if a third state considers it has an interest in the issue, it may request the court to permit it to intervene,[15] and if the construction of a multi-lateral convention is involved, the other parties to the convention must be notified that they have this right.[16] Similarly, the court may request information from international organizations if this is relevant to a case before the court and if the constituent instrument of such an organization is in issue, the organization must be so informed.[17] While the decisions of the court are final and without appeal, in the event of a dispute as to their meaning any party may request an interpretation.[18] Moreover, if some new fact of a decisive character is discovered after the judgment has been delivered, the party discovering that fact may request a revision of the judgment, provided that its ignorance of the fact was not due to negligence.[19] While all members of the United Nations have undertaken to carry out the decisions of the Court,[20] if the party against which a judgment has been delivered fails to carry out that judgment, the successful party may refer the matter to the Security Council, "which may, if it deems necessary, make recommendations or decide upon measures to be taken to give effect to the judgment."[21] Should the Council decide, for whatever reason, to take no action, and this is a question which is subject to the veto,[22] the effect may be the same as if the decision had been reversed on appeal.

13. Art. 34(1).

14. Art. 59. Thus, there is no rule of precedent in the practice of international judicial tribunals. However, since such courts regularly refer to and apply earlier decisions rendered by themselves or other tribunals there is in fact a jurisprudence constante.

15. Art. 62; the application by Fiji to intervene in the *Nuclear Tests Cases* (Australia/France; N.Z./France), [1974] I.C.J. 253, 457 failed since the cases themselves lapsed: see pp. 530, 535.

16. Art. 63; Cuba exercised this right in the *Haya de la Torre Case* (Colombia/Peru), [1951] I.C.J. 71 at 76. In the *Nuclear Tests Cases ante,* at pp. 255, 459, all parties to the General Act for the Pacific Settlement of International Disputes, 1928, to which Canada is a party, were notified and Fiji, Peru and Argentina asked for all pleadings and documents to be made available to them. In the United States declaration of 1946 accepting compulsory jurisdiction it stated that in the case of a multi-lateral treaty, 'all parties to the treaty affected by the decision' must be parties to the case. The

meaning of this phrase was considered in *Military and Paramilitary Activities in and against Nicaragua* (Nicaragua/U.S.), [1984] I.C.J. 392, 424-426.

17.   Art. 34(2), (3).

18.   Art. 60; see *Asylum Case (Interpretation)* (Colombia/Peru), [1950] I.C.J. 395, in which the court held its original judgment to be clear ([1950] I.C.J. 266), and that the request for interpretation only arose because the parties had failed to submit the proper question. See also, *Application for Revision and Interpretation of the Continental Shelf Case* (Tunisia/Libyan Arab Jamahiriyah), [1985] I.C.J. 192, partially granting the request and partially interpreting the earlier ([1982] I.C.J. 18) judgment.

19.   Art. 61; in the advisory opinion on *Effect of Awards of Compensation made by the U.N. Administrative Tribunal,* [1954] I.C.J. 47 at 55, the Court said that the rule that a judgment was final and without appeal "cannot be considered as excluding the Tribunal from itself revising a judgment in special circumstances when new facts of decisive importance have been discovered. . . . Such a strictly limited revision by the Tribunal itself cannot be considered as an 'appeal' . . . and would conform with rules generally provided in statutes or laws for courts of justice, such as for instance in Article 61 of the Statute of the International Court of Justice."

20.   Charter of the U.N., Art. 94(1). Since any non-member authorized to appear before the Court shall in no case be in a position of inequality, it follows that such a state is equally obliged to carry out the decision: Statute of the International Court of Justice, Art. 35(2).

21.   Charter, Art. 94(2).

22.   Charter, Art. 27(3); see §418.

§403   While only states may be parties to a dispute before the court, the United Nations and the specialized agencies are able to request an advisory opinion on any legal question.[23] In fact, since the proposal that such an opinion be requested will invariably come on a motion first mooted by a member of the organization, this means in practice that states, too, can secure such an opinion. While such an opinion lacks obligatory force,[24] practice by the various organizations concerned indicates that such opinions are invariably accepted as authoritative and acted upon.[25] However, an international organization may itself undertake to recognize such an opinion as binding.[26]

23.   Charter of the U.N., Art. 96; Statute, Art. 65.

24.   See, e.g., *Interpretation of Peace Treaties, ante,* at p. 71: "The Court's reply is only of an advisory character; as such it has no binding force." In *Status of Eastern Carelia* (1923), 1 W.C.R. 191 at 205, the Court said: "The Court is aware of the fact that it is not requested to decide a dispute, but to give an advisory opinion. . . . Answering the question [put to the Court] would be substantially equivalent to deciding the dispute between the parties. The Court, being a Court of Justice, cannot, even in giving advisory opinions, depart from the essential rules guiding their activity as a Court."

25.   Thus, as a result of the opinion on *Effect of Awards of Compensation made by the U.N. Administrative Tribunal, ante,* the General Assembly amended the Statute of

the Administrative Tribunal of the U.N., Res. 957 (X). See, 2 Rosenne, The Law and Practice of the International Court (1965), pp. 747-754, for a number of examples.

26.   Thus by Art. 12 of the Statute of the Administrative Tribunal of the International Labour Organisation, which serves the whole international civil service (see §§428-435) other than the Secretariat of the U.N., if the Executive Board of the organization challenges a decision of the Tribunal confirming its decision or on the ground that there was a fundamental fault in the procedure followed, the Executive Board is to refer the question to the I.C.J. for an advisory opinion, and "the opinion given by the Court shall be binding." On this Art., the Court has said: "Such effect of the Opinion goes beyond the scope attributed by the Charter and by the Statute of the Court to an Advisory Opinion": *Judgments of the Administrative Tribunal of the I.L.O. Upon Complaints Made Against UNESCO*, [1956] I.C.J. 77 at 84. See also §431.

§404   Although the jurisdiction of the court depends on consent and the parties appear before it on a basis of equality, the court will give a judgment in absentia if the defendant fails to appear when it has accepted a prior obligatory commitment to accept the jurisdiction[27] or if, in its refusal, it in fact appears to have accepted it.[28] On the other hand, no judgment will be rendered if it appears to the court that the interests of a non-party are directly involved and that party does not appear.[29] Similarly, the court will not deliver an advisory opinion if it appears that this is really an indirect way of securing a judgment on a disputed matter and one of the parties in the dispute does not recognize the jurisdiction.[30]

27.   See *Case Concerning U.S. Diplomatic and Consular Staff in Tehran, ante*. After the court asserted its competence to hear the Nicaraguan accusations concerning *Military and Paramilitary Activities in and against Nicaragua* (Nicaragua/U.S.), [1984] I.C.J. 392, the United States contested that jurisdiction and refused to participate further. The I.C.J., however, proceded with the hearing and delivered judgment [1986] I.C.J. 14.

28.   See *Corfu Channel Case (Preliminary Objection)* (G.B./Albania), [1948] I.C.J. 15, in which Albania unsuccessfully objected to the procedure adopted by G.B. in instituting proceedings, and the Court went on to deliver judgment on the *Merits*, [1949] I.C.J. 4.

29.   See *Monetary Gold* (Italy/France, G.B., U.S.), [1954] I.C.J. 19.

30.   See *Status of Eastern Carelia, ante*.

§405   The clearest expression of consent to the acceptance of the jurisdiction of the World Court is by way of a declaration made under Article 36 of the Statute: "2. The parties to the present Statute may at any time declare that they recognize as compulsory ipso facto and without special agreement, in relation to any other state accepting the same obligation, the jurisdiction of the Court in all legal disputes concerning: a. the interpretation of a treaty; b. any question of international law; c. the existence of any fact which, if established, would constitute a breach of an international obligation;[31] d. the nature or extent of the reparation to be made for the breach of an international obligation.[32] 3. The declarations referred to above may be made unconditionally[33] or on condition of reciprocity[34] on the part of several or certain states, or for a certain time. ... 5. Declarations made under Article 36 of the Statute of the Permanent Court of International Justice and which are still in force[35] shall be deemed, as between the parties to the present Statute, to be acceptances of the compulsory jurisdiction of the International Court of Justice for the period which they still have to run and in accordance with their terms."

31. See §§316-328.

32. See §319. In the *Corfu Channel Case (Merits), ante.*, the court held that if it was eligible to decide on the nature of compensation due, it was also competent to assess that compensation.

33. See §408.

34. See §407.

35. In the *Aerial Incident of July 27, 1955 (Israel v. Bulgaria)*, [1959] I.C.J. 127 at 143-144, it was held that the non-membership of Bulgaria in the United Nations between 1945 and 1955 terminated the existence of its declaration with the extinction of the Permanent Court: "[Art. 36(5)] laid upon the States to which it applied an obligation, the obligation to recognize, ipso facto and without special agreement, the jurisdiction of the new Court. This constituted a new obligation which was, doubtless, no more onerous than the obligation which was to disappear but it was nevertheless a new obligation. ... Until its admission, [a non-signatory] was a stranger to the Charter and to the Statute. What has been agreed upon between the signatories of these instruments cannot have created any obligation binding upon it [see §308], in particular an obligation to recognize the jurisdiction of the Court [see *Status of Eastern Carelia, ante*]. This was the position of Bulgaria. Art. 36(5), could not in any event be operative as regards that State until ... its admission to the United Nations [in] 1955. At that date, however, the Bulgarian Declaration ... was no longer in force in consequence of the dissolution of the Permanent Court. ... The acceptance set out in that Declaration ... was therefore devoid of object since the Court was no longer in existence. The legal basis for that acceptance ... [under] the former Statute ... ceased to exist with the disappearance of the Statute. Thus, the Bulgarian Declaration had lapsed. ... [Art. 36(5) in the present Statute] determines, in respect of a State to which it applies, the birth of the compulsory jurisdiction of the new Court. It makes that subject to two conditions: (1) that the State having made the declaration should be a party to the Statute, (2) that the declaration of that State should still be in force. Since the Bulgarian Declaration had lapsed before Bulgaria was admitted to the United Nations, it cannot be said that, at that time, that declaration was still in force. ..." On the other hand, after being admitted to the United Nations in 1946 Thailand in 1950 made a declaration which appeared to be a mere renewal of one no longer valid, and the court's jurisdiction was objected to on the same basis as in the Bulgarian case. However, in the *Case Concerning the Temple of Preah Vihear* (Cambodia/Thailand), [1961] I.C.J. 17 at 29, the court held that "this Declaration was a new independent instrument and has to be dealt with as such. It was not, and could not have been, made under Art. 36(5)."

§406 A declaration made under Article 36 has to be lodged with the Secretary-General of the United Nations who transmits copies to the parties to the Statute as well as to the Registrar of the court.[36] Such notification gives immediate effect to the Declaration and renders it operative even against a party similarly bound which has not yet received the notification,[37] and despite the fact that this might result in the respondent state being unable to make use of a reservation attached to its Declaration by the plaintiff state.[38]

36. Statute of the International Court of Justice, Art. 36(4). Problems arose in the case concerning *Military and Paramilitary Activities in and against Nicaragua, ante.* Nicaragua became a member of the League of Nations in 1920 and made its declaration in 1929, making it subject to ratification, intimating this would follow. No ratification was ever submitted and Nicaragua's withdrawal from the League became effective in 1938, although in 1939 it informed the Secretary-General that ratification had ensued and the instrument would be forwarded. The court had accepted the validity of the Nicaraguan declaration when seised of the *Arbitral Award made by the King of Spain in 1906,* [1960] I.C.J. 192, and Nicaragua argued that para. 5 (see note 35 *ante*) only related to declarations that had actually expired, and not to one which 'had not been perfected'. The court examined the facts and concluded that the declaration was valid, at 401-413. For a comprehensive survey of Nicaragua's standing and the Optional Clause in general, see Judge Oda's Separate Opinion, 471-513.

37. *Right of Passage over Indian Territory (Preliminary Objection)* (Portugal/India), [1957] I.C.J. 125 at 145-146: "The principle of reciprocity forms part of the system of the Optional Clause by virtue of the express terms both of Art. 36 ... and of most Declarations of Acceptance.... However, ... the Court considers that, by the deposit of its Declaration of Acceptance with the Secretary-General, the accepting State becomes a Party to the system of the Optional Clause in relation to the other declarant States [see §301], with all the rights and obligations deriving from Art. 36. The contractual relation between the Parties and the compulsory jurisdiction of the Court resulting therefrom are established, 'ipso facto and without special agreement', by the fact of the making of the Declaration. Accordingly, every State which makes a Declaration of Acceptance must be deemed to take into account the possibility that, under the Statute, it may at any time find itself subjected to the obligations of the Optional Clause in relation to a new Signatory as the result of the deposit by that Signatory of a Declaration of Acceptance. A State accepting the jurisdiction of the Court must expect that an Application may be filed against it before the Court by a new declarant State on the same day on which the State deposits with the Secretary-General its Declaration of Acceptance. For it is on that very day that the consensual bond, which is the basis of the Optional Clause, comes into being between the States concerned. ..." See also, *Military and Paramilitary Activities in and against Nicaragua, ante,* at 417, re the U.S. attempt to exclude jurisdiction from issues concerning Central America after Nicaragua had filed its case.

38. *Right of Passage over Indian Territory (Preliminary Objection), ante,* at pp. 146-7. As to the issue of reciprocity, see §407.

§407 Most declarations accepting the compulsory jurisdiction of the court are based on the principle of reciprocity, that is to say, the declarant state indicates that it is accepting such jurisdiction automatically only in respect of states which have made a similar declaration of acceptance.[39] As a result, a party to a dispute is entitled to take advantage of any reservation[40] attached to the other party's declaration, even though it has not itself made any such reservation.[41]

39. In *Military and Paramilitary Activities in and Against Nicaragua, ante,* the U.S. argued that since the Nicaraguan declaration lacked any provision for notice of termination it could be terminated at any time and that, on a reciprocal basis, the U.S. could do the same regardless of the presence of a term prescribing the method of unilateral termination in its own declaration. The court said (at 419) "The notion of reciprocity is concerned with the scope and substance of the commitment entered into, including reservations, and not with the formal conditions of their creation, duration or extinction. It appears clearly that reciprocity cannot be invoked in order to excuse departure from the terms of a State's own declaration, whatever its scope, limitations or conditions."

40. See Statute of the International Court of Justice, Art. 36(3) (§405).

41. See *Case of Certain Norwegian Loans* (France/Norway),[1957] I.C.J. 9 at 23-24: "... The jurisdiction of the Court depends upon the Declarations made by the Parties ...;... since two unilateral declarations are involved, such jurisdiction is conferred upon the Court only to the extent to which the two Declarations coincide in conferring it. A comparison between the two Declarations shows that the French Declaration accepts the Court's jurisdiction within narrower limits than the Norwegian Declaration; consequently, the common will of the Parties, which is the basis of the Court's jurisdiction, exists within these narrower limits. ... In accordance with the condition of reciprocity to which acceptance of the compulsory jurisdiction is made subject in both Declarations ..., Norway, equally with France, is entitled to except from the compulsory jurisdiction of the Court disputes" excepted by France. See §408.

§408 Among the reservations attached to declarations accepting the jurisdiction of the World Court is that concerning domestic jurisdiction.[42] In the days of the Permanent Court of International Justice, such declarations were expressed in a form that acknowledged that the reservation was subject to interpretation in accordance with international law.[43] However, since these limiting words have been omitted from Article 2, paragraph 7, of the Charter of the United Nations,[44] a number of states making declarations accepting the Court's compulsory jurisdiction have reserved to themselves the decision whether an issue falls within domestic jurisdiction or not.[45] Despite the fact that Article 36 of the Statute specifically states that "in the event of a dispute as to whether the Court has jurisdiction, the matter shall be settled by the decision of the Court",[46] the Court has held that such a reservation is valid, enabling the state party to the dispute which has not made such a reservation to take advantage of it on the basis of reciprocity[47] and to deny that the Court has jurisdiction.[48]

42. See §§83-85.

43. See, e.g., Canadian Declaration, 20 Sept. 1929: ". . . other than . . . disputes with regard to questions which by international law are essentially within the domestic jurisdiction [— these are the words of the League Covenant, Art. 15(8) —] of Canada", Rosenne, Documents on the International Court of Justice (1979), p. 352.

44. "Nothing contained in the present Charter shall authorize the United Nations to intervene in matters which are essentially within the domestic jurisdiction of any state or shall require the Members to submit such matters to settlement under the present Charter." Judicial settlement is one of the procedures of pacific settlement by which states are bound to have recourse by Art. 33 of the Charter.

45. See U.S. Declaration, 14 Aug., 1946: ". . . this declaration shall not apply to . . . disputes with regard to matters which are essentially within the domestic jurisdiction of the United States of America as determined by the United States of America . . .": Rosenne, p. 415; see also Y.B.I.C.J. 1981-1982, p. 92. In October 1985, the United States, because of its disagreement with the I.C.J.'s 1984 decision affirming its jurisdiction in the *Military and Paramilitary Activities in and against Nicaragua, ante,* gave six months notice terminating its acceptance of jurisdiction. This, or course, does not affect any other state's declaration, nor discussion as to the validity or otherwise of this type of declaration. The current declarations are to be found in the latest issue of the Yearbook of the International Court of Justice. See Crawford, "The Legal Effect of Automatic Reservations to the Jurisdiction of the International Court," (1979) 50 B.Y.B.I.L. 63.

46. Art. 36(6).

47. See §407.

48. *Case of Certain Norwegian Loans, ante,* at p. 24. The court also stated at p. 27: "The validity of the reservation has not been questioned by the Parties. It is clear that France [which had made the reservation] maintains its Declaration, including the reservation, and that Norway relies upon the reservation." Guerrero J. regarded such a reservation "as devoid of all legal validity", at p. 69, while Lauterpacht J. considered that the reservation went to the root of the Declaration rendering the entire French acceptance invalid, at p. 66: ". . . the French Declaration is invalid. . . . (1) it is contrary to the Statute of the Court; (2) it is incapable of giving rise to a legal obligation inasmuch as it claims, and effectively secures, the right of unilateral determination of the extent and of the existence of the obligation of judicial settlement with regard to a comprehensive and indefinite category of disputes covering potentially most disputes which may come before the Court; (3) the particular qualification of the reservation in question forms an essential part of the Acceptance and it is not possible to treat it as invalid and at the same time to maintain the validity of the reservation to which it is attached or of the Acceptance as a whole. Accordingly, . . . the entire French Declaration of Acceptance must be treated as devoid of legal effect and as incapable of providing a base for the jurisdiction of the Court. It is for that reason that the Court has no jurisdiction over the dispute. The majority of the Court has reached the same result by acting upon the 'automatic reservation' [claimed by Norway] and the French Declaration of Acceptance — both of which I consider to be invalid. . . ."

§409 Some declarations of acceptance are limited temporally, only accepting jurisdiction in respect of disputes arising after a certain date. Occasionally this raises questions as to when the dispute actually arose.[49] If, however, the temporal reservation relates to termination of acceptance, this cannot operate retroactively so as to affect cases of which the court is already seised.[50]

49.   See *Interhandel Case* (Switzerland/U.S.), [1959] I.C.J. 6 at 22, ". . . the facts and situations which have led to a dispute must not be confused with the dispute itself. . . . The point here in dispute is the obligation of the Government of the United States to submit to arbitration or to conciliation an obligation the existence of which is asserted by Switzerland and denied by the United States. This part of the dispute can only have arisen subsequently to that relating to the restitution of Interhandel's assets in the United States, since the procedure proposed by Switzerland and rejected by the United States was conceived as a means of settling the first dispute. [Since] the Swiss Government put forward this proposal first in . . . 1956, and the Government of the United States rejected it . . . [in] 1957", it clearly arose after the date mentioned in the U.S. declaration of 1946. See, also, *Right of Passage over Indian Territory (Merits)* (Portugal/India), [1960] I.C.J. 6 at 33-34: India's declaration of acceptance only applied to "all legal disputes arising after Feb. 5, 1930, with regard to situations or facts subsequent to the same date," and India argued that since Portugal's execution of passage predated this, the issue was outside the jurisdiction. The court pointed out that the subject of the dispute was "the conflict of views which arose between the two States when, in 1954, India opposed the exercise of Portugal's right of passage. If this were the subject of the dispute referred to the Court, the challenge to the jurisdiction could not be sustained. But it appeared from the Application [submitting the case] and it was fully confirmed by the subsequent proceedings, the Submissions of the Parties and statements made in the course of the hearings, that the dispute submitted to the Court had a threefold subject: (1) the disputed existence of a right of passage in favour of Portugal; (2) the alleged failure of India in July 1954 to comply with its obligations concerning that right of passage; (3) the redress of the illegal situation flowing from that failure. The dispute before the Court, having this three-fold subject, could not arise until all its constituent elements had come into existence. . . ." See, also, Rosenne, The Time Factor in the Jurisdiction of the International Court of Justice (1960), and Gross, "The Time Element in the Contentious Proceedings in the International Court of Justice," (1969) 63 A.J.I.L. 74.

50.   *Right of Passage over Indian Territory (Preliminary Objection), ante*, at p. 142: "It is a rule of law generally accepted, as well as one acted upon in the past by the Court, that, once the Court has been validly seised of a dispute, unilateral action by the respondent State in terminating its Declaration, in whole or in part, cannot divest the Court of jurisdiction [even if the Declaration itself provides for termination 'with effect from the moment of such notification']." See also, *Military and Paramilitary Activities in and against Nicaragua, ante* at 419.

§410   Canada first accepted the compulsory jurisdiction of the World Court in 1929 when its reservations were those common to all members of the Commonwealth: "disputes in regard to which the Parties to the dispute have agreed or shall agree to have recourse to some other method of peaceful settlement; disputes with any other Member of the League which is a member of the British Commonwealth of Nations, all of which disputes shall be settled in such manner as the Parties have agreed or shall agree;[51] and disputes with regard to questions which by international law fall within the jurisdiction of the Dominion of Canada. . . ."

> 51. This reflects the view that the relations between members of the Commonwealth were more in the nature of quasi-international law and amenable to what was then thought might be a jurisdiction enjoyed by the Judicial Committee of the Privy Council.

§411   Since judicial settlement is a matter of pacific relations, it is not surprising that, in exercise of the principle rebus sic stantibus,[52] Canada added the following reservation in 1939:[53] ". . . the Canadian Government will not regard the acceptance of the Optional Clause as covering disputes arising out of events occurring during the present war." In 1970, at the time of Canada's proposed legislation on Arctic pollution, the territorial sea and fishing zones, Canada replaced its earlier declaration:[54] "(2) . . . the Government of Canada accepts as compulsory ipso facto and without special convention, on condition of reciprocity,[55] the jurisdiction of the International Court of Justice, in conformity with paragraph 2 of Article 36 of the Statute of the Court, until such time as notice may be given to terminate the acceptance, over all disputes arising after the present declaration with regard to situations or facts subsequent to this declaration,[56] other than: (a) disputes in regard to which the parties have agreed or shall agree to have recourse to some other method of peaceful settlement; (b) disputes with the Government of any other country which is a member of the Commonwealth of Nations, all of which disputes shall be settled in such manner as the parties have agreed or shall agree; (c) disputes with regard to questions which by international law fall exclusively within the jurisdiction of Canada; (d) disputes arising out of or concerning jurisdiction or rights claimed or exercised by Canada in respect of the conservation, management or exploitation of the living resources of the sea, or in respect of the prevention or control of pollution or contamination of the marine environment in maritime areas adjacent to the coast of Canada.[57] (3) The Government of Canada also reserves the right at any time, by means of a notification addressed to the Secretary-General of the United Nations[58] and with effect as from the moment of such notification,[59] either to add to, amend or withdraw any of the foregoing reservations, or any that may hereafter be added."[60] Despite this Declaration of Acceptance, and even though the United States had made its own similar Declaration,[61] Canada and the United States entered into a Special Agreement[62] with regard to the submission to the Court of their dispute concerning delimitation of the maritime boundary in the Gulf of Maine area.[63] After the decision of the court in the *Gulf of Maine* case, Canada amended its Declaration cancelling paragraph (d) just referred to.[64]

52.   See §314.

53.   Rosenne, *op. cit.*, p. 353.

54.   7 Apr. 1970, Rosenne, 353-354; Y.B.I.C.J. 1981-1982, 62-63.

55.   See §407 and §406 note 37.

56.   See §409.

57.   See McRae and Goundray, "Environmental Jurisdiction in Arctic Waters", (1982) 16 U.B.C.L.R. 197.

58.   See §406. Such a notice was delivered on 10 Sept. 1985 amending the Declaration of 1970, I.C.J.Y.B. 1985-1986, 64. In its 1984 decision on the *Military and Paramilitary Activities in and against Nicaragua, ante* the I.C.J. held that notice terminating acceptance of jurisdiction had to be in accord with the terms of the original declaration of acceptance, overruling the contention of the United States that reciprocity enabled it to do so with immediate effect since there was no period of notice specified in the Nicaraguan declaration, "on the contrary it is Nicaragua that can invoke the six months' notice against the United States — not of course on the basis of reciprocity, but because it is an undertaking which is an integral part of the instrument that contains it" (at 419).

59.   For an assessment of the contribution to international judicial settlement by the Canadian member of the Court, 1946-1958, see Rosenne, "Judge John E. Read and the International Court of Justice", (1979), 17 C.Y.B.I.L. 3.

60.   See §406 note 37. See also Macdonald, "The New Canadian Declaration of Acceptance of the Compulsory Jurisdiction of the I.C.J.", (1970) 8 C.Y.B.I.L. 3.

61.   See §408 note 45.

62.   20 I.L.M. 1373 at 1377.

63.   See McRae, "Adjudication of the Maritime Boundary on the Gulf of Maine", (1979), 17 C.Y.B.I.L. 292. *Gulf of Maine Case* (Canada/U.S.), [1984] I.C.J. 246; Legault and McRae, "The Gulf of Maine Case", (1984) 22 C.Y.B.I.L. 267.

64.   U.N. Doc. C.N. 257 1985. Treaties — 3 (Annex).

§412   It has sometimes been contended that not all disputes are amenable to jurisdiction and it is argued that a distinction must be drawn between those issues which are political and those which are legal, with only the latter being considered justiciable. This, however, is a false distinction. Any international issue may be subjected to legal determination, although in a particular instance one or other of the states in dispute may consider that the matter touches issues of prestige or security[65] and is, as a result, not amenable to third party adjudication. The decision to have recourse to a judicial process is political. However, once this decision has been made, the issue becomes legal and justiciable, subject to determination in accordance with legal principles.[66]

65.   In connection with the *Military and Paramilitary Activities in and against Nicaragua* the United States argued that since allegations of aggression had been

made and met by pleas of self-defence, the issue was one for the Security Council, but the court stated, at 434-435: "The Charter does not confer *exclusive* responsibility upon the Security Council for the purpose. While in Article 12 there is a provision for a clear demarcation of functions between the General Assembly and the Security Council, in respect of any dispute or situation, that the former should not make any recommendation with regard to that dispute or situation unless the Security Council so requires, there is no similar provision anywhere in the Charter with respect to the Security Council and the Court. The Council has functions of a political nature assigned to it, whereas the Court exercises purely judicial functions. Both organs can therefore perform their separate but complementary functions with respect to the same events."

66. See Rosenne, The Law and Practice of the International Court (1965), pp. 2-4.

2. THE UNITED NATIONS AND SPECIALIZED AGENCIES

§413 The United Nations is a treaty-created body which has an international personality of its own,[67] enjoying such immunity and privileges for itself, its officials,[68] and the representatives of members as are necessary to fulfil its purposes.[69] But it is not a super-state nor does it constitute a government exercising authority over its members.[70] It is a political organization which reaches political decisions through the votes of the representatives of its member states.[71] Nevertheless, since its constituent instrument is a treaty, it is subject to the rules of interpretation of treaties[72] and its competence is determined by such interpretation. The Charter is, therefore, an instrument of international law and although its members act in accordance with political reasons, a number of legal problems inevitably arise.

67. Charter, Art. 104. See *Reparation for Injuries Suffered in the Service of the U.N.*, [1949] I.C.J. 174. See also §53.

68. See §§428-435.

69. Charter, Art. 105. See also Privileges and Immunities (International Organizations) Act., R.S.C. 1970, c. P-22.

70. *Reparation for Injuries Suffered in the Service of the U.N., ante*, at p. 179: ". . . the Organization is an international person. That is not the same as saying that it is a State, which it certainly is not, or that its legal personality and rights and duties are the same as those of a State. Still less is it the same thing as saying that it is a 'super State'. . . . It is a subject of international law and capable of possessing international rights and duties, and it has capacity to maintain its rights by bringing international claims." See also *A.G. v. Nissan*, [1970] A.C. 179 at 222 per Lord Borth-y-Gest: "The United Nations is not a State or a sovereign: it is an international organisation formed to maintain international peace and security and to take effective collective measures for the prevention and removal of threats to peace; it is based on the principle of sovereign equality of all its members [Charter, Art. 2(1)]: it does not intervene in matters which are essentially within the domestic jurisdiction of a State [Art. 2(7)]."

71. *Reparation for Injuries Suffered in the Service of the U.N., ante*, at p. 179: ". . . the Organization is a political body, charged with political tasks of an important

character, and covering a wide field, namely, the maintenance of international peace and security, the development of friendly relations among nations, and the achievement of international co-operation in the solution of problems of an economic, social, cultural or humanitarian character (Art. 1); and in dealing with its Members it employs political means." See also *Mosul Case* (1925), 1 W.C.R. 722 at 740: the League Council is "composed of representatives of Members, that is to say, of persons delegated by their respective Governments, from whom they receive instructions and whose responsibility they engage."

72. See §310.

§414 Membership in the United Nations is of two kinds. In the first instance there are the original members,[73] those who had participated in the drafting Conference at San Francisco, as well as those who had signed the Declaration by United Nations of January 1, 1942.[74] Secondly, there are the new members who are subsequently admitted to membership. The qualification for admission is that the applicant be a "peace-loving state which accept[s] the obligations contained in the present Charter and, in the judgment of the Organization, [is] able and willing to carry out these obligations".[75] Provided these qualifications are satisfied, admission is "effected by a decision of the General Assembly upon the recommendation of the Security Council."[76] This means that both organs of the United Nations must be in agreement, so that the General Assembly cannot decide to admit if the recommendation of the Security Council is negative.[77] The conditions laid down for membership are exhaustive, so that neither the General Assembly nor the Security Council may stipulate any additional requirements.[78] However, since the United Nations is a political body, with decisions made for political reasons, there is nothing to prevent a state from considering other factors, and allowing these factors to condition its vote provided it does so in good faith.[79]

73. Art. 3.

74. 9 Hudson, Int. Leg. 1. 'United Nations' is the name of the alliance opposed to the Axis Powers during World War II.

75. Art. 4(1).

76. Art. 4(2).

77. *Competence of General Assembly for the Admission of a State to the United Nations,* [1950] I.C.J. 4 at 7: ". . . the text . . . requires two things to effect admission: a 'recommendation' of the Security Council and a 'decision' of the General Assembly. The word 'recommendation' and the word 'upon' preceding it, imply the idea that the recommendation is the foundation of the decision to admit, and that the latter rests upon the recommendation. Both these acts are indispensable to form the judgment of the Organization. . . ."

78. *Admission of a State to Membership in the United Nations,* [1948] I.C.J. 57 at 62-63: "The natural meaning of the words used [in Art. 4(1)] leads to the conclusion that these conditions constitute an exhaustive enumeration and are not merely stated

by way of guidance or example. The provision would lose its significance and weight, if other conditions, unconnected with those laid down, could be demanded. The conditions stated . . . must therefore be regarded not merely as the necessary conditions, but also as the conditions which suffice. . . . Moreover, the spirit as well as the terms of the paragraph preclude the idea that considerations extraneous to these principles and obligations can prevent the admission of a State which complies with them."

79. *Admission of a State to Membership in the United Nations, ante;* see joint dissenting opinion by Basdevant, Winiarski, McNair and Read JJ., 82 at pp. 90-92: "It is the function of the Security Council to reject an application or to recommend its admission. On the one hand, this fact indicates the discretionary nature of this function of the Security Council, while, on the other hand, the freedom of the General Assembly either to accept the recommendation and admit the applicant or to reject the application indicates that the function of the German Assembly in this matter is also discretionary. . . . [A] member of the United Nations remains legally entitled, either in the Security Council or in the General Assembly, during the discussion upon the admission of a new Member, to put forward considerations foreign to the qualifications specified in Art. 4(1), and, assuming these qualifications to be fulfilled, to base its vote upon such considerations. . . . When a Member . . . imports into the examination of an application for admission a consideration which is foreign to the qualifications of [the] paragraph . . ., what he does is not the same thing as it would be if the Charter made such a consideration a qualification additional to those already required. That would involve amending the Charter, and there can be no question of that. [The procedure for amendment is laid down in Arts. 108 and 109.] The Member is merely introducing into the discussion . . . a political factor which he considered of importance and on which he is entitled to rely but which the other Members are equally entitled to consider and decide whether to accept or reject, without being legally bound to attach any weight to it. . . . While the Members of the United Nations have thus the right and the duty to take into account all the political considerations which are in their opinion relevant to a decision whether or not to admit an applicant for membership . . ., it must be remembered that there is an overriding legal obligation resting upon every Member of the United Nations to act in good faith . . . and with a view to carrying out the Purposes and Principles of the United Nations [as laid down in Arts. 1 and 2], while at the same time the members of the Security Council . . . are participating in the action of an organ which in the discharge of its primary responsibility for the maintenance of international peace and security is acting on behalf of all the Members of the United Nations [*Admission of a State to Membership in the United Nations, ante,* at p. 92]. . . . A member . . . called upon . . . to pronounce itself by its vote . . . on the admission of a State which possesses the qualifications specified . . ., is participating in a political decision and is therefore legally entitled to make its consent to admission dependent on any political consideration which seems to it to be relevant. In the exercise of this power the Member is legally bound to have regard to the principle of good faith, to give effect to the Purposes and Principles of the United Nations and to act in such a manner as not to involve any breach of the Charter."

§415 There is no provision in the Charter of the United Nations permitting a member to resign. However, in accordance with the principle that restrictions on sovereignty must be expressed and will be narrowly interpreted,[80] and in view of a decision at the San Francisco drafting Conference,[81] it is clear that this right exists. In practice, the United Nations has been most unwilling to accept notice of withdrawal and has sought every means to suggest that it has not taken place.[82] In this connection, it must be remembered that it is states that are members of the United Nations, while it is the governments which appoint the representatives. A change in government, as extensive or revolutionary this might be, does not affect the membership of the state.[83] The normal procedure for terminating membership is expulsion. This occurs[84] when a member "has persistently violated the Principles contained in the present Charter" and is effected "by the General Assembly upon the recommendation of the Security Council." This means that positive action to this effect is necessary, with the recommendation of the Security Council preceding the decision of the Assembly.[85]

80. See *The S.S. Lotus* (France/Turkey) (1937), 2 W.C.R. 20 at 35. See §310 note 62.

81. 7 U.N. Conference on Int. Organization Documents 263-7.

82. See, with reference to Indonesian withdrawal and return, and the disappearance and reappearance of Syria occasioned by its membership in and withdrawal from the United Arab Republic, Green, "The Dissolution of States and Membership in the United Nations", (1967) 32 Sask. L.R. 93.

83. See Green, "Representation v. Membership: The Chinese Precedent in the U.N.", (1972) 10 C.Y.B.I.L. 102.

84. Art. 6.

85. For the meaning of these terms see note 77 *ante*.

§416   If the Security Council does not recommend expulsion, it may, in respect of a member against which it has taken preventive or enforcement action,[86] recommend to the General Assembly that the member "be suspended from the exercise of the rights and privileges of membership".[87] It is clear, therefore, that the General Assembly does not have the legal power to suspend or expel any member by action taken by that organ alone. However, the Assembly has the power to "discuss any questions or any matters within the scope of the present Charter or relating to the powers and functions of any organs . . . and . . . may make recommendations to the . . . Security Council . . . on any such questions or matters".[88] It may initiate such processes by asking the Council to make the necessary recommendation. Moreover, since the General Assembly has adopted its own rules of procedure[89] and provided therein for the appointment of a credentials committee which examines the credentials of all representatives before the sessions of the Assembly open, it is possible for the Assembly, by rejecting such credentials, to achieve the same effect as it would if it had the power to suspend. This in fact happened in the case of Hungary in 1965 and, since its credentials were rejected in 1974 and 1979, South Africa has not presented its credentials nor tried to participate in Assembly discussions.

86. See Charter of the United Nations, Ch. VII.

87. Art. 5.

88. Art. 10.

89. Art. 22.

§417 Every member of the United Nations is a member of the General Assembly and entitled to vote therein.[90] Every member may vote on every issue. Unlike the Assembly of the League of Nations, the General Assembly does not decide by unanimity. Instead, it depends on whether an issue is regarded as important or not. If so considered, the vote is by two-thirds of those present and voting,[91] while on other issues, including a decision as to whether an issue is in fact important, the vote is by simple majority.[92] Except on those matters which may be regarded as of a house-keeping character,[93] most of the 'decisions' of the General Assembly are actually 'recommendations' and as such lack binding force.[94] However, in the practice of the United Nations 'recommendations,' if repeated frequently, are often considered to be obligatory.[95] Moreover, those described as 'Declarations',[96] are considered as being of greater significance and authority.[97]

90. Arts. 9, 18(1).

91. Art. 18(2). The Art. indicates some of the issues which are to be decided in this way.

92. Art. 18(3).

93. It does make 'decisions' re membership, elections to subsidiary organs, the budget, and the like.

94. See *South-West Africa — Voting Procedure,* [1955] I.C.J. 67, separate opinion by Lauterpacht J., 90 at pp. 115: "Although decisions of the General Assembly are endowed with full legal effect in some spheres of the activity of the United Nations and with limited legal effect in other spheres, it may be said by way of broad generalisation, that they are not legally binding upon the members of the United Nations. . . . [I]n general, they are in the nature of recommendations and it is in the nature of recommendations that, although on proper occasions they provide a legal authorisation for members determined to act upon them individually or collectively, they do not create a legal obligation to comply with them. This is so although . . . the General Assembly's request for the present Opinion . . . refer[s] to 'decisions' which, in ordinary connotation, signif[ies] binding expression of will. In fact, the request contemplate[s] decisions in their wider, somewhat non-technical sense. . . . The intended reference is to Resolutions generally, a generic term which, although it does not appear in the Charter, has found an accepted place in the practice of the United Nations. . . . [T]he discretion which is vested in the Members . . . in respect of the Resolutions of the General Assembly, is not a discretion tantamount to unrestricted freedom of action. It is a discretion to be exercised in good faith. Undoubtedly, the

degree of application of good faith in the exercise of full discretion does not lend itself to rigid legal appreciation. This fact does not destroy altogether the legal relevance of the discretion thus to be exercised. This is particularly so in relation to a succession of recommendations on the same subject ... solemnly reaffirmed by the General Assembly."

95.   See e.g., Bleicher, "The Legal Significance of Re-Citation of General Assembly Resolutions", (1969) 63 A.J.I.L. 444: the Declaration on Colonialism 95 times, that on Human Rights 75 times.

96.   See Universal Declaration on Human Rights, 1948 (Res. 217-IIIA); Declaration on the Granting of Independence to Colonial Countries and Peoples, 1960 (Res. 1514-XV); Declaration on Principles of International Law concerning Friendly Relations and Co-operation among States in accordance with the Charter of the United Nations, 1970 (Res. 2625-XXV, Annex).

97.   See statement of Legal Dept. of U.N. Secretariat, Apr. 2, 1962, Doc. E/CN. 4/L610 (cited in 2 Schermers, International Institutional Law (1972), p. 500): ". . . in view of the greater solemnity and significance of a declaration, it may be considered to import, on behalf of the organ adopting it, a strong expectation that Members of the international community will abide by it. Consequently, in so far as the expectation is gradually justified by State practice, a declaration may by custom become recognized as laying down rules binding upon States. In conclusion, it may be said that in United Nations practice, a declaration is a solemn instrument resorted to only in very rare cases relating to matters of major and lasting importance where maximum compliance is expected." It is now increasingly common for the General Assembly to describe its Resolutions as Declarations. For Canadian view of the significance of declarations see §§24 and 26.

§418   In contrast to the General Assembly, the Security Council does not comprise all the members of the United Nations. There are fifteen members, of whom five — China, France, the Union of Soviet Socialist Republics, the United Kingdom and the United States — are permanent members, while the other ten are elected for two-year terms, "due regard being specially paid to the maintenance of international peace and security and to the other purposes of the Organization, and also to equitable geographical distribution."[98] In fact, far more attention is paid to geographic distribution than to any other consideration.[99] Each member of the Security Council has one vote, with decisions on procedural matters made by an affirmative vote of nine.[1] On matters of substance, the affirmative vote of nine is to include the votes of the five permanent members.[2] This means that, regardless of the size of the majority, if any one of these five fails to concur there is no decision. However, in practice there has been what may be called a de facto revision of the Charter,[3] so that if a permanent member abstains from the vote or is absent, there is considered to have been a sufficient majority for the vote to be carried, and the United Nations has accepted such votes as legal[4] and obligatory, for unlike the recommendations of the General Assembly the decisions of the Security Council are true decisions and are binding.[5] Again, unlike the position in the General Assembly, a member of the Council which is a party to an issue being considered by the Council under Chapter VI relating to the pacific settlement of disputes is not permitted to vote.[6]

98. Charter of the United Nations, Art. 23.

99. See Green, "Gentlemen's Agreements and the Security Council", (1960) 13 Current Legal Problems 255; "Representation in the Security Council — A Survey", (1962) 11 Ind. Y.B.I.L. 48. When it was agreed to increase the number of non-permanent members in 1963 (Res. 1991-XVIII), it was decided that the 10 seats should be alloted — 5 to Africa and Asia, 1 to Eastern Europe, 2 to Latin America and 2 for Western Europe and 'other States'.

1. Art. 27(1), (2).

2. Art. 27(3), This is the 'veto' Article.

3. See also the decision of the General Assembly that the elected members might serve for only one instead of the two-year period stipulated in the Charter. This was done because of the difficulties in distribution that arose before the Security Council was enlarged: see Green, "Gentlemen's Agreements and the Security Council", (1960) 13 Current Legal Problems 255.

4. Thus Israel was admitted to membership by a decision of the General Assembly upon a recommendation of the Security Council on which the United Kingdom abstained. The Security Council continued to function during the period that the Soviet Union absented itself and while, according to the Soviet Union, China was improperly represented.

5. Charter, Art. 25: "The Members of the United Nations agree to accept and carry out the decisions of the Security Council in accordance with the present Charter."

6. Charter, Art. 27(3).

§419   Problems arise when the United Nations is called upon to fulfil some obligation which it has inherited from the League of Nations. This is particularly so when the procedures or competences of the two organizations differ. In such cases, the organ of the United Nations concerned will operate in accordance with the Charter procedures provided they achieve the purpose of the original League obligation, even though the procedure by which this is done may differ radically from that prescribed in the document originally embodying the function.[7] Since the Organization has to be able to carry out its functions, it has a budget which is approved by the General Assembly,[8] and the Organization's expenses are to be met by the members in a manner determined by the Assembly.[9] The concept of 'expenses' includes not merely the 'regular expenses,' but also any 'extraordinary expenses' which might arise to enable the Organization to carry out its functions, and such 'extraordinary expenses' constitute part of the budget and are to be apportioned in the same way among all members.[10]

7. See, e.g., *South-West Africa — Voting Procedure, ante*, at p. 76, which concerned voting procedures in relation to Petitions relating to the operation of the Mandate and the 'degree of supervision' to be exercised by the General Assembly". "The words 'the degree of supervision' relate to the extent of the substantive supervision to be exercised, and not to the manner in which the collective will of the General Assembly is expressed. . . . [I]t follows that the General Assembly, in adopting a method of reaching decisions [on this matter] . . . should base itself exclusively on the Charter. . . . It is from the Charter that the General Assembly derives its competence to exercise its supervisory functions; and it is within the framework of the Charter that the General Assembly must find the rules governing the making of its decisions in connection with those functions. It would be legally impossible for the General Assembly . . . to rely on the Charter in receiving and examining reports and petitions concerning South-West Africa [*South-West Africa — Hearing of Petitioners*, [1956] I.C.J. 23], and . . . to reach decisions relating to [them] with a voting system entirely alien to that prescribed by the Charter."

8. Art. 17(1).

9. Art. 17(2).

10. See *Certain Expenses of the United Nations*, [1962] I.C.J. 151 at 167-169: ". . . In determining whether the actual expenditures authorized constitute 'expenses of the Organization within the meaning of Art. 17(2)', the Court agrees that such expenditures must be tested by their relationship to the purpose of the United Nations in the sense that if an expenditure were made for a purpose which is not one of the purposes of the United Nations, it could not be considered an 'expense of the Organization'. . . . These purposes are broad indeed, but neither they nor the powers conferred to effectuate them are unlimited. Save as they have entrusted the Organization with the attainment of these common ends, the Member States retain their freedom of action. But when the Organization takes action which warrants the assertion that it was appropriate for the fulfilment of one of the stated purposes of the United Nations the presumption is that such action is not ultra vires the Organization. . . . If the action was taken by the wrong organ, it was irregular as a matter of . . . internal structure, but this would not necessarily mean that the expense incurred was not an expense of the Organization. . . . [E]ach organ must . . . determine its own jurisdiction. If the Security Council, for example, adopts a resolution purportedly for the maintenance of international peace and security and if, in accordance with a mandate or authorization in such resolution, the Secretary-General incurs financial obligations, these amounts must be presumed to constitute 'expenses of the Organization'. . . . The obligation is one thing: the way in which the obligation is met — that is from what source the funds are secured — is another. . . . [I]t is of no legal significance whether, as a matter of book-keeping or accounting, the General Assembly chooses to have the item in question included under one of the standard established sections of the 'regular' budget or whether it is separately listed in some special account or fund. The significant thing is that the item is an expense of the Organization. . . ."

§420 Problems may arise when the United Nations, either as an original party or by succession from the League of Nations, purports to terminate an agreement between itself and a member. If the member has been in breach of its obligations under the agreement, then, in accordance with the general rules of the law concerning treaties,[11] the United Nations has the power of repudiation whether the agreement so provides or not[12] and in this field a recommendation[13] of the General Assembly may well have some legal effect.[14] If the Security Council acting upon this recommendation decides that compliance is necessary for the maintenance of international peace and security, the combined effect of the two resolutions is to create a binding legal obligation.[15] Moreover, despite the normal rule that non-parties to a treaty are not affected by decisions taken under that treaty, and the Charter of the Nations is a treaty, in circumstances of the kind herein mentioned, the World Court has held[16] that such decisions of the United Nations are binding even upon a non-member.

11. See text to §311 note 70.

12. *Namibia (South-West Africa) Opinion,* [1971] I.C.J. 16: "... The silence of a treaty as to the existence of a right [to terminate on account of a breach] cannot be interpreted as implying the exclusion of a right which has its source outside of the treaty, in general international law, and is dependent on the occurrence of circumstances which are not normally envisaged when a treaty is concluded [for the doctrine rebus sic stantibus, see §314]. To contend, on the basis of the principle of unanimity which applied in the League of Nations [Covenant, Art. 5(1)], that in this case revocation could only take place with the concurrence of the Mandatory, would not only run contrary to the general principle of law governing termination on account of breach, but also postulate an impossibility. For obvious reasons, the consent of the wrongdoer to such a form of termination cannot be required." See also *Mosul Case* (1925), 1 W.C.R. 722 at 743 in which the P.C.I.J. had to construe the unanimity rule in the League Covenant: "... it may perhaps be well to observe that since the Council consists of representatives of States or Members, the legal position of the representatives of the Parties upon the Council is not comparable to that of national arbitrators upon courts of arbitration [whose votes are of significance]. The votes of the representatives of the Parties are not, therefore, to be taken into account in ascertaining whether there is unanimity. But the representatives will take part in the vote, for they form part of the Council and, like the other representatives, they are entitled and are in duty bound to take part in the deliberation of that body. ... [T]he representatives of the Parties may take part in the voting, and it is only for the purpose of determining whether unanimous agreement has been reached that their votes are not counted."

13. See §417.

14. *Namibia (South-West Africa) Opinion, ante,* at pp. 50-51: "... the General Assembly declared that the Mandate having been terminated 'South Africa has no other right to administer the Territory'. This is not a finding on facts, but the formulation of a legal situation. For it would not be correct to assume that, because the General Assembly is in principle vested with recommendatory powers, it is debarred from adopting, in specific cases, within the framework of its competence, resolutions which make determinations or have operative design. ... However, lacking the necessary powers to ensure the withdrawal of South Africa from the Territory, it enlisted the co-operation of the Security Council by calling the latter's attention to the resolution, thus acting in accordance with Art. 11(2) of the Charter."

15. *Namibia (South-West Africa) Opinion, ante,* at pp. 51-54: "... The Security Council, when it adopted these resolutions, was acting in the exercise of what it

deemed to be its primary responsibility, the maintenance of international peace and security, which, under the Charter, embraces situations which might lead to a breach of the peace. . . . As to the legal basis of the resolution, Art. 24 . . . vests in the Security Council the necessary authority to take action such as that taken in the present case. . . . It would be an untenable interpretation to maintain that, once such a declaration had been made by the Security Council under Art. 24 . . ., on behalf of all member States, those Members would be free to act in disregard of such illegality or even to recognize violations of law resulting from it. When confronted with such an internationally unlawful situation, Members of the United Nations would be expected to act in consequence of the declaration made on their behalf. . . . In view of the nature of the powers under Art. 25, the question whether they have been in fact exercised is to be determined in each case, having regard to the terms of the resolution to be interpreted, the discussions leading to it, the Charter provisions invoked and, in general, all circumstances that might assist in determining the legal consequences of the resolution of the Security Council. . . . Thus when the Security Council adopts a decision under Art. 25 in accordance with the Charter, it is for member States to comply with that decision, including those members of the Security Council which voted against it and those Members of the United Nations who are not members of the Council. To hold otherwise would be to deprive the principal organ of its essential functions and powers under the Charter."

16. *Namibia (South-West Africa) Opinion, ante,* at p. 56: "As to non-member States, although not bound by Arts. 24 and 25 . . . they have been called upon in the [Security Council] resolution to give assistance to the action which has been taken by the United Nations with regard to Namibia. . . . [T]he termination of the Mandate and the declaration of the illegality of South Africa's presence in Namibia are opposable to all States in the sense of barring erga omnes the legality of a situation which is maintained in violation of international law: in particular, no State which enters into relations with South Africa concerning Namibia may expect the United Nations or its Members to recognize the validity or effects of such relationship, or of the consequences thereof. The Mandate having been determined by decision of the international organization in which the supervisory authority over its administration was vested, and South Africa's continued presence in Namibia having been declared illegal, it is for non-member states to act in accordance with those decisions." See dissenting opinion of Schwebel J. in *Military and Paramilitary Activities in and against Nicaragua,* [1984] I.C.J. 392 at 615 re effect of Charter, Art. 2(4), non-use of force, on non-members.

§421 On occasion, it is necessary for state members of the United Nations to enact legislation to give effect to decisions of the United Nations. This was the case in Canada after the Security Council adopted its resolution providing for comprehensive trade and financial sanctions against Rhodesia.[17] By Order in Council,[18] Canada made it "illegal for Canadians to send money to Rhodesia unless it was for the purpose of a pension or annuity benefit or for medical, educational or humanitarian purposes. Another provision . . . was designed to prevent flights by Canadian aircraft to Rhodesia and the coordination of air services between Canadian and Rhodesian aircraft. The Government also intended by administrative action[19] . . . to implement the Security Council's prohibition on the entry to Canada of persons travelling on Rhodesian passports and of persons, other than Canadians, who have assisted, or may assist, the unlawful actions of the illegal régime."[20]

17. Security Council Resolution 253-1968.

18. PC 1968-2339 SOR/69-14, summarized in Castel, International Law Chiefly as Applied and Interpreted in Canada (1976), p. 1223. See also Macdonald, "Economic Sanctions in the International System", (1969) 7 C.Y.B.I.L. 61.

19. Taken under authority of United Nations Act, R.S.C. 1970, c. U-3.

20. The British authorities brought a number of alleged violations to the attention of the Canadian government which found all to be unfounded: Castel, 1223. See also *Diggs v. Schultz* (1972), 470 F. 2d 461 (U.S. C.A.). See, for action under the U.K. Sanctions Order, 1968, S.I. No. 1020, *A.G.'s Reference (No. 2 of 1977)*, [1978] 1 W.L.R. 29.

§422 As to the imposition of sanctions as a response to illegal actions by a state, the Legal Bureau of the Canadian Department of External Affairs has stated[21] "In general international law accords states a wide latitude to implement economic measures in retaliation against objectionable conduct of other states, providing such measures do *not* violate specific international legal obligations, such as treaty commitments. However, the traditional Canadian view has been that, as a matter of legal and commercial policy, economic sanctions should only be imposed pursuant to (a) a resolution of the Security Council under Chapter VII of the United Nations Charter dealing with threats to the peace, or (b) collective action by States designed to deal with fundamental violations of international law and threats to the peace, taken pursuant to a UN resolution that could be assimilated to a Chapter VII resolution described in (a) above (e.g. Uniting for Peace Resolution taken by the General Assembly).[22] The traditional Canadian approach is based on the view that economic sanctions are a derogation from the general principle of friendly relations among states and, therefore, are not to be instituted lightly, or in reaction to every act by other States that we may disapprove of or may even violate international law." In 1977, the Security Council imposed an arms embargo on South Africa,[23] and the Legal Bureau explained in a memorandum[24] the legal significance of this decision for Canada: "Security Council Resolution 418 is binding on Canada as a matter of international law. By virtue of this fact, Canada is under an obligation not to sell or transfer arms and ammunition, military vehicles and equipment, and related spare parts and manufacturing and maintenance equipment to South Africa. Committee Report S/14179 may be viewed as an aid to interpreting the extent to which 'dual-purpose' items are considered to be within the ambit of SC 418. The report suggests that, in general, goods not consigned to the military are to be considered as of military character within the meaning of SC 418 if there is a potential for diversion or conversion to military use. More specifically, however, it suggests that aircraft and related parts, as well as electronic and telecommunications and computer equipment, may be considered to be prima facie of a military character. . . . In sum, under SC 418 . . . no military equipment should be exported to any consignee in South Africa, and second, no dual-purpose items should be exported to South Africa in any manner that presents a risk of diversion or conversion to military use . . ."

21. Memo, 22 Nov. 1983, (1984) 22 C.Y.B.I.L. 328.

22. 1950, Res. 377(V).

23. Security Council Res. 418, 16 I.L.M. 1548.

24. 9 Apr. 1984, (1985) 23 C.Y.B.I.L. 336. See §183.

§423 A number of international organizations have been established and brought into relationship with the United Nations for the purpose of fulfilling certain specialised functions. Left over from the days of the League of Nations is the International Labour Organization intended to regulate the conditions of labour and this purpose has been interpreted in a functional fashion.[25] Moreover, in seeking the true functional purpose of the Organization in question it may be necessary to look at substantial rather than formal fact.[26] On the other hand, if the wording of the constitution in question is specific, it must be given effect to, even if by so doing the requirements laid down are only apparently complied with.[27]

25. See *Agricultural Labour and Production* (1922), 1 W.C.R. 124; *Personal Work of Employers* (1926), 1 W.C.R. 746; *Employment of Women During the Night* (1932), 3 W.C.R. 100. See also §425.

26. See *Nomination of the Netherlands Wkrs. Delegate to the Third Session of the Int. Labour Conference* (1922), 1 W.C.R. 115, when the court held that in seeking the representative of labour a party is entitled to ignore the largest trade union organization in order to find the true representative of the majority of the workers.

27. See *Constitution of the Maritime Safety Ctee. of the Inter-Governmental Maritime Consultative Organization,* [1960] I.C.J. 150: the Intergovernmental Maritime Consultative Organization (I.M.C.O.) Convention (1948, 289 U.N.T.S. 48), which is the Constitution of the Organization, provides that the Maritime Safety Committee is to include not less than eight of 'the largest ship-owning nations'. In the 1959 election Liberia and Panama, both flag of convenience states, were ignored, but the court held, at p. 171: ". . . the determination of the largest shipowning nations depends solely upon the tonnage registered in the countries in question, any further examination . . . based on a genuine link is irrelevant. . . ."

§424 The International Civil Aviation Organization has its headquarters in Montreal and there has been no problem between it and Canada as the host state.[28] This has not been so in the case of the Regional Office for the Eastern Mediterranean Region of the World Health Organization in Alexandria and the host state Egypt. Problems arose in 1979 when some members of the Region sought the transfer of the Office from Egypt.[29] The principles laid down by the World Court when consulted on this matter[30] are probably applicable to every organization in its relations with its host state, subject to any provisions in the agreement between them: ". . . the mutual obligations of the Organization and the host State to co-operate under the applicable legal principles and rules are as follows: 1. Those obligations place a duty both upon the Organization and upon [the host] to consult together in good faith as to the question under what conditions and in accordance with what modalities a transfer of the Office from [the host State] may be effected. 2. In the event of its being finally decided that the Office shall be transferred from [the host], their mutual obligations to co-operate place a duty upon the Organization and [the host] to consult together and to negotiate regarding the various arrangements needed to effect the transfer from the existing to the new site in an orderly manner and with a minimum of prejudice to the work of the Organization and the interests of [the host]. 3. Those mutual obligations place a duty upon the party which wishes to effect the transfer to give a reasonable period of notice to the other party for the termination of the existing situation regarding the Office [in the host state], taking due account of all the practical arrangements needed to effect an equitable and orderly transfer of the Office to its new site. Those . . . are the implications of the general legal principles and rules applicable in the event of the transfer of the seat of a[n Organization] from the territory of a host State. Precisely what periods of time may be involved in the observance of the duties to consult and negotiate, and what period of notice of termination should be given, are matters which necessarily vary according to the requirements of the particular case. In principle, therefore, it is for the parties in each case to determine the length of those periods by consultation and negotiation in good faith. . . . [W]hat is reasonable and equitable in any given case must depend on its particular circumstances. Moreover, the paramount consideration both for the Organization and the host State in every case must be their clear obligation to co-operate in good faith to promote the objectives and purposes of the Organization as expressed in its Constitution; and this too means that they must in consultation determine a reasonable period of time to enable them to achieve an orderly transfer of the Office from the territory of the host State."

28. See Dai, "The HQ Agreement between Canada and the ICAO", (1964) 2 C.Y.B.I.L. 205.

29. This was a consequence of Egypt's signature of a Peace Treaty with Israel, a policy not approved by the majority of the members of the Region. Problems arose in 1988 between the U.S. and the U.N., when the former, in apparent breach of the Headquarters Agreement, 1947, 11 U.N.T.S. 11, ordered the Palestine Liberation Organization, which enjoyed observer status, to close its U.N. office.

30. *Interpretation of the Agreement between the W.H.O. and Egypt,* [1980] I.C.J. 73 at 95-96.

§425 Some of the specialized agencies are authorized to draw up Conventions, as is the case with the International Labour Organization. These Conventions differ from those normally regarded as such, which are binding treaties.[31] With regard to the Organization, the Conventions are proposals which it is incumbent upon the members to submit to their legislatures. In addition, states are expected to carry out their obligations as members in good faith, paying due attention to the fact that ". . . labour should not be regarded merely as an article of commerce, [and] there are methods and principles for regulating labour conditions which all industrial communities should endeavour to apply, so far as their special circumstances will permit. Among these methods and principles, the following seem to be of special and urgent importance: . . . 2. The right of association for all lawful purposes by the employed as well as by the employers. . . . 8. The standard set by law in each country with respect to the conditions of labour should have due regard to the equitable treatment of all workers lawfully resident therein."[32] Canada is a member of the International Labour Organization and as such must in good faith seek to give effect to these principles. Canada is also a party to the I.L.O. Convention concerning the Freedom of Association and Protection of the Right to Organize,[33] which guarantees to workers and employers, 'without distinction whatever', the right to join organizations of their own choosing, but in exercising their rights they 'shall respect the law of the land', which, 'shall not be such as to impair . . . the guarantee provided' in the Convention.[34]

31. See §299 note 3.

32. Treaty of Versailles, Art. 427, 1919, (1919) 13 A.J.I.L. 1.

33. I.L.O. Convention 87, 1948, 68 U.N.T.S. 17, ratified by Canada in 1973, Can. T.S. 1973/14.

34. In the case of *Young, James and Webster* (1981), 62 I.L.R. 359 (European Ct. of Human Rights) the court held that the 'right to associate' included the right not to join a trade union.

§426 By the International Covenant on Economic, Social and Cultural Rights,[35] to which Canada acceded in 1976, the right to form trade unions is confirmed, with "the right to strike, provided that it is exercised in conformity with the laws of the country [, but] this article shall not prevent the imposition of lawful restrictions on the exercise of these rights by members of the armed forces or of the police or of the administration of the State." In accordance with the Public Service Employee Relations Act of Alberta,[36] broadly speaking strikes by public employees are forbidden and the right to arbitrate limited, and the Canadian Labour Congress complained to the I.L.O. contending the legislation to be contrary to international law. The I.L.O. made a number of criticisms of the legislation and recommended a variety of amendments. In *Re Alberta Union of Provincial Employees and the Crown in Right of Alberta*[37] it was decided that there is no "universal consent on the subject of the right to strike in the public service . . . [and] that it is not, and never has been, part of the customary international law that public servants have the right to strike. . . . [Moreover,] the right to strike in the public service is not expressly mentioned in any of the conventions to which Canada is a party." As to the recommendations of the I.L.O. directed to the government on the matter, "from a legal point of view . . . the Government of Alberta is in no way bound by the I.L.O. recommendations which do not and have never formed part of the law of Alberta."

35.   1966, 993 U.N.T.S. 3, Art 8(1)(*d*), (2).

36.   R.S.A. 1980, c. P-33.

37.   [1980] 120 D.L.R. (3d) 590 at 620-621 (Alta. Q.B.), per Sinclair C.J.Q.B. See also Bendel, "The International Protection of Trade Union Rights: A Canadian Case Study", (1981) 13 Ottawa L.R. 169; *Ref. re Public Service Employees Relations Act*, [1985] 2 W.W.R. 289 (Alta. C.A.); affirmed [1987] 3 W.W.R. 577 (S.C.C.), especially dissent by Dickson C.J.

§427   It may happen that a group of states within a region set up an organization with comprehensive powers within specific areas. In such a case the decisions of some or all of its organs may be obligatory upon the members which are then obliged to give effect to them, even though national law is prima facie to the contrary. This is the case with the European Community, whose decisions override national law. Moreover, within the field of competence of the Treaty of Rome, 1957, national courts are subordinate to the decisions of the European Court.[38] In fact, if the court of a member country is faced with conflicting interpretations of a provision of the Rome Treaty, the issue should be referred to the European Court of Justice before considering the merits.[39] Such an organization may be described as supra- rather than international.

395

38. *Costa v. E.N.E.L.*, [1946] C.M.L.R. 429 (request for preliminary ruling by Milan court); *Application des Gaz S.A. v. Falks Veritas Ltd.*, [1974] 3 W.L.R. 235 (C.A.); see, however, *Internationale Handelsgesellschaft mbH v. Einfuhr-und Vorratsstelle für Getreide und Futtermittel* (Fed. Const. Ct. Germany), [1974] 2 C.M.L.R.Z. 540.

39. *R. v. Pharmaceutical Society of Great Britain; ex parte Association of Pharmaceutical Importers* (1987), The Times, 15 Sept. 1987. (C.A.).

3. THE INTERNATIONAL CIVIL SERVICE

§428 International organizations operate through their secretariats, the officials of which form collectively an international civil service. Members of the United Nations and the specialized agencies have undertaken to recognize the inviolability of the members of the respective secretariats[40] and Canada has enacted the Privileges and Immunities (United Nations) Act, 1952.[41] If a member of a national civil service is appointed to the staff of an international organization, the practice is that his home state will discharge him or he will resign from his national appointment, and problems may arise if he is only seconded.[42]

40. See, U.N. Charter, Art. 100: 1. In the performance of their duties the Secretary-General and the staff shall not seek or receive instructions from any government or from any other authority external to the organization. 2. Each member of the United Nations undertakes to respect the exclusively international character of the responsibilities of the Secretary-General and the staff and not to seek to influence them in the discharge of their responsibilities"; UNESCO Constitution, 1945, 4 U.N.T.S. 275, Art. 6(5): ". . . In the discharge of their duties [the Director-General and the staff] shall not seek or receive instructions from any government or from any authority external to the Organization. They shall refrain from any action which might prejudice their position as international officials. Each state Member of the Organization undertakes to respect the international character of the responsibilities of the Director-General and the staff, and not to seek to influence them in the discharge of their duties." See also Convention on Privileges and Immunities of the United Nations, 1946, 1 U.N.T.S. 15, ratified by Canada in 1948; Convention on Privileges and Immunities of the Specialised Agencies of the U.N., 1947, 33 U.N.T.S. 262, acceded to by Canada 1966, but since the Canadian legislation (see note 41) and the instrument of accession contain a reservation in respect of taxes, this instrument was rejected by the Secretariat and Canada is not included in the list of parties.

41. R.S.C. 1970, c. P-22, amended by S.C. 1974-75, c. 69 to deal with the European Economic Communities; see also Privileges and Immunities (North Atlantic Treaty Organization) Act, R.S.C. 1970, c. P-23. See also Dai, "The Headquarters Agreement between Canada and the International Civil Aviation Organization", (1964) 2 C.Y.B.I.L. 205. For a collection of texts of treaties and national legislative measures on this matter, see U.N., Legislative Texts and Treaty Provisions concerning the Legal Status, Privileges and Immunities of International Organizations 1959, 1961; later texts appear in the annual volumes of the U.N. Juridical Yearbook. See *M. (K) v. Provincial Revenue Office for Vienna* (1970), 71 I.L.R. 573 (Austria Admin. Ct.) (Mrs.

M. was employed by the International Atomic Energy Agency and her salary was tax free; Karl M.'s application for tax-free allowance due to sole earners under Austrian tax law on the ground that his wife had 'no income' was rejected).

42. *Levcik v. Secretary-General of the United Nations* (1974), U.N. Admin. Trib., Judgment No. 192. Problems arose in Nov. 1983 after the U.S. invasion of Grenada, when the Gov. Gen. Sir Paul Scoon sought to appoint as chairman of his advisory council Mr. Alister McIntyre, then deputy Secretary Gen. of the U.N. Ctee. of Trade and Development. Mr. McIntyre ultimately declined the offer.

§429 The treaty-guaranteed immunity for an international civil servant extends to all acts done in his official capacity[43] and, unless the organization of which he is a member waives that immunity, it protects him in respect of acts done in his official capacity even after he has ceased to hold that position, and even though he is a national of the country in which he is being sued.[44] However, his status and immunity as an official of an international organization does not make him a diplomat entitled to the immunities of a diplomat,[45] unless the local law prescribes otherwise. The mere fact that the official is acting in his capacity does not serve to give him the requisite immunity. What is required is that at the time of the act in question, the undertaking should be of importance to the success of the Organization.[46]

43. In *International Atomic Energy Agency Representative Immunity Case* (1971), 70 I.L.R. 413 (Fed. German Rep. Prov. S.C.) a plea of immunity was rejected since the issue did not relate to the applicant's acts in his representative capacity.

44. See, e.g., *Zoernsch v. Waldock*, [1964] 1 W.L.R. 675 (C.A.). See *European Space Operations Centre (ESOC) Official Immunity Case* (1973) 73 I.L.R. 683 (German Fed. Labour Ct.).

45. See, e.g., *U.S. v. Coplon* (1949), 84 F. Supp. 472 at 473: "At the time of his arrest he was employed as a member of the staff of the Headquarters Planning Office of the Secretariat of the United Nations. Such status does not per se confer diplomatic immunity under generally accepted principles of international law. Nor does the defendant, by reason of such employment, possess immunity from prosecution for the offense charged by virtue of any law or treaty of the United States. . . . [T]he International Organizations Immunities Act (22 U.S.C.A.S. 288) . . . does not avail the defendant. It does not confer diplomatic status or immunity. It does confer immunity on United Nations officers and employees for the category of acts performed by them in their official capacity and falling within their functions as such officers or employees. . . . It seems clear that unlawful espionage is not a function of the defendant as an employee of the United Nations. Freedom from arrest for such conduct, it would seem, is not a privilege or immunity necessary for the independent exercise of defendant's functions in connection with the United Nations."

46. *County of Westchester v. Ranollo* (1946), 67 N.Y.S. 2d 31 at 33-34: the defendant was chauffeur to the Secretary-General of the U.N., and was charged with speeding while the Secretary-General was in the car: "To recognize the existence of a general and unrestricted immunity from suit or prosecution on the part of the personnel of the U.N., so long as the individual is performing in his official capacity, even though the individual's function has no relation to the importance or the success

of the organization's deliberations, is carrying the principle of immunity completely out of bounds. . . . There can be no disputing of the proposition that if these international legislative bodies are to function properly within the borders of the particular nation that may be housing their activities, a certain amount of immunity, exemption and privilege is necessary to insure their necessary personnel against harassment by way of court proceedings, civil or criminal. . . . This assurance can be given . . . [by limiting] the application of the principle of immunity to those personnel whose activities are such as to be necessary to the actual execution of the purposes and deliberations of the U.N. as distinguished from those household servants and personnel who merely serve the personal comfort, convenience of luxury of the delegates and Secretariat who actually perform the true functions of the organization."

§430　In view of the special relationship that exists between members of the international civil service and their employers, and the absence while in that position of the normal close relationship that exists between a state and its nationals, there exists a type of functional protection, somewhat similar to diplomatic protection, between the Organization and its employees.[47]

47.　See *Reparation for Injuries in the Service of the U.N.*, [1949] I.C.J. 174 at 184: "Upon examination of the character of the functions entrusted to the Organization and of the nature of the missions of its agents, it becomes clear that the capacity of the Organization to exercise a measure of functional protection of its agents arises by necessary intendment out of the Charter."

§431　The relations between the members of the international civil service and the organization by which they are employed are governed by Staff Rules and Regulations, together with an Administrative Tribunal to deal with such staff and contract issues which might arise. In the event of the Administrative Tribunal of the United Nations awarding damages for wrongful dismissal, the General Assembly is obliged to adjust its budget to meet the financial responsibilities thus created, even though some members of the United Nations might disagree with the ruling or the award,[48] and even though the employees in question might be nationals of the objecting state.[49] In fact, it amounts to breach of contract and wrongful dismissal on the part of the Organization if the dismissal is based on complaints from a member state regarding the relations of that state with employees possessing its nationality.[50] The staff of the United Nations has access to the United Nations Administrative Tribunal, while the employees of other specialised agencies make use of the facilities of the Administrative Tribunal of the International Labour Organization. If any international organization wishes to challenge the competence of the relevant Administrative Tribunal, it may do so by requesting an advisory opinion from the International

Court of Justice. Moreover, even though the decisions of the Administrative Tribunals are judgments and definitive,[51] in the case of the United Nations, provision has now been made whereby a member state,[52] the Secretary General or the civil servant[53] involved may request a review of the award by the International Court "on the ground that the Tribunal has exceeded its jurisdiction or competence or that the Tribunal has failed to exercise jurisdiction vested in it, or has erred on a question of law relating to the provisions of the Charter of the United Nations, or has committed a fundamental error in procedure which occasioned a failure of justice. . . ."

48. *Effect of Awards of Compensation made by the U.N. Administrative Tribunal,* [1954] I.C.J. 47 at 53: ". . . a contract of service is concluded between the staff member concerned and the Secretary-General in his capacity as the chief administrative officer of the United Nations Organization, acting on behalf of the Organization as its representative. When the Secretary-General concludes such a contract of service with a staff member, he engages the legal responsibility of the Organization, which is the juridical person on whose behalf he acts. If he terminates the contract of service without the assent of the staff member and this action results in a dispute which is referred to the Administrative Tribunal, the parties to this dispute before the Tribunal are the staff member concerned and the United Nations Organization, represented by the Secretary-General, and these parties will become bound by the judgment of the Tribunal. This judgment is, according to the Tribunal's Statute, final and without appeal. The Statute has provided for no kind of review [this has now been changed]. As this final judgment has binding force on the United Nations Organization as the juridical person responsible for the proper observance of the contract of service, that Organization becomes legally bound to carry out the judgment and to pay the compensation awarded to the staff member. It follows that the General Assembly, as an organ of the United Nations, must likewise be bound by the judgment." See Cohen, "The U.N. Secretariat: Some Constitutional and Administrative Developments", (1955) 49 A.J.I.L. 295, and Green, "The Status of the International Civil Service", (1954) 7 Current Legal Problems 192. The Organization must carry out any judgment that has been reviewed by the Court, in accordance with the review.

49. *Judgments of the Administrative Tribunal of the I.L.O. Upon Complaints Made Against UNESCO,* [1956] I.C.J. 77 at 98-99. Since an award of the Tribunal was only open to challenge on the ground of jurisdiction or for a fundamental fault in procedure, the Court refused to answer whether "the Administrative Tribunal [was] competent to pronounce on the attitude which the Director-General, under the terms of the Constitution of UNESCO, ought to maintain in its relations with a Member State, particularly as regards the execution of the policy of the Government authorities of that Member State". See Green, "The International Civil Servant, His State and His Employer", (1956) 40 Grotius Transactions 147.

50. *Hickel v. Int. Institute of Intellectual Co-op.* (1947), 18 Ann. Dig. 460; *McIntire v. Food & Agriculture Organization* (1954), 21 I.L.R. 356; *Leff v. UNESCO* (1954), 21 I.L.R. 349, (1955), 22 I.L.R. 783; *Duberg v. UNESCO* (1955), 22 I.L.R. 768. See Green, "The Status of the International Civil Service", (1954) 7 Current Legal Problems 192 and "The International Civil Servant, His State and His Employer,"

(1956) 40 Grotius Transactions 147. See also Langrod, The International Civil Service (1963). See also *Rosescu v. Int. Atomic Energy Agency* (1980), Admin. Trib. I.L.O. Judgment 431, p. 7: "The executive head of an organization is bound at all times to safeguard its interests and, where necessary, give them priority over others. One area in which the rule applies is staff recruitment. If a director-general intends to appoint to the staff someone who is a government official in a member State [and most of those recruited from Communist states are government officials] he will normally consult the member State, which may wish to keep the official in its service. Similarly, if such a government official's appointment is to be extended, it is reasonable that the organization should again consult the member State, which may have good reason to re-employ him. *This does not mean that the director-general must bow unquestioningly to the wishes of the government he consults.* He will be right to accede where sound reasons for opposition are expressed or implied. But he may not forego taking a decision in the organization's interests for the sole purpose of satisfying a member State. *The organization has an interest in being on good terms with all member States, but that is no valid ground for a director-general to fall in with the wishes of every one of them*" (italics added). The Tribunal concluded that in his ruling the Director-General had allowed the interests of the government to prevail over those of the Agency for no valid reason and so misused his authority. The Tribunal awarded Rosescu *ex aequo et bono* $50000 U.S.. and 15000 French francs costs. See Adv. Op., *Application for Review of Judgment 333 of the U.N. Administrative Trib.,* [1987] I.C.J. General List No. 72.

51. *Effect of Awards of Compensation Made by the U.N. Administrative Tribunal, ante,* at pp. 52-53: "Art. 2(3) [of the Tribunal's Statute] prescribes: 'In the event of a dispute as to whether the Tribunal has competence, the matter shall be settled by the decision of the Tribunal.' Art. 10 contains the following provision: '(2) The judgments shall be final and without appeal (3) The judgments shall state the reasons on which they are based.' These provisions and the terminology used are evidence of the judicial nature of the Tribunal.... The provisions ... are of an essentially judicial character and conform with rules generally laid down in statutes or laws issued for courts of justice.... The Statute ... contains no provisions attributing an advisory character to its functions, nor does it in any way limit the independence of its activity. The independence of its members is ensured. ... [Art. 9] prescribe[s] ... that the Tribunal shall, if it finds that the application is well founded, order the rescinding of the decision contested or the specific performance of the obligation invoked. As the power to issue such orders to the chief administrative officer of the Organization could hardly have been conferred on an advisory organ or a subordinate committee, these provisions confirm the judicial nature of the Tribunal...."

52. See, e.g., *Application for Review of Judgment 273 of the U.N. Administrative Trib.* [1982] I.C.J. 325 at 335: "... although a member State of the U.N. be not a party to a judgment rendered by the Administrative Tribunal in a dispute between a staff member and the Organization, it may well have a legal interest in giving rise to a review of the judgment. This is certainly so, where, as in the present case, the Judgment in question is challenged on the ground that an error has been committed on a question of law relating to the provisions of the Charter, that is to say of a treaty to which this State is a party. Secondly, the Court notes that the respective roles of a member State which submits an application to the Committee [on Applications for Review of Administrative Tribunal Judgments] and of the Committee itself are precisely defined by the Statute of the Administrative Tribunal. Admittedly, it is the member State which, by submitting its application to the Committee, gives rise to the

Committee's discussion of that application. Nevertheless, once the Committee has decided that there is a substantial basis for the application, the request for advisory opinion comes from the Committee and not from the member State. The origin of the application which the Committee has to consider, be it the initiative of a member State, of the Secretary-General or of a staff member party to the judgment in question, does not affect the formal origin of the request submitted to the Court: it is always from the Committee that this request emanates. Besides, if that were not so, as neither a member State nor the Secretary-General nor a staff member is authorised to request an advisory opinion of the Court, their request would not be admissible"; see §403.

53. See *Application for Review of Judgment 158 of the U.N. Administrative Trib.* [1973] I.C.J. 166 at 171-4, 182, 187-8: ". . . doubts have been voiced regarding the legality of the use of the advisory jurisdiction for the review of judgments of the Advisory Tribunal. The contentious jurisdiction of the Court, it has been urged, is limited . . . to disputes between States [see §376]; and it has been questioned whether the advisory jurisdiction may be used for the judicial review of contentious proceedings which have taken place before other tribunals and to which individuals were parties. However, the existence, in the background, of a dispute the parties to which may be affected as a consequence of the Court's opinion, does not change the advisory nature of the Court's task, which is to answer the questions put to it with regard to a judgment. . . . If the request for advisory opinion emanates from a body duly authorized in accordance with the Charter to make it, the Court is competent under Art. 65 of its Statute to give such opinion on any legal question arising within the scope of the activities of that body. The mere fact that it is not the rights of States which are in issue in the proceedings cannot suffice to deprive the Court of a competence expressly conferred on it by its Statute. . . . [T]he General Assembly's power to regulate staff regulations also comprises the power to create an organ designed to provide machinery for initiating the review by the Court of judgments of such a tribunal. . . . [T]he Committee's activities . . . have to be viewed in the larger context of the General Assembly's function in the regulation of staff relations of which they form a part. This is . . . the creation of a subsidiary organ having a particular task and invested with the power to request advisory opinions in the performance of that task. The mere fact that the Committee's activities serve a particular, limited, purpose in the General Assembly's performance of its function in the regulation of staff relations does not prevent the advisory jurisdiction of the Court from being exercised in regard to those activities. . . . In fact, the primary function of the Committee is not the requesting of advisory opinions, but the examination of objections to judgments in order to decide in each case whether there is a substantial basis for the application so as to call for a request for an advisory opinion. If it finds that there is not such a substantial basis for the application the Committee rejects the application without requesting an opinion of the Court. When it does find that there is a substantial basis for the application, the legal questions which the Committee then submits to the Court clearly arise out of the performance of this primary function of screening the applications presented to it. They are therefore questions which . . . arise within the scope of the Committee's own activities. . . . [T]he Tribunal's Statute provides that the Secretary-General shall either give effect to the opinion of the Court or request the Tribunal to convene specially in order that it shall confirm its original judgment, or give a new judgment, in conformity with the opinion of the Court. Nevertheless, the proceedings before the Court are still advisory proceedings, in which the task of the Court is not to retry the case but to reply to the questions put to it regarding the objections which have been raised to the Judgment of the Administrative Tribunal. . . . Again, the fact that . . . the opinion given by the Court is to have a conclusive effect with respect to the matters in

litigation in that case does not constitute any obstacle to the Court's replying to the request for an opinion. Such an effect, it is true, goes beyond the scope attributed by the Charter and by the Statute of the Court to an advisory opinion. It results, however, not from the advisory opinion itself but from a provision of an autonomous instrument having the force of law for staff members and the Secretary-General. . . . [T]he task of the Court is not to retry the case but to give its opinion on the questions submitted to it concerning the objections lodged against the Judgment. The Court is not therefore entitled to substitute its own opinion for that of the Tribunal on the merits of the case adjudicated by the Tribunal. Its role is to determine if the circumstances of the case, whether they relate to merits or procedure, show that any objection made to the Judgment on one of the grounds mentioned in [the Statute] is well founded. In so doing, the Court is not limited to the contents of the challenged award itself, but takes under its consideration all relevant aspects of the proceedings before the Tribunal as well as all matters submitted to the Court itself by the staff member and by the Secretary-General with regard to the objections raised against the judgment. These objections the Court examines on their merits in the light of the information before it. . . . [A] challenge to a decision for alleged failure to exercise jurisdiction or fundamental error in procedure cannot properly be transformed into a proceeding against the absence of the decision. This does not mean that in an appropriate case, where the judgment has been challenged on the ground of an error on a question of law relating to the provisions of the Charter, the Court may not be called upon to review the actual substance of the decision. . . ."

§432 Failing such a request, the award of the Tribunal becomes final. However, "in any case in which a request has been made for an advisory opinion [for review], the Secretary-General shall either give effect to the opinion of the Court or request the Tribunal to convene specially in order that it shall confirm its original judgment, or give a new judgment, in conformity with the opinion of the Court. If not requested to convene specially the Tribunal shall at its next session confirm its judgment or bring it into conformity with the opinion of the Court".[54] Any award so confirmed is a burden upon the budget of the Organization.

54. Statute of the Administrative Tribunal of the U.N., Art. 11.

§433 Not only the specialized agencies and the United Nations have established tribunals to which their staffs may apply in the event of a labour dispute. However, in some cases the appellate body concerned does not consider that it has the power to overrule or review a decision based, for example, on an action by the employee's national state. Thus, if an employee of NATO has his security clearance removed by his state and is thereupon dismissed by NATO, that decision is final.[55]

55. See, e.g., *NATO Appeals Board Decision No. 18* (1970), 44 I.L.R. 423 at 424: ". . . under . . . the NATO Civilian Personnel Regulations an Appeals Board only has jurisdiction to decide 'any individual dispute arising out of a decision taken by the head of a NATO body'; it is not . . . competent to appraise the lawfulness of decisions

taken by the authorities of a member State; it follows that it is not for the Board to rule on the lawfulness of the withdrawal of the security clearance certificate by the [national] authorities; [and] the [national] courts alone would be competent to do so in the appropriate circumstances."

§434 While international institutions recognize that the international civil service has rights and may even be permitted to organize, it depends on the institution in question whether such professional bodies enjoy legal personality or can be said to have sufficient legal interest to intervene when the rights of individual servants may be infringed.[56] On the other hand, there is some evidence to suggest that in their dealing with their officials international institutions must operate on a basis of fairness, non-discrimination,[57] natural justice and the provision of some type of effective remedy.[58]

56. See, e.g., *Lasalle v. European Parliament*, [1964] C.M.L.R. 267 (Ct. of Justice of the European Communities).

57. *Lasalle v. European Parliament, ante; Prais v. Council of the European Communities*, [1976] 2 C.M.L.R. 708 (Ct. of Justice of the European Communities).

58. See *Gadhok v. Commonwealth Secretariat* (1977), 12 I.T.R. 440.

§435 With regard to the European institutions, the law of the institution overrides that of the national member so that if, for example, a member of the European Parliament receives a sum by way of expenses larger than the amount he actually expends, national revenue authorities are not entitled to tax the excess as if it were a normal emolument.[59] This supremacy of the law of the institution only operates in relation to organizations which may be described as supranational, as is the European Community.[60]

59. *Lord Bruce of Donington v. Aspen, H.M. Inspector of Taxes* (1981), The Times (London), Oct. 5, 1981 (Ct. of Justice of the European Communities): "... the [European] Parliament's view is that by virtue of the principle of the independence of the European Parliament with regard to provisions concerning the internal functioning of the institution . . ., and independence which the members are bound to respect . . ., the national tax provisions do not apply to Community payments which are necessary for the functioning of the institution. Community law lays down certain limits, which the member states must observe in the enactment of taxation laws applicable to members of the Parliament. . . . A review by national revenue authorities, such as the one provided for by the U.K. legislation, constitutes an interference in the internal functioning of the Parliament resulting in a substitution by the national authorities for the one undertaken by the European Parliament in the exercise of its powers. It would therefore be likely to impair the effectiveness of the action of the Parliament and be incompatible with its autonomy. . . . Community law prohibits the imposition of national tax on lump-sum payments made by the European Parliament to its members from Community funds by way of reimbursement of

travel and subsistence expenses, unless it can be shown in accordance with Community law that such lump-sum reimbursement constitutes in part remuneration."

60. Thus, in *Porrini v. Euratom, Comont. S.p.A.* (1975), 60 I.L.R. 494 at p. 510, the European Court examined the basis of the service relationship between the Community and its staff other than local staff: "The national Court [which had asked what competence it possessed] has no jurisdiction in disputes between the Community and persons who claim the status of officials or that of establishment staff. The European Court of Justice has exclusive jurisdiction to decide such cases."

Index to International Law

All references are to paragraph numbers.